Theoretical Comparative Syntax

Theoretical Comparative Syntax brings together, for the first time, profoundly influential essays and articles by Naoki Fukui, exploring various topics in the areas of syntactic theory and comparative syntax. The articles have a special focus on the typological differences between English (-type languages) and Japanese (-type languages) and abstract parameters that derive them. Linguistic universals are considered in the light of cross-linguistic variation, and typological (parametric) differences are investigated from the viewpoint of universal principles.

The unifying theme of this volume is the nature and structure of invariant principles and parameters (variables) and how they interact to give principled accounts to a variety of seemingly unrelated differences between English and Japanese. These two types of languages provide an ideal testing ground for the principles and their interactions with the parameters since the languages exhibit diverse superficial differences in virtually every aspect of their linguistic structures: word order, *wh*-movement, grammatical agreement, the obligatoriness and uniqueness of a subject, complex predicates, case-marking systems, anaphoric systems, classifiers and numerals, among others. Detailed descriptions of the phenomena and attempts to provide principled accounts for them constitute considerable contributions to the development of the principles-and-parameters model in its exploration and refinement of theoretical concepts and fundamental principles of linguistic theory, leading to some of the basic insights that lie behind the minimalist program. The essays on theoretical comparative syntax collected here present a substantial contribution to the field of linguistics.

Naoki Fukui is Professor of Linguistics and Chair of the Linguistics Department at Sophia University, Tokyo. He is the author of several books and has been an editorial board member of various international journals.

Routledge leading linguists
Series editor Carlos P. Otero
University of California, Los Angeles, USA

1 **Essays on Syntax and Semantics**
   James Higginbotham

2 **Partitions and Atoms of Clause Structure**
   Subjects, agreement, case and clitics
   Dominique Sportiche

3 **The Syntax of Specifiers and Heads**
   Collected essays of Hilda J. Koopman
   Hilda J. Koopman

4 **Configurations of Sentential Complementation**
   Perspectives from Romance languages
   Johan Rooryck

5 **Essays in Syntactic Theory**
   Samuel David Epstein

6 **On Syntax and Semantics**
   Richard K. Larson

7 **Comparative Syntax and Language Acquisition**
   Luigi Rizzi

8 **Minimalist Investigations in Linguistic Theory**
   Howard Lasnik

9 **Derivations**
   Exploring the dynamics of syntax
   Juan Uriagereka

10 **Towards an Elegant Syntax**
   Michael Brody

11 **Logical Form and Linguistic Theory**
   Robert May

12 **Generative Grammar**
   The theory and its history
   Robert Freidin

13 **Theoretical Comparative Syntax**
   Studies in macroparameters
   Naoki Fukui

Theoretical Comparative Syntax
Studies in macroparameters

Naoki Fukui

Routledge
Taylor & Francis Group
LONDON AND NEW YORK

First published 2006 by Routledge

Published 2017 by Routledge
2 Park Square, Milton Park, Abingdon, Oxon OX14 4RN
711 Third Avenue, New York, NY 10017, USA

Routledge is an imprint of the Taylor & Francis Group, an informa business

Copyright © 2006 Naoki Fukui

First issued in paperback 2013

Typeset in Garamond by Wearset Ltd, Boldon, Tyne and Wear

The Open Access version of this book, available at
www. tandfebooks. com, has been made available under a Creative
Creative Commons Attribution-Non Commercial-No Derivatives
4.0 license.

British Library Cataloguing in Publication Data
A catalogue record for this book is available from the British Library

Library of Congress Cataloging in Publication Data
A catalog record for this book has been requested

ISBN 978-0-415-34103-5 (hbk)
ISBN 978-0-415-86012-3 (pbk)

Contents

Original publication details	viii
Introduction	1
1 Specifiers and projection	9
2 LF extraction of *naze*: some theoretical implications	38
3 Strong and weak barriers: remarks on the proper characterization of barriers	55
4 Parameters and optionality	69
5 A note on improper movement	87
6 The principles-and-parameters approach: a comparative syntax of English and Japanese	100
7 Symmetry in syntax: Merge and Demerge	132
8 Order in phrase structure and movement	179
9 An A-over-A perspective on locality	209
10 The uniqueness parameter	224
11 Nominal structure: an extension of the Symmetry Principle	229
12 Phrase structure	258
13 The Visibility Guideline for functional categories: verb-raising in Japanese and related issues	289
Appendix: on the nature of economy in language	337
Notes	354
References	392
Index	415

Original publication details

Chapter 1 "Specifiers and projection" is reprinted from N. Fukui, T. Rapoport, and E. Sagey (eds) *MIT Working Papers in Linguistics: Papers in Theoretical Linguistics*, 8: 128–172, 1986.

Chapter 2 "LF extraction of *naze*: some theoretical implications" is reprinted from *Natural Language and Linguistic Theory* 6: 503–526, 1988, by permission from Kluwer Academic Publishers.

Chapter 3 "Strong and weak barriers: remarks on the proper characterization of barriers" is reprinted from H. Nakajima (ed.) *Current English Linguistics in Japan*, 1991: 77–93, by permission from Mouton de Gruyter.

Chapter 4 "Parameters and optionality" is reprinted from *Linguistic Inquiry* 24: 399–420, 1993, by permission from MIT Press.

Chapter 5 "A note on improper movement" is reprinted from *The Linguistic Review* 10: 111–126, 1993, by permission from Walter de Gruyter.

Chapter 6 "The principles-and-parameters approach: a comparative syntax of English and Japanese" is reprinted from M. Shibatani and T. Bynon (eds) *Approaches to Language Typology*, 1995: 327–372, by permission from Oxford University Press.

Chapter 7 "Symmetry in syntax: Merge and Demerge" is reprinted from *Journal of East Asian Linguistics* 7: 27–86, 1998, by permission from Kluwer Academic Publishers.

Chapter 8 "Order in phrase structure and movement" is reprinted from *Linguistic Inquiry* 29: 439–474, 1998, by permission from MIT Press.

Chapter 9 "An A-over-A perspective on locality" is reprinted from E. Iwamoto and M. Muraki (eds) *Linguistics: In Search of the Human Mind*, 1999: 109–129, by permission from Kaitakusha.

Chapter 10 "The uniqueness parameter" is reprinted from *Glot International* 4, 9/10: 26–27, 1999, by permission from Blackwell Publishers.

Chapter 11 "Nominal structure: an extension of the Symmetry Principle" is reprinted from P. Svenonius (ed.) *The Derivation of VO and OV*, 2000: 219–254, by permission from John Benjamins.

Chapter 12 "Phrase structure" is reprinted from M. Baltin and C. Collins (eds) *The Handbook of Contemporary Syntactic Theory*, 2001: 374–406, by permission from Blackwell Publishers.

Original publication details ix

Chapter 13 "The Visibility Guideline for functional categories: verb-raising in Japanese and related issues" is reprinted from *Lingua* 113: 321–375, 2003, by permission from Elsevier.

Appendix "On the nature of economy in language" is reprinted from *Cognitive Studies* 3: 51–71, 1996, by permission from the Japanese Cognitive Science Society.

Introduction

This volume is a collection of articles I have written over the years concerning linguistic theory and comparative syntax. The study of the principles of Universal Grammar (UG), as they have been discovered in the tradition of modern generative grammar, has always been the major object of my research. Given the diversity of natural languages, however, the discovery of the principles of UG cannot be the sole object of inquiry in linguistic theory, a situation which makes the field more challenging and even more interesting, at least to me, than, say, arithmetic or physics. Thus, comparative syntax comes into play. Comparative syntax is concerned with the properties of languages that are not universal, and it attempts to discover "natural classes" of syntactic properties that can be traced back to a single (usually quite abstract) parameter that yields observed differences among target languages. In the principles-and-parameters model assumed throughout the whole book, the study of comparative syntax proceeds hand in hand with the study of general principles of UG that interact with language-specific parameters to induce observed variation. All of the essays contained in this volume deal with comparative syntax as it pertains to the study of invariant principles of UG, with a special focus on the in-depth comparative analyses of English (-type languages) and Japanese (-type languages).

Before giving a summary of the articles, let me briefly sketch the development of my thought on the issues of comparative syntax and syntactic theory over the period in which the articles were written. (References to important work by others are largely omitted in the following discussion. See the original articles in this volume for detailed references.) The peculiar properties of subjects in Japanese, as compared to those in English, first attracted my attention. On the one hand, they behave like subjects of noun phrases in English, in that they are truly optional and can be syntactically absent (unlike subjects of clauses in English, which cannot be completely absent but require an empty category). In this respect, subjects in Japanese seem to be more closely connected to a lexical category. On the other hand, a subject in Japanese shares certain properties with a topic and the head of a relative clause. For example, the subject is a default candidate for a topic, and all three elements (subject, topic, and relative head) can bind an anaphor-like element *zibun* "self". In the terms in which I thought about these problems at the time, the subject position in Japanese shares certain properties with so-called "A′-positions" while at the same time it exhibits some "A-position" characteristics. I proposed a preliminary analysis of these peculiar properties of the Japanese subject position (Fukui, N. 1984. "The adjunct subject hypothesis and *zibun*", MS, MIT; not included in this volume), but the fundamental problems concerning the differences between English and Japanese in the relevant respects were largely left open.

Pursuing the same intuitions that I had gained from the considerations of Japanese subjects (as compared to English subjects), I developed, in collaboration with Margaret Speas, a system of phrase structure that I later dubbed "relativized X′ theory" (Chapter 1 of this volume). Relativized X′ theory is further refined and developed in my dissertation (Fukui, N. 1986. *A Theory of Category Projection and Its Applications*, Ph.D. dissertation, MIT; a revised version was published by CSLI Publications in 1995). The basic ingredients of this system are the following: (i) the distinction between lexical and "functional" elements (supplemented with the so-called "DP-analysis"), (ii) the denial of X′ schema widely assumed at the time, (iii) the "predicate-internal" subject hypothesis, and (iv) the characterization of specifiers (Specs) in terms of agreement. As noted in the original publications, most of these ideas had important predecessors or were being explored in different orientations by other linguists, but putting these perspectives together into a single system of phrase structure seems to have been unique to the approach I was taking at that time. It seems fair to say that all of the basic ideas mentioned above (perhaps with the exception of (iv)) have been refined in various forms and have now been incorporated, in one way or another, into "mainstream" syntactic theory.

As for the comparative syntax of English and Japanese, I came up with the parametric statement that Japanese lacks active (i.e., agreement-inducing) functional elements (while languages like English do have active functional elements). This parametric hypothesis, through interactions with the general principles of UG (relativized X′ theory being one of the principles), was shown to derive a clustering of hitherto unrelated differences between the two types of languages. The properties that were given a principled account include the existence of overt *wh*-movement, multiple subject (multiple nominative and genitive) constructions, scrambling, expletives, complex predicate formation, and so on. English and Japanese behave exactly the opposite way with respect to these properties, and this fact, so it was demonstrated, follows naturally from the existence of agreement in English and the lack thereof in Japanese (Chapters 1, 6, 7, 8, 11).

As I worked on the comparative syntax of English and Japanese, I was led to a general hypothesis concerning the locus of parametric variation. It was suggested in my dissertation (mentioned above), but a more explicit formulation of this hypothesis was stated in my 1988 article (Fukui, N. 1988. "Deriving the differences between English and Japanese: a case study in parametric syntax", *English Linguistics* 5: 249–270; not included in this volume), according to which parametric differences in UG are restricted to either the functional domain of the lexicon or those conditions having to do with linear order (the head-parameter and the like). The rationale behind this proposal was to severely restrict the class of possible parameters (and hence the class of available grammars), and, given the nature of functional elements (i.e., they are mostly responsible for the computational aspects of UG), it seemed plausible to attribute the sources for parametric variation to these elements (apart from linear order) (cf. Chapter 6).

With regard to linear order, English and Japanese are taken to be representative cases of the two opposite values for the head-parameter: English is uniformly head-initial, whereas Japanese is strictly head-last. I tried to find out how (or whether) this fact correlates with other typological properties of these languages. That the value for the head-parameter is somehow related to the existence of overt *wh*-movement was relatively well known. Then, does the head-parameter value correlate with, say, the possibility of scrambling? I argued that it does, which implies that linear order somehow plays a role in the computational component of the language faculty (Chapters 4, 8, 12). In fact, three features of Japanese grammar seem to conspire in such a way as to make scrambling possible in the language: (i) the head-last value for the head-parameter, (ii) the existence of overt Case particles, and (iii) the lack of active functional elements (hence the lack of formal agreement (ϕ-features)). Several of the articles included in this volume approach these properties and their interactions from various perspectives (Chapters 4, 6, 7, 8, 9, 11).

The system of functional elements has always been one of my central concerns, since these elements play prominent roles in the theory of phrase structure and movement. Properties of functional elements will have a variety of consequences and ramifications for the theory of locality, movement, phrase structure, and comparative syntax (Chapters 1, 2, 3, 5, 8, 9, 11, 13). Given their usefulness as a descriptive tool, however, functional elements have sometimes been overused in syntactic analyses, particularly in the late 1980s, a situation that is reminiscent of the overuse of grammatical transformations in the 1970s or parameters in the early 1980s. Some of my articles argue against the inflation of functional categories, and propose a restrictive theory of these elements both in UG and in particular grammars (Chapters 6, 13).

Turning now to a more detailed description of each of the articles collected in this volume, Chapter 1 ("Specifiers and projection") proposes a system of phrase structure which departs from standard X' theory in several important respects. In particular, it denies the existence of X' schema and claims that phrase structures in natural languages are built in a bottom-up fashion, based on inherent properties of lexical items, where the lexical-functional distinction plays an important role in determining the characteristics of phrase structure. Corollaries of this claim include the hypothesis that the concept of maximal projection cannot be defined in terms of bar levels; rather, it must be defined as a projection that does not further project in a given configuration. The article contains other novel proposals regarding specific aspects of phrase structure, particularly the parametric statement that Japanese lacks the class of active functional categories, from which various typological properties of the language are shown to follow.

Chapter 2 ("LF extraction of *naze*: some theoretical implications") explores the intuition obtained from my earlier work (discussed above) that constituents in Japanese clauses are linked to the predicate in a "closer" way than corresponding elements in, say, English, while, in certain respects, the elements in clauses and noun phrases in Japanese are more remote from the head than the corresponding elements in English. The notion of "L-containment" is introduced to capture the necessary distinctions, and the discussion is extended to the relation between subjacency and the ECP (Empty Category Principle).

Extensions of the proposed system of projection to the theory of locality (namely, the "barriers" system) are briefly touched on in Chapter 1. Chapter 3 ("Strong and weak barriers: remarks on the proper characterization of barriers") further explores this possibility. It is proposed that the notion of barriers in syntactic computation ought to be refined by using the distinction (made available only in the proposed system of phrase structure) between "maximal projection" and "XP" (the double-bar level). A maximal projection becomes a weak barrier if not L-marked (not a complement of a lexical head). When a maximal projection happens to be an XP, it becomes a strong barrier, "strong" in the sense that its effect as a barrier is stronger than a non-L-marked maximal projection that is not an XP, and that it functions as a barrier regardless of whether it is L-marked or not. It is also hypothesized that given the lack of active functional elements in the language, Japanese lacks strong barriers, which accounts for the weaker effect of subjacency observed in various places in the syntax of Japanese.

Chapter 4 ("Parameters and optionality") takes up the problems of scrambling. Scrambling in Japanese is generally considered to be an optional movement. However, the status of optionality, particularly the status of optional movement, under the general economy approach has been quite unclear, since economy conditions tend to eliminate the possibility of optionality in derivation quite strongly, thereby characterizing movement operations as a last resort. An optional rule is allowed only if its application is "costless", where the cost of rule application is calculated by a certain algorithm. This chapter proposes one specific measure of the cost of formal operations in a grammar, under which optional movement is allowed. The measure, called the "parameter value preservation (PVP) measure", dictates that the chosen value for a parameter in a given language must be maximally preserved throughout the derivation, and that optionality is allowed only when this requirement is met. Thus, optional scrambling is allowed in Japanese, because the Japanese value for the head-parameter, i.e., "head-last", is preserved under the application of leftward scrambling. Such is not the case in "head-initial" English. Hence the impossibility of optional scrambling in the latter type of languages. Thus, the PVP measure imposes a necessary (but perhaps not sufficient) condition for a possibility of scrambling.

Chapter 5 ("A note on improper movement") argues that the then standard account of improper movement in terms of Condition C of the Binding Theory cannot be maintained under the Uniformity Condition on Chains, and suggests two alternative approaches to improper movement. One approach, a reformulation of the Uniformity Condition as a derivational constraint, makes certain significant predictions concerning the theory of movement in general. The second approach, based on an economy condition on adjunction, provides a unified account of improper movement and the *that*-trace effect, offering novel accounts of other hitherto unexplained facts such as subject-nonsubject asymmetries with respect to topicalization and scrambling.

My general views on the theory of comparative syntax and the comparative syntax of English and Japanese are stated in a relatively comprehensive fashion in Chapter 6 ("The principles-and-parameters approach: a comparative syntax of English and Japanese"). In addition to specific parametric statements about Japanese (e.g., the head-last order, the lack of active functional elements, etc.), a restrictive theory of parameters and functional elements is proposed. Functional categories are classified in terms of [±N] and [±V] features, and certain generalizations are drawn from the proposed classification of functional categories. A number of typological properties of Japanese are shown to derive from a single parameter (or as the interaction of a couple of parameters).

Chapter 7 ("Symmetry in syntax: Merge and Demerge") puts forth the hypothesis that the computations in the overt syntax and the computations in the (pre-morphology) phonological component are "symmetric" in the sense that they form mirror images of each other. This "Symmetry Principle" is couched in a restrictive theory of parameters proposed in Chapter 6, and plays an important role in explaining the major properties of phrase structure in an elegant way. Thus, the Symmetry Principle accounts for the apparently universal leftness property of Spec in a straightforward way by attributing its leftness to the fact that a Spec, by definition, is the first maximal projection in a given phrase that the top-down computation (Demerge) encounters. With respect to the order between a head and its complement, which allows for cross-linguistic variation (head-first v. head-last), the principle predicts that the head-last order reflects the "base" order involving no relevant movement whereas the head-initial order is derived by movement. Various other theoretical and empirical consequences are also shown to follow under the Symmetry Principle, coupled with a few parametric statements about Japanese.

Chapter 8 ("Order in phrase structure and movement") further pursues a proper analysis of Japanese scrambling, with a special focus on the role of linear order in the theory of phrase structure and movement. A parametrized version of Merge incorporating the effect of the head-parameter is proposed, and it is argued that under the parametrized Merge, traditional "adjunction" operations are characterized as substitution in the sense that they always accompany the projection of the target structure, whereas traditional "substitution" operations are analysed as genuine adjunction. It is then shown that a number of empirical consequences follow from this theory of phrase structure and movement, including (i) the nature and distribution of optional movements, (ii) an elegant account of some peculiar properties of Specs, and (iii) a new unification of adjunct and subject condition effects (two central cases of the Condition on Extraction Domain, CED), with a natural explanation of the parametric variation associated with the latter effect.

Chapter 9 ("An A-over-A perspective on locality") argues that the basic insights of Attract can actually revive the A-over-A principle as a minimum principle, in such a way that the principle is relativized as to the relevant features (not the categories). The feature version of the A-over-A principle accounts for the major portion of the classical island constraints, except for the CED cases for which an independent explanation is available (see Chapter 8). Whether this version of the A-over-A principle should be stipulated as an independent principle, or ought to be incorporated into the functioning of the Attract operation itself remains to be seen. It is also an interesting related open problem whether the notion of "c-command" (utilized in Attract) exists without reference to "domination" (which plays a crucial role in the A-over-A principle), or whether these structural notions should be somehow reshuffled.

A macroparameter called the "uniqueness parameter" is suggested in Chapter 10 ("The uniqueness parameter"). The basic idea behind this "parameter" is that language can be taken as a procedure for providing a solution to an equation. UG assures the "existence" of a solution, but it does not guarantee the "uniqueness" of such a solution. (An analogy can be made to differential equations in mathematics.) The uniqueness can be obtained under certain conditions which are regulated, but not directly provided, by UG. English fulfills these conditions, while Japanese does not, from which a variety of cases of non-uniqueness in the latter type of languages follow. It is also suggested in this short paper that the scope of the uniqueness parameter goes well beyond English/Japanese comparative syntax.

Chapter 11 ("Nominal structure: an extension of the Symmetry Principle") is an extension of Chapter 7. By applying the Symmetry Principle proposed in Chapter 7 to the analysis of nominal structures (in particular, relative clauses), it is argued that a variety of differences between, say, English and Japanese fall out in a simple and elegant fashion, based solely on the single parametric difference between the languages: English exhibits N-to-D raising, while Japanese does not. It is then demonstrated that the existence of a rich classifier system in Japanese (and the "floatability" of numerals), as opposed to the non-existence of classifiers in a language like English, is just another consequence of the lack of N-raising in the language.

Chapter 12 ("Phrase structure") discusses the development of the theory of phrase structure in modern generative grammar, and tries to situate various proposals in my earlier work in the context of the broader theoretical setting. In particular, issues of linear order are taken up again, and pieces of evidence that seem to be indicative of the visibility of linear order in narrow syntax are presented.

In line with my long-term critical view on the unconstrained postulation of functional categories, Chapter 13 ("The Visibility Guideline for functional categories: verb-raising in Japanese and related issues") proposes the "Visibility Guideline for functional categories", according to which functional elements are required to be (directly or indirectly) "detectable" in the primary linguistic data. Various candidates for functional categories in Japanese are examined in light of this guideline, and it is concluded that none of them is qualified as an active functional category inducing formal and mechanical computations in Japanese grammar. An alternative view of the relevant phenomena in terms of "PF reanalysis" is put forward, and the analysis is extended to the case-marking mechanism in Japanese. The general perspective on the grammar of Japanese that emerges from the critical discussion on functional elements in the language is that, in many areas of Japanese grammar, PF and semantic mechanisms are at work in place of mechanical computations in narrow syntax, although the core computational machineries in UG (such as Merge and Agree) are also available in the grammar of Japanese.

The Appendix deals with somewhat different issues than those extensively discussed in other chapters of this volume. It argues that there are rather unexpected fundamental connections to be made between the principles of language and the laws governing the physical world. More specifically, it is suggested that the economy principles explored in theoretical linguistics are comparable to the Principle of Least Action in physics, which in turn suggests that, given the status of language as a discrete system, economy principles built in the language mechanisms could turn out to be a reflection of natural laws that require computational efficiencies. Exactly what mathematical or physical laws lie behind the principles of UG remains an extremely important problem for linguistics.

As is clear from the summaries of the articles, my research on parameters has so far been almost solely on the issues of what the possible parameters permitted in UG are and how they are organized in such a way as to deduce, by interacting with invariant principles of UG, the observed typological properties of languages. The fundamental problem, that is, why do parameters exist in the first place, has almost never been touched upon. This is because I thought it was simply premature to ask such a question. With the recent development of minimalism, however, it now seems possible to address such questions in a meaningful way. There have been a few recent attempts (most notably by Mark Baker and Noam Chomsky) to tackle the problem of why parameters exist in UG, but the issue still seems quite open. My own view on this issue is that the fundamental difference between language and other cognitive capacities (such as vision and arithmetic) boils down to the fact that growth of the language faculty requires "society" (i.e., human interactions), and this somehow leads to the emergence of parameters in UG. That is, a language is, after all, "un produit social de la faculté du langage" (Ferdinand de Saussure). As the theory of generative grammar has convincingly demonstrated, the faculty of language is a biological endowment, but, as it is "designed" to go through social interactions, parameters come into play. Modern generative grammar has taken language as a natural object, and has refrained from incorporating the factors having to do with interpersonal interactions. Rightly so, in my opinion, since, above all, it is not even clear whether science can actually approach complex social phenomena. Recent developments in game theory, however, have opened up a promising way to approach the problem of language growth. In game-theoretic terms, a steady state of the faculty of language (I-language) can be regarded as an equilibrium of some sort that the faculty of language reaches through social interactions. The problem of parameters, then, amounts to the conditions under which more than one equilibrium is allowed, given the faculty of language (which is itself an equilibrium in a different dimension). It seems to me that the fundamental problem of parameters can be approached along these lines. This will set a research agenda for my work on parameters that follows this volume.

I would like to take this opportunity to thank Carlos Otero (the editor of the *Routledge Leading Linguists* series) and Juan Uriagereka for their encouragement in this project. Next I offer deep thanks to my co-authors for their kind permission to reprint their co-authored articles in this volume. I am also grateful to Noriko Kobayashi for her indispensable help with the preparation of the manuscript, and Hironobu Kasai and Takaomi Kato for their excellent job of proofreading and indexing. As always, I have benefited a lot from comments and suggestions by Teresa Griffith and Mihoko Zushi, to whom I am grateful. The completion of this book was supported in part by a research grant from the Kozo Keikaku Engineering Inc.

Naoki Fukui
Summer 2005

1 Specifiers and projection

with Margaret Speas

The overlap between the constraints imposed at the level of D-structure by the Projection Principle and those imposed by X' theory has been noticed by various linguists, including Hale (1978, 1980b), Chomsky (1981a), Stowell (1981b), Marantz (1984), and Emonds (1985). As long as no empirical generalization is lost, we may wish to attribute this overlap to inherent redundancy in cognitive mechanisms. However, if there are linguistic generalizations which are obscured by this redundancy, then it is appropriate to investigate the properties of the two systems of constraints, in order to isolate the unique properties of each, so that the observed generalizations will be expressible.

In this paper, we will argue that there are certain important generalizations which cannot be expressed in terms of X' theory and the Projection Principle as they are currently conceived. We will propose a theory of well-formed D-structures which captures these generalizations. Our theory is based on what we take to be a fundamental asymmetry between lexical categories and functional (non-lexical) categories: functional categories project to X'', and are limited to a single specifier position and a single complement position, while all projections of lexical categories are X', which is indefinitely iterable (in the sense of Harris 1951), limited only by the Projection Principle and other independent principles of licensing.

After having introduced this "non-uniform" bar level hypothesis in section 1, we will argue in the following sections that various desirable consequences follow from this hypothesis: (1) The so-called "implicit argument" (Roeper 1983), whose syntactic characterization has been the subject of much recent discussion, can now be explicitly represented in the phrase structure under this hypothesis; (2) We can capture certain typological variations which are not expressible in other theories; (3) We can predict which positions will be iterable and which will not; (4) We can simplify the principles of θ-marking (especially θ-marking for "external arguments"); (5) We can eliminate the need for "VP-adjunction" in syntax, and can also simplify the definition of "barrier"; and finally (6) We can eliminate the undesirable overlap between constraints on possible D-structures imposed by the Projection Principle and those provided by X' theory.

1 Projection of lexical and functional categories

Following Chomsky (1970), we will assume that the primitive vocabulary of the grammar includes the category features [±N] and [±V], and that these features allow a partition of lexical items into four categories. It is not clear to what extent the above features may be labels for some semantic or other property of the categories, but there is an important distinction between categories which bear these features and those which do not: the categories bearing these features are those which may take arguments. In the theory of Higginbotham (1985), these and only these are the categories which have a θ-grid as part of the lexical entry. Following the longstanding tradition, we will call these four categories the lexical categories.

Lexical Categories: [+N −V]   (noun)
                      [−N +V]   (verb)
                      [+N +V]   (adjective)
                      [−N −V]   (preposition)

In the framework of Chomsky (1986a, b), the relationship between the lexicon and the syntactic level of D-structure is one of projection; properties of lexical items, including θ-marking properties, are projected from the lexicon into syntax, constrained by the Projection Principle and the schematic "X'" well-formedness conditions on phrase markers.

The Projection Principle (informal statement): lexical properties are maintained at all syntactic levels.

The X' Schema:
(i) X' = X X"*   (order irrelevant)
(ii) X" = X"* X'

> where X"* stands for zero or more occurrences of some maximal projection.
> (Chomsky 1986a: 2–3)

In English at least, the lexical categories do not exhaustively partition the set of items in the lexicon. In particular, the items such as Comp and Infl, which have been called non-lexical or minor categories, act as heads but do not appear to bear the N and V features.[1] Since these categories are projected from the lexicon and have independent lexical entries, we will avoid the term non-lexical, and will refer to these categories as functional categories.

It has long been observed that the cross-category generalizations captured by the X' schema were fuzzy with respect to the functional categories; even Jackendoff (1977) resorted to some extra features to get the generalization to work out right. (Specifically, to the features [±subject], [±object], he added [±comp] and [±det].) Until Chomsky (1986a), it was thought that the categories IP and CP were defective in some way; Chomsky suggests extending the X' schema so that CP and IP would both have specifier positions.

We would like to propose a different view, in which functional categories have a unique specifier position, but lexical categories may iterate "specifiers", as long as all "specifiers" are fully licensed and can be interpreted at LF. We maintain that only the specifiers of functional categories close off projections, therefore the node dominating the maximal projection of a functional category should be X'' (or XP), while all projections of a lexical category are X', since there is no inherent limit to their iteration.

Before we proceed, let us be clear about exactly what we mean by "specifier". Chomsky emphasizes that the notion "specifier" is strictly a relational one, used as a label for whichever maximal projections happen to appear in a given category as immediate daughters of X''. However, this version of the X' schema does not give us an explanation for the contrast between (1) and (2).

(1) a. the very very old man
    b. Mary's big red book
    c. Susan never could have been eating cabbage.

(2) a. *the the old man
    b *yesterday's Chomsky's book.
    c. *It Mary ate a bagel.
    d. *the John's cat
    e. *What who did buy?

These data show that there are some types of "specifiers" which may iterate and others which may not. Of course, it is not a priori necessary that the ungrammatical cases be ruled out by X' theory alone. For example, some of the ungrammatical examples might be ruled out by other principles, such as the θ-Criterion. However, these data are important because it is routinely assumed in current theory that cases like (2) are ruled out by the supposed fact that there is only one available specifier position, yet X' theory as it is formulated in the most recent treatments provides no such restriction. Chomsky's formulation of X' theory allows any number of specifiers for each category.

It should also be pointed out that the presence of apparent subjects across categories (cf. Stowell 1982) does not provide evidence that each category has some unique subject position given by X' theory, since extraction data reveal an underlying difference in the status of the "subject" from category to category, as shown by the examples below:

(3) a. We saw Bill's book.
    b. We saw Bill drunk.
    c. *Whose did you see book?
    d. Who did you see drunk?
    e. Whose book did you see?
    f. *Who drunk did you see?

12 Specifiers and projection

The subject of the adjective can be extracted (d), while the subject of the noun cannot (c). The noun plus its subject can move as a constituent (e), while the adjective plus its subject cannot (f). These examples indicate that the status of the "subject" of the adjective *drunk* in (b), (d) and (f) differs in some fundamental way from the status of the "subject" of the noun *book* in (a), (c) and (e).

In order to avoid terminological confusion, we will henceforth use the term specifier to mean an element that closes off a category projection.

In the theory which we propose, we will be taking the position that the determiners found in NPs are functional heads, on a par with the functional heads Comp and Infl. To our knowledge, the first to advocate such a view of determiners was Brame (1981, 1982), who developed the idea within his own framework. (Brame called determiners "head selectors".) Reuland (1983) proposes that NPs, in particular, gerunds, contain an Infl-like element, and Abney (1986) argues within GB theory that determiners can be considered heads of a constituent Determiner Phrase (DP).

The proposal that Det, Comp and Infl[2] constitute a natural class of functional categories allows parallel structures to be assigned to DP (=Determiner Phrase), IP and CP. We propose the following structures for IP, CP and DP.

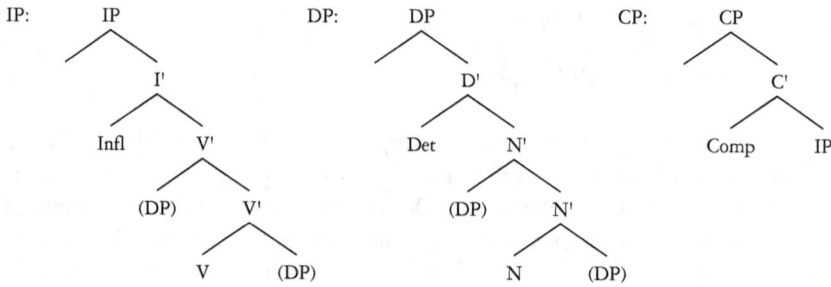

In the above structures, we are suggesting that Brame's proposal that the determiner heads a constituent DP be adopted in a GB framework, and we are proposing that the maximal projection of a lexical category is X'.

Notice that CP is distinguished from the other two by the fact that its complement is the projection of a functional category. This is a property that Comp shares with the lexical categories.

Our proposal is based on a number of empirical observations about structure across categories.

1 Functional heads have one and only one (i.e., non-iterable) specifier, while the specifiers of lexical heads may be iterable ones.
2 The specifiers of functional heads are often (in our model, always – see below) moved from within their complement.
3 All functional heads have specifier positions; it is not at all clear that all lexical heads have Spec positions.

4   Languages which lack functional heads also lack specifier positions.
5   Functional heads are special in that they are closed-class items.
6   Functional heads lack the sort of semantic value associated with lexical categories.
7   Functional heads always select a unique complement.³

The claim that lexical categories project to X′ while functional categories can project to X″ is substantiated by data from Japanese. Japanese lacks the functional categories Det, Infl and Comp,⁴ so our theory of projection makes the prediction that all Japanese constituents are X′ and not X″. Below we will give evidence involving NP structure, pro-forms, subjects and scrambling that the prediction is correct; Japanese phrases should be considered X′ projections, because they do not contain the position which would close off a projection, yielding X″ categories. For a more detailed discussion of evidence that Japanese phrases also behave as X′ and not XP with respect to extraction, see Fukui (1986).

1.1 *Japanese NPs are N′s*

Given an "NP", it is always possible in Japanese to attach another modifying phrase to it, as long as certain semantic conditions governing the mutual order among prenominal elements are met. In Japanese, the phrases which may be iterated include not only modifying adjectives and the like, but also *-no* genitive phrases.

(4) a. ko-no hon   "this book"
        this   book
    b. John-no ko-no hon   Lit. "John's this book"
    c. kireina John-no ko-no hon   Lit. "beautiful John's this book"
        beautiful

In these examples we see that *John-no* "John's" and *kono* "this" do not close off a projection of N; rather, they are iterable, parallel to those modifiers in English which under our account are projected under a projection of a lexical category.

A second piece of evidence that Japanese has no NP projection is the fact that even pro-forms like *sore* "it", *kare* "he", *zibun* "self" can be modified. (Note incidentally that the relative clause in (5) which modifies a pro-form *sore* "it" clearly has a restrictive meaning rather than an appositive one.)

(5) Tokyo-no   biru-no   okuzyoo kara mita Haree-suisei-wa
        -GEN building-GEN top   from (I)saw Halley's Comet-TOP
    smog-no   tame bonyarito nigotte ita ga,
    smog-GEN   due to faintly blurred was but
    Okinawa-no Naha-de mita sore-wa   yozora-ni   kukkirito kagayaite-ita.
        -GEN   -in saw it -TOP   night sky-in vividly   shining-was

Lit. "Halley's Comet that (I) saw from the top of a building in Tokyo was blurred by the smog, but *it that (I) saw from Naha City in Okinawa* was vividly shining in the night sky."

(6) Kinoo   Taroo-ni   atta ka-i?
    yesterday Taro -with met Q

   "Did you meet with Taro yesterday?"

   Un, demo *kinoo-no*   *kare*-wa sukosi   yoosu-ga
   Yes but   yesterday-GEN he-TOP somewhat state-NOM
   hendat-ta.
   be strange-PAST

   Lit. "Yes, but *yesterday's he* was somewhat strange."

(7) Kukyoo-ni tatasare-ta   Saburoo-wa   nanno   kuroo-mo
    hardship-in forced to face-PAST -TOP   not any sufferings-even
    siranakat-ta   *mukasi-no*   *zibun*-ni modoritai-to   omotta.
    not know-PAST old day-GEN self-to   wanted to go back-that thought

   Lit. "Saburo, who was stranded in hardships, wanted to go back to *old days' himself* who did not know any sufferings."

In English, pro-forms cannot be further modified,[5] but in Japanese they can be. This fact is predicted if we assume that Japanese pro-forms are N' rather than NP. In fact, there seem to be no NP pro-forms in this language comparable to English *it*, *he*, etc.

1.2 Japanese S is V'

Unlike English, in Japanese the subject, marked by the suffix -*ga*, may be iterated (again, provided that certain semantic conditions are met).

(8) heikin-zyumyoo-ga   mizikai.
    average-lifespan-NOM is short

   "The average lifespan is short."

   dansei-ga   heikin-zyumyoo-ga   mizikai.
   male -NOM average-lifespan -NOM is short

   "It is men that their average lifespan is short."

   bunmei koku-ga   dansei-ga heikin-zyumyoo-ga   mizikai.
   civilized countries-NOM male-NOM average -lifespan-NOM is short

   "It is civilized countries that men, their average lifespan is short in."

   (Kuno 1973)

This fact can be explained if we assume that Japanese S's are not only headed by V (cf. Whitman 1984, Fukui 1986), but that all projections of V are V' (not V"), a category within which iteration is permitted.

Data concerning "multiple" scrambling provides further support for this claim. As shown in the following examples, "multiple" scrambling is possible in Japanese. That is, having moved a category to the initial position of the embedded sentence ((9b)), we can further front another category to the initial position of the entire (matrix) sentence (9c).

(9) a. Boku-wa [$_S$Taroo-ga   Hanako-ni sono kireina hon-o
       I-TOP   Taro-NOM Hanako-to that pretty book-ACC
       watasita (no da)]-to omou
       handed   that think

   "I think that Taro handed that pretty book to Hanako."

   b. Boku-wa [$_S$sono kireina hon-o$_i$ [$_S$ Taroo-ga   Hanako-ni t_i
      I-TOP   that pretty book-ACC Taro-NOM Hanako-to
      watasita (no da)]]-to omou
      handed   that think

   c. [$_S$Hanako-ni$_j$ [$_S$ boku-wa [$_S$sono kireina hon-o$_i$ [$_S$Taroo-ga t_j t_i
      Hanako-to]   I-TOP   that pretty book-ACC Taro-NOM
      watasita (no da)]]-to omou]]
      handed   that think

If scrambling involves an adjunction operation to a sentence, as argued in Saito (1985), and Japanese sentences are X" (V" or I"), the "multiple" scrambling exemplified by the examples above should not be possible, since a non-structure-preserving operation such as adjunction generally creates an island from which nothing can be extracted (basically a "freezing" effect as observed, for example, by Culicover and Wexler 1973, Wexler and Culicover 1980, etc.). On the other hand, under our hypothesis, "adjunction" to a sentence is always structure-preserving because Japanese sentences are V's, and V's, being a projection of a lexical category, permit free iteration. Thus, the possibility of "multiple" scrambling provides further evidence for our claim that Japanese S is V' rather than V" or I".

1.3 *The structure of IP and DP*

The Projection Principle allows any number of arguments (and modifiers) to project, as long as they are all fully licensed and can be interpreted at LF. The X' schema, on the other hand, restricts the projections of functional categories to one specifier and one complement. This move captures the fact mentioned above that functional categories differ from lexical categories in that they take unique complements. Further, it allows us to encode the distinction between iterable and non-iterable specifiers: the elements in lexical categories which are neither heads nor complements are iterable if they meet all licensing conditions of other modules of the grammar, while functional categories have a unique specifier.

1.4 Function features

We adopt the standard analysis of the elements of the category Infl: i.e., that tense/Agr assigns nominative Case, while *to* does not. We further extend this analysis, proposing that each functional category includes some elements which assign what we will call function features, or F-features, and other elements which do not assign these features. F-features include nominative Case, assigned by tense/Agr, genitive Case, assigned by *'s*, and +*wh*, assigned by a *wh*-Comp (for the latter two cases, see below). We now introduce the term Kase to mean both Case in the standard sense (i.e., Case assigned by lexical categories, in particular objective Case assigned by V) and F-features assigned by functional categories. The Spec position of a functional category can appear only when Kase is assigned to that position. Otherwise, the projection of a functional category stops at the single-bar level. The Kase assignment which licenses the element in Spec position may come either from the functional head itself (this would be licensing by F-features), or, as in Exceptional Case Marking environments, from a lexical element (this would be licensing by Case assignment). (See section 3.1 for details on ECM.)

In Det position, articles are in complementary distribution with *'s*, the genitive Kase assigner. Therefore, we will suppose that *'s*, like tensed Infl, assigns Kase, and that *the*, *a*, etc., like *to*, do not assign Kase. The only possible filler for the Spec of Comp is a *wh*-word, so we suggest that the feature [+*wh*] be considered an F-feature, a member of the set of Kase, so that the alternation between +*wh* and *that* in Comp is parallel to the tense/*to* alternation in Infl and the article/genitive alternation in Det. This gives us the following paradigm:

	CP	IP	DP
Kase assigner	*wh*	tense/Agr	's
non-Kase assigner	that	to	the

We now have a way of explaining the doubly filled Comp effect, which, as Abney (1985) points out, seems to be parallel to the fact that articles do not appear with other specifiers. The reason that (10a–c) are all ungrammatical is that the functional heads underlined in these examples do not have F-features to assign, so the pre-head position is unlicensed.

(10) a. *I wonder who *that* arrived.
 b. *I think that Susan *to* leave.
 c. *I enjoyed Mary *the* book.

By associating the presence of an element in the Spec of a functional category with the presence of Kase, we are disassociating totally the existence of specifiers from the Projection Principle. This means that the "Extended" part of the Extended Projection Principle really has nothing to do with the Projection Principle, if the former is interpreted as a requirement that IP have a Spec position. We differ, then, from Rothstein (1983), who suggests that the requirement that the Spec of IP be filled (in English) can be explained in terms of a general requirement that predicates must be predicated of something and thus must have subjects. In our view, this condition on predication may be true, but since saturation of a predicate takes place within the projection of a lexical head, the condition on predication has nothing directly to do with the licensing of the Spec of IP position. The requirement that we adopt, which is also independently necessary in Rothstein's theory, is the following:

The Saturation Principle: All positions in a grid must be discharged.

Here, "grids" include not only the θ-grid of a lexical entry, but also Kase grids (F-features and Case). When all positions in a given grid are discharged, that grid is saturated. Thus, the Saturation Principle collapses the θ-Criterion with a requirement that, if an element has a Kase to discharge, the feature must be discharged. Higginbotham (1985) states the θ-Criterion as in (11).

(11) a. Every thematic position is discharged.
 b. If X discharges a thematic role in Y, then it discharges only one.
 (Higginbotham 1985: 561)

As we have stated previously, functional heads do not have θ-grids, while lexical heads do have θ-grids. Both may have Kase grids. Notice that the assumption that lexical items have Case grids is not an innovation; in fact it is implicit in most theories of lexical representation and explicit in most studies of languages with richer overt case marking than English. (In such work, what we are calling a "Case grid" is usually called a "case array".) See, for example, Ostler (1979), Levin (1983), Nash (1980), and Simpson (1984). See also Fukui (1986) for some evidence that Japanese verbs must have Case grids which are, although related, independent of their θ-grids.

A slight modification to Higginbotham's statement of the θ-Criterion gives us the appropriate Saturation Principle:

18 Specifiers and projection

(12) a. Every position in a grid is discharged.
   b. If X discharges a position in a grid of Y, then it discharges only one.

1.5 Deriving the surface order

There are several ways that we might derive the surface order of English from the D-structures which we are proposing. We suggest adopting the standard assumption that nominative and genitive Kase are assigned leftward, so one of the categories under V'/N' must move to get Kase. This property of assigning Kase leftward extends to all functional categories, and is one of the properties which distinguish functional categories from lexical ones. Under such an analysis, a movement operation parallel to that in the standard raising cases takes place in ordinary tensed sentences.[6]

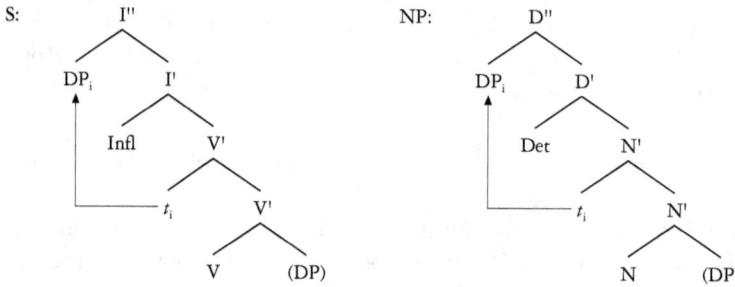

An interesting difference between S and NP is captured under this analysis: since the verb may assign structural Kase (recall that in our terms, Kase includes Case as well as F-features) to its sister the direct object, only the subject may raise to get Kase from Infl, since the movement of the object to a Kase-marked position results in a violation of (some) condition on chains which would rule out Case (and Kase) conflict (Chomsky 1986a). Nouns, on the other hand, do not assign structural Case, according to Chomsky (1986a), therefore either argument may move, and the other argument will be Kase-marked by an inserted preposition.

(13) a. [$_{DP}$ the Roman$_i$ [$_{D'}$ s' [$_{N'}$ t_i destruction of the city]]]
   b. [$_{DP}$ the city$_i$ [$_{D'}$ s' [$_{N'}$ destruction t_i of the Romans]]]

Since nouns do not assign structural Kase, any NP (in our system, these are actually DPs) may move to receive the Kase assigned by D, regardless of whether that NP (DP) is an argument of N.

(14) a. The city's destruction by the Romans
   b. The Romans' destruction of the city
   c. Yesterday's destruction of the city by Romans.[7]

Under our system, the subject of a clause is required in Spec of IP position only by the Saturation Principle. If Infl has F-features to discharge, some DP must move to the sister of I' position so that those features may be discharged. We can also explain ECM in terms of the Saturation Principle. An ECM verb has accusative Kase to discharge, so the argument of a subordinate verb which does not otherwise get Kase is moved into a position where it may get that accusative Kase. Notice that another difference between lexical and functional heads is that lexical heads may govern and Kase-mark into their complements, while a functional head may not. We speculate that this difference is attributable to the directionality of F-feature assignment: the direction of F-feature assignment (at least in English) is uniformly to the left.

Our elimination of the Extension of the Projection Principle in favour of a unified theory of F-feature assignment has a rather unexpected result: we now predict that languages which lack functional categories will lack *wh*-movement in syntax. This is because the *wh* feature is an F-feature, encoded in the grid of a functional head. In a language which does have functional heads, *wh*-movement is obligatory, because F-features must be discharged. In languages which lack functional heads, there is neither a motivation (assuming that the scope assignment of *wh* elements takes place in LF) nor a landing site for *wh*-movement in syntax. Thus, the lack of syntactic *wh*-movement in languages like Japanese can be derived from the lack of functional categories. See Fukui (1986) for details.

An alternative possibility for deriving the correct order of the subject and predicate at PF (suggested to us by Noam Chomsky, personal communication) would be to assume that there is a rule of PF which fronts the subject, and that Infl is allowed to assign Kase rightward to the subject within V'. One advantage of this approach is that Case assignment (in the standard sense) may be considered to be uniformly rightward, under government defined in terms of c-command rather than m-command (see below for definitions of these notions). Disadvantages include the following:

- We must assume an equivalent PF rule within NP, which may only apply if the Det is the genitive Kase marker.
- We must stipulate that the PF rule must apply to one and only one constituent.
- We must extrinsically order the "subject-fronting" rule to apply before *wanna*-contraction,[8] in order to block derivations such as (15).

(15) Mary might want [$_{CP}$ [$_{C'}$ [$_{IP}$ [$_{I'}$ to [$_{V'}$ Sue win]]]]] →
     *Mary might wanna Sue win.

1.6 The Spec position

In our proposal as well as in the other proposals involving some "subject raising" operation in simple transitive sentences, it seems to be the case that the position into which the subject is moved is an A'-position, with the result that all traces are A'-bound traces. We might stipulate that the Spec of I" and the Spec of D" are A-positions, since elements with argumental status may appear in these positions, but such a stipulation would obscure the fact that these positions are always empty at D-structure. In our theory, the crucial distinction is between θ-positions and non-θ-positions, and A-positions are equivalent to θ-positions.

It is not a straightforward matter to conclude that all traces are A'-bound. For one thing, movement of an NP does not show crossover effects in sentences like (16a), as contrasted with (16b), in which an operator has moved.

(16) a. John$_i$ seems to his$_i$ friends to be t_i intelligent.
　　 b. *Who$_i$ does it seem to his$_i$ friends that Sue likes t_i?

If we are right that all movement is to an A'-position, this will necessitate that we adopt a theory of chains in which the content of the head rather than the position of the head is what distinguishes different type of chains. A variable might be defined in such a theory as an element that is operator-bound (and perhaps Case-marked). Thus, the A/A' distinction would have no real content.

The result that all movement is to an A'-position is complemented by several recent proposals. Kayne (class lectures, MIT) and Barss (1986) give evidence that the content of the head of the chain rather than the position of the head is the relevant factor in defining empty categories. Also, Saxon (1986) and Bergvall (1987) argue that some languages have a base-generated reflexive empty category, i.e., a +anaphoric empty category which is distinct from NP-trace. Saxon investigates the consequences of the existence of this element, proposing that traces are contextually defined while other empty elements possess inherent features. In her system, as in ours, it seems to be the case that the only property distinguishing *wh*-trace from NP-trace is the content of their antecedent.

We may ask at this point why it should be the case that the functional categories have one and only one Spec position. Why not two, five, any odd number etc.? While our answer to this question at this point can be little more than speculation, we can make some observations. As we pointed out above, the only elements which seem to appear in the unique Spec position of a functional category are elements which have moved into the position at S-structure. This suggests that the landing site might actually be an adjunction site, and the fact that a barrier is formed when an element moves to receive F-features may be a subcase of the more general constraint on non-structure-preserving movement known as the Freezing Principle, which states (at this point in our theoretical knowledge, stipulates) that when one element is adjoined to another, the structure is "frozen", i.e., no further movement may take place out of it. The view that all movements are adjunctions has a vast number of consequences which we are not prepared to address at this point,[9] so, for the moment, we will refer to the Spec of a functional category as a position which is optionally present, and leave open the question of how exactly to distinguish adjunction from substitution to an optional position. The core of our proposal is that positions at D-structure must be licensed by independent principles of Universal Grammar; no positions are licensed by well-formedness conditions on phrase markers.

In part, the ultimate answer to the question of why there can be one and only one Spec for functional categories may parallel Chomsky's (1986a) answer to a similar question about bounding nodes for subjacency: if we assume that Universal Grammar contains no counting mechanisms, then we might expect that the functional categories, whose purpose, intuitively, is to connect parts of the sentence,[10] would appear in construction with only two constituents of the sentence in any given structure, hence its unique Spec (and unique complement).

2 Some consequences of the proposal

In the theory that we are proposing, A-positions are equivalent to θ-positions, and all θ-positions appear at D-structure inside of X'.[11] Consequently, the position of Spec of IP is a θ', and hence an A', position. We believe that there is evidence that this is correct, as we will outline below.

Furthermore, projection from X' to X'' is licensed only if Kase is discharged to the Spec of X'. Hence, the projection of a functional category is X'' iff an element in its Spec receives Kase. One result of this is that the only "truly empty" positions at D-structure are those licensed by Kase principles.[12] In fact, the Spec of a functional category is always empty at D-structure. We take this to be due to the fact that assignment of Kase takes place at S-structure, while θ-assignment takes place at D-structure.

We will adopt the definitions of basic configurational relations given in Chomsky (1986a). These definitions, coupled with our proposed system of projection, yield various interesting results.

C-Command
A *c-commands* B iff A does not dominate B and every G that dominates A dominates B.
M-Command
A *m-commands* B iff A does not dominate B and every G, G a maximal projection, that dominates A dominates B.
Dominance
A is *dominated* by G only if it is dominated by every segment of G.

Government
A *governs* B iff A m-commands B and every barrier[13] for B dominates A.[14]
(cf. Chomsky 1986a: 8)

2.1 θ-marking is simplified

Among other results, we may now simplify the definitions of θ-marking and sisterhood. θ-marking takes place only within the projection of a lexical head. We retain the definition of direct θ-marking from Chomsky (1986a), and define sisterhood in the most restricted sense, in terms of mutual c-command.

A directly θ-marks B only if A and B are sisters.

Under our system, L-marking is equivalent to direct θ-marking. Functional heads do not have θ-grids, therefore they do not θ-mark their sisters.[15] Indirect θ-marking is defined as:

A indirectly θ-marks B only if B is a sister of A'.

Under earlier conceptions of the position of the subject argument, it has not been clear how the verb assigns a θ-role to the subject. If the subject is generated under a projection of the verb, there is no longer any need to posit some method of composite θ-role assignment for an argument external to the verbal projection. We may interpret the suggestion of Williams (1981) and others that the θ-grid of a lexical category includes some inherent distinction among the arguments as meaning that one argument is marked as discharging the final or outermost θ-role in the grid. The discharge of θ-roles is sequential, beginning with the sister of X^0 and working outward. That is, θ-role assignment takes place "from the bottom up", and does not skip over non-θ-marked positions to assign a θ-role to a higher position. We will continue to refer to the subject θ-role as the "external" one, on the assumption that we may interpret "external" as meaning "outermost".

2.2 PRO and passive

In our system, PRO may be in a position within X'. We may express this possibility in one of two ways. We might elevate Chomsky's (1986a: 8) observation that "it seems that for binding theory, [the relevant requirement] should be taken to be any branching category, along the lines of Reinhart (1976)" to the status of an axiom of the theory. The PRO Theorem, which requires PRO to be ungoverned, is a theorem derived from the binding theory, therefore we can expect the definition of government used in the statement of the PRO Theorem to use the structural relation appropriate for binding theory. If PRO is a sister of V', it is not strictly c-commanded by the verb, therefore it would be ungoverned in the relevant sense.[16]

Another possible approach is based on the definition of "dominates" given above. If all projections of a lexical category are X', then the node dominating the verb and its complement is identical to the next projection up. In other words, in (17), V' [1] and V' [2] are segments of the same category.

(17)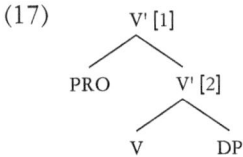

Since PRO is not dominated by all segments of V', it is not actually dominated by a maximal projection of V'. Therefore, there is a maximal projection that dominates V but not PRO, namely V'. Hence, V does not even m-command and consequently does not govern PRO.

The proposal that PRO is within the projection of a lexical category has various consequences. Among these is the fact that we now may make overt the representation of those "implicit arguments" which behave as though they were syntactically present. Consider in particular the passive. Under previous frameworks, if the passive morphology absorbed accusative Kase, it was necessary to assume that it also (mysteriously) absorbed the subject θ-role, so that the subject position could be an available landing site for NP movement. Under our proposal, this is not necessary; the passive morphology absorbs accusative Kase, but it does not absorb the subject θ-role. Thus, there must be a position to which the subject θ-role is assigned. PRO appears in that position, receiving the external (subject) θ-role from the verb. This PRO is what has been called the "implicit argument". PRO remains in its D-structure position in a passive and the object moves to be assigned Kase by Infl, yielding the following structure:

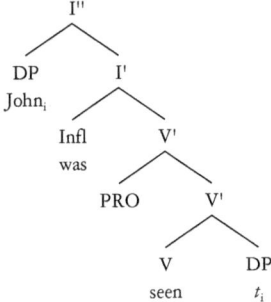

PRO in this structure is ungoverned by the verb, as explained above. PRO is not governed by Infl, since, following Chomsky (1986a), only lexical categories can govern across maximal projections. The status of implicit arguments is now no longer a mystery; they are overtly represented under the projection of a lexical category.

One interesting result of this approach to implicit arguments[17] is that we now predict in structural terms the fact, pointed out by Williams (1985), that the implicit argument in a passive is obligatorily disjoint from the overt argument. Coindexing the object with PRO in the structure above would result in a strong crossover violation, since the specifier of IP is an A' position. Williams uses the obligatory disjointness of implicit arguments as evidence that binding theory must refer only to θ-structure and not to syntactic configuration, but, under our analysis, binding theory may be formulated in purely structural terms.

One might suspect that the postulation of PRO inside V' would result in a violation of the Specified Subject Condition (SSC), with PRO failing to bind the trace of *John*, under the assumption that this trace is an anaphor. This is not the case, however. First, recall that we have maintained in section 1 that it is not entirely clear that the trace of *John* is an anaphor in the standard sense, and therefore we do not necessarily expect this trace to be subject to Principle A of the Binding Theory. In our system, movement to the Spec of IP could be regarded as a movement to an A' position, or, more precisely put, the status of the trace cannot be characterized solely in terms of the landing site of the antecedent. Secondly, even if the trace does turn out to be an anaphor, a violation of the SSC would not arise on the rather reasonable assumption that the Binding Theory (at least, Principle A), being a theory of syntax (rather than LF), refers to X". That is, we may assume that only X" can be a potential binding domain with respect to the Binding Theory, and therefore, V' cannot even constitute a binding domain for the trace of *John*. This is a natural extension of our approach to the notion of "barrier" as defined in section 3.

2.3 Wanna-*contraction*

Notice further that the availability of a position within a lexical projection for PRO gives us a simple explanation for the phenomenon of "*wanna*-contraction". Instead of having to stipulate that *wh*-t is visible at PF and PRO is not,[18] or that PRO can be to the right of I',[19] we can simply say that *want* + *to* contract only if they are adjacent.[20]

(18) a. Who do you want [$_{IP}$ *t* to [$_{V'}$ *t* visit Bill]] (no contraction)
 b. Who do you want [$_{I'}$ to PRO visit *t*]   (contraction OK)

In the case where contraction is possible, no empty categories intervene between *want* and *to*, while in the cases where contraction is blocked, there is a *wh*-trace intervening.[21] Hence, we can say that any intervening terminal element blocks contraction, and that all phonetically null categories are equally visible at PF.

2.4 Adverbs as Spec of N'

If PRO is within X', then we can also correctly predict the following contrast. (See Yamada 1983 and Chomsky 1986b, for arguments that PRO should be optionally present within a noun phrase in order to account for various binding facts. Cf. also Williams 1985 for some counterarguments.)

(19) a. The men read the stories about them.
b. The men read the stories about each other.
c. The men read Mary's stories about them.
d. *The men read Mary's stories about each other.
e. (?)The men read yesterday's stories about each other.

If we assume that the noun *stories* has one and only one θ-role (specifically, the external-θ role) to assign, then (19d) cannot contain a PRO within the N', while (19b) and (19e) may contain PRO.

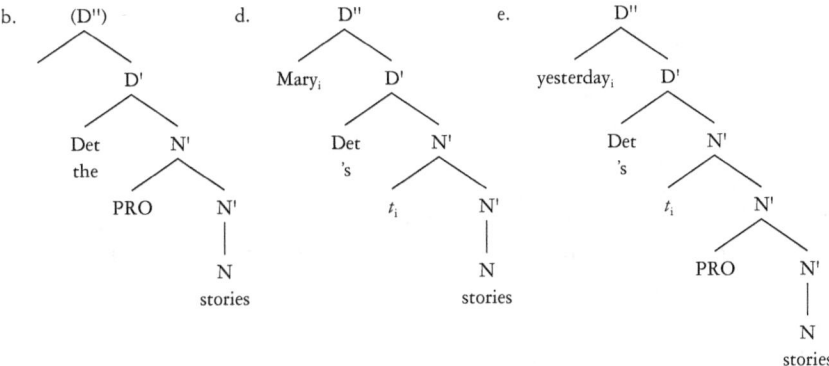

The reason that (19d) is ungrammatical is that, as shown above, since *stories* has only one external θ-role to assign, and that θ-role has been assigned to *Mary*, there can be no PRO within N'. Therefore, there is no antecedent for the anaphor within the DP.[22]

2.5 Small clauses

It may be possible within our system to give an account of small clauses as maximal projections of X', as shown in (20).

(20)

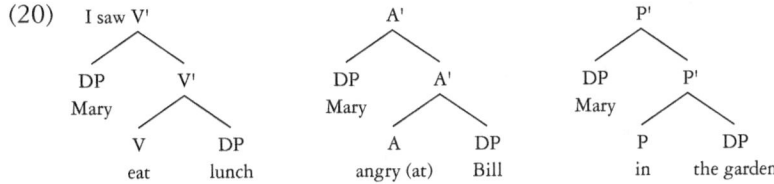

26 Specifiers and projection

This analysis is not completely straightforward. For one thing, small clauses involving predicate nominals apparently cannot be considered projections of X′ (this was pointed out to us by Ken Hale).

(21) a. I made Mary the chief.
     b. I consider Mary our best student.
     c. We appointed John Mary's assistant.

If these examples are fully grammatical, then this constitutes evidence that both the subject and the predicate in a small clause are some sort of maximal projection.

A further issue which must be ironed out is that, in the case of a verbal small clause, we must distinguish two different projections of V′:

(22)
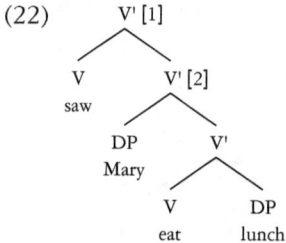

If small clauses are to be a maximal projection of X′, then we must be sure that our definition of "maximal projection" can distinguish between V′ [1] and V′ [2] above.

3 Long-distance movement and barriers

The view of phrase structure which we are proposing allows us to suggest a revision to Chomsky's (1986a) definition of "barrier" which we believe to have various advantages over the original version.

As outlined in the sections above, we suggest that syntactic positions must be licensed by some independent module of the Grammar; no positions are licensed by well-formedness conditions on phrase markers. Double-bar level projections are created only when some element moves into a position to which Kase is discharged. We have proposed the following general principle:

(25) *The Saturation Principle*
     a. Every grid position is discharged.
     b. If X discharges a grid position in Y, then it discharges only one.

As a direct consequence of the Saturation Principle and the hypothesis that no positions in syntactic structure are licensed by well-formedness conditions on phrase-markers, we have the following condition on the projection of functional categories:

(24) *Functional Projection Theorem*
A functional head projects to the X″ level iff there is Kase to be discharged to its Spec position. Otherwise, it projects only to X′.

In our theory, the Spec position exists only if some Kase features are discharged onto an element in that position. As we will show below, the Functional Projection Theorem leads to a reformulation of the definition of "barrier" which avoids the stipulation that IP does not count as a barrier (or "Blocking Category", to be precise; see below).

The crucial assumptions of our theory which bear on the definition of barrierhood are these:

1 Only X″ can be a blocking category.
2 Lexical heads project only to X′.
3 Functional heads project to X″ iff some Kase must be discharged to an element in their Spec position. Otherwise they project only to X′ (Functional Projection Theorem).

Chomsky (1986a) proposes the following definition of a barrier:

α is a Blocking Category (BC) for β iff α is not L-marked and α dominates β.
α is a barrier for β iff (i) or (ii):

(i) α immediately dominates γ, γ a BC for β
(ii) α is a BC for β, α not equal to IP.

(Chomsky 1986a: 14)

L-marking is defined as direct θ-marking by a lexical head. We suggest revising the definition of "barrier" along the following lines:

(25) 1. α is a *BC* for β iff

   (i) α dominates β
   (ii) $\alpha = X''$
   (iii) α is not L-marked and
   (iv) α does not m-command the antecedent of β

2. α is a *barrier* for β iff (i) or (ii)

   (i) α is a BC for β
   (ii) α immediately dominates a BC for β.

We adopt the definitions of m-command, c-command, and dominance given by Chomsky, which we outlined in section 2.

In our model, there is a distinction between "maximal" projection of G in the sense of the highest occurring token of G, and "maximal" in the sense of XP (X″). Our proposal therefore predicts that different principles and rules of the Grammar might refer to different types of maximality. Henceforth, when we mean to refer to X″, we will refer to X″, and we define "maximal projection" as follows:

α^n is the *maximal projection* of α iff it is immediately dominated by β^m, where $\alpha \neq \beta$.[23]

We will show how these definitions work with some simple cases, and then go on to discuss the advantages that we believe they have over the original definition. For ease of exposition, we will show only the relevant bracketing, and we will also omit the traces of moved elements other than the ones under discussion.

(26) $[_{C″}$ Who$_i$ $[_{C′}$ does $[_{I″}$ Mary $[_{I′}$ $[_{V′}$ believe $[_{I″}$ $t′_i$ $[_{I′}$ to be $[_{A′}$ t_i intelligent[24]

(27) $[_{I″}$ Mary$_i$ $[_{I′}$ $[_{V′}$ seems $[_{I′}$ to be considered $[_{I′}$ to be $[_{A′}$ t_i intelligent.

In (26), *who* originates under A′, and moves to the Spec of I″ in order to be assigned Kase by the verb *believe*. Because Kase is assigned to this Spec, there is an I″ node dominating the trace and I′, by the Functional Projection Theorem. This I″ is not a BC for t_i because it is L-marked by the verb *believe* (see (25iii) above). From this position, *who* moves directly to its S-structure position, where it is assigned the *wh*-F-feature by the head Comp. The only X″ crossed in this step is the I″ which dominates *Mary* and I′. This node is not a BC for t_i because it m-commands *who*, the antecedent of t_i (see (25iv) above).

In the raising case, (27), no barriers are crossed at all. Since the passive morphology has absorbed the Case features of the verb *consider*, no Spec position is licensed for its complement, therefore its complement is I′ and not I″. Thus, there is no X″, a potential candidate for a BC, between t_i and its antecedent *Mary*.

Let us now compare these cases with similar ones which are not grammatical.

(28) *$[_{C″}$ Who$_i$ $[_{C′}$ does $[_{I″}$ Mary $[_{I′}$ $[_{V′}$ wonder $[_{C″}$ why $[_{C′}$ $[_{I″}$ $t′_i$ $[_{I′}$ is $[_{A′}$ t_i intelligent?

(29) *$[_{I″}$ Mary$_i$ $[_{I′}$ $[_{V′}$ seems $[_{I″}$ it $[_{I′}$ is $[_{V′}$ considered $[_{I′}$ $t′_i$ to be $[_{A′}$ t_i intelligent.

These differ minimally from the ones above, in that there is an intervening barrier, by the definition (25) given above. In (28), the complement of *wonder* is C″, projected from C′ because of the presence of the *wh*-word *why*.[25] Here, two X″s intervene between the trace within I″ and its antecedent *who* (namely, I″ and C″). Although it may be that *wonder* L-marks its complement (C″), inheritance of barrierhood from I″, which is not L-marked, would override the L-marking exception (cf. (25ii)).

As for (29), *seems* does not L-mark its complement (see Chomsky 1986a). Thus, the I″ immediately dominating *it* and I′ is a BC and hence a barrier for t_i, as this I″ also does not m-command the antecedent of t_i.

It is clear that clause (iv) of our definition of barrier, i.e., the exception for nodes which m-command the trace's antecedent, is the part of our definition which allows successive cyclic movement. Since Comp is the only functional category which takes a functional category as its complement,[26] the configuration in which an XP m-commands the antecedent of a trace within it will arise only when the antecedent is in the Spec of Comp. Thus, clause (iv) of our definition is our suggestion for formalizing the fact noticed by Bresnan (1972) that Comp functions as an "escape hatch" for movement.

We are maintaining the idea that barrierhood should be inherited, but it is not entirely clear whether this gives the right results. In our system, since V′ is never a barrier, the only configuration in which barrierhood may be inherited is the configuration in which I″ m-commands the Spec of C″. Since this is suspiciously close to the configuration in our clause (iv) of the definition of barrier, it seems that more research is needed to find the correct generalization.

3.1 Long-distance raising and passive v. wh-*movement*

As long as no Case (Kase) or θ-violation results, long-distance raising and passive are possible, by extension of the above structures. In previous accounts, these were distinguished from long-distance *wh*-movement by the fact that NP movement involved movement into an A-position, while *wh*-movement involved movement to an A′-position. In our system, it is not clear that this distinction is available, as discussed in section 1.[27] How, then, are we to distinguish between long-distance raising and passive from *wh*-movement? The crucial cases are the following.

(30) a. Who did they wonder whether to consider to be intelligent?
     b. *John seems that it is considered to be intelligent.

These are the cases that lead Chomsky (1986a) to propose that we allow adjunction to VP (as a particular case of the allowable adjunction to non-arguments). For Chomsky, in sentence (30a), the *wh*-element may first adjoin to the VP node dominating *consider*. Given his definition of "dominates", the node adjoined to and the node created by adjunction are segments of the same category, therefore the adjoined element is not "dominated" by VP, so VP is not a barrier for it. This adjunction to VP is licit in (30a), because the trace at the adjunction site is A′-bound, and properly governed by its antecedent. In (30b), however, no such adjunction is possible, because the head of the chain is in an A-position. Adjunction to VP in (30b) would result in a violation of general principles forbidding movement from an A'-position to an A-position (cf. Chomsky 1986b). In the system that we are proposing, there is no movement to an A-position; indeed, there are no base-generated empty A-positions. So far, nothing in our system rules out adjunction to X'. If the adjunction analysis turns out to be correct, we might explain it in terms of the iterability of X' in general, rather than by stipulating, as does Chomsky (1986a), that adjunction is permitted to non-arguments. However, we think that our system captures the facts without the option of such non-structure-preserving syntactic movement.

(31) a. [$_{C''}$ Who$_i$ [$_{C'}$ did [$_{I''}$ they [$_{I'}$ Infl [$_{V'}$ wonder [$_{C''}$ whether [$_{I'}$ to [$_{V'}$ PRO consider [$_{I''}$ t'_i [$_{I'}$ to be [$_{A'}$ t_i intelligent.
b. *John$_i$ [$_{I'}$ [$_{V'}$ seems [$_{C'}$ that [$_{I''}$ it [$_{I'}$ is [$_{V'}$ considered [$_{I'}$ to be [$_{A'}$ t_i intelligent.

In (31a), the *wh*-movement case, three X''s are crossed, but none of them are barriers:[28] the I'' complement of *consider* and the C'' complement of *wonder* are L-marked, and the highest I'' m-commands the antecedent, *who*. Contrast this situation with that in (32), where there is an I'' which counts as a barrier by (25).

(32) *[$_{C''}$ Who [$_{C'}$ did [$_{I''}$ they [$_{I'}$ Infl [$_{V'}$ wonder [$_{C''}$ whether [$_{I''}$ John [$_{I'}$ [$_{V'}$ considers [$_{I''}$ t [$_{I'}$ to be [$_{A'}$ t intelligent.

Raising verbs do not assign Kase and do not select *wh*-complements, so there is no way that a Spec position can be licensed for the complement of a raising verb. (A passive verb's Kase assigning properties have been absorbed by the passive morphology, so they also cannot license a Spec position in their complement.) Therefore, in (31b), the complement of *seems* has no Spec. The I'' dominating *it* and I' is a BC and hence a barrier, by our definition. Clause (iv) cannot apply to this example, because the absence of the Spec position for Comp rules out the possibility of an intermediate trace m-commanded by the I''. Compare (31b) with (33), in which there are no barriers:

(33) John$_i$ [$_{I'}$ [$_{V'}$ seems [$_{C'}$ [$_{I'}$ to [$_{V'}$ be considered [$_{I'}$ to be [$_{A'}$ t_i intelligent.

We notice that raising verbs differ from ECM verbs in that raising verbs do not assign any Kase, and do not L-mark their complement, while ECM verbs do assign Kase, and do L-mark their complement. Since raising verbs never assign Kase, they cannot license the Spec position of their complement. Therefore, their infinitival complement will be I', not I'', and thus not a BC, and hence not a barrier. The infinitival complement of an ECM verb will be

I″, because the verb assigns Kase to the Spec of I. This I″ will be L-marked, however, and thus not a BC, hence not a barrier, resulting in the following pair:

(34) a. Mary$_i$ seems [$_{I'}$ to be t_i intelligent.
     b. Who$_i$ does Anne believe [$_{I''}$ t_i to be t_i intelligent?

3.2 Relative clauses v. complex DPs

In our theory, the structural differences between complex DPs like (35a) and relative clauses like (35b) are minimal.

(35) a. [$_{D'}$ the [$_{N'}$ claim [$_{C'}$ that [$_{I''}$ Mary [$_{I'}$ [$_{V'}$ likes Bill]]]]]]
     b. [$_{D'}$ the [$_{N'}$ man [$_{C''}$ who$_i$ [$_{C'}$ [$_{I''}$ Mary [$_{I'}$ [$_{V'}$ likes t_i]]]]]]]

The differences which result when we attempt to extract out of each are due to the fact that the projection of Comp which appears in a relative clause is C″, while that which appears as the complement of an N like *claim, fact*, etc. is C′, since the latter includes no *wh*-feature to license the Spec position. Extraction out of (35a) yields a subjacency violation, because there is an I″ which counts as a barrier. But extraction out of (35b) is much worse; in this case, there are two barriers (C″ and I″).

(36) a. *Who do you believe the claim that Mary likes *t*
     b. **Who did you see the woman who likes *t*

We further predict a contrast between extraction out of a complex DP like (35a) and extraction out of a complex DP which has a subject.

(37) a. *Who do you believe the claim that Mary likes.
     b. **Who do you believe Susan's claim that Mary likes.[29]

In (37a), the complex DP *the claim that Mary likes t* is actually only a D′, since *the* is a non-Kase-assigning functional category, so no Spec appears as a sister to D′. In (37b), on the other hand, *Susan* has been moved to receive Kase from '*s*, so the complex DP in (37b) is D″, which is a barrier by inheritance.

3.3 Some advantages over Chomsky (1986a)

In addition to the empirical coverage outlined above, we believe our theory to have certain advantages over that of Chomsky (1986a), since it allows a simpler definition of what counts as a barrier, and it restricts the number of devices needed in the Grammar, eliminating several of those proposed by Chomsky which lack convincing motivation.

First of all, we have eliminated the need to stipulate that I″ exceptionally does not count as a barrier (cf. clause (ii) of Chomsky's definition). In our system, when I″ is L-marked or when it m-commands the antecedent, it does not count as a barrier; otherwise I″ does count as a barrier. Evidence that I″ can count as a barrier came from the ungrammatical super-raising cases, such as (31b).

Second, we have eliminated the need to incorporate feature sharing (agreement) into the definition of chain coindexing, which Chomsky finds necessary in order to explain why VP is not a barrier in simple raising cases, like (38) (Chomsky's (169)).

(38) John$_i$ [seem$_V$ -I] [$_{VP}$ t_V [$_{IP}$ t_i to be intelligent]].

For these simple cases, Chomsky claims that t_i is properly governed by t_V because the verb *seem*, which has raised to Infl, shares features, or agrees, with *John*. By coindexing the subject-Infl agreement chain with the v-to-Infl movement chain, the trace of the verb will have the features necessary to be a proper governor.

In our system, it is not necessary to coindex agreement chains with movement chains. There is no VP, only V′, which is never a barrier (cf. 25.1 (ii)), so no extra mechanism is needed for simple raising sentences.

Notice that the configuration under which chain coindexing will create a proper government environment is exactly the one stated in clause (iv) of our definition of barrier. Under Chomsky's system, coindexing between an agreement chain and a movement chain seems to be a special device needed for raising cases, but potentially available for any agreement configuration. In our system, because only functional categories can have Spec positions, clause (iv) turns out to be restricted to cases of movement to the Spec of Comp. Such a restriction yields both a way of formalizing the statement that Comp is an "escape hatch" for movement, and a way of deriving rather than stipulating that I″ does not count as a barrier in certain configurations.

The third device of Chomsky's which we have eliminated is the use of adjunction in syntax, in particular the VP-adjunction. The fact that in Chomsky's system the VP does not count as a barrier in the simple raising case suggests that Chomsky's use of VP-adjunction to distinguish long-distance raising from long-distance *wh*-movement is on the wrong track. In our system, all syntactic movements are structure-preserving.

3.4 A problem

In the system that we have proposed, we lack an explanation for why extraction out of adjunct clauses is far worse than a simple subjacency violation. There is only one barrier in (39a), so its degree of ungrammaticality should be about equal to that of (39b).

(39) a. Who did you leave before John met *t*
     b. Who do you believe the claim that John met *t*

(40) a. Who did you [$_{V'}$ [$_{V'}$ leave [$_{C'}$ before [$_{I''}$ John [$_{I'}$[$_{V'}$ met *t*]]]]]]
     b. Who do you [$_{V'}$ believe [$_{D'}$ the [$_{N'}$ claim [$_{C'}$ that [$_{I''}$ John [$_{I'}$ [$_{V'}$ met *t*]]]]]]

Judgments vary on (39a). D. Feldman (personal communication), for example, suggested that something is wrong with the focus relations in this example, pointing out that given a more plausible context, the sentence does improve, possibly to the level of (39b):

(41) Who did you blush after John kissed?

However, if examples like (39a) are really worse than (39b), we need an explanation. We need to do more research on the status of adjoined modifiers in our system in order to come up with a satisfactory account of these cases.

4 The role of the X′ schema in restricting projection

If the phrase structures which we have proposed in this paper conform to some version of X′ theory, it is a quite different version from the version which is generally assumed. In this section, we will discuss the role, if any, of the X′ schema in restricting phrase markers at D-structure.

Pullum (1985), pointing out that the correctness of the restrictions which the X′ schema is supposed to encode has not been very thoroughly investigated, expresses the claims made by X′ theory as follows:

Lexicality: Every nonterminal is a projection of some lexical[30] category.
Succession: The bar level of a head is one less than the bar level of its mother.
Uniformity: The maximum permitted bar level is the same for every lexical category.
Maximality: Non-heads in a rule are either maximal projections or minor lexical categories.[31]
Centrality: The initial symbol is the maximal projection of some (lexical) category.
Optionality: Every non-head daughter in a rule is optional.

We have suggested a theory in which succession and uniformity do not hold. It should be pointed out that we are not the first to suggest that these two conditions do not hold. Pullum (1985) argues against succession, concluding that the correct condition is one which says that the bar value of a head is the same as that of its mother unless a rule or constraint determines otherwise. Fabb (1984) and Travis (1984) both argue that there is no distinction among intermediate nodes in a projection. We have proposed that, in lexical categories, the only bar level distinction is between the head and all projections, while, in functional categories, succession is related to the discharge of Kase features. We believe that this system captures the insights of Pullum as well as those of Fabb and Travis.

It has never been clear that uniformity captured a correct generalization. Those who have argued against uniformity include George (1980), di Sciullo (1980), Williams (1981), Muysken (1982), Stuurman (1985), and Emonds (1985). If one adopts the assumptions of Travis and Fabb, then the uniformity condition becomes trivial, simply stating that a maximal projection is a maximal projection (distinguished by definition from an intermediate projection). We have disputed the hypothesis that all maximal projections are identical with respect to the number of bars, suggesting instead that functional categories which are closed off by a specifier are structurally different from the maximal projection of a lexical category.

What remains, then, of X′ theory within our system? We are working within a theory in which D-structures are projected from lexical items, so we would retain a form of lexicality, in which every nonterminal is a projection of a lexical or functional category. However, notice that the condition that all structure is projected from lexical items is a definitional condition on D-structures, and not a well-formedness condition. Lexicality is simply another way of stating the Projection Principle, which is independently needed to constrain the relations among various levels of syntax.

Under the definition which we have given for "maximal projection", the maximality condition on structures is analytic, since we are defining maximal projections relative to an existing structure. Therefore, maximality cannot be considered to be a well-formedness condition on phrase markers.

Centrality follows trivially from lexicality, except perhaps in the case of the S node. We are assuming that lexicality holds of all categories, so in a sense we are adopting the centrality condition, but only as a subpart of lexicality, which, as we pointed out above, is a definitional condition on D-structures, not a well-formedness condition.

As for optionality, such a condition is also definitional, since in the theory within which we are working (GB), every element in a structure must be independently licensed in order to appear. Otherwise, it will not appear.

We may summarize our position by saying that what remains of X′ theory in our system is some statement that projection from the lexicon into D-structure involves the formation of constituent structures which are labelled by feature percolation from lexical items. No well-formedness conditions on phrase markers beyond this very general statement are included in the Grammar.

Speas (1984, 1986) argues that even the percolation of features follows automatically from the formal properties of the representation of the lexical item. She points out that, within many theories of the relationship between the lexicon and syntax, there is an overlap between headedness and possession of an unsaturated θ-grid. She goes on to suggest that, at least from the simplest examples, we can define head as follows:

(42) X is the *head* of Y in the configuration

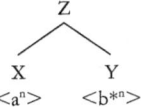

A similar proposal is made by Flynn (1983), who proposes, within the framework of Montague Grammar, that the building of a constituent from a head plus its complement can be viewed as a simple arithmetic cancellation operation, so that the label on the dominating node necessarily "percolates" from the item whose lexical representation includes terms other than its own category label. Informally, we can say that if the lexical representation of some lexical item, for example, a verb, includes the information that that verb requires a particular complement in order to be complete, or saturated, in our terminology, then adding that complement yields a (partially) saturated verb. The nature of the lexical representation dictates the label on the node dominating a head and its complement, without stipulation.

If some way of building constituents along these lines turns out to be correct, then even the residue of X' theory which remains in the system we have proposed in this paper may be dispensed with.

5 Projection typology

Since we are claiming that only functional categories project to X'', one obvious prediction of our proposal is that, in languages which lack functional categories, all constituents will behave like X'. According to Fukui (1986), Japanese lacks functional categories. As predicted, Japanese constituents never seem to behave as X''.

Some of the evidence that Japanese X^{max} is X' was given in section 1, where we showed that *-ga* and *-no* marked NPs may iterate in sentences and N^{max}, respectively. Another piece of evidence comes from extraction facts, in particular, from the fact that Japanese does not exhibit island effects for syntactic movement (see Fukui 1986 for details). This is exactly what we expect if the notion of barrier for syntactic movement is defined on the basis of the X'' status of a category and Japanese does not have X''s as English does.

A third piece of evidence is found in the facts of Japanese long-distance binding. This evidence requires that we make the assumption that the binding domain for Principle A of the Binding Theory is universally stated in terms of syntactic X''.

36 Specifiers and projection

Principle A: an anaphor must be bound in its minimal X".

If this assumption is right, then we predict that languages which lack functional categories will have long-distance anaphor of the sort exemplified by Japanese *zibun*, because these languages will not have any X" categories. The minimal domain in such a language would always be the entire sentence.[32]

So far, we have been referring to "languages which lack functional categories", but there is no a priori reason that a language must have all or none of the functional categories. Japanese and English seem to represent the extremes in this regard. It should also be pointed out that while we have related the surface word order in English to an interaction between Case (Kase, in our terms) theory and the presence of functional categories, the two modules are probably distinct. We would expect, then, to find languages which have functional categories, but which realize Case (and perhaps also F-features) by means of overt case markers. The surface effect of such a system would be that any constituent could move into the position of Spec of the functional category. While this speculation is vastly oversimplified, the system we have proposed may lead to a new analysis of general Aux-second phenomena.

6 Conclusion

We have proposed a theory of projection in which the presence of a position which closes off a category syntactically is directly related to the existence of a functional head. The property of a functional head which allows a specifier position to be licensed follows from a principled extension of the θ-Criterion, namely, our Saturation Principle.

Our proposal is intended to further the transition from rules to principles in the Grammar, in particular, to eliminate the residue of Phrase Structure rules which remained in Stowell's (1981b) X′ schema. We have rejected the uniform bar level hypothesis and have outlined a theory in which those elements in a constituent which are neither heads nor complements are not cross-categorially uniform. It should be emphasized that, by rejecting these aspects of X′ theory, we are not sacrificing the ability to express the cross-categorial generalizations which were the original motivation for the X′ theory. In fact, we are moving closer to capturing the true nature of what is general about the structure of syntactic categories. Two core aspects of X′ theory remain in our proposal. First and foremost, we retain a conception of syntactic structure as projected from lexical items; thus, the arbitrary structures like those in (43) which were in principle generable by Phrase Structure rules cannot arise.

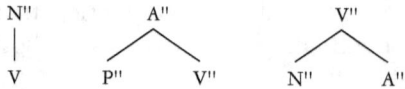

Second, we take the head-complement relation and the modifier-modifiee relation to hold within any category. Since θ-role assignment must take place under sisterhood, and modifiers may iterate, the internal structure of the categories turns out to be quite similar.

Our reinterpretation of the nature of projection has various consequences. First, it allows us to express several generalizations which were not previously expressible. Further, it allows us a vocabulary in which the definition of which nodes constitute barriers to local and long-distance dependencies may be simplified. In addition, it reduces the principles licensing empty positions at D-structure to a minimum.

2 LF extraction of *naze*
Some theoretical implications

1 Introduction

This paper investigates various facts, all of which are related to *Logical Form* (LF) extraction of *naze* "why" in Japanese. The *wh*-phrase *naze* has been assumed to be a typical adjunct *wh*-element in Japanese, i.e., the counterpart of English *why*, and consequently, its behaviour with respect to the *Empty Category Principle* (ECP) has been examined in the literature (cf. in particular, Lasnik and Saito 1984).

In what follows, I will present various new facts concerning LF extraction of *naze*, all of which point to the same conclusion – that the notion of *barrier* relevant to antecedent-government in particular, and to antecedent-trace relations in general, must be defined in terms of L-marking rather than in terms of category types such as NP, S', etc. This argument provides new empirical evidence for Chomsky's (1986a) approach to the proper characterization of the concept of barriers in syntax (narrowly understood) and LF. Furthermore, I will argue that the facts presented in this paper cast doubt on the standard characterization of Japanese *naze* as a well-behaved adjunct with respect to the ECP, and lead us to the rather surprising conclusion that Japanese lacks true adjuncts in the sense relevant to the ECP.

The organization of the paper is as follows. Section 2 introduces very briefly the relevant part of Chomsky's (1986a) barriers theory. In section 3, I will present a set of Japanese data concerning LF extraction of *naze*. Section 4 shows how the data presented in section 3 can be handled naturally within Chomsky's (1986a) framework, in which the relevant notion of barriers is defined in terms of L-marking. Section 5 investigates theoretical implications of the facts about *naze* extraction for linguistic theory, particularly for the theory of subjacency/ECP and the typology of English and Japanese.

2 Barriers

I will very briefly summarize in this section the relevant part of the barriers theory developed by Chomsky (1986a). Chomsky's theory of barriers has a much broader perspective than the present paper, including e.g., the nature of parasitic gaps and thus contains various technical details beyond the scope of this paper. I will introduce only a small part of the entire barriers theory developed by Chomsky (1986a), putting many potentially relevant technical problems aside. The reader is referred to Chomsky's original work for fuller exposition.

The basic idea behind the barriers theory is that essentially the same concept of barriers constrains both movement and (antecedent-) government, and that any maximal projection, irrespective of its category type, can be a potential barrier. Furthermore, a potential barrier may be exempted from barrierhood if it is L-marked by a lexical head:[1]

(1) α L-*marks* β if β is a complement of α, and α is lexical.

Before defining the notion of barrier in terms of L-marking, however, it is appropriate at this point to make it clear that L-marking as construed in (1) above is different from the widely-used notion of lexical government, which is defined as follows.

(2) α *lexically governs* β iff α governs[2] β and α is lexical.

L-marking and lexical government are closely related, but they are nevertheless two distinct notions. In fact, as can easily be seen from statements (1) and (2), L-marking is a narrower notion than lexical government, since complementhood always requires government by the head, but the converse is not always true. Thus, for example, the specifier position is lexically governed by a head (if the head is lexical), but it is not L-marked by the head, because the specifier, by definition, is not a complement, as illustrated by the following schematic representation.

(3) 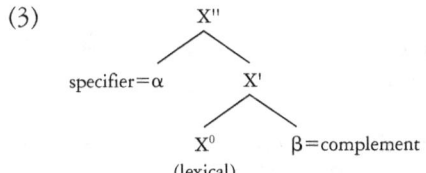   α: lexically governed (but not L-marked) by X^0
   β: lexically governed and L-marked by X^0

Given the notion of L-marking, we may now turn to the definition of barrier. Barrier is defined in two steps: We first define *Blocking Category* (BC) as in (4) and then define barrier in terms of BC as in (5).

(4) γ is a *Blocking Category* for β iff γ is not L-marked and γ dominates β.

(5) γ is a *barrier* for β iff (a) or (b):
   a. γ immediately dominates δ, δ a BC for β; or
   b. γ is a BC for β, γ ≠ IP

(Chomsky 1986a: 14)

We understand γ in these definitions to be a maximal projection. Also "immediately dominates" in (5) is restricted to a relation between maximal projections, so that γ immediately dominates δ even if a nonmaximal projection intervenes between them. Condition (5a) is a case of *inheritance*, i.e., the category γ inherits barrierhood from a BC that it immediately dominates; in case (5b), γ is a barrier intrinsically, being a BC in itself.

Extending the analysis put forth in Huang (1982) and Pesetsky (1982b), Chomsky (1986a) proposes that the scope of X' theory be extended to all categories, including the nonlexical categories C(omp) and I(nfl), which have hitherto been more or less exceptions to the general X' schema (Chomsky 1981a). Thus, the basic clausal structure (for English) should look like the following, where XP stands for X" (e.g., CP = C", IP = I", etc.).

(6) [$_{CP}$ Spec [$_{C'}$ C [$_{IP}$ Spec [$_{I'}$ I [VP . . .]]]]]

Under this conception of phrase structure, the traditional categories S' and S are regarded as the maximal projections of C and I, respectively. Thus, the symbol IP used in (5b) above, for example, corresponds to S. Chomsky further proposes that a *wh*-element is moved into the specifier of CP position, rather than into the C (complementizer) position as has been widely assumed in the literature.

In the following discussion, I will essentially adopt these proposals, though I will rather freely use the traditional symbols S' and S when their exact categorial status and internal (X' theoretic) structures are not directly relevant to our present concern.

We now define government, including antecedent-government (Chomsky 1986a), in the following way.

(7) α *governs* β if α m-commands β and there is no γ, γ a barrier for β, such that γ excludes[3] α. (Chomsky 1986a: 9)

(8) α *m-commands* β iff α does not dominate β and every γ, γ a maximal projection, that dominates α dominates β. (cf. Chomsky 1986a: 8)

Notice that Chomsky's (1986a) intention was to unify subjacency (Bounding Theory) and government, including antecedent-government. That is, the same notion of barrier as defined in (5) above plays a role in the proper characterization of the locality requirement for movement and government. We can formulate this idea in a natural way as follows, using the notion of barrier defined in (5) (Chomsky 1986a: 30). We first define *n*-subjacency.

(9) β is *n*-subjacent to α iff there are fewer than $n+1$ barriers for β that exclude α.

Then, the relevant locality requirement for movement and government (antecedent-government) can be expressed in a general way as follows:

(10) If (α_i, α_{i+1}) is a link of a chain, then α_{i+1} is m-subjacent to α_i.
   a. subjacency (movement): $m = 1$,
   b. antecedent-government: $m = 0$.

Note incidentally that condition (10) clearly captures the generalization that the same notion of barrier is involved both in subjacency and antecedent-government, the only difference being that the latter imposes a stricter requirement (0-subjacency) than the former (1-subjacency). This fact makes Chomsky's (1986a) theory conceptually more attractive than earlier theories of antecedent-government in which the barriers relevant to antecedent-government and to movement (subjacency) are unrelated. We will see in what follows that Chomsky's (1986a) approach is not only conceptually attractive, but also is empirically supported by data from Japanese *naze* extraction.

3 The relevant data

3.1 Nonbridge verb cases

Let us first consider the nonbridge verb cases. Stowell (1981a, b) claims that *bridge* verbs such as *say, think, believe*, etc. and *nonbridge* verbs such as *whine, whisper, murmur*, etc., are different in that the former class of verbs lexically governs the Comp position of their clausal complements (and hence the clausal complements themselves), whereas the latter class of verbs does not. Thus, according to Stowell, the following contrast with respect to the possibility of an empty complementizer can be accounted for in terms of the ECP.

(11) a. Bill says [$_{S'}$ [$_{COMP}$ e][$_S$ Mary likes John]].
   b. *Bill whined [$_{S'}$ [$_{COMP}$ e][$_S$ Mary likes John]].

   (Stowell 1981a: 350)

In (11a), the empty complementizer is lexically governed by the higher verb *says*; thus the structure satisfies the ECP. In (11b), the empty complementizer is not lexically governed because the higher verb is a nonbridge verb; thus the structure is ruled out by the ECP. (See Stowell 1981a for details.)

In our terms, Stowell's observation can be interpreted as follows. Bridge verbs take clauses as their complements. Thus, they L-mark and lexically govern their clausal complement; they also lexically govern (but do not L-mark) the head of the clausal complement, namely Comp.[4] Nonbridge verbs, on the other hand, do not take the associated clauses as their complements; these clauses are a kind of adjunct of the nonbridge verbs. Therefore, nonbridge verbs neither L-mark nor lexically govern the associated clauses.[5]

A somewhat similar contrast between bridge and nonbridge verbs can be observed in the case of antecedent-government. Consider the following examples, in which extraction of adjuncts out of the clausal complements of nonbridge verbs takes place in LF.

(12) a.   ??Bill-wa [$_{S'}$ John-ga   naze kubi-ni natta tte]   sasayaita   no?
           -TOP   -NOM why was fired   COMP whispered Q

"Why did Bill whisper that John was fired *t*?"

b.   ??Bill-wa [$_{S'}$ John-ga naze kubi-ni natta tte] tubuyaita no?
                                                        murmured Q

"Why did Bill murmur that John was fired *t*?"

With nonbridge verbs such as *sasayaita* "whispered" and *tubuyaita* "murmured", in place of a bridge verb *itta* "said", the acceptability of the sentence is considerably decreased. Thus, just as in the English counterparts, the sentences in (12) are significantly worse than (13).

(13)   Bill-wa [$_{S'}$ John-ga   naze kubi-ni natta tte]   itta no?
       -TOP   -NOM why was fired   -COMP said Q

"Why did Bill say that John was fired *t*?"

(Lasnik and Saito 1984: 244)

3.2 Noun-complement constructions v. relative clauses

Another set of data is concerned with noun-complement constructions such as *the fact that* ... and relative clauses such as *the man who* ... with respect to the possibility of extraction of an adjunct out of these noun phrases. Consider the following examples from Japanese.

(14) Noun-complement constructions
   a.   *?[$_{NP}$ [$_{S'}$ Taroo-ga   naze sore-o te-ni ireta] koto]-o   sonnani
                      -NOM why it-ACC obtained fact -ACC so much
        okotteru no?
        be angry Q

"Why are you so angry about the fact that Taro obtained it *t*?"
(Lasnik and Saito 1984: 244; judgment is mine)

   b.   *?Kimi-wa [$_{NP}$ [$_{S'}$ Taroo-ga girlfriend-to naze wakareta] koto]-ni
            you   -TOP   with   broke up   at
        sonnani odoroite-iru no?
              be surprised

"Why are you so surprised at the fact that Taro broke up with his girlfriend *t*?"

(15) Relative clauses
 a. *[NP [S' Taroo-ga sore-o naze watasita] otoko]-o sitte-iru no?
                                   handed   man   know

   "Why do you know the man to whom Taro handed it *t*?"

 b. *Kimi-wa [NP [S' Taroo-ga naze wakareta] onnanoko]-ni
                                       broke up girl   with
   kinoo   party-de atta-no?
   yesterday   at   met

   "Why did you meet the girl at the party yesterday whom Taro broke up with *t*?"

Judgments are subtle, but there is a clear contrast between the examples in (14) and those in (15); examples in the latter are almost unintelligible and much worse than the examples in the former, though examples of both kinds are fairly unacceptable. This contrast in acceptability between noun-complement constructions and relative clauses in regard to adjunct extraction suggests that some notion of L-marking plays a role in forming a relevant barrier to antecedent-government, since it is widely assumed that a relative clause does not involve the head-complement relation that a noun-complement construction generally involves (cf. Chomsky 1986a, among others). It is clear that in earlier theories of antecedent-government in which the relevant barrier is defined in terms of category types (NP, S'), the contrast between (14) and (15) cannot be accounted for, because noun-complement constructions and relative clauses both have the structure [NP ... [S' ...]] (English) or [NP [S' ...] ...] (Japanese), whatever the internal structure of the NP may be. Thus, it is predicted, contrary to fact, that adjunct extraction out of noun-complement constructions and out of relative clauses will produce equally bad sequences with the same grammatical status, due to the presence of the NP node.

3.3 Extraction of adjuncts out of adjunct clauses

A third piece of evidence can be obtained from the facts concerning extraction of an adjunct out of an adjunct clause. A contrast between complements and adjuncts, which is similar to the complex NP case discussed in Lasnik and Saito (1984), can also be obtained in adjunct clauses. Lasnik and Saito (1984: 267, fn. 41) observe this contrast and give the following examples:

(16) a. ?*What did you leave [before buying t]?
    b. *Why did you leave [before buying it t]?

Example (16a) shows the unacceptability of the normal subjacency violation, while (16b) is significantly worse than the normal subjacency violation and seems to be an ECP violation. The adjunct clause in (16b) is assigned the following structure by Lasnik and Saito (p. 267):

(17) [$_{PP}$ before [$_{NP}$ [$_{S'}$ [$_S$ PRO buying it t]]]]

Thus, the total ungrammaticality of (16b) is attributed to the fact that even if *why* is moved successive-cyclically, the intermediate trace in Comp of the adjunct S' is not antecedent-governed by its antecedent outside the adjunct clause, owing to the existence of the intervening NP node, which is widely assumed to be a barrier to antecedent-government. Although it is not unreasonable to assume an NP node dominating the adjunct S' in gerundive cases like (16), it seems implausible to postulate the existence of an NP node in the case of tensed adjunct clauses such as the following:

(18) I got angry [because John kicked my dog].

Since *because* generally requires *of* when it takes an NP object, if S' (or S) following it is dominated by an NP node, *of* should appear between *because* and the S' (or S). However, this is not the case as can be seen in the following example:

(19) *I got angry [because of [John kicked my dog]].

Thus, it seems reasonable to assume that when *because* takes a tensed S' (or S) as its complement, there is no NP node dominating that S' (or S).

Bearing this in mind, consider the following contrast:

(20) a. ?*What did you get angry because Mary bought t?
    b. *Why did you get angry because Mary bought it t?

The examples in (20) exhibit the same contrast we observed in (16). The unacceptability of (20a) appears to be due to a mere subjacency violation while (20b) is much worse and appears to contain an ECP violation. However, the explanation given by Lasnik and Saito for the contrast in (16) cannot apply to the one in (20), since in this case there is no NP node dominating the S' (or S) complement of *because* as we have argued above. The representation of (20b) can be one of the following.

(21) a. [$_{S'}$ why$_i$ [$_S$ did you get angry [$_{PP}$ because [$_{S'}$ t'_i [$_S$ Mary bought it t_i]]]]]
    b. [$_{S'}$ why$_i$ [$_S$ did you get angry [$_S$ t'_i because [$_S$ Mary bought it t_i]]]]

In either case, i.e., whether or not *because* is in Comp and whether or not there is a PP node, nothing would prevent the intermediate trace t'_i from being antecedent-governed by why_i, since PP is not generally assumed to be one of the potential barriers (see Lasnik and Saito 1984 for discussion). Therefore, there appears to be no straightforward way of accounting for the total ungrammaticality of (20b) within a theory in which the barriers relevant to antecedent-government are restricted to NP and S'.[6]

A similar contrast can be obtained in Japanese. Consider the following.

(22) a. Kimi-wa [$_{S'}$ [$_S$ Mary-ga   nani-o   katta] kara][7] sonnani
        you -TOP   -NOM what -ACC bought because so much
        okotteru? no
        angry   Q

   "What are you so angry because Mary bought *t*?"

   b. *?Kimi-wa [$_{S'}$ [$_S$ Mary-ga naze sore-o katta] kara] sonnani
        okotteru no?
                        why it-ACC

   "Why are you so angry because Mary bought it *t*?"

In these Japanese examples, it is clear that there is no NP node in the relevant position. First, case particles in Japanese (*-o* "ACC", *-ga* "NOM", etc.) can always be attached to NPs, but they can never be attached to the clausal complement of *kara* ("because") or to the *kara* clause as a whole.

(23) *... [Mary-ga sore-o katta kara] $\begin{Bmatrix} \text{-ga} \\ \text{-o} \end{Bmatrix}$ ...

Second, demonstratives such as *kono* "this", *ano* "that", etc. can generally be attached to any NP (or a noun), but they can never be attached to *kara* "because".

(24) *kono kara, *ano kara, etc.

These facts clearly show that *kara* "because", unlike, say, *koto* "fact", is not a nominal, and consequently that it is extremely implausible to postulate an NP node dominating the *kara* clause. Thus, these Japanese facts constitute evidence in favour of Chomsky's (1986a) approach to antecedent-government, in which any maximal projection can be a potential barrier.

3.4 Empty complementizers

A final piece of evidence in favour of the theory of antecedent-government that defines the relevant barriers in terms of L-marking has to do with a rather subtle difference with respect to the interaction between the extraction of an adjunct out of a complex NP and the possibility of an empty complementizer appearing in the complex NP.

Recall that we assume with Stowell (1981a, b) that the possibility of an empty complementizer is closely related to the existence of (in our terms) L-marking of the clause by the X^0 element to which it is a complement, i.e., in order for a complementizer to be empty, it must be the case that the clause of which it is a head is L-marked.[8]

Notice now that the nominal head *koto* "fact" in Japanese generally allows an empty complementizer in its clausal complement:

(25) [$_{NP}$ [$_{S'}$ [$_S$ Taroo-ga   sore-o   te-ni ireta] $\left\{\begin{array}{c} \text{to-yuu} \\ e \end{array}\right\}$] koto]
    -NOM   it   -ACC obtained   COMP   fact

the fact that Taro obtained it

In (25), the structure is well-formed with or without an overt complementizer *to-yuu* "that".[9] This is what we expect, since we are assuming that *koto* is a nominal head and the preceding clause is its complement. Therefore, *koto*, by definition, L-marks the preceding clause, and Stowell's theory (now reinterpreted in our terms) correctly predicts the possibility of an empty complementizer.

In contrast, there is a class of nouns in Japanese which do not allow such an empty complementizer.[10] The following is a typical example.

(26) [$_{NP}$ [$_{S'}$ [$_S$ Taroo-ga sore-o te-ni ireta] $\left\{\begin{array}{c} \text{to-yuu} \\ *e \end{array}\right\}$] uwasa]

the rumour that Taro obtained it

If our discussion so far is correct, *uwasa* "rumour" must not L-mark its clausal complement, while *koto* "fact" does L-mark its clausal complement. This situation is not so puzzling as first appears, in view of the fundamental semantic difference between these two nominals. The noun *uwasa* "rumour" has a clear meaning in itself and the associated clause can be interpreted as a statement about the content of the idea expressed by the nominal head. For instance, in (26), the associated clause "that Taro obtained it" is a statement about the content of the rumour. Therefore it is not unnatural to assume, following Stowell (1981b), that a construction such as (26) is a kind of appositive construction, rather than a pure noun-complement construction.[11,12] On the other hand, the noun *koto*, despite the tentative English gloss "fact" assigned to it, has no semantic content comparable to that possessed by *uwasa*; rather, its sole function is to form a syntactic unit – noun phrase – accompanying an associated clause (or any other prenominal modifiers). Traditional Japanese grammarians have noticed this property of *koto*, and have given it an appropriate name *keisiki meisi* "formal noun" (cf. Tokieda 1950 and references therein). Thus it is not plausible to claim that *koto* and its associated clause form an appositive structure as in the case of *uwasa*, since it is impossible to interpret the associated clause as being a statement about the content of *koto*. However we can still claim, relying on Stowell's (1981b) analysis, that the associated clause is a complement of (and thus L-marked by) *koto*, "complement" being a purely X'-theoretic notion.

We have argued on the basis of the possibility of an empty complementizer that the clause associated with *koto* is a complement of (and thus L-marked by) the head noun *koto*, while the clause associated with *uwasa* is not a complement (and thus not L-marked by) the noun *uwasa*. Let us now consider the following example (27) in which an adjunct is extracted in LF out of a clausal complement of *koto*, and compare it with (28), in which an adjunct is extracted out of a clausal complement of *uwasa*.

(27) *?Kimi-wa [$_{NP}$ [$_{S'}$ [$_S$ Taroo-ga naze sono   onnanoko-to
    -TOP   -NOM why that/the girl   with
    kekkon sita]] koto]-ni sonnani hara-o tatete iru no?
    married   at so much be angry   Q

"Why are you so angry about the fact that Taro married the girl *t*?"

(28) *Kimi-wa [$_{NP}$[$_{S'}$[$_S$Taroo-ga naze sono onnanoko-to kekkon
                                                                    married
    sita] to-yuu] uwasa]-ni sonnani hara-o tatete iru no?
         COMP   rumour at

"Why are you so angry about the rumour that Taro married the girl *t*?"

Here the judgment of relative acceptability is extremely subtle; it is therefore not entirely clear at this point whether the contrastive judgments assigned to the examples in (27) and (28) above are observationally justified. Let us suppose, however, that there is indeed a real contrast between (27) and (28), as indicated by my judgments. This then constitutes another piece of evidence for Chomsky's (1986a) theory of barriers for the now familiar reason. That is, the contrast between (27) and (28) shows that the notion of L-marking enters into the determination of the barrier relevant to antecedent-government.

4 The relevant data recapitulated

Let us first summarize the Japanese data that have been presented so far.

A. Bridge v. nonbridge verbs

(13) Bill-wa [$_{S'}$ John-ga   naze kubi-ninatta tte]   itta no?
     -TOP   -NOM why was fired   COMP said Q

"Why did Bill say that John was fired *t*?"

(12a) ??Bill-wa [$_{S'}$ John-ga naze kubi-ni natta tte] sasayaita no?
      -TOP   -NOM why was fired   COMP whispered Q

"Why did Bill whisper that John was fired *t*?"

B. Noun-complement constructions v. relative clauses

(14b) *?Kimi-wa [$_{NP}$ [$_{S'}$ Taroo-ga girlfriend-to naze wakareta] koto]-ni
      you -TOP   with broke up   at
sonnani odoroite-iru no?
       be surprised

"Why are you so surprised at the fact that Taro broke up with his girl-friend *t*?"

(15b) *Kimi-wa [$_{NP}$ [$_{S'}$ Taroo-ga naze wakareta] onnanoko]-ni kinoo-party-de
                                broke up girl   yesterday at
atta-no?
met

"Why did you meet the girl at the party yesterday whom Taro broke up with *t*?"

C. Extraction of adjuncts out of adjunct clauses

(22a) Kimi-wa[$_{S'}$ [$_S$ Mary-ga nani-o katta] kara] sonnani
       you -TOP   -NOM what-ACC bought because so much
okotteru no?
angry Q

"What are you so angry because Mary bought *t*?"

(22b) *?Kimi-wa [$_{S'}$ [$_S$ Mary-ga naze sore-o katta] kara] sonnani okotteru no?

"Why are you so angry because Mary bought it *t*?"

D. *Koto* v. *uwasa*

(27) *?Kimi-wa [$_{NP}$ [$_{S'}$ [$_S$ Taroo-ga naze sono onnanoko-to
     you -TOP   why that/the girl   with
kekkon sita]] koto]-ni sonnani hara-o tatete iru no?
married   at so much be angry   Q

"Why are you so angry about the fact that Taro married the girl *t*?"

(28) *Kimi-wa [$_{NP}$ [$_{S'}$ [$_{S'}$ Taroo-ga naze sono oonanoko-to
kekkon sita] to-yuu] uwasa]- ni sonnani hara-o tatete iru no?
married   COMP rumour at

"Why are you so angry about the rumour that Taro married the girl *t*?"

Recall that all of these data are problematic for earlier theories of antecedent-government in which the relevant notion of barrier is defined solely on the basis of category types (NP, S′). In these theories it is not possible in principle to make the distinction needed, with respect to the barrierhood of a category, to account for the Japanese data. Adopting Chomsky's (1986a) theory of barriers, in which the notion of barrier is defined in terms of a category-neutral "maximal projectionhood" and the concept of "L-marking", we can now make this necessary distinction.

Consider first the case of the bridge v. nonbridge distinction. We are assuming with Stowell (1981a, b) that the associated clause of a bridge verb such as *itta* "said" is a complement of the verb, while the associated clause of a nonbridge verb like *sasayaita* "whispered" is not its complement. In other words, the clausal complement in (13b) is L-marked by the verb *itta* "said", whereas the one in (12a) is not L-marked. Therefore, the S′ node in (13b) does not constitute a barrier for the intermediate trace of *naze* "why" in LF, which is in the specifier of S′ (CP), so that no violation of the ECP results, and the structure is well-formed. On the other hand, the S′ node in (12a) is a barrier for the intermediate trace of *naze* "why" since it is not L-marked, and the chain link between the intermediate trace and its potential antecedent-governor does not satisfy the 0-subjacency requirement imposed by condition (10). Thus, the contrast between (13b) and (12a) is successfully accounted for.

Let us consider next case B. It is widely assumed that the associated clause in a relative clause structure is not the complement of the relative head. Rather, the relationship between a head noun phrase and the associated clause is that of *predication* in the sense of Williams (1980). Then the S′ node in (15b), a maximal projection, is a barrier for the initial trace and for the intermediate trace in its specifier position. In addition, by the inheritance mechanism introduced in (5a) in section 2 above, the NP node immediately dominating the S′ node in (15b) is also a barrier for the intermediate trace in the specifier of S′ node, even if it is L-marked by the verb *atta* "met". Thus, (15b) is extremely ungrammatical, with two barriers intervening between the intermediate trace and its potential antecedent-governor outside the NP. In contrast, the S′ node in (14b) is a complement of the nominal head *koto* "fact", as we have argued before. It thus does not constitute a barrier for the intermediate trace of *naze* "why" in its specifier position. Furthermore, the entire noun phrase in (14b) is not a barrier for the intermediate trace, since it is a complement of, and thus L-marked by, the predicate *odoroite-iru* "be surprised". We now face the problem of how to account for the grammatical status of (14b), since, as it stands, the barriers theory of Chomsky (1986a) predicts that it is perfectly grammatical as far as the ECP is concerned. Noting a similar problem concerning noun-complement constructions in English, Chomsky (1986a) suggests the following two possible ways to resolve this problem. The first possibility is to assume that oblique Case assigned by the noun *koto* "fact" to its associated clause makes that clause a "weak" barrier which cannot be inherited by a noun phrase dominating it (cf. Chomsky 1981a, 1986a, for relevant discussion of Case). Another possibility is to invoke the *Minimality Condition* given below which Chomsky (1986a) argues to be independently necessary in the theory of government.

(29) γ is a barrier for β if γ is the immediate projection of δ, a zero-level category distinct from β.

(cf. Chomsky 1986a: 42)

Technical details aside (see Chomsky 1986a), the intuitive idea behind the Minimality Condition is clear: β cannot be governed by α, a potential governor, if there is a "closer" governor δ. If the Minimality Condition is, as Chomsky (1986a) argues, independently motivated in the theory of government and if, in addition, the Minimality Condition applies to antecedent-government as well, as seems plausible, then it becomes possible to account for the grammatical status of (14b). That is, in (14b), the noun *koto* "fact" is a zero-level category distinct from the intermediate trace in the specifier of S', and thus the N' node, which is the immediate projection of *koto* "fact", is a barrier for the trace.

(30) ... [$_{NP}$ [$_{N'}$ [$_{S'}$ ... t_i] koto]] ...
　　　　　　↑
　　　　barrier for t_i

We now have an account of the contrast between (14b) and (15b): (14b) is bad because the chain link between the intermediate trace and its potential antecedent-governor outside the noun phrase does not satisfy the 0-subjacency requirement, since the Minimality barrier N' intervenes between them. The relative clause case (15b) is even worse, because the number of barriers intervening between the intermediate trace and its potential antecedent-governor outside the NP is two, viz., S' and NP. Thus, condition (10) on chain links is more severely violated.

Let us now consider the case of adjunct extraction out of an adjunct clause. Here the explanation is rather straightforward. The adjunct *kara* "because" clause in (22) is not a complement of a verb, and hence is not L-marked. Therefore, it constitutes a barrier for the intermediate trace, and thus a violation of condition (10) results, as desired.

Assuming that the contrast between (27) and (28) is a real one (see the discussion in section 3), let us finally consider the case of *koto* "fact" v. *uwasa* "rumour". The grammatical status of (27) is accounted for in exactly the same way as that of (14b) – in terms of the Minimality Condition. And (28) can be explained in the same way as (15b), a case of relative clauses. That is, we argued in section 3 that the noun *uwasa* "rumour" does not L-mark its associated clause; instead, the relationship between the noun and its associated clause is that of apposition. Thus, the S' node in (28) counts as a barrier for the intermediate trace in its specifier position, and the NP node immediately dominating the S' node also becomes a barrier for the intermediate trace by the inheritance mechanism in (5a). The chain link between the intermediate trace and its potential antecedent-governor outside the entire noun phrase does not satisfy the 0-subjacency requirement with two intervening barriers, and thus constitutes a more "severe" violation than *koto* "fact" examples, in which the single Minimality barrier N' intervenes between the intermediate trace and its potential antecedent-governor outside of the phrase, as explained above.

5 Theoretical implications

I have argued that the facts concerning LF extraction of *naze* "why" in Japanese present a cluster of properties that cannot be accounted for by earlier theories of antecedent-government, in which the relevant notion of barriers is defined solely on the basis of category types, and that we can readily handle the set of properties of *naze* "why" extractions within the theory of barriers developed in Chomsky (1986a), thus providing further empirical support for this approach. In this section, I will discuss the implications of the results we have achieved in the preceding discussion for the theory of antecedent-government in general.

Most importantly, the data concerning *naze* "why" extraction in Japanese LF presented above suggest the overall similarities between LF movement of *naze* "why" and overt movement of *wh*-complements in English. Specifically, I have shown that LF extraction of *naze* "why" is affected by a number of factors all of which are more or less related to the concept of L-marking, e.g., (i) the bridge v. nonbridge verb distinction, (ii) noun-complement constructions v. relative clauses, (iii) the *Condition on Extraction Domain* (CED) effect (Huang 1982), in particular, the impossibility of extraction from adjunct clauses (cf. (22)), etc. It is well known that all of these factors enter into acceptability judgments with respect to subjacency violations as well.[13] Thus, as I have argued above, given Chomsky's (1986a) theory of barriers, it is, in a sense, quite natural that LF extraction of *naze* "why" in Japanese and syntactic movement of complement *wh*-elements in English are both sensitive to the same set of factors, resulting in a gradation of acceptability judgments. For, in Chomsky's (1986a) theory, essentially the same notion of barriers is involved both in subjacency and antecedent-government (the ECP). However, it is at the same time somewhat surprising because it is generally assumed in the literature that adjunct extractions, which have to do with the ECP, do not exhibit the same gradation of acceptability as complement extractions having to do with subjacency. An ECP violation, or for that matter, a violation of the government requirement in general, is supposed to result in total ungrammaticality. Therefore, the observed acceptability gradation with respect to *naze* "why" extraction in Japanese calls for some explanation. In what follows, I would like to make some suggestions on this problem.

52 LF extraction of naze

In Fukui (1986), I argued that Japanese lacks specifiers in the sense that the language does not have elements that "close off" category projections. Hence category projections in Japanese stop at the single-bar level, allowing free recursion at that level of projection as permitted by the version of X′ theory proposed there, but they never reach the double-bar level (see Fukui 1986, for details). Under this conception of Japanese phrase structure, every category projection in the language is of the following form, where X^0 appears phrase-finally because Japanese is a head-final language.

(31)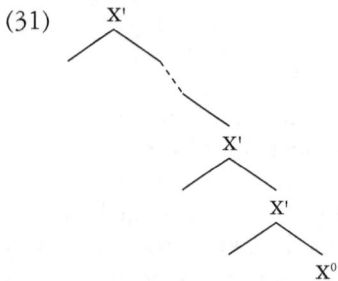

Suppose now that the existence of adjuncts (or *D-structure A′-position*) is somehow contingent on the existence of the XP level, in particular, the existence of the nodes VP and IP.[14] This assumption makes much intuitive sense, since it is generally assumed that XPs constitute upper boundaries for government by their (lexical) heads from inside, and that adjuncts could be characterized as elements that are not under the influence of any (lexical) heads, or, in other words, elements that are not governed by (lexical) heads, in the sense relevant to the ECP. Thus, in English, we assume that *why* is adjoined to IP, and *how* is adjoined to VP, for example, at D-structure.

(32)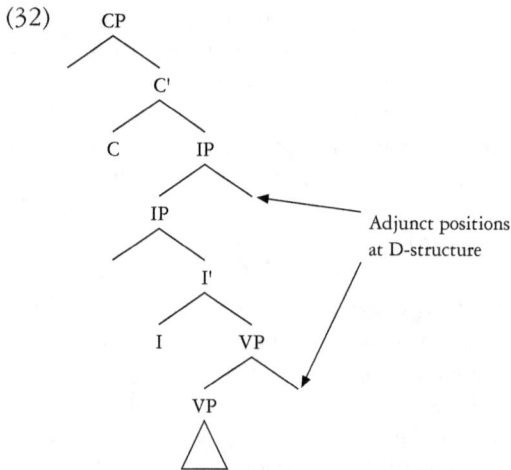

Therefore, *why* and *how* behave like real adjuncts with respect to extraction.

Putting this idea in a somewhat more formal way, we say, following Noam Chomsky (personal communication), that, in the following configuration, a category δ *contains* α, β, and γ:

(33)

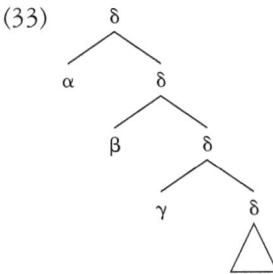

If δ in (33) is an immediate projection of a lexical head, namely, X' (X lexical), we say that δ *L-contains* α, β, and γ. For example, in the following hypothetical configuration, α, β, and γ are all L-contained by V'.

(34)

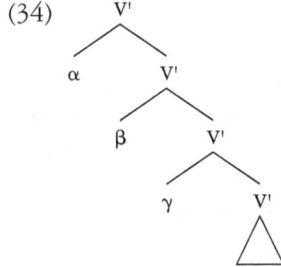

On the other hand, the adjunct positions in (32) above are not L-contained; they are, so to speak, completely outside the influence of a lexical head, as far as projection of a head is concerned. We can now characterize the D-structure non-adjunct positions as follows.[15]

(35) α is a *non-adjunct* at D-structure iff (i) or (ii):
   i. α is L-marked,
   ii. α is L-contained.

Then, non-adjuncts include not only "real" complements, which are L-marked, but also other elements appearing in the positions L-contained by some lexical category, the latter perhaps being interpreted as a kind of quasi-argument.

If (35) is essentially right, and if, in addition, the general phrase structure configuration (31) for Japanese proposed in Fukui (1986) is correct, then we now have a principled reason for the fact that even extraction of *naze* "why", which has been regarded as the only "well-behaved" adjunct in Japanese, is subject to a gradation of acceptability judgments, being affected by a number of factors. That is, owing to the general nonexistence of XPs in Japanese, *naze* "why", unlike *why* in English, is L-contained by V′, thus acting like a quasi-argument with respect to the ECP. In fact, if the line of argument just presented is right, it is predicted that nothing in Japanese, including a subject, will behave like a real adjunct as far as the ECP is concerned, and that the ECP, in this respect, applies only vacuously in Japanese, since everything in a Japanese clause is L-contained (or otherwise L-marked).

Notice, however, that to say that everything in Japanese is L-contained does not mean that everything is L-marked in the language. Specifically, we should note that different relations enter into the determination of *extraction site* and *extraction domain*. Though I am claiming that every position in Japanese is properly governed in the sense relevant to the ECP, I am not claiming that there is no domain in Japanese out of which extraction is inhibited. There is certainly such a domain in the language, for example, *kara* "because" clauses (cf. (22)), or for that matter adverbial clauses in general. Therefore, it should be the case that L-marking is the relevant concept for the determination of whether or not a given domain induces the CED effect, while L-containment is the relevant notion for whether or not a given element is licensed in situ. Note in this connection that the status of subject in Japanese poses an interesting question, because the subject position in this language not only behaves like a complement as an extraction site, as is well known, but also it does not, as a domain, induce the CED effect, unlike adverbial clauses such as *kara* clauses. This might mean that we should incorporate the θ-marking property into the proper characterization of extraction domain, as proposed by Koopman and Sportiche (1986a), or into the definition of L-marking. Various interesting consequences come to mind, especially those concerning the so-called *multiple subjects* in Japanese, but I leave this important problem open here for future research.[16]

Be that as it may, the next question in the present context is: what is responsible for the locality requirement imposed on extraction of *naze* "why" in Japanese LF? A natural candidate is obviously subjacency. If subjacency applies in LF, as well as in syntax, then it is not necessary to invoke an extra device to account for the properties of *naze* "why" extraction. Moreover, the similarities between overt *wh*-movement in English and LF extraction of *naze* "why" in Japanese pointed out in this paper are exactly what we expect under this approach, since these two processes are constrained by the same condition. On the other hand, it is well known that there are crucial open problems for the applicability of subjacency in LF.[17] Thus, the present paper is noncommittal with respect to the issue of subjacency (as it is currently formulated) in LF. However, the results we have achieved in this paper strongly suggest the fundamental commonalities between overt *wh*-movement and LF *wh*-movement (in particular, *naze* "why" extraction), and thus provide further empirical support for the approach taken by Chomsky (1986a), in which it is proposed that theories of (antecedent-) government and movement (subjacency) should be somehow unified.

3 Strong and weak barriers
Remarks on the proper characterization of barriers

1 Introduction

This paper attempts to construct a system in which the notion of "barriers" in syntax is properly characterized. Specifically, it will be argued that the effects of some stipulative statements made within the system of barriers proposed by Chomsky (1986a), in particular his constraints on adjunction, can be derived as consequences of interactions of general principles if we adopt a certain version of X' theory, namely, the "relativized" X' theory proposed in Fukui (1986).

After outlining the relevant part of Chomsky's (1986a) system of barriers in section 2, we will, in section 3, point out some problems left open in his system, and suggest how these problems should be addressed. Section 4 very briefly summarizes "relativized" X' theory and explains in what respects it differs from "standard" X' theory such as that formulated in Chomsky (1986a). Assuming relativized X' theory as a module of phrase structure, we will, in section 5, explore a way to derive the effects of the constraints on adjunction operation made within the Chomsky (1986a) system while avoiding some conceptual and empirical problems raised by the original constraints. Section 6 summarizes our discussion and draws some conclusions.

2 The Chomsky (1986a) system

One of the central goals of the barriers system proposed in Chomsky (1986a) is, among many others, to unify the locality constraint on movement and that on antecedent-government in such a way that essentially the same notion of barrier can capture the fundamental similarities of locality constraints in both movement and antecedent-government cases, incorporating, in particular, the classical cases of the subjacency condition, namely Complex NP Constraint (CNPC) and the *wh*-island constraint, and the cases falling under Huang's (1982) Condition on Extraction Domain, i.e., Subject Condition and Adjunct Condition. In order to achieve this goal, the following concepts are introduced. The basic idea behind the barriers theory of Chomsky (1986a) is that any maximal projection can be a potential barrier.

However, a potential barrier may be exempted from barrierhood if it is L-marked by a lexical head:[1]

(1) α *L-marks* β if β is a complement of α, and α is lexical.

Given this notion of L-marking, we may now turn to the definition of barrier. Barrier is defined in two steps: we first define Blocking Category (BC) as in (2) and then barrier in terms of Blocking Category as in (3):

(2) γ, an X^{max}, is a Blocking Category (BC) for β iff γ is not L-marked and γ dominates β.

(3) γ is a barrier for β if and only if:
 a. γ immediately dominates δ, δ a BC for β; or
 b. γ is a BC for β, $\gamma \neq$ IP

(Chomsky 1986a: 14)

We understand "immediately dominates" in (3) to be restricted to a relation between maximal projections, so that γ immediately dominates δ even if a nonmaximal projection intervenes between them. Condition (3a) is a case of "inheritance"; i.e., the category γ inherits barrierhood from a Blocking Category that it immediately dominates; in case (3b), γ is a barrier intrinsically, being a Blocking Category itself.

Extending the analysis put forth in Huang (1982) and Pesetsky (1982b), Chomsky (1986a) proposes that the scope of X′ theory be extended to all categories, including the non-lexical (functional) categories C(omp) and I(nfl), which have hitherto been more or less exceptions to the general X′ schema. Thus, basic clausal structure looks as follows, where XP stands for X″ (e.g., CP = C″, IP = I″, etc.).

(4) [$_{CP}$ Spec [$_{C'}$ C [$_{IP}$ Spec [$_{I'}$ I [$_{VP}$ ...]]]]]

Under this conception of clausal structure, the traditional categories S′ and S are regarded as the maximal projections of C and I, respectively. Chomsky further proposes that a *wh*-phrase is moved into the Spec of CP position, rather than into the C position as has been widely assumed in the literature.

Now the notion of subjacency is formulated as follows:

(5) β is *n*-subjacent to α iff there are fewer than $n+1$ barriers for β that exclude α.

(Chomsky 1986a: 30)

The definition of exclusion is given as follows:

(6) α *excludes* β if no segment of α dominates β.

(Chomsky 1986a: 9)

Notice that in Chomsky's theory (cf. also May 1985), a category β consists of a sequence of nodes (segments) $(\beta_1, \ldots, \beta_n)$, where β_i immediately dominates β_{i+1}. Though in most cases a category consists of only one segment, i.e., n = 1, a structure of the form (7), a typical adjunction structure in which α is adjoined to β, presents a crucially differentiating case:

(7) $[\beta_1 \, \alpha \, [\beta_2 \ldots]]$

The distinction becomes most relevant when the notion "dominate" is considered. May (1985) proposes the definition of "dominate" in (8) in order to ensure that α is not dominated by β in an adjunction structure such as (7):

(8) α is *dominated by* β only if it is dominated by every segment of β.

Thus, in (7), α is not dominated by β, which consists of two segments β_1 and β_2, since there is a segment of β, namely β_2, that does not dominate α. The term "dominate" used in the definitions of barrier and exclusion in (3) and (6) should be understood in this sense.

The subjacency condition is now formulated as in (9).

(9) If (α_i, α_{i+1}) is a link of a chain, then α_{i+1} is 1-subjacent to α_i.[2]

The subjacency condition (9), coupled with the system of barriers briefly outlined above, handles all of the major cases of the "classical" subjacency condition and the cases of Huang's (1982) Condition on Extraction Domain (see Chomsky 1986a for exposition). More specifically, the subjacency condition (9), which is based on the notion of barrier defined in terms of L-marking, brings the Condition on Extraction Domain, which prohibits movement out of subject or adjunct, under the subjacency condition, thereby giving a unified account of island effects.

However, in order for the whole system of barriers to work properly in all the relevant cases, certain additional assumptions need to be made. Consider first the following example:

(10) $[_{CP}$ who$_i$ did $[_{IP}$ John $[_{VP}$ see $t_i]]]$

(10) is a perfectly grammatical sentence. However, if the movement of *who* in (10) takes place in one step from the position of t_i to its surface position, then it violates the subjacency condition, since it crosses two barriers, VP and IP. Chomsky (1986a) assumes that VP is not L-marked. Thus, VP is a barrier for t_i, since it is not L-marked and is not IP. Furthermore, IP is another barrier for t_i because it immediately dominates VP, a Blocking Category for t_i. Therefore, the movement of *who* in (10) may not be in one step, but, rather, it must take place in two steps. Chomsky (1986a) proposes that

a *wh*-phrase first adjoins to VP and then moves to the Spec of CP, as shown in (11):

(11) [$_{CP}$ who$_i$ did [$_{IP}$ John [$_{VP}$ t'_i [$_{VP}$ see t_i]]]]

Here, the definition of "exclusion" given above becomes relevant. In (11), VP is a barrier for t_i for the reasons stated above. But this is irrelevant for the subjacency relation between t_i and t'_i since the VP in (11) does not exclude t'_i, given that its lower segment does not dominate t'_i. As for the subjacency relation between *who*$_i$ and t'_i in (11), VP is not a barrier for t'_i since it does not dominate t'_i, for the reason just given. IP is a BC for t'_i, but it is not a barrier due to (3b). Thus, the movement of *who* in (11) does not cross any barriers, obeying the subjacency condition.

The "VP-adjunction" operation employed in the derivation of (11) is a kind of null hypothesis under a theory of movement that allows both adjunction and substitution (Chomsky 1986a) and therefore does not pose a conceptual problem. However, if we allow adjunction of a *wh*-phrase to any maximal projection, then the definition of the subjacency condition becomes too permissive. Take, for example, the case of Subject Condition, a subcase of the subjacency condition:

(12) a. *who$_i$ did your interest in t_i surprise Bill?
      b. [$_{CP}$ who$_i$ did [$_{IP}$ t''_i [$_{IP}$ [$_{NP}$ t'_i [$_{NP}$ your interest in t_i]] surprise Bill]]]

(12a) involves extraction out of a subject phrase and needs to be excluded in terms of the subjacency condition. However, if a *wh*-phrase can freely adjoin to any maximal projection, then it should be possible to derive (12a) as in (12b), with *who* adjoining first to the subject NP, and then to IP, and finally moving into the Spec of CP. This derivation does not violate the subjacency condition, since each maximal projection (NP, IP) neither dominates nor excludes the trace adjoined to it. Essentially, the same situation arises in all the other subcases of the subjacency condition (i.e., Complex NP Constraint, *wh*-island constraint, etc.). In short, if adjunction creates an escape hatch and its application is unconstrained, then it will void virtually all the effects of the subjacency condition. Noting this problem, Chomsky proposes the following constraint on adjunction:

(13) Adjunction is possible only to a maximal projection that is a non-argument.

(Chomsky 1986a: 6)

The constraint (13) correctly allows adjunction to VP, which is necessary as we saw in (11), since VP, being a predicate, is clearly not an argument while it prohibits adjunction to a subject NP as in (12). However, adjunction to IP, which is another problematic operation in (12), cannot be excluded by

(13), since IP is not an argument there. The following example shows that adjunction of a *wh*-phrase to IP needs to be prohibited in other cases as well (only relevant portions are represented):

(14) a. ?? what$_i$ did John wonder where$_j$ Bill put t_i t_j ?
 b. [$_{CP}$ what did [$_{IP}$ t'''_i [$_{IP}$ John [$_{VP}$ t''_i [$_{VP}$ wonder [$_{CP}$ where$_j$ [$_{IP}$ t'_i [$_{IP}$ Bill put t_i t_j] ...]]]]]]]

(14a) is a typical *wh*-island case and therefore should be treated as involving a violation of the subjacency condition. However, if the movement of *what* can proceed via adjunction to IP (as well as via adjunction to VP) as shown in (14b), then it will cross no barrier in the derivation of (14a). Chomsky (1986a) therefore proposes the following additional constraint on adjunction:

(15) *wh*-phrases cannot be adjoined to IP.

(cf. Chomsky 1986a: 5)

Given the constraints on adjunction (13) and (15), Chomsky's (1986a) system of barriers works quite nicely in almost all cases of the "classical" subjacency condition as well as of the Condition on Extraction Domain, providing a general and unified account of these island phenomena.

3 Posing the problem

The system of barriers outlined in the preceding section is very attractive in that it gives a unified account of both the "classical" subjacency cases and Huang's (1982) cases of Condition on Extraction Domain. There are, however, some problems still left open in the Chomsky (1986a) system, to which we now turn.

The problems we will discuss in the following have to do with the constraints on adjunction (13) and (15) discussed above. There are two kinds of problems concerning the two proposed constraints on adjunction. One is of a conceptual nature. The constraint (13), for example, still leaves us with the question: why is it that only non-arguments allow adjunction? An analogous problem arises for the constraint (15): it gives us no explanation as to why movement of a *wh*-phrase should be constrained in such a way that it cannot adjoin to IP. In short, the constraints on adjunction as they are formulated in (13) and (15) bear a highly stipulative flavour and do not seem to qualify as principles of Universal Grammar. The other problem has to do with the empirical predictions made by the constraint (13). If we interpret the term "non-argument" used in (13) literally, the constraint would predict, as pointed out by many linguists including Chomsky, that adjunction to adjunct clauses is possible, thereby voiding the Adjunct Condition effect, since adjuncts are, by definition, non-arguments. The same problem arises in the case of relative clauses, since CP in relative clause structures is clearly a non-argument and hence should allow adjunction to it. We thus lose an explanation for half the cases of Complex NP Constraint. The relevant structures are schematically represented as follows (intermediate adjunctions that are not relevant here are omitted):

(16) a. adjunct:[3] $[_{CP}\ wh_i\ [_{IP}\ [_{I'}\ I\ [_{VP}\ \ldots\ ][_{CP}\ t_i^!\ [_{CP}\ \ldots\ t_i\ \ldots\ ]]]]]$

b. relative clause: $[_{CP}\ wh_i\ [_{IP}\ \ldots\ V\ [_{NP}\ \ldots\ [_{CP}\ t_i^!\ [_{CP}\ \ldots\ t_i\ \ldots\ ]]]]]$

How do we approach these problems? Let us consider the conceptual problem first. In order to solve the conceptual problem associated with the constraint (13), Chomsky (1986a: 16) proposes, on the basis of a suggestion made by Kyle Johnson, that it be derived from the θ-Criterion. In particular, he proposes that adjunction to a category makes the category "invisible" to θ-marking, changing the status of the original category as "head" into "non-head" with respect to θ-marking. Thus, adjunction to an argument will always yield a violation of the θ-Criterion. As for the constraint (15), Chomsky (1986a: 5) also suggests that the effect of this constraint is derivable from the general property of *wh*-phrases, which states that these elements have clausal scope. Thus, they must move to a pre-IP position and cannot be adjoined to IP. While these suggestions seem plausible and therefore are certainly worth pursuing, it is also true at this point that they can hardly be more than suggestions, and it is not at all clear precisely how these ideas can be worked out.

Turning to the empirical problems, one possibility to solve the problems along the lines of Chomsky's suggestions discussed above is to assume that adjuncts and clauses in relative clauses are θ-recipients. The idea that adjuncts receive a certain kind of θ-role has already been suggested in the literature (Zubizarreta 1982), and this idea can easily be extended to CP in relative clauses, i.e., clauses in relative-clause structure are assigned some type of θ-role, perhaps via predication. If this approach is tenable, then adjunction to adjuncts and CP in relative clauses will always yield a θ-Criterion violation, and will thus be disallowed by θ-theory.

All of the suggested solutions to the conceptual and empirical problems raised by the constraints (13) and (15) on adjunction are based on the fundamental assumption adopted in Chomsky (1986a) that every maximal projection is equal with respect to its potential barrierhood, and that only contextual factors such as L-marking are relevant to the determination of barriers. In what follows, I will explore a different approach in which, in addition to contextual factors, some category-inherent factors are involved in characterizing barriers to movement. It is important to bear in mind when taking this approach that the class of potential barriers should not be simply stipulated in terms of category types such as NP or S. This would take us back to the "classical" subjacency condition, where just this is done with the class of "bounding nodes". Rather, it would be desirable to derive the categorial asymmetry with respect to barrierhood from some general principles of grammar.

To start our exploration, let us first clarify the kind of problem we are to solve. We saw above that if we interpret the constraint (13) literally, some unwanted derivations will be permitted. From our present perspective, the problem lies in our interpretation of the concept of "arguments" used in (13). The term "argument" has two different meanings. Firstly, the term "argument" is used as a notion contrary to "adjunct". We have so far interpreted the term in this sense. However, the concept "argument" is also used as an opposing notion to the concept of "predicate", as is customary in predicate logic. Notice that "argument" in the first sense, i.e., "argument" as opposed to "adjunct", is a relational notion. The same category (CP, for instance) may or may not be an argument, depending on the syntactic configuration in which it appears. On the other hand, the term "argument" in the second sense, i.e., "argument" as opposed to predicate, is an absolute notion. A given category is an argument or a non-argument (predicate) inherently and independently of context. We have already seen that if the notion of "argument" is used in the first sense, then the constraint (13) will face certain empirical problems. This suggests that the concept of "argument" in the absolute (category-inherent) sense might be the relevant notion to the proper characterization of barriers. If this idea is correct, then the intuition behind Chomsky's constraint (13) on adjunction can be rephrased as follows:

(17) Only potential arguments can be barriers (or more or less equivalently, "predicates are not barriers").

In the remainder of this paper, we will explore a natural way of capturing the intuition expressed in (17) within the framework of the "relativized" X' theory proposed in Fukui (1986).

4 Relativized X' theory

In this section, we will very briefly introduce the relevant part of relativized X' theory. The basic idea of this version of X' theory is that the fundamental difference between the two distinct lexical classes, viz., lexical categories (N, V, etc.) v. functional (non-lexical) categories (C, I, etc.), should be reflected in the ways they project in accordance with X' theory. Lexical categories have "meaning", however this term is to be defined precisely, so that they play a role of being the core of any thought expression. Functional categories, on the other hand, do not have comparable "meaning", at least to a large extent.[4] Their function in syntactic structure is basically to associate syntactic categories via relations such as "agreement". This fundamental difference between lexical and functional categories is represented in the following scheme of projection (linear order is irrelevant):

(18) Lexical projection: [$_{L'}$ X [$_{L'}$ ... [$_{L'}$ X [$_{L'}$ L⁰ complement]] ...]]

(L^0 = N, V, A, etc.)   selection

Functional projection: [$_{F''}$ Spec [$_{F'}$ F⁰ complement]]

(F^0 = C, I, D, etc.)   agreement selection

Thus, a lexical head projects to the single-bar level, taking a complement as its lexical property, and at that level it allows free recursion.[5] A functional head also projects to the single-bar level in the same way as a lexical head. However, a functional projection differs from a lexical projection in that it can project up to the double-bar level with the help of its agreement features. The status of a "specifier" in the functional projection calls for some clarification. The basic role of a specifier in a functional projection is clearly that it "closes" the projection. This characterization of specifiers can be interpreted in two slightly different ways. One is to assume that the specifier position must be licensed by some syntactic relation, typically by an agreement relation with its head (F^0), and that therefore a functional projection stops at the single-bar level when the head has no agreement features. The other way is to assume that the specifier position is freely generated with an empty category underneath it, but that the actual occurrence of some maximal projection in the specifier position must be licensed by some principle (such as the "agreement principle" of Fukui 1988a), in which case a functional projection can optionally project up to the double-bar level with an empty specifier position even when its head bears no agreement features. Though the latter approach seems to have some desirable consequences, including a fairly straightforward account of successive cyclic movement into the specifier of CP, and thus would be worth pursuing, I will, in what follows (leaving the ultimate choice between the two approaches open), assume the first approach simply for the sake of exposition, and state the following condition:

(19) A functional category projects to XP (i.e., to the double-bar level) if and only if its Spec is licensed.

The relativized X' theory briefly outlined above differs from "standard" versions of X' theory such as that formulated in Chomsky (1986a) in a number of respects. One crucial difference which is relevant to our present concern is that while the notion of "maximal projection" is equivalent to a certain number of bars in the standard X' theory (in Chomsky's (1986a) version of X' theory, the number is two), these two notions are dissociated in relativized X' theory, where the maximal projection is defined as being, roughly, the top node of a given projection. Thus, while the maximal projections of lexical categories are always X's, the maximal projections of functional categories are either X's or XPs, depending on whether or not Spec is licensed. For a fuller exposition of relativized X' theory, the reader is referred to Fukui (1986, 1995a).

5 Toward a solution of the problem

Assuming the relativized X' theory briefly outlined in the preceding section, let us now explore a way of capturing the intuition stated in (17).

Let us first consider the class of potential Blocking Categories (and barriers) in relation to the lexical v. functional distinction. V^{max} is a typical category that does not function as a Blocking Category, and is a lexical projection. CP and IP are typical Blocking Categories and are functional projections. The parallelism between Blocking Categories and functional categories breaks down when we consider "NP", which is a typical Blocking Categories but is assumed to be a lexical projection. This problem is resolved, however, if we adopt the "DP analysis", according to which noun phrases are analysed as determiner-headed DPs, determiners being a functional category (cf. Brame 1981, 1982; Fukui and Speas 1986; Abney 1987 for relevant discussion). Thus, assuming the DP analysis, we have the following generalization:

(20) functional categories = potential Blocking Categories
     lexical categories   = non-Blocking Categories

This generalization is clearly in accord with our earlier statement (17), since functional categories (CP, IP, DP, etc.) are typical arguments and lexical categories, particularly VPs and APs, generally function as predicates.

One possible way to derive the distinction stated in (20) within relativized X' theory is to assume the following condition:

(21) Only an XP can be a Blocking Category (and hence a barrier).

This approach is taken by Fukui and Speas (1986) and is further explored, with considerations of cross-linguistic data, by Uriagereka (1988: Chapter 2). Under this approach, lexical categories are never barriers, because their projections never reach the double-bar (XP) level. Some of the consequences of this approach are summarized below:

(22) a. "VP-adjunction" is not necessary.
     b. No lexical projection (in particular, V') can be a barrier.
     c. A functional category that projects only to X' cannot be a barrier.
     d. A language that has no XPs would have no barriers (in D- to S-structure mapping).

64 Strong and weak barriers

Some problems arise with respect to (22b–d). First, (22b) would imply that the "zero-subjacency" approach to parasitic-gap construction proposed by Chomsky (1986a) cannot be maintained. Consider the following contrast taken from Chomsky (1986a: 64):

(23) a. what$_i$ did you file t_i [$_{PP}$ O_i [$_{PP}$ before [t_i [you read e_i]]]]?
     b. *who$_i$ [t_i [$_{VP}$ spoke to you [$_{PP}$ O_i [$_{PP}$ before [t_i [you met e_i]]]]]]?

Putting aside the problem arising from adjunction of an operator to PP,[6] a plausible candidate for the explanation of the contrast under the "zero-subjacency" approach is the existence of an intervening VP between t_i and O_i in (23b) and the lack thereof in (23a). That is, in (23a) the operator O_i is "zero-subjacent" to the trace t_i, whereas in (23b) the intervening maximal projection VP breaks such a "zero-subjacency" relation, thereby making the sentence ungrammatical (see Chomsky 1986a for discussion). Thus, if we want to maintain the "zero-subjacency" analysis of parasitic gaps, then V^{max} should count as a barrier at least in the cases where no adjunction to V^{max} is involved. Second, (22c) makes wrong predictions concerning some cases of the Subject Condition. Consider the following:

(24) a. *?who$_i$ did a picture of t_i please her?
     b. [$_{CP}$ who$_i$ [$_{C'}$ did [$_{IP}$ [$_{D'}$ a [$_{N'}$ picture of t_i]] please her]]]

(24a) is a typical case of the Subject Condition violation. Therefore, we would expect the movement of *who* from its original position indicated by t_i to its surface position to cross more than one barrier. However, as (24b) shows, there is no barrier between the two positions. The crucial factor here is that the subject does not have a Spec position due to the lack of agreement features, and hence projects only up to the single-bar level. Thus, D′ in (24b) does not count as a Blocking Category, and hence not as a barrier, and consequently the IP dominating the D′ does not inherit barrierhood. In short, (22c) would make it impossible to account for the Subject Condition effect when the subject phrase does not contain a specifier position. As for (22d), Japanese is a case in point. It has been argued in Fukui (1986, 1988a) that Japanese lacks specifiers and therefore, given the statement (19), is a single-bar language. If this is correct, then (22d) would predict that the language does not exhibit any island effects. This prediction is not borne out, as the following scrambling facts show (Saito 1985):[7]

(25) a. ?Bill-o$_i$ [$_S$ John-ga [$_{NP}$ [$_{S'}$ Mary-ga t_i sakete-iru to-yuu] uwasa]-o
        -ACC   -NOM   is avoiding that   rumour
        kiita (koto).
        heard that

    "John heard the rumour (which says) that Mary is avoiding Bill."

b. ??ano hon-o$_i$ [$_S$ John-ga [$_{NP}$ [$_S$ e_j [t_i katta]   hito$_j$]-o sagashite-iru
      that book   bought person   is looking for
    rashii.
    seems

    "It seems that John is looking for the person who bought that book."

c. ?sono-hon-o$_i$ John-ga [$_{S'}$ Mary-ga t_i yomi-oete   kara]
    that/the   finish-reading after
    dekaketa (koto).
    went out

    "John went out after Mary finished reading that/the book."

All of these examples involve scrambling out of alleged islands: (25a) involves scrambling out of a complex (non-relative) NP; (25b) scrambling out of a relative clause; and (25c) scrambling out of an adjunct clause. As indicated, (25a–c) are not perfect, and, in conjunction with other relevant phenomena, including *naze* "why" extraction (Fukui 1988b) and the comparative construction (Kikuchi 1989), suggest the following observational generalization regarding extraction phenomena in Japanese:

(26) Japanese does exhibit some island effects, but they are, in many cases, "milder" than those found in languages like English.

Obviously, this observational generalization poses some problems for the prediction made by (22d).

Based on these considerations, we would now like to explore an alternative way of capturing the intuition stated in (17) and its restatement in (20). The basic idea behind this approach can be stated as follows:

(27) The strength of a barrier depends on the "depth" of projection.
An XP is a "strong" barrier, whereas an X', when it is not L-marked, is a "weak" barrier.

Incorporating this idea into the characterization of Blocking Categories, we have the following definition of BC:

(28) γ, an X^{max}, is a BC for β if and only if γ dominates β and:

   (i) γ is an XP (strong barrier); or
   (ii) γ is an X' that is not L-marked (weak barrier).

The terms "strong" and "weak" used in this definition have dual sense: an XP is a "strong" barrier in that it functions as a barrier in its own right, independently of the syntactic context, and also in that it is "strong" in its effect as a barrier. Likewise, an X' is a "weak" barrier in the sense both that its barrierhood depends on the configuration in which it appears, and that its effect as a barrier is relatively "weak".

Notice that under this approach lexical projections can be (weak) barriers when they are not L-marked. However, in cases where movement is involved, their barrierhood will always be voided by adjoining a phrase to them. Such an adjunction operation is available, since relativized X' theory permits free recursion at the single-bar level of a lexical projection. When movement is not involved, on the other hand, lexical projections function as a barrier (when they are not L-marked). This distinguishes the case of the parasitic gap construction where V^{max} functions as a barrier, from the cases of extraction out of V^{max} where V^{max} should not function as a barrier. In the case of functional projections, no such option is available, since relativized X' theory allows recursion neither at the single-bar nor at the double-bar level in this case. The desired result can be obtained without further stipulation by assuming relativized X' theory to hold at both D- and S-structures:

(29) Relativized X' theory holds at both D-structure and S-structure.[8]

If this approach is correct, then it might be that there is no "true" (i.e., structure-creating) adjunction operation in D- to S-structure mapping, and that processes such as extraposition and Heavy NP Shift should be reanalysed in one of the following ways: (i) as belonging to PF-component, (ii) as substitution into Spec of a functional category, (iii) as "adjunction" to a lexical category, or (iv) as being base-generated in one of the positions permitted by the X' theory. One potential problem for this approach is topicalization of the following kind:

(30) I believe that [this book$_i$ [you should read t_i]].

If this type of topicalization involves adjunction to IP, as argued by Baltin (1982) and Lasnik and Saito (1992), then it poses a problem, since adjunction to a functional projection is prohibited under the approach we are exploring. One possibility (suggested to me by Noam Chomsky) is to assume that IP is "lexical" in the relevant sense, owing to its close relation to a verb. Thus, IP, unlike other functional categories such as CP and DP, exceptionally allows adjunction to it. However, a problem with this solution is that it requires us to re-adopt the constraint (15) until we find satisfactorily general reasons for disallowing such adjunction. Another possibility is to analyse topicalization of the above kind as substitution into the specifier position of TP (Tensed Phrase), on the assumption that subject appears in the specifier of AgrP (Agreement Phrase), modifying slightly the analysis of clause structures proposed in Pollock (1989) and Chomsky (1991b). This analysis would capture the relationship between topicalization (in the embedded context) and tensed elements. Specifically, the analysis accounts for the impossibility of topicalization in infinitival complements:

(31) a. *I believe [Mary$_i$ [Bill to have met t_i]].
 b. *John tried [the exam$_i$ [PRO to pass t_i]].

To the extent that there are alternative accounts, however, this fact does not in itself constitute supporting evidence for the suggested analysis of topicalization. For example, (31a) is independently excluded as a violation of the adjacency requirement on Case-marking, with *Bill* being Caseless. The treatment of (31b) is not as straightforward as that of (31a), but, as Mamoru Saito has suggested to me, it might be possible to rule out (31b) as a violation of control theory. In the absence of conclusive evidence, we will leave open the choice between the two possible analyses of topicalization in the embedded context illustrated in (30).

Let us now turn to some further consequences of our current approach. The definition of Blocking Category given in (29) predicts that in a language that has no XP projections, like Japanese, there are only weak barriers. And as we have already seen above, this prediction is fulfilled. Thus, we now have a principled way, though at a rather speculative level, to explain our general intuition that island effects in Japanese are "milder" than those found in English, as far as movement between D-structure and S-structure is concerned.

Another consequence of our approach is that it opens up a possibility of explaining the well-known difference between "syntactic" *wh*-movement and *wh*-movement in LF. That is, as has been pointed out in the literature (cf. Huang 1982), it seems that *wh*-movement in LF is less constrained by the subjacency condition than "syntactic" *wh*-movement. If our approach is on the right track, then this difference between "syntactic" *wh*-movement and LF *wh*-movement could be an automatic consequence of the fact that X$'$ theory holds at S-structure, but not at LF. That is, in LF a *wh*-phrase can freely escape from an island by adjunction without being constrained by relativized X$'$ theory. Though there are various important questions regarding *wh*-movement in LF, particularly ones concerning the "pied-piping" analysis (Nishigauchi 1986; Pesetsky 1987), the possibility mentioned above appears worth exploring.

A further consequence of the approach being explored here is that at least some aspects of the so-called "specificity" phenomena could be handled as falling under the theory of barriers. Consider the following contrast:

(32) a. Who$_i$ did you see [a picture of t_i]?

 b. *?Who$_i$ did you see [John's picture of t_i]?

(33) a. [$_{CP}$ who$_i$ [$_{IP}$ did [$_{IP}$ you [$_{V'}$ t_i'' [$_{V'}$ see [$_{D'}$ a [$_{N'}$ t_i' [$_{N'}$ picture of t_i] ...]]]]]]]

 b. [$_{CP}$ who$_i$ [$_{IP}$ did [$_{IP}$ you [$_{V'}$ t_i'' [$_{V'}$ see [$_{DP}$ John's [$_{N'}$ t_i' [$_{N'}$ picture of t_i] ...]]]]]]]]

Under our analysis, the examples (32a) and (32b) have the derivations (33a) and (33b), respectively. In (33a), the movement of *who* crosses no barrier. The likeliest candidate for a barrier, D', is L-marked by the verb *see* and thus is not a barrier. In (33b), on the other hand, the object phrase projects up to the double-bar level owing to the presence of *John's* in its specifier position. Therefore, the DP in the object position functions as a strong barrier even though it is L-marked by *see*. We thus account for the difference in grammaticality between (32a) and (32b) in terms of the theory of barriers. There are of course various other factors involved in the "specificity" phenomena, and most of them perhaps fall outside the scope of the barriers theory. Our approach, however, suggests that at least some factors involved in the phenomena can be handled in terms of the theory of barriers. Incidentally, the approach to the "specificity" phenomena discussed above could possibly be extended to the well-known distinction between tensed clauses and infinitivals with regard to extraction, by utilizing the difference in the "depth" of projection between the two cases, i.e., tensed clauses are IPs and infinitivals are generally I's. We will not explore this possibility here, leaving it for future research.

6 Summary and conclusion

In this paper, we have explored a general way of deriving the effects of the two constraints on adjunction operation proposed in Chomsky (1986a), and have made, among others, the following claims.

(i) In addition to contextual factors such as L-marking (Chomsky 1986a), there is a category-inherent asymmetry with respect to barrierhood.
(ii) Given relativized X' theory (Fukui 1986), with the assumption that it holds both at D- and S-structures, such an asymmetry does not have to be stipulated. Rather, it is a reflection or a fundamental categorial distinction: lexical v. functional categories.
(iii) Data from Japanese (and other data as well) suggest that the strength of a barrier depends on the "depth" of projection. Thus, there are two types of barriers: (1) strong barriers (XPs), which are independent of the context, and (2) weak barriers (X's), which are sensitive to the syntactic environment in which they appear.

4 Parameters and optionality

Chomsky (1991b) proposes general principles of economy that require derivations and representations to be minimal in cost. To provide the economy principles with full empirical content, it is of course necessary to characterize precisely the notion of "cost" in a grammar. Among other things, the status of optionality, particularly the status of optional movement, has been quite unclear under the general economy approach, which "tends to eliminate the possibility of optionality in derivation" (Chomsky 1991b: 433). Under the economy approach, "choice points will be permissible only if the resulting derivations are all minimal in cost" (p. 433). It then follows that an optional rule is allowed only if its application is "costless", the "cost" of rule application being calculated by a certain algorithm defined in the theory of grammar. However, no concrete measure of cost of rule application has been proposed in the literature, thereby rendering the algorithm almost undefined. The purpose of this article is to propose one specific measure of the cost of formal operations in a grammar in an attempt to clarify the conditions under which optional movement is allowed in natural languages.

The article is organized as follows. Section 1 proposes a measure of cost of rule applications, the parameter value preservation (PVP) measure, which essentially states that an application of Move α is costless in a language only if it results in a structure that is compatible with the parameter value for the language. Section 2 summarizes the basic facts about English and Japanese with regard to their respective values for the head parameter. Section 3 discusses in detail the distribution of optional movement in English and Japanese, and argues that the PVP measure proposed in section 1 straightforwardly accounts for the hitherto unexplained asymmetry between the two languages with respect to the distribution of optional movement. Section 4 extends the discussion beyond English and Japanese and briefly discusses other languages such as Chinese and some of the "VSO" languages (Chamorro and Irish). It is shown that facts in these languages receive a natural explanation under the PVP measure and thus support its general validity. Finally, section 5 summarizes the discussion and points towards future research topics.

1 The parameter value preservation measure

I would like to propose the following measure of the cost of formal operations in a grammar:

(1) *The Parameter Value Preservation (PVP) Measure*

A grammatical operation (Move α, in particular) that creates a structure that is inconsistent with the value of a given parameter in a language is costly in the language, whereas one that produces a structure consistent with the parameter value is costless.

The PVP measure claims that the fixed parameter value for a language must be maximally maintained and states that an application of Move α whose resulting structure is consistent with the parameter setting for the language is costless, whereas one that destroys the canonical structure determined by the parameter setting for the language is more costly in the language. One specific interpretation of this measure is that a costly application of Move α requires some driving force, such as the Case Filter or Spec(ifier)-head agreement (i.e., it displays the "last resort" characteristic), whereas a costless application does not need such a driving force and can in principle be truly optional. In what follows, I will explore some of the implications of the PVP measure pertaining to this interpretation. First, however, I should emphasize that the PVP measure provides only a necessary condition for optionality of Move α. That is, if an application of Move α is evaluated as costless by the PVP measure, then it can in principle be an optional operation, but this does not necessarily mean that the application of Move α in question is actually optional; other principles and conditions may interact to make it a "forced" (obligatory) application. On the other hand, if an application of Move α is evaluated as costly by the PVP measure, then this application must be "forced" (obligatory) and cannot be optional. Thus, the PVP measure provides a necessary (but not necessarily sufficient) condition for optionality of Move α, as we will see.

2 The head parameter: English versus Japanese

The PVP measure proposed in section 1 makes an interesting prediction about the existence of "optional" movement in a language. A case in point is the "head-initial/final" parameter (or simply "head parameter"; Chomsky 1981a)[1] associated with X' theory. As is widely assumed, although X' theory, like other principles of Universal Grammar, is formulated in a "linear order free" fashion, the value of the head parameter must be fixed on the basis of the available data in order to obtain a core grammar of a particular language. (See Chomsky 1986a and Chomsky and Lasnik 1993, for the latest versions of X' theory.) Thus, if the value is set as head-initial, the particular realization (2a) of the X' schema becomes available, whereas if it is set as head-final, the realization (2b) becomes available. (Y^{max} is a maximal projection that is relationally defined as a "complement" of X^0.)

(2) a. $[_{X'} X^0 Y^{max}]$
    b. $[_{X'} Y^{max} X^0]$

Representative examples from English and Japanese are given in (3a) and (3b) (in the case where X = V).

(3) a. $[_{V'} [V^0$ eat$][_{Y^{max}}$ an apple$]]$
    b. $[_{V'} [_{Y^{max}}$ ringo-o$]$ $[V^0$ tabe-ru$]]$
            apple-ACC   eat -NONPAST

"eat an apple"

Thus, the value for the head parameter can be fixed locally by looking at the linear order between X^0 (=a verb) and its complement, head-initial for English and head-final for Japanese. Now it is quite natural to suppose that, although the parameter setting itself is done quite locally (which is desirable from the point of view of learnability), once the value is set, the linear order between a head and its complement determined by that particular value is extended to nonlocal domains. That is, the *canonical precedence relation* (CPR), an "extended" parameter value, between a head and its complement is established on the basis of the particular parameter setting for the language.[2] Thus, the CPRs between, say, a verb (V^0) and its object (Y^{max}) for English and Japanese are as follows (">" means "precedes"):

(4) a. English: $V^0 > Y^{max}$
    b. Japanese: $Y^{max} > V^0$

The PVP measure now predicts that grammatical operations (in particular, movement operations) that destroy the CPRs determined as in (4) on the basis of the parameter setting for these languages are more costly than those preserving the CPRs, which are costless. More specifically, the PVP measure states that in English leftward movement of an object over the verb is more costly than rightward movement, whereas in Japanese leftward movement of an object is costless, but rightward movement of an object over the verb is always costly. Under the interpretation of the PVP measure discussed above, this means that in English leftward movement of an object always requires some driving force, thus having "last resort" status, whereas rightward movement need not have a driving force and can be optional. By contrast, in Japanese leftward movement of an object need not have any driving force and can be optional, whereas rightward movement does need some grammatical factor that makes it forced (or obligatory). In the next section I will show that this prediction is borne out.

3 Leftward and rightward movement in English and Japanese

Let us first consider Japanese. Two cases of movement in Japanese have been argued for in the literature: scrambling (see Harada 1977, Saito 1985, and references cited in these works) and (direct) passive (see Saito 1982 and Miyagawa 1989, among others). These are illustrated in (5).

(5) *Scrambling*
    a. John-ga   sono-hon-o   katta   (koto).[3]
        John-NOM that-book-ACC bought (the-fact-that)

        "John bought that book."

    b. Sono-hon$_i$-o John-ga t_i katta (koto).

        "John bought that book."

    Passive
    c. (Mary-ni) John(-ga)   nagur-rare   -ta (koto).
        Mary-by John -NOM hit   -PASSIVE-PAST

        "John was hit (by Mary)."

    d. John$_i$-ga (Mary-ni) t_i nagur-rare-ta (koto).

        "John was hit (by Mary)."

It has been argued in the above-mentioned literature that (5a) represents the underlying structure and (5b) is created by an application of Move α that fronts the object to a presubject position. And it is generally assumed that the fronting process ("scrambling") in Japanese is truly optional. This is exactly in conformity with the PVP measure, since in (5b) the CPR between a verb and its object, which is determined on the basis of the head-final value for Japanese, is still maintained. That is, in both (5a) and (5b) the object *sono-hon-o* "that book-ACC" precedes the verb *katta* "bought", in accordance with the $CPR = Y^{max} > V^0$. Thus, the PVP measure predicts that unless some independent factor (the Case Filter, etc.) forces Move α to apply, its application can remain optional; and the measure therefore successfully accounts for the optionality of scrambling.

The authors cited above have also argued that the (direct) passive in Japanese involves an application of Move α. According to this analysis, (5d) is produced from an underlying structure like (5c) by an application of Move α. Again, the $CPR = Y^{max} > V^0$ is maintained in (5d). Therefore, the PVP measure predicts that an application of Move α involved in the (direct) passive construction in Japanese can in principle be optional. Whether it is actually optional or is forced to apply is not so obvious here, unlike the case of scrambling, which is universally assumed to be optional. The issue involves what type of Case-marking system one assumes for Japanese. If the

Case-marking system allows the D-structure object in the passive construction to be assigned nominative Case (*ga*) in place, then it need not move and the application of Move α involved in the passive construction in Japanese will be optional. On the other hand, if the Case-marking system does not allow the D-structure object in the passive construction to receive nominative Case in its original position, then it will have to move to some other position to receive nominative Case, just like its counterpart in English passive constructions.[4] I leave this particular issue open here, but would like to reiterate the point: the PVP measure predicts that in Japanese any leftward movement, including scrambling, passive, and even possible S-structure *wh*-movement (see Takahashi 1991, Watanabe 1992), can in principle be optional, unless some other factor requires it to apply.

Turning to rightward movement in Japanese, it has been widely observed that Japanese has no rightward movement of Y^{max} that moves a maximal projection over the verb to its right and that consequently the language is strictly head-final (see, for example, Saito 1985 and references cited there). Until now this fact has received no principled account. However, the PVP measure offers the following straightforward explanation. First, any operation that moves a maximal projection over the verb in Japanese creates the precedence relation $V^0 > Y^{max}$, which is inconsistent with the CPR determined by the head-final value for the language, $Y^{max} > V^0$. Therefore, the PVP measure marks it as a costly movement and states that it cannot be optional but instead must be forced by some grammatical factor. We have been assuming that the Case Filter and Spec-head agreement are such grammatical factors. The Case Filter is irrelevant here since the maximal projections in question will somehow be Case-marked either in their original position or in some position on the left side of a verbal head (see references cited in note 4). As for Spec-head agreement, if we assume with Fukui (1988a) that Japanese generally lacks Spec-head agreement in all the relevant cases, then there will be no Spec-head agreement requirement that forces rightward movement to apply. Or even if we assume some Spec-head agreement (which may exist in the case of C^0) in Japanese, the position of a specifier (or the "directionality" of agreement) is required, as pointed out independently by Jim Huang and Mamoru Saito (personal communications), to be always to the left of its immediate head in the language.[5] Thus, under this assumption, too, no rightward movement is justified. Hence, there is no rightward movement of a maximal projection over a head in Japanese.

Now let us consider English. Typical cases of leftward movement in English are *wh*-movement and NP-movement. We will restrict our attention here to movement of objects, since that is the clearest case where the head parameter plays a role. Both *wh*-movement and NP-movement produce as their output structures that are clearly not consistent with the CPR = $V^0 > Y^{max}$ determined for English on the basis of its head-initial value of the head parameter:

(6) a. What$_i$ did John buy t_i? (*wh*-movement)
b. John$_i$ was killed t_i. (NP-movement)

In (6a) the *wh*-phrase *what*, which is an object of the verb *buy*, is moved from its original position to clause-initial position, destroying the CPR in English, $V^0 > Y^{max}$. In (6b) *John* is also moved from its D-structure position (indicated by t_i) to initial position, again destroying the CPR between the verb *killed* and its (D-structure) object, *John*. Thus, the PVP measure predicts that leftward movement in these cases cannot be optional. A convincing argument that leftward object movement in general cannot be optional in English can be made on the basis of the following examples (see Chomsky 1986b):

(7) a. It strikes John that the directed Hamilton problem is NP-complete.
b. *John$_i$ strikes t_i that the directed Hamilton problem is NP-complete.

In (7a) *it* in the matrix subject position is an expletive, nonthematic subject. Thus, if leftward object movement were optional, then it would be possible to move *John* to the position of the matrix subject, since such a derivation would not violate the θ-Criterion. To do so, however, results in ungrammaticality, as shown by (7b). Lasnik and Saito (1992) tentatively attribute the ungrammaticality of examples like (7b) to the ban on Case conflict. Assuming the economy principles coupled with the PVP measure, however, it is possible to explain the contrast between (7a) and (7b) in terms of the principle of Last Resort, one of the general economy principles (Chomsky 1991b), without recourse to an additional condition such as the ban on Case conflict. First, leftward movement of *John* over its head *strikes* destroys the $CPR = V^0 > Y^{max}$ and hence is marked as costly by the PVP measure. The economy principles then dictate that, in order for *John* to move over the verb, there must be some factor that forces such a movement. However, there is no such factor here; *John* is already Case-marked in place, and the Spec-head agreement in the matrix clause can be independently satisfied by inserting an expletive *it*. Therefore, *John* is prohibited from moving and (7b) is correctly ruled out as a violation of Last Resort. The contrast in (7) can thus be taken as a piece of evidence that leftward object movement in English cannot be optional.

Since leftward object movement in English necessarily destroys the CPR in that language and the PVP measure therefore predicts it to be nonoptional, such movement cannot be truly optional, but must always be forced to apply by some grammatical factors, exhibiting the "last resort" characteristic. And in fact, it is widely assumed that obligatory Spec-head agreement is involved in all of the leftward movement cases we have considered so far: *wh*-movement is obligatorily triggered by a [+wh]-feature associated with C^0 (complementizer), and NP-movement is obligatorily caused by Agr$_s$

(subject agreement) or its equivalent (see Chomsky 1986a, 1991b, for relevant discussion). Thus, the prediction made by the PVP measure that leftward movement in English cannot be optional conforms precisely with the facts.

One might now wonder about the status of topicalization in English, which has generally been assumed to be optional. Let us focus on the type of topicalization that has been argued to involve movement (see Baltin 1982, Lasnik and Saito 1992).

(8) a. This book$_i$, John wanted t_i most.
    b. I think that this book$_i$, John wanted t_i most.

Clearly, an application of topicalization destroys the CPR between a verb and its object ($V^0 > Y^{max}$), moving the object to the left side of the verb. Thus, the PVP measure predicts that it cannot be optional, but must be forced to apply by some grammatical factor. In fact, if we look closely at topicalization and compare it with scrambling in Japanese, which is clearly optional, then the facts seem to support this claim. To see this, let us consider some of the differences between the two grammatical processes. Saito (1989) argues that there are at least two crucial differences between topicalization in English and scrambling in Japanese. First, it is clearly possible to apply scrambling more than once within a single clause, whereas multiple applications of topicalization always result in marginality (also see Fukui 1988a for relevant discussion):[6]

(9) a. John-ga   Mary-ni sono-hon-o   watasita.
       John-NOM Mary-to that-book-ACC handed
       "John handed that book to Mary."

    b. Sono-hon$_i$-o John-ga Mary-ni t_i watasita.
    c. Mary$_j$-ni John-ga t_j sono-hon-o watasita.
    d. Sono-hon$_i$-o Mary$_j$-ni John-ga t_j t_i watasita.
    e. Mary$_j$-ni sono-hon$_i$-o John-ga t_j t_i watasita.

(10) a. John handed that book to Mary.
     b. That book$_i$, John handed t_i to Mary.
     c. To Mary$_j$, John handed that book t_j.
     d. ??That book$_i$, to Mary$_j$, John handed t_i t_j.
     e. ??To Mary$_j$, that book$_i$, John handed t_i t_j.

Second, topicalization and scrambling differ with respect to whether or not they can be "undone" in LF. Because Saito's (1989) arguments showing the crucial difference between the two operations are too complicated to reproduce here in detail, I will merely summarize relevant parts of those arguments in what follows.

First consider (11a–b) (Saito's (18)).

(11) a. Who$_i$ t_i knows [[which picture of whom]$_j$ [Bill bought t_j]]?
    b. ??[Which picture of whom]$_j$ do you wonder [who$_i$ [t_i bought t_j]]?

Based on an observation by Van Riemsdijk and Williams (1981), Saito claims that (11a) is ambiguous in that *whom* can take either matrix or embedded scope. On the other hand, (11b) is clearly unambiguous: it has only the reading in which *whom* takes matrix scope. (Here I put aside the marginal status of (11b), due to Subjacency, as irrelevant.) The interpretation in which *whom* takes embedded scope is simply impossible. This indicates that (11b) cannot have the following LF representation:

(12) [$_{C^{max}}$ [which picture of t_k]$_i$ [$_{I^{max}}$ do you wonder [$_{C^{max}}$ [whom$_k$ who$_j$][$_{I^{max}}$ t_j bought t_i]]]]

Saito argues that the contrast between (11a) and (11b) is due to the Proper Binding Condition (Fiengo 1977, May 1977):

(13) Traces must be bound.[7]

(11a) is ambiguous because *whom* can stay in the embedded C^{max}, taking scope there, or it can raise in LF to the Spec of the matrix C^{max}, taking wide scope. In either case there will be no unbound trace. (11b), on the other hand, lacks the narrow scope reading, because if *whom* lowers in LF to take narrow scope, the resulting LF representation will be (12), which contains an unbound trace, t_k, in violation of the Proper Binding Condition. In order for this explanation to be possible, however, it must be the case that *wh*-movement cannot be undone in LF. This is so, because, if *wh*-movement can be undone in LF, then the *wh*-phrase *which picture of whom* can move back to its original position and *whom* can take narrow scope without leaving an unbound trace. We then lose a plausible explanation for the contrast between (11a) and (11b).

Exactly the same point can be made with respect to topicalization. Consider (14a–b) (Saito's (21)).

(14) a. ??Who$_i$ t_i said that [the man that bought what]$_j$, John knows whether Mary likes t_j?
    b. *Mary thinks that [the man that bought what]$_j$, John knows who$_i$ t_i likes t_j.

Both (14a) and (14b) violate Subjacency, since the embedded topic *the man that bought what* is moved out of a *wh*-island in both cases. (14a) is only marginal, and hence does not seem to violate any principle other than Subjacency. Note that the only possible interpretation for (14a) is the one in which *what* takes matrix scope. This means that its LF representation is (15).

(15) [$_{C^{max}}$ [what$_k$ who$_i$][$_{I^{max}}$ t_i said [$_{C^{max}}$ that [$_{I^{max}}$ [the man that bought t_k]$_j$, John knows [$_{C^{max}}$ whether [$_{I^{max}}$ Mary likes t_j]]]]]]

In (15) all the traces are bound in obedience to the Proper Binding Condition; in particular, the trace t_k is bound by *what*$_k$, as the condition requires. On the other hand, (14b) is totally ungrammatical and clearly does not merely violate Subjacency. Since *what* must move to the Spec of a [+wh] C⁰ in LF, the LF representation of (14b) is (16). (Notice that the matrix C⁰ in (14b), unlike that in (14a), is not [+wh], so that *what* cannot move to its Spec.)

(16) [$_{C^{max}}$ Mary thinks [$_{C^{max}}$ that [$_{I^{max}}$ [the man that bought t_k]$_j$, John knows [$_{C^{max}}$ [what$_k$ who$_i$][$_{I^{max}}$ t_i likes t_j]]]]]

Here the trace of *what*$_k$ (t_k) is not bound at all, violating the Proper Binding Condition; hence the total ungrammaticality of (14b). Again, for this plausible explanation for the contrast between (14a) and (14b) to be possible, it must be the case that topicalization cannot be undone at LF, just as with *wh*-movement.

Let us now turn to scrambling. In Japanese an embedded C⁰ must be [+wh] if and only if it contains the Q-morpheme *ka*, and a *wh*-phrase must move into the Spec position of a [+wh] C⁰ in order to take scope there.[8] Thus, (17a) and (17b) must have the LF representations (18a) and (18b), respectively.

(17) a. [$_{I^{max}}$ John-ga [$_{C^{max}}$ [$_{I^{max}}$ *dare-ga*   sono-hon-o   katta] ka]
         John-NOM   who-NOM that-book-ACC bought Q
    siritagatte-iru] (koto).
    want-to-know

    "John wants to know Q who bought that book."

   b. *[$_{I^{max}}$ *Dare-ga* [$_{C^{max}}$ [$_{I^{max}}$ John-ga   sono-hon-o   katta]
         who-NOM   John-NOM that-book-ACC bought
    ka] siritagatte-iru] (koto).
    Q   want-to-know

    "Who wants to know Q John bought that book?"

(18) a. [$_{I^{max}}$ John-ga [$_{C^{max}}$ *dare$_i$-ga* [$_{I^{max}}$ t_i sono-hon-o katta](ka)] siritagatte-iru]
    b. [$_{I^{max}}$ t_i [$_{C^{max}}$ *dare$_i$-ga* [$_{I^{max}}$ John-ga sono-hon-o katta](ka)] siritagatte-iru]

In (18a) the trace of *dare-ga* "who-NOM" is bound, satisfying the Proper Binding Condition, whereas the corresponding trace in (l8b) is clearly not bound by *dare-ga*, violating the condition. Thus, the contrast between (17a) and (17b) indicates that LF *wh*-movement in Japanese is constrained by the Proper Binding Condition. Now consider (19a–b) (Saito's (35)).

(19) a. [$_I$max Mary-ga [$_C$max [$_I$max minna-ga [$_C$max [$_I$max John-ga
Mary-NOM   all-NOM   John-NOM
dono hon-o tosyokan-kara karidasita] to] omotteiru] ka]
which book-ACC library-from checked-out that think   Q
siritagatteiru] (koto).
want-to-know

"Mary wants to know Q everyone thinks that John checked out which book from the library."

b. ??[$_I$max [$_C$max [$_I$max John-ga *dono hon-o* tosyokan-kara karidasita] to]$_i$ [$_I$max Mary-ga [$_C$max [$_I$max minna-ga t_i omotteiru] ka] siritagatteiru]] (koto).

(19b) is derived from (19a) by scrambling the most deeply embedded C^{max} *John-ga dono hon-o tosyokan-kara karidasita to* "that John checked out which book from the library" to sentence-initial position. The fronted C^{max} contains a *wh*-phrase, *dono hon-o* "which book-ACC" and is moved out of the c-command domain of the C^0 (=*ka*) at which it takes scope at LF. (19b) is not perfect for some independent reasons, but it is significantly better than (17b), which violates the Proper Binding Condition. This indicates that (19b) does not violate the condition, which in turn implies that scrambling, unlike *wh*-movement and topicalization, can be undone in LF. (See Saito 1989 for more detailed discussion.)

We have seen that topicalization in English differs crucially from scrambling in Japanese, and patterns with *wh*-movement in English, in two important respects: (i) it is restricted in such a way as to apply only once per clause,[9] and (ii) it cannot be undone at LF. In view of these important differences between topicalization (and *wh*-movement) in English and scrambling in Japanese, we are naturally led to conclude that topicalization in English, like *wh*-movement, is actually an obligatory operation forced by some grammatical factor, perhaps by Spec-head agreement of some sort – exactly as the PVP measure predicts.

The next question is, What is the Spec-head agreement relation that triggers topicalization in English? A natural answer would be to analyse the type of English topicalization we are considering (the one that involves movement) as a kind of "focalization" process triggered by the Spec-head agreement between a [+focus] head and its specifier. This is a natural extension of Chomsky's (1977) proposal according to which topicalization is analysed as an operator movement into C^0 ([Spec, C^0], under our current assumptions; see Chomsky 1986a). There are many ways to work out this intuitive idea, but I leave a detailed analysis of topicalization for future research, noting that, to the extent that topicalization in English is triggered by some grammatical factor (Spec-head agreement of some sort), it is quite consistent with the PVP measure.

Assuming that topicalization is triggered by some Spec-head agreement, it is now possible to explain the two crucial differences between topicalization (and *wh*-movement) in English and scrambling in Japanese. Topicalization, as well as *wh*-movement, can apply only once per maximal projection in English, since Spec-head agreement in the language requires a one-to-one relationship between a functional head and its specifier. Also, topicalization in English, like *wh*-movement, cannot be undone in LF because the relevant Spec-head agreement must be checked at LF.

On the other hand, scrambling in Japanese can apply more than once per clause and can be freely undone in LF. One might account for these properties by assuming, with Fukui (1988a), that in Japanese functional heads do not induce Spec-head agreement (perhaps with the exception of C^0; see Takahashi 1992) and that a subject can stay in its D-structure position; that is, it can stay within V^{max}, being Case-marked in place differently from the way nominative Case is assigned in English. (See Saito 1982, Fukui 1986, 1988a, Takezawa 1987, and Kuroda 1988 for relevant discussions.) Thus, scrambling can either be adjunction to V^{max} (V' in Fukui's system of projection), as schematically represented in (20a), or adjunction to T^{max} (T' in Fukui's system), as in (20b) (scrambling, of course, can be successive cyclic; I omit the possible intermediate steps here).

(20) a. $[_{T^{max}} [_{V'} X_i^{max} [_{V'} \text{subject } t_i V^0] T^0]]$

b. $[_{T'} X_i^{max} [_{T'} [_{V^{max}} \text{subject } t_i V^0] T^0]]$

In either case scrambling is not triggered by Spec-head agreement, but is truly optional. Since scrambling is an optional adjunction operation and is not triggered by Spec-head agreement, the LF checking of Spec-head agreement, which prevents a topicalized/*wh*-moved phrase from moving back to its D-structure position in LF, simply does not apply. Consequently, scrambling can be freely undone in LF. The possibility of multiple scrambling is also straightforwardly accounted for, because in Fukui's system the single-bar level of X' projection allows recursion, and multiple adjunction is possible to X'. (See Fukui 1986, 1988a for detailed discussion.)

I have argued that the PVP measure dictates that no leftward movement in English can be truly optional and have suggested that topicalization in English should be analysed as a process triggered by Spec-head agreement of some sort, essentially along the lines put forth by Chomsky (1977). I have also shown that the crucial differences discussed by Saito (1989) between topicalization/*wh*-movement in English and scrambling in Japanese follow naturally if we analyse the former type of movement as triggered by Spec-head agreement and the latter as an adjunction operation.

Finally, let us turn to rightward movement in English. Two typical cases of rightward movement in English are extraposition and Heavy NP Shift, both instances of Move α. These operations are illustrated in (21) and (22), respectively.

(21) a. I read a review of John's book last week.
b. I read a review t_i last week [of John's book]$_i$.

(22) a. They brought the beautiful pink dress into my room.
b. They brought t_i into my room [the beautiful pink dress]$_i$.

The PVP measure predicts that extraposition and Heavy NP Shift can be truly optional here, because the CPR between the moved elements and their heads is maintained in both cases. In (21) the CPR is N^0 (*review*) > Y^{max} ((*of*) *John's book*), and in (22) it is V^0 (*brought*) > Y^{max} (*the beautiful pink dress*), both of which are preserved through an application of Move α. And indeed it is fairly uncontroversial that extraposition and Heavy NP Shift in English are optional rules, certainly not obligatorily triggered by Spec-head agreement, thereby lacking the "last resort" characteristic (though of course their actual application is constrained by various conditions, which I will not go into here).[10] See, among many others, Ross 1967, Rochemont 1978, Baltin 1982, 1983, and Johnson 1992, for much detailed discussion.

I have shown in this section that the PVP measure predicts that in English, a typical head-initial language, leftward movement (of object) cannot be truly optional since it destroys the CPR = X^0 > Y^{max}, whereas rightward movement can be optional, unless forced by some grammatical factor, because it maintains the CPR. On the other hand, in Japanese, a typical head-final language, exactly the reverse is true: leftward movement can be truly optional since it preserves the CPR = Y^{max} > X^0, whereas rightward movement cannot be optional and must have some driving force in order to apply. Since Japanese, as its parametric property, does not have such a driving force for rightward movement, there is no rightward movement (over a head) in the language. Thus, the strict head-final character of Japanese, which has been widely noticed but has hitherto remained unaccounted for, naturally follows. I have examined the major cases of leftward and rightward movement in English and Japanese and have argued that all of the predictions made by the PVP measure are confirmed.

4 Further cross-linguistic considerations

In this section I will extend our discussion of the PVP measure beyond English and Japanese and consider some relevant facts from other languages.

Recall that the PVP measure allows Move α to apply optionally only if its application preserves the CPR in a language determined on the basis of the parameter value for the language. So far we have considered two extreme cases, where the CPR is either uniformly X^0 > Y^{max} (English) or uniformly

$Y^{max} > X^0$ (Japanese). However, if a language has different parameter values for different categories, then the PVP measure will make different predictions about optionality for different categories in a single language. Chinese provides an interesting test case. Huang (1982) argues that categories other than N are head-initial in Chinese, whereas noun phrases are rather strictly head-final. (We restrict our attention for the moment to the lowest level of X′ projection, that is, to the relation between X^0 and its complement; see Huang 1982, especially chapter 2, for much detailed discussion.) Thus, Chinese clauses, like those in English, exhibit an SVO pattern, as in (23) (abstracting away from the distribution of adverbial elements; see Huang 1982 for discussion), whereas noun phrases in Chinese, like those in Japanese, exhibit a typical head-final pattern, as in (24).

(23) Zhangsan zuotian zai xuexiao kanjian-le Lisi.
Zhangsan yesterday at school see-ASPECT Lisi

"Zhangsan saw Lisi at school yesterday."

(Huang 1982: 26)

(24) [N^{max} [ta de]¹¹ [neishuang][hui shuohua de][piaoliang de][N^0 yenjing]]
s/he DE that-pair can speak DE pretty DE eye

"that pair of pretty eyes of hers that can speak"

(Huang 1982: 28, with modifications)

Now the PVP measure predicts that optional leftward movement (of a complement) is possible in noun phrases but is not allowed in clauses, since in noun phrases leftward movement of a complement of N will preserve the CPR = $Y^{max} > N^0$, which is determined on the basis of the parameter value fixed for a category N in this language, whereas the CPR in clauses is $V^0 > Y^{max}$ and leftward movement of an object over the head verb will necessarily destroy this canonical pattern. In other words, the PVP predicts that Chinese can have "scrambling" in noun phrases but not in clauses. This is exactly what happens. Consider the following examples:¹²

(25) a. Zhangsan zuotian [zai New York de] ke
Zhangsan yesterday at/in New York DE lecture

"Zhangsan's lecture in New York yesterday"

b. Zhangsan [zai New York (de)] zuotian de ke
c. zuotian Zhangsan [zai New York de] ke
d. zuotian [zai New York (de)] Zhangsan de ke
e. [zai New York] Zhangsan zuotian de ke
f. [zai New York] zuotian Zhangsan de ke

(26) a. Zhangsan xie-le nei-fong-xin gei Lisi.
Zhangsan write-ASPECT that-CLITIC-letter to Lisi

"Zhangsan wrote that letter to Lisi."

b. Nei-fong-xin$_i$, Zhangsan xie-le t_i gei Lisi.
c. Gei Lisi$_j$, Zhangsan xie-le nei-fong-xin t_j.
d. *Nei-fong-xin$_i$, gei Lisi$_j$, Zhangsan xie-le t_i t_j.
e. *Gei Lisi$_j$, nei-fong-xin$_i$, Zhangsan xie-le t_i t_j.

In a noun phrase structure (25), prenominal modifiers may occur essentially in "free word order" among themselves, though, as is usually the case, each difference in order almost always entails a difference in meaning (with respect to scope and binding relations, in particular; see Huang 1982), and the actual possibility of "free word order" (or the actual application of Move α (scrambling), if the "free word order" in this case can be argued to involve movement) is governed by other, independent conditions. Thus, the phrases in (25) pattern exactly with their Japanese counterparts in (27).

(27) a. John-no   kinoo-no   New York-de-no   koogi
         John-GEN yesterday-GEN New York-in-GEN lecture

   "John's lecture in New York yesterday"

   b. John-no New York-de-no kinoo-no koogi
   c. kinoo-no John-no New York-de-no koogi
   d. kinoo-no New York-de-no John-no koogi
   e. New York-de-no John-no kinoo-no koogi
   f. New York-de-no kinoo-no John-no koogi

On the other hand, (26) shows that multiple fronting in a clause is impossible in Chinese, just as in English but in clear contrast to Japanese. (26), then, patterns with the English paradigm (10) and differs from the Japanese paradigm (9), reproduced here as (28) and (29).

(28) a. John handed that book to Mary.
   b. That book$_i$, John handed t_i to Mary.
   c. To Mary$_j$, John handed that book t_j.
   d. ??That book$_i$, to Mary$_j$, John handed t_i t_j.
   e. ??To Mary$_j$, that book$_i$, John handed t_i t_j.

(29) a. John-ga   Mary-ni sono-hon-o   watasita.
        John-NOM Mary-to that-book-ACC handed

   "John handed that book to Mary."

   b. Sono-hon$_i$-o John-ga Mary-ni t_i watasita.
   c. Mary$_j$-ni John-ga t_j sono-hon-o watasita,
   d. Sono-hon$_i$-o Mary$_j$-ni John-ga t_j t_i watasita.
   e. Mary$_j$-ni sono-hon$_i$-o John-ga t_j t_i watasita.

I have argued that the PVP measure makes specific predictions about the possibility of optional movement in general, and about the possibility of "scrambling" in particular, in languages like Chinese where the parameter values are not uniform across categories, and I have shown that the Chinese data confirm the predictions. Thus, the PVP measure naturally explains the otherwise mysterious fact about Chinese that it resembles Japanese in that noun phrases exhibit "scrambling" phenomena,[13] whereas it resembles English in that clauses do not allow scrambling-type multiple fronting.

Let us now turn to the so-called VSO languages and consider briefly what the facts in this type of language can tell us about the validity of the PVP measure.[14] There has been much discussion in the literature about how to analyse surface VSO order in the context of the current grammatical theory. One account that has been widely supported is to assume that languages with surface VSO order in fact have underlying SVO order and that the surface VSO order is derived via leftward verb movement – arguably movement of V^0 to I^0 (see, among others, Emonds 1979, Koopman 1984, Travis 1984, Sproat 1985, McCloskey 1990, and references cited in these works). According to this analysis, the Irish sentence (30), taken from McCloskey 1983: 10, has the underlying structure (31) and is derived by leftward movement of a verb (perhaps to the position of I^0) as depicted there.

(30) Thug me ull donghasur sin inne.
    gave I an-apple to-that-boy yesterday
    "I gave that boy an apple yesterday."

(31) [$_{I^0}$] me *thug* ull donghasur sin inne

Chung (1990), however, claims that leftward movement of a verb (into I^0) is not the only way to derive the surface VSO order. She argues that Chamorro, a surface VSO language (with an alternative VOS order) spoken in the Mariana Islands, has the underlying order VOS, rather than SVO as advocated previously. Slightly modifying Choe's (1987a) analysis of Berber, she proposes that the surface VSO order in Chamorro is derived by optional adjunction of the subject to the right of V^0. In this analysis, the surface VSO order in (32) (Chung's (3a)) is derived from the underlying VOS structure (33) (Chung's (5a)), which also represents an alternative surface order, via adjunction of the subject *si Maria* "Maria" to the right of the verb *ha-fahan* "bought".

(32) Ha-fahan si Maria i bistidu-na gi tenda.
    Infl(3S)-buy Maria the dress-Agr(3S) LOCATIVE store
    "Maria bought her dress at the store."

(33) [[$_{V^0}$ ha-fahan]] i bistidu-na gi tenda [*si Maria*]

If Chung's analysis is correct, then there are two different classes of languages that exhibit the surface VSO order. One class has the underlying SVO order, surface VSO order being derived by leftward verb movement (e.g., Irish and Welsh; for relevant discussion see McCloskey 1990 on Irish, and Sproat 1985 on Welsh); the other class has the basic VOS structure, surface VSO order being derived by optional adjunction of the subject to the right of the verb (e.g., Chamorro (Chung 1990) and, conceivably, Berber (Choe 1987a)). This situation is schematically represented as follows (details are omitted; V_I stands for an inflected verb):

(34) Type I: ($[_I\ ]$) SVO → ($[_{I_\blacktriangle}]$) S VO → V_I SO

   Type II: (I) VOS → (I) V O S → (I) [[V] S] O

The situation described in (34) is entirely consistent with the PVP measure. Restricting our attention to the relation between a verb and its object and subject, one particular prediction made by the PVP measure is that if the parameter value set for a language states that subject and object appear on the same side of a verb in the language, then, speaking at the phenomenal level, "free word order" between the subject and the object may arise (unless other independent conditions prevent it), since the reordering of the two phrases – in particular, movement of object to the opposite side of subject – will not destroy the CPR between a head verb and its complement. Thus, among the most salient underlying word order types (see Greenberg 1963 for some preliminary discussion), only SOV- and VOS-type languages are predicted by the PVP to allow optional reordering of subject and object. We have already seen that this prediction is confirmed on the basis of English (SVO) and Japanese (SOV); optional movement of object to the presubject position ("scrambling") is not allowed in the former, but occurs quite freely in the latter. Now we have an instance of "free word order" between subject and object in the other case, that is, in a VOS language (Chamorro).

Note incidentally that Chung's (1990) analysis has one technical problem with respect to the theory of movement. As Chung herself notes (1990: sec. 4.2), the proposed adjunction of subject (X^{max}) to a verb (X^0) violates the general constraint on adjunction espoused by Chomsky (1986a), which dictates essentially that only X^0 can adjoin to X^0 and only X^{max} can adjoin to X^{max}. (See Chomsky 1986a for discussion.) An alternative analysis of Chamorro word order that is more consistent with Chomsky's constraint might be to claim that what is involved in deriving the surface VSO order from the underlying VOS order is not adjunction of a subject to a verb, but (rightward) "scrambling" of object to postsubject position, perhaps an adjunction to some projection of V or I:

(35) VOS → VOS → VSO
         └─↑
          scrambling

Although this alternative analysis seems plausible from a theoretical point of view, I will not pursue it further here since it is not clear at this point whether it is consistent with the facts reported by Chung, especially those having to do with coordination (1990: secs 8 and 9). Whichever analysis may turn out to be correct, however, the Chamorro facts described by Chung (1990) are quite consistent with the PVP measure.[15] Note finally that at this point the PVP measure makes no specific predictions and thus is neutral with regard to the mechanism of deriving the surface VSO order in Type I languages in (34), where the SVO structure is assumed to be underlying. This is so, because the PVP measure makes predictions in accordance with the formulations of parameters, and it remains to be seen what parameters, if any, are associated with head movement.

5 Concluding remarks

The status of optionality, particularly the status of optional movement, has not been clear under the general economy approach put forth by Chomsky (1991b), which "tends to eliminate the possibility of optionality in derivation". The economy principles require all derivations to be minimal in cost. Therefore, optional rules are allowed only when their applications are considered to be costless, by certain measures of cost. In this article I have attempted to provide one specific measure of cost of movement in a grammar, thereby defining the conditions under which optional applications of rules are allowed. The proposed parameter value preservation (PVP) measure sets a necessary – though certainly not sufficient – condition for the existence of scrambling-type optional movement in a language (see Fukui 1988a, Saito 1989, Miyagawa 1991, Webelhuth 1992, for discussion of other potentially relevant conditions). The PVP measure states that the parameter value that is fixed for a language should be maximally maintained. Thus, in a given language only an application of Move α that results in a structure consistent with the parameter value for that language is evaluated as costless; otherwise, an application of Move α is costly and therefore requires a special "reason" to apply (the "last resort" property).

I have shown that the PVP measure naturally explains, on the basis of fixed values of the head parameter, the overall asymmetry in directionality of optional movement between English and Japanese, including the long-noted but hitherto unexplained fact that there is no rightward movement over a head in Japanese (its strict head-final nature). I have also suggested that analysing topicalization in English as a forced process (as the PVP measure predicts to be the case) nicely accounts for the two important differences pointed out by Saito (1989) between topicalization/*wh*-movement in English and scrambling in Japanese, namely, that topicalization/*wh*-movement in English cannot be undone in LF and multiple applications of topicalization/*wh*-movement are generally not allowed, whereas both are quite possible in the case of scrambling in Japanese. I also considered facts about Chinese and some of the so-called VSO languages, arguing that they provide further evidence in support of the PVP measure. In particular, it accounts naturally for the curious fact that Chinese allows "scrambling" in noun phrases but not in clauses, by capitalizing on the different parameter values the language sets for nouns and other categories.

In closing, I would like to point out two topics for future research along the lines suggested in this article. The first is whether the PVP measure is confirmed by the facts of a wider variety of languages than those considered here. Preliminary indications on this point seem favourable. To the best of my knowledge, most of the well-known "scrambling" languages (e.g., Korean (Lee 1991), German (Webelhuth 1989, Santorini 1991), Dutch (Den Besten and Webelhuth 1987), Tagalog (Schachter 1976), Papago (Hale 1990)) conform to the pattern predicted by the PVP measure. More specifically, no instance of "scrambling" in those languages involves movement of a complement over its head.[16]

The second issue concerns what empirical predictions the PVP measure makes with respect to other possible parameters in a grammar. I have focused on a single parameter, the head parameter (or its equivalent; see note 1), mainly because the nature of other proposed "parameters" is not clear enough at this point to enable us to consider specific predictions the PVP measure makes with respect to each "parameter". If the approach to optionality in grammar suggested here is on the right track, there will certainly be fruitful interactions, as the theory of parameters advances, between the theory of parameters and the theory of cost of derivations.

5 A note on improper movement

The purpose of this note is to argue that the "standard" account of improper movement in terms of Condition C of the Binding Theory (cf. May 1979) is no longer available if we assume Chomsky and Lasnik's (1993) version of the Uniformity Condition, and to suggest two alternative accounts of improper movement each of which has some interesting theoretical consequences.

1 A problem with the standard account of improper movement

Chomsky and Lasnik (1993) propose the Uniformity Condition on Chains as a condition on legitimate objects in Logical Form (LF) (cf. also Browning 1987), stating that the chain C of (1) is a legitimate LF object only if C is "uniform".

(1) $C = (\alpha_1, \ldots, \alpha_n)$

Uniformity here is defined as a relational notion, that is, "the chain C is *uniform with respect to P* (UN[P]) if each α_i has property P or each α_i has non-P" (Chomsky and Lasnik 1993: 58). If we take "L-relatedness" (Chomsky and Lasnik 1993; Chomsky 1992) which grounds the distinction between A- and A′-positions to be the property P, then we can say that a chain is UN [L-relatedness] (or, roughly, UN [A/A′], "A" corresponding to "L-related", and "A′" to "non-L-related") if it is uniform with respect to L-relatedness. The Uniformity Condition then dictates that only chains that are UN [L-relatedness] are legitimate LF-objects. Assuming that the operation of deletion is a last resort mechanism, Chomsky and Lasnik (1993) propose that deletion is impermissible in a uniform chain (since it is already legitimate), whereas deletion is permissible "for α_i in an A′ position, where $i > 1$ and α_n is in an A-position; that is, the case of successive-cyclic movement of an argument" (Chomsky and Lasnik 1993: 59). An immediate consequence of this proposal is a new account of the argument-adjunct asymmetry with respect to the Empty Category Principle (ECP) and subjacency. It is a well-known fact that movement of an adjunct over a barrier yields a much greater deviance (triggering both ECP and subjacency violations) than the corresponding movement of an argument (triggering a subjacency violation). See Chomsky (1981a), Huang (1982), Lasnik and Saito (1984, 1992), Rizzi (1990), among many others. Thus, in the following examples, adapted from Chomsky and Lasnik (1993: 56), the first example, (2), in which an adjunct *how* is extracted out of a *wh*-island, is almost unintelligible, whereas the second example, (3), with movement of an argument (subject) *who*, is much less severely deviant.

(2) *how$_i$ do you wonder [$_{CP}$ whether [$_{IP}$ John said [$_{CP}$ t_i' [$_C$ e] [$_{IP}$ Mary solved the problem t_i]]]]

(3) ??who$_i$ do you wonder [$_{CP}$ whether [$_{IP}$ John said [$_{CP}$ t_i' [$_C$ e][$_{IP}$ t_i solved the problem]]]]

Chomsky and Lasnik's (1993) account of the contrast is as follows. Suppose that when a chain link is formed by movement, the trace created is assigned a * if a barrier is crossed as it is created (more precisely, if the economy condition *Minimize chain links* is violated; see Chomsky and Lasnik 1993: 58 for details). An expression induces a subjacency violation if its derivation forms a starred trace. It shows the additional effect of an ECP-violation if the starred trace remains at LF. In (2), the intermediate trace t_i' is starred when it is created, and, furthermore, it remains at LF since deletion is impermissible because the chain C = (*how*$_i$, t_i', t_i) is already UN [L-relatedness] with all members of the chain in A$'$-positions. Therefore, (2) exhibits the effect of an ECP violation (in addition to a subjacency violation). On the other hand, the corresponding starred trace t_i' in (3) is deletable since the chain C = (*who*$_i$, t_i', t_i) is not, as it stands, uniform with respect to L-relatedness: while t_i' is in an A$'$-position, t_i is in an A-position. Thus, the offending trace t_i' deletes in LF and the resulting LF-representation for (3) does not contain any starred trace. Hence (3) shows only the effect of a subjacency violation.

Note, however, that once we assume the Uniformity Condition on Chains and trace-deletion, we can no longer maintain the account of improper movement cases in terms of Condition C of the Binding Theory. Thus, consider the following examples taken from Chomsky and Lasnik (1993) (*e* represents an empty complementizer, functioning as a proper governor to license the initial trace; see Chomsky and Lasnik 1993 for details).

(4) *John$_i$ was decided [$_{CP}$ e [$_{IP}$ t_i to leave at noon]]

(5) who$_i$ did you say [$_{CP}$ t_i' e [$_{IP}$ t_i left yesterday]]

According to Chomsky and Lasnik (1993), the difference in grammaticality between these examples can be attributed to the fact that in (4) the head of the chain, *John*, is in an A-position, whereas in (5), the head of the chain, *who*, is in an A'-position. Thus, in (4) the trace t_i is starred when it is created because the economy principle (*Minimize chain links*) is violated (see above); and since the trace is not deletable, as the chain is uniform (both *John* and t_i are in A-positions), the starred trace remains at LF, yielding an ECP violation. In (5), on the other hand, no violation of the economy principle is involved with each chain link being minimal, and therefore the sentence is grammatical. Crucial for this account is the assumption that there is no derivation similar to that in (5) available for (4), in which no violation of the economy condition is involved.

(6) *John$_i$ was decided [$_{CP}$ t_i' e [$_{IP}$ t_i to leave at noon]]

Chomsky and Lasnik (1993) claim that a derivation such as (6) is impossible, since movement to an A-position cannot proceed through the specifier of C (Spec of C) because such movement results in an illegitimate A-bound variable (in this case, the initial trace t_i) in violation of Condition C of the Binding Theory (a special case of their principle Command). Notice however that the chain C = (*John$_i$*, t_i', t_i) in (6) is not a uniform chain, with *John$_i$* and t_i being in A-positions and the intermediate trace t_i' in an A'-position. Therefore, given the Uniformity Condition on Chains, the deletion of t_i' should be possible as a last resort to change an illegitimate LF object to a legitimate one, yielding an LF representation with no starred trace. On the assumption that the Binding Theory applies at LF (cf. Chomsky 1992), then, there is no way to rule out a derivation like (6) in terms of the Binding Theory.

2 Alternative accounts

In the following, I would like to suggest two alternative ways to handle the cases of improper movement without recourse to Condition C of the Binding Theory and explore their consequences.

2.1 *A uniformity condition on Form-Chain*

The first possibility to handle cases of improper movement such as (6), while expressing the basic insight behind the standard account of those cases, that is, the idea that A- and A'-movement cannot both occur in the same chain, seems to be to reformulate the Uniformity Condition as a derivational condition; that is, as a condition on the operation Form-Chain (Chomsky 1992) itself, rather than a condition on the resulting LF-representation.

(7) *The Uniformity Condition on Form-Chain*
Form-Chain must apply to form a uniform chain.

Form-Chain is an operation that applies to, say, a structure like (8a) to form (8b) in a single step, yielding the chain C of (8c) (the successive-cyclic mode of its application is required by the economy condition *Minimize chain links*):[1]

(8) a. seems [to be likely [John to win the race]]
 b. John$_i$ seems [t_i' to be likely [t_i to win the race]]
 c. C = (John$_i$, t_i', t_i)

Note that the position of *John*, the target of Form-Chain, in the representation (8a) is already given in the input structure for the operation, thereby falling outside of the scope of the operation Form-Chain itself. Thus, we must exempt the property of the given element, that is, the tail of the chain to be formed by Form-Chain, from those properties determining the uniformity status of a chain relevant for the condition in (7) above, which is a condition on Form-Chain itself. We therefore define the notion of *uniform chain* as follows.

(9) Chain C = (α_1, ..., α_n) is *uniform with respect to the property P* (UN[P]) iff: For each i, j < n, α_i has P ≡ α_j has P

Notice that in Chomsky and Lasnik's account, operator-variable constructions (especially when a variable is in an A-position) fall outside the scope of their Uniformity Condition on Chains (see Chomsky and Lasnik 1993: 58). By excluding the property of the tail of a chain from those contributing to the uniformity status of the chain, we can now treat the operator-variable construction in the same way as other chains, that is, as an LF-object created by the computation Form-Chain in accordance with the Uniformity Condition.[2] Given the Uniformity Condition (7), trace-deletion becomes irrelevant as "the means to make a chain uniform". Non-uniform chains will simply not be created by Form-Chain, because of the Uniformity Condition (7).

The cases of improper movement such as (6) can now be straightforwardly ruled out without appealing to Condition C of the Binding Theory. The chain in (6), C = (*John$_i$*, t_i', t_i), is not a uniform chain with *John* in an A-position and t_i' in an A'-position. Form-Chain simply cannot apply to create such a non-uniform chain. An application of Form-Chain skipping the intermediate Spec-of-C position will violate the economy condition, inducing an ECP violation with a starred trace in the embedded subject position at LF. The problem associated with trace-deletion discussed above does not arise.

The Uniformity Condition (7) has one important consequence for the theory of movement. The condition requires that all intermediate members of a chain created by Form-Chain share the same positional property, say, L-relatedness, with the head of the chain. Thus, in the case of *wh*-movement, in which the head of a chain is in a "non-L-related position" (Spec of C), the Uniformity Condition requires all intermediate positions of the chain to be also non-L-related. This virtually excludes the possibility of "intermediate adjunctions", in particular, adjunction to VP, rendering the classical "Comp-to-Comp" successive-cyclic application as the only option for *wh*-movement (cf. also Takano 1992).[3] The various problems discussed in

Chomsky (1986a) concerning how to constrain possible adjunction sites essentially disappear, while the spirit of the Free Movement Hypothesis is maintained.

The Uniformity Condition proposed above has one apparent drawback in that it makes it impossible to maintain the account for the argument-adjunct asymmetry in terms of trace-deletion proposed by Chomsky and Lasnik (1993), since, under the approach just suggested, a non-uniform chain cannot be created by Form-Chain in the first place, thereby rendering the trace-deletion mechanism irrelevant. A new account for the asymmetry is thus called for under the approach we are considering. I do not intend to offer a fully adequate account here, but would like to suggest a few possibilities that seem worth exploring.

The first possibility, suggested by Chomsky (1993b), is that the apparent argument-adjunct asymmetry is just a matter of parsing: adjunct extraction exhibits less acceptability than argument extraction because it shares some features with garden path sentences. If this is indeed the case, about which I am neutral at this point, then grammar does not have to (in fact should not) offer an account for the asymmetry.

Another possibility, still on the assumption that the argument-adjunct asymmetry is a matter of grammar, is as follows. Suppose, extending slightly a suggestion made by Jim Huang (personal communication), that all operators must head a non-trivial chain at LF. We assume that this requirement also holds for the copy (i.e., the trace) of an operator that has already been moved prior to Spell-Out (Chomsky 1992). In the case of argument (subject and object) *wh*-phrases, such a requirement can be locally satisfied. Thus, in English, a *wh*-phrase in the subject position (or its copy) moves locally to Spec of Agr_s, thereby heading a non-trivial chain at LF. A *wh*-phrase in the object position can also head a non-trivial chain at LF by moving into the local Spec of Agr_O in LF, satisfying the requirement. Hence, to the extent that their scopal properties are expressed in some other way (cf. Chomsky 1992), argument *wh*-phrases need not be subject to LF *wh*-movement.

By contrast, such a local way of fulfilling the requirement is not available to adjunct *wh*-phrases, because adjunct *wh*-phrases do not have Case features to check. Therefore, in order to satisfy the requirement, they have to move farther (to Spec of C), leaving a starred trace which induces an ECP-violation if there is a non-minimal chain link in the chain formed by such movement.

The account just given makes crucial use of whether or not a phrase to be *wh*-moved can be (and has to be) Case-checked. This distinction also plays a role in solving another apparent problem under the current approach. That is, as pointed out by a reviewer, it seems to be the case that *wh*-movement from an A'-position to an A-position is impossible, which is not excluded by the Uniformity Condition (7) itself. However, if we look at the Case properties of arguments and adjuncts, it is clear that arguments are all noun phrases with Case features to be checked, whereas adjuncts either are not noun phrases (e.g., *how*) or are Case checked in the base-generated position (e.g., *in which city*). Thus, owing to the principle of Last Resort, an adjunct cannot move into an A-position, which is typically a Case-checking position.

2.2 An economy condition on adjunction

Another possibility is to analyse the cases of improper movement as involving a violation of economy principles. Noam Chomsky (personal communication) has suggested the possibility that whatever is responsible for improper movement is also responsible for the *that*-trace effect. Suppose so. Then, a natural way to implement the idea is to disallow adjunction from a subject position to Agr_SP. Consider the following paradigm.

(10) a. *who$_i$ do you think [$_{CP}$ t_i' that [$_{AgrSmP}$ t_i left]]
 b. who$_i$ do you think [$_{CP}$ t_i' e [$_{AgrSmP}$ t_i left]]
 c. how$_i$ do you think [$_{CP}$ t_i'' that [$_{AgrSmP}$ t_i' [$_{AgrS-P}$ John fixed the car t_i]]]

Assuming with Fukui and Saito (1993; cf. also Takahashi 1993a) that the S-adjoined position is an A′-position (or an operator position, depending on the nature of S in a given language; see Fukui and Saito 1993 for more details), the economy condition *Minimize chain links* requires that a movement that moves a phrase to Spec of C, which is an A′- (or operator) position, must go through an Agr_SP-adjoined position, a closer A′-position. However, we are assuming that adjunction from the subject position to Agr_SP is disallowed. Then, (10a) is ruled out as a violation of the economy condition.

The reason why (10b) is grammatical has to do with the possibility of head movement from Agr_S to C.[4] In (10b), head movement from Agr_S to C is possible, and because of this head movement, Spec of C and Agr_S-P-adjoined positions become equidistant (cf. Chomsky 1992). Thus, the movement from the subject position to Spec of C does not violate the economy condition. Note that in (10a), head movement from Agr_S to C is blocked by the presence of *that*, and, therefore, the movement from the subject position (Spec of Agr_S) to Spec of C, skipping over the Agr_SP-adjoined position, violates the economy condition, as discussed above. The reason why (10c) is grammatical, or in other words, why adjunct extraction does not exhibit the *that*-trace effect, is that adjunction from the base-generated position of an adjunct to Agr_SP is somehow allowed. Thus, the movement of the adjunct to Spec of C can be mediated by adjunction to Agr_SP, and therefore does not violate the economy condition.

The cases of improper movement can be accounted for in essentially the same way as (10a) is handled. Consider the typical case of improper movement (6), repeated here as (11) with adaptations.

(11) *John$_i$ was decided [$_{CP}$ t_i' e [$_{AgrSP}$ t_i to leave at noon]]

(11), like (10a), violates the economy condition on chain links, since adjunction from the subject position to Agr_SP is prohibited, as we just discussed. The crucial difference between the *that*-trace phenomenon and the cases of improper movement is that the head movement from Agr_S to C, which saves (10b), making Spec of C and Agr_SP-adjoined position equidistant, is not available in (11) even though *that* is not present in C. I have no principled answer to the question of why that should be the case, but my speculation is that in infinitivals, Agr_S is too "weak" to warrant its movement into C. Put it another way, we may say, following a suggestion made by Kyle Johnson, that, in finite clauses, it is the presence of the verb in Agr_S that allows I-to-C-movement at LF. This amounts to saying that English is essentially a verb-second language at LF, and thereby more like the other Germanic languages. Then, because of the presence of *to*, "V-to-I-to-C" is blocked in infinitivals. Note incidentally that in the case of A-movement, the Agr_S-adjoined position does not function as a closer, potential landing side, simply because it is not an A-position. Thus, the intuition behind the standard account of improper movement, i.e., that A- and A'-movements cannot co-occur in a single chain, is incorporated into this account.

We have been assuming that a certain condition on adjunction plays a role in handling in a unified way various hitherto unrelated phenomena. Now the question is: What is the relevant condition on adjunction? The condition should allow adjunction from object/adjunct position to Agr_SP (objects and adjuncts do not induce the *that*-trace effect), but should disallow adjunction from subject position to Agr_SP. It is generally assumed that adjuncts like *how* are in a position that is structurally lower in a sentence than subject. Let us assume for the sake of concreteness that adjuncts are adjoined either to T' or to V'/V^{max}. Now the relevant condition should be such that adjunction to Agr_SP is possible from T'-adjoined position (adjunct) and from within VP (object) (or from Spec of Agr_O if the raising of object has already taken place), but it is impossible from Spec of Agr_S. Takahashi (1993a) suggests a condition, attributing it to Mamoru Saito (class lectures, University of Connecticut), that adjunction to X^{max} is possible only from a position c-commanded by the head of X^{max}.[5] This condition correctly allows adjunction to Agr_SP from object and adjunct positions, both c-commanded by Agr_S, while disallowing adjunction from subject (Spec of Agr_S), which is not c-commanded by Agr_S. I will return to further elaborations on this formulation below.

The condition on adjunction just discussed has a number of desirable consequences. First, as pointed out by Jim Huang (personal communication), the impossibility of topicalization of subject in English, which is discussed in detail by Lasnik and Saito (1992), can now be automatically accounted for by the condition.

(12) a. $[_{CP}$ Mary$_i$ $[_{Agr_SP}$ t_i' $[_{Agr_SP}$ John loves t_i]]]
 b. *$[_{CP}$ John$_i$ $[_{Agr_SP}$ t_i loves Mary]]

For the sake of exposition, let us assume with Chomsky (1977) that topicalization is a movement into Spec of C, when movement is actually involved (i.e., in non-base-generated topicalization cases). In (12a), a case of topicalization of object, the movement of object can go through adjunction to Agr_SP and end up in Spec of C, as required by the economy condition *Minimize chain links*. On the other hand, in (12b), a case of topicalization of subject, movement of the subject, *John*, cannot be mediated by adjunction to Agr_SP, owing to the condition on adjunction just proposed, and the example is ruled out as a violation of the economy condition. The same account can easily be extended to the cases of long-distance topicalization of subject. Thus, the subject-object asymmetry with respect to topicalization is naturally accounted for.

Second, the condition on adjunction also gives a natural account to a certain subject-object asymmetry with regard to scrambling in Japanese. Saito (1985) argues that while other arguments can freely scramble (short-distance or long-distance) in Japanese, as is well-known, subject NPs cannot be scrambled long-distance. The following examples (13c, d), adapted from Saito (1985: 193), illustrate this point. (Judgments are Saito's.)

(13) a. sono hon -o_i John-ga [Mary-ga Bill-ni t_i watasita to]
    that book-ACC -NOM -NOM -to handed that
    omotte-iru (koto).[6]
    thinks

   "John thinks that Mary handed that book to Bill."

   b. Bill-ni_i John-ga [Mary-ga t_i sono-hon-o watasita to] omotte-iru (koto).

   "John thinks that Mary handed that book to Bill."

   c. *kono giron-ga_i John-ga [t_i omosiroi to] omotte-iru (koto).
      this argument   interesting

   "John thinks that this argument is interesting."

   d. *kono giron-ga_i Mary-ga John-ni [t_i okasii to] itta (koto).
                                         -to strange said

   "Mary said to John that this argument is funny."

It is well known, as exemplified by (13a, b), that direct and indirect objects can be freely scrambled across a clause boundary. On the other hand, the ungrammaticality of (13c, d) shows, as Saito argues, that the subject cannot be scrambled long-distance.[7]

This asymmetry, again, receives a natural account under the approach we are pursuing. Let us assume with much recent work (in particular, Saito 1985 and Fukui and Saito 1993) that scrambling in Japanese is an adjunction operation, and that scrambling must proceed through successive adjunctions, in obedience to economy conditions. It then follows that long-distance scrambling of a phrase is possible only if it can be adjoined to a clause, which we assume with Fukui and Saito (1993) to be T^{max} in Japanese.[8] Such adjunction to T^{max} is possible in the case of a nonsubject argument, but is disallowed in the case of subjects, owing to the condition on adjunction. Hence, the impossibility of long-distance scrambling of subjects is naturally accounted for without recourse to other factors such as Case (cf. Saito 1985). And the same analysis can be straightforwardly extended to the impossibility of scrambling of genitive NPs, assuming that nominative (subject) phrases and genitive phrases are immediately dominated by sentences and noun phrases, respectively.

Third, the condition on adjunction we are considering essentially forces the Vacuous Movement Hypothesis, according to which *wh*-movement takes place except for the subject (George 1980; Chomsky 1986a), in the case of infinitivals. This is so, because the Agr_sP-adjoined position, which is a necessary path for a phrase to reach Spec of C, is not available to the subject, owing to the adjunction condition. The only way to make a direct movement from the subject position to Spec of C, that is, the I-to-C-movement, is not available in infinitivals, as we discussed above. Thus, *wh*-movement of the subject in infinitivals will necessarily violate the economy condition (*Minimize chain links*). Hence, *wh*-movement must not take place in the case of subjects in infinitivals. This in turn implies that Spec of C is available for further *wh*-movement in infinitivals but it is not available in finite clauses, since, in the latter case, the subject has already moved into the Spec-of-C-position. It is interesting to see how this difference may account for the well-known difference between finite clauses and infinitivals with respect to "degrees" of *wh*-island effect, that is, the effect of the *wh*-island constraint seems stronger in finite clauses than in infinitives. But the relevant examples are almost impossible to construct in English, owing to the fact that *wh*-phrases can never appear in the subject position of an infinitive for Case reasons, and I would like to refrain from discussing this point further here.

We have seen that the condition on adjunction, which dictates that adjunction to X^{max} is possible only from a position c-commanded by the head of X^{max}, has several interesting consequences. Let us now elaborate the characterization of the condition in the light of economy considerations. Fukui and Saito (1993) argue that the difference between English and Japanese with respect to the Subject Condition effect – English exhibits the subject condition effect, whereas Japanese does not – can be explained if we assume that the subject in English does not allow adjunction to itself, whereas the subject in Japanese does allow adjunction to itself, which in turn is derived from a more fundamental difference between the two languages, namely the existence versus the nonexistence of agreement. In Japanese, then, a phrase occurring inside a subject can first adjoin to the subject, then to a clause, and go on to a higher clause, whereas in English, the first step is prohibited due to Spec-head agreement, yielding the Subject Condition effect (see Fukui and Saito 1993 for details). If their explanation is correct, then adjunction to a clause (T^{max} in Japanese; cf.

note 9) is impossible from the position of the subject, as we discussed above, but is possible from a position that is adjoined to the subject (the case of extraction out of the subject), as well as from other positions that are structurally lower than the subject. This situation is schematically represented as follows. While the condition on adjunction as formulated above in terms of c-command of the relevant head successfully distinguishes adjunction to T^{max} from the subject and that from within V^{max}, it cannot distinguish adjunction to T^{max} from the subject and that from a position adjoined to the subject. Therefore, a further refinement of the condition is necessary.

(14)

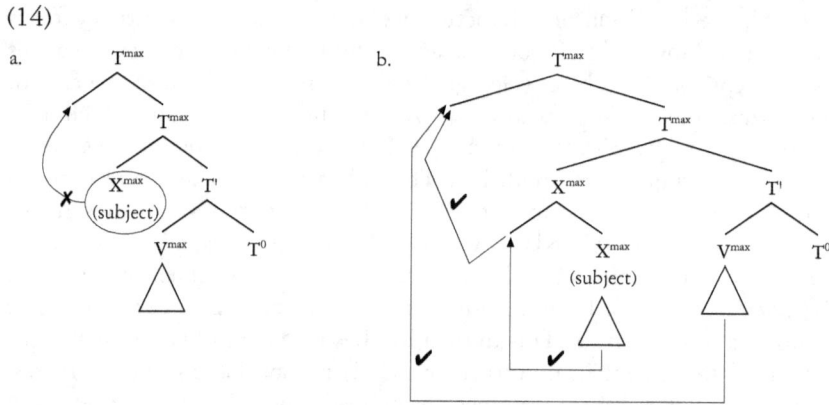

Notice that the intuition behind the proposed condition is that in an adjunction operation from the position x to the position y, x and y must not be "too close". Let us now state this intuition as follows.

(15) Adjunction cannot be vacuous.

The condition (15) should ultimately be motivated by economy considerations, though I can only speculate on what seems to me a plausible reasoning here: vacuous adjunction is a kind of operation that one does not have to perform, since it is not motivated by any grammatical principle and is "invisible" in any significant sense to the eye that scans the derivation; it is a superfluous step in a derivation, and hence prohibited by economy conditions.

Leaving for future research the problem of appropriately motivating the condition (15) in terms of economy of derivation, an immediate problem here is how to characterize the notion *vacuous*. Obviously, linear adjacency is irrelevant for the proper characterization of vacuousness here. Adjunction from subject and adjunction from a position adjoined to subject are both vacuous in terms of linear order, but, as we saw above (cf. 14a, b), the former is banned while the latter is allowed. Thus, we have to characterize the notion in terms of abstract hierarchical structure. If we look at all the relevant cases considered so far, we arrive at the following descriptive statement.

(16) Adjunction is vacuous if it crosses only one node.

Consider again the cases we have discussed so far, which are schematically summarized in (17). (Linear order is irrelevant.)

(17) a. adjunction to X^{max} from its complement/adjunct position[9]

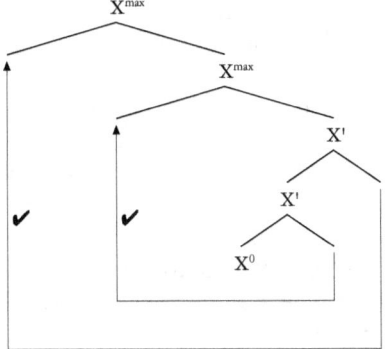

b. adjunction to X^{max} from the position adjoined to its subject

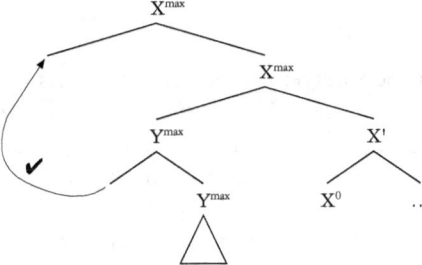

c. adjunction to X^{max} from its subject position

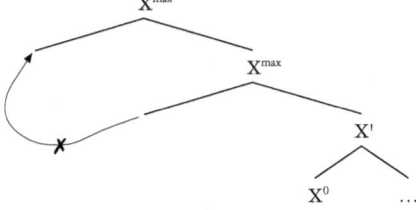

In (17a) and (17b), in which adjunctions are all allowed, two nodes are crossed in each adjunction, that is, there are (at least) two nodes between the two structural positions involved in each adjunction operation (x and y in the discussion above). Thus, in the case of adjunction to X^{max} from the adjunct position inside it, X^{max} (the lower segment of X^{max}) and X' are crossed, and in the case of adjunction to X^{max} from its complement position, X^{max} (the lower segment of X^{max}) and X' (two X's if an adjunct is present) intervene between x and y. By contrast, in (17c), in which adjunction is disallowed, only one node, namely the lower segment of X^{max}, is crossed by adjunction. Therefore, according to the characterization (16), adjunction operations in (17a) and (17b) are all non-vacuous, whereas adjunction in (17c) is vacuous. The condition (15) then dictates that adjunctions in (17a) and (17b) are licit operations, but adjunction in (17c) is banned as illicit, in conformity with the facts.

One of the predictions that the condition on adjunction (15) makes is that if sufficient distance is created between x and y, then an otherwise impossible adjunction operation becomes possible. This is exactly what happens in the case of the *that*-trace phenomenon. It is a long-noted observation (Bresnan 1977; cf. Culicover 1993 for more recent discussion)[10] that when another phrase intervenes between the complementizer *that* and the trace of moved subject, the *that*-trace effect disappears. Consider the following examples from Bresnan (1977: 194).

(18) a. who$_i$ did she say [that [*tomorrow* t_i would regret his words]]
    b. which doctor$_i$ did you tell me [that [*during an operation* t_i had had a heart attack]]

In these examples, owing to the intervening phrases (in italics in (18)), the expected *that*-trace effect is not induced. This is exactly what is predicted by the condition on adjunction just proposed. The intervening phrases have the effect of making the distance between subject and the Agr$_S$P-adjoined position "far enough", so that adjunction to Agr$_S$P becomes possible, avoiding a violation of the economy condition. For concreteness, let us assume that the intervening phrase is adjoined to Agr$_S$P. Then the relevant portion of the structure of examples in (18) should be as follows.

(19)

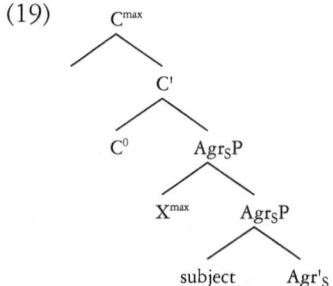

In (19), the subject phrase can first adjoin to Agr$_S$P and then move into Spec of C, obeying the economy condition. The first step should be possible because, thanks to the intervening phrase, adjunction crosses two nodes, namely two segments of Agr_SP, and thus is not vacuous. The otherwise mysterious fact about the *that*-trace effect is straightforwardly accounted for under the approach advocated here.

We have seen that the cases of improper movement and the *that*-trace effect stem from the same fundamental factor, and have proposed a condition on adjunction operation which should ultimately be derived from some kind of economy condition. The proposed condition seems to have a number of interesting consequences, as we have shown, though many details remain to be spelled out and the condition should be formulated in a more elegant way.[11]

3 Summary

In this note, I have argued that the standard account of improper movement in terms of Condition C of the Binding Theory cannot be maintained if we assume Chomsky and Lasnik's (1993) version of the Uniformity Condition. I have suggested two alternative approaches to the problem of improper movement, each of which seems to have a number of theoretical and empirical consequences. The first approach, a reformulation of the Uniformity Condition as a derivational constraint, makes interesting predictions about the theory of movement. The second approach, based on an economy condition on adjunction, provides a unified account of improper movement and the *that*-trace effect, offering novel accounts of other hitherto unexplained facts such as the subject-nonsubject asymmetries with respect to topicalization and scrambling. The choice between the two approaches would require much extensive work on the theory of movement, and would go far beyond the scope of this note. I would like to leave it for future research.

6 The principles-and-parameters approach
A comparative syntax of English and Japanese

1 Introduction

Since around 1960, constant efforts have been made in the theory of generative grammar to factor out certain general principles that govern rule application in the grammars of particular languages, attributing them to the initial state of the language faculty, i.e., Universal Grammar (UG), thereby allowing the rules of the language to remain in the simplest form. The extracted general principles gradually eliminated the need for rules of particular languages entirely, deducing the effects of the apparent rules in the sense that the interaction of these invariant principles yields the phenomena of particular languages which the rules were constructed to describe. Around 1980, work along these lines converged to form a conception of the nature of language called the "principles-and-parameters" theory in which the biologically determined mental organ UG is conceived as the set of principles each of which is associated with an open parameter whose value is to be set by experience (cf. Chomsky 1981a, b). The postulation of such parameters in UG is mainly motivated by the fact that there are various superficially diverse languages in the world, a fact that is fairly obvious but none the less is rather surprising under the biological approach towards the human language faculty assumed in generative grammar, since there is no known biological reason why the mental organ UG, unlike other organs such as the faculty of number, the faculty of spacio-temporal perception, etc., should end up with different steady states (different core grammars) as it grows through experience. See Chomsky (1988) for some interesting discussions on this general question.

At any rate, we know that there are a number of different languages (core grammars) and this fact has led to the emergence of a rather new area of inquiry in which attempts have been made to "explain", rather than just to "describe", why such and such differences exist among languages. This new area of linguistic inquiry is sometimes called "parametric syntax" or "comparative syntax", which shares a lot of its scope with typological studies but departs from most of the traditional studies in its pursuit of genuine "explanations" in the sense just described. In this paper, I will present a case study of comparative/parametric syntax in the case of English and Japanese within the general principles-and-parameters theory.

The organization of this paper is as follows. Section 2 presents an overview of the studies of cross-linguistic variation within the principles-and-parameters theory, and proposes a hypothesis that possible sources for cross-linguistic variation must be limited to differences in the properties of certain lexical items ("functional elements") in the lexicon or to those in ordering restrictions ("linearity"). The case study of the English/Japanese comparative syntax that follows will be carried out under this hypothesis. Section 3 briefly introduces a version of X' theory, "relativized X' theory", developed in my earlier work (Fukui 1986, 1988a). In section 4, some of the major typological differences between English and Japanese will be summarized and illustrated. Then, in section 5, I will show how relativized X' theory makes it possible, under the restrictive theory of parametric variation introduced in section 2, to derive the superficially diverse differences between the two languages from a few fundamental differences in a quite natural and straightforward way. Section 6 summarizes our discussion and makes some concluding remarks.

2 Cross-linguistic variation in the principles-and-parameters theory: functional categories and ordering restrictions

Within the principles-and-parameters framework, the essential properties of a language are determined by the way the language fixes the values of parameters associated with invariant principles of UG, along with the properties of lexical items in the language which are an ineliminable part of language acquisition in any theory of language; without the knowledge of lexical items and their properties, the entire computational system (a language) simply cannot start functioning. Ever since the principles-and-parameters theory emerged around 1980, numerous parameters have been proposed to account for cross-linguistic variation. I will briefly discuss some of them.

One parameter that has been widely assumed and discussed in the literature is the "head-parameter" (Chomsky 1981a) which is associated with X' theory. As is widely assumed, while X' theory, like other principles of UG, is formulated in a "linear order free" fashion, one has to fix, on the basis of the data available, the value of the head-parameter in order to obtain a core grammar of a particular language. (See Chomsky 1993a for the latest version of X' theory; see also the discussion in the next section.) Thus, if the value is set as "head-initial", the particular realization of X' schema becomes available as in (1a), while if the value is fixed as "head-last", it takes the form of (1b). (Y^{max} is a maximal projection which is relationally defined as "complement" of X^0.)

(1) a. $[_{X'} X^0 Y^{max}]$
     b. $[_{X'} Y^{max} X^0]$

Representative examples of (1a) and (1b), respectively, are English and Japanese (in the case where X = V).

(2) a. English: $[_{V'} [_{V^0}$ eat$] [_{Y^{max}}$ an apple$]]$
    b. Japanese: $[_{V'} [_{Y^{max}}$ ringo-o$] [_{V^0}$ tabe-ru$]]$
                    apple-ACC eat-NONPAST
      "eat an apple"

In this way, the value for the head-parameter can be fixed locally by looking at the linear order between X^0 (=a verb) and its complement, "head-initial" for English and "head-last" for Japanese. In the case of English and Japanese, the parameter value for the head-parameter is uniform across categories. Thus, English has head-initial structure for a noun phrase (e.g. *a* $[_{\text{Noun Phrase}}$ $[_N$ *student*$]$ *of physics*$]$), it has prepositions (e.g. *a letter* $[_{\text{Prepositional Phrase}} [_P$ *from*$]$ *John*$]$), etc., while Japanese has head-last structure for a noun phrase (e.g. $[_{\text{Noun Phrase}}$ *buturigaku-(senkoo)-no* $[_N$ *gakusei*$]]$ "(a) student of/majoring in physics"), it has postpositions (e.g. $[_{\text{Postpositional Phrase}}$ *John* $[_P$ *kara*$]]$ *no tegami* "(a) letter from John"), etc. The traditional observation concerning "word order" variation among languages, for example that English has SVO word order and Japanese has SOV word order, is now placed in broader cross-categorial perspective in terms of the head-parameter associated with X' theory.

Another parameter that has been proposed with respect to phrase structure is the "configurationality parameter". After examining various types of languages most of which had not hitherto attracted much attention from theoretical linguists, Ken Hale discovered that certain features of language "cluster" cross-linguistically (see Hale's series of works; Hale 1980a, 1982, 1983). Hale calls this cluster of properties the "diagnostics of nonconfigurationality". Hale's diagnostics of nonconfigurationality include the following:

(3) a. free word order
    b. the use of discontinuous expressions
    c. free or frequent pronoun drop
    d. lack of NP movement transformations
    e. lack of pleonastic NPs
    f. use of a rich Case system
    g. complex verb words or verb-cum-Aux systems

Although this clustering of properties should be considered as a rough approximation and is by no means "defining", as Hale himself notes (Hale 1982), it is certainly beyond the level of accident and therefore calls for some principled explanation. To do this, Hale (1983) proposes, following the suggestion made by Chomsky (1981a) which in turn is inspired by Hale's earlier work (Hale 1980a), that the structure projected from the lexicon is a pair (LS, PS), where LS = Lexical Structure, PS = Phrase Structure, and that languages may vary with respect to the way they relate the two representations and which of the two provides the domain in which various principles of grammar are stated. He then formulates the "configurationality parameter" in the following way (Hale 1983: 26).

(4) *The Configurationality Parameter*:
   a. In configurational languages, the Projection Principle holds of the pair (LS, PS).
   b. In nonconfigurational languages, the Projection Principle holds of LS alone.

The Projection Principle is an overarching principle postulated in the theory of generative grammar which states that subcategorization properties of each lexical item be preserved in the course of derivation (cf. Chomsky 1981a for detailed discussion). Hale assumes the following restricted version of the Projection Principle (Hale 1983: 25).

(5) *The Projection Principle*
   If *verb* selects *arg*(ument) at L_i, then *verb* selects *arg* at L_j (where L_i, L_j range over the "levels" L(ogical) F(orm), D-structure, S-structure in the syntactic representations of clauses).

According to Hale's proposal, the Projection Principle (5) holds of both LS and PS in "configurational" languages such as English, French, etc., so all arguments of the predicate (verb) must be represented in both LS and PS, and thus both must be hierarchically structured (on the assumption that LS must be hierarchically structured in any language; see Hale (1983) for justification of the assumption). In "nonconfigurational" languages such as Warlpiri, Navaho, Winnebago, Japanese, etc., in contrast, since the Projection Principle does not hold of PS, PS may lack arguments of the predicate (verb) and it need not be hierarchically structured, with LS and PS being related by "linking rules" (see Hale 1983 for further details). Thus, the Warlpiri sentence (6) has the representation (7) with each predicate and arguments being connected by linking rules (these examples are taken from Speas 1990: 141).

(6) wawirri   kapi-rna   panti-rni   yalumpu.
    kangaroo AUX I PERSON SUBJ spear NONPAST that
    "I will spear that kangaroo."

(7)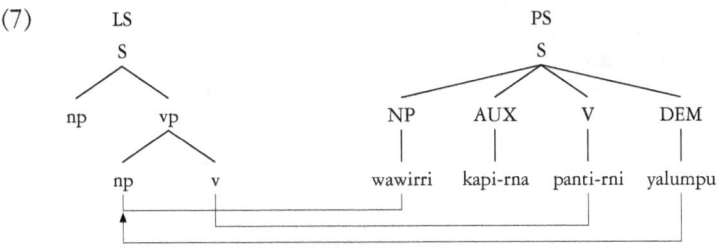

(AUX = auxiliary element; DEM = demonstrative; SUBJ = subject)

Hale then argues that the cluster of typological properties listed in (3) follow as consequences of being "nonconfigurational" in the sense just defined. It is, however, beyond the scope of our present discussion to show how, according to Hale, the properties in fact follow from the "nonconfigurational" value for the configurationality parameter. The reader is referred to Hale (1983) for detailed exposition. In the following sections, I will present an alternative way of deriving (some of) the typological properties listed in (3) in the case of English and Japanese. But it should be stressed that Hale's "configurationality parameter" has set an important research program for any cross-linguistic studies carried out in the principles-and-parameters framework; in fact, virtually all the work that has been done in the 1980s concerning the comparative grammar of European languages and non-European languages has been inspired in one way or another by the "configurational parameter" research program. For more detailed discussions on this issue, see, among others, Saito (1985), Speas (1990), and references cited in these works.

Parameters have also been proposed in other domains of grammar. Languages differ in whether or not a question phrase ("*wh*-phrase") is obligatorily displaced from its original position when an interrogative sentence is formed. For example, a *wh*-phrase must move to the clause-initial position to form an interrogative sentence in English (except for "echo-questions"), whereas, in Chinese, a *wh*-phrase need not move to the clause-initial position and can stay in its original position (t is trace of a displaced phrase, indicating its original position):

(8) who$_i$ did you see t_i? (cf. *did you see whom?)

(9) ni   kanjian-le   shei?
     you see -ASP   who (ASP = aspectual element)

   "who did you see?"

(Huang 1982: 253)

In English, a *wh*-phrase must move overtly as in (8); otherwise a sentence becomes ungrammatical. By contrast, a *wh*-phrase in Chinese need not move overtly to form an interrogative sentence, as shown by (9). Huang (1982) argues that it is a universal requirement that quantificational phrases, including *wh*-phrases, must move in LF to a position at which they take scope (cf. also May 1977), but languages differ in whether they require *wh*-movement to take place before S-structure, as well as in LF. English and languages of similar type impose such a requirement, whereas Chinese and other East Asian languages do not. In this view, languages do not differ with respect to whether they have a particular instance of Move α, a *wh*-movement rule, or not; rather, all languages incorporate such a process as part of the properties of UG, but they may differ in where in the grammar such a rule applies. In English, *wh*-movement applies both before S-structure and in LF, while in Chinese it applies only in LF.

(10) *English*: D-structure → S-structure → LF
                    ↖_____↗
                     wh-movement

Chinese: D-structure → S-structure → LF
                                ↑
                          wh-movement

Thus, according to Huang, languages are "parametrized" with respect to the level at which Move α (*wh*-movement, in particular) applies.

One other well-known parameter in relation to Move α is Rizzi's (1982) proposal that the choice of "bounding nodes" for the subjacency condition is parametrized. The subjacency condition is a universal locality condition on application of Move α. Roughly, it states that movement cannot cross "more than one bounding node" at a time (see Chomsky 1973 for more detailed and technical discussions; see also Chomsky 1986a for more recent development of this principle). The set of bounding nodes is usually assumed to be [NP, S] (cf. Chomsky 1977). Thus, the subjacency condition subsumes, among others, Ross's (1967) Complex NP Constraint, Chomsky's (1964) *wh*-island constraint, and Chomsky's (1973) Subject Condition (a generalized version of Ross's 1967 Sentential Subject Constraint). Movement crosses NP and S at one go in the cases of the Complex NP Constraint and the Subject Condition, and it crosses two instances of S in the case of *wh*-island violations (see any textbook on the theory of generative grammar, e.g., van Riemsdijk and Williams 1986, for illustrations of how exactly the subjacency condition works in each of these cases). Rizzi observes that Italian exhibits the effects of Complex NP Constraint, but does not seem to obey the *wh*-island constraint and the Subject Condition. To solve this problem, Rizzi proposes that the choice of bounding nodes is subject to parametric variation, and that the choice ("value") for Italian is [NP, S′], as opposed to the "English-value" [NP, S]. He also argues that with this hypothesis it becomes possible to explain the otherwise mysterious fact about Italian that, despite the lack of the normal *wh*-island effect in it, the language shows the "double *wh*-island" effect – that is, the extraction of a phrase out of a clause headed by a *wh*-phrase which is embedded in another *wh*-headed clause is impossible even in Italian. Thus, Rizzi's parametric analysis of apparently problematic facts of Italian provides interesting cross-linguistic evidence for the subjacency condition, instead of falsifying it. See Rizzi (1982) for further details.

Perhaps the most widely discussed parameter in principles-and-parameters theory is the "null subject" (or "pro-drop") parameter, which has to do with the occurrence of covert (empty) pronouns in the subject position of the finite clause. It is a well-known fact that some languages allow a pronominal subject to be left unexpressed (unpronounced), while others do not; the former type of languages are called "null subject" languages. For example, Italian and Spanish are null subject languages, but English and

French are not. Thus, the following Italian sentences are all grammatical with pronominal subjects (indicated by *pro*) unpronounced, whereas the corresponding English sentences are ungrammatical (Italian examples are taken from Haegeman 1991: 415).

(11) *Italian*:
    a. *pro* ho   telefonato.
             have telephoned

       "I have telephoned."

    b. Giacomo$_i$ ha detto che *pro*$_i$ ha telefonato.
                   has said   that (he) has telephoned

       "Giacomo$_i$ has said that he$_i$ has telephoned."

English:
    a. **pro* have telephoned.
    b. *John$_i$ said that *pro*$_i$ has telephoned.

Various proposals have been made in the literature with respect to the nature of the null subject parameter (see, among many others, Taraldsen 1978; Chomsky 1981a; Rizzi 1982, 1986a; Borer 1984, 1986; Jaeggli and Safir 1989; and references cited in these works). Virtually all of the proposals made thus far are, no matter how details are executed, based on the central idea that a rich (or "strong") agreement system plays a vital role in allowing the pronominal subject to remain unpronounced. Thus, the subject-agreement element ("Agr$_s$" in Chomsky's 1991b terminology) in Italian is "strong enough" to license an empty pronoun *pro* in the subject position, whereas the Agr$_s$ in English is not "strong enough" to allow *pro* to occur in the subject position. However, Huang (1984) argues that this parameter alone cannot account for the fact that East Asian languages such as Chinese, Korean, and Japanese, which can arguably be said to lack Agr$_s$ entirely (see the discussion in section 5), nevertheless allow empty subject quite regularly. He proposes, partly on the basis of Tsao's (1977) "discourse-oriented" v. "sentence-oriented" distinction, that there is another relevant parameter, the "zero topic" parameter, according to which languages are parametrized as to whether or not they allow a zero topic; for example, English does not allow zero topics, whereas Chinese (and other East Asian languages) allows the occurrence of zero topics. Huang then argues that interactions of the two parameters (the null subject parameter and the zero topic parameter), coupled with his "generalized control rule" which essentially states that an empty pronoun must be controlled by the closest possible nominal element, yield the right cross-linguistic generalization that an empty pronoun *pro* is possible either in languages with "strong enough" Agr$_s$ (e.g., Italian, Spanish, etc.) or no Agr$_s$ at all (e.g., Chinese, Japanese, etc.), but not in languages like English which have meagre Agr$_s$. (See Huang 1984 for detailed discussions.)

We have briefly reviewed some of the major parameters that have been proposed in principles-and-parameters theory.[1] Those parameters are placed in various components of grammar. The head-parameter has to do with the ordering restriction on D-structures ("head-initial" or "head-last"); the configurationality parameter is stated in terms of the way in which the Projection Principle governs the lexical structure (LS) and the phrase structure (PS) of a particular language; Huang's (1982) parameter on *wh*-movement states that languages differ as to which linguistic level *wh*-movement applies at; Rizzi's (1982) "bounding node parameter" claims that the choice of S' or S as one of the bounding nodes for the subjacency condition is open to cross-linguistic variation; the null subject parameter centres around the properties of agreement elements; and the zero topic parameter states that languages are parametrized as to whether or not they choose an option for an empty topic. It is clear that the proposed parameters couched in principles-and-parameters theory have played important roles in making quite interesting cross-linguistic generalizations which had never been made before. However, an instance of the classical tension between descriptive and explanatory adequacy (cf. Chomsky and Lasnik 1977) also arises, as well as other domains of grammar, with respect to the theory of parametric variation. That is, to attain explanatory adequacy it is in general necessary to restrict the class of permissible grammars, whereas the pursuit of descriptive adequacy often requires elaboration of the mechanism available, thus extending the class of permissible grammars. Thus, our task is to construct a constrained theory of parametric variation in the principles-and-parameters framework that is compatible with the existing cross-linguistic diversity. Several attempts have already been made to achieve this goal. One particularly interesting hypothesis that was first proposed by Borer (1984) based on the detailed study of properties of inflectional elements, and has been advanced as the "lexical parametrization hypothesis" by Manzini and Wexler (1987), is stated as follows (Manzini and Wexler 1987: 424):

(12) *Lexical Parametrization Hypothesis*
Values of a parameter are associated not with particular grammars but with particular lexical items.

This hypothesis is theoretically attractive in that it reduces the language learner's task of fixing the parameter values of the language to which he or she is exposed, to the learning of lexical items, which is ineliminable anyway. If this hypothesis is maintained, then there is only one human language outside of the lexicon, and language acquisition can be regarded as a matter of determining lexical idiosyncrasies. Fukui (1988a) argues, however, that the lexical parametrization hypothesis probably cannot be maintained in its strongest form, and claims that parameters which have to do with ordering restrictions should be postulated outside of the lexicon. Then, Fukui proposes the following restriction on the possible parameters outside of the lexicon (adapted from Fukui 1988a: 267):

(13) Parameters are restricted to ordering restrictions.

Under this view, while the principles of UG are stated in an abstract form independent of linear order, the language learner must determine, on the basis of available data, particular instantiations of the principles in a language by fixing the values for ordering parameters, if the principles in question are associated with such parameters (cf. the head-parameter associated with X' theory). As for parametric variation in the lexicon, Fukui (1988a) proposes a more restrictive version of the lexical parametrization hypothesis. Let us assume, as in the standard literature, that the universal lexicon is divided into two distinct subsets: the set of lexical categories (substantive elements) which are defined in terms of the primitive features [±N] and [±V], and the set of functional categories which, we assume, includes C(omplementizer), Agr_S (subject-agreement elements), Agr_O (object-agreement elements), T(ense), and D(eterminer).[2] We state this by postulating a universal feature [±F(unctional)].

(14) [±F]→[+F]: functional categories (C, Agr, T, etc.)
       →[−F]: lexical categories (N, V, A, etc.)

Then, Fukui's (1988a) hypothesis, which we call the "functional parametrization hypothesis", can be stated as follows.

(15) *Functional Parametrization Hypothesis*:
   Only [+F] elements in the lexicon are subject to parametric variation.

This hypothesis is based on the following considerations. Lexical categories have their own "meaning", however this term should be characterized precisely (perhaps by θ-theory). These categories, then, constitute the basic units for the expression of thought. It is quite inconceivable that a language without lexical categories as the basic units of expression can serve as a free instrument of thought and self-expression, an oft-cited function of human language. Functional elements, on the other hand, do not have their own "meaning" comparable to the one associated with lexical categories. The basic role of functional elements is, as pointed out in Fukui (1986), to connect syntactic constituents via some purely syntactic relationship such as "agreement". It would still be possible to form a "basic unit of thought" without these categories. In fact, as we will see in the following sections, Japanese lacks some of the functional categories attested in other languages, but it can still serve as a free instrument of thought and self-expression. See Fukui (1988a) for more discussion.

Under the functional parametrization hypothesis, then, parametric variation in the lexicon is restricted to how properties of functional elements are realized in particular languages,[3] with substantive elements (lexical categories) drawn from essentially the same universal vocabulary across languages, apart from some limited variety in their choice.

From the point of view of learnability, however, the functional parametrization hypothesis becomes meaningful only if the class of possible functional elements in human language is constrained in a principled way (cf. the discussion above on explanatory adequacy); otherwise, the class of possible grammars would be left unconstrained with arbitrary additions of "functional elements". One possible way, suggested in my earlier work (Fukui 1990), to impose such a required constraint on the class of functional elements is to characterize the items in the class in terms of features [±N] and [±V]. This approach predicts that there are essentially four functional categories, just as there are essentially four lexical categories (N, V, A, and P), in human language. I will call these functional categories *the major functional categories*, corresponding to *the major lexical categories* N, V, A, and P. Thus, the representative functional elements Agr, T, D, and C can be defined in the following way.

(16) *Feature specifications of the major functional categories*
Agr = [+F, +N, +V]
T = [+F, −N, +V]
D = [+F, +N, −V]
C = [+F, −N, −V]

These feature specifications capture a number of interesting generalizations. For example, the [+V] specification for T and Agr explicitly expresses the fact that these functional elements are very closely related to a verbal head and thus are called "features" of a verb (Chomsky and Lasnik 1993). The [−N, −V] feature specification for C expresses its property as being "unrelated" to either a verb or a noun. Thus, elements inside the C-projection (but outside the Agr_S-projection) are not "L-related", that is, not related to a verb, a lexical head, in the clausal structure (cf. Chomsky and Lasnik 1993). Also, the common feature specification for C and P, i.e., [−N, −V], captures the basic similarities of these categories (see, for example, Emonds 1985), thereby explaining the fact that post/prepositions sometimes function as complementizers in many languages (cf. *for* in English, *to* "that" in Japanese, etc.). The [+N, −V] specification for D clearly captures the intuitively obvious fact that determiners are closely related to nouns, but are unrelated to verbs. Agr is specified as [+N], as well as [+V]. The [+N] value assigned to Agr not only captures the fact that Agr is "nominal" in its nature (cf. Chomsky 1981a), but also suggests that there may be some relationship between Agr and a noun, just as there is a strong relationship between Agr and a verb (cf. the discussion above). If this intuition is correct, then the internal structure of nominal expressions will be essentially parallel to that of clauses. Thus, putting aside the possibility of C in nominal phrases (cf. Szabolcsi 1987), the internal structure of what has traditionally been called "NP" (noun phrase) should look like the following:

(17) $[_{Agr^{max}} [_{Agr'} \text{Agr} [_{D^{max}} [_{D'} \text{D} [_{N^{max}} [_{N'} \text{N} \ldots]]]]]]$

Note that replacing D and N in (17) with T and V, respectively, we have essentially the structure of a clause, putting aside for the moment the existence of Agr_O.

(18) $[_{Agr^{max}} [_{Agr'} Agr [_{T^{max}} [_{T'} T [_{V^{max}} [_{V'} V \ldots]]]]]]$

We can thus capture the basic similarities between clauses and noun phrases under this approach. We will briefly discuss this topic in the next section.

Returning to our main discussion, we might narrow down the range of parametric variation in the lexicon even further, based on the invariant nature of LF. It is widely assumed that the basic properties of LF are the same across languages and that there is no cross-linguistic difference at this level (cf. Chomsky and Lasnik 1993). If this is true, then it must be the case that the elements attested in some language, say, in English, at the level of LF must be in the universal lexicon, and therefore their existence in the lexicon of a particular language must be assured, although languages may differ in whether or not these elements enter into PF: that is, whether or not they have phonetic features. Chomsky (1991b: 440) argues that the following elements are permitted at LF:

(19) 1. Arguments: each element is in an A-position, α_1 Case-marked and α_n θ-marked, in accordance with the Chain Condition.
2. Adjuncts: each element is in an A'-position.
3. Lexical elements: each element is in an X^0-position.
4. Predicates, possibly predicate chains if there is predicate raising, VP-movement in overt syntax, and other cases.
5. Operator-variable constructions, each a chain (α_1, α_2), where the operator α_1 is in an A'-position and the variable α_2 is in an A-position.

According to this proposal, the necessity for lexical categories at LF is obvious: they are heads, and form core units for arguments, adjuncts, and predicates. Among the functional elements we are considering in this paper, it can arguably be claimed that T must be present at LF, since it is often argued that T functions as an operator binding a certain position in the θ-grid of a predicate (cf. Higginbotham 1985). The status of D at LF is less clear, but we tentatively assume that D is "visible" in LF, functioning as a kind of operator. C and Agr (Agr_S and Agr_O) do not seem to play any role in LF, although the status of C in LF is not entirely clear at this point. This is in fact the intuitive reason for the proposals that, under certain conditions, these elements are erased in LF (see Lasnik and Saito 1984 for C-deletion (*that*-deletion), and Chomsky 1991b for the process of deleting Agr in LF). We may, therefore, conclude that the existence of T (and D) must be assured in the lexicon of any language, that is, these elements cannot be absent in the lexicon, whereas functional elements such as Agr (and C) can be absent in the lexicon of a particular language, that is, some languages may in fact lack these functional elements. Notice that this restriction is only on the "existence" (or "absence") of certain functional elements. For example, even though the existence of T is assured according to this hypothesis, its properties may vary from language to language. Functional elements like Agr, on the other hand, may be entirely lacking in the lexicon of certain types of language (see the discussion below).

If the approach outlined above towards a more restrictive theory of parametric variation is generally correct, various "parameters" that have been proposed so far in the literature should be re-examined to see whether they are in fact possible "parameters", or whether their effect should be further derived from some other factor(s) in a grammar in a way consistent with the restrictive theory of parametric variation. Among the "parameters" we have summarized in this section, the head-parameter and the null subject parameter are certainly within the range of the "possible parametric variation" determined by the theory suggested above. The head-parameter is an instance of "ordering restrictions" in (13), and hence should be a permissible parameter. The null subject parameter has to do with the properties of Agr (especially Agr_s) which is one of the functional elements ([+F] elements in (15)) permitted in UG; thus, the parameter is in accordance with the functional parametrization hypothesis (15), no matter how details are going to be worked out. Other "parameters" that we have discussed, on the other hand, are all outside the range of possible parametric variation in one way or another. The "configurationality parameter", which is stated in terms of the way the Projection Principle is satisfied in a given language, that is, whether it must be satisfied by both of LS and PS or by LS only (cf. (4)), cannot qualify as an independent parameter under our current approach. Thus, the important descriptive generalizations captured by the "configurationality parameter" must be explained by some other way which is consistent with our hypothesis. I will make some proposals concerning this issue in the case of English and Japanese. It appears that Huang's (1982) parameter with respect to overt/covert *wh*-movement also needs to be reformulated, since it neither has to do with ordering restrictions nor is related to the properties of functional elements. An alternative account in terms of different properties of C will be presented in section 5. The "choice of the bounding nodes" parameter proposed by Rizzi (1982) regarding the differences in effects of the subjacency condition between English and Italian should also be reinterpreted for the same reason. It may be that the differences between English and Italian with respect to the *wh*-island constraint reported in Rizzi's work can be derived from some factor involving non-realized subject, which in turn derives from the different properties of the functional category Agr_s (and possibly C) in these languages. The "zero topic" parameter, which also seems to require a reinterpretation, can be restated along the following lines. Suppose that clauses in "zero topic" (topic-prominent) languages are essentially projections of V, as argued for Japanese in Fukui (1986) (see also the discussion in section 5).[4] It is well known that projections of V are generally characterized as predicates. Being predicates, they require a target element to be predicated of. Even though such an element does not overtly exist, they nevertheless require the target element of predication. A "zero topic" is therefore required as a consequence of the basic property of clauses as predicates in "zero topic" (topic-prominent) languages. On the other hand, clauses in "non-zero-topic" (non-topic-prominent) languages such as English are projections of Agr, which is a nominal element (cf. (16)), and their basic property is being an argument, predication being already carried out within it. Therefore, clauses in this type of language do not further require the target element of predication. Hence, the non-topic-prominence of, say, English.

Summing up, we have briefly overviewed how cross-linguistic variation has been studied in the principles-and-parameters framework, summarizing some of the major "parameters" proposed in the literature. We have also pointed out that, although the proposed "parameters" have inspired much cross-linguistic work and have enhanced current research leading to illuminating results, a more restrictive theory of parametric variation is certainly needed to achieve explanatory adequacy. In an attempt to achieve this goal, we have suggested the following constraints on possible parametric variation:

(20) a. Parametric variation outside of the lexicon must be limited to ordering restrictions ("linearity").
b. Inside the lexicon, only [+F] elements ("functional elements") are subject to parametric variation ("functional parametrization hypothesis").
c. Among the functional elements, only those that do not play any role in LF can be absent in the lexicon of a particular language.

What follows is a case study of comparative (or parametric) syntax in the case of English and Japanese within this restrictive theory of parametric variation.

3 Relativized X′ theory

In this section, I will briefly outline a particular theory of phrase structure, the relativized X′ theory, which gives us a theoretical apparatus for the comparative studies of English-type languages and Japanese-type languages in the following sections. I will focus on the aspects of the relativized X′ theory as they pertain to the comparative syntax of English and Japanese; the reader is referred to Fukui (1993b), Fukui and Speas (1986), and Fukui and Saito (1994) for more comprehensive discussions of the relativized X′ theory and its implications for other areas of grammatical theory.

The fundamental difference between the standard X′ theory (Chomsky

1970, 1986a, 1993a; Chomsky and Lasnik 1993) and the relativized X′ theory is that while it is assumed in the former that all the major properties of phrase structure are determined solely by X′ theory, it is claimed in the latter framework that there is at least one property of phrase structure that is not totally determined by X′ scheme, namely, the "closure property" of phrase structure: that is, whether or not a given projection is "closed" is determined not by the X′ scheme *per se*, but by the "agreement" (or "Spec-head agreement") relation holding between a head and a maximal projection in the specific structural configuration. Thus, in structures of the form (21) (order irrelevant),

(21)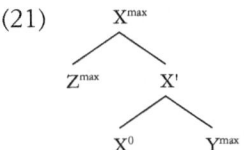

X^{max} is "closed" if and only if there is an agreement relation between X^0, the head of X^{max}, and Z^{max}, the Spec(ifier) of X^{max} (or of X^0), which I will henceforth notate as Spec-XP (or Spec-X^0). In other words, agreement is taken to be a basic relation determining whether or not a projection is closed: if there is an agreement relation, then the projection is closed; otherwise, the projection is not closed. I will use the notation "XP" to stand for a "closed projection" of X^0. The notion of Spec, then, is derivatively defined as a maximal projection participating in agreement (or, equivalently, as a maximal projection that is immediately dominated by a closed category XP). Whether Spec must be unique per projection or multiple Specs are allowed depends on the nature of agreement. I assume here that in unmarked cases, agreement is generally one-to-one, and hence Spec is unique per projection, putting aside for the moment cases where a maximal projection which is adjoined to Z^{max} in (21) also participates in agreement relation with the head X^0.

In the relativized X′ theory, then, a structure like (21) has two instantiations, depending on whether or not an agreement relation holds between X^0 and Z^{max}. If the agreement relation holds, the structure should look like (22); if there is no such relation between X^0 and Z^{max}, the structure will be (23).[5]

(22)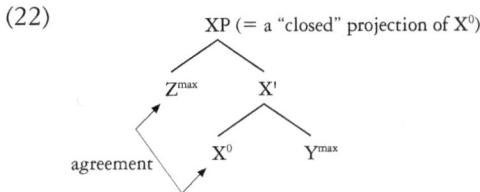

(23)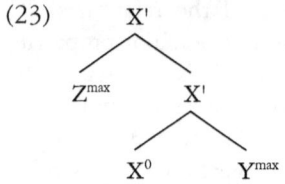

The point here is that the concept of "maximal projection" and the number of bars are completely dissociated in the relativized X' theory, while in the standard X' theory, these two notions are closely connected. In the standard X' theory, the maximal projection of X^0 is, by definition, X'' regardless of what syntactic relation is obtained inside it, thereby predicting that all maximal projections behave in the same way. In the relativized X' theory, on the other hand, the maximal projection of a head X^0 is defined relative to a given head, as being, roughly, the top node of its actual projection, which is quite independent of the bar level: it is X' if X^0 has no agreement features; it is XP if X^0 induces agreement. Let us assume that, among lexical items, only functional elements can have agreement features (cf. Fukui 1986; 1995a and the references cited there). It thus follows that maximal projections of lexical categories are always X', whereas maximal projections of functional categories are either XP or X' depending on whether a given functional head induces agreement, as is illustrated in (24) and (25) (order irrelevant, as usual). A lexical head projects to the single-bar level, taking a complement as its lexical property, and at that level it allows free recursion as shown in (24); a lexical projection is never closed, owing to the lack of agreement relation. A functional head also projects to the single-bar level in the same way as a lexical head, allowing recursion.[6] If the functional head induces agreement, as in (25b), its projection is closed and its maximal projection is XP (FP in (25b)); if the functional head does not induce agreement, as in (25a), then its projection is not closed and the top node of its projection, F', becomes the maximal projection.

(24)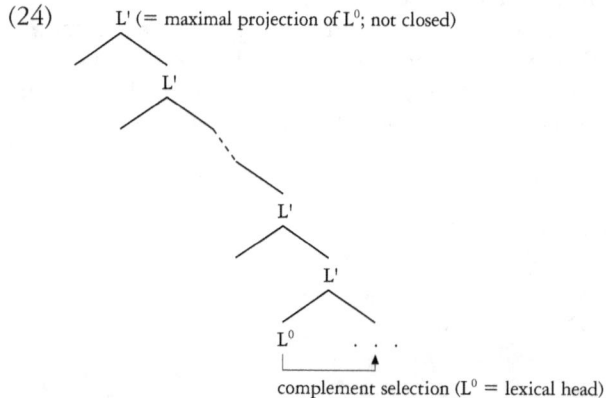

(25)
a. F' (= maximal projection of F⁰; not closed)

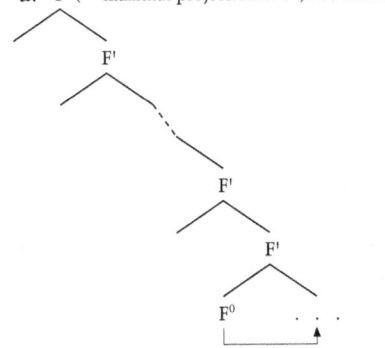

complement selection (F⁰ = functional head without agreement features)

(25)
b. FP (= maximal projection of F⁰; closed)

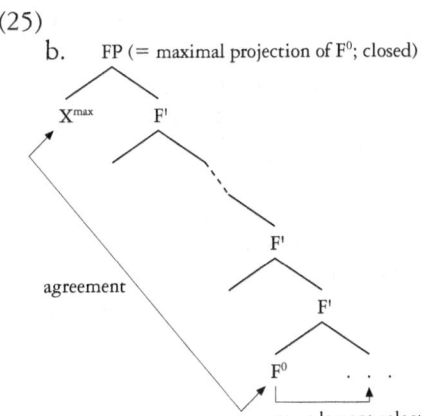

complement selection (F⁰ = functional head with agreement features)

One consequence of this version of X′ theory that is particularly relevant to the discussion that follows is that the theory of movement can be significantly simplified. Specifically, substitution, which is, along with adjunction, one of the two standardly assumed movement operations, can now be entirely dispensed with in the theory of movement.[7] In the standard literature (cf. Chomsky 1986a, 1993a; Chomsky and Lasnik 1993, etc.), a substitution operation replaces an "empty category" Δ either with X^{max}, when it is in the "Spec" position, or with X^0 when it is in the head position, in accordance with a version of the structure-preserving constraint. There are at least two problems with this theory. First, the concept of "Spec" in the standard theory represents a set of rather heterogeneous entities and thus does not constitute a well-defined natural class. For example, the "Spec of C^{0}" is an operator position and an A′-position, and cannot be a θ-position; the "Spec of Agr_S^0 (or T^0)" is a non-operator position and an A-position, but cannot be a θ-position (under the "VP-internal subject hypothesis"; see below); the "Spec of V^{0}" is a non-operator position and an A-position, and can be a θ-position; etc. Notice incidentally that under this approach there is no principled explanation for the fact that no substitution is ever possible into "Specs" of lexical categories. If we define the notion of Spec in terms of agreement, as we do in the relativized X' theory, the notion receives a natural interpretation and constitutes a well-defined natural class, with the result that only functional categories, and no lexical categories, can have Specs, thereby explaining the impossibility of substitution into "Specs" of lexical categories.

Second, the status of "empty category" Δ utilized by substitution is rather unclear. Unlike other empty categories proposed in the literature, Δ is postulated solely for the purpose of movement; it has no semantic content and plays no role in syntactic representations other than serving as a target for movement. Thus, it does not satisfy the principle of Full Interpretation and is not licensed at any level of derivation. Chomsky and Lasnik (1993) assume that Δ is a "fourth type of empty category" and that it is "inserted in the course of derivation" only as "a position to be filled or otherwise eliminated". Chomsky (1993a: 31) claims that Δ represents "the inner workings of a single operation", and thus it is "invisible to the eye that scans only the derivation itself" and therefore is "subliminal".[8] It is then clear that Δ has quite peculiar properties that are not shared by other empty categories, and the sole reason for postulating such an "empty category" is to maintain substitution as a possible option for movement. If we dispense with substitution, then, the need for the peculiar "empty category" Δ will also be eliminated and we will have a simple theory of movement which consists of adjunction only. Empirical differences that have been attributed to the substitution/adjunction dichotomy will then be handled in terms of whether the moved element participates in agreement ("substitution") or not ("adjunction") in the case of X^{max}-movement,[9] or in terms of a proper mechanism of feature percolation for cases of X^0-movement. In the following discussion, I will assume the relativized X' theory coupled with the theory of movement in which adjunction is the only formal operation.

Together with the relativized X' theory, I will also assume the so-called "VP-internal subject hypothesis" (or, more appropriately, the "predicate-internal subject hypothesis", since the analysis should apply to any predicate phrase and not be limited to VP), according to which all of a predicate's arguments, including, crucially, its "external" ("subject") argument, are initially generated within its own projection. Thus, clauses and noun phrases have the following basic predicate structures (as indicated, clauses can be headed by either a verb or an adjective, and the existence of subject is optional in noun phrases; linear order irrelevant):

(26) *Clauses*   *Noun phrases*

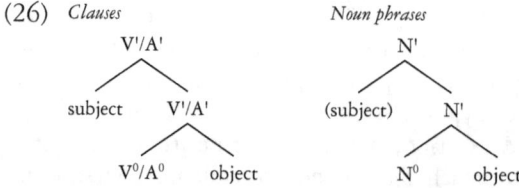

These structures are embedded in higher structures projected from functional heads (cf. (17) and (18)), and subject (and object) may move, depending on the properties of functional heads upstairs, out of a predicate phrase and adjoin to a functional projection, attracted by agreement features associated with the functional head. See Fukui (1986; 1995a) for further details.

The idea that subject is located within a predicate's own projection is a rather traditional one. In earlier literature on X' theory (cf. Chomsky 1970, Jackendoff 1977, etc.), clauses are assumed to be projections of a verb, i.e., $S = V^{max}$, with subject located inside its projection. In traditional studies of Japanese, it is a commonly held assumption that subject is located inside the predicate phrase. For example, Motoki Tokieda (1941: 370–371) claims that "in Japanese, subject contrasts with predicate in the form that the former is contained in the latter".[10] He further argues that "subject in Japanese, when overtly expressed in a sentence, is extracted from predicate in which it was embedded or included" (Tokieda 1941: 371; cf. also Tokieda 1978: 226). The problem, then, is how to accommodate this intuitive idea that subject is located inside the predicate to increasing evidence that, at least in the English-type languages, clauses are headed by inflectional elements (Chomsky 1981a, Huang 1982, Stowell 1981b). The solution was first proposed, on independent grounds having to do with the subject-Aux inversion structure, by Hale (1978), who proposes that subject in English is generated inside VP and then later optionally "raised" to a position higher than inflectional/modal elements. If the movement occurs, a regular sentence surfaces (e.g. *John will hit the road*); if the movement does not apply, the subject-Aux inversion sentence obtains (e.g. *will John hit the road?*).[11] Recently, many linguists have revived Ken Hale's original analysis with prospects for numerous interesting theoretical and cross-linguistic implications. For those contemporary versions of the "VP-internal subject hypothesis" see Fukui and Speas (1986), Kitagawa (1986), Koopman and Sportiche (1988), Kuroda (1988), and Zagona (1988).

In this section, I have summarized the basic tenets of the relativized X' theory with some of the associated hypotheses, viz., the hypothesis that adjunction is the only possible movement ("no substitution hypothesis") and the "VP-internal subject hypothesis". I will assume them in the discussion that follows.

4 Typological differences between English and Japanese

The major typological differences between English and Japanese of which I would like to give a unified account in the following discussion are summarized and illustrated below in (27)–(32).

(27) *The existence of obligatory syntactic* wh-*movement*
English: has obligatory syntactic *wh*-movement
Japanese: no obligatory syntactic *wh*-movement
a. English: I don't know *what*$_i$ John bought t_i.

b. Japanese:
Boku-ga   John-ga   *nani* -o   katta   ka siranai (koto).[12]
I   -NOM   -NOM   what-ACC   bought   Q do not know
"I don't know what John bought."

(28) *The existence of overt "expletive" elements*
English: has overt expletive elements
Japanese: no overt expletive elements
a. English: *It* seems that John is competent.
b. Japanese: no corresponding constructions

(29) *The existence of "scrambling"*
English: no "scrambling"
Japanese: has "scrambling"
a. English:
   (i) John put that book on the table.
   (ii) that book$_i$, John put t_i on the table.
   (iii) on the table$_j$, John put that book t_j.
   (iv) *? on the table$_j$, that book$_i$, John put t_i t_j.
   (v) *? that book$_i$, on the table$_j$, John put t_i t_j.
b. Japanese:
   (i) Mary-ga   John-ni so-no hon -o   watasita.
        -NOM   -to that book-ACC handed
        "Mary handed that book to John."
   (ii) John-ni$_i$ Mary-ga t_i so-no hon-o watasita.
   (iii) so-no hon-o$_j$ Mary-ga John-ni t_j watasita.
   (iv) so-no hon-o$_j$ John-ni$_i$ Mary-ga t_i t_j watasita.
   (v) John-ni$_i$ so-no hon-o$_j$ Mary-ga t_i t_j watasita.

(30) *The existence of "multiple subject" constructions*
English: no multiple subject constructions
Japanese: has multiple subject constructions
a. English:
   (i) *civilized countries, male, the average lifespan is short.
        (with the intended meaning "it is civilized countries that men, their average lifespan is short in")
   (ii) *Tokyo's last week's John's that lecture
b. Japanese:
   (i) bunmeikoku-ga   dansei-ga   heikinzyumyoo-ga
        civilized countries-NOM   male-NOM   average lifespan-NOM
        mizikai.
        is short

        "It is civilized countries that men, their average lifespan is short in."

(Kuno 1973)

(ii) Tokyo-(de)-no sensyuu-no John-no so-no koogi
at-GEN last week-GEN -GEN that lecture

Lit. "Tokyo's last week's John's that lecture"

(31) *The existence of subject-Aux inversion*
English: has subject-Aux inversion
Japanese: no subject-Aux inversion

a. English:
(i) John will come home early this evening.
(ii) Will John come home early this evening?
b. Japanese:
(i) John-wa kyoo ie -ni hayaku kaette-kuru.
-TOP today home-to early come back

"John will come home early today."
(ii) John-wa kyoo ie-ni hayaku kaette-ki-masu-ka?
Q

"Will John come home early today?"

(32) *The existence of productive "complex predicate" formation*
English: no productive complex predicate formation
Japanese: has productive complex predicate formation

a. English: no word-level complex predicates
b. Japanese:
tabe-sase -rare
eat -CAUSE-PASSIVE
"to be caused to eat"
nagur-(r)are-ta -gar -are
hit -PASSIVE-DESIDERATIVE-PASSIVE
"to be shown a sign of wanting to be hit", etc.

These typological differences between the two languages have been noted quite widely in the literature, but so far no systematic account has been given in order to derive them from a more general typological character of the language in question. Given the principles-and-parameters approach adopted in the present paper, coupled with the relativized X' theory briefly summarized above, a question can now be addressed as to what are the fundamental parametric differences between English and Japanese which explain the typological differences summarized above (and possibly others) that have hitherto been regarded as unrelated to one another. In the following section, I will try to give a possible answer to this question.

5 Explanations for the typological differences

If the restrictive theory of parametric variation proposed in section 2 (cf. (20)) is on the right track, the place where we should look for the fundamental differences between English and Japanese is either the properties of functional elements in these languages, or the difference in ordering restrictions between them.

Let us consider first the difference in ordering restrictions. As we discussed in section 2, it is a well-known fact that English and Japanese choose different values for the head-parameter: English is "head-initial", and Japanese is "head-last". Thus, English exhibits the head-complement order in every phrase and Japanese shows the reverse, complement-head order everywhere.

Consider next the properties of functional elements. I will confine the discussion to the four "major functional categories" (cf. section 2) Agr, T, D, and C. Assuming an earlier system of functional categories where I(nflection) is yet to be decomposed into two independent functional elements Agr and T, Fukui (1988a) argues that Japanese lacks all of the functional categories attested in, say, English: that is, Japanese lacks C, D, and I altogether.[13] Given the restrictive theory of parametric variation discussed in section 2, it is not possible to maintain Fukui's (1988a) hypothesis in its strongest form, if we interpret Fukui's claim that Japanese lacks I to mean that it lacks both Agr and T, since T plays a role at LF, and we propose that "only those functional elements that do not play any role in LF can be absent in the lexicon of a particular language" (cf. (20c)). Therefore, we must interpret Fukui's (1988a) claim to mean that Japanese lacks Agr, D, and C, which is essentially the hypothesis put forth in Fukui (1986). The lack of Agr receives initial support from the fact that Japanese entirely lacks subject-verb and object-verb agreement.[14] Also, if nominative Case (in English) is assigned by Spec-head agreement between Agr_s and a noun phrase in its Spec position (cf. Chomsky and Lasnik 1993), and if agreement is generally one-to-one, then nominative Case in Japanese (*ga*) cannot be assigned by Agr_s since, unlike in English, there is no requirement in Japanese that nominative noun phrase be unique per sentence, as evidenced by the existence of so-called "multiple subject constructions" (cf. (30)). Note that the point remains the same even under the assumption that nominative Case is assigned to Spec-T (and agreement to Spec-Agr_s),[15] as long as the relevant Spec-head agreement is assumed to be one-to-one. That is, nominative Case in Japanese is assigned (or "realized") by some mechanism other than Spec-head agreement. See Fukui and Saito (1994) and Fukui and Nishigauchi (1992) for relevant discussion.

What about the other two functional heads, D and C? Let us consider C first. By the criterion (20c), C can be lacking in Japanese (see the discussion in section 2). In fact, Fukui (1986) shows that *to* "that", which has been assumed without argument to be the Japanese counterpart of *that* in English, does not exhibit the same properties as *that*. On top of the differences pointed out by Fukui (1986), we may add several others here. First, clauses headed by *that* can be passivized, whereas those headed by *to* cannot.

(33) a. John claims that Mary proved the Church-Turing thesis.
 b. that Mary proved the Church-Turing thesis is claimed by John.

(34) a. John-ga [Mary-ga   Church-Turing-no   teeze -o
      -NOM   -NOM   -GEN thesis-ACC
    syoomei sita to] syutyoosite-iru (koto).
    proved   "that" claims   (fact)

    "John claims that Mary proved the Church-Turing thesis."

 b. *[Mary-ga Church-Turing-no teeze-o syoomei sita to]-ga
    John-niyotte syutyoos-are-te-iru.
       -by   is claimed

    "that Mary proved the Church-Turing thesis is claimed by John."

In fact, *to*-headed clauses can never appear in subject position, in contrast to *that*-clauses.[16]

(35) that the doctor came so early surprised John.

(36) *[isya-ga   sugoku hayaku kita to] -ga   John-o
      doctor-NOM so   early   came "that"-NOM   -ACC
    odorok-ase-ta.
    surprised

    "that the doctor came so early surprised John."

Second, *to* can co-occur with direct quotation marks, but *that* cannot.

(37) John-wa   "boku-ga   saisyoni sono   teeri   -o
      -TOP   I   -NOM   first   the/that theorem-ACC
    syoomei-sita-nda!"   to   itta.
    proved   -PARTICLE "that" said

    "John said, 'I proved the theorem first!'"

(38) *John said that, "I proved the theorem first!"

That and *to* also differ in other respects concerning the direct quote. Kuno (1972) observes that certain verbs such as *claim*, *think*, etc. allow what he calls "direct discourse" representations, that is, representations that contain direct quotes, while verbs such as *deny*, *forget*, etc. do not allow such representations (see Kuno 1972 for more detailed discussion). Thus, while the examples in (39) are grammatical, those in (40) are ill-formed.

(39) a. John claims, "Mary proved the theorem."
 b. John thinks, "Mary is a genius,"

(40) a. *John denies, "Mary is sick."
 b. *John forgot, "Mary came to my office yesterday."

Now, notice that verbs that do not allow direct discourse representations are exactly those that do not take *to* in Japanese. This can be shown by looking at the Japanese examples corresponding to the English ones in (39) and (40).

(41) a.   John-wa [Mary-ga sono   teeri   -o   syoomei sita to]
                      the/that theorem-ACC proved   "that"
     syutyoosite-iru.
     is claiming

     "John claims that Mary proved the theorem."

   b. John-wa [Mary-ga tensai da to]   omotte-iru.
                        genius is "that" is thinking

     "John thinks that Mary is a genius."

(42) a. *John-wa [Mary-ga byooki da to]   hiteisite-iru.
                          sick is   "that" denies

     "John denies that Mary is sick."

   b. *John-wa [Mary-ga kinoo   zibun/kare-no   office-ni kita
                         yesterday self/his   -GEN   -to came
     to]   wasureta.
     "that" forgot

     "John forgot that Mary came to his office yesterday."[17]

These facts strongly suggest that *that* and *to* have quite different properties, and that the basic function of *to* is largely, if not entirely, to introduce direct quotations. If the basic function of *to* is to introduce a direct quote, we may also be able to account for another difference between *that* and *to*, namely the fact that while *that* can appear in relative clauses, *to* never appears in relative clauses, since it is independently known that relative clauses do not allow direct quotations.

(43) [the man [that I saw in the park]]

(44) [[boku-ga   kooen-de atta (*to)] otoko]
       I   -NOM park   -in met   "that" man

   "the man that I saw in the park"

It may also be possible to account for the fact that *to* can never be optionally deleted, whereas *that* can be optionally deleted under certain conditions (cf. Stowell 1981b).

(45) I think (that) Mary is a genius.

(46) Boku-wa [Mary-ga tensai da *(to)] omou.
　　　　　　　　　 genius is "that" think

"I think (that) Mary is a genius."

Optional deletion of *to* is impossible just as optional deletion of the quotation marks is impossible.[18]

(47) *John said, I am a genius. (with the meaning "John said that he, John, is a genius")

It should be clear from these considerations that merely identifying *to* as the Japanese counterpart of *that* does not solve various empirical problems; in particular, it does not explain numerous differences between *that* and *to*. The situation seems to be the same in the cases of other candidates for C in Japanese, such as *ka* (Question marker), *no* (Nominalizer), etc., where these elements simply do not have counterparts in English or, even if there are some similar elements in English, their properties are quite different. It is of course quite possible that all of these elements constitute the single, well-defined functional category C, with relatively minor idiosyncrasies being exhibited by each element. To draw such a conclusion, however, seems quite premature at this point. Thus, I will tentatively assume in the following discussion the hypothesis put forth in my earlier writings (Fukui 1986, 1988a) that Japanese lacks C with the same properties as the English complementizers, putting aside for the moment the determination of the exact categorial nature of such elements as *ka*, *no*, etc. in Japanese (cf. Fukui 1986 and 1995a for some discussion on this matter).

Let us now consider the status of D in Japanese. Fukui (1986, 1995a) argues that demonstratives such as *kono* "this", *sono* "that", and *ano* "that" in Japanese, which have long been assumed to be "determiners" in the language, do not share the crucial properties of determiners in English (*the*, *a*, etc.), and that they therefore do not qualify as D in Japanese (see Fukui 1986, 1995a for detailed discussions). In the absence of any other plausible candidates for D in Japanese, Fukui (1986, 1988a) concludes that the language lacks D in its lexicon.[19] However, given the restrictive theory of parametric variation discussed in section 2 (cf. (20c)), we are now forced to assume that every language has D in some form or another, if D indeed plays a role in LF just as T is visible in LF. Thus, I will tentatively assume that Japanese has D (or something equivalent to it in function, perhaps a non-major functional head "Quantifier" (Q^0) if the internal structure of noun phrases contains such a functional phrase outside of N^{max}), which has no phonetic content and also does not induce agreement,[20] though the issue here is far from being settled and needs much further research.

Summing up our discussion so far, we have looked at the differences between English and Japanese with respect to (i) ordering restrictions, and (ii) properties of functional elements, the two domains in which all the major cross-linguistic variations are supposed to be explained, according to the restrictive theory of parametric variation proposed in section 2. In the domain of ordering restrictions, we have recapitulated the well-known fact that English is a head-initial language, while Japanese is a head-last language. As for properties of functional elements in the two languages, we have concluded that English has Agr, C, T, and D, all of which are active and can induce agreement. Japanese, on the other hand, lacks Agr and (possibly) C; it has T and D, as required by (20c), but these functional heads seem to play no active role in syntax (narrowly construed, excluding LF and PF) and do not induce agreement. We will now see how the typological differences between English and Japanese summarized in the preceding section can be explained on the basis of these few fundamental differences between the two languages.

Let us first consider scrambling (cf. (29)). First of all, the status of optional movement in general, and scrambling in particular, has been rather unclear under the "economy" approach first explicitly put forth by Chomsky (1991b). The general principle of economy, which has been proposed by Chomsky as an overarching principle deriving some of the existing principles of UG, requires derivations and representations to be minimum in cost. One specific property of the economy principle is that it has the "tendency" to eliminate the possibility of optionality in derivation (cf. Chomsky 1991b: 433). Under the economy approach, a choice point will be permissible only if the resulting derivations are all minimum in cost. It then follows that an optional rule such as scrambling is allowed only if its application is "costless", the "cost" of rule application being calculated by a certain algorithm defined in the theory of grammar. Fukui (1993b) proposes one specific measure to compute the cost of rule application, the parameter-value preservation (PVP) measure, which states that a grammatical operation (movement, in particular) that creates a structure which is inconsistent with the parameter-value for a language is costly in the language, whereas one which produces a structure consistent with the parameter-value is costless (cf. Fukui 1993b for more detailed discussion). A case in point here is the head-parameter. English sets the value for the head-parameter as "head-initial", while Japanese sets it as "head-last". Restricting our attention to the linear order between a verb and its object, this means that English has the canonical order (called the "canonical precedence relation" (CPR) in Fukui 1993b) $V > X^{max}$, whereas Japanese has $X^{max} > V$. Now the PVP measure predicts that optional movement of object (X^{max}) destroying the CPR is not allowed in a language. Therefore, in English, any leftward optional movement of object over verb is prohibited, while rightward optional movement of object should be permitted. In Japanese, where the CPR is $X^{max} > V$, any optional rightward movement of object over verb is disallowed, whereas optional leftward movement of object is permitted. This situation is schematically represented as follows.

(48) *Distribution of optional movement*

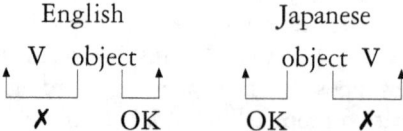

Thus, English does not have leftward optional movement of object (scrambling), but Japanese allows such optional movement.[21] As for rightward optional movement, English exhibits some instances of rightward optional movement of object (e.g., Heavy NP Shift), whereas Japanese does not allow rightward optional movement of object over verb; hence, the well-known strict "head-last" status of Japanese clauses (see Fukui 1993b for more detailed explanations). Note incidentally that, under this account, topicalization in English cannot be a truly optional movement, since its application destroys the CPR in the language. Topicalization, therefore, should be analysed as a kind of "focalization" process triggered by some functional head, perhaps along the lines suggested by Chomsky (1977). See Fukui (1993b) and Fukui and Saito (1994) for extensive discussion on this and related matters. Note also that multiple applications of scrambling should be possible because the relativized X' theory allows recursion at the single-bar level and T in Japanese does not induce agreement and its projection is never closed. Scrambling in Japanese, then, can be analysed as (possibly multiple) adjunction to T'.[22]

(49) $[_{T'} Y^{max} [_{T'} X^{max} [_{T'} [_{V'} \ldots t_x \quad t_y] V] T]]]$

Note finally that the analysis of scrambling (and optional movement) just presented makes a cross-linguistic prediction beyond English and Japanese. That is, it is predicted under this analysis that only (underlyingly) SOV and VOS languages can have scrambling-type optional movement of object. See Fukui (1993b) for further discussion.

Let us consider next the existence of overt expletives. English has overt expletives; Japanese doesn't (cf. (28)). This difference can be explained on the basis of Agr in English and the lack of such an element in Japanese. Let us assume with Fukui (1988a) (cf. also Kuroda 1988) that the agreement relation must be satisfied before the process of Spell-Out (i.e., the process which leads to PF: cf. Chomsky 1993a) applies. It follows then that in English, a language with an active Agr, a phonetically non-null element must be present in an adjoined position to Agr' before Spell-Out, to satisfy the agreement relation induced by the functional head Agr, even if no θ-role is assigned to that position. On the other hand, such a requirement does not hold in Japanese, simply because this language does not have Agr. Therefore, Japanese need not, and by the principle of economy cannot, have overt expletives.[23] Note, incidentally, that our account of overt expletives in English just given implies that the so-called "extended" part of the Extended Projection Principle (cf. Chomsky 1982) does not have to be stipulated. Rather, it should be dissociated from the Projection Principle and be derived from some independent principles having to do with the functional head Agr (cf. Borer 1986, Fukui and Speas 1986, and references cited in these works for detailed discussion).

Multiple subjects, that is, multiple occurrences of nominative and genitive noun phrases, are allowed in Japanese, but are prohibited in English

126 *The principles-and-parameters approach*

(cf. (30)). This again is due to the existence of Agr in English and lack thereof in Japanese. In English, subject ends up in the Spec-Agr position, participating in the agreement relation.

(50) $[_{\text{AGRP}} \text{ subject}_i \, [_{\text{AGR}'} \text{Agr}^0 \ldots [_{V'} t_i \ldots] \ldots]]$

  agreement

Owing to the one-to-one nature of agreement, subject must be unique in English. Japanese, on the other hand, lacks Agr. Nominative Case must be assigned in some other way. I assume here with Kuroda (1978), Saito (1982), and Fukui (1986) that nominative Case is in fact not "assigned", by anything, but it is a kind of "default" mechanism to license a non-Case-marked phrase. To work out the Kuroda-Saito-Fukui view of nominative Case in Japanese, I assume, essentially along the lines of Fukui and Nishigauchi (1992), that non-Case-marked phrases are licensed by T^0 (which has no features other than its own categorial features) under government which is based on "c-command" (not on a looser notion of "m-command");[24] the so-called "nominative Case-marker" *ga* is realized on a phrase, indicating that it has been licensed. Thus, subject in Japanese need not move and can stay inside the projection of a predicate, since it is governed by T^0 in its original place; there is no Case-theoretic reason for subject to move.[25]

(51) $[_{T'} \, [_{V'} \text{ subject } [_{V'} \ldots V^0]] \, T^0]$

  government

Now notice that the position of subject in Japanese, namely a position adjoined to V', can freely iterate, according to relativized X' theory. Therefore, there can in principle be any number of phrases in V'-adjoined positions, being all governed by T^0 because government, unlike agreement, need not be generally one-to-one. Hence, they are all marked with *ga*, quite independently of their status with respect to argumenthood.

(52) $[_{T'} \, [_{V'} X^{\max} \, [_{V'} X^{\max} \, [_{V'} \ldots [_{V'} X^{\max} \, [_{V'} \ldots V^0]] \ldots]]] \, T^0]$

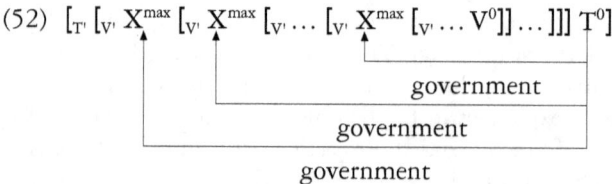

Multiple occurrences of genitives can be accounted for in a similar way. In English, genitive Case is assigned via agreement either with Agr, if English indeed has Agr in noun phrases (cf. (17)),[26] or with D^0, if English lacks Agr in noun phrases. In either case, genitive Case must be unique owing to the one-to-one nature of agreement. Japanese, by contrast, lacks Agr, and D^0, if any, lacks agreement features. Genitive Case in Japanese, i.e., *no*, exactly like nominative Case in this language (*ga*), is not assigned by anything, but is a "default" marker to license a non-Case-marked phrase under government by D^0 (or its equivalent; see above). Again, as government need not be one-to-one, and as relativized X' theory allows free recursion at the single-bar level, here at the level of N', multiple occurrences of genitive phrases are allowed.

Note, incidentally, that under our analysis of *ga*-marking just presented, the (final) landing site for scrambling should be an adjoined position to T', rather than an adjoined position to V' as assumed in my earlier writings (cf. Fukui 1988a). The positions for scrambled phrases and those for multiple subjects are thus structurally distinguished under our current analysis. Whether or not this distinction can be empirically supported must await future research.

Note also that our analysis of *ga/no*-marking, coupled with our analysis of scrambling, gives an interesting account of the Case-conversion phenomenon, called "*ga/no* conversion" in Japanese (cf. Harada 1971, Bedell 1972, etc.). *Ga-no* conversion is a process in which the Case-particles *ga* and *no* convert optionally in relative clauses and noun-complement constructions. Thus, in the following examples, the subject of a relative clause, *John*, can appear either in the nominative (with *ga*) or in the genitive (with *no*).

(53) a. John-ga   yonda hon
         -NOM read book
     b. John-no   yonda hon
         -GEN

   "the book that John read"

Details aside, the underlying structure of the examples in (53) is as follows (O is an abstract relative clause operator):[27]

(54)

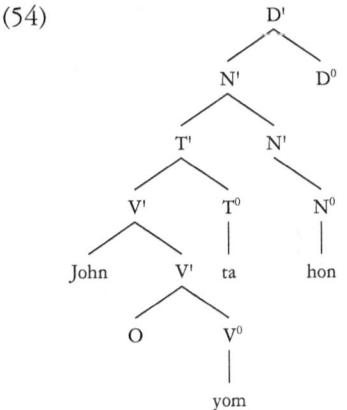

If *John* does not move and stays in its original position, as in normal independent clauses, then it will be governed by T^0 and *ga* is realized on it, yielding (53a). Recall now that Japanese has scrambling, and nothing prevents *John* from adjoining to N' (via successive adjunctions to V' and T'), producing the following structure (we ignore as irrelevant adjunction of O to T'; cf. note 27).

(55)

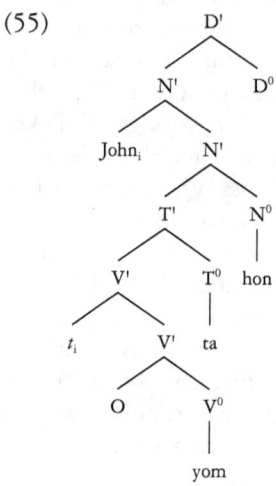

In (55), *John*, a non-Case-marked phrase, is governed by D^0. Thus, a "default" Case-marker *no* is realized on *John* to license it. In this way, our analysis clearly captures an important generalization that the existence of scrambling and the existence of *ga/no* conversion are fundamentally related, a generalization which has never been made in previous analyses. The reason why these two Case-particles (*ga* and *no*) can only convert with each other but cannot convert with other Case-particles (e.g. *o* "ACC") is that these are the only two "default" markers in Japanese and that other Case-particles are really "assigned" by some head. See Fukui and Nishigauchi (1992) for more detailed discussion on this matter.

Consider next the case of *wh*-movement. English has an obligatory process of *wh*-movement before Spell-Out; Japanese does not (cf. (27)). It is widely assumed that *wh*-movement in syntax is a process triggered by C^0 (+*wh* Comp) (cf. Bresnan 1972, Chomsky 1986a, etc.). The obligatory nature of syntactic *wh*-movement in English can then be accounted for in terms of the requirement we have already discussed that the agreement relation (Spec-head agreement) be satisfied before Spell-Out applies (Fukui's 1988a "principle of agreement"): a *wh*-phrase must adjoin to C' and participate in the agreement relation with C^0 before Spell-Out in order to fulfill the requirement. Japanese, on the other hand, either completely lacks C; or even if it has some kind of C, it does not induce agreement. Thus, a *wh*-phrase in Japanese need not move in overt syntax,[28] and, if it has to move for scopal reasons, it moves in LF.[29]

Turning to the last two differences between English and Japanese, let us assume that subject-Aux inversion and "complex predicate" formation are both instances of head-movement (Chomsky 1986a, Baker 1988). Subject-Aux inversion can be viewed as a movement of an inflected verb to the position of C (cf. Chomsky 1986a). The "lack" of this process in Japanese can be explained in either of the following two ways: (i) Japanese does not have subject-Aux inversion just because it does not have C, which is a triggering element and also a landing site of the movement; or (ii) even if Japanese does have such a process, its effect is invisible owing to the head-last character of the language. In the absence of decisive evidence between these two accounts, I simply leave the issue open here.

As for the case of "complex predicate" formation, the process in Japanese can be schematically represented as follows.

(56) $\ldots V_{1\,V_{1'}}]\,V_{2\,V_{2'}}]\,V_{3\,V_{3'}}]]\,T^0{}_{T'}]$

Each movement operation in (56) does not violate any principles of UG. Therefore, "complex predicate" formation freely takes place in Japanese as a series of successive movements of a verb into the next higher one. Regarding the impossibility of "complex predicate" formation in English, Fukui (1988a) proposes an account based essentially on the head-parameter: in Japanese, successive movement can take place between two adjacent verbs because of the language's strict head-last character, whereas, in English, verbs cannot be adjacent to each other, being separated by subject, owing to the language's head-initial value for the head-parameter. However, Shibatani (1990a) points out, citing examples from Baker (1988), that the value for the head-parameter and the existence of "complex predicate" formation do not generally correlate. Thus, languages like Chichewa and Southern Tiwa, which are apparently head-initial, display rich arrays of "complex predicates", allowing verb movement over an intervening subject. Shibatani argues that the existence of "complex predicate" formation is attributable to the presence of bound form predicates. Japanese exhibits the process of "complex predicate" formation since the language has bound verbs which trigger verb movement; English lacks such a process simply because it has no available bound verbs in the lexicon. This explanation is plausible, but may be inconsistent with our restrictive theory of parametric variation, which states that, in the lexicon, only functional elements are subject to cross-linguistic variation (cf. (20b)). One way to resolve this potential difficulty is to state the relevant condition in terms of different properties of T.[30] Exactly how the condition should be stated, however, is not a trivial matter, and I would like to leave it to future research. See Kuno (1978), Saito (1985), and Fukui (1986) for some relevant discussions of the differences between English and Japanese tense elements.

6 Concluding remarks

We have seen that some of the major typological differences between English and Japanese can be explained in a highly deductive and modular manner, if we assume a certain version of X' theory (relativized X' theory), coupled with a few fundamental parametric properties of the languages. In section 2, we argued that, to achieve explanatory adequacy, the theory of parametric variation must be narrowly constrained. Specifically, we suggested a restrictive theory of parametric variation in which the following constraints are imposed:

(57) (=(20)) *A restrictive theory of parametric variation*
 a. Parametric variation outside of the lexicon must be limited to ordering restrictions ("linearity").
 b. Inside the lexicon, only [+F] elements ("functional elements") are subject to parametric variation ("functional parametrization hypothesis").
 c. Among the functional elements, only those that do not play any role in LF can be absent in the lexicon of a particular language.

In an attempt to make the functional parametrization hypothesis restrictive, we also proposed that the "major functional categories" (Agr, T, D, and C) in human language should be specified in terms of the primitive features [±N] and [±V], just like the "major lexical categories" (A, V, N, and P), the difference between these two classes of categories being different values for the feature [±F].

(58) (=(16)) *Feature specifications of the major functional categories*
 Agr = [+F, +N, +V]
 T = [+F, −N, +V]
 D = [+F, +N, −V]
 C = [+F, −N, −V]

After briefly outlining, in section 3, the relativized X' theory in which "agreement" is taken to be a basic notion, we illustrated some of the major typological differences between English and Japanese in section 4. Then, in section 5, we argued that these typological differences, as well as a few others mentioned in the course of our discussion, can be explained naturally in a deductive way, if we assume, in accordance with the restrictive theory of parametric variation proposed in section 2, (i) different values for the head-parameter (English, "head-initial"; Japanese, "head-last"), and (ii) that Japanese does not have Agr (and possibly, C) and existing functional elements in the language do not induce agreement.

The research on comparative syntax presented in this paper is couched within the principles-and-parameters approach. One of the characteristics of this approach that distinguishes it from most of the traditional typological studies is its abstractness. In the principles-and-parameters theory, attempts have been made to give deductive explanations to the observed linguistic phenomena on the basis of certain abstract features of language. We have tried to show that such an abstract approach towards explanations of observed cross-linguistic differences, as well as striking commonality, opens up a refreshingly new way of looking at them. The abstract approach represented by the principles-and-parameters theory has not only presented a new way of looking at the phenomena that have been observed in the traditional literature, but also facilitated discoveries of new phenomena that call for novel explanations. For example, English and Japanese also show quite different properties with respect to some of the general conditions postulated in the theory of UG. Thus, English exhibits the "Subject Condition" effect, that is, the effect that extraction out of subject results in ungrammaticality, as illustrated by (59), while Japanese does not show such an effect, as shown by (60), which is taken from Saito (1985).[31]

(59) a. [pictures of Bill] pleased John.
 b. *?who$_i$ did [pictures of t_i] please John?
 c. [that John will win the race] is likely.
 d. *?which race$_i$ is [that John will win t_i] likely?

(60) a. John-ga [[Mary-ga nani-o   katta koto] -ga   mondai -da
        -NOM   what-ACC bought fact   -NOM problem-is
     to]   omotteru no?
     "that" think   Q

   "John thinks that [the fact that Mary bought what] is a problem."

 b. ?nani$_i$-o John-ga [[Mary-ga t_i katta koto]-ga mondai-da to] omotteru no?

   "what$_i$, John thinks that [the fact that Mary bought t_i] is a problem."

Examples (59b) and (59d) are derived from (59a) and (59c), respectively, by *wh*-movement, showing the typical Subject Condition effect, which is a subcase of the subjacency condition (cf. Kayne 1981, Huang 1982). On the other hand, the scrambling of a phrase out of subject does not exhibit a similar effect in Japanese. Example (60b) is derived from (60a) by scrambling *nani-o* "what-ACC" out of the subject phrase [*Mary-ga nani-o katta koto*]-*ga*. The result is a little bit awkward, but is much better than normal subjacency violations.[32] There have been several proposals to account for this difference between English and Japanese that I am not going into here (see Kayne 1983b, Ueda 1991, Saito 1992b, among others), but the point is that this kind of difference among languages can be unveiled only under a rather abstract approach to cross-linguistic variation with an articulated theory of UG. The principles-and-parameters theory presents one such approach, and the hypotheses made under this abstract approach should be tested against a wider range of cross-linguistic data, as in the traditional studies of typology.

7 Symmetry in syntax
Merge and Demerge

with Yuji Takano

1 Introduction

The theory of phrase structure has been playing an increasingly important role in the theory of grammar as one of the few remaining core components of the human language faculty. As the "minimalist program" (Chomsky 1993a) has been developed, a variety of the subcomponents of grammar that had been assumed in earlier work have been critically scrutinized in light of minimalist assumptions and, in many cases, eliminated from grammar as conceptually unwarranted from the strictly minimalist viewpoint. However, to the extent that linguistic expressions in human languages have hierarchical structures, not just strings of words and formatives, which is a fairly well-established point, the theory of Universal Grammar (UG) must have a procedure that is responsible for the "structures" embodied in human languages. Of course, the theory of phrase structure itself has to be subjected to minimalist scrutiny, as it has been in recent works (Chomsky 1995a, b, Kayne 1994; see also Fukui 1986). It should not contain any stipulations that are not motivated by such considerations as economy/optimality or by properties of the interface levels (conceptual/intentional ("LF") and articulatory/perceptual ("PF"); see Chomsky 1993a for detailed discussion).

The theory of language variation also has to be narrowly constrained. We assume in this article the "principles-and-parameters" approach in which the theory of UG is viewed as a system of invariant principles with parameters that are to be fixed by experience. Recent work within this framework (Borer 1984, Chomsky 1995b, Fukui 1988a, 1995b, among others) has proposed that the locus of language variation and typology be found either with respect to linear order or in a certain subcomponent of the lexicon ("functional categories"). If so, a restrictive theory of linear order and functional categories is certainly called for, to obtain a minimalist theory of comparative syntax.

The goal of this article is to develop a theory of phrase structure which is free from unmotivated stipulations as much as possible and which is also compatible with the most restrictive theory of parametric variation currently available, with a special focus on the nature and role of linear order and functional categories. The organization of the article is as follows. In section 2, we will go over some of the most important recent works on parametric variation and the status of linear order, in an attempt to set the theoretical background for our main proposal. We will then present the major hypothesis of this article, the "Symmetry" principle of derivation, in section 3 and discuss some of the most immediate consequences of the hypothesis. Section 4 discusses further consequences of our proposal, focusing on its implications for the theory of language variation and typology. Through the discussion, special attention is paid to the comparison of Japanese (and other East Asian languages) and English (and other Indo-European languages). Section 5 summarizes the discussion and makes concluding remarks.

2 Theoretical background: the status of linear order in phrase structure

In an attempt to construct a restrictive theory of comparative syntax, Fukui (1995b), on the basis of his earlier works (Fukui 1986, 1988a), proposes the following constraints on the parametric options available to UG and the components of language in which they are to be found.

(1) *A restrictive theory of parametric variation* (adapted from Fukui 1995b, 342–343)
   a. Parametric variation outside of the lexicon must be limited to ordering restrictions (linear order).
   b. Inside the lexicon, only [+F] elements ("functional categories") are subject to parametric variation ("functional parametrization hypothesis").
   c. Among the functional categories, only those that do not play any role in LF can be absent in the lexicon of a particular language.

Along similar lines, Chomsky (1995b) suggests that parametric variation be restricted to formal features of functional categories (with no interpretation at the interface). There can be other variants of essentially the same thesis, but it is now widely assumed that something of this sort must be correct. If so, then the sources of language variation must be found either in terms of linear order or in the domain of functional categories, though too little is known at this point to become more specific about, say, exactly what properties of functional categories are subject to parametric variation.

Of the two sources of parametric variation, linear order and functional categories, the latter seems to be ineliminable, given the crucial role played by lexical acquisition in the process of language growth or acquisition. It is plainly impossible to acquire a language without acquiring its lexicon. By contrast, the status of linear order in parametric variation, or in the computation of human language more generally, is not so obvious. In fact, although the role of linear order in language was never questioned in earlier work of generative grammar, it has been increasingly less obvious that linear order plays a role at all in language computation, apart from phonology. Thus, virtually all the principles and conditions assumed in the principles-and-parameters theory in the 1980s are formulated purely in hierarchical terms (in terms of domination and c-command), without referring to linear order. The "head-parameter" (and its variants) seems to be the only notion in linguistic theory which crucially refers to linear order.[1]

Kayne (1994) challenges this notion of head-parameter. He proposes a universal principle, the Linear Correspondence Axiom (LCA), which states essentially that asymmetric c-command imposes a linear ordering of terminal elements. More specifically, the LCA requires that if a nonterminal X asymmetrically c-commands a nonterminal Y in a given phrase marker P, then all terminals dominated by X must precede or follow all terminals dominated by Y in P. Kayne takes the relevant ordering to be precedence, rather than subsequence (following), based on his assumptions about the relation between terminals and "time slots" (see Kayne 1994 for details). Thus, within Kayne's theory, asymmetric c-command relations uniquely map into precedence relations: all terminals dominated by X precede all terminals dominated by Y, in the configuration stated above. It then follows, given Kayne's formulation, that there is a universal S(pecifier)-H(ead)-C(omplement) order (in particular, S(ubject)-V(erb)-O(bject)), with other orders (S-O-V, for example) being derived via movement. With the universal S-H-C order, the head-parameter is entirely eliminated.

Note that in Kayne's theory, linear order still plays a role in the core computation of language, though redundantly, because it is entirely determined by asymmetric c-command relations. In other words, Kayne proposes that linear order is not parametrized and that it is uniquely determined by asymmetric c-command relations, given his LCA, which he claims to apply at every syntactic level. But linear order is still defined and remains visible throughout the derivation and could conceivably play a role in the core computation of language.

Chomsky (1994, 1995b), adopting and incorporating the basic insights of Kayne's LCA into his "bare phrase structure theory", makes a step further towards complete elimination of linear order from the core of language computation. Working under minimalist assumptions, he points out that X' theory specifies much redundant information and ought to be eliminated altogether.[2] Chomsky claims that the only structural information that is needed in phrase structure theory is that head and non-head combine to form a unit. He then proposes that phrase structure is constructed in a bottom-up fashion by an operation called *Merge*, which takes a pair of syntactic objects (elements in syntax) and replaces them by a new combined syntactic object. More formally, "syntactic objects" are defined as follows in Chomsky's bare theory.

(2) *Syntactic objects*
    a.   Lexical items

b. K = [γ, [α, β]],
where α, β are objects and γ is the label of K, γ ∈ [α, β]

Objects of type (2a) are complexes of features, the smallest functioning units in syntax. Merge is the recursive step represented by (2b). Applied to two objects α and β, Merge forms a new object K, with α and β the *constituents* of K and γ the *label* of K. When α and β merge, either one of the two, say α, *projects* and becomes the *head* of the newly created unit. This is illustrated informally in (3).[3]

(3)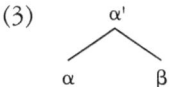

Chomsky claims that, with this simple bare theory, various properties stipulated in the traditional X' theory can be straightforwardly derived and consequently that X' theory can be totally dispensed with. (See Chomsky 1994, 1995b for much detailed discussion.) Note that the definition of syntactic objects given in (2) is stated purely in set-theoretic terms, and hence no linear order is introduced. According to Chomsky, there is no clear evidence that linear order plays a role at LF or in the core computation of human language. Thus, he assumes that linear order is not defined and hence does not play a role in the core computation of language, and he suggests that ordering is a property of the phonological component, a proposal that has been occasionally made in various forms in the literature. Specifically, he claims that a modified version of the LCA applies as a principle of the phonological component to the output of Morphology, a subcomponent of the phonological component (see Chomsky 1995b for detailed discussion). Thus, under Chomsky's proposal, syntactic objects are defined without reference to linear order (as in (2)) in the core computational part of human language and will later be assigned linear order by (a modified version of) the LCA in the phonological component.

On the other hand, Fukui and Saito (1992, 1996) (see also Fukui 1993b) claim that linear order indeed plays an important role in the core computational part of human language and argue that the head-parameter, or more precisely a modified version of it, should be maintained. One way, proposed in Fukui and Saito (1996), to incorporate the head-parameter into the bare phrase structure theory is to replace the set notation [α, β] in (2) by an ordered pair <α, β> thereby specifying which of the two elements projects in a given language. Thus, we have (4) instead of (2b) (the qualifications are the same, omitted here):

(4) K = [γ, <α, β>]

If γ takes the value α, we have a "head-initial/left-headed" language such as English, whereas if γ = β, a "head-last/right-headed" language like Japanese obtains. Fukui and Saito argue that given the modified version of Merge, it is possible to characterize the traditional "adjunction" operations, viz., scrambling in Japanese and Heavy NP Shift in English, as paradigm cases of Merge. Hence, given the costless nature of Merge (Chomsky 1995b; but see Chomsky 1995a for a different view), the optionality of these operations, a matter that has been quite disturbing for the general economy approach to movement (Chomsky 1991b), is also straightforwardly accounted for. Further, they point out that the "directionality" of these optional movements correlates with the "directionality" of projection in the language. Thus, head-initial/left-headed English has rightward Heavy NP Shift whereas head-last/right-headed Japanese exhibits leftward scrambling, but no other combination is allowed. It is clear that such a correlation can be captured only by a parametrized Merge embodying linear order, as in (4). Fukui and Saito show that a number of other differences between English and Japanese also follow from their theory of phrase structure.

While all these approaches have their attractiveness, none of them is free from problems. The biggest problem for those approaches abandoning the head-parameter,[4] as discussed extensively in Takano (1996), arises with respect to the explanation of word order variation. As stated above, Kayne's LCA (or Chomsky's modified version of it) predicts the universal S-H-C order. Thus, the word order observed in, say, English follows directly from the LCA. However, the word order in Japanese (the S-C-H order) is inconsistent with the LCA and therefore needs explanation. Kayne proposes to account for this fact by appealing to "hypothetical" functional categories in Japanese. Let us consider the S-O-V order in Japanese for illustration. To derive this order from the underlying S-V-O order, Kayne suggests that Japanese has a functional category which always forces the object to move overtly to its Spec, crossing the verb. After the overt movement, the object is in the position asymmetrically c-commanding the verb, and hence the LCA maps the resulting structure into the O-V order. If the subject in Japanese appears in a position still higher than the raised object, the correct surface S-O-V order follows. The same account carries over to the other "head-last" structures in Japanese, with an associated functional category in each case, triggering movement of a complement to the Spec position of the functional category.

The plausibility of this account hinges on the nature and justification of the postulated functional category in Japanese. Some non-trivial problems arise in this regard, however. The exact nature of the postulated functional category that Kayne suggests for languages like Japanese is quite obscure. Note that the functional category in question must force all complements to move past the verb, given that all complements, regardless of their categorial status, appear to the left of the verb in Japanese.[5]

(5) a. John-ga [hon-o] yonda (koto).
 -NOM book-ACC read

"John read a book."

b. John-ga   [gakkoo-e] itta (koto).
   -NOM school-to   went

"John went to school."

c. John-ga   [Bill-ga   tensai da to] omotte-iru(koto).
   -NOM   -NOM genius is   that thinks

"John thinks that Bill is a genius."

d. [Bill-ga   tensai da]-to
   -NOM genius is   that

"that Bill is a genius"

The categorial status of the complements (bracketed above) in (5) are all different: in (a), it is a noun phrase; in (b), the complement is a postpositional phrase; in (c), it is a clausal complement (at a "CP" level); and in (d), it is an "IP" clausal complement. In all of these cases, the complements precede the heads, and the opposite order is never allowed. Kayne's suggestion would lead us to postulate a functional category in each case which triggers movement of the complement from a lower position to the position of Spec, which asymmetrically c-commands the head. What is the nature of the functional category, and what motivates movement of the complements? Notice that in all well-known cases where functional categories are postulated, they are selective as to the elements that they force to move. Thus, [+Q] C triggers movement of categories that function as operators at LF, a finite T is associated with categories having nominative Case, and so on. The situation seems to be totally different with the postulated functional category for the examples in (5). It is associated with all sorts of complements, regardless of their categorial status, their Case-theoretic properties, and their status with respect to interpretation at LF. We cannot think of any independent motivation for movement of complements other than the very reason for getting the surface order right (the C-H order), and it looks as though the postulated functional category attracts complements of any type just to ensure the correct word order under the LCA.

A related question arises as to the plausibility of the general approach taken under the LCA with respect to the comparative syntax of English and Japanese. As discussed above, in the LCA account, an "active" functional category triggering overt movement is postulated in Japanese whereas the corresponding functional category in English should be "inactive", forcing no movement. This is exactly the opposite of the widely assumed, if not universally accepted, view represented by Fukui (1986, 1988a), that functional categories in Japanese, if any, are "inactive" as compared to those in English, in that they do not induce overt movements of the kind attested in English, e.g., *wh*-movement and NP-movement. (See also Kuroda 1988 for a proposal that could be interpreted in these terms.) While it is logically possible that the same functional categories are "active" in certain domains and "inactive" in certain others (for example, T in Japanese forces movement of object but never triggers subject-raising (NP-movement), etc.), careful empirical justifications are required before such a claim is actually made. See Takano (1996) for much detailed discussion on this point.

As it maintains the head-parameter, Fukui and Saito's (1996) approach is free from the kind of problems associated with the H-C v. C-H variation, as exemplified by English and Japanese. However, it faces a different problem, i.e., the positioning of Specs. It seems almost universally true, as Kayne (1994) claims, that a Spec of the head H precedes rather than follows H and its complement, regardless of the relative order between H and its complement. (See Greenberg 1966 for classical observations relevant for this point.) If this is indeed a universal property of phrase structure of human language, it has to be somehow accounted for. In the LCA-based approach, this is nicely done because a Spec of H always asymmetrically c-commands H and its complement and therefore must precede them. In the Fukui-Saito approach, on the other hand, nothing would predict this apparently universal "leftness" property of Specs since their modified version of the head-parameter is restricted, just like the classical head-parameter, to the relative ordering of a head and its complement, with specifiers falling outside of the domain of the parameter. Fukui and Saito (1996) notice this point and attribute it to the universal directionality of agreement, leaving open the ultimate explanation of this important fact.[6]

To sum up, Kayne's and Chomsky's LCA-based approaches face a nontrivial problem of accounting for the word order variation observed between, say, English and Japanese. The LCA dictates that H-C order be the only order made available by UG. Therefore, it has to come up with a way of deriving the C-H order from the underlying H-C order. To do so, however, requires postulation of functional categories inducing overt movement in a language like Japanese, contrary to traditional observations about the language. The nature of the postulated functional categories is not clear, and the motivations for required overt movement are quite obscure. Unless compelling independent evidence is found, it is very hard to accept postulation of such "active" functional categories in Japanese. Fukui and Saito's (1996) approach is free from this particular problem because it maintains the head-parameter, as discussed above. But it faces the problem of accounting for the apparent universality of the "leftness of Specs", which is, as Kayne (1994) argues, nicely accounted for under the LCA approach. In this article, we would like to explore a theory of phrase structure which does not involve either of these problems. Specifically, we will put forth a hypothesis, a hypothesis we will call the "Symmetry Principle of Derivation", by which we can account for the word order variation without postulating dubious functional categories in Japanese, and, at the same time, we can explain the universal positioning of Specs in a natural way.

3 Proposal

We will assume the following view, proposed by Chomsky (1993a, 1995a, 1995b, among others), on the structure of language.[7] The cognitive system of UG consists of a computational system and a lexicon. The computational system is regarded as a generative procedure, mapping some array of lexical choices to the pair (π, λ), where π is taken to be a PF representation, and λ an LF representation, the representations at the two "interface levels". Following Chomsky, let us take "some array of lexical choices" to involve (at least) the information on what the lexical choices are and how many times each lexical item is selected by computation in forming (π, λ), and call it a *numeration* N. Thus, N is a set of pairs (LI, i), where LI is an item of the lexicon and i is its index, indicating the number of times the LI is selected. The computational system applies to N and forms a sequence S of symbolic elements S = (σ_1, σ_2, ..., σ_n) terminating only if σ_n is a pair (π, λ) and N is reduced to zero. S formed in this way is called a *derivation*, which may or may not *converge* depending on whether the *(bare) output conditions*, the conditions imposed on π and λ, are met at PF and LF. If the output conditions are met at PF/LF, the derivation converges at PF/LF; if not, it *crashes* at PF/LF.

Output conditions show that the interface representations at PF and LF, i.e., π and λ, respectively, are constituted in a very different way. Elements that are interpretable and legitimate in π at PF are not interpretable and legitimate in λ at LF, and conversely. Thus, at some point, a derivation (computation) splits into two parts, one leading to a PF representation π and the other forming an LF representation λ. We assume, then, that there is an operation *Spell-Out* at some point of a derivation that applies to the structure Σ already formed. Spell-Out strips away those elements of Σ that are relevant only to π, leaving the residual structure, which is mapped to π by operations of the kind that formed Σ. The modified Σ (by Spell-Out) is mapped to π, by operations in the subsystem of human language computation, called the *phonological component*, whose properties are apparently quite different from the "core" part of the computation (the N $\to$ λ mapping). The relevant portions of inner workings of language computation can thus be graphically represented as follows.

(6)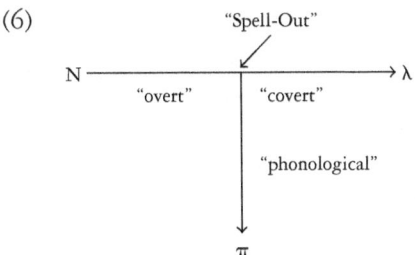

As indicated in (6), we call the pre-Spell-Out computation the *overt* component, and the computation from Spell-Out to λ the *covert* component. Now the major hypothesis we would like to put forth is as follows.

(7) *The Symmetry of Derivation*
Computations in the overt (pre-Spell-Out) component and computations in the phonological component are symmetric.

Given that Merge, an operation that combines two objects forming a larger object, is the basic operation of overt computations, the hypothesis in (7) essentially states that the basic computation in the phonological component is characterized as an operation reversing the effects of Merge, i.e., breaking a single object into two objects. As discussed in the preceding section, syntactic structures are built in a bottom-up fashion by Merge in the overt component. At the point of Spell-Out, the structure Σ, created by successive applications of Merge, enters into the phonological component. One of the central properties of the phonological component is to break down the input structure Σ and map it into an unstructured (linearized) sequence of elements (cf. Chomsky 1995b). We call a formal operation responsible for breaking down the structures *Demerge*, implying that it is an operation undoing the result of Merge. And our hypothesis is that human language is designed in such a way that Merge and Demerge are in a symmetric relation with respect to their applications. In what follows, we will go into a more precise and detailed exposition of this hypothesis and its ramified implications for linguistic theory and comparative syntax.

3.1 Linearization

To start our discussion, let us essentially adopt the bare phrase structure theory of Chomsky (1994, 1995a, 1995b) and a proposal about linear order made by Takano (1996). As stated in (2), in the bare theory, syntactic objects available for the core part of the human language computation (i.e., the N→λ computation) are either lexical items or set-theoretic objects constructed from them, both lacking ordering properties. Chomsky (1994, 1995a, 1995b) suggests that order plays no role in the N→λ computation (see also Marantz 1989 and Halle and Marantz 1993), and that a modified version of Kayne's LCA applies to the syntactic object Σ in the phonological component (i.e., the computation from Spell-Out to π). Adapting this idea, Takano (1996) proposes that there is a process, called *Linearization*, that applies to Σ in the phonological component and assigns Σ a linear order, interpreted as a temporal order at PF. If Σ has some structural property that prevents it from being linearized, the derivation yielding Σ crashes at PF, on the assumption that the output conditions at PF include something like (8).

(8) At the PF interface, all elements must be linearly ordered.

On this view, the N→λ computation and the Spell-Out→Linearization computation are strictly hierarchical, having no ordering properties, whereas the Linearization→π computation is strictly linear, having no hierarchical properties (in a syntactic sense).

As we will see in detail below, Linearization determines the S-C-H order for Σ if no movement is involved in Σ, and the H-C order results when H undergoes head movement to a higher head position in Σ, a situation exactly opposite to the one under Kayne's proposal. Thus, under this alternative, the O-V order of Japanese reflects the "base" structure that involves no movement, whereas the V-O order of English reflects the "derived" structure that involves verb-raising, triggered by a higher functional head. Notice that this is well in accord with the general view on the differences between English and Japanese that Japanese lacks "active" functional categories that English has, so that movement processes that are attested in the latter do not occur in the former. Accordingly, we do not have to postulate "abstract" functional categories in Japanese of the kind needed under Kayne's approach, in order to get the right surface order.

Recall that Kayne's LCA-based theory makes crucial reference to asymmetric c-command, which is a derivative notion defined in terms of the structural properties of syntactic objects (see Epstein 1995 for relevant discussion on the nature of c-command). Instead of appealing to asymmetric c-command, we propose to capitalize on a more fundamental property of syntactic objects. As we saw in the preceding section, the basic operation of the core part of human language computation is Merge (note that Move is a combination of movement and Merge; see Chomsky 1995a, 1995b). Applied to two objects α and β, Merge forms a new object K that is a projection of either α or β (but not both). The resulting object K thus created is inherently asymmetric: if α projects, K is a projection of α but not of β. Thus, the core computation forms syntactic objects in a bottom-up fashion, and the syntactic objects formed in this way necessarily have intrinsic asymmetric properties.

The basic idea we would like to pursue here is that Linearization essentially does the *reverse* of the computation N→Spell-Out (i.e., Merge), in the sense that it "breaks down" the syntactic object K, making crucial reference to the inherently asymmetric properties of K just discussed, to eventually yield a linear sequence of the terminals of K.[8] Thus, Linearization consists of two basic operations: one that breaks down K into smaller pieces and another that puts the pieces into linear sequence. The former operation is called *Demerge* and the latter *Concatenate*. The operation Concatenate is to be understood in the usual sense, namely as a binary operation with the property of being associative but not commutative.

Merge and Demerge are the two basic operations that affect syntactic objects in the computation that yields (π, λ). Given that Merge always combines two root elements and creates a single root, it is natural to assume that Demerge always applies to a single root element and breaks it into two roots. Thus, we have the following characterization of Linearization:

142 *Symmetry in syntax*

(9) Linearization is a top-down process.

By virtue of the nature of Demerge, then, Linearization breaks down syntactic objects from the top down.

To illustrate how Linearization works, let us look at the following structure.

(10) K = VP

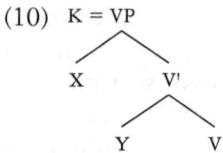

The tree diagram in (10) is an informal representation. A more formal and precise representation of the syntactic object K represented in (10) under the bare theory is given in (11).

(11) K = [V, [X, [V, [Y, V]]]]

We continue to use informal tree diagrams as in (10) for ease of exposition. As an informal notation, the tree diagram in (10) should be understood to express only hierarchical relations among the elements appearing in it and imply nothing about the linear order of those elements.

Now suppose that K in (10) is subjected to Linearization. Since Linearization is a top-down process, it must apply to the root K, not to any other element internal to K. As stated above, Demerge breaks K into two root elements. Note that K consists of two constituents: X and V'. In principle, Demerge can affect either X or V' or both. Crucially, however, the two elements do not have the same status in K because of the asymmetric nature of the syntactic object created by Merge: K is a projection of V' but not of X. Chomsky (1994, 1995b) claims that in the bare theory, the notions of "minimal" and "maximal" projections should be understood relationally (cf. Muysken 1982).

(12) A category that does not project any further is a maximal projection X^{max} (or XP), and one that is not a projection at all is a minimal projection X^{min} (or X^0). A category that is neither maximal nor minimal is an X' (intermediate category).

(Adapted from Chomsky 1995b, 242)

Under this conception of minimal and maximal projections, X in (10) is a maximal projection whereas V' is not.

Note now that Merge always combines two maximal projections. Given this, it is natural to carry that property over to Demerge so that Demerge affects only maximal projections. In general, (13) holds:

(13) Only maximal projections are visible to Merge and Demerge.

It follows from (13) that in (10) Demerge can affect only X in K, V' being invisible to the operation. Thus, Demerge detaches X from K, breaking down the latter into two pieces, X and V'. This yields the following two objects (note that after an application of Demerge, V' is now a maximal projection because there is no further projection of V in K').

(14) X   K' = V'(=V^{max})
          /\
         Y   V

Note that once X is detached from K, the projection of V' (VP in the tree diagram (10)) can no longer exist since there is no such thing as a non-branching projection in the bare phrase structure theory. As a result, Demerge breaks K into two root elements, X and K' (=V'). Thus, in more general terms, applied to a single object Σ, Demerge detaches a constituent of Σ, a maximal projection, from Σ, yielding two objects: the detached constituent α (an X^{max}) and the residue of Σ, Σ' (=Σ − α).

X and K' in (14) are two independent root elements. To form an ordered object from them, Linearization must have another operation, Concatenate, that applies to two independent roots created by Demerge and forms an ordered sequence of the two. Applied to [X, K'] in (14), Concatenate determines linear order between them, which is ultimately mapped into temporal precedence at PF. Specifically, Concatenate chooses between X + K' (X precedes K') and K' + X (K' precedes X) ("+" indicates concatenation). Precedence is an asymmetric property (if α precedes β, β never precedes α). It will be most desirable if Concatenate makes reference only to some asymmetric property inherent to the relation between X and K' and maps that asymmetric property into temporal precedence. In fact, there *is* such an asymmetry inherent to the relation between X and K'. Consider again how the two roots X and K' result from K. Because of the nature of Demerge, K' becomes an independent root only "after" X becomes an independent root: It is the detachment of X that makes K' (=V') an independent root element, a maximal projection. But the reverse relation does not hold. X in (10) is a maximal projection quite independently from an application of Demerge. This means that X becomes available for Concatenate "before" K' does. In other words, X "precedes" K' in becoming available for Concatenate. Of course, the "precedence relation" here has nothing to do with temporal order but is an abstract relation inherent to the computation. Let us then assume that Concatenate retains this abstract "precedence relation" inherent to the computation and maps it to a temporal precedence relation at the PF interface.

(15) If α "precedes" β in becoming available for Concatenate, α precedes β in temporal order.

Thus, what is directly affected by Demerge comes first in temporal order. In the case of (14), for example, Concatenate turns [X, K'] into X + K', which is eventually interpreted at PF as "X temporally precedes K'".

We can summarize the basic workings of Linearization as in (16), where $(\Sigma - \alpha)$ indicates the object resulting from detachment of α from the syntactic object Σ.

(16) *Linearization*
Applied to Σ, Demerge yields [α, [$\Sigma - \alpha$]], α an X^{max} constituent of Σ, and Concatenate turns [α, $(\Sigma - \alpha)$] into $\alpha + (\Sigma - \alpha)$.

Having fixed the order X + K' for (14), Linearization next applies to X and K'. In this way, Linearization recursively applies in a top-down fashion to the newly created root elements until all elements become terminals. Thus, if Linearization goes on to apply to K' in (14), which has Y and V as its constituents, Demerge detaches Y (an X^{max}) from K', yielding two separate root elements Y and V. (Recall that V is not a maximal projection and hence is not visible to Demerge.) Concatenate then applies to the two, forming Y + V, in accordance with (15). Thus, after two successive applications of Linearization, we obtain the sequence X + Y + V. If X and Y are nonterminals, Linearization will apply to each of them in the same way.

X and Y of K in (10) are the specifier and the complement of V, respectively. Notice here that K reflects the "base" structure, involving no movement. Therefore, contrary to Kayne's theory, the Linearization mechanism just presented predicts that the syntactic object Σ yields an S-C-H order if Σ involves no movement.[9]

Summing up, we have proposed a mechanism of Linearization (Demerge and Concatenate) applying in the phonological component. Linearization applies to a set-theoretic, unordered syntactic object Σ and maps it to an unstructured sequence, assigning it a fixed linear order. The resulting sequence will then be converted (via other processes of the phonological component) into a PF representation. While Merge applies recursively in a bottom-up fashion, Demerge and Concatenate apply recursively in a top-down fashion. Both processes are strictly derivational, carrying out admissible computations step by step. Taken together, we have a kind of a "symmetry of derivation", stated in (7), with its "global" character completely reduced to properties of strictly local operations. More specifically, Demerge essentially does the reverse of what Merge does in the N → Spell-Out computation, undoing the result of Merge in a top-down fashion. Concatenate then linearizes the result of Demerge, mapping the inherently asymmetric relation embedded in the structures created by Merge to linear precedence, yielding the "basic" order S-C-H (as opposed to the S-H-C order predicted by the LCA). Thus, the apparent universality of the "leftness of Specs", which is a problem for Fukui and Saito's (1996) approach as we saw above, is accounted for in a principled way: Spec is the first maximal projection that Demerge "encounters" when it applies in a top-down fashion. Therefore, it must be put into an ordered sequence prior to any other elements in the phrase: that is, it precedes the rest of the phrase. Likewise, the complement, which is a maximal projection, must precede the head, yielding the S-C-H order. The only remaining problem, then, is how to derive the H-C order in a natural way, to which we will turn in the next subsection.

3.2 Order of head and complement

As we have just seen, the proposed Linearization mechanism always imposes the S-C-H order on all VP structures. Let us now turn to larger structures. Essentially following Hale and Keyser's (1993) "configurational approach" to θ-marking, Chomsky (1995b) argues that the external argument of a transitive verb occupies a specifier position of v, a "light verb" taking a VP as its complement. On this view, the core proposition of a ditransitive structure is represented as follows:

(17)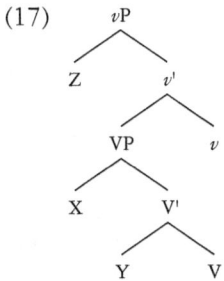

Here Z is an external argument, X is an indirect internal argument, and Y is a direct internal argument. Applied to vP, Linearization yields $Z + v'$.[10] Applied to v', it yields $VP + v$. We have already concluded that the order among the VP-internal elements is $X + Y + V$. Thus Linearization assigns the structure in (17) the surface order $Z - X - Y - V - v$. Takano (1996) argues that this is exactly what happens in Japanese. Thus, the SOV order in Japanese reflects in a straightforward way the order assigned by Linearization to the structure in (17). The conclusion remains the same if the subject raises out of vP, say, to Spec, T.

Chomsky (1995b) argues that V raises overtly to v in English. On the widely-accepted view of head movement as adjunction to a head, the structure resulting from movement of V is (18).

(18)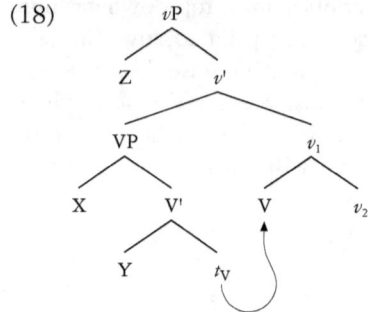

Nothing changes from (17) regarding the order between Z and v'. Thus, we have (19) after Linearization has applied to vP.

(19)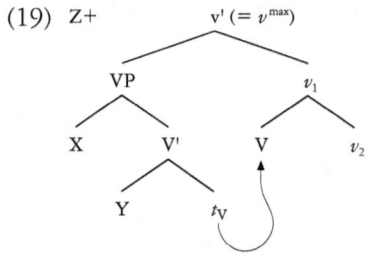

Suppose that Linearization applies to v' in (19). The situation here is different from that in (17). Here, one constituent of v' is a two-segmented category [v_1, v_2], formed by adjunction of V to v.[11] Takano (1996) argues that, in this structure, the raised V is a constituent of v' and hence can be a target of Demerge. He further claims that if Linearization applies to v', detachment of VP prior to V causes the derivation to crash at PF, and hence that detachment of V from v' is the only possibility that yields a convergent derivation (see Takano 1996 for details). If so, (19) yields the surface order Z + V + VP + v, which corresponds to the English order (note that v is phonetically null and thus has no effects at PF).

Here we depart from Takano's (1996) rather complicated account and explore another possibility. Recall that the basic intuition we are pursuing is that Linearization breaks down the given syntactic object from the top down. In the account of (19), however, this intuition is not reflected in a straightforward way because of the structure formed by V-raising. We cannot avoid this situation as long as we keep to the traditional assumption that head movement is "adjunction to head". In an earlier framework, this assumption was well-motivated by X' theory. However, under the bare phrase structure theory, assumed here, nothing seems to block V-raising from taking place in the following manner.

(20)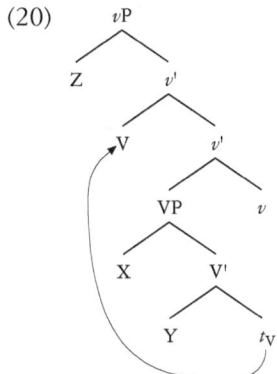

In (20), V has undergone "substitution into Spec", rather than "adjunction to head" though the traditional term "substitution" is not appropriate any more in the bare theory to represent this type of operation since nothing is "substituted" for by the moved element (see Chomsky 1995b, Fukui and Saito 1996 for relevant discussion).[12] Chomsky (1994, 1995b) argues that this type of head movement is blocked by the uniformity condition that requires chain to be uniform with regard to phrase structure status. Thus, in (20), V is an X^{min} in its original position and is both an X^{min} and X^{max} in its landing site (recall (12)). The chain formed by the movement of V is non-uniform with respect to phrase structure status and is hence excluded by the uniformity condition. However, the same problem arises with head movement of the usual kind shown in (18). There, too, the chain formed by the movement of V has an X^{min} in its tail and an X^{min}/X^{max} in its head. Noting this problem, Chomsky suggests that, at LF, elements internal to X^{min} are submitted to independent word interpretation processes that ignore principles of the core computation and are thus exempt from the uniformity condition.

There is, however, another possible direction to take, namely to assume that head movement of the kind described in (20) is indeed permitted in principle. This move dispenses with the special word interpretation at LF that Chomsky postulates. Regarding the uniformity condition, we might either eliminate it entirely or adopt it in a weaker form, so that "uniformity" is defined in terms of "nondistinctness". The chain resulting from the V-raising in (20) meets the weaker version of uniformity, given that both the head and the tail of the chain have the X^{min} status.

Thus, we propose that head movement for checking purposes always takes the form of "substitution into Spec", eliminating traditional "adjunction to head" as an unnecessary (and hence undesirable) option. In fact, this proposal is motivated on independent grounds, to which we will return in 3.3. For the moment, let us assume that English has the structure in (20) after V-raising. Disregarding Z (if it is a trace of the subject, it is "invisible" on the surface in any case), let us consider what happens if Linearization applies to the upper v'. Since the raised V is an X^{max}, while the lower v' is not, only the former is visible to Demerge. Therefore, Demerge breaks down the higher v', detaching V from it. After detachment of V from v' and concatenation of the resulting objects, we have (21).

(21)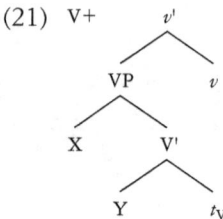

This ensures that V precedes all VP-internal elements when it raises out of VP, that is, the "head initial" order. Further applications of Linearization give rise to the ultimate surface order $V + X + Y + t_v + v$ (with t_v and v invisible).

Thus, our reanalysis of head movement as a "substitution" operation makes it possible to represent the basic intuition we mentioned before in a straightforward way: the simple process of breaking down a syntactic object in a top-down fashion yields its surface order. We attribute the VO/OV distinction between English and Japanese to the presence or absence of verb-raising. We claim that the VO order in English results from overt verb-raising while the OV order in Japanese reflects the "base properties" of the verb phrase, involving no verb-raising.[13] We also claim that the relevant difference ultimately arises from a parameter associated with the "functional head" v. We thus make the following hypothesis about the fundamental difference between English and Japanese with respect to word order.

(22) v has the property of attracting V in English but not in Japanese.

Note that this type of parametrization is quite consistent with the restrictive theory of parametric variation of the kind discussed in section 2 in that the relevant parametric factor is reduced to properties of functional elements and also is in line with the "traditional" view on the English/Japanese comparative syntax that functional categories in Japanese, if any, are not "active", compared to corresponding elements in English.

3.3 Feature checking and head movement

Let us now discuss the nature of head movement in more detail. In the preceding subsection, we noted that the VO/OV distinction follows straightforwardly from the Demerge plus Concatenate approach to linear order if head movement is analysed as "substitution into Spec" rather than "adjunction to head". There are several independent reasons to believe that this is indeed a desirable move.[14]

First of all, under the traditional conception, head movement must be treated as an exception to Chomsky's (1993a) "extension condition" on phrase structure construction. In the terms of the bare theory, this condition can be stated as the "root condition" that requires that Merge always apply at the root. According to Chomsky (1994, 1995b), root merger is the simplest form of Merge, and hence minimalist considerations should allow only this type of merger. Recall that Move is just a special case of Merge (Move = movement + Merge). Thus, Move must also meet the root condition, given that it is a condition on Merge. However, head movement in the traditional sense never satisfies it since the target of head movement (i.e., an X^{min} element) is always internal to the root element at the stage of the derivation where head movement occurs. Since other types of movement do meet the root condition, the question arises as to why only head movement is exceptional in this regard.

This problem simply does not arise if head movement is analysed as "substitution", as we have proposed: it merges at the root, just like other types of Move and Merge. Thus, our analysis of head movement resolves the paradoxical situation associated with the root condition under the traditional analysis of head movement.

Furthermore, the traditional "adjunction-to-head" approach to head movement does not fit well into the theory of feature checking that we assume. Chomsky (1993a, 1995b) claims that all movement takes place because of the necessity of feature checking. Thus, the element α moves to the domain of the head H to enter into a checking relation with some feature F of H and eliminates F. According to Chomsky, feature checking between α and F of H takes place in a local relation, namely when α enters the "checking domain" of H. The checking domain of H is defined as the set consisting of specifiers of H and positions adjoined to H (Chomsky 1995b). Thus, in (23), the checking domain of H is [Y, W]. X, an adjunct to HP, and Z, the complement of H, are not in the checking domain of H (see Chomsky 1993a for a different view). Notice now that the checking domain thus defined is a heterogeneous set, in the sense that it includes positions for "substitution" (Y) and adjunction (W). Given that the checking domain of H does not include positions adjoined to HP (i.e., X in (23)), it is conceptually more desirable if we can eliminate adjoined positions altogether from the checking domain.

(23)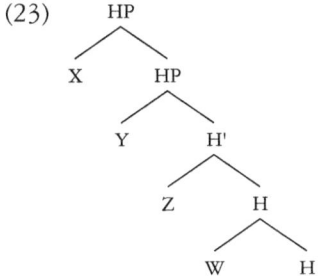

Note that the inclusion of W in the checking domain of H is necessary because head movement is considered to be driven by the necessity of feature checking and is assumed to be adjunction to head. On the other hand, we can achieve the unification of the domain for feature checking if we analyse head movement as substitution.

Chomsky (1995a, 1996) suggests a further revision of the checking theory, to the effect that all movement for checking purposes involves movement of formal features, regardless of whether the relevant movement takes place overtly or covertly. Let us consider the following structure:

(24)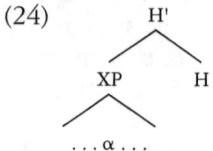

Suppose that some feature of H is to be in a checking relation with some feature of α. In this situation, the former "attracts" the latter so that the set of all formal features of α, FF(α), raises and attaches to H (Chomsky calls this operation "Attract-F"), yielding (25).

(25)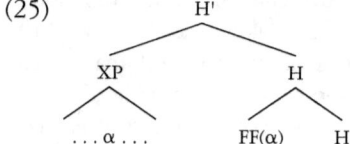

As stated above, this happens to all movement for feature checking, regardless of whether it is overt or covert.[15] If it is covert, nothing more happens. If it is overt, Chomsky claims that the rules in the phonological component cannot interpret a feature chain that extends beyond a minimal domain (note that in (25) there is a trace in α of the raised FF(α), thus FF(α) and its trace in α form a feature chain) and hence that the structure in (25) causes the derivation to crash if it enters the phonological component.[16] He further suggests that for convergence, α must be placed in the minimal domain of H to make the feature chain shorter. This is essentially the mechanism responsible for the "generalized pied-piping" (or category movement) that is observed in overt movement. If this happens, (26) results:

(26)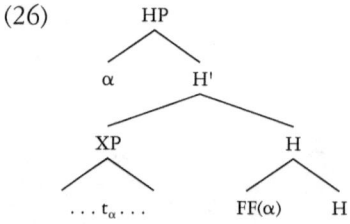

Now the feature chain exists only within the minimal domain of H, and the structure yields a convergent derivation at PF.

On this view of movement and feature checking, the core part of movement is always attachment of formal features to the head H, namely Attract-F, and placement of a categorial element in the minimal domain of H, which Chomsky calls Merge, takes place only when it is necessary to make shorter the feature chain formed by Attract-F. The simplest assumption, then, is that Attract-F is always feature adjunction to H whereas Merge is always substitution into the minimal domain of H. If so, overt head movement must be analysed in the following way. Suppose that the head H has a feature that overtly attracts a feature of α, α an X^{min}. Then Attract-F attaches FF(α) to H before Spell-Out. After this, Merge puts the category α in Spec, H, creating the structure in (26) with $\alpha = X^{min}$. Thus, head movement is treated in exactly the same way as XP-movement.

This approach to head movement also has desirable consequences for certain empirical phenomena. One consequence has to do with the VSO order in Irish. Bobaljik and Carnie (1994) show that the Irish VSO order cannot be analysed in terms of V-to-C movement or subject in situ. They observe that the raised V is lower than C and further that the object always moves overtly to Spec, Agr_o for Case checking. From this, they conclude that the Irish VSO order results when the verb raises to Agr_s and the subject moves to Spec, T, with the object sitting in Spec, Agr_o.

Their proposal cannot be maintained in the original form under the Agr-less system of Chomsky (1995b), which we adopt here. In the Agr-less system, there is no functional projection between C and T nor is there any functional projection between T and v (see Chomsky 1995b for arguments for this move; see also Fukui 1995b for relevant discussion). However, given our conception of head movement, Bobaljik and Carnie's observations fall into place. We can say that the Irish VSO order results from the following:

(27)

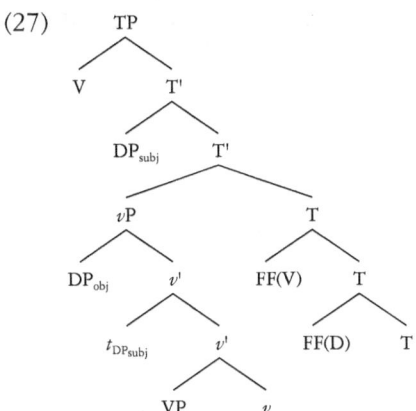

The object DP is in the outer Spec, v, the position for accusative checking (Chomsky 1995b). What is special about Irish is that T has the property of attracting FF(D) first and then FF(V). Accordingly, Merge places the subject DP in Spec, T when T attracts FF(D), and after that, it places V in Spec, T when T attracts FF(V). The resulting structure is linearized into $V + DP_{subj} + vP + T$.

Under this analysis, French differs from Irish in that T attracts FF(V) first. This results in a structure where DP_{subj} occupies the higher Spec, T, while V occupies the lower Spec, T, yielding the surface SVO order. This analysis can also maintain the difference between French and English with respect to raising of the finite verb noted and discussed by Emonds (1978) and Pollock (1989). Both languages have the SVO order, and this follows from verb-raising. French differs from English in that the French finite verb moves to Spec, T past negation (assuming that negation is located somewhere between T and vP) whereas the English finite V moves only to Spec, v. The difference is due to different properties of the two functional categories, T and v, in the two languages.[17]

The substitution approach to head movement has a further consequence for French. Pollock (1989) notes that the French infinitival V behaves like the English finite V in that it cannot appear to the left of negation. However, Pollock further notes that the French infinitival V can appear either in the order "adjunct-V-DP_{obj}" or in the order "V-adjunct-DP_{obj}" while the English finite V can appear only in the form "adjunct-V-DP_{obj}". These observations lead Pollock to conclude that the French infinitival V "optionally" moves to Agr, located between T and V (v in our terms), whereas the English finite V never moves to Agr (Pollock assumes that negation is located between T and Agr and that adjuncts are adjoined to VP). We cannot account for Pollock's observations under the Agr-less system if we assume the traditional "head-adjunction" analysis of head movement. The reason is simple: there is no functional projection between T and v, and hence there is no place for the French infinitival V to move to. The substitution analysis of head movement, on the other hand, opens up a new way of accounting for the relevant facts in terms of different properties of the functional category v in the two languages. Let us consider (28).

(28)
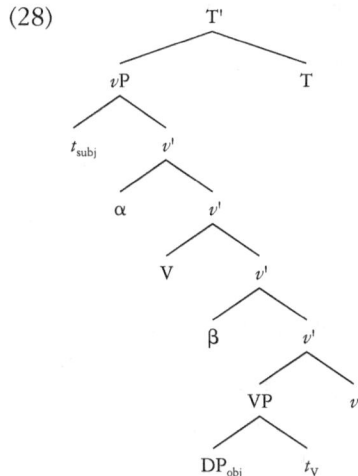

Both the French infinitival V and the English finite V move to Spec, v. French differs from English in that its v allows an adjunct to appear in the positions of α and β. This explains why the French infinitival V can appear in alternating orders "adjunct-V-DP_{obj}" and "V-adjunct-DP_{obj}" but cannot appear to the left of negation. Note that under this analysis, we need not posit "optional" verb-raising, as Pollock does. English v allows an adjunct to appear only in the position of α, and hence V never appears in the order "V-adjunct-DP_{obj}".

These considerations show that the substitution analysis of head movement is well-motivated on both conceptual and empirical grounds. As we discussed in section 3.2, it also makes it possible to deduce the VO/OV distinction from the presence/absence of V-raising in a straightforward way under the theory of phrase structure and linear order adopted here.[18]

3.4 Verb-raising and language typology

It has been noted in the traditional literature that some cases of language variation can be analysed in terms of verb movement. For example, Emonds (1978) and Pollock (1989) argue that certain word order differences between English and French follow if we assume that V raises in French but not in English. Travis (1984, 1991) also proposes that V-2 phenomena in several Germanic languages should be analysed as involving V-raising. As James Huang (personal communication) points out, our approach further develops this way of looking at language variation, in such a way as to accommodate Japanese and Chinese.

Our discussion so far shows the following: V stays in place in Japanese, raises to Spec, v in English, raises to "lower" Spec, T (i.e., lower than subject) in French, and raises to "higher" Spec, T (i.e., higher than subject) in Irish. In our terms, V-2 phenomena result from V raising to "lower" Spec, C (i.e., lower than topic). Putting these together, we have the following result, arranged in order of the "height/length" of verb-raising:

(29) Japanese: V stays in place
      English: V raises to Spec, v
      French: V raises to lower Spec, T
      Irish: V raises to higher Spec, T
      German: V raises to lower Spec, C

We may interpret this in terms of "degrees of markedness" (i.e., degrees of "departures" from the basic order determined by Linearization) among these languages, Japanese being the most unmarked. James Huang further suggests that Chinese may fall between Japanese and English. On independent grounds, Huang (1992, 1997) shows that Chinese does have verb-raising to the "light verb". In our terms, this means that Chinese V raises out of VP, thereby yielding the surface VO order. On the other hand, adjuncts always appear to the left of V in Chinese. Thus, Chinese is like English with respect to the VO order but is like Japanese in other respects.[19] To account for this observation, Huang suggests that V-raising in Chinese should be shorter than that in English. One way of incorporating his suggestion is to suppose that the "light verb" in Huang's (1992, 1997) sense is located between v and VP, and that adjuncts appear at least higher than Spec of this "light verb". We then have the following spectrum of languages.

(30) Japanese < Chinese < English < French < Irish < German

In terms of "degrees of markedness", Japanese is the most unmarked, having no verb-raising at all, thereby retaining the "basic" order, and German is the most marked, having the longest verb-raising within a clause.

3.5 Other cases of head-complement order

So far, we have restricted our attention to head-complement order where the relevant head is V and have seen that given Linearization, the OV order results when the structure involves no movement, while the VO order arises when V undergoes head movement. We can generalize the conclusion to other cases. Thus, Linearization assigns the C-H order to structures that have H in place and the H-C order to structures that involve movement of H.

Japanese has the C-H order in NP, AP, and PP whereas English has the H-C order in those categories. The Japanese cases fall out straightforwardly. The relevant structures have the heads (N, A, and P) in place, and therefore Linearization forces them to follow their complements.

What about the English cases? Abney (1987) proposes that NP and AP are structurally parallel in that they are complements to functional heads D and Deg, respectively. Thus, under Abney's proposal, "noun phrase" and "adjective phrase" have the following structures:

(31)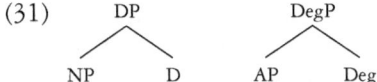

Adopting this proposal, we must address the question of where in these structures determiners (*the*, *a*, *this*, *that*, etc.) and degree words (*so*, *as*, *too*, *very*, etc.) appear. Given that these elements appear to the left of NP and AP, they cannot themselves be D and Deg (Linearization would then dictate that D and Deg follow NP and AP, respectively, on the surface). Since we adopt the substitution analysis of head movement, a natural extension of it is to say that determiners and degree words are Spec elements, entering into a checking relation with (features of) D and Deg, respectively.[20] On this view, the structures of, say, *the picture* and *too big* are as in (32).

(32)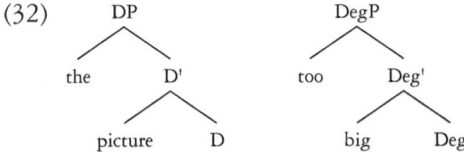

We thus claim that determiners and degree words are not functional heads themselves, as is currently assumed, but are elements that check features of functional heads.

Let us turn now to the H-C order in these categories. As stated above, the H-C order results if H undergoes head movement. Assuming the substitution analysis of head movement, we claim that *the picture of John* and *too proud of Bill* have the following structures.

(33)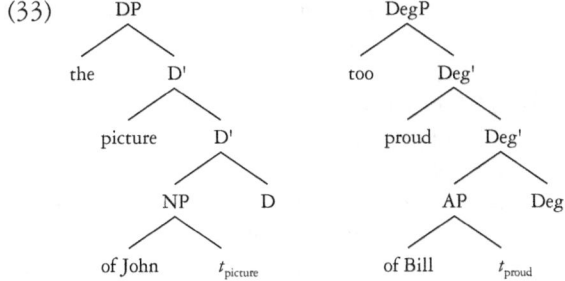

Here *picture* and *proud*, both X^{min} elements, move to Spec, D and Spec, Deg, respectively, for the purpose of checking. D has the property of checking

FF(N) prior to FF(*the*), thereby yielding the surface order we observe.[21] Similarly, Deg checks FF(A) before it checks FF(*too*).

Finally, let us turn to order in PP. English has prepositions, yielding the H-C order. There are two possible ways of accounting for it in our system. One possibility, entertained by Takano (1996), is to extend to this case the account of the H-C order in VP, NP, and AP and claim that there is some functional head above PP to whose Spec the head P raises overtly. However, our present assumption that X^{min} elements can occupy Spec positions leads us to another possibility that does not have to posit such a functional category. It has been noted that there is some parallelism obtaining between P and C (cf. Emonds 1985). For example, *for* in English functions as P as well as C. Heads like *before* and *after* can take both nominal and clausal complements, suggesting that they have the dual status of P and C. Let us take these observations to suggest that P is both lexical and functional, in the sense that P can be a θ-marker and at the same time can enter into feature checking (in this sense, P is similar to *v*). Then, the English PP *in the house*, for example, can be analysed in the following way.

(34)

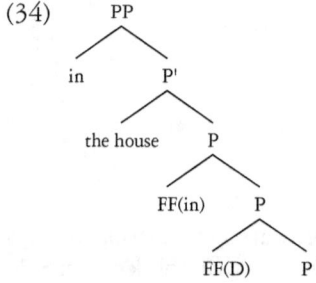

Suppose that FF(D) is first attached to P by direct merger to enter into a checking relation with (a Case feature of) P and that the DP *the house* is merged with P. Notice that the resulting feature chain of FF(D) is short enough here, staying in the minimal domain of P. Thus, no category movement of *the house* is necessary in this case. Assuming that P has a feature that attracts FF(in), FF(in) is attached by direct merger to P to check this feature, and the category *in* is merged with P', creating a short feature chain. In this structure, P also θ-marks its DP complement, showing its hybrid character. The structure yields the surface H-C order when Linearization applies to it.

Note that this analysis of PP in English amounts to saying that prepositions such as *in* in English are not Ps themselves, as assumed in the current literature, but rather are elements that check (a feature of) P, which has no phonetic content, an analysis somewhat reminiscent of the standard analysis of [+*wh*] C and nominative-assigning T in English, in which the triggering heads are assumed to have no phonetic content. Thus, the status of prepositions is parallel to that of determiners and degree words in English, which are also analysed here as elements that check (features of) D and Deg, respectively. On the other hand, postpositions in Japanese are genuine Ps, occupying the position of P in (34) without inducing feature checking. In section 4.5 we will extend this analysis to complementizers in English and Japanese.

An interesting question arises in this connection as to the relation between the existence of phonetic content of a functional head and the possibility of feature checking by the functional head. Fukui (1986) considers the correlation with respect to (then available) functional heads C, I (T, in current terms), and D in English and suggests that it might not be an accident that all "agreement-inducing" (feature checking, in our terms) functional heads in English are null ([+wh] C, nominative-assigning I/T, and genitive-assigning D), while all "non-agreement-inducing" functional heads have phonetic content ([−wh] C (e.g., *that*), an infinitive marker *to*, and determiners such as *the/a*). As a reviewer points out, this observation can be extended to the light verb *v*: the Japanese light verb *v* tends to have phonetic content distinguishing transitive verbs and their unaccusative counterparts (e.g., *akeru* "to open/transitive" v. *aku* "to open/unaccusative", *simeru* "to close/transitive" v. *simaru* "to close/unaccusative", *kowasu* "to destroy" v. *kowareru* "to break down", etc.) whereas the English light verb *v* is always null. The same pattern seems to carry over to other functional heads, including Deg and P, as discussed above. If this is true, then we might make the following generalization with respect to the correlation between the existence of phonetic content of a functional head and the possibility of feature checking by the functional head.

(35) A functional head H enters into feature checking only if H lacks phonetic content.

It is possible, as the reviewer suggests, that the generalization (35) receives support from considerations of language acquisition: feature checking is a necessary factor during the language acquisition process in ensuring visibility of null heads.

In short, we derive the systematic differences regarding the order of head and complement between English and Japanese by appealing to the basic idea going back to Fukui (1986, 1988a) that functional heads require checking in English but not in Japanese. The requirement for checking in English is satisfied by head movement in the case of V, N, and A and by direct merger in the case of P.

3.6 Merger in the phonological component

As we have seen, our symmetry hypothesis predicts that Japanese does not have overt verb-raising of any sort, contrary to claims made by Otani and Whitman (1991) and Koizumi (1995), among others. Otani and Whitman argue that the verb raises to I/T in Japanese and that it makes "VP-ellipsis" possible in the language. Koizumi presents empirical observations involving cleft formation and coordination to show that the verb raises up to C in Japanese.

However, Hoji (1995) refutes Otani and Whitman's arguments and demonstrates that the Japanese construction that they analyse as involving VP-ellipsis does not in fact have the properties characteristic of the VP-ellipsis construction in English. Also, Koizumi's arguments for verb-raising in terms of cleft and co-ordinate constructions do not seem decisive owing to the rather obscure nature of these constructions in Japanese. Furthermore, Kim (1996) argues, on the basis of data from Korean, that neither Otani and Whitman's nor Koizumi's observations can be maintained as decisive evidence for the existence of verb-raising.[22] Thus, it seems to us that there is no compelling evidence at this point that Japanese indeed has overt verb-raising, a situation that is quite consistent with our conclusion. Moreover, we will argue in section 4 that a wide range of empirical consequences can be derived if we hypothesize that Japanese lacks verb-raising. Since those consequences cannot be obtained if Japanese has verb-raising, the whole discussion in section 4 provides a strong empirical argument for our position.

One question immediately arises if there is no overt verb-raising in Japanese. Japanese has various types of complex predicates, and such complex predicates have usually been analysed as resulting from overt verb-raising (cf. Baker 1988). One such example is a causative construction, as in (36).

(36) John-ga   Mary-ni   hon-o   yom-ase-ta   (koto).
     -NOM   -DAT book-ACC read-make-PAST

"John made Mary read a book."

The question is how the separate morphemes can be combined to give the surface form. Given that overt head movement is not an option here, we claim, following Takano (1996), that the complex form is in fact created in the phonological component; more specifically, that the two syntactically separate verbal morphemes undergo "phonological merger", or "cliticization", carried out by phonological rules under adjacency, which we assume to be a necessary condition for this process (see Marantz 1989 for a similar analysis of clitics).

We might analyse the surface form of tense inflection in the same way. Thus, in the case of (36), the past tense *ta* is a phonetically realized T and is thus separated from the matrix verb *(s)ase* "make". After Linearization, since *ta* is adjacent to *(s)ase*, satisfying the condition, it "cliticizes" onto the latter in the phonological component, yielding the surface form in (36).

4 Further consequences: verb-raising and its implications

The symmetric view on derivation that we have advanced in the preceding section has further consequences for the study of parametric variation. In particular, the hypothesis that English has overt verb-raising whereas Japanese lacks it, a hypothesis that derives from the general Symmetry Principle, opens up a new way of looking at typological differences between the two languages. In particular, given the basic assumptions of the minimalist program, this hypothesis allows us to link ordering properties to other syntactic properties. We will discuss some of the major consequences in this section.

4.1 Case systems

One of the central claims of the minimalist program concerning the nature of lexical items is that certain "formal features" (features that are accessible to recursive operations in the $N \rightarrow \lambda$ mapping, e.g., Case features), must be eliminated before the derivation containing them reaches LF. More specifically, Chomsky (1995b) claims that those formal features that are not subject to interpretation at LF must be eliminated by the time the derivation reaches the LF interface. For example, the Case feature of D (nominative, accusative, etc.) is uninterpretable at LF, and hence if it survives to LF, the derivation containing it crashes at LF. Therefore, it must be eliminated for the derivation to converge.[23] Similarly, finite T and transitive verbs have the features [assign nominative Case] and [assign accusative Case], respectively, and these features, too, must be eliminated if the derivation is to converge at LF. Formal features are generally eliminated by checking, and checking always takes place within the domain of a functional head (see Chomsky 1993a for detailed discussion on the mechanism). Under Chomsky's (1995b) Agr-less clausal structure, which we assume here, finite T provides the domain for nominative checking and the light verb v for accusative checking. If so, then while [assign nominative Case] of finite T can itself enter into a checking relation with $FF(D_{nom})$ (=a formal nominative Case feature of D), [assign accusative Case] of the transitive verb must raise to v to enter into a checking relation with $FF(D_{acc})$ (=a formal accusative Case feature of D).[24]

The condition that [assign accusative Case] enters into a checking relation with $FF(D_{acc})$ only if [assign accusative Case] raises to v has an immediate consequence for Japanese. Given this condition coupled with our hypothesis that verbs do not raise in Japanese, it follows that accusative features cannot be eliminated by checking in Japanese.[25] Thus, Japanese must appeal to an alternative way of eliminating accusative features so that the derivation will not crash at LF. Note, in this connection, that Japanese has a rich system of overt Case particles. Essentially along the lines of Kuroda (1988), who argues that noun phrases can be licensed either by abstract Case (feature checking in our terms) or by morphological case (Case particles), we claim that the existence of such a rich system of Case particles correlates with the impossibility of eliminating Case features in terms of checking (due to the lack of verb-raising; cf. note 25) and hypothesize that those overt

Case particles in fact contribute to eliminating Case features. Specifically, we assume that a Case particle is a morphological realization of a Case feature and heads its own projection. Following a suggestion made by Kenneth Hale dating back to the mid-1980s (see Bittner and Hale 1996 for a written version; see also Lamontagne and Travis 1987), let us call the relevant head "K". Then, the Japanese noun phrases in (37) have the structures in (38).[26]

(37) John-ga   Mary-o   mita (koto).
     -NOM   -ACC   saw

"John saw Mary."

(38)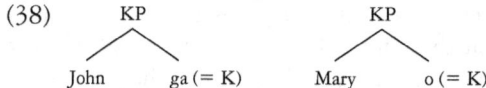

With respect to the elimination of Case features in Japanese, we claim that they are eliminated by the operation Spell-Out. Spell-Out is an operation that applies freely to a syntactic object Σ in the computation from N and strips away from Σ those elements relevant only to π, leaving the residue Σ_L (Chomsky 1995b). After Spell-Out, Σ_L and Σ are further mapped to λ and π, respectively. In other words, Spell-Out removes all phonological features from Σ. Now, given our assumption that Case particles are morphological realizations of Case features, it is natural to assume that Case features are linked to phonological features when Case particles are present. Thus,

(39) Case particles make Case features visible to Spell-Out.

Recall that Case features are formal features and therefore are usually invisible to Spell-Out. But the presence of Case particles has the effect of making Case features visible to Spell-out, by linking them to phonological features. When they are visible, Spell-Out removes (and hence eliminates/deletes) Case features from Σ, and the derivation forming Σ yields λ without crashing at LF. Note that Case features removed by Spell-Out enter the phonological component. This does not cause a problem since the Case features are linked to phonological features and therefore are interpretable at PF.

Transitive verbs also have Case features ([assign accusative Case]) that are uninterpretable at LF. For derivations containing them to converge at LF, they must be either eliminated or rendered interpretable. Here we pursue the latter possibility, by adopting Takahashi's (1993d) claim (based on a suggestion made by Mamoru Saito) that accusative Case in Japanese is inherent Case. We can interpret this claim as follows. In Japanese the feature [assign accusative Case] of the transitive verb is always linked to a particular θ-role (typically theme/patient) of the verb. Since θ-roles are interpreted at

LF, the linking between the Case feature of the verb and a θ-role renders the former interpretable at LF. As a result, the Case feature of the verb need not be eliminated.

Thus, the Japanese accusative Case has the following properties:

(40) a. The Case particle makes the Case feature of a noun phrase visible to Spell-Out.
 b. Linking to a particular θ-role makes the Case feature of a transitive verb interpretable at LF.

We assume that property (40a) also holds for Japanese postpositions in general. That is, Japanese postpositions are morphological realizations of Case features of their complement NPs and thus make the Case features visible to Spell-Out. As a result, the Case features of NP complements of postpositions need not undergo checking. The only difference between postpositions and Case particles is that postpositions θ-mark their complement whereas Case particles do not. We also assume that (40b) is a property of inherent Case in general.

Note that we must ensure the correct matching between verbs and Case particles. Thus, we must exclude cases like (41b).

(41) a. John-ga   Mary-o   mita (koto).
      -NOM   -ACC saw

 "John saw Mary."

 b. *John-ga   Mary-ni   mita (koto).
     -NOM   -DAT saw

Here we tentatively adopt Chomsky's (1995a) suggestion that Merge as well as Move is driven by some property of a head (see Ishii 1997 for a similar proposal and its extension to the theory of barriers). The relevant property of a head may be a property of feature checking or a "selectional" property (including θ-marking). Now let us consider (41) in this light. The verb *mita* "saw" has the property of assigning a patient/theme role to its complement. Recall that this θ-role is linked to accusative Case. Suppose now that *Mary-ni* "Mary-DAT" merges with the verb *mita* "saw". According to Chomsky's suggestion, this operation is valid only if it meets a selectional property of the latter. In other words, *Mary-ni* "Mary-DAT" must be compatible with the relevant property of the verb; otherwise, this application of Merge fails. In fact, *Mary-ni* "Mary-DAT" cannot satisfy the relevant property of the verb since it has dative Case, and the patient/theme role of the verb is linked to accusative Case. This "mismatch" of the properties of the object and the verb blocks the application of Merge. Hence (41b) is never created by Merge. The problem does not arise for (41a), where the object satisfies the relevant property of the verb. Details aside, we can generally avoid mismatch cases in this way.

These considerations indicate that UG must have (at least) two ways of eliminating Case features: checking and Spell-Out. Elimination by Spell-Out requires the presence of an overt particle. The lack of verb-raising in Japanese forces the language to develop and make use of the overt particle system. Generalizing this, we have the following conclusion.

(42) If a language lacks verb-raising, it must invoke the overt particle system for accusative Case.[27]

English has verb-raising and uses the checking system to eliminate accusative Case feature. But notice that (42) does not say anything about languages *with* verb-raising. Thus, in principle, languages with verb-raising could deploy either the checking system or the particle system. It may be that languages with verb-raising just arbitrarily choose between the two available options. If that is the case, there will be no interesting connection to be made between the fact that English has verb-raising and the fact that it has the checking system. Another, more interesting, possibility is that economy considerations in fact play a role here, as expressed, for example, by generalization (35) in section 3.5. Since the checking system is already built into the computational system of human language, it should be available for free to languages with verb-raising. On the other hand, adding overt Case particles to the lexicon is arguably an additional task for the language learner. Given these "economy" considerations, it seems natural to claim that languages with verb-raising must use the checking system as a costless option unless some language-particular factor forces otherwise. On this view, therefore, the particle system functions as a kind of last resort (cf. Chomsky 1991b for some related discussion), and the fact that English uses the checking system rather than the particle system will follow from economy.

As stated, (42) does not hold for nominative Case. This is because nominative checking is carried out by finite T and hence is not contingent on verb-raising. That this is empirically correct can be seen by considering the fact that there are OV languages like Turkish and Tamil that have particles for accusative Case but not for nominative Case:

(43) a. Ahmet gazete-yi   oku-yor.
         newspaper-ACC read-PRES PROG

    "Ahmet is reading the newspaper."

                                          (Turkish; Kornfilt 1991)

   b. Kumaar Raajaav-ai   ati-tt-aan.
                -ACC beat-PAST-3sg.m

    "Kumar beat Raja."

                          (Tamil; Lehmann 1993, cited by Ura 1996)

Under our assumptions, these languages have the particle system for accusative Case, as in Japanese, but the checking system for nominative Case, as in English. The fact that Turkish and Tamil have subject-verb agreement also supports this claim. The existence of these languages thus supports the general view that there is an asymmetry between nominative checking and accusative checking, as implied by the Case theory of Chomsky (1995b).

Note that Japanese uses the particle system for nominative Case as well as accusative Case, as evidenced by the fact that there is a particle for nominative Case (and that there is no subject-verb agreement).

(44) John-ga   Mary-o   mita (koto).
     -NOM   -ACC   saw

"John saw Mary."

Given the conclusion just reached that there is no inherent connection between nominative and accusative systems, the fact that Japanese differs from Turkish and Tamil in this respect is not surprising.[28]

Extending the claim made above about accusative Case, let us say that the nominative Case particle in Japanese renders the noun phrase to which it is attached visible to Spell-Out. The question that arises now is whether or not finite T in Japanese has the feature [assign nominative Case]. Finite T in English has this feature and triggers movement of the subject noun phrase for checking. Suppose that finite T in Japanese has [assign nominative Case]. This feature must be either eliminated by Spell-Out or rendered interpretable; otherwise, the derivation crashes at LF. It is impossible to make the feature interpretable as in the case of the feature [assign accusative Case] since T is not a θ-marker (recall that the feature [assign accusative Case] is made interpretable by linking it to a particular θ-role of the verb). The only other choice is elimination by Spell-Out. This is also impossible, however, since elimination by Spell-Out requires the Case feature to be linked to phonological features, realized as an overt particle, but T has no such particle (Case particles are a property of noun phrases). Thus, the Case feature of T can be neither eliminated nor rendered interpretable. Therefore, we arrive at the conclusion that T in Japanese cannot have the feature [assign nominative Case].[29]

This conclusion is exactly in line with Kuroda's (1983) (see also Saito 1982) observation that nominative Case in Japanese, unlike nominative Case in English, is not contingent on the presence of tense. In fact, this property of Japanese nominative Case has led Saito (1982), Fukui (1986, 1988a), and Fukui and Nishigauchi (1992) to propose that nominative *ga* is a default Case in Japanese.[30] In our terms, both *ga* and *o* are morphological realizations of the nominative feature and the accusative feature, respectively, of noun phrases. In the case of accusative Case, transitive verbs have the feature [assign accusative Case] linked to a particular θ-role. Therefore, *o* must appear on the noun phrase that receives this θ-role. On the other hand, as we have seen, T in Japanese cannot hold the feature [assign nominative Case] for principled reasons. As a result, all that is necessary to "license" nominative Case in Japanese is elimination of the nominative feature of noun phrases by Spell-Out, for which the presence of *ga* is sufficient. Hence *ga* behaves like a default Case.

4.2 Multiple subjects and objects

We have so far argued that English and Japanese employ different mechanisms for Case licensing: English uses the checking system whereas Japanese makes use of the particle system. This difference immediately accounts for another difference between the two languages.

It is well known that Japanese, but not English, allows multiple occurrences of nominative Case in a single sentence.

(45) bunmeikoku-ga   dansei-ga heikin-zyumyoo-ga   mizikai.
     civilized country-NOM male-NOM average-lifespan-NOM short

"It is civilized countries that men, their average lifespan is short in."
(Kuno 1973)

(46) *Civilized countries, men, their average lifespan is short.

Various proposals have been made, centring on basically the same intuition, to account for this property of Japanese. Thus, Saito (1982) argues that the nominative Case in Japanese is "structurally" assigned to an element immediately dominated by S. Fukui (1986, 1988a) proposes to derive this phenomenon from his hypothesis that Japanese lacks the active, "agreement-inducing" I, which is widely assumed to be responsible for nominative Case assignment in English, and that nominative Case in Japanese, unlike nominative in English, is assigned by a rule similar to "*of*-insertion" in English, which applies in the phonological component. Kuroda (1988) claims to attribute the construction to his hypothesis that Japanese is not a "forced Agreement" language.

Basically in line with these previous works, our current approach derives it from the hypothesis that Case features are eliminated by Spell-Out rather than by checking in Japanese. In the checking system it is impossible for T to check more than one nominative noun phrase because feature elimination by checking takes place as soon as the proper configuration is formed so that the nominative feature of T is eliminated when one noun phrase is inserted in the checking domain of T and becomes unavailable for further checking (hence the "one-to-one convention" for checking/agreement). Therefore, English does not allow multiple subjects. On the other hand, elimination by Spell-Out applies to any feature that is linked to phonological features when

Spell-Out applies. Thus, in principle, Spell-Out can eliminate any number of features. As a result, multiple occurrences of nominative phrases as in (45) are possible in Japanese.

Thus our account is well in accord with the "traditional" intuition (represented by the works just cited) that Japanese nominative Case marking is not based on agreement/checking and supports it by claiming that Japanese relies on Spell-Out, rather than checking, for elimination of Case features.[31]

It is interesting to note in this connection that Turkish patterns with English in that it does not allow multiple occurrences of nominative phrases, as pointed out by Kornfilt (1989, 1991). Compare (47) with (45).

(47) *[medeni: ülke-ler]   [erkek-ler]   [ortalama hayat
     civilized country-PL (NOM) man-PL (NOM) average life
     süre-si]   kisa
     span-Cmpd (NOM) short

As noted before, Turkish has a particle for accusative Case but not for nominative Case, which, under our assumptions, implies that it deploys the particle system for accusative Case, like Japanese, but the checking system for nominative Case, like English. It is in fact expected under our approach that Turkish does not allow multiple subjects.

The analysis of multiple nominative constructions presented above predicts that multiple objects with accusative Case will also be allowed in Japanese, since Spell-Out should be able to eliminate multiple accusative features as long as they are realized by overt particles. As Kuroda (1988) claims, Japanese indeed seems to allow multiple objects, although a cursory look at relevant cases suggests otherwise:

(48) a. ??John-ga   Mary-o   atama-o   nagutta (koto).
             -NOM   -ACC   head-ACC hit

   "John hit Mary on the head."

   (cf. Kuroda 1988)

   b. ??keisatu-ga   sono ziken-o   nyuunenni   tyoosa-o
         police-NOM that case-ACC carefully   investigation-ACC
         sita (koto).
         did

   "The police investigated the case carefully."

   (cf. Hoshi and Saito 1993)

These examples have two accusative phrases in a single clause. Cases like (48a) are reported to be fully grammatical in Korean, which also uses the particle system for accusative Case (see Choe 1987b for relevant discussion).

Thus, Korean confirms our prediction. By contrast, the Japanese examples in (48) are clearly degraded.

However, these examples improve if the two accusative phrases are separated by, say, cleft formation, as Kuroda (1988) and Hoshi and Saito (1993) observe (in (49), NM = nominalizer):

(49) a. John-ga   Mary-o   nagutta no   wa   atama-o   da.
     -NOM   -ACC hit   NM TOP head-ACC is

"It is on her head that John hit Mary."

b. keisatu-ga   nyuuenni tyoosa-o   sita no   wa
   police -NOM carefully investigation-ACC did NM TOP
   sono ziken-o   da.
   that case-ACC is

"It is that case that the police investigated carefully."

Following Kuroda (1988), we assume that the deviance of (48) can be attributed to the so-called Double-*o* Constraint operative in Japanese (see Harada 1973b, Kuroda 1978, and Poser 1981, among others, for discussion of the nature of this constraint). When the effect of the Double-*o* Constraint is somehow circumvented, as in (49), multiple occurrences of accusative noun phrases become acceptable. Thus, we conclude that Japanese does indeed allow multiple objects with accusative Case, exactly as expected under our approach.

On the other hand, the checking system in English will never allow multiple objects as seen in (48), for the same reason as we have seen for the case of multiple subjects. As is well known, this prediction is clearly borne out.

(50)   *John hit Mary her/the head.
       cf. John hit Mary on the head.

Thus, the multiple-object phenomenon, too, provides direct empirical support for our non-checking Case system in Japanese.

4.3 *Adjacency effects*

The claim that English and Japanese employ different systems for accusative Case because of the presence or absence of verb-raising also accounts for another well-known difference between the two languages, the difference with regard to adjacency effects. (See Hinds 1973 for relevant discussion.) Let us consider the following.

(51)   a.   Mary gave books to John.
       b.   Mary put books on the table.
       c.   Mary borrowed books from John.

(52) a. *Mary gave to John books.
b. *Mary put on the table books.
c. *Mary borrowed from John books.

(53) a. Mary-ga   hon-o   John-ni   ageta.
         -NOM book-ACC   -DAT gave
b. Mary-ga   hon-o   teeburu-ni   oita.
         -NOM book-ACC table   -DAT put
c. Mary-ga   hon-o   John-kara karita.
         -NOM book-ACC   -from borrowed

(54) a. Mary-ga John-ni hon-o ageta.
b. Mary-ga teeburu-ni hon-o oita.
c. Mary-ga John-kara hon-o karita.

The cases in (53) and (54) are Japanese equivalents of those in (51) and (52), respectively. Note that English requires the accusative object to be adjacent to the verb whereas Japanese does not. Takano (1996) argues that, when two internal arguments appear in the same structure, the theme argument is always interpreted (at LF) in a lower position than the other internal argument. This implies that the cases in (52) and (54) reflect the "base structure" and that those in (51) and (53) involve movement of the theme phrase within VP.[32]

We can derive the adjacency effects in English by appealing to the checking system and Attract-F (see Chomsky 1995b for much relevant discussion on this operation). The accusative feature in English is eliminated by checking. In order to be eliminated by checking, the accusative feature must be attracted by the FF(V)-v complex, formed as a result of attraction of FF(V) by v. Chomsky (1995b) argues that the head H always attracts the closest features, "close" here being defined in terms of c-command. According to this idea, FF(V)-v in (52) cannot attract the accusative feature since the other internal argument c-commands the accusative object and hence is closer to FF(V)-v than the accusative object (see Takano 1996 for more technical details). Therefore, the accusative feature cannot be checked, and the derivation crashes at LF. On the other hand, Japanese employs the particle system owing to the absence of verb-raising. Given the particle system, the accusative feature is subject to elimination by Spell-Out rather than checking and hence does not have to move. Attract-F is simply irrelevant here. Thus, the accusative phrase in Japanese does not show adjacency effects. See Fukui (1986) for a similar account within an earlier framework.

4.4 Wh-*movement*

Let us now turn to still another well-known difference between English and Japanese, namely, the existence of overt *wh*-movement in English and the lack thereof in Japanese, as illustrated below.

(55) a. Tell me [what$_i$ John bought t_i].
 b. [John-ga   nani-o   katta (no) ka] osiete kudasai.
         -NOM what-ACC bought   Q   tell   please

"Tell me what John bought."

Fukui (1986, 1988a, 1995b) argues that this difference follows from his hypothesis that English has an active ("agreement-inducing", in his terms) functional element C, which triggers overt *wh*-movement, whereas Japanese lacks it. Kuroda (1988) claims that English has overt *wh*-movement because "Agreement" (a technical notion in his system, which includes agreement in the usual sense as a special case; see Kuroda 1988 for details) is forced whereas Japanese lacks it because Agreement is not forced.[33]

Here, too, our approach deduces the relevant difference from the fundamental difference concerning verb-raising. Recall that the lack of verb-raising in Japanese leads the language to use the particle system for accusative Case, in which the accusative particle is a morphological realization of the accusative feature of a noun phrase and heads its own projection KP (see the discussion in section 4.1). Thus, the accusative *wh*-phrase in (55b) has the following structure.

(56)

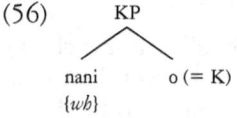

Let us assume that the embedded C in (55a, b) has the feature [+Q] (a question marker/feature). Suppose that Japanese [+Q] C required overt checking. Under our assumptions about feature checking, [+Q] C would have to attach FF(*nani*) to C, and the category *nani* "what", containing the "trace" of FF(*nani*), would have to raise to Spec, C to make the feature chain shorter. However, the latter operation is impossible simply because K cannot be stranded. Movement of the whole KP is also impossible, given the ungrammaticality of cases like (57).

(57) *I wonder [pictures of who] John saw.

Just like *who* in (57), *nani* "what" is too deeply embedded in the raised category KP. For category movement to be successful, the head of the moving category must contain the trace of the feature movement. Hence movement of KP fails, too. These considerations indicate that the presence of KP prevents [+Q] from being eliminated by overt checking.

Assuming that [+Q] must be eliminated for a derivation containing it to converge at LF, Japanese must deploy an alternative way of eliminating the feature [+Q].[34] We have already seen a similar situation. That is, the lack of verb-raising in Japanese forces the language to adopt a non-checking system that eliminates Case features, and that is the particle system. Here, a natural extension of this idea suggests itself, given the fact that interrogative clauses in Japanese always have the question particle *ka* at the end (see Cheng 1991 for an original proposal to link the presence of a question particle and the absence of overt *wh*-movement).[35] Let us then assume that Japanese uses the particle system for elimination of [+Q], more specifically, that (58) holds:

(58) Question particles make [+Q] of C visible to Spell-Out.

We now see a clear parallelism holding between the role of Case particles and that of question particles: both have the effect of rendering the formal features linked to them visible to Spell-Out. Given (58), [+Q] of the embedded C in (55b) is eliminated by Spell-Out, and the derivation converges at LF without overt *wh*-movement.[36]

The situation differs in English. Since English has the checking system for Case, the accusative *wh*-phrase in (55a) is a DP whose head has the *wh*-feature (Chomsky 1993a, 1995b). Thus, [+Q] of C can be eliminated by overt checking, that is, by attaching FF(D) to C and raising *wh*-DP (whose head contains the trace of FF(D)) to Spec, C.[37] In short, the distribution of overt *wh*-movement in English and Japanese clearly confirms the pattern expected by the generalization (35) put forth in section 3.5: English has overt *wh*-movement, and its [+Q] C lacks phonetic content whereas Japanese lacks overt *wh*-movement, and its [+Q] C has phonetic content.

In this connection, one might wonder how an interrogative clause is interpreted as such after [+Q] is eliminated (either by checking or by Spell-Out). Here it is important to distinguish formal features from other features. [+Q] is a formal feature of C. The same C has semantic features as well. It is such semantic features of C that are relevant to LF interpretation. We might assume that there is some correspondence relation between formal features and semantic features so that [+Q] C has the semantic feature [interrogative], [−Q] C has [declarative], and so on. The feature [interrogative] remains as part of C after the elimination of [+Q] and provides the basis for interpretation at LF.

Given the analysis of the lack of overt *wh*-movement in Japanese just proposed, a question naturally arises as to why English allows pied-piping of the following kind.

(59) In which house did John live?

How does the *wh*-phrase within the preposed PP contribute to making the feature chain shorter? Recall that in our analysis of the H-C order in PP, PP has the following structure (see the discussion in section 3.5):

(60)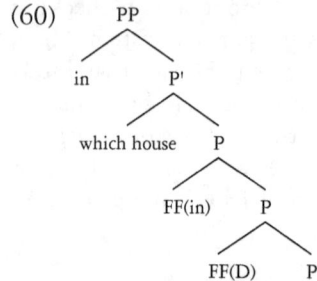

Here FF(D) is attached to P to enter into a checking relation with the latter. In the case of *wh*-checking, as in (59), this FF(D) is attracted by [+Q] C and leaves a "trace" in its original position within the "extended" P. In this situation, pied-piping of the whole PP is valid: the "extended" head of the PP contains the trace of FF(D). Thus, this case contrasts with the case in (56), where the head of KP cannot contain a trace of FF(*nani*) owing to the lack of feature checking by K.

In short, under our approach, Japanese must make use of the particle system for elimination of [+Q] because of the lack of verb-raising whereas the presence of verb-raising (and checking by P) allows English to adopt the checking system.

Before closing the discussion on *wh*-movement, let us briefly see how the following generalization, a generalization often referred to as "Bach's generalization" (Bach 1971), can be accounted for under the approach we're exploring.

(61) *Wh*-movement never occurs in SOV languages.

Note that German and Dutch do not quite fall under this generalization, given that they show the SVO order as well as the SOV order (and that they exhibit overt *wh*-movement). Japanese clearly falls under this generalization; it is a pure SOV language and does not have overt *wh*-movement. We can easily generalize the account proposed above for the lack of *wh*-movement in Japanese to other (pure) SOV languages, including Tamil and Turkish, given our hypothesis that SOV languages lack verb-raising. Note that languages like Turkish and Tamil have the checking system for nominative Case and hence do not have a nominative particle. This means that the nominative phrase in those languages is NP (or DP) rather than KP. But this fact does not enable those languages to invoke the checking system for [+Q] since the checking option is not available for the accusative *wh*-phrase, and hence the *wh*-in-situ option must be adopted in any case. Once the language L employs the non-checking strategy for elimination of [+Q] of C, it becomes a property of the C-system of L. As a result, L uses the same strategy for all cases relevant to the C-system.[38] Thus, Bach's generalization in

(61) can ultimately be attributed to the lack of head movement in SOV languages, a natural result under the approach explored here.

4.5 Complementizers

Let us turn now to the properties related to complementizers. English and Japanese differ with respect to the position of complementizers. A complementizer appears in a clause-initial position in English and in a clause-final position in Japanese.

(62) a. John thinks [that Mary left].
    b. John-ga   [Mary-ga   kaetta to]   omotteiru (koto).
       -NOM   -NOM left   that   think

"John thinks that Mary left."

The embedded clause for the Japanese case in (62b) can be analysed as follows:

(63)
```
        CP
       /  \
      TP   to (= C)
```

When Linearization applies to this structure, it yields the sequence TP + *to*, and hence everything dominated by TP precedes *to* on the surface. The same story holds for the question particle *ka* in Japanese, which can be taken to be an interrogative complementizer.

(64) John-ga   [Mary-ga   kaetta ka] tazuneta (koto).
      -NOM   -NOM left   Q   asked

"John asked whether/if Mary left."

What about the English case? The C-TP order in (62a) cannot be attributed to movement of the complementizer simply because the complementizer does not originate in a lower position. Therefore, we have to look for another explanation that is consistent with our basic assumptions.

Recall that we argued in section 3.5 that determiners, degree words, and prepositions in English are not functional heads themselves but are elements that check (features of) D, Deg, and P. We can extend this idea to the case in question. That is, the so-called complementizer *that* is in fact an element in Spec, C that checks [−Q] of C.[39] Similarly, *whether* and *if* are analysed as elements that occupy Spec, C, checking [+Q] of C (cf. Chomsky 1986a). Linearization gives the correct head-initial order for these cases, as in the cases of determiners, degree words, etc. discussed in section 3.5.

In effect, this analysis claims that clause-final *to* and *ka* in Japanese are morphological realizations of [−Q] and [+Q], respectively, which render [−Q] and [+Q] visible to Spell-Out whereas clause-initial *that* and *whether/if* are elements introduced by direct merger to check [±Q] of a phonetically null C. In other words, on this analysis, *that* and *whether/if* are not Cs but rather "C-checkers".

This difference between English *that* and Japanese *to* follows from our hypothesis that English has verb-raising whereas Japanese does not. Recall that the lack of verb-raising leads Japanese to invoke the particle system for elimination of accusative Case, which in turn is responsible for the particle system for elimination of [+Q]. It is reasonable, then, to assume that once a language adopts a particle system for some feature of a functional head F, it must be led to use the particle system for other features of F as well. Since Japanese adopts a particle system for [+Q] of C, it also employs a particle system to eliminate [−Q] of C. On the other hand, the existence of verb-raising allows English to use a checking system for accusative Case and [+Q]. Therefore, English adopts a checking system for [−Q] as well. The whole pattern is, again, consistent with the generalization (35) discussed in section 3.5.

The claim that *that* in English and *to* in Japanese are different in nature has certain immediate consequences. First, it provides a theoretical basis for Fukui's (1986, 1995b) observation that *that* and *to* have rather different properties. Among other things, Fukui (1995b) points out that *to* in Japanese can be used to introduce direct quotations (in fact, the particle *to* is called a "quotative" particle in the traditional literature) whereas *that* in English can never be, as shown below.

(65) a. John-wa "boku-ga   sono teeri-o   saisyoni
         -TOP I   -NOM that theorem-ACC first
         syoomeisita-nda!" *to*   itta.
         proved-PART   that said.

   "John said, 'I proved the theorem first!'"

   b. *John said *that*, "I proved the theorem first!"
      cf. John said, "I proved the theorem first!"

(Fukui 1995b, 354–355)

As we have seen above, C in English always lacks phonetic content. Japanese *to* corresponds to this phonetically null C (with [−Q]), rather than *that*, in English. Then it is not surprising that *to* and *that* behave differently. Suppose that the feature [−Q] is divided into two: [−Q, +DQ] for direct quotation and [−Q, −DQ] for indirect quotation. Now the fact in (65b) indicates that English *that* cannot check [−Q, +DQ]. Given (65a), Japanese *to* is a morphological realization of [−Q] in general, compatible with both [−Q, +DQ] and [−Q, −DQ]. In other words, we claim that *that* is a particular C-checker whereas *to* is a "general subordinator".

These characterizations of *that* and *to* can be extended to an account of the distribution of the so-called "*that*-trace" effects. Kayne (1994) makes the following conjecture about the cross-linguistic distribution of *that*-trace effects:

(66) *That*-trace effects are found only in languages with clause-initial complementizers.

Kayne suggests that this asymmetry between languages with clause-initial complementizers and those with clause-final complementizers follows under the assumptions (i) that the whole TP is always moved into Spec, C in languages with clause-final complementizers (of which Japanese is an example) and (ii) that a necessary condition for *that*-trace violations is that the overt complementizer asymmetrically c-commands the subject position. Assumption (i) is independently necessary in his theory to derive the correct TP-C order for languages like Japanese.

Kayne's conjecture (66) can be easily derived under the present approach. In any theory, the core of the account of *that*-trace effects is the distinction between the presence of *that* (or its equivalent) and its absence.[40] In our terms, *that* is an overt C-checker. Then we can say that *that*-trace effects arise only if an overt C-checker is present (and asymmetrically c-commands the subject position if Kayne is right). Recall now that Japanese *to* is a morphological realization of $[-Q]$ and is not a C-checker. Given this, it follows that Japanese *to* does not meet the necessary condition for *that*-trace violations. Generalizing this reasoning to all clause-final complementizers, we derive Kayne's conjecture.

4.6 Complementizer Substitution Universal

The claim that the clause-initial complementizer is a C-checker, whereas the clause-final complementizer is a morphological realization of $[-Q]$, also derives Bresnan's (1970) Complementizer Substitution Universal, which is an alternative to Baker's (1970) proposal formulated in terms of "Q-morpheme". The core of the Complementizer Substitution Universal can be stated as follows.

(67) Only languages with clause-initial complementizers permit overt *wh*-movement.[41]

The clause-final complementizer makes $[-Q]$ visible to Spell-Out. This means that languages with clause-final complementizers use the particle system for elimination of the features of C. It then follows that such languages never eliminate $[\pm Q]$ by feature checking and hence never have overt *wh*-movement, given that overt *wh*-movement takes place for the purpose of checking $[+Q]$ of C. In contrast, the clause-initial complementizer is a

4.7 Summary: verb-raising and typological differences

To sum up the results so far, we have arrived at the following conclusion for Japanese:

(68) The lack of verb-raising in Japanese accounts for:
  (i) OV order;
  (ii) the existence of a particle for accusative Case;
  (iii) the existence of multiple objects (and subjects);
  (iv) the lack of adjacency effects;
  (v) the lack of overt *wh*-movement (Bach's generalization);
  (vi) the existence of a clause-final particle for [±Q];
  (vii) the occurrence of complementizer *to* in direct quotation;
  (viii) the lack of *that*-trace effects; and
  (ix) the Complementizer Substitution Universal.

The contrasting properties of English also fall out from our hypothesis that English, unlike Japanese, exhibits verb-raising.

Some of the properties listed above are discussed by Fukui (1986, 1988a, 1995b) and Kuroda (1988). On the basis of the idea that a "specifier" is licensed only through agreement with a head, Fukui proposes that Japanese lacks "active" (i.e., "agreement-inducing") functional categories, whereas English has them, and deduces from this difference the properties related to multiple Case, scrambling, *wh*-movement, and others.[42] Kuroda (1988) also proposes to derive those properties from the alternative hypothesis that "Agreement" is not forced in Japanese whereas it is forced in English. Our approach unifies those properties with the other properties in (68) under the hypothesis that English has verb-raising whereas Japanese does not (the difference is ultimately attributed to different properties of v in the two languages; see (22)). Furthermore, our approach allows us to connect word order differences to other syntactic differences, which has been impossible in the previous approaches.

5 Conclusions

In this article, we have attempted to develop a theory of phrase structure that is both theoretically desirable ("minimalist" in spirit) and empirically viable in accounting for cross-linguistic word order variation in a principled way without postulating obscure extra machinery. The intuition we have pursued throughout this study is that language computation maps an array of linguistic elements (a numeration, N) to an interface representation in such a way that it starts with a lexical item (a head) proceeding in a bottom-up fashion and, at some point of this step-by-step derivational process, starts "decomposing" the structure already formed in a top-down way until the derivation reaches a completely unstructured sequence with a fixed linear order. The bottom-up part of the computation is generally called Merge, the "turning point" is called Spell-Out, and we call the decomposition part of the computation Demerge (a part of the process of Linearization), implying it does the "reverse" of what Merge does. Thus, we have in effect proposed a kind of "Symmetry Principle" governing human language computation, as stated in (7), reproduced here as (69).

(69) *The Symmetry of Derivation*
Computations in the overt (pre-Spell-Out) component and computations in the phonological component are symmetric.

We have shown that this Symmetry Principle explains the major properties of phrase structure in an elegant way. More specifically, the principle accounts for the apparently universal "leftness" property of Specs in a straightforward way, by attributing its leftness to the fact that a Spec, by definition, is the first maximal projection in a given phrase that the top-down computation Demerge encounters.

With respect to the order between a head and its complement, which allows for cross-linguistic variation (H-C v. C-H), the proposed Symmetry Principle predicts that the "head-last" C-H order reflects the "base" order involving no relevant movement whereas the "head-initial" H-C order is the result of some movement operation, in clear contrast with Kayne's LCA approach, under which exactly the opposite is predicted. Thus, under our approach, no abstract "functional categories", which are crucially needed in the LCA-based theory, have to be postulated to derive, say, the Japanese order (C-H). The H-C order, on the other hand, must be derived by movement in our system, and we have proposed, following Chomsky (1995b), that a "light verb" v (a kind of functional element) is responsible for deriving the head-initial V-O order and suggested that extensions of this analysis, in conjunction with some reanalyses of lexical categories, can account for other "head-initial" structures. The fundamental difference between, say, English and Japanese, with respect to word order (in a sentence) would, then, be reduced to the property of this light verb. We have proposed the following hypothesis in this regard.

(70) (=(22)) v has the property of attracting V in English, but not in Japanese.

This hypothesis is quite consistent with the restrictive theory of parametric variation discussed in section 2 in that it reduces the parametric differences to the property of a "functional" element and is also in line with the "traditional" view on the English/Japanese comparative syntax that functional categories in Japanese are "inactive" compared to those in English in the sense that they do not induce overt movement operations.

The hypothesis (70) entails the lack of overt verb-raising in Japanese. The lack of verb-raising in Japanese, in fact, has a number of desirable consequences, as we extensively discussed in section 4. We have argued that it has direct and important implications for a variety of phenomena, including the nature of Case systems, (particularly the role of overt Case particles), the (non)existence of overt *wh*-movement, the nature of particles, and the cross-linguistic distribution of *that*-trace effects, among many others. What is noteworthy here is that unlike earlier approaches to the comparative syntax of English and Japanese, our approach makes clear the status of the ordering factor and how it relates to other typological properties.

The symmetry view on derivation advocated in this article also has potentially important implications for the theory of human language computation. First, recall that the intuition we have pursued is that the $N \rightarrow$ Spell-Out computation and the Spell-Out $\rightarrow \pi$ computation[43] are symmetric in the sense that the step-by-step computations in these components form mirror-images of each other, implying that Merge is a bottom-up operation and Demerge is a top-down operation, doing the reverse of what Merge has done. It is clear that this intuition can be stated only under the assumption that language computation is "derivational", in the sense that it involves successive operations leading, if it converges, to (π, λ). Thus, to the extent that the intuition pursued in this article is well-grounded and the symmetry principle we have proposed is tenable, our approach supports the controversial derivational view on language computation currently assumed in the minimalist program (see Chomsky 1995b and references cited there for relevant discussion on the general controversy over the derivational or representational view on language computation).

Second, as James Huang (personal communication) has pointed out to us, the architecture of language computation implied by the Symmetry Principle is quite reminiscent of the classical pushdown automaton. Technical details aside, the pushdown automaton is a finite automaton with an additional property of having control of both an input tape and a "first in-last out/last in-first out" list, usually called a *stack*. Utilizing this stack, the machine works in such a way that the most recently added item is the first one to be removed; when an item at the top is removed, the item previously second from the top becomes the top item, and so on. We cannot go into further formal details of the pushdown automaton here, but the similarity between the pushdown automaton and the model of language computation we have proposed in this article should be clear.[44] If human language computation can indeed be formalized as a pushdown automaton, then further interesting questions arise. For example, we can ask whether language computation should be formalized as a deterministic pushdown automaton or as a nondeterministic one. Depending on the answer to this question, a question of "context-freeness" of natural language might receive a new light (if such a question is in fact relevant for linguistics; see Chomsky 1986b for relevant discussion). Also, the stack associated with the pushdown automaton is known to have a property of "globality"; more specifically, it has the "look-ahead" property by consuming an input item ahead of time and incorporating the information into its state. Yet it is also known that the "language" accepted by the pushdown automaton is within the class of context-free languages, a class of languages that are assumed to be "efficiently parsable". If language computation can be modelled upon the pushdown automaton equipped with a stack, these facts will have some important implications for the theory of economy, which is currently facing the problem of "globality" and potential computational intractability.

On a more empirical side, we have assumed with Chomsky (1995b) that linear order is not defined in the core $N \rightarrow$ Spell-Out ($\rightarrow \lambda$) computation and that order is fully determined by Linearization applying in the phonological component. This assumption, however, is incompatible with the evidence presented by Fukui and Saito (1996). As briefly discussed in section 2, Fukui and Saito (1996) presents evidence that linear order does indeed play a role in the core part of language computation. The presented evidence has to do with (i) the nature and the distribution of optional movements and (ii) the unification of the cases of the Condition on Extraction Domain (CED) (cf. Huang 1982). One possibility to accommodate Fukui and Saito's evidence under our approach is to incorporate the head-parameter in the theory. Notice that there is no inherent contradiction between our theory and the head-parameter. If linear order is already defined between a head and its complement in the $N \rightarrow$ Spell-Out computation, that information can be carried over to the phonological component, and the scope of Linearization is, in effect, limited to the positioning of Specs. This move, however, is not only theoretically undesirable (we add one extra factor, the head-parameter, to determine the order of elements) but also rips some consequences away from our theory. For instance, under the mixed theory of head-parameter and Linearization, most of the consequences regarding verb-raising that we discussed in section 4 will be lost. Thus, we would like to look for other possible ways of accommodating the evidence for linear order.

Recall that the evidence presented by Fukui and Saito is divided into two categories: (i) optional movement and (ii) CED. Chomsky (1995b) suggests that instances of optional movement such as scrambling and Heavy NP Shift may well be processes in the phonological component (similar suggestions have been made in various forms in the past). If this suggestion is on the right track, the evidence provided by Fukui and Saito can be reinterpreted as the evidence for linear order in the phonological component, with the implication that economy considerations of the kind discussed by Fukui and Saito do play a role even in (a certain portion of) the phonological component (see Fukui and Saito 1996 for details). The reinterpretation of the evidence (ii) would suggest a more radical departure from the standard assumptions.

That is, if CED should be analysed along the lines of Fukui and Saito (1996) and if we are to maintain our assumption that linear order is restricted to the phonological component, then the effect of CED must be located not in the core N→Spell-Out computation but rather in the phonological component. In fact, Fukui (1996b) (cf. also Fukui 1997 for some related discussion) suggests that portions of the Barriers system (Chomsky 1986a) that cannot be reduced to the properties of Attract (or to the Minimal Link Condition, depending on one's theory of locality) ought to be located in the phonological component.[45] These include the cases of CED (Subject Condition and Adjunct Condition). If this is a correct move, then it is exactly consistent with the reinterpretation of Fukui and Saito's evidence regarding the unification of CED though much more extensive work will be required to fully determine the status of "island constraints" in language.

The nature and status of linear order is a complex matter and is far from being settled. We have tried to develop a theory which requires a minimal and natural mechanism in accounting for linear order in human language, including its cross-linguistic variation. To determine whether or not our approach will eventually turn out to be on the right track, accounting for all the important evidence, should await future research.

8 Order in phrase structure and movement

with Mamoru Saito

1 Introduction

In this article we aim to develop the theory of phrase structure and movement, focusing in particular on parametric differences between English and Japanese. We adopt and argue for Chomsky's (1994) proposal to eliminate X' theory. At the same time, we maintain that the head parameter, or more precisely a modified version of it, plays a crucial role in syntax. We propose that the traditional "adjunction" operations – that is, scrambling and Heavy NP Shift – should be considered to be *substitution* in the sense that their landing site is completely within a projection of the target. We argue further that classical cases of "substitution" including NP-movement and *wh*-movement involve genuine *adjunction* in that they create a multisegmented category out of the target. We show that a number of differences between English and Japanese follow from this theory.

The article is organized as follows. Sections 2–3 are concerned with the issue of optionality. We first briefly discuss some phenomena that show that scrambling and Heavy NP Shift are indeed optional and are not subject to Last Resort (Chomsky 1986b, 1993a). Then, developing ideas in Fukui (1986, 1993b), Saito (1985, 1994b), Fukui and Saito (1992), and Murasugi and Saito (1995), we argue that the optionality is best explained if these operations necessarily accompany the projection of the target structure in the sense of Chomsky (1994). The theory of scrambling proposed here is intended to be an alternative to that proposed by Kuroda (1988). Section 4 deals with "movement to specifier position" (hereafter, Spec). We argue on both conceptual and empirical grounds that it is adjunction coupled with agreement with the head, along the lines suggested by Kayne (1994), Takahashi (1994a), and others. The empirical arguments rely heavily on Lee's (1994) analysis of certain cases of specifier-head agreement. The discussion in sections 2–4 is based on the hypothesis that nominative Case is not licensed via specifier-head agreement in Japanese. In section 5 we discuss some peculiar properties of the subject position in this language and provide further evidence for this hypothesis. Section 6 concludes the article and contains a brief discussion of some remaining issues.

2 The optionality of scrambling and Heavy NP Shift

Scrambling and Heavy NP Shift have been considered paradigm cases of optional movement. The most detailed discussion of their optional characteristics is found in Tada (1990, 1993).[1] In this section we discuss two pieces of evidence that they are not motivated by any sort of feature checking and hence are indeed optional.

2.1 Radical reconstruction

First, as discussed in detail in Saito (1986, 1989), scrambling, as opposed to English *wh*-movement and topicalization, is subject to "radical reconstruction". The following examples from Harada (1972) show that *wh*-phrases in Japanese must be within a CP headed by a Q morpheme ($=[+wh]$ C):[2]

(1) a. [$_{IP}$ John-ga [$_{CP}$[$_{IP}$ dare-ga sono hon-o katta] ka]
John-NOM who-NOM that book-ACC bought Q
siritagatteiru] (koto).
want-to-know fact

"[John wants to know [Q [who bought that book]]]."

b. *[$_{IP}$ Dare-ga [$_{CP}$[$_{IP}$ John-ga sono hon-o katta] ka]
who-NOM John-NOM that book-ACC bought Q
siritagatteiru] (koto).
want-to-know fact

"[who wants to know [Q [John bought that book]]]."

The relevant constraint, which we call the *wh*-Q Constraint following Harada (1972), is plausibly an LF condition, since it directly relates to interpretation.

However, as shown in (2)–(3), a *wh*-phrase, or a phrase containing a *wh*-phrase, can be rather freely scrambled to a position outside the CP headed by the relevant Q morpheme.

(2) a. [$_{IP}$ John-ga [$_{CP}$[$_{IP}$ Mary-ga dono hon-o yonda] ka]
John-NOM Mary-NOM which book-ACC read Q
siritagatteiru] (koto).
want-to-know fact

"[John wants to know [Q [Mary read which book]]]."

b. ?[$_{IP}$ Dono hon-o$_i$ [John-ga [$_{CP}$[$_{IP}$ Mary-ga t_i yonda] ka]
which book-ACC John-NOM Mary-NOM read Q
siritagatteiru]] (koto).
want-to-know fact

"[which book$_i$, John wants to know [Q [Mary read t_i]]]."

(3) a. [IP John-ga   [CP[IP minna-ga [CP Mary-ga   dono hon-o
         John-NOM   all-NOM   Mary-NOM which book-ACC
    yonda to] omotteiru] ka] siritagatteiru] (koto).
    read   that think   Q want-to-know fact

    "[John wants to know [Q [everyone thinks [that Mary read which book]]]]."

  b. ??[IP[CP Mary-ga   dono hon-o   yonda to]ᵢ [John-ga
          Mary-NOM which book-ACC read   that John-NOM
    [CP[IP minna-ga tᵢ omotteiru] ka] siritagatteiru]] (koto).
        all-NOM   think   Q want-to-know fact

    "[[that Mary read which book]ᵢ, John wants to know [Q [everyone thinks tᵢ]]]."

In (2b) a *wh*-phrase is scrambled to a position outside the CP headed by the associated Q morpheme; and in (3b) a CP containing a *wh*-phrase is scrambled so that the question CP no longer contains the *wh*-phrase. These examples are slightly marginal, but they clearly do not have the ungrammatical status of (1b).

Given examples of this kind, it is proposed in Saito (1986, 1989) that scrambling is "semantically vacuous" in the sense that it need not be represented at LF. Then, the scrambled phrases in (2b) and (3b) can be "moved back" to their original positions in LF, and these examples need not violate the *wh*-Q Constraint.[3] Note that this radical reconstruction property is not observed with the typical cases of A'-movement that are motivated by feature checking. Let us first consider the following examples of *wh*-movement:

(4) a. [CP Whoᵢ [IP tᵢ wonders [CP whatⱼ [IP John gave tⱼ to whom]]]]?
    b. [CP Whoᵢ [IP tᵢ asked whom [CP whatⱼ [IP John bought tⱼ]]]]?

The in-situ *wh*-phrase *whom* in (4a) can take matrix scope or embedded scope. (See Baker 1970.) On the other hand, *whom* in (4b) can take only matrix scope. This indicates, as noted in Chomsky (1973), that an in-situ *wh*-phrase can be interpreted at [Spec, CP] only if it is contained within the CP. That is, the *wh*-Q Constraint holds not only in Japanese but also in English.

The following examples, then, show that *wh*-movement does not have the radical reconstruction property:

(5) a. [CP Whoᵢ [IP tᵢ wonders [CP [which picture of whom]ⱼ [IP Bill bought tⱼ]]]]?

b. ??[$_{CP}$[Which picture of whom]$_j$ does [$_{IP}$John wonder [$_{CP}$who$_i$[$_{IP}$ t_i bought t_j]]]]?

As noted in van Riemsdijk and Williams (1981), *whom* in (5a) can be interpreted either at the embedded CP or at the matrix CP. *Whom* in (5b), on the other hand, can have only matrix scope.[4] This contrast is straightforwardly predicted by the *wh*-Q Constraint, but only if *wh*-movement is not subject to radical reconstruction. If the *wh*-phrase *which picture of whom* in (5b) can be moved back to its original position in LF, the *wh*-Q Constraint does not prevent *whom* from taking embedded scope.

The same kind of argument can be constructed for English topicalization.[5] Examples such as (6a) are marginally allowed by those who accept embedded topicalization quite generously.

(6) a. ??[$_{CP}$ Who$_i$ [$_{IP}$ t_i said [$_{CP}$ that [[the man that bought what]$_j$ [$_{IP}$ John knows [$_{CP}$ whether [$_{IP}$ Mary likes t_j]]]]]]]?
    b. *[$_{IP}$ Mary thinks [$_{CP}$ that [[the man that bought what]$_j$ [$_{IP}$ John knows [$_{CP}$ who$_i$ [$_{IP}$ t_i likes t_j]]]]]].

But even these speakers reject (6b). As these examples both violate Subjacency, the contrast must be attributed to an independent condition. The *wh*-Q Constraint makes the desired distinction if a topic cannot be moved back in LF to its original position. The *wh*-in-situ *what* in (6a) can be interpreted at the matrix interrogative CP since it is contained within this CP. On the other hand, *what* in (6b) cannot take scope at the most deeply embedded interrogative CP, because it is moved out of this CP. As there is no other interrogative CP in the example, the *wh*-phrase fails to receive an interpretation. Note that if topicalization is subject to radical reconstruction, (6b) is incorrectly predicted to be only marginal. The *wh*-phrase *what* could then be contained within the most deeply embedded CP at LF.

We have shown that scrambling has a property not shared by those A'-movement operations that are forced by the necessity of feature checking through specifier-head agreement. As discussed in detail in Lee (1994), one plausible hypothesis is to attribute the absence of radical reconstruction with the latter operations precisely to their feature-checking property. That is, a chain created for the purpose of feature checking must be retained at LF.[6] If this approach is on the right track, it follows that scrambling is not motivated by any sort of feature checking and hence, by definition, is an optional operation.[7]

2.2 The absence of relativized minimality effects

The second phenomenon has to do with the multiple application of scrambling. As is well known, multiple scrambling is freely allowed in Japanese. Thus, (7b) and (7c) are both perfectly grammatical.

(7) a. [$_{IP}$ Mary-ga   John-ni sono hon-o   watasita] (koto).
       Mary-NOM John-to that book-ACC handed

   "Mary handed that book to John."

   b. [$_{IP}$ Sono hon-o$_i$ [John-ni$_j$ [Mary-ga t_j t_i watasita]]] (koto).
       that book-ACC John-to Mary-NOM   handed
   c. [$_{IP}$ John-ni$_j$ [sono hon-o$_i$ [Mary-ga t_j t_i watasita]]] (koto).
       John-to that book-ACC Mary-NOM   handed

Further, it is not only clause-internal scrambling that allows multiple application; long-distance scrambling does so as well, as shown in (8).

(8) a. [$_{IP}$ Bill-ga   [$_{CP}$[$_{IP}$ Mary-ga   John-ni sono hon-o   watasita]
       Bill-NOM   Mary-NOM John-to that book-ACC handed
       to] itta] (koto).
       that said fact

   "Bill said that Mary handed that book to John."

   b. [$_{IP}$ Sono hon-o$_i$ [John-ni$_j$ [Bill-ga [$_{CP}$[$_{IP}$ Mary-ga t_j t_i
       that book-ACC John-to Bill-NOM   Mary-NOM
       watasita] to] itta]]] (koto).
       handed that said fact
   c. [$_{IP}$ John-ni$_j$ [sono hon-o$_i$ [Bill-ga [$_{CP}$[$_{IP}$ Mary-ga t_j t_i
       John-to that book-ACC Bill-NOM   Mary-NOM
       watasita] to] itta]]] (koto).[8]
       handed that said fact

As discussed in Takano (1995), this fact is significant when it is considered in the light of Rizzi's (1990) Relativized Minimality and Chomsky and Lasnik's (1993) Minimal Link Condition. (See also Abe 1993 for much relevant discussion.) The latter condition, in particular, requires movement to proceed through every possible landing site and is designed to block *wh*-island violations like the one in (9).

(9) ??[$_{CP}$ What$_i$ does [$_{IP}$ John wonder [$_{CP}$ where$_j$ [$_{IP}$ Mary put t_i t_j]]]]?

The embedded [Spec, CP], being an A'-Spec, is a possible landing site for the *wh*-phrase *what*, but the *wh* is unable to move through this position because of the presence of *where*. The Minimal Link Condition is thus violated in (9). The marginality of multiple topicalization, discussed in Lasnik and Saito (1992), can be accounted for in a similar way.

(10) a. Mary handed that book to John.
    b. ??That book$_i$, to John$_j$, Mary handed t_i t_j.
    c. ??To John$_j$, that book$_i$, Mary handed t_i t_j.

In (10b–c) the sentence-initial topic skips the position of the second topic, a potential landing site, in violation of the Minimal Link Condition.

Examples (7b–c) and (8b–c) are in clear contrast with (10b–c). But if scrambling is movement to an A'-Spec, then (7b–c) and (8b–c) should violate the Minimal Link Condition in the same way as (10b–c). The sentence-initial phrase in (8b–c), for example, should have moved across an A'-Spec occupied by the second phrase. Thus, the grammaticality of these examples indicates that scrambling is not triggered by feature checking through specifier-head agreement. Examples such as (12), which contrast with (9) and (11), also point to the same conclusion.

(11) ??To Mary$_j$, Bill thinks that that book$_i$, John handed t_j t_i.

(12) [$_{IP}$ Mary-ni$_j$ [Bill-ga [$_{CP}$[$_{IP}$ zibun-o$_i$ [John-ga$_i$ t_i t_j urikonda]] to]
     Mary-to Bill-NOM self-ACC John-NOM   advertised that
omotteiru]] (koto).
think   fact

"To Mary$_j$, Bill thinks [that [himself$_i$, John$_i$ advertised t_i t_j]]."

(9) and (11) are marginal since A'-movement takes place across an A'-spec. In contrast, (12) is fine since scrambling is not motivated by feature checking and hence is not movement to an A'-Spec.

So far we have shown evidence that scrambling does not take place for the purpose of feature checking, and this implies that it is optional. If feature checking is not the motivation for scrambling, the operation cannot be subject to Last Resort. It should be noted here that the difference between scrambling and *wh*-movement/topicalization illustrated above is not a parametric difference between Japanese and English. English Heavy NP Shift in fact shares the basic properties of scrambling. First, as noted by Webelhuth (1989), among others, multiple Heavy NP Shift is possible, as shown in (13).

(13) John told t_i t_j yesterday [a most incredible story]$_i$ [to practically everyone who was willing to listen]$_j$.

This indicates that the landing site of Heavy NP Shift, like that of scrambling, is not a Spec, and that Heavy NP Shift is not motivated by feature checking via specifier-head agreement. Second, the following examples indicate that Heavy NP Shift, like scrambling and unlike topicalization, applies to *wh*-phrases:

(14) Who$_i$ t_i borrowed t_j from the library [which book that David assigned in class]$_j$?

(15) a. John-ga [$_{CP}$[$_{IP}$ nani-o   [Mary-ga t_i katta]] to] itta no?
      John-NOM what-ACC Mary-NOM bought that said Q

"John said that [what$_i$, Mary bought t_i]."

b. *Who$_i$ t_i said that what$_j$, Mary bought t_j?

Intuitively, (15b) is ruled out because a *wh*-phrase cannot be interpreted as a topic. This kind of incompatibility in interpretation does not arise in the case of (15a), since scrambling is "semantically vacuous" in the sense that the scrambled phrase need not be interpreted as any kind of operator. The grammaticality of (14), then, is consistent with the hypothesis that Heavy NP Shift is "semantically vacuous" exactly like scrambling. We will henceforth assume that English Heavy NP Shift is not movement to a feature-checking position and that it is to be treated on a par with scrambling.

3 Optional movement and the theory of phrase structure

Having established the optionality of scrambling and Heavy NP Shift, we now present our hypothesis regarding how they are licensed. We first discuss their basic structural properties and briefly go over the analysis proposed in Fukui and Saito (1992). We then develop this analysis adopting Chomsky's (1994) bare phrase structure theory, along the lines suggested in Saito (1994b). We argue that scrambling and Heavy NP Shift are not subject to Last Resort precisely because each follows the basic pattern of phrase structure building of its respective language.

3.1 *The directionality of adjunction*

It is suggested in Saito (1985) that the directionality of "adjunction", in the traditional sense, covaries with the value for the head parameter. Suppose that scrambling and Heavy NP Shift are adjunction operations, as has been widely assumed in the literature. Then, as illustrated in (16)–(18), adjunction always takes place to the side opposite from the head.

(16) *IP-adjunction scrambling*
 [$_{IP}$ Sono hon-o$_i$ [$_{IP}$ Mary-ga [$_{VP}$ John-ni t_i watasita]]] (koto).
   that book-ACC Mary-NOM John-to   handed   fact

 "[$_{IP}$ That book$_i$ [$_{IP}$ Mary handed t_i to John]]."

(17) *VP-adjunction scrambling*
 [$_{IP}$ Mary-ga [$_{VP}$ sono hon-o$_i$ [$_{VP}$ John-ni t_i watasita]]] (koto).
   Mary-NOM that book-ACC John-to   handed   fact

 "[$_{IP}$ Mary [$_{VP}$ that book$_i$ [$_{VP}$ handed t_i to John]]]."

(18) *Heavy NP Shift*
 [$_{IP}$ Mary [$_{VP}$[$_{VP}$ handed t_i to John] [the book she brought back from China]$_i$]].

Since English is head-initial, Heavy NP Shift moves elements to the right. On the other hand, since Japanese is a strict head-final language, scrambling always moves elements to the left.

The relativized X' theory developed in Fukui and Speas (1986) and Fukui (1986) captures this directionality in an elegant way.[9] The basic proposals made in these works are stated in (19).

(19) a. Free recursion is allowed at the X' level.
 b. [Spec, X^0] is the maximal projection that agrees with the X^0.
 c. An X' projects to X'' when and only when it is combined with Spec.

The X' schema for English-type languages (specifier-initial, head-initial languages) is then as shown in (20).

(20) a. $X'' = Y^{max} X'$
 b. $X' = X/X' \ Y^{max}$
 where $X/X' = X$ or X', and Y^{max} (YP) is the highest projection of Y^0.[10]

Given (19b), (20a) applies only when Y^{max} agrees with X^0. The structure of (21a) is illustrated in (21b).[11]

(21) a. Mary handed that book to John.

 b.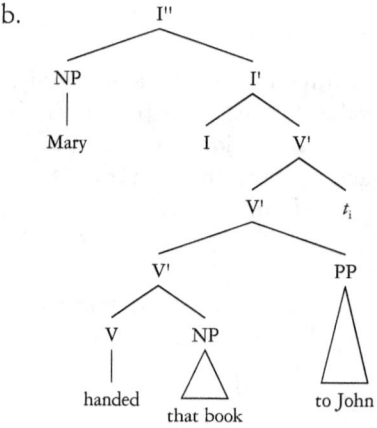

Here, as V does not agree with the VP-internal subject, it is projected only to V'. On the other hand, since the raised subject and I agree, the topmost node is I''. In this theory, the movement of the subject to [Spec, IP] can be viewed as adjunction to I' followed by specifier-head agreement, which results in the projection of I' to I''.[12] (19a) allows free recursion at the X' level, but not at the X'' level. Thus, we obtain the following generalization:

(22) Specifier-head agreement closes off the projection. (See Fukui 1986.)

Given this theory of phrase structure, the following simple hypothesis captures the distribution of adjunction operations:

(23) Adjunction is constrained by X' theory. (See also Saito 1985.)

Here, we will present a modified version of the account proposed in Fukui and Speas (1986) and Fukui (1986). First, since the I projection in English is closed off by specifier-head agreement, we predict that there is no "IP-adjunction scrambling" in this language. On the other hand, the V projection projects only to V'. As X'-recursion is allowed, "adjunction to VP" should be possible. Further, the adjunction must take place to the right because English is head-initial as specified in (20b). This case is instantiated by Heavy NP Shift.

Japanese sentence structure differs from English sentence structure in two important respects. First, Japanese is head-final. Thus, it has the X' schema (24) instead of (20b).

(24) $X' = Y^{max} X/X'$

Second, as discussed in detail in Saito (1982, 1983), and subsequent works, nominative Case in this language does not seem to be licensed via specifier-head agreement. One piece of evidence for this claim is the existence of the multiple-subject construction, exemplified in (25).

(25) [Boston-ga [susi-ga   umai]].
     Boston-NOM sushi-NOM tasty

"It is Boston where sushi is good."

If specifier-head agreement is one to one, as is widely assumed, then the two nominative Case markers in (25) cannot be both licensed at [Spec, IP]. Given this and other types of evidence, it is proposed in the works cited above that nominative Case in Japanese is licensed contextually on any argument phrase immediately dominated by a projection of I.[13] This hypothesis is consistent with the general absence of subject-verb agreement in the language.[14]

Given these facts and proposals about Japanese, the structure of (26a), for example, will be as shown in (26b).

(26) a. Mary-ga   John-ni sono hon-o   watasita.
         Mary-NOM John-to that book-ACC handed

     "Mary handed that book to John."

b.

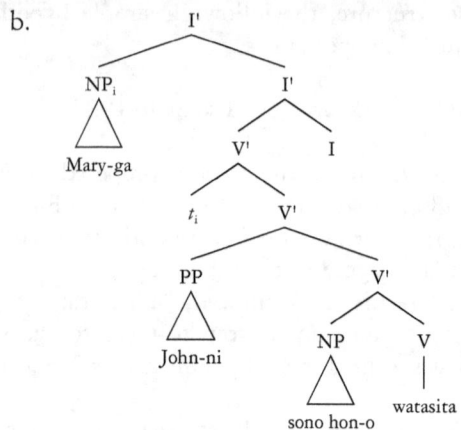

Since the subject does not close off the projection of I by specifier-head agreement, the head can be projected further, consistently with X′ theory. This has two effects: first, the multiple-subject construction becomes possible; and second, adjunction to the highest projection of I is allowed by (23), in contrast to the situation in English. We thus account for the difference between English and Japanese with respect to "IP-adjunction scrambling". "VP-adjunction" is allowed in Japanese, exactly as in English. The direction, however, must be leftward, since the adjunction structure is constrained by (24).[15]

The basic idea we proposed in Fukui and Saito (1992) is to attribute the optionality of scrambling and Heavy NP Shift to their "X′ compatible" property. Note first that the relativized X′ theory reduces the role of X′ schemata drastically.[16] It allows adjunction as a way of projecting the head. The directionality of adjunction is specified basically by the head parameter; that is, an adjoined phrase follows the head in head-initial languages and precedes the head in head-final languages. The only exception with respect to directionality is observed when agreement forces adjunction to the opposite side. Recall here that movement of α to [Spec, X] can be viewed as adjunction of α to X′, followed by agreement between α and X and projection of X′ to X″. If this is the correct interpretation, the subject in English, for example, must adjoin to the left of I′, contrary to the head parameter, and create the configuration in (20a). This apparently is forced by the "directionality of agreement"; that is, only a YP left-adjoined to a projection of X agrees with X. The phrase structures of English and Japanese can then be schematized as in (27)–(28).

(27) *Basic phrase structure*
    a.   English (head-initial): $X' = X/X'\ X^{max}$
    b.   Japanese (head-final): $X' = X^{max}\ X/X'$

(28) *Agreement*

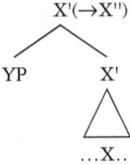

Here, (27) and (28) clearly have different status: the configuration in (28), as opposed to those in (27), is created only by movement. For example, a *wh*-phrase left-adjoins to C′ and agrees with a [+wh] C, as illustrated in (29a).

(29) a. [$_{C''}$ wh [$_{C'}$ [+wh] [$_{I''}$ ... *t* ...]]]
    b. [$_{D''}$ DP [$_{D'}$'s [$_{N'}$ ... *t* ...]]]
    c. [$_{I''}$ XP [$_{I'}$ [+agr] [$_{V'}$ ... *t* ...]]]

Similarly, according to the DP hypothesis (Abney 1985, Fukui and Speas 1986), a genitive phrase moves to the D projection as in (29b) to have its Case licensed.[17] And given the VP-internal subject hypothesis (Kuroda 1988, among others), the subject of a finite clause moves to the I projection as in (29c). Hence, if X′ theory reflects the basic pattern of phrase structure construction at D-Structure, then the X′ schemata should be limited to those in (27).

Given this conclusion, the difference between the traditional "adjunction" operation and the traditional "substitution" operation can be reduced to "X′ compatibility". As noted above, the latter can be considered adjunction followed by agreement. Thus, formally, both movement types can be considered adjunction operations. But scrambling and Heavy NP Shift create adjunction structures consistent with the X′ schemata in (27), as shown above. On the other hand, *wh*-movement and NP-movement result in configurations not allowed by (27). This is forced by the directionality of agreement.[18] It is therefore possible to characterize optional movement as X′ compatible movement. As long as it creates an X′ compatible structure, movement need not have a driving force. But movement is allowed to create a structure that diverges from the X′ schema only as a last resort for the purpose of feature checking.[19]

3.2 Adjunction in bare phrase structure

The hypothesis outlined above distinguishes adjunction and substitution in a principled way. But it poses one major conceptual problem. According to the hypothesis, all cases of movement are formally adjunction. Further, as specified in (27), adjunction is allowed as a way to build a phrase structure independently of movement. The agent and the goal arguments in (21) and (26), for example, are base-generated in V′-adjoined positions. Then, virtually all cases of syntactic operations, basic phrase structure construction or movement involve adjunction. It is thus clearly desirable to be able to maintain that adjunction is the only form of syntactic operation. However, there is one outstanding exception: the head-complement relation. As this configuration cannot be created by adjunction, a generalization seems to be missed here.

This problem seems unsolvable with the X' theory in (27). However, Chomsky's (1994) bare phrase structure theory provides a straightforward solution. The X' theory in (27) is already quite impoverished. But Chomsky (1994) proposes further that X' theory should be eliminated altogether. He argues that it specifies much redundant information when in fact the only structural information needed is that a "head" and a "nonhead" combine to create a unit. He then proposes that a phrase structure is constructed in a bottom-up fashion by an operation called Merge, which combines two elements – say, α and β – and projects one of them as the "head". This is illustrated in (30).[20]

(30)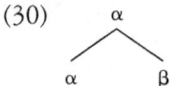

Since Merge does not specify the linear order of α and β, the tree structure in (30) can be more formally (and more accurately) represented as in (31).

(31) $K = [\alpha, [\alpha, \beta]]$

The structure in (30)–(31) corresponds roughly to those specified in (27). As β does not project, it is construed as a maximal projection; and, as α is the projecting head, its projection is not "closed off". Given Chomsky's (1994) theory of phrase structure, the difference between the head-complement structure and the "base-generated adjunction structure" (as opposed to the structure created by genuine adjunction) disappears. The theme argument and the goal argument in (21) and (26), for example, have the same status: both are combined with a (projection of) V and the V projects further as the head. Thus, the problem noted above does not arise.[21]

One way to incorporate the head parameter into this theory is to replace [α, β] in (31) by an ordered pair <α, β>, thereby specifying whether the left element projects as in English, a head-initial language, or whether the right one projects as in the head-final Japanese. This is illustrated in (32).

(32) $K = [\gamma, <\alpha, \beta>]$, where $\gamma \in [\alpha, \beta]$.
    a. $\gamma = \alpha$: head-initial, left-headed
    b. $\gamma = \beta$: head-final, right-headed

We will assume (32) in place of (31) in the following discussion.[22]

According to Chomsky (1994), the operation Move is a special case of Merge: if β in (31) is taken from within α, the result is a case of movement as in (33).[23]

(33)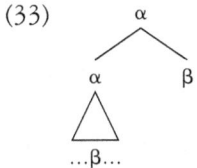

Given (32), then, scrambling and Heavy NP Shift are the paradigm cases of Move. As seen above, they are X' compatible with respect to (27). This means that they preserve the "head parameter value" specified in (32): scrambling creates a "right-headed" structure and Heavy NP Shift a "left-headed" one. Thus, they are in fact special cases of Merge. The basic phrase-structure-building operation and the traditional adjunction operation, then, can be treated uniformly: they both involve Merge as specified in (32).

The analysis of traditional adjunction outlined above is in fact suggested in Saito (1994b) with conceptual and empirical arguments. Conceptually, it not only is consistent with the elimination of X' theory, but also allows the optionality of scrambling and Heavy NP Shift to be characterized in a more straightforward way. The operation Merge is not subject to Last Resort, in the sense that it is "costless" and thus need not be motivated by any kind of feature checking (Chomsky 1995b: 226). Hence, if scrambling and Heavy NP Shift are instances of Merge, it is not at all surprising that they are optional. As we will discuss in detail in section 4, we claim then that only those instances of Move that do not conform to (32) need to be triggered by feature checking.

The empirical evidence comes from the dual status of the "VP-adjoined position", which is discussed in detail in Murasugi and Saito (1995). Roughly put, "VP-adjunction scrambling", as opposed to "IP-adjunction scrambling", shows the locality of A-movement in that it cannot take place across a CP. The following examples illustrate this generalization:

(34) a. [$_{IP}$ John-ga [$_{VP}$ Bill-ni [$_{CP}$ Mary-ga sore-o motteiru to] itta]]
          John-NOM Bill-to   Mary-NOM it-ACC have   that said
       (koto).
       fact

    "John said to Bill that Mary has it."

   b. [$_{IP}$ Sore-o$_i$ [John-ga [$_{VP}$ Bill-ni [$_{CP}$ Mary-ga t_i motteiru to] itta]]] (koto).

   c. ??[$_{IP}$ John-ga [$_{VP}$ sore-o$_i$ [Bill-ni [$_{CP}$ Mary-ga t_i motteiru to] itta]]] (koto).

(35) a. [IP John-ga [VP Bill-ni [CP Mary-ga   soko-ni sundeiru to] itta]]
       John-NOM Bill-to   Mary-NOM there-in reside   that said
       (koto).
       fact

   "John said to Bill that Mary lives there."

   b. [IP Soko-ni$_i$ [John-ga [VP Bill-ni [CP Mary-ga t_i sundeiru to] itta]]] (koto).
   c. ??[IP John-ga [VP soko-ni$_i$ [Bill-ni [CP Mary-ga t_i sundeiru to] itta]]] (koto).

A similar effect is observed – and even more clearly – with Heavy NP Shift. It has been well known since Ross (1967) that rightward movement is in general "clause-bound". Thus, Heavy NP Shift out of an embedded CP is ruled out, as the following example from Postal (1974) shows:

(36) *I have expected [CP that I would find t_i] since 1939 [NP the treasure said to have been buried on that island]$_i$.

Given these facts, it was proposed in Tada and Saito (1991) that the VP-adjoined position is an A-position.[24]

However, this analysis is apparently inconsistent with the strong derivational interpretation of the Minimal Link Condition, argued for convincingly in Takahashi (1993b, 1994a). According to this view, A'-movement must proceed through every possible landing site including adjoined positions. In particular, the moved phrase must adjoin to each XP that dominates the initial position and excludes the final landing site. Then, the *wh*-movement in (37) as well as the "IP-adjunction scrambling" in (34b) and (35b) must proceed via adjunction to the matrix VP.

(37) What$_i$ have you expected [CP that you would find t_i]?

If the VP-adjoined position is an A-position, this step should be ruled out exactly like the VP-adjunction in (36), (34c), and (35c).

But if scrambling and Heavy NP Shift are instances of Merge, this contradiction can be avoided. In this case "VP-adjunction scrambling" and Heavy NP Shift are not adjunction operations, but they induce the projection of the target VP. The final landing site is thus completely within the V projection, and it is reasonable to suppose that this is necessarily an A-position.[25] On the other hand, it is quite plausible that Merge allows only one of the elements combined (α or β in (31)), and no subparts of them, to project in phrase structure construction. (See Chomsky 1993a, 1994 for detailed discussion of this point.) Then, only the matrix I projects with the scrambling in (34b) and (35b), and only the matrix C with the *wh*-movement in (37). Consequently, the intermediate VP-adjunction in (37), (34b), and (35b) cannot involve a projection of the VP and hence must be genuine adjunction. If a genuine VP-adjoined position (or more generally, any adjoined position) can be an A′-position, no problem arises with these examples.[26]

The analysis of the traditional adjunction operations presented above implies that they are, in a sense, substitution operations. The term *substitution* loses its traditional meaning since the dubious empty category "Δ" is eliminated from the theory of movement in the bare phrase structure theory. (See note 12.) But substitution, as opposed to adjunction, can be characterized as movement to a position completely inside a projection of the target. Scrambling and Heavy NP Shift have this property, since they accompany the projection of the "landing site" (the "target"). They are not adjunction operations, since they do not create a two-segment maximal projection as in (38).

(38)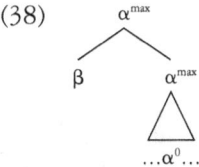

In the following section we argue that the traditional "substitution" operations (i.e., movement to [Spec, CP] and [Spec, IP]) do create the structure in (38) and therefore ought to be analysed as genuine adjunction operations.

4 Spec and adjunction

We have just argued that the traditional "adjunction" operations are genuine subcases of Merge and hence are the paradigm cases of Move. In this section we argue that the traditional "substitution" operations do not have this property and must involve extra machinery. We propose that they involve real adjunction as in (38) and agreement between the adjoined phrase β and the head $α^0$.[27]

4.1 Conceptual argument

We have proposed that the operation Merge creates the structures in (32), repeated in (39).

(39) $K = [γ, <α, β>]$, where $γ ∈ [α, β]$.
    a. $γ = α$: head-initial, left-headed
    b. $γ = β$: head-final, right-headed

As scrambling and Heavy NP Shift also create these structures, we considered them subcases of Merge. However, movement to Spec in English clearly does not have this property. As English is specifier-initial, the resulting configuration is not of the form in (39a). That is, in the terms used in Fukui and Saito (1992), it is not "X' compatible". Hence, movement to Spec, unlike scrambling and Heavy NP Shift, cannot be a subcase of Merge in the strict sense. This conclusion is in accord with the analysis of optionality suggested above. We attributed the optionality of scrambling and Heavy NP Shift to the property of Merge itself. Since they are subcases of Merge, they need not be triggered by feature checking, exactly like the nonmovement case of Merge. If this is correct, then movement to Spec, which is subject to Last Resort, cannot be a subcase of Merge in the strict sense.

Then, what configuration does movement to Spec create? If the form of "head" projection is constrained by the head parameter as in (39), movement to Spec in English cannot induce the projection of the target. For example, when an NP moves to the subject position, the target I' cannot project to I". (39) allows the moved phrase, instead of the target, to project, but this is clearly undesirable. A sentence, for example, is a projection of I, not of the subject. Only one option seems to be left: that is, movement to Spec involves adjunction and creates a multisegmented category out of the target.

As far as we can see, this hypothesis faces no conceptual difficulty. It simply states that the configuration of specifier-head agreement is as in (38), repeated in (40a), instead of as in (40b).

(40) a.   b.

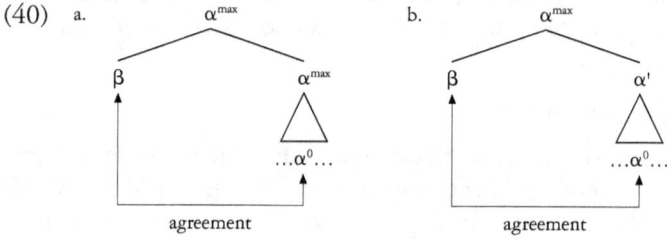

The adjoined phrase is defined as Spec when it agrees with the head of the target phrase. We continue to assume, as in Fukui and Saito (1992), that the directionality of specifier-head agreement forces left-adjunction instead of right-adjunction. But the last resort property of movement to Spec no longer needs to be stated in terms of directionality. Given (39), no adjunction operation can be a straightforward instantiation of Merge, which necessarily induces the projection of the head. Hence, if any operation that diverges from (39) requires a trigger, all adjunction operations must be subject to Last Resort.[28] In the following subsections we will discuss some desirable empirical consequences of this adjunction analysis of movement to Spec.

4.2 Empirical consequences

A number of phenomena indicate that the adjoined position "counts as" Spec. Lee (1994) discusses these phenomena in detail and suggests that the adjoined position can be "reanalysed" as Spec. Our hypothesis makes it possible to express her insight more straightforwardly without "reanalysis". Spec is in fact an adjoined position in our system. In this section we will briefly go over some of the phenomena that Lee considers.

The first case is simple successive-cyclic movement as in (41).

(41) [$_{IP}$ John$_i$ [$_{I'}$ is [$_{VP}$ t_V [$_{AP}$ likely [$_{IP}$ t_i' [$_{I'}$ to [$_{VP}$ win the race t_i]]]]]]].

It has been standardly assumed that the matrix subject *John* moves successive-cyclically through the embedded [Spec, IP].[29] This analysis implies that the embedded I' projects and creates the embedded [Spec, IP] as part of this movement operation. However, it is clearly more conceptually desirable if "Project" can be constrained so that it applies only to the top node of the target phrase structure. The purpose of the movement in (41) is to combine *John* with the matrix I' and not with the embedded I'. And the operation "Project" as a part of Merge applies only to one of the two elements combined, namely, the head. Hence, it is not clear how the embedded [Spec, IP] can be created by the movement in (41).

The adjunction analysis of movement to Spec straightforwardly solves this problem. According to this analysis, the NP *John* adjoins to the matrix I' (=I^{max}) and agrees with the head I. The Minimal Link Condition forces this movement to proceed through all possible adjunction sites, including the embedded I'-adjoined position. The trace adjoined to the embedded I' (=I^{max}) agrees with the Extended Projection Principle feature of the embedded I and thus counts as the embedded [Spec, IP]. No device is necessary to create the embedded [Spec, IP] position for the intermediate trace t_i'.

The second case concerns Bošković's (1993) analysis of some apparent exceptions to superiority. Chomsky (1973) characterizes the superiority phenomenon roughly as in (42).

(42) If two *wh*-phrases X and Y take scope at the same CP, and X asymmetrically c-commands Y, then X moves to the [Spec, CP].

The examples in (43) illustrate this generalization.

(43) a. Who$_i$ t_i bought what?
 b. ?*What$_i$ did who buy t_i?

Since *who* asymmetrically c-commands *what* prior to movement, the former must move to [Spec, CP]. However, there are notable exceptions to this generalization. For example, an object *wh* can move to [Spec, CP] "across" an adjunct *wh*, as shown in (44b).

(44) a. Where$_i$ did you buy what t_i?
 b. What$_i$ did you buy t_i where?

Bošković (1993) points out that this problem is resolved if the Minimal Link Condition forces *what* to go through [Spec, Agr$_O$] in (44b). Then, the initial part of the movement to [Spec, Agr$_O$] takes place for Case-checking purposes, and the *wh*-movement starts from this position. As the object *wh* in [Spec, Agr$_O$] c-commands *where*, it must move to [Spec, CP]. On the other hand, in (44a) *what* stays in the object position; hence, *where* asymmetrically c-commands this *wh* when it moves to [Spec, CP]. Bošković notes that this account generalizes to another apparent exception to (42), discussed in detail in Jaeggli (1982). As shown in (45b), an object *wh* can move "across" a postverbal subject *wh* in Spanish.

(45) a. Juan sabe quién dijo qué.
      Juan knows who said what
    b. Juan sabe qué dijo quién.
      Juan knows what said who

(45a) is expected to be grammatical since *quién* asymmetrically c-commands *qué* before movement. (45b) also poses no problem as long as the postverbal subject is VP-internal or at least in a position lower than [Spec, Agr$_O$]. The landing site for the first part of the movement of *qué* is [Spec, Agr$_O$], and the *wh*-movement originates in this position.

One question that remains in this elegant account is why the *wh*-movement of an object, an A'-movement, must (or at least can) go through [Spec, Agr$_O$], an A-position. Lee (1994) discusses this problem and suggests that the object *wh* must adjoin to Agr$_O$P on the way to [Spec, CP], and the adjoined position is reanalysed as (or counts as) [Spec, Agr$_O$]. This analysis becomes much more straightforward if movement to Spec is adjunction, as we argued above. The position adjoined to Agr$_O$P is Spec by definition, as long as the moved phrase agrees with the Agr$_O$ head. Thus, Lee's analysis succeeds without any stipulation.[30]

As Lee notes, her refinement of Bošković's analysis is quite similar to the analysis of French participle agreement proposed by Kayne (1989). French participles show object agreement only when the object is moved to an A'-position. The example in (46) is from Branigan (1992).

(46) la letter qu'il a écrite
     the letter that he has written-FEM-SING

    (cf. *Joséphe a écrite cette lettre)

Kayne proposes that the moved object goes through the Agr$_O$P-adjoined position and agrees with the Agr$_O$ head there. Branigan, on the other hand, points out that the Agr$_O$P-adjoined position cannot always be in an agreement relation with the Agr$_O$ head. The following example shows that a participle can agree only with its own object:

(47) *la lettre qu'il   a   dite   que Claire lui   a
    the letter that he has said-FEM-SING that Claire to him has

envoyée
sent-FEM-SING

The Minimal Link Condition forces the embedded object to adjoin to the higher Agr$_O$P in (47). Thus, given Kayne's proposal that adjunction to Agr$_O$P triggers object agreement, the contrast between (46) and (47) is surprising.

Lee (1994) proposes a refinement of Kayne's account that avoids this problem. As in the account for (44b) and (45b), she suggests that the Agr$_O$P-adjoined position is reanalysed as Spec. Then, the object operator forms two chains in (46): an A'-chain between [Spec, CP] and [Spec, Agr$_O$], and an A-chain between [Spec, Agr$_O$] and the object position. This reanalysis is blocked in the case of (47), since the resulting A-chain would violate a locality condition. That is, the head and the tail are separated by a CP node. Thus, Lee successfully explains the contrast between (46) and (47).

Lee's insight is that when an adjoined phrase agrees with the head, the adjoined position *counts as* Spec and hence as an A-position. This, again, is a straightforward consequence of the hypothesis that movement to Spec is indeed adjunction. Given this hypothesis, the adjoined position *is* Spec when the adjoined phrase agrees with the head.

4.3 The reunification of Condition on Extraction Domain effects

Cases where the adjoined position counts as Spec provide strong empirical support for our hypothesis that Spec is in general created by adjunction. Before we close this section, we will point out a possible consequence of this hypothesis for bounding theory.

It has been known since Cattell (1976), Kayne (1981), and Huang (1982) that a noncomplement maximal projection forms an island for movement, a generalization that led to Huang's (1982) Condition on Extraction Domain (CED), which, in effect, bans extractions from subjects and adjuncts. Thus, extraction out of subjects and adverbial adjuncts results in ungrammaticality, as shown in (48).

(48) a.   ?*Who$_i$ did [a picture of t_i] please John?
    b.   ?*Who$_i$ did John go home [because he saw t_i]?

Takahashi (1994a), extending Chomsky (1986a) and Chomsky and Lasnik (1993), proposes to derive these facts from the Minimal Link Condition and constraints on adjunction sites. The former condition, when interpreted derivationally, requires that movement go through every possible landing site. If any XP dominating the moved element is a potential adjunction site in the case of A'-movement, this implies that the *wh*-phrases in (48) must adjoin to every maximal position that intervenes between their initial positions and the matrix [Spec, CP]. In particular, *who* must adjoin to the subject NP in (48a) and the adverbial CP in (48b). But if adjunction to subjects and modifiers is prohibited, as argued in Chomsky (1986a), then the moved *wh*-phrase must skip a possible landing site in these examples. Hence, (48a–b) both violate the Minimal Link Condition.

The remaining problem is to derive the constraints on adjunction sites. Some proposals have treated the subject case and the adjunct (modifier) case separately. (See, for example, Chomsky 1986a and Takahashi 1994a.) However, our analysis of Spec opens up a way to unify these two cases. Suppose, following a standard assumption, that an adjunct (modifier) appears in a position adjoined to a maximal projection.[31] Then, descriptively, what is prohibited in the adjunct (modifier) case is adjunction to an adjoined phrase. This extends automatically to the subject case, since a subject is in [Spec, IP], and hence, under our hypothesis, it is in an adjoined position. The question thus reduces to why adjunction to an adjoined position is disallowed.

We suggest that this is due to the indeterminacy of the adjunction site that arises in the relevant case. Consider the configuration in (49).

(49)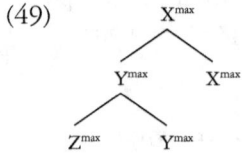

Both X^{max} and Y^{max} neither dominate nor exclude Z^{max}. Hence, if adjunction is defined as in (50), then Z^{max} is adjoined simultaneously to X^{max} and Y^{max}.

(50) α *is adjoined to* $\beta =_{def}$ neither α nor β dominates the other and β does not exclude α.

Adjunction to adjoined phrases, then, is excluded by the following plausible condition:

(51) An adjunction site must be unique.[32]

This condition can be generalized as a licensing condition for all nonroot constituents or positions. The intuition here is that every nonroot constituent must be adjoined to, or be sister to, a unique node. Suppose that α and β merge as in (52).

(52)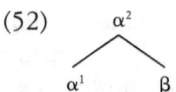

Order in phrase structure and movement 199

Here, α^1 and α^2 are independent categories, each consisting of a single segment. Hence, the first segment dominating α^1 is a segment of α^2 (i.e., the first category dominating α^1). The same is true of β. Thus, we may define projection licensing as follows:

(53) α *projection-licenses* $\beta =_{def} \alpha$ dominates β, and the first segment dominating β is a segment of α.

Then, α^1 projection-licenses both α^1 and β in (52). On the other hand, an adjoined element is not projection-licensed, because the first segment dominating it is not a segment of a category that dominates it. This is so since by definition adjunction creates a multisegmented category, and also by definition the category does not dominate the adjoined element.[33]

The uniqueness condition in (51) can now be generalized to the case of Merge as in (54).

(54) *Principle of Unique Licensing*
   a. α *licenses* $\beta =_{def} \alpha$ projection-licenses β or β is adjoined to α.
   b. Every nonroot constituent (or position) must have a unique licenser.

It is natural that a root constituent is exempted from this licensing condition, if the condition applies to operations, as opposed to representations, as suggested in note 32. The condition, then, states that Merge and Adjoin apply to a constituent – say, α – so that α has a unique licenser in the resulting structure. The resulting structure itself is not subject to the condition.

We have shown in this section that our adjunction analysis of movement to Spec not only receives conceptual and empirical support, but also opens a way to unify the subject condition and the adjunct condition.[34] This unification itself has a desirable empirical consequence: it makes it possible to provide a principled account for the absence of subject condition effects in Japanese, as we will show in the next section.

5 The absence of specifier-head agreement in Japanese

In our account of scrambling in section 3, we relied on the hypothesis that there is no specifier-head agreement in Japanese IPs. In English the subject agrees with I and closes off the projection as in (55).

(55)
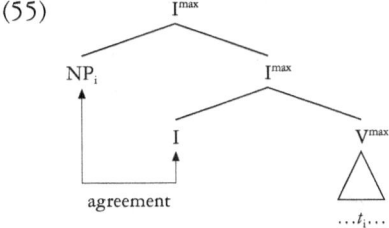

As I cannot project further, English lacks "IP-adjunction scrambling".[35] On the other hand, in Japanese a subject does not agree with I, and nominative Case is licensed on any argument immediately dominated by an I projection. Thus, I can project beyond the subject NP, and both multiple subjects and "IP-adjunction scrambling" are allowed in this language, as in (56).

(56)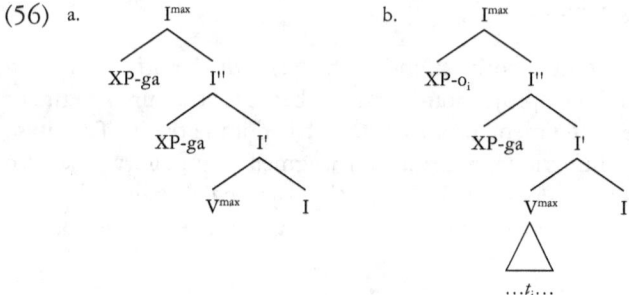

Under the VP-internal subject hypothesis, not only the accusative XP but also the nominative XP move from within VP, for example, in (56b). But note that this movement also can be a subcase of Merge, exactly like scrambling. The nominative XP only needs to be immediately dominated by an I projection and hence need not be adjoined to I^{max}. Further, the movement is in accord with the basic phrase-structure-building pattern of the language and creates a "head-final" structure. Thus, even if Japanese subjects are moved from within VP, they still can be contained completely within the I projection. In this section we present data indicating that subjects in Japanese have properties quite different from those of English subjects, and we show how these properties can be analysed within the system we have developed so far.

First, as pointed out in Kayne (1983a), Japanese, unlike English, seems to allow extraction out of subjects. The examples in (57) show that scrambling out of a complex NP or an adjunct (modifier) induces degradation.

(57) a. ??Nani-o$_i$ [John-ga   [$_{NP}$[$_{IP}$ e_j t_i katta] hito$_j$]-o   sagasiteru]
         what-ACC John-NOM   bought person-ACC looking-for
         no?
         Q

   "What$_i$, John is looking for [the person that bought t_i]."

   b. ?Nani-o$_i$ [John-ga   [$_{PP}$ Mary-ga t_i katta   kara] okotteru]
         what-ACC John-NOM   Mary-NOM   bought since angry
         no?
         Q

   "What$_i$, John is angry [because Mary bought t_i]."

For some reason, these examples are probably not as bad as similar Subjacency violations with English *wh*-movement; but they clearly contrast with the perfect (58).

(58) Nani-o$_i$ [John-ga [$_{CP}$ Mary-ga t_i katta to] omotteru] no?
　　　what-ACC John-NOM　　Mary-NOM bought that think　　Q

　　　"What$_i$, John thinks that Mary bought t_i."

However, scrambling does not distinguish between extraction out of a subject and extraction out of an object, as illustrated in (59).

(59) a.　?Nani-o$_i$　[John-ga　[$_{NP}$[$_{IP}$ Mary-ga　t_i katta] koto]-o
　　　　　what-ACC John-NOM　　Mary-NOM　bought fact-ACC
　　　　　mondai-ni　siteru] no?
　　　　　problem-into making Q

　　　　　"What$_i$, John is making an issue out of [the fact that Mary bought t_i]."

　　 b.　?Nani-o$_i$　[John-ga　[$_{CP}$[$_{NP}$[$_{IP}$ Mary-ga t_i　katta] koto]-ga
　　　　　what-ACC John-NOM　　Mary-NOM bought fact-NOM
　　　　　mondai-da to] omotteru] no?
　　　　　problem-is that think　　Q

　　　　　"What$_i$, John thinks that [the fact that Mary bought t_i] is a problem."

These examples are both slightly degraded since they involve extraction out of a pure complex NP. Crucially, though, (59b) is no worse than (59a). It seems, then, that subjects do not form islands for movement in Japanese.[36]

In section 4, we followed Takahashi (1994a) in attributing the subject condition effect in English to the impossibility of adjunction to a subject. As adjunction to a subject is impossible, extraction out of a subject necessarily results in a violation of the Minimal Link Condition. Given this, the absence of subject condition effects in Japanese implies that Japanese subjects, unlike English ones, allow adjunction. And there is in fact independent evidence from the "additional-*wh* effect" that this is correct.

As has been well known since Huang (1982), an adjunct (modifier) *wh*, as opposed to an argument *wh*, cannot appear in situ within an island in Japanese. Thus, (60a) is perfect, but (60b) is significantly degraded.

(60) a.　John-wa [$_{NP}$[$_{IP}$ nani-o　　katta] hito]-o　　sagasiteru no?
　　　　　John-TOP　　what-ACC bought person-ACC looking-for Q

　　　　　"John is looking for [the person that bought what]."

b. *John-wa [$_{NP}$[$_{IP}$ Mary-ga naze katta] hon]-o sagasiteru no?
   John-TOP   Mary-NOM why bought book-ACC looking-for
   Q

"John is looking for [the book that Mary bought why]."

Here, we follow Tsai (1994) and assume that an argument *wh* can be unselectively bound in situ by a [+wh] C, but an adjunct (modifier) *wh* can be licensed only via specifier-head agreement with a [+wh] head. *Naze* "why" in (60b), then, must move out of the island to adjoin to the matrix CP in LF.

However, there are some cases where an adjunct (modifier) *wh* is marginally allowed in an island. The examples in (61) show that the relevant cases improve drastically when there is an argument *wh* in a position c-commanding the adjunct *wh*.

(61) a. ??John-wa [$_{NP}$[$_{IP}$ dare-ga naze katta] hon]-o sagasiteru
        John-TOP   who-NOM why bought book-ACC looking-for
        no?
        Q

    "John is looking for [the book that who bought why]."

    b. *John-wa [$_{NP}$[$_{IP}$ naze dare-ga katta] hon]-o sagasiteru
        John-TOP   why who-NOM bought book-ACC looking-for
        no?
        Q

The "saving" argument *wh* must not only c-command *naze* but also be contained within the island, as shown in (62).

(62) *Dare-ga [$_{NP}$[$_{IP}$ Mary-ga naze katta] hon]-o sagasiteru no?
     who-NOM   Mary-NOM why bought book-ACC looking-for Q

"Who is looking for [the book that Mary bought why]?"

Given this kind of data, it is proposed in Saito (1994a) that *naze* can be licensed at [Spec, CP] or by adjoining to an independently licensed *wh*-phrase. (See also Sohn 1993, 1994 for much relevant discussion.) Then, *naze* in (61a) can adjoin to *dare* "who" and be licensed without moving out of the complex NP. Note here that this form of adjunct *wh* licensing may also involve specifier-head agreement with a [+wh] head. If the *wh*-phrase *dare* is headed by a D with the feature [+wh], then the adjunction of an adjunct *wh* to this DP creates the configuration of specifier-head agreement with a [+wh] head.

Order in phrase structure and movement 203

If correct, this analysis of (61a) implies that adjunction to a subject is possible in Japanese. In this example *naze* is licensed by adjoining to *dare* in the subject position. On the other hand, (63)–(64) from Huang (1982) indicate that English does not allow adjunction to a subject, as expected.

(63) a. Why$_i$ did you say [that John left early t_i]?
     b. *Who$_i$ t_i said [that John left early why]?

(64) a. ?Who$_i$ t_i said [that who left early]?
     b. *Who$_i$ t_i said [that who left early why]?

The contrast between (63a) and (63b) shows that *why* is licensed only through specifier-head agreement with a [+wh] head. As the matrix [Spec, CP] is already occupied by *who* in (63b), *why* cannot be licensed in this position at LF. (64a) shows that *who*, an argument *wh*, can be unselectively bound in situ by a [+wh] C. Now, if *why* in (64b) can be licensed, like its Japanese counterpart in (61a), by adjoining to *who*, then we predict incorrectly that this example should be far better than (63b). Thus, the contrast between (61a) and (64b) provides independent evidence that adjunction to a subject is possible in Japanese, but not in English.

In Saito (1994a) this difference between English and Japanese was attributed directly to the presence versus absence of specifier-head agreement in IP. It was suggested there that adjunction to an agreeing Spec forces the adjoined phrase to participate in the specifier-head agreement. As *why* in (64b) cannot agree with I, its adjunction to the subject is barred. On the other hand, the subject *dare* in (61a) does not agree with I, and *naze* can therefore freely adjoin to this phrase. But given the theory developed here, a more principled account based on phrase structure becomes possible. We suggested in section 4 that adjunction to a subject is illicit in English because, more generally, adjunction to an adjoined phrase is prohibited. If this is correct, then we automatically predict that adjunction to a subject should be possible in Japanese. As there is no subject-verb agreement in this language, the subject is not adjoined to IP but is contained completely within the projection of I as illustrated in (56). Thus, nothing blocks adjunction to a subject.

This account extends straightforwardly to the nonislandhood of scrambled phrases in Japanese. As noted in Saito (1985), scrambling out of scrambled phrases is allowed quite freely. The following examples illustrate this generalization:

(65) a. [$_{IP}$ John-ga   [$_{CP}$[$_{IP}$ Bill-ga   [$_{CP}$ Mary-ga   sono hon-o
         John-NOM   Bill-NOM   Mary-NOM   that book-ACC
         katta   to] itta] to] omotteiru].
         bought that said that think

    "John thinks that Bill said that Mary bought that book."

b. [$_{IP}$ John-ga   [$_{CP}$[$_{IP}$[$_{CP}$ Mary-ga   sono hon-o   katta to]$_i$
   John-NOM   Mary-NOM that book-ACC bought that
   [Bill-ga t_i itta]] to] omotteiru].
   Bill-NOM said   that think

"John thinks that [that Mary bought that book]$_i$, Bill said t_i."

c. [$_{IP}$ Sono hon-o$_j$ [John-ga [$_{CP}$[$_{IP}$[$_{CP}$ Mary-ga t_j katta   to]$_i$
   that book-ACC John-NOM   Mary-NOM bought that
   [Bill-ga t_i itta]] to] omotteiru]].
   Bill-NOM said   that think

"That book$_j$, John thinks that [that Mary bought t_j]$_i$, Bill said t_i."

All of these examples are complex since they involve double embedding of CPs. In (65b) the most deeply embedded CP is scrambled to the initial position of the middle clause. In (65c) the object NP is scrambled out of the scrambled CP to the initial position of the matrix clause. This example, although complex, has no flavour of a Subjacency violation.

The grammaticality of (65c) is surprising if scrambling is an adjunction operation. In that case the scrambled CP should be in an adjoined position, and the example should therefore be as bad as those with extraction out of an adverbial adjunct. But the grammatical status of this example is correctly predicted by our analysis of scrambling. Extraction out of an adjunct (modifier) is ruled out, since an adjunct (modifier) is in an adjoined position and adjunction to an adjoined phrase is prohibited. On the other hand, scrambling is not adjunction, but involves the projection of the target structure. Hence, the scrambled CP in (65c) is not adjoined to, but is completely contained within, the middle IP, exactly like the scrambled object XP in (56b). Therefore, a scrambled phrase is a possible adjunction site and does not constitute an island for movement.[37]

This account of (65c) makes a clear prediction regarding the "additional-*wh* effect" discussed above. Since a scrambled phrase is a possible adjunction site, a scrambled argument *wh* should be able to save *naze* contained within an island. This prediction is borne out, as shown in (66)–(67).

(66) a. *John-wa [$_{NP}$[$_{IP}$ sono hon-o$_i$ naze t_i katta] hito]-o
        John-TOP   that book-ACC why   bough person-ACC
        sagasiteru   no?
        looking-for Q

"John is looking for [the person that bought that book why]."

b. ??John-wa [$_{NP}$[$_{IP}$ nani-o$_i$ naze t_i katta] hito]-o
   John-TOP   what-ACC why   bought person-ACC
   sagasiteru   no?
   looking-for Q

"John is looking for [the person that bought what why]."

(67) a. *John-wa [$_{NP}$[$_{IP}$ naze nani-o katta] hito]-o
John-TOP　　　why what-ACC bought person-ACC
sagasiteru no?
looking-for Q

"John is looking for [the person that bought what why]."

b. *John-wa nani-o$_i$ [$_{NP}$[$_{IP}$ sono hon-o naze katta] hito]-ni
John-TOP what-ACC　　　that book-ACC why bought person-to
t_i watasita no?
handed Q

"John handed what to [the person that bought that book why]."

(66a–b) demonstrate that a scrambled object *wh*, *nani* "what", can save *naze*. (67a–b) show that this is the same effect as the one observed in (61)–(62). The "additional-*wh*" *nani* must be contained within the island and at the same time c-command *naze*. This pattern is exactly what we expect, since *nani* in (66b) is a possible landing site for *naze*. The adjunct (modifier) *wh* can adjoin to *nani* and can be licensed without moving out of the island.[38]

We have shown in this section that our analysis of subjects and scrambling leads to a rather straightforward account for certain facts concerning the island phenomenon and the "additional-*wh* effect". The data considered here thus constitute further evidence for our theory of multiple subjects and scrambling in Japanese.

6 Conclusion and further issues

In this article we argued for a theory of phrase structure in which the operation Merge is constrained by the head parameter, as in (39), repeated in (68).

(68) $K = [\gamma, <\alpha, \beta>]$, where $\gamma \in [\alpha, \beta]$.

　　a.　$\gamma = \alpha$: head-initial, left-headed
　　b.　$\gamma = \beta$: head-final, right-headed

We showed that this theory provides an explanation for the existence and distribution of optional movements, scrambling and Heavy NP Shift. We presented arguments that those movement operations are genuine subcases of Merge. The theory, then, provides a straightforward account for their directionality. It also explains their optionality, provided that the operation Merge is not subject to Last Resort. When analysed in this way, scrambling and Heavy NP Shift necessarily involve the projection of the target structure. In this sense, they are characterized as "substitution" rather than adjunction.

We then examined a consequence of this theory for the analysis of movement to Spec. We showed that movement to Spec cannot be a subcase of

Merge and must involve adjunction as in (69). We argued that this adjunction analysis itself has a number of desirable consequences. It allows a straightforward account for those cases where the adjoined position counts as Spec. This is so because Spec *is* an adjoined position in our system. It also opens up a way to unify the subject condition and the adjunct condition, because the subject position and the adjunct (modifier) position are both adjoined positions. We suggested a unified explanation, based on our theory of phrase structure and movement.

(69)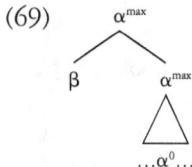

Finally, we re-examined our basic assumption that there is no specifier-head agreement in Japanese IPs. We showed that our theory, coupled with this assumption, automatically explains the absence of subject condition effects in Japanese. We also demonstrated that the distribution of "additional-*wh* effects" also follows as a consequence.

Before concluding the article, we would like to briefly mention two remaining issues. The first involves comparing our theory of scrambling with that of Kuroda (1988). We initially motivated our theory in part on the basis of the fact that Japanese allows "IP-adjunction scrambling" and the multiple-subject construction. We maintained that this is due to the absence of specifier-head agreement in Japanese IPs and the contextual licensing of nominative Case in this language. The former allows I to project beyond the regular subject position, and the latter enables more than one subject to have nominative Case. We presented our analysis with extensions of the proposals in Fukui (1986) and Fukui and Speas (1986), where it is argued that Japanese lacks functional categories, apart from the "defective" I that does not induce agreement. We assumed in this article that Japanese has other functional categories. But we maintained the proposal in the works just cited that Spec is the XP that agrees with a head. Thus, as Japanese does not have subject-verb agreement, it does not have [Spec, IP]. As noted in the preceding paragraph, we showed that this hypothesis has a number of desirable consequences.[39]

However, it should be noted also that this analysis is difficult to distinguish from that of Kuroda (1988), who proposes that Japanese allows multiple Specs. This is so especially when we limit the scope of investigation to "IP-adjunction scrambling" and the multiple-subject construction. Kuroda suggests that specifier-head agreement, which is a one-to-one relation, is obligatory in English, but is optional in Japanese. As the subject XP necessarily agrees with I in English, there cannot be any more Specs in the structure. If there is an additional Spec, it must – but fails to – agree with the head I. On the other hand, as the phrase in Spec need not agree with the head in Japanese, an IP can have more than one Spec in this language. Those extra Specs, according to Kuroda, are the landing sites of scrambling. (See Ura 1994a for a more recent analysis based on similar ideas.) Further, Kuroda assumes, as we do here, that nominative Case in Japanese need not be licensed by specifier-head agreement with I, and that this is part of the reason why the multiple-subject construction is possible. Although Kuroda's analysis and ours differ, they both successfully accommodate the differences between English and Japanese with respect to multiple subjects and "IP-adjunction scrambling".

The only way to distinguish our theory from Kuroda's, then, is to compare their overall success on both empirical and conceptual grounds. This would involve, for example, a detailed examination of how "VP-adjunction scrambling" and Heavy NP Shift would be analysed in Kuroda's theory and of how the difference between English and Japanese with respect to subject condition effects can be best captured within his theory. Unfortunately, this kind of detailed comparison is beyond the scope of this article, and we must leave it for future research.

The second, related issue concerns the analysis of ellipses in Japanese. Although Japanese lacks subject-verb agreement, evidence has been presented that specifier-head agreement takes place in this language. One outstanding case has to do with the licensing of ellipses. On the basis of the theory presented in Fukui and Speas (1986), it is argued in Lobeck (1990) and Saito and Murasugi (1990) that a functional head allows ellipsis of its complement only when it agrees with its Spec. Thus, "N'-deletion" is possible only when there is a genitive phrase in [Spec, DP], as shown in (70).

(70) a.   I read [$_{DP}$ John's book], and now, I want to read [$_{DP}$ Mary's e].
     b.   *I read about [$_{DP}$ that person], and now, I want to see [$_{DP}$ the e].

It is argued further in Saito and Murasugi (1990) that Japanese has "N'-deletion", as in (71).

(71) [$_{DP}$ Gakubusei-no   sensei-e-no   izon]-wa   ii   ga,
         undergraduates-GEN teacher-on-GEN reliance-TOP good   though
     [$_{DP}$ insei-no e]   -wa   yokunai.
         grad. students-GEN-TOP good-not

"The undergraduates' reliance on the faculty is OK, but not the graduate students."

The conclusion drawn there is that specifier-head agreement takes place (at least optionally) in Japanese DPs.[40]

As we only argued above that specifier-head agreement is absent in Japanese IPs, it may seem possible to maintain both conclusions. That is, specifier-head agreement takes place in DPs but not in IPs in Japanese. But scrambling is allowed in DPs exactly as in IPs. Further, "N'-deletion" is possible even when "DP-adjunction scrambling" applies. Relevant examples are shown in (72).

(72) a. [$_{DP}$ oya-e-no$_i$ [kodomo-no t_i izon]]
         parents-on-GEN child-GEN   reliance

   "the child's reliance on (his/her) parents"

   b. [$_{DP}$ Kodomo-e-no$_i$ [oya-no t_i izon]-wa   ii   ga,
       child-on-GEN parents-GEN   reliance-TOP good though
       [$_{DP}$ oya-e-no   [kodomo-no e]-wa yokunai.
       parents-on-GEN child-GEN-TOP good-not

   "The parents' reliance on (their) child is OK, but not the child's reliance on (his/her) parents."

It appears that given the analysis in Saito and Murasugi (1990), *kodomo-no* "child-Gen" in the second conjunct of (72b) must be in [Spec, DP], agreeing with the D head, so that the ellipsis is licensed. But if this is the case, then according to the analysis presented in this article, the scrambling of *oya-e-no* "parents on-Gen" should be impossible exactly like "IP-adjunction scrambling" in English.[41]

If we maintain our analysis of scrambling, then there should be no specifier-head agreement in (72b). This, in turn, implies that ellipses are licensed under a slightly weaker environment than specifier-head agreement. We must leave the detailed examination of ellipses for future research as well.

9 An A-over-A perspective on locality

It is proposed by Chomsky (1995b), on the basis of a suggestion made by John Frampton, that the operation of movement be reinterpreted as "attraction": "movement" of α to the neighbourhood of K should be thought of as K attracting the relevant feature(s) of α for the latter to enter into a checking relation with K, rather than α moving to the neighbourhood of K to get its relevant features checked off. Chomsky (1995b) defines this basic operation of human language computation in the following form, incorporating the effect of the Minimal Link Condition (MLC) of Chomsky and Lasnik (1993) into the definition of the operation itself, to avoid the well-known problem of computational complexity arising with respect to economy considerations (see Chomsky 1995b for a fuller discussion on these matters, as well as expositions of technical concepts of the minimalist program).

(1) Attract
     K attracts F if F is the closest feature that can enter into a checking relation with a sublabel of K (where a sublabel of K is a feature of the zero-level projection of the head H(K) of K).
     (Adapted from Chomsky 1995b: 297)

The purpose of this article is to explore further consequences of Attract for the theory of movement, suggesting, in a preliminary form, what seems to be a promising direction to take. More specifically, I will argue that Attract revives the A-over-A Principle in the form that is sensitive to relevant features (section 1). I will then show that the "feature version" of the A-over-A Principle accounts for not only the Relativized Minimality cases, but also for the major portions of the classical island constraints (section 2.1). It is also shown that the A-over-A Principle so reformulated can handle some disturbing cases for the Proper Binding Condition without any problem (section 2.2). I will then make some concluding remarks in the final section (section 3).

1 Attract and the A-over-A Principle

The A-over-A Principle, ever since it was first introduced by Chomsky (1964), has been formulated in various ways (see Chomsky 1964, 1968, 1973, Bresnan 1976, among many others; see in particular Hasegawa 1974 for an approach that could be, in certain respects, interpreted as an important precursor for the approach to be presented below), but the basic idea of the principle seems to be pretty much the same: that no phrase can be extracted from within another phrase of the same "type". Chomsky (1968: 51) formulates the A-over-A Principle as follows:

(2) *The A-over-A Principle*
If a transformation applies to a structure of the form
$[_S \ldots [_A \ldots]_A \ldots]_S$
for any category A, then it must be so interpreted as to apply to the maximal phrase of the type A.

From this formulation (and from other variants as well), it is clear that the A-over-A Principle has been characterized as a *maximum* principle which dictates that computations in human language (transformations in this case) apply in such a way as to "maximize" their target structures. However, this type of *maximum* principle is not well attested in linguistic theory. In fact, empirical considerations accumulated so far strongly suggest that language computation is subject to fundamental *minimum* principles ("economy principles"), showing striking similarities with properties of the inorganic world (see Chomsky 1995b for relevant discussion; see also Fukui 1996a for an attempt to situate the discussion of economy principles of language in a wider intellectual context). This peculiar status of the A-over-A Principle (*vis-à-vis* other principles of Universal Grammar (UG)) seems to be at least partially responsible for the fact that the principle, despite its naturalness and attractive generality, has been largely ignored or even forgotten in the subsequent development of the theory of locality, such as subjacency, the Barriers system, etc.

Given the idea of Attract, however, the A-over-A Principle can now be reformulated as a minimum principle (rather than a maximum principle), in harmony with other economy considerations in UG. Notice that there are two crucial ingredients of Attract, which distinguish this operation from the earlier conception of Move (see Chomsky 1995b: chapter 4 for detailed discussion). One is that what is subject to a movement operation is not a syntactic category, as has been assumed, but rather a feature/features that will enter into checking relation with a functional element triggering the movement. The other is the idea that calculation of "distance" should be carried out from the position of the triggering element (the "attractor"). It is not that the element to be moved must move to the closest position, but that the element triggering movement must pick the closest element (feature) that is to be checked off by the triggering element.

Chomsky (1995b) argues that the notion of Attract (involving the two modifications just mentioned) successfully accounts for the representative cases of Relativized Minimality (*wh*-island and superraising), which have been handled by the MLC (Chomsky and Lasnik 1993) in an earlier framework where Move is assumed, inducing serious problems of computational intractability (see Chomsky 1995b for much detailed discussion on this matter). Consider the following schematic structure (nonessential factors are all omitted, focusing on the relevant point):

(3)
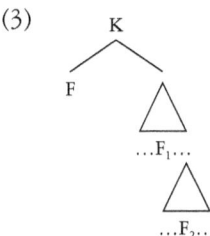

Suppose that the sublabel of K, designated as F in (3), has a feature that checks off the feature of the type F, and that there are two features in the structure, F_1 and F_2 as indicated. Then, Attract dictates that K attract F_1 but cannot attract F_2, since F_1 is clearly closer to K than F_2 in the obvious sense (and α, the minimal element containing F_1, merges with K; see Chomsky 1995b for more details of how Attract exactly works). Depending on the kind of F, we have cases of *wh*-island and superraising: if F = [+wh], the case of *wh*-island results; if F = [D/φ-features], we have the case of superraising. The representative examples are adapted below from Chomsky (1995b) (the relevant elements are italicized):[1]

(4) a. wh-*island*
(guess) [Q' (F = [+wh]) they remember [*which book* (F = [+wh])
Q [John gave t_{which book} [*to whom*] (F = [+wh])]]]
b. *superraising*
I/T (F = [D-feature, φ-features]) seem [that it (F = [D-feature, φ-features]) was told *John* (F = [D-feature, φ-features]) [that IP]]

In (4a), a case of *wh*-island, *to whom* cannot be attracted by the matrix +*wh* Q, because there is a closer element bearing a +*wh* feature, *which book*. The matrix I/T in (4b) cannot attract *John* bearing F_2, since *it*, which bears the same features (D and φ) is closer to the attractor I/T. In this way, the Relativized Minimality cases can be straightforwardly handled by Attract.

Although Chomsky (1995b) considers only those cases having to do with Relativized Minimality, where there is assumed to be no dominance relation between F_1 and F_2 (but see below), nothing precludes F_1 from dominating F_2 (Chomsky's 1995b definition of "distance" in terms of c-command will have to be redefined accordingly). Thus, in the following configuration, where F_1 dominates F_2:

(5)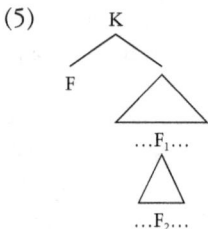

Attract dictates that K attract F_1, a more inclusive element, but not F_2, an element that is more distant from (the sublabel of) K than F_1 is. This is exactly the effect of the A-over-A Principle, now taking A to be some relevant feature, not limited to the categorial type assumed in the classical formulation of the principle. Thus, Attract resurrects the A-over-A Principle as a kind of minimum principle and in the form relative to features.

We have seen that the cases of Relativized Minimality (*wh*-island and superraising, the two major cases that have been handled by the MLC) are basic motivations for the minimality/locality requirement incorporated into Attract (cf. (1)). A closer look at the cases, however, suggests that these are actually the cases of the A-over-A Principle as well, conforming to the schema (5), where F_1 dominates F_2, rather than (3) in which there is no dominance relation between F_1 and F_2. To see this, let us consider what is involved in "feature-checking". The discussion of checking/agreement in the current literature still remains rather intuitive and there have been controversies over its nature, including the one whether it is a symmetric relation or an asymmetric relation (see Chomsky 1995b for relevant discussion). But for any theory of checking, the bottom line is that there is some exchange of relevant features between a head H and an element in its neighbourhood (i.e., in its "checking domain", normally in its Spec position), attracted for the purpose of checking; otherwise, it is not clear even how to formulate the notion of checking/agreement.[2] Let us suppose so, leaving aside other details of the theory of checking.

Then, it is natural to assume that the agreeing features in a given checking/agreement environment are shared by the head and an element in its Spec. For example, φ-features and D-feature are shared by the I/T head and an element (a DP) in its Spec, and a *wh*-feature is shared by a +*wh* C and a *wh*-phrase in its Spec, and so on. And if a head assumes the relevant agreeing features, they automatically project along with other formal features of the head (for example, categorial features), in accordance with the fundamental nature of the notion of "projection" (which is pretty much constant from the classical X′ theory to the current "bare phrase structure" theory). Thus, the relevant portions of Relativized Minimality cases can be now schematically represented as follows:[3]

(6) a. *wh-island*

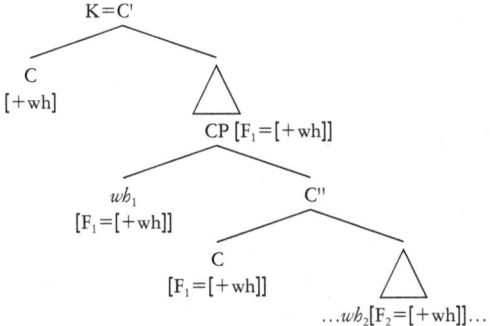

b. *superraising*

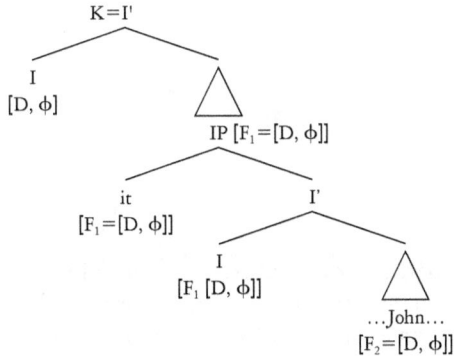

In (6a), the matrix +*wh* C cannot attract wh_2 (=F_2) because the latter is dominated by a more inclusive F_1, the intermediate CP, which obtains the feature F_1 from the agreeing wh_1 through agreement/checking and a subsequent projection. The same account carries over to the case of superraising (6b). The matrix I/T cannot attract F_2 (=[D, φ]) of *John*, since the intermediate IP, which dominates F_2, has the feature F_1 (=[D, φ]), inheriting from *it* via agreement/checking and projection. In both cases, an A-over-A configuration is formed, with A = [+wh] in the case of *wh*-island, and A = [D, φ] in the superraising case.

Notice that in both *wh*-island and superraising cases, attraction of wh_1 and *it*, respectively, is allowed as a legitimate operation. This is because the "dominating" F_1 is their "own" features, so that CP/IP immediately dominating them is rendered transparent with respect to the A-over-A Principle, not forming a genuine A-over-A structure with wh_1 and *it*.[4]

Note incidentally that an alternative way to achieve the same result without appealing to the feature-sharing mechanism is explored in detail by Agbayani (1998). Suppose, following Chomsky (1995b), that movement of a category α forms a separate chain (CH_{CAT}) from the chain formed by movement of the formal features (CH_{FF}). CH_{FF} consists of the set of formal features FF[F] and its trace (cf. Chomsky 1995b: 265). CH_{CAT} is formed by raising of a category α carried along by generalized pied-piping. CH_{FF} is always constructed, whereas CH_{CAT} is constructed only when required for PF convergence.

Chomsky then claims that FF(α) (the set of formal features of α) adjoins to the head containing the relevant feature to be checked, whether the movement is overt or covert. Let us now assume, following Saito and Fukui (1998), that the category α adjoins to the maximal projection of the relevant head to be in the same minimal domain as FF(α), when movement of FF(α) is overt. The category and the formal features must be in the same minimal domain for PF convergence (see Fukui and Takano 1998 for a similar proposal):

(7)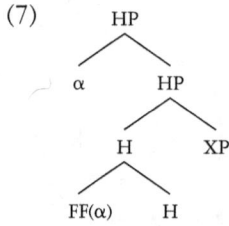

Given this possibility in the overt syntax, then, an additional feature-sharing mechanism between a head and its Spec employed above may become unnecessary. The formal features of α are literally contained in the head H, so, by assumption, they automatically project with the other features of H. The category adjoined to HP is not relevant for feature-sensitive operations/principles (Attract and the A-over-A Principle), but is only there for PF convergence. This alternative seems to work nicely for the cases discussed above (the Relativized Minimality cases) without positing an additional Spec-head agreement/feature-sharing mechanism. See Agbayani (1998) for more details of this approach, including its various other consequences.

We have shown that the Relativized Minimality cases, which are major motivations for the minimality/locality requirement incorporated into the definition of Attract, can in fact be successfully handled by the feature-version of the A-over-A Principle. Since the Relativized Minimality effects are almost exhaustively the motivations for the minimality/locality portion of Attract,[5] this result strongly suggests that the A-over-A Principle, although its resurrection is made possible under the Attract approach toward movement, is nevertheless an independent principle of UG, and that the minimality/locality part can be eliminated from the definition of Attract. Thus, we have the following notions of Attract and the A-over-A Principle.

(8) *Attract*
K attracts F if F is a feature that can enter into a checking relation with a sublabel of K.

(9) *The A-over-A Principle*
If a transformation (i.e., Attract) is to apply to a phrase-maker Σ which contains the following configuration, where A ranges over a set of features:
...[$_{A1}$ ... [$_{A2}$ ...] ...]...
it must apply to A_1.

In fact, the dissociation of the minimality/locality part from the definition of Attract itself is theoretically desirable. Note that in an attempt to achieve explanatory adequacy, generative grammar has always (since the early 1960s) taken an approach, which has proven to be very fruitful, that tries to factor out certain general principles which govern rule application and attribute them to the theory of UG, rather than stipulating them as specific properties of each rule, thereby allowing the actual "rules" to be formulated in the simplest possible form. Then, these UG principles interact in such a way as to explain the observed phenomenal complexity that the "rules" are initially designed to account for. Thus, the apparent complexity of application and interaction of, say, transformational rules, has been largely deduced from deeper principles of UG, leading, eventually, to the simple notion of Move α in the principles-and-parameters theory. It is, then, clear that adding a stipulated property to the formulation of a (transformational) rule is against the research spirit of this approach and, therefore, should be regarded as a step backward. For this reason, adding the "closest" proviso to the definition of Attract (see (1)) is certainly not a theoretically desirable move.[6]

There are of course compelling reasons for Chomsky (1995b) to propose that the locality/minimality requirement be incorporated into the definition of Attract itself, rather than attribute the property to economy of derivation. First, Chomsky argues that there is an inherent computational problem about economy of derivation in the form that the most optimal derivation is to be selected among convergent derivations. In particular, he points out that "if the MLC is an economy condition selecting among derivations, [an operation] OP will be permissible only if no other convergent derivation has shorter links. It is hard to see even how to formulate such a condition, let alone apply it in some computationally feasible way; for example, how do we compare derivations with shorter links in different places? But the question does not arise if violation of the MLC is not a legitimate move in the first place" (Chomsky 1995b: 267–268). Hence, the MLC has to be stated as part of the definition of Attract, in the form of the locality/minimality proviso, to avoid inducing excessive computational complexity.

Secondly, there is a more specific problem having to do with an account of superraising (or the difference between *wh*-island and superraising) that requires the MLC to be part of the definition of Attract. Suppose, at some stage of a derivation, we have constructed the structure (4b), reproduced here as (10).

(10) I/T (F = [D-feature, φ-features]) seem [that it (F = [D-feature, φ-features]) was told John (F = [D-feature, φ-features]) [that IP]]

Raising of *John* in (10) to the matrix [Spec, IP/TP] is an MLC violation, since there is a "shorter move" option which raises *it* to the same position. However, if, as Chomsky (1995b) argues, economy of derivation involves comparison of convergent derivations, this account does not hold. For raising of *it* will not lead to convergence, and therefore, cannot count as a competing, more economical move that bars raising of *John*. This is so, because raising of *it*, even though it satisfies the EPP (Extended Projection Principle) feature and the φ-features of the matrix I/T, does not satisfy the Case feature of the I/T (*it* has already had its Case feature checked in the embedded clause), which, being uninterpretable, causes the derivation to crash if not checked (and erased). Therefore, "For the account of the superraising to go through, we must take the MLC to be part of the definition of Move [Attract], hence inviolable, not an economy condition that chooses among convergent derivations" (Chomsky 1995b: 296).

Neither of these problems, however, arises under the A-over-A approach we are pursuing. The A-over-A Principle is an independent principle of UG that regulates application of transformations. Transformations simply cannot apply if they violate the A-over-A Principle. Whether or not an application of a transformation violates the A-over-A Principle can be fully determined by looking at the single phrase-marker at a given stage of a derivation, without any need for comparing (convergent) derivations. Thus, no serious problem of computational complexity arises. As for the account of superraising, we have already discussed how the A-over-A Principle handles it. Raising of *John* is an A-over-A violation, and hence is barred. Raising of *it* is a legitimate operation as far as the A-over-A Principle is concerned, but it will eventually lead to nonconvergence of the derivation, for reasons just discussed. This account, incidentally, carries over to the case of *wh*-island, the only difference being that, unlike superraising, the movement allowed by the A-over-A Principle will lead to convergence of the derivation (due to the difference in interpretability between *wh*-feature and Case feature; see Chomsky 1995b for detailed discussion).

Thus, no problems, empirical or theoretical, arise with postulating the A-over-A Principle as an independent principle of UG, rendering unnecessary the locality/minimality requirement in the definition of Attract. Furthermore, on conceptual grounds, adding such a stipulated property to Attract/transformations has an undesirable effect, as we just discussed. We conclude, therefore, that the locality/minimality requirement should be

2 Extensions of the A-over-A Principle

The scope of the A-over-A Principle, revived under the new light provided by Attract, can be extended well beyond the MLC. These consequences, then, lend further support for the status of the A-over-A Principle as an independent principle of UG, not reducible as part of the definition of Attract.

2.1 Island constraints

Let us consider the major cases of island constraints, the Complex NP Constraint (CNPC) (Ross 1967) and the cases of Condition on Extraction Domain (CED) (Huang 1982), illustrated by the following examples:[7]

(11) CNPC
    a. ??Who$_i$ did he believe [$_{NP/DP}$ the claim [$_{CP}$ that John killed t_i]]
                                                                             (the noun-complement case)
    b. *Who$_i$ did he read [$_{NP/DP}$ the book [$_{CP}$ that criticized t_i]]
                                                                             (the relative clause case)

(12) CED
    a. *Who$_i$ did you think that [$_{NP/DP}$ pictures of t_i] would be on sale
                                                                             (the Subject Condition effect)
    b. *?Who$_i$ did they leave the party [$_{PP}$ before meeting t_i]
                                                                             (the Adjunct Condition effect)

It is clear that the CNPC cases fall under the A-over-A Principle (in fact, these are the classical cases of the A-over-A Principle discussed in earlier literature), with A = categorial features. Extraction of *who*, a NP/DP, from within a more inclusive NP/DP (a noun-complement phrase (11a) or a relative clause (11b)) is a straightforward violation of the A-over-A Principle.[8] Notice that for this account of CNPC in terms of the A-over-A Principle to hold, the A-over-A must be an independent principle and not merely a part of the definition of Attract, since "A" in this case, that is, categorial features, are, unlike *wh*-feature and D and φ-features discussed above, not the features to be attracted by K.

The treatment of the CED cases requires caution. The Subject Condition case appears to be handled by the A-over-A Principle, as involving extraction of a NP/DP (*who*) from within a more inclusive NP/DP (the subject phrase). But this account does not hold of the Adjunct Condition case, where there is no obvious A-over-A structure involved. Thus, if we want to keep the unification of these cases as established by the CED, an alternative explanation must be called for. In fact, Saito and Fukui (1998) argue that the account of the CED effect should be divorced from other cases of island, and propose that the CED effect is best accounted for in terms of phrase structural properties.

Saito and Fukui (1998) (see also Fukui 1993b) claims that linear order plays an important role in the core computational part of human language, and argues that the head parameter, or more precisely a modified version of it, should be maintained. One way to incorporate the head parameter into the bare phrase structure theory is to replace the set notation [α, β] in Chomsky's original formulation of Merge (an operation responsible for building phrase structure) by an ordered pair <α, β>, thereby specifying which of the two elements projects in a given language. Thus, we have (14) instead of (13).

(13) Chomsky's Merge:
 K = [γ, [α, β]], where γ ∈ [α, β]

(14) Saito and Fukui's parametrized Merge:
 K = [γ, <α, β>], where γ ∈ [α, β]

If γ takes the value "α", we have a "head-initial/left-headed" language such as English, whereas if γ = β, a "head-last/right-headed" language like Japanese is defined. Thus, in left-headed English, elements can be merged only on the *right* side of a head, whereas in right-headed Japanese, Merge occurs only on the *left* side of a head. If something is to be introduced on the opposite side of the structure (i.e., on the left side of a head in English, and on the right side of a head in Japanese), it must be "adjoined" to the target, creating a multisegment structure (see Chomsky 1986a, 1995b for relevant discussion on substitution v. adjunction; see also the discussion below). A case in point is the status of subjects in these languages. The subject in English is in an adjoined position because it appears on the left side of the head, where projection of the target is prohibited by (14) as it is parametrized for English. The subject in Japanese, on the other hand, is introduced into phrase structure by Merge (i.e., substitution; see below), since it shows up on the left side of the head, where merger is possible (Japanese is a right-headed language). See Saito and Fukui (1998) for more detailed discussion, as well as illustrations of this point.

Saito and Fukui argue that given the parametrized version of Merge (14), it becomes possible to characterize the traditional "adjunction" operations, that is, scrambling in Japanese and Heavy NP Shift in English, as paradigm cases of Merge (i.e., as substitution, in the sense that they always accompany projection of the target), and hence, given the costless nature of Merge (Chomsky 1995b: 226), the optionality of these operations, a matter that has been quite disturbing for the general economy approach to movement, is also straightforwardly accounted for. On the other hand, traditional "substitution" operations (*wh*-movement and NP-movement) are analysed in this system as genuine adjunction since they never induce projection of the target, creating a multisegment structure of the target (see Saito and Fukui 1998 for much detail). Further, they point out that the "directionality" of these optional movements correlates with the "directionality" of projection in the language. Thus, head-initial/left-headed English has rightward Heavy NP Shift, whereas head-last/right-headed Japanese exhibits leftward scrambling, but no other combination is allowed. It is clear that such a correlation can only be captured by a parametrized Merge embodying linear order, as in (14). Saito and Fukui show that a number of other differences between English and Japanese also follow from their theory of phrase structure.

Returning to our main point of discussion, Saito and Fukui's parametrized Merge has an important implication for the theory of locality on movement, in particular, the treatment of Subject and Adjunct Condition effects (the two major cases of CED). There are two important problems with respect to these effects. One is how to unify these effects in a natural way. The other problem has to do with the cross-linguistic considerations of these effects. The Adjunct Condition effects are generally assumed to be universal, whereas the Subject Condition effects are known to show cross-linguistic variation. Specifically, it appears that while SVO languages generally exhibit the Subject Condition effects, SOV languages systematically lack the effects (Kayne 1983b; see also Aissen 1996 for related discussion). As is well known, Huang (1982) proposes his CED, which unifies the Subject and Adjunct Condition effects in terms of the notion of "proper government", and suggests a possible way of accounting for the observed cross-linguistic difference with respect to the Subject Condition effects (see Huang 1982 for details). Huang's CED was later incorporated into Chomsky's (1986a) barriers theory as a central ingredient of the latter system.

Takahashi (1994a), working under the general "economy" guidelines and extending Chomsky (1986a), and Chomsky and Lasnik (1993), proposes to derive these effects from the MLC and constraints on adjunction sites. The former condition, when interpreted derivationally, requires that movement go through every possible landing site. If any XP dominating the moved element is a potential adjunction site in the case of A′-movement, this implies that the *wh*-phrases to be moved into Spec positions must adjoin to every maximal position that intervenes between their initial positions and the Spec. In particular, *who* must adjoin to the subject DP in (12a), and the adverbial PP in (12b). But if adjunction to subjects and adjuncts or modifiers is prohibited, as argued in Chomsky (1986a), then the moved *wh*-phrase must skip a possible landing site in these examples. Hence, (12a, b) both violate the MLC.

The remaining problem is to derive the constraints on adjunction sites. There have been some proposals that treat the subject case and the adjunct (modifier) case separately. (See, for example, Chomsky 1986a and Takahashi 1994a.) However, Saito and Fukui argue that their parametrized Merge approach opens up a refreshingly new way to unify these two cases. Suppose, following a standard assumption, that an adjunct (modifier) appears in a position adjoined to a maximal projection. Then, descriptively, what is prohibited in the adjunct (modifier) case is adjunction to an adjoined phrase. And this extends automatically to the subject case, since a subject in English (or SVO languages generally) is in an adjoined position, as we discussed above. The explanation for the lack of the Subject Condition effects in Japanese (or SOV languages generally) is straightforward: subjects in this language are not in an adjoined position, but rather are introduced into structure by Merge (substitution). The question, thus, reduces to why adjunction to an adjoined position is disallowed.

Saito and Fukui propose that this is due to the indeterminacy of the adjunction site that arises in the relevant case. Consider the following configuration:

(15)

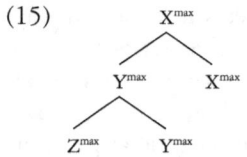

Both X^{max} and Y^{max} neither dominate nor exclude Z^{max} (see Chomsky 1986a for the definitions of these structural notions). Hence, if "adjunction" is defined as in (16), then Z^{max} in (15) is adjoined simultaneously to X^{max} and Y^{max}.

(16) α is adjoined to $\beta \equiv_{def}$ neither α nor β dominates the other and β does not exclude α.

Adjunction to adjoined phrases, then, is excluded by the following plausible condition:

(17) An adjunction site must be unique.

Saito and Fukui argue that the condition (17) need not be stipulated as an independent condition on adjunction site, but rather is an instance of the general uniqueness condition on the licensing of (nonroot) elements in a phrase marker. (See Saito and Fukui 1998 for a precise formulation of the principle as well as much detailed discussion on relevant points.) Thus, their parametrized Merge which incorporates the notion of linear order (the head parameter, in particular) unifies, without having recourse to such notions as "proper government" (Huang 1982) and "L-marking" (Chomsky 1986a), the classical cases of CED (the Subject and the Adjunct Condition effects), offering a natural explanation for the parametric variation associated with the Subject Condition effects.

If this account is on the right track, then the CED cases should indeed be attributed to properties of phrase structure and, therefore, should be independent from the A-over-A Principle.[9] I will assume so, referring the reader to Saito and Fukui (1998) for an extensive discussion.

Thus, the major cases of the classical island constraints are handled in the following way, if the line of research pursued in this paper is correct:

(18) • Relativized Minimality
  (wh-island/superraising) } → The A-over-A principle
 • CNPC
 • CED → Phrase Structure

This picture suggests that the theory of locality should basically go back to the classical version of the 1960s, where the A-over-A Principle is the unifying principle accounting for wh-island and CNPC (with an addition of superraising). Of course, the empirical coverage of the relevant data has been significantly widened since then, and numerous important new phenomena have been discovered, including superraising and CED effects.

But if the A-over-A Principle can be revived as a general minimum principle with due attention to relevant features and if the CED cases can be successfully handled by a natural principle of phrase structure (as Saito and Fukui 1998 argue), then it seems that the subsequent development of the locality theory in the 1970s and 1980s (the subjacency condition and its various modifications) may turn out to be a long way back to the original insight of the 1960s. Owing to space limitations, I must leave further discussion of this important subject for future research.

2.2 The proper binding condition

The feature version of the A-over-A Principle also has nice consequences for phenomena outside of the theory of locality on movement. Consider the following well-known contrast, taken from Saito (1992a):

(19) a. ?who$_i$ do you wonder [$_{CP}$[which picture of t_i]$_j$ [$_{IP}$ John likes t_j]]
   b. *[which picture of t_i]$_j$ do you wonder [$_{CP}$ who$_i$ [$_{IP}$ John likes t_j]]

The standard account given to the contrast in (19) is that (19b) contains an unbound trace t_i in the fronted phrase, in violation of the Proper Binding Condition (PBC) that requires traces to be bound (Fiengo 1974, May 1977), yielding total ungrammaticality, whereas (19a) does not contain any unbound trace, satisfying the PBC, but involves only a violation of wh-island constraint that is responsible for its mild deviance.

There are, however, at least two problems in this account, as noted in the literature (Collins 1994, Takano 1995, among others). First, the status of the PBC in the current minimalist program is not entirely clear. In particular, the condition does not seem to be motivated by bare output conditions (cf. Chomsky 1995b for relevant discussion). Thus, economy alternatives have been proposed to replace the PBC (see Collins 1994). Secondly, the PBC erroneously excludes examples such as the following (taken from Takano 1995), which are in fact grammatical:

(20) How proud of Bill is John?
(21) $[_{CP} [_{Pred} t_i$ how proud of Bill$]_j$ is $[_{IP}$ John$_i$ $t_j]]$

(21) is the relevant structure of (20) under the predicate-internal subject hypothesis, now widely assumed. In (21), there is an unbound trace, t_i of the subject *John*$_i$, in violation of the PBC. But the sentence is actually grammatical.

The feature version of the A-over-A Principle gives the following straightforward account to all these cases, without appealing to the PBC, whose status, as we just pointed out, is rather dubious in the current theoretical framework. In deriving (19a), *which picture of who* first moves to the embedded [Spec, CP] to check off its *wh*-feature. This is a legitimate operation. Then, from the embedded [Spec, CP] position, *who* moves to the matrix [Spec, CP] position to check off its *wh*-feature. This operation violates the A-over-A Principle, with A = categorial features. Hence, the "??" status of (19a). Note that for the matrix +*wh* C to attract *who* in the embedded [Spec, CP], there is no violation of the A-over-A Principle with A = [+wh], since the *wh*-feature of the entire phrase *which picture of who* has already been checked at the embedded [Spec, CP].[10] The derivation of (19b), on the other hand, violates the A-over-A Principle more than once. The attraction of *who* by the embedded +*wh* C violates the principle both with A = categorial features and A = [+wh]. (In addition, the attraction of *which picture of* t_i to the matrix [Spec, CP] may violate the A-over-A Principle with A = [+wh], if the *wh*-feature percolated up to the embedded CP remains accessible/visible after checking; see our discussion of *wh*-island. See also note 10.) Therefore, (19b) shows complete ungrammaticality. Turning to (20), there is simply no violation of the A-over-A Principle in its derivation. The attraction of *John* by the embedded I/T violates no principle. Further attraction of *how proud of Bill* is of no problem, with the matrix +*wh* C attracting the most inclusive *wh*-phrase. Thus, (20) is fully grammatical, without violating the A-over-A Principle at all.

Note that this account captures the insight of various past attempts to handle examples like (20) under the PBC (see Takano 1995 and references therein). The insight is that when two instances of the same type of movement (say, A'-movement) are involved, a violation of the condition occurs, whereas if the types of movement involved are different, say, one is NP-movement and the other is *wh*-movement, no violation of the PBC is induced. In our terms, if one feature is included by another feature of the same type (say, [+wh]), extraction is impossible (as in (19b)), while if the two features are of different types, for example, one is [+wh] and the other is D/φ-features, then no violation occurs (as in (20)).

3 Conclusion

I have argued that the basic ideas of Attract can revive the A-over-A Principle as a minimum principle, in such a way that the principle is relativized as to the relevant features. Given the independent A-over-A Principle, there is no need to stipulate that Attract picks the "closest" feature that can enter into checking relation, and the locality/minimality part of the definition of Attract seems to be rendered unnecessary and can be done away with. I have also shown that the feature version of the A-over-A Principle accounts for the major portion of the classical island constraints, except for the CED cases for which an independent explanation is available (Saito and Fukui 1998).

An interesting question arises with respect to the nature of the revived A-over-A Principle. The Principle clearly bears a flavour of "economy", though applying only to a specific configuration, that is, a "self-embedding" configuration. It remains to be seen how this principle is related to other economy considerations in UG.

Finally, as is well known, there are classical problems of (the traditional version of) the A-over-A Principle that have to be dealt with (see Chomsky 1964, 1968, Ross 1967), before the principle can be fully revived. I simply leave this matter open for more comprehensive future research.

10 The uniqueness parameter

This squib proposes, in a preliminary fashion, a kind of macro parameter, the "uniqueness" parameter, which is to derive various properties of languages over a wide range of phenomena. I will focus on the comparative syntax of English and Japanese, since these two languages exhibit clear and almost across-the-board contrasts with respect to what one might call the uniqueness effect.

There are two well-known phenomena in which English and Japanese show a clear contrast: the multiple subject construction and scrambling. Japanese has a multiple subject (or more accurately, "multiple nominative") construction, while English does not. (A familiar qualification about the Japanese examples with respect to the "topic-orientation" of the language is in order.)

(1) a. Irvine-ga susi-ga umai (koto)
       -NOM sushi-NOM delicious

   "In Irvine, sushi is delicious."

   b. *Irvine, sushi is delicious.

The same pattern is observed with other types of Case. Thus, Japanese exhibits multiple genitive constructions as in (2a), whereas English disallows them, as in (2b).

(2) a. John-no sensyuu-no koogi
       -GEN last week-GEN lecture

   Lit. "John's last week's lecture"

   b. *John's last week's lecture

The pattern can possibly be extended even to accusative Case, as discussed in Kuroda (1988) (see also Fukui and Takano 1998), though other factors intervene in this case, blurring the effect. Regardless of the particular analyses, it is clear that the syntax of Japanese allows multiple occurrences of Case, while the syntax of English disallows them.

It is also well known that there is a tremendous freedom in ordering arguments in Japanese sentences, a phenomenon called "scrambling", whereas English word order is fixed to a large extent. For example, while the Japanese examples (3b) and (3c) are perfectly grammatical with essentially the same meaning as (3a), the English counterparts in (4), i.e., (4b) and (4c), which alter the "basic word order" Subject-Verb-Direct Object-Indirect Object in the language, are highly marginal, if not totally ungrammatical, even under the focus/topic interpretation.

(3) a. Mary-ga   John-ni sono hon-o   watasita (koto).
       Mary-NOM John-to that book-ACC handed

   "Mary handed that book to John."

   b. Sono hon-o John-ni Mary-ga watasita (koto).
   c. John-ni sono hon-o Mary-ga watasita (koto).
(4) a. Mary handed that book to John.
   b. ??That book, to John, Mary handed.
   c. ??To John, that book, Mary handed.

These are two well-known factual differences between English and Japanese, and it has been attempted to seek a way to derive these differences from a single source.

One such attempt is a proposal made independently by Fukui (1986) and Kuroda (1988). Both Fukui and Kuroda try to construct a deductive model of an English/Japanese comparative syntax by which a variety of differences between the two (types of) languages, including scrambling and multiple nominative constructions, can be derived from a few, hopefully a single, irreducible fundamental difference(s) between English and Japanese. Ignoring the differences between Fukui's approach and Kuroda's, we note that they share the fundamental assumption that the notion of "agreement" (or "feature-checking" in more recent terms) plays a crucial role, and that this notion requires a one-to-one relation between a head and the phrase that agrees with the head. English agrees, whereas Japanese does not; in the latter, phrases are licensed by some other way than agreement/feature-checking, not requiring a one-to-one relationship. Therefore, the nominative phrase in English has to be unique per sentence in English, while there can be more than one in a Japanese sentence (this account straightforwardly carries over to other cases of multiple Case). Furthermore, the position that can be characterized roughly as SpecTP must be unique in English, but there can be, under certain assumptions of the theory of phrase structure (see Fukui 1986), more than one such position in Japanese, thereby allowing "scrambled phrases" to occupy these positions.

However, two questions are raised by the Fukui/Kuroda approach. First, the one-to-one nature of agreement/feature-checking is simply stipulated: it may have been a standard assumption in the mid-1980s, but the assumption does not seem to be innocuous now. Secondly, if we extend our observation beyond these particular phenomena (multiple Case and scrambling), it appears that the existence of the "uniqueness" effect in English and the lack of such uniqueness in Japanese constitute a rather consistent pattern, and an appeal to agreement/feature checking is simply not sufficient.

In particular, the lack of uniqueness is pervasive in a variety of domains of Japanese grammar, not restricted to those where the notion of agreement/feature-checking is directly relevant. For instance, it has been observed that Japanese generally allows "multiple foci" structures (see Hoji 1987, among others). Along with (5a), where a single phrase *gengogaku-no hon-o (san-satu)* "three books on linguistics-Acc" is focalized, (5b) is also possible with more than one phrase (*John-ga* "John-Nom" and *gengogaku-no hon-o san-satu* "three books on linguistics-Acc") being focalized (NM = nominalizer, CL = classifier).

(5) a. John-ga   Mary-ni ageta no-wa   gengogaku-no hon-o
       John-NOM Mary-to gave NM-TOP linguistics-GEN book-ACC
       san-satu   da.
       three-CL is

   "It is three books on linguistics that John gave to Mary."

   b. Mary-ni ageta no-wa   John-ga   gengogaku-no hon-o
      Mary-to gave NM-TOP John-NOM linguistics-GEN book-ACC
      san-satu   da.
      three-CL is.

   Lit. "It is John, three books on linguistics that gave to Mary."
   That is: John gave three books on linguistics to Mary.

English does not allow multiple foci constructions such as (5b).

Takeda (1999) argues that the lack of uniqueness can be observed in various other constructions in Japanese as well, presenting evidence from multiple-headed relative clauses, multiple-sluicing, multiple-topics, etc., all possible in Japanese, but not in English. To give just one of Takeda's many examples, given the context described in the statement in the parentheses, the relative clause construction in (6) (adapted from Takeda 1999, chapter 4) seems to be quite naturally allowed in Japanese.

(6) (Mary-wa   hon-no   genkoo-o   iroirona syuppansya-ni
     Mary-TOP book-GEN manuscript-ACC various publishers-to
     saikin   okutteirurasii.
     recently send-seems

   "It seems that Mary has recently sent (her) book manuscripts to various publishers."

[[Mary-ga   kono nikagetu-de e_1 e_2 okutta] [hon-no
   Mary-NOM this   two months-in   sent   book-GEN
genkoo$_2$ to syuppansya$_1$]]-o osiete kudasai.
manuscripts and publishers-ACC tell   please

Lit. "Please tell me the book manuscripts and the publishers that Mary has sent for the past two months."

In (6), the conjoined structure *hon-no genkoo to syuppansya* "the book manuscripts and the publishers" functions as the head of a relative clause in which the associated clause *Mary-ga kono nikagetu-de okutta* "Mary has sent for the past two months" modifies the head noun. Such a double-headed relative clause is not allowed in English (cf. **the book manuscripts and the publishers that Mary has sent for the past two months*). We might add in this connection another fact about Japanese grammar, the existence of "mixed type" categories such as adjectival nouns (or *keiyoo-doosi* "adjectival verbs" as traditional Japanese grammarians call them) and verbal nouns. As their names suggest, these types of categories exhibit mixed properties of nouns and adjectives/verbs. (See Martin 1975; for a general description, see Shibatani 1990b; for more technical discussion; see, for instance, Harada 1998, Nishiyama 1998, Urushibara 1993.) The existence of these "mixed type" lexical heads can be taken as another instance of a "double-headed" structure in Japanese. English lacks these types of categories altogether.

We have briefly glanced at several phenomena in Japanese which seem to exhibit, in a certain sense, the effect of the lack of uniqueness. Accounts have been offered (or can be offered) for each phenomenon, on a case by case basis. However, by treating these phenomena on a case by case basis, we fail to capture the general pattern that holds throughout: Japanese lacks "uniqueness" consistently over a wide range of phenomena, where "uniqueness" is obtained in a language like English. Thus, the hypothesis that suggests itself is that "uniqueness" itself can be somehow "parametrized". Japanese lacks uniqueness in large measure, whereas English fulfills the uniqueness condition, from which a variety of differences between the languages, including those phenomena discussed above, follow in a deductive way.

Language can be regarded as a generative procedure for providing a "solution" to the equation defined by the legibility (or "bare output") conditions imposed by the performance systems in which language is embedded (Chomsky 1995b, 1998). If so, we can make the following analogy between the theory of equations and the case of language. It is a rather well established point in the theory of differential equations that the "existence" of a solution to a given equation and the "uniqueness" of such a solution to the equation are two separate matters, each to be proven independently. Thus, while the ordinary differential equation of first order $y' = 1$, $y(0) = 0$ has the unique (trivial) solution $y = x$, the ordinary differential equation $dx/dt = |x|^\alpha$, $x(0) = 0$, $0 < \alpha < 1$ (where t: variable; x is a function of t

($x = x(t)$) has more than one solution (in fact, infinitely many): the equation has a solution $x(t) = 0$, and then, given a, $b > 0$, $x(t) = -[(1-\alpha)|t+a|]^{1/1-\alpha}$ (if $t \leq -a$), $x(t) = 0$ (if $-a \leq t \leq b$)), $x(t) = [(1-\alpha)(t-b)]^{1/1-\alpha}$ (if $t \geq b$). Therefore, $x(t)$ satisfies the equation, with infinitely many solutions. Furthermore, there are cases where solutions do not even exist (e.g., the partial differential equation $\partial z/\partial x = y$, $\partial z/\partial y = 0$, where x, y = variables and z is a function of (x, y), does not have a solution at all).

Correspondingly, if language can be taken as a procedure for providing a solution to an equation, Universal Grammar (UG) assures the "existence" of a solution (even this has to be proven, since equations may not have solutions), but it does not guarantee the "uniqueness" of such a solution. The "uniqueness" can be obtained under certain conditions which are regulated, but not directly provided, by UG. If this idea is on the right track, our next task is, obviously, to discover the empirical conditions under which the uniqueness of a solution is guaranteed in the case of language. English fulfills these conditions, while Japanese does not, from which a variety of cases of nonuniqueness follow.

The scope of the "uniqueness parameter" suggested here, if it is real, seems to go well beyond English/Japanese comparative syntax. Note that effects of the existence/non-existence of uniqueness may be exhibited totally or partially depending on the inner mechanisms of each language. English and Japanese present fairly across-the-board contrasts with respect to the uniqueness effect, but there are other more mixed cases (e.g., Hungarian, as pointed out by a reviewer). Phenomena that show a "flavour" of the lack of uniqueness abound cross-linguistically. For example, serial verb constructions, multiple *wh*-movement phenomena, and multiple agreement immediately come to mind as salient cases of nonuniqueness. Explorations of all of these possibilities, as well as a more accurate formulation of the uniqueness parameter, must be left for future research.

11 Nominal structure

An extension of the Symmetry Principle

with Yuji Takano

1 Introduction

This article extends the scope of the "Symmetry Principle of Derivation" proposed in our previous work (Fukui and Takano 1998) to the study of the internal structure of noun phrases. The Symmetry Principle dictates that the pre-Spell-Out derivational computations and the post-Spell-Out (pre-Morphology) derivational computations form mirror images of each other. More specifically, we argued in Fukui and Takano (1998) that language computation maps an array of linguistic elements to a PF representation in such a way that it starts with a lexical item (a head) proceeding in a bottom-up fashion (Merge) and at some point of a derivation, starts "decomposing" the structures already formed in a top-down fashion (Demerge) until the derivation reaches a completely unstructured sequence with a fixed linear ("temporal") order. The central tenet of the Symmetry Principle is that Demerge, which is an operation undoing the result of Merge, abstractly reflects and reverses the order in which Merge has applied, thereby rendering the applications of these operations "symmetric" with respect to the point of Spell-Out.

Fukui and Takano (1998) argue that the Symmetry Principle, when coupled with a parametric statement about the nature of a "light verb" v, derives in an extremely elegant way numerous cross-linguistic differences observed among a variety of languages. There, we focused our discussion primarily on the analyses of various phenomena as they pertain to the clausal structure, paying only limited attention to internal structures of other categories, in particular, noun phrases, although it was clear that the effects of the Symmetry Principle could be readily and straightforwardly extended to the analyses of nominal structures.

Thus, this article can be regarded as a sequel to Fukui and Takano (1998), exploring the consequences of the Symmetry Principle for the analysis of nominal structures, with a special focus on relative clause structures. The organization of the paper is as follows. Section 2 discusses general issues of linear order in the theory of grammar and summarizes the basic claims of the theory of phrase structure proposed in our previous work. Section 3 is mainly concerned with cross-linguistic variation in relative clauses. The section takes up such issues as the order of elements in nominal structures, the existence or lack of relative pronouns, the properties of relative complementizers, the nature of internally headed relative clauses that are attested in some types of languages but not in others, etc., and argues that the Symmetry Principle offers a unifying account of all of these phenomena. Section 4 extends the discussion to the analysis of classifiers in human languages, in an attempt to account for the existence/non-existence of classifier systems on principled grounds. Section 5 makes some concluding remarks.

2 Phrase structure and linear order

This section first presents general discussions on the nature of "linear order"[1] in the theory of grammar (subsection 2.1) and then summarizes the framework within which our analysis of nominal structures in the following section is to be presented (subsection 2.2).

2.1 Issues of linear order

The concept of linear order in a phrase marker was never questioned in an earlier framework of generative grammar.[2] In fact, it was one of the few crucial primitive concepts in the theory of phrase structure, and a variety of grammatical rules were formulated with crucial reference to linear order (see, for example, the "pronominalization" transformation in the 1960s). However, it has been increasingly less obvious that linear order plays a role at all in language computation, apart from phonology. Thus, virtually all the principles and conditions assumed in the principles-and-parameters theory in the 1980s are formulated purely in hierarchical terms (in terms of domination and c-command), without referring to linear order. The "head parameter" (and its variants) seems to be the only notion in linguistic theory which crucially refers to linear order.

Kayne (1994) challenges this notion of head parameter. He proposes a universal principle, the Linear Correspondence Axiom (LCA), which states essentially that asymmetric c-command imposes a linear ordering of terminal elements. More specifically, the LCA dictates that if a nonterminal X asymmetrically c-commands a nonterminal Y in a given phrase marker P, then all terminals dominated by X must precede or follow all terminals dominated by Y in P. Kayne takes the relevant ordering to be precedence, rather than subsequence (following), based on his assumptions about the relation between terminals and "time slots" (see Kayne 1994 for more details). Thus, within Kayne's theory, asymmetric c-command relations uniquely map into precedence relations: all terminals dominated by X precede all terminals dominated by Y, in the configuration stated above. It then follows, given Kayne's formulation, that there is a universal S(pecifier)-H(ead)-C(omplement) order (in particular, S(ubject)-V(erb)-O(bject)), with other orders (S-C-H/S-O-V, for example) being derived via movement. With the universal S-H-C order, the head parameter is entirely eliminated.

Note that in Kayne's theory, linear order still plays a role in the core computation of language (albeit redundantly, because it is entirely determined by asymmetric c-command relations). Kayne proposes that linear order is not parametrized and that it is uniquely determined by asymmetric c-command relations, given his LCA which he claims to apply at every syntactic level. Thus, linear order is still defined and remains visible throughout the derivation and could conceivably play a role in the core computation of language.

Chomsky (1994, 1995b), adopting and incorporating the basic insights of Kayne's LCA into his "bare phrase structure" theory, makes a step further toward complete elimination of linear order from the core of language computation. In Chomsky's bare theory, the recursive procedure Merge, in particular, does not encode any information regarding linear order of syntactic elements. This is based on his understanding that there is no clear evidence that linear order plays a role at LF or in the core computation of human language. Thus, he assumes that linear order is not defined and hence does not play a role in the core computation of language, and suggests that ordering is a property of the phonological component, a proposal that has occasionally been made in various forms in the literature. Specifically, he claims that a modified version of the LCA applies as a principle of the phonological component to the output of Morphology, a subcomponent of the phonological component (see Chomsky 1995b for detailed discussion). Thus, under Chomsky's proposal, phrase structure is defined without reference to linear order in the core computational part of human language, and will be assigned a linear order later by (a modified version of) the LCA in the phonological component. The status of the head parameter, however, is not entirely clear in Chomsky's approach. While, as we just saw, linear order is not even defined in the core language computation, leaving no room for the head parameter, it could still be possible to formulate the head parameter as a parameter in the phonological component, something similar to a parameter in stress assignment proposed in phonology. See Fukui and Takano (1998: 78) for much relevant discussion.

On the other hand, Saito and Fukui (1998) (see also Fukui 1993b and Fukui and Saito 1992) claim that linear order indeed plays an important role in the core computational part of human language, and argue that the head parameter, or more precisely a modified version of it, should be maintained. One way to incorporate the head parameter into the bare theory, as Saito and Fukui propose, is to replace the set notation $[\alpha, \beta]$ in Chomsky's formulation of Merge by an ordered pair $<\alpha, \beta>$, thereby specifying which of the two elements is to "project" (in the usual sense of the term in the theory of phrase structure) in a given language. Thus, we have (2) instead of (1):

(1) *Chomsky's Merge*: $K = [\gamma, [\alpha, \beta]]$, where $\gamma \in [\alpha, \beta]$

(2) *Saito and Fukui's parametrized Merge*: $K = [\gamma, <\alpha, \beta>]$, where $\gamma [[\alpha, \beta]$

If γ takes the value "α", we have a "head-initial/left-headed" language such as English, whereas if $\gamma = \beta$, a "head-last/right-headed" language like Japanese is defined. Thus, in left-headed English, elements can be merged only on the right side of a head, whereas in right-headed Japanese, Merge occurs only on the left side of a head. If something is to be introduced on the opposite side of the structure (i.e., on the left side of a head in English, and on the right side of a head in Japanese), it must be "adjoined" to the target without inducing projection, i.e., creating a multisegmented structure (see Chomsky 1986a, 1995b for relevant discussion on substitution v. adjunction). A case in point is the status of subjects in these languages. The subject in English is in an adjoined position because it appears on the left side of the head, where projection of the target is prohibited by (2) as it is parametrized for English. The subject in Japanese, on the other hand, is introduced into the phrase structure by Merge (i.e., substitution; see below), since it shows up on the left side of the head, where merger is possible (Japanese is a right-headed language). See Saito and Fukui (1998) for more detailed discussion, as well as illustrations of this point.

Saito and Fukui argue that given the parametrized version of Merge (2), it becomes possible to characterize the traditional "adjunction" operations, viz., scrambling in Japanese and Heavy NP Shift in English, as paradigm cases of Merge (i.e., as substitution, in the sense that they always accompany projection of the target), and hence, given the costless nature of Merge (Chomsky 1995b), the optionality of these operations, a matter that has been quite disturbing for the general economy approach to movement, is also straightforwardly accounted for. On the other hand, traditional "substitution" operations (*wh*-movement and NP-movement) are analysed in this system as genuine adjunction since they never induce projection of the target, creating a multisegmented structure of the target (see Saito and Fukui 1998 for much detail). Further, they point out that the "directionality" of these optional movements correlates with the "directionality" of projection in the language. Thus, head-initial/left-headed English has rightward Heavy NP Shift, whereas head-last/right-headed Japanese exhibits leftward scrambling, but no other combination is allowed. It is clear that such a correlation can only be captured by a parametrized Merge embodying linear order, as in (2). Saito and Fukui show that a number of other differences between English and Japanese also follow from their theory of phrase structure.

2.2 *The Symmetry Principle*

Fukui and Takano (1998) develop a theory of phrase structure and linear order based on the intuition captured by Saito and Fukui's (1998) proposal, while maintaining the basic insights of Kayne (1994) and Chomsky (1995b).

The intuition behind Saito and Fukui's proposal (cf. also Fukui 1993b) is that as long as projections (applications of Merge) consistently occur on the same side of a head, they are "unmarked" and "costless", whereas if Merge is to apply on the other side of a head, it is "costly", and hence requires a driving force, i.e., feature-checking. As we saw above, Saito and Fukui propose that there is a choice (the head parameter) as to which side of the head we start applying Merge.

Kayne rejects the postulation of the head parameter, claiming that his LCA uniquely determines the linear ordering of elements based on asymmetric c-command, with the universal S-H-C order. Chomsky claims that linear order does not play a role in the core (pre-Spell-Out) computation of human language, and that a modified version of Kayne's LCA applies in the "phonological component", determining the linear order of elements (with potential room for the "head parameter in the phonological component", in our opinion; see the discussion above).

Fukui and Takano adopt the basic intuition of Saito and Fukui that, putting it in slightly different terms, maximal projections occurring on the same side of a head are "unmarked". However, we reject postulating the head parameter in the core computational part and claim, following Chomsky (1995b), that linear order is determined in the phonological component. Thus, we propose the following *Symmetry Principle of Derivation*:

(3) *The Symmetry Principle of Derivation*
Pre-Spell-Out computations and post-Spell-Out (and pre-Morphology) computations are "symmetric", in the sense that they form mirror-images of each other.

We refer the reader to Fukui and Takano (1998) for detailed discussion, but the general idea presented in our previous work, in a nutshell, is as follows. In the pre-Spell-Out portion of the derivation, Merge, as is standardly assumed, applies in a bottom-up fashion, combining two syntactic objects (both maximal projections) to form a new, larger syntactic object; Merge continues to apply recursively until there is no object available for further merger. Spell-Out then applies to the structure Σ formed by successive applications of Merge, sending the relevant portions of Σ into the phonological component. This much is a "standard" view presented in, say, Chomsky (1995b) (but see Chomsky 1998 for a different view on Spell-Out).

The modified Σ (by Spell-Out) is then mapped to π, a linguistic expression at the "PF" interface, by operations in the phonological component. We propose that in the pre-Morphology portion of the phonological component, the process of *Linearization* takes place. The structure Σ that enters into the phonological component first undergoes this process of Linearization. The process of Linearization consists of two distinct operations: (i) *Demerge*, and

234 *Nominal structure*

(ii) *Concatenate.* Demerge is a kind of a "reverse" operation of Merge. It applies to the structure Σ in a top-down fashion (recall that Merge applies from the bottom up), applying to a single root element and breaking it into two roots. The resulting two roots are of course both maximal projections, but it is important to note that it is always the case, given the nature of Merge, that one of them is already a maximal projection when Demerge applies, whereas the other *becomes* a maximal projection only "as a result of" an application of Demerge (see Fukui and Takano 1998: 40 for much more detailed discussion). Like Merge, Demerge applies only to maximal projections. Concatenate then applies to assign the linear order of the two maximal projections made available by Demerge, making reference to the inherent asymmetry of the maximal projection status between them just mentioned: of the two root elements, the one that is already a maximal projection at the point of an application of Demerge always "precedes" the other. We can thus summarize the basic workings of Linearization as follows, where (Σ − α) indicates the object resulting from detachment of α from the structure Σ.

(4) *Linearization*
Applied to the structure Σ, Demerge yields [α, [Σ − α]], α an X^{max} constituent of Σ, and Concatenate turns [α, [Σ − α]] into α + (Σ − α).

To illustrate briefly how Linearization works, let us look at the following structure, where X, Y are maximal projections (as well as VP).

(5)   Σ =

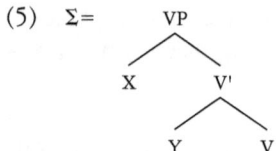

Demerge applies to Σ (=VP) and breaks it into two root elements, X and V'. X is already a maximal projection when Demerge applies whereas V' becomes a maximal projection as a result of an application of Demerge. Thus, Concatenate puts them in a sequence (X + V'). Now V' is a maximal projection to which Demerge applies, yielding two root elements Y and V, both maximal projections. Y is a maximal projection independently of the application of Demerge, while V becomes a maximal projection only as a result of Demerge. Concatenate, then, assigns them the order (Y + V). Taken together, the output of the Linearization process applying to the structure in (5) is the sequence (X + Y + V). X and Y are conventionally called Specifier and Complement of the head V, respectively. Therefore, Fukui and Takano's Linearization process, based on their Symmetry Principle, predicts that S-C-H (S-O-V, in particular) is the "basic" order, as opposed to the S-H-C/S-V-O order which is claimed to be basic by Kayne's LCA.

Nominal structure   235

Then, how do we get the S-H-C/S-V-O order, as exemplified by, say, English? The S-H-C/S-V-O order is the result of movement. Fukui and Takano assume with Chomsky (1995b) that the external argument of a transitive verb occupies a specifier position of v, a "light verb" taking a VP as its complement. On this view, the core proposition of a ditransitive structure should look like the following.

(6)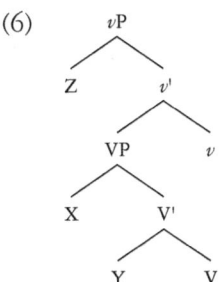

In (6), Z is an external argument, X is an indirect internal argument, and Y is a direct internal argument, all maximal projections. Applied to this structure in the way already described before, Linearization assigns the surface order Z-X-Y-V-v, if no movement is involved. This is exactly what happens in, say, Japanese, where no V-raising takes place (see Fukui and Takano 1998 for supporting arguments for this hypothesis). In languages like English, where overt V-raising takes place (see Chomsky 1995b), the structure to which Linearization applies is different. Fukui and Takano (1998, section 2.2) argue in this connection (but on independent grounds) that head movement should be analysed as "substitution into Spec", rather than as "adjunction to head" as has been standardly assumed. Under this analysis of head movement, the V-to-v movement (V-raising) which takes place in English can be depicted as follows (t_V is the trace left by the V-to-v movement).

(7)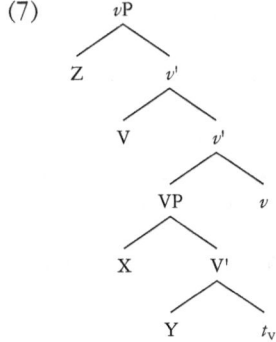

If Linearization applies to the structure (7), it first yields the sequence Z + v' (i.e., the upper v'), and then linearizes the latter as V + v' (i.e., the lower v';

note that V in (7) is a maximal projection (and also a minimal projection), under the assumptions of bare phrase structure theory assumed here, and hence is visible to Demerge). Linearization eventually gives rise to the surface order $Z + V + X + Y + t_{V+v}$ (with t_V and v invisible). This is essentially how we get the S-H-C/S-V-O order.

Thus, Fukui and Takano (1998) attribute the VO/OV (i.e., head-initial v. head-last) distinction between, say, English and Japanese, to the presence/absence of V-raising. The VO order (in English) results from overt V-raising while the OV order (in Japanese) reflects the "base properties" of the verb phrase, involving no V-raising. The relevant difference ultimately arises from a parameter associated with the "functional head" v. It was then hypothesized in our previous work that the fundamental difference between the head-initial English and the head-last Japanese with respect to word order is the following.[3]

(8) v has the property of attracting V in English but not in Japanese.

The hypothesis (8) is consistent with the restrictive theory of parameters (cf. Fukui 1988a, 1995b) according to which the locus of parametric variation must be limited to the "functional domain" of the lexicon. Furthermore, the hypothesis is in line with the "traditional" view on English/Japanese comparative syntax (see Fukui 1986; Kuroda 1988; among others) that functional categories in Japanese, if any, are "inactive/inert" (triggering no movement), as compared to corresponding elements in English, a view that is incompatible with Kayne's way of obtaining the S-C-H/S-O-V order (see Fukui and Takano 1998 for much detailed discussion).

Summarizing, the Symmetry Principle of Fukui and Takano (1998) dictates that pre-Spell-Out computations in syntax and post-Spell-Out computations in the phonological component form mirror images of each other. More specifically, the Linearization process consists of two operations, Demerge and Concatenate, the former of which does exactly the reverse of what Merge does, reversing the order of operations of Merge in a step-by-step manner. Thus, the Symmetry Principle predicts that Spec always comes first in a given maximal projection, since it is the first element that Demerge encounters. Similarly, the second element that is to linearize has to be the complement of a head, because that is the next maximal projection that Demerge detects. Finally, the head of a phrase (which becomes a maximal projection after its specifier and complement have been demerged) is to be linearized by Demerge and Concatenate. The Symmetry Principle, therefore, claims that the S-C-H/S-O-V order, having S and C/O on the same side of the head, represents the "basic" order, contrary to the LCA, which states that the S-H-C/S-V-O order is the "basic" order.[4] Fukui and Takano then go on to argue that the S-H-C/S-V-O order is indeed a "derived" order, involving V-raising triggered by the "light verb" v. Thus, the difference between, say Japanese (S-O-V) and English (S-V-O) is reduced to the lexical property of v: v attracts V in English, resulting in the S-V-O order, whereas it does not attract V in Japanese, leading to the "basic" S-O-V order.

Fukui and Takano further argue that if this approach is correct, then it becomes unnecessary to postulate a number of hypothetical "functional categories" triggering overt movements in languages like Japanese (S-O-V languages generally), a necessity under the LCA approach to get the right surface order, thereby getting along quite nicely with the "traditional" view of comparative Japanese/English syntax that the "movement portion" of the Japanese grammar is very inactive, if not completely inert, compared to the English counterpart.

In the remainder of this article, we will attempt to extend the scope of the Symmetry Principle to the analysis of nominal structures, with a special focus on relative clauses and classifiers.

3 Variation in relative clauses

3.1 Order in nominal structure

As is well known, Japanese is a consistent head-last language and English is a fairly consistent head-initial language. Thus, just as English and Japanese differ in the location of V in the clausal/verbal structure, they also differ in the location of N in the nominal structure. English places N before its complement, whereas Japanese puts it after its complement:

(9) the student of physics

(10) buturigaku-no   gakusei
     physics   -GEN student

    "the/a student of physics"

According to Fukui and Takano's theory of phrase structure and linear order summarized in the preceding section, this difference between English and Japanese should be explained in terms of different positions that the nominal head occupies within the noun phrase structure. Specifically, the Japanese case involves the nominal head N in situ, that is, it stays in its original position. The English case, by contrast, involves raising of the nominal head to SpecD.[5] The difference can be schematically shown as in (11).[6]

(11)
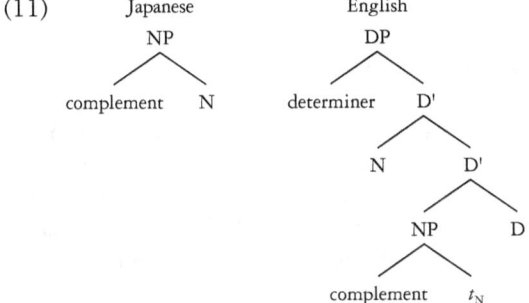

238 *Nominal structure*

Given Fukui and Takano's system of Linearization (which we described briefly in the preceding section), the Japanese structure is linearized into the sequence "complement + N", while the English structure is linearized into the sequence "determiner + N + complement".[7]

Note that, in this theory, the difference in linear order is directly correlated with the difference in hierarchical structure, much in the spirit of Kayne's (1994) approach based on his LCA. Thus, the nominal head is within NP in Japanese and follows its complement, while it is raised out of NP and precedes the complement in English. Given this fundamental parametric difference in the syntactic structure, we naturally expect to see other differences that could be shown to correlate with the position of the nominal head N. In particular, it will be interesting if we are able to deduce some properties of nominal structure in the two languages from this single difference in the structural position of N, much in the same way that we have done in the case of verbal/clausal structure.

In the remainder of this section, we will explore this possibility for an empirical domain related to relative clauses in English and Japanese.[8] We will show that a number of different properties concerning relative clauses in the two languages follow rather straightforwardly from the hypothesized single parametric difference in the position of N within the nominal structure.

3.2 Relative pronouns

First, we look at the difference between English and Japanese with respect to the presence v. absence of relative pronouns. English relative clauses have relative pronouns (as underscored in (12)), whereas Japanese equivalents do not:

(12) a. a picture *which* John saw yesterday
     b. a student *who(m)* John met yesterday
(13) a. John-ga   kinoo   mita syasin
         John-NOM yesterday saw   picture
         "the/a picture that John saw yesterday"

     b. John-ga   kinoo   atta gakusei
         John-NOM yesterday met student
         "the/a student who(m) John met yesterday"

If we compare (12) and (13), we see that they differ in two ways: (i) in the position of the relative head and (ii) in whether or not the relative pronoun is present. English places the relative head (*picture* in (a) and *student* in (b)) before the relative clause and has relative pronouns (*which* in (a) and *who(m)* in (b)), whereas Japanese places the relative head (*syasin* in (a) and *gakusei* in (b)) after the relative clause and has no relative pronouns.

Under Fukui and Takano's theory, it is actually possible to deduce the two differences in a unified way from the hypothesis that the nominal head stays in its original position in Japanese, but is raised to Spec(D) in English. Let us first look at the English case, taking (12a) as an example. We claim that (12a) has the following structure:

(14)
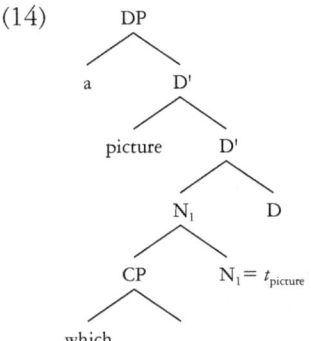

Here the relative head is raised to Spec(D) in accordance with our basic claim about the parametric property of the English nominal structure. Following the traditional intuition, we assume that a relative clause is always adjoined to the maximal projection of N. Under the bare phrase structure theory, this means that if there is no complement of N, the relative clause is adjoined to N, because there is no such thing as a "non-branching projection" in the bare theory. Thus, in (14), the upper N_1 and the lower N_1 form a two-segmented category.[9] Notice that the two-segmented category $[N_1, N_1]$ is maximal, in the sense that they do not project any further (Chomsky 1995b). Therefore, the relative clause CP in (14) is properly adjoined to the maximal projection of N.[10]

Another common assumption about relative clauses is that the relative pronoun is referentially identified with the relative head. Suppose that there is a general requirement on the licensing of the relative pronoun of the following kind:

(15) The relative pronoun must be bound by the relative head.

Thus, the proper relation between the relative head and the relative pronoun is established through the syntactic relation of binding.[11] Now let us look at the structure in (14) in this light. There the relevant requirement on the relative pronoun is met: the raised N *picture* c-commands the relative pronoun *which* in CP and thus the former can bind the latter. The relative pronoun is then correctly licensed in the English relative clause.[12]

The structure in (14) also yields the correct surface order under our Linearization procedure. Disregarding elements lacking phonetic content, this structure yields the surface order "*a* + *picture* + CP", with the relative head preceding the relative clause, which is a consequence of the supposed raising of the relative head.

Now, let us turn to the Japanese case. Recalling that the nominal head stays in place in Japanese, we see that the Japanese relative clause in (13a) has the following structure:

(16)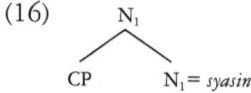

As in the English case, the relative clause is adjoined to a maximal minimal category N_1, forming the two-segmented category $[N_1, N_1]$. The difference is that in the Japanese case, the nominal head N does not raise but stays put. The system of Linearization in Fukui and Takano (1998) correctly assigns the structure in (16) the linear order "CP + N_1" on the assumption that Demerge always affects only a maximal projection/category.[13] In (16), CP is a maximal category, whereas the lower N_1 is not (it is a segment), and hence, when Linearization applies in the phonological component, Demerge detaches CP from the structure, thereby sending CP into Concatenate prior to N_1.

Now, let us suppose that the relative clause in (16) contained a relative pronoun. Recall that, in order to be licensed, the relative pronoun must satisfy the condition in (15), which dictates that it be bound by the relative head. However, in the structure in (16), this condition cannot be met if we assume the following definition of c-command, adapted from Kayne (1994):

(17) X c-commands Y iff X excludes Y and every element that dominates X dominates Y.

(18) X excludes Y iff no segment of X dominates Y.

Suppose that the two-segmented category $[N_1, N_1]$ is the relative head. Then, it does not c-command CP, since $[N_1, N_1]$ does not exclude CP with the upper N_1, a segment of $[N_1, N_1]$, dominating CP. Even if we assume that the lower N_1 alone is the relative head, it does not c-command CP either, given that the upper N_1, which is a segment of the category $[N_1, N_1]$, dominates CP, thereby failing to satisfy the exclusion condition in (17). As a result, if the relative clause in (16) contained a relative pronoun, the relative pronoun would fail to satisfy the condition in (15) and hence could not be properly licensed.

This explains why the Japanese relative clause lacks a relative pronoun, in contrast to the English relative clause. The Japanese relative clause cannot have a relative pronoun since the latter can never satisfy the licensing condition on relative pronouns (15).

3.3 Properties of relative clauses

We have just reached the conclusion that the Japanese relative clause cannot contain a relative pronoun. What exactly does this mean for the syntax of relative clauses in Japanese? This means that Japanese cannot have an "operator-oriented" relative clause, which is licensed as a modifier of the relative head through the mediation of a relative pronoun functioning as an operator creating an open position within the relative clause. In the case of the operator-oriented relative clause, the relation between the relative head and its associated relative clause is established in a syntactic way, namely, by binding of the relative pronoun by the relative head (and by a predication relation between the relative head and the relative clause; see note 11), as we have seen in the English case.

The question then is how the relative clause in Japanese is licensed. Since it lacks an operator, syntactic binding (and predication) is not an option. The only remaining option, then, is licensing the relative clause semantically. In fact, Kuno (1973) and Murasugi (1991), among others, have already addressed this problem and reached the conclusion that the relative clause in Japanese is licensed by a semantic relation with the relative head. More specifically, the Japanese relative clause is licensed by an "aboutness" relation with the relative head. The "aboutness" condition is not peculiar to the licensing of the Japanese relative clause; it can also be seen in the licensing of certain topic constructions in Japanese and in English (see Kuno 1973 and Saito 1985 for extensive discussion on this):

(19) Sakana-wa tai   -ga   ii.
     fish   -TOP red snapper-NOM good

   "As for fish, red snapper is the best."

(Kuno 1973)

(20) As for sports, I like baseball best.

(Lasnik 1989)

Thus, in both cases, the topic construction is licensed to the extent that the sentence following the topic is interpreted as being relevant to, or about, the topic. Kuno (1973) and Murasugi (1991) argue that this is also true of the Japanese relative construction. Consider the following example.

(21) John-ga   kinoo   mita syasin
     John-NOM yesterday saw picture

   "the/a picture John saw yesterday"

In (21), the relative clause can be interpreted as being about a picture. Since the relative clause is in an "aboutness" relation with the relative head, it is properly licensed.

If the Japanese relative clause is licensed by "aboutness", the question arises as to the status of the object in the relative clause in (21). Murasugi (1991), adopting Perlmutter's (1972) proposal, claims that the gap in the Japanese relative clause is a *pro* (see also Oka 1988). In the case of (21), then, the *pro* in the object position in the relative clause is interpreted as referring to the relative head *syasin* "picture" and this interpretation makes the relative clause compatible with the "aboutness" condition on the relative clause.[14]

Given that the gap in the Japanese relative clause is a *pro* and that the relative clause is licensed by an "aboutness" relation with the relative head, we can naturally account for the well-known fact that in Japanese, the relation between the gap and the relative head can be unbounded, showing no island effects, as Kuno (1973), Oka (1988), and Murasugi (1991) observe. Compare (22) and (23), taken from Kuno (1973).

(22) *a gentleman [who$_i$ the suit that t_i is wearing is dirty]

(23) [*pro*$_i$ kiteiru   yoohuku-ga   yogoreteiru] sinsi$_i$
     is.wearing suit   -NOM is.dirty   gentleman

Lit. "the/a gentleman who the suit that is wearing is dirty"

Unlike its English counterpart in (22), the Japanese example in (23) is fully grammatical, despite the fact that the gap in the relative clause and the relative head are separated by a complex NP.

The existence of the so-called gapless relative clauses in Japanese, also discussed by Kuno (1973), follows as well from the fact that the Japanese relative clause is licensed by the aboutness relation with the relative head:

(24) [syuusyoku -ga   taihen na] buturigaku
     employment-NOM difficult is   physics

Lit. "physics (that) finding a job is difficult"

The English equivalent is simply impossible, since the English relative clause must be licensed by a binding relation between the relative head and the relative pronoun.

So far we have observed (i) that the Japanese relative clause is licensed by an "aboutness" relation with the relative head, (ii) that the gap in the relative clause is a *pro*, (iii) that the gap can be related to the relative head in an unbounded manner, and (iv) that the relative clause can be gapless. As we have noted, these observations are far from new and have been discussed in the traditional literature on Japanese syntax. Our claim here is that the theory of phrase structure and linear order developed by Fukui and Takano (1998) can deduce these properties from the fundamental property of the nominal head staying in situ in Japanese. Because of this fundamental property, the relative clause cannot contain a relative pronoun and hence cannot be "operator-oriented". Since it cannot be operator-oriented, the relative clause must be licensed semantically, namely, by an "aboutness" relation with the relative head. One way to satisfy the aboutness condition is for the relative clause to contain a pronominal which is co-referential with the relative head. Since the relation between the pronominal in the relative clause and the relative head does not involve movement, the lack of island effects within the relative clause and the existence of gapless relative clauses also follow. In this way, we derive the four well-known properties of the Japanese relative clause from the single parametric property concerning the location of the nominal head.

Notice, incidentally, that in our account of the presence of a pronominal element within the relative clause just mentioned, we did not make any specific reference to a *pro*, a pronominal without phonetic content. This is because the relevant pronominal can be an overt element, as noted by Kuno (1973):

(25) watakusi-ga *sono hito*-no/ *kare*-no namae-o wasuretesimatta
I-NOM that person-GEN/he-GEN name-ACC have.forgotten
okyakusan
guest

"a guest whose name I have forgotten"

On the other hand, the overt pronominal is not always allowed in the relative clause:

(26) ?*John-ga kinoo *sore*-o mita syasin
John-NOM yesterday it-ACC saw picture

"the/a picture John saw yesterday"

The example (26) is extremely awkward. This observation is reminiscent of the well-known restriction on the distribution of resumptive pronouns in questions and relative clauses in other languages (Chao and Sells 1983), and Japanese seems to exhibit similar effects in the form of the distribution of overt pronominal elements within the relative clause, though we do not go into any further details on this matter (see Ishii 1991 for extensive discussion on this point).

Whatever the exact restriction, we hold that the availability of *pro* is not directly relevant to the fundamental parametric property that is responsible for the Japanese relative clause, unlike Murasugi (1991), who, following Perlmutter's (1972) original claim, argues that the presence of *pro* is part of the necessary condition that accounts for the properties of the Japanese relative clause. In our account, what is fundamental is the absence of N-raising in Japanese.

In contrast to Japanese, the English relative clause has the following properties: (i) it is "operator-oriented", licensed by syntactic binding of the relative pronoun by the relative head, (ii) the gap in the relative clause is a trace/copy of the moved relative pronoun, (iii) the relation between the relative pronoun and the gap shows island effects, and (iv) the relative clause always contains a gap. Properties (ii) and (iv) follow from (i), and property (iii) is a direct consequence of (ii). The reason why English can (and in fact does) have a relative pronoun is that English has N-raising. Thus, the four properties follow from this single property.

3.4 Relative complementizers

Another property that follows from our basic parameter is the presence v. absence of a complementizer in relative clauses. English has such a complementizer, whereas Japanese lacks it:

(27) a picture that John saw yesterday

(28) John-ga   kinoo   mita syasin
     John-NOM yesterday saw picture

  "the/a picture that John saw yesterday"

In explaining this difference, we follow Murasugi (1991) and Sakai (1994) and assume that the English relative clause is CP, whereas the Japanese relative clause is TP (we also assume, contra Kayne (1994), that the English relative clause in (27) involves a phonetically null counterpart of the relative pronoun *which*). On different grounds, Murasugi and Sakai independently argue that the Japanese relative clause lacks the CP level (though some of their arguments are based on assumptions that are not adopted in the current framework and their validity can thus be questioned now). If the Japanese relative clause is TP, the absence of a complementizer in the relative clause follows straightforwardly, on the standard assumption that complementizers appear exclusively in CP (as heads of CPs).

Here, we might ask why the Japanese relative clause lacks the CP level altogether. In contrast to the relative clause, subordinate clauses in Japanese do have complementizers (or, at least, equivalents of *that* and *whether* in English; see Fukui 1995b for relevant discussion):

(29) a. John-wa   Mary-ga   kuru to   omotteiru.
         John-TOP Mary-NOM come that think

  "John thinks that Mary will come."

   b. John-wa   Mary-ga   kuru ka   siritagatteiru.
       John-TOP Mary-NOM come whether want to know

  "John wants to know whether Mary will come."

Apparently, then, in Japanese, the subordinate clause has a CP projection, while the relative clause lacks it.

In this connection, we would like to adopt Diesing's (1990) basic idea about the presence of functional projections in the structure. To account for a certain asymmetry between matrix and embedded questions in Yiddish with respect to where the fronted *wh*-phrase moves, Diesing proposes that embedded questions, being selected by matrix predicates, have a CP node, while matrix questions have only an IP (=TP) node, and suggests that this will follow if we assume that only the minimal amount of A′ structure is generated. Slightly modifying Diesing's suggestion, let us adopt the following condition:

(30) A functional category is present in the structure only when it is necessary.

In effect, this condition requires every syntactic structure to contain only necessary functional projections. This condition allows subordinate clauses in English and Japanese to have CP, since the subordinate clauses are always marked for the declarative/interrogative distinction and this marking is carried out by [±Q] features of C (Fukui and Takano 1998). The relative clause in English is also allowed to have CP, given that it is "operator-oriented" and thus contains a relative pronoun, which follows from the presence of N-raising, and that CP is necessary to hold the overtly raised relative pronoun.[15]

Turning to the Japanese relative clause, we see that it does not need CP: because of the lack of N-raising, the Japanese relative clause cannot be operator-oriented but is licensed by the "aboutness" relation with the relative head, and for this purpose, the functional category C is not necessary. Therefore, given condition (30), it follows that the Japanese relative clause lacks CP.[16]

In this way, we can derive the difference between English and Japanese with respect to the presence/absence of a relative complementizer in a relative clause from the fundamental difference we are pursuing.

3.5 *Internally headed relative clauses*

Let us move on to still another difference between English and Japanese: the presence or absence of the so-called internally headed (or head-internal) relative clause. The following is an example of the internally headed relative clause in Japanese:

(31) Susan-wa [Mary-ga sandoitti-o tukutta no]-o tabeta.
Susan-TOP Mary-NOM sandwich-ACC made NM-ACC ate
(NM = nominalizer)

"Susan ate a sandwich Mary had made."

In (31), the object of *tabeta* "ate" is an internally headed relative clause where the "internal head" *sandoitti* "sandwich" is located in the object position of the verb *tukutta* "made" in the relative clause. Unlike Japanese, English does not have this construction.

Cole (1987) argues that internally headed relative clauses are allowed only in languages with left-branching structure in noun phrases. He then claims that this restriction on the distribution of internally headed relative clauses follows if it is assumed (i) that internally headed relative clauses in fact have heads that are null pronominals co-referential with the internal heads (the "anaphoric head analysis") and (ii) that an anaphoric element cannot both precede and c-command its antecedent. Given these assumptions, the difference between Japanese and English can be seen in the structures in (32).

(32)

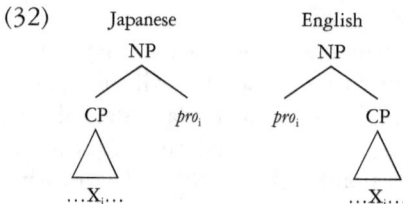

In (32), X is the internal head and *pro* is the "hidden external head". In the English structure, pro_i both precedes and c-commands X_i. As a result, English cannot have internally headed relative constructions. On the other hand, the Japanese structure does not violate the condition, since pro_i does not precede X_i.

Incorporating Cole's anaphoric head analysis of internally headed relative clauses, Kayne (1994) argues that his "antisymmetric view" of syntax allows us to dispense with specific reference to precedence in the account of the distribution of internally headed relative clauses. This is because the antisymmetric view ensures that if some element c-commands another and not vice versa, then the former necessarily precedes the latter on the surface.

Essentially following Kayne's reinterpretation of Cole's idea, we analyse the internally headed relative clause in (31) as follows:[17]

(33)

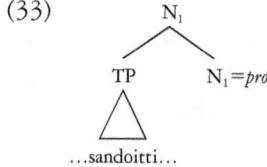

At LF, the external head *pro* is interpreted as co-referential with the internal head *sandoitti* "sandwich", which is allowed, given that neither [N_1, N_1] nor the lower N_1 c-commands the internal head (recall discussion in 3.2).

Suppose that English has an internally headed relative clause. The structure would be as in (34).

Nominal structure 247

(34)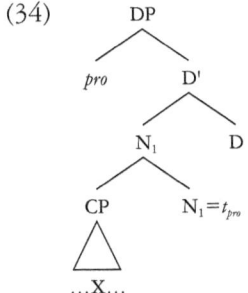

Because of raising of the nominal head, the external head *pro* is located in SpecD. Imagine now that the external head *pro* were co-referential with the internal head X. This would violate condition (C) of the Binding Theory, which dictates that a referential expression not be bound. This shows that English cannot have an internally headed relative clause, because of the existence of N-raising.

Note that on this analysis, the existence of a relative pronoun and the lack of an internally headed relative in English are treated as essentially the same effect, caused by the existence of N-raising. Since N raises to SpecD, it c-commands the relative clause CP, and as a result, the relative pronoun is licensed and the internal head is banned. In the same vein, the lack of a relative pronoun and the existence of an internally headed relative in Japanese follow. This kind of unification of the two phenomena has been impossible in traditional approaches but becomes a natural consequence of our approach.

3.6 Properties unified

Summarizing so far, we have shown that the theory of phrase structure and linear order proposed by Fukui and Takano (1998) deduces the differences concerning relative clauses given in (35) between English and Japanese from the single fundamental parametric property in (36).

(35)

	English	Japanese
order	N-initial	N-final
relative pronoun	present	absent
licensing of relative clause	syntactic: binding (and predication)	semantic: aboutness
gap in relative clause	trace/copy	*pro*
island effects	present	absent
gapless relative clause	absent	present
relative complementizer	present	absent
internally headed relative	absent	present

248 *Nominal structure*

(36) The nominal head overtly raises to Spec(D) in English but stays in place in Japanese.

Thus, our approach provides a unified account of the phenomena given in (35) under the hypothesis in (36). Unification of these properties has not been discussed in traditional literature. In this sense, the present proposal offers significant insights into the nature of parametric variation and lends further support to Fukui and Takano's (1998) theory.

3.7 *Comparison with Kayne's (1994) proposal*

Before closing this section, let us compare the present proposal with Kayne's (1994), which is also intended to explain some of the properties discussed above.[18] Unlike Fukui and Takano (1998), Kayne proposes (via his LCA) that UG allows only S-C-H order, and offers an analysis of the English relative clause compatible with this claim, as in (37).

(37)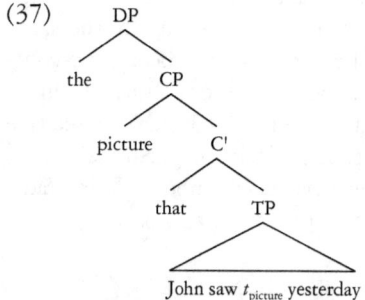

In this analysis, the relative clause CP is a complement of D and the relative head *picture* is moved from within the relative clause and occupies Spec(C). For cases where the relative clause involves a relative pronoun, Kayne suggests the following analysis:

(38)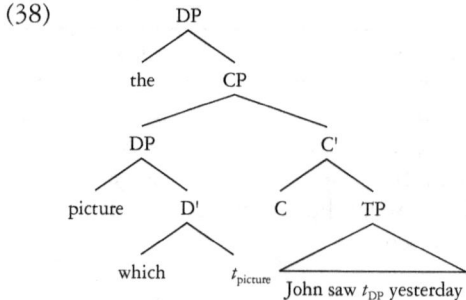

Here, what moves to Spec(C) is the DP *which picture* and within the raised DP, the NP *picture* moves to Spec(D).

Kayne further proposes to analyse N-final relatives as in Japanese as involving overt movement of the relative head to Spec(C) followed by overt movement of TP (IP in Kayne's terms) to Spec(D). The resulting structure is shown in (39).

(39)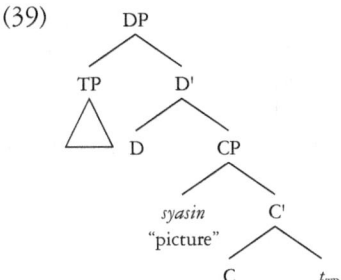

This structure yields the observed N-final order. Further, Kayne argues that the lack of a relative pronoun and of a relative complementizer in N-final relatives follow from this analysis. For Kayne, the relative pronoun is the D head of the raised DP, as in (38), and hence does not form a constituent with TP. As a result, moving TP with the relative pronoun, which would yield the surface form "relative clause + relative pronoun + relative head", is simply impossible. However, as Kayne himself notes (Kayne 1994: 158, note 29), it is not clear why N-final languages do not show the order "relative clause + relative head + relative pronoun", which would result if the DP headed by the relative pronoun raised to Spec(C), the relative head moved to Spec(D) of the raised DP, and TP moved to Spec(D) (of the entire DP).

As for the lack of a relative complementizer in N-final relatives, Kayne claims that it follows directly from the fact that what moves to SpecD is TP, a category which cannot contain a complementizer. Here, too, the question remains as to why C in (39) must be empty (if it were overt, the relative complementizer would follow the relative head, which never happens in N-final relatives). Kayne suggests that this may be treated on a par with *that*-trace effects, given that in his analysis, TP necessarily moves in N-final relatives, as shown in (39), thereby creating a configuration similar to that which induces *that*-trace effects. However, in a different context in which he discusses the lack of *that*-trace effects in complementizer-final languages, Kayne also suggests that it is due to TP movement to Spec(C), which yields C-final order, as shown in (40).

(40)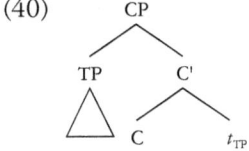

Kayne suggests that *that*-trace effects arise only when an overt complementizer c-commands a trace in Spec(T), so that the lack of *that*-trace effects in C-final languages follows from the structure in (40). If so, one cannot have recourse to *that*-trace effects to account for why C cannot be overt in (39).

Also potentially problematic is Kayne's claim that N-final relatives necessarily involve overt movement of TP. As discussed in Takano (1996) and Fukui and Takano (1998), there is no independent evidence internal to Japanese for the existence of such obligatory movement in the language. In order to maintain Kayne's proposal, a general theory of movement that tells us which element moves where for what reason would need to be constructed.

Finally, Kayne's analysis of N-final relatives makes wrong predictions for cases where the relative head and the gap in the relative clause are separated by an island. Recall that under Kayne's analysis, the relative head always moves from within the relative clause to Spec(C). This predicts that the relation between the gap in the relative clause and the relative head should be bounded in N-final relatives, as in N-initial relatives. However, as we have seen in 3.3, this is not the case. The relevant examples are repeated here:

(22) *a gentleman [who$_i$ the suit that t_i is wearing is dirty]

(23) [*pro*$_i$ kiteiru   yoohuku-ga yogoreteiru] sinsi$_i$
    is.wearing suit-NOM is.dirty   gentleman

The Japanese counterpart of (22) is fully grammatical, showing that the gap in the relative clause (i.e., *pro* in (23)) and the relative head can be separated by an island. This fact stands as a problem for Kayne's analysis, which takes the gap to be a trace or copy of the relative head.

These problems do not arise in our approach, as is clear from the discussion in the previous subsections. The lack of a relative pronoun and a relative complementizer in the N-final relative clause follows from the lack of N-raising. We do not invoke TP movement to derive the observed N-final order; in fact, the crucial part of our claim is that no movement is involved in the head-final structure. The lack of island effects in the Japanese relative clause is attributed to the gap in the relative clause being a *pro*, which in turn is ultimately attributed to the lack of N-raising.

4 Classifiers

As in many other languages, Japanese has a classifier system. Thus, when a numeral and a noun co-occur, a classifier, which expresses the kind of objects that the noun refers to, is attached to the numeral.

(41) san-nin   no   gakusei
      three-CL("person") GEN student (CL = *classifier*)

   "three students"

san-satu   no   hon
three-CL("volume") GEN book

"three books"

go-dai   no   kuruma
five-CL("body") GEN car

"five cars"

With "*no*-insertion", whose nature does not concern us here, a noun phrase with a numeral in Japanese comes out as "numeral-classifier-*no* + noun" (e.g., *san-nin-no gakusei* "three students"). English does not have a classifier system of this sort.

The question to be addressed is, of course, why Japanese has classifiers, while English lacks them. Again, we claim that this difference between English and Japanese derives from the existence or non-existence of N-raising in these languages. Our basic idea is that classifiers are on a par with Case-particles in the relevant respects. Thus, as argued by Fukui and Takano (1998), Japanese lacks V-raising and therefore invokes overt Case-particles, whereas English has V-raising, thereby rendering overt Case-particles unnecessary (and thus impossible). Similarly, Japanese lacks overt N-raising (owing to the lack of D in its lexicon; see above), thus requiring classifiers, while English exhibits overt N-raising, which makes classifiers unnecessary (hence impossible, under minimalist assumptions).

Let us illustrate how this intuition can be worked out. Assume first that prenominal numerals have the following structure (see Fukui and Takano 1998: 2.5 for relevant discussion):

(42)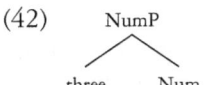

Num(eral) is a functional head that takes a numeral as its complement. Num has a formal feature that needs to be eliminated before the derivation reaches LF. Given that numerals are necessarily related to nominals, we call the feature [nominal]. In English, this feature gets eliminated by entering into a checking relation with the nominal head N that has raised to D. The exact derivation proceeds as follows. First, D attracts FF(N) (the set of formal features of N),[19] inducing overt movement of the category N to Spec(D) (see Fukui and Takano 1998):

252 *Nominal structure*

(43)

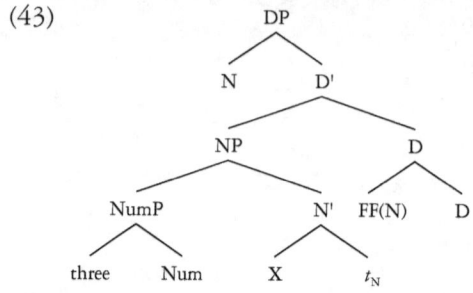

Then, FF(N) attached to D attracts FF(Num), which includes [nominal], and as a result, NumP moves to Spec(D) (NumP becomes an outer Spec of D in a multiple specifier configuration):

(44)

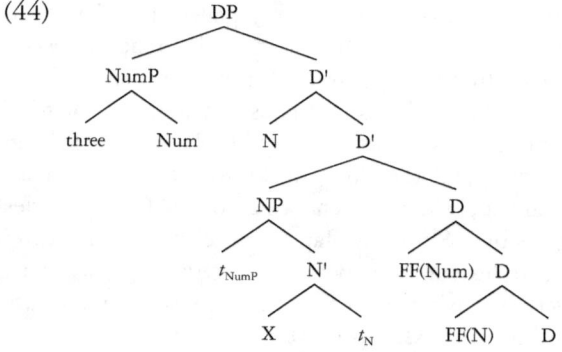

The whole process occurs before Spell-Out. After Spell-Out, the structure (44) is subject to the process of Linearization (Demerge and Concatenate) and is linearized into the sequence "*three + books + about John*" if N = *books* and X = *about John*.

On the other hand, Japanese has no N-raising and thus cannot eliminate the feature [nominal] of Num by checking (note that FF(N) can attract FF(Num) only when it is attached to a functional head such as D). Therefore, Japanese invokes the other strategy for eliminating a formal feature proposed by Fukui and Takano (1998), namely, elimination by Spell-Out: the feature [nominal] of Num gets eliminated from the derivation going to λ (a linguistic expression at LF) when Spell-Out strips away phonological features from the structure Σ. To make this possible, [nominal] of Num must be linked with phonological features, and this is exactly what classifiers are for. Thus, a classifier is a phonological/morphological realization of the [nominal] feature of Num. Because of the presence of a classifier, the formal feature [nominal] of Num gets eliminated by Spell-Out from the derivation going to λ:

(45)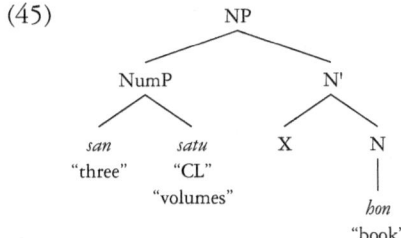

With *no*-insertion, this structure yields the surface form "*san-satu-no* + X + *hon*" (X a complement of N).

This analysis deduces the presence/absence of classifiers from the existence/nonexistence of N-raising, much in the same way that the presence/absence of Case-particles are derived from the existence or nonexistence of V-raising (as argued in detail in Fukui and Takano 1998). Furthermore, the analysis just presented also explains why Japanese allows numerals to "float", while English does not. As is well known, the distribution of numerals in Japanese is much freer than that in English: a numeral in Japanese can appear either inside a noun phrase with the noun it modifies, or outside of the noun phrase, without significantly changing the meaning of a sentence. Thus, along with (46a), (46b) is also grammatical with essentially the same meaning.

(46) a. [San -nin -no gakusei]-ga sono hon-o katta (koto).
three-CL("person")-GEN students-NOM that book-ACC bought

"Three students bought that book."

b. [Gakusei]-ga san-nin sono hon-o katta (koto).
students -NOM three-CL("person") that book-ACC bought

"Three students bought that book."

Obviously, English does not allow its numerals to float in this way.

(47) a. Three students bought that book.
b. *Students three bought that book.

Extensive research has been done on the nature and characteristics of this phenomenon in Japanese (called "Quantifier Float", somewhat misleadingly so, because some quantifiers, such as *all*, do float even in English; it is numerals that can never float in English), particularly in connection with its implications for the movement analysis of scrambling (see Kuroda 1983; Miyagawa 1989; among many others). However, it still remains open why Japanese exhibits this phenomenon while English does not. The obvious intuition is that the existence of overt classifiers in Japanese somehow makes it possible for a numeral to be associated with a noun it modifies, thereby allowing it to float rather freely.[20] Our explanation straightforwardly captures this intuition.

Thus, unlike in Japanese where the feature [nominal] gets eliminated by being linked with phonological features (i.e., overt classifiers), the feature [nominal] of Num in English must enter into a checking relation with N attached to D and, therefore, NumP can only appear where it is c-commanded by the N. This is the reason why NumP can never appear outside a DP in English. By contrast, NumP in Japanese does not have such a restriction. The feature [nominal] of Num does not enter into a checking relation at all, so it can appear anywhere in the structure, to the extent that it meets the conditions on its interpretation (which have been extensively investigated in the literature on Japanese syntax). As a result, numerals can freely appear outside a noun phrase in Japanese.

In summary, we have shown in this section that given the parametric statement that English has N-raising while Japanese lacks it, the existence of classifiers in Japanese and the lack thereof in English receives a straightforward account. We have also seen that our approach explains why numerals can "float" in Japanese, whereas they are not allowed to do so in English, a problem that has remained unexplained thus far. The reason, again, has to do with the lack of N-raising (hence the lack of feature-checking) in Japanese on the one hand, and the existence of feature-checking (hence the lack of overt classifiers) in English.

5 Concluding remarks

In this article, we have tried to extend the scope of the Symmetry Principle put forth in our previous work (Fukui and Takano 1998) to the structure of noun phrases. We focused on the major differences between English and Japanese with respect to their nominal structures, and argued that the Symmetry Principle, coupled with the parametric statement that N raises into D in English but not in Japanese, straightforwardly accounts for the differences. More specifically, we have demonstrated that the following differences fall out rather elegantly under our symmetry approach: (i) Japanese noun phrases are head-last, whereas English noun phrases are head-initial, (ii) there is no relative pronoun in Japanese, but English has them, (iii) the licensing of relative clauses involves the "aboutness" condition in Japanese, while English licenses its relative clauses via binding (and predication), (iv) the gap in relative clauses in Japanese is *pro*, in English, it is a trace or copy, (v) island effects are not observed with respect to Japanese relative clauses, whereas they are clearly attested in English, (vi) Japanese exhibits gapless relative clauses, but English does not, (vii) Japanese does not have a "relative complementizer", while English possesses it, and (viii) so-called "internally headed" relative clauses exist in Japanese, but not in English.

We then discussed the issue of overt classifiers: Japanese numerals are always accompanied by overt classifiers which "agree with" the kind of nouns that are counted, whereas English does not have such elements. We argued that this difference, too, can be deduced from the lack of N-raising in Japanese as opposed to the existence of such an operation in English. We also claimed that this analysis accounts for the "floatability" of numerals in Japanese. Japanese numerals are always accompanied by classifiers, as an alternative means to eliminate the [nominal] feature of Num, inducing no feature-checking. English numerals, on the other hand, have to be in the c-command domain of an N, since the [nominal] feature has to be eliminated via feature-checking. Thus, Japanese numerals freely "float" (under certain conditions on interpretation), occurring outside of a noun phrase, while English numerals can only occur within a noun phrase.

All these differences between English and Japanese follow from the hypothesis that N raises into D in English, but not in Japanese (see (36)), which in turn derives from the lack of the functional head D in Japanese (see note 7). This situation is slightly different from the one with respect to verbal or clausal structures. In Fukui and Takano (1998), we argue that a number of differences between English and Japanese in the domain of verbal/clausal structure follow straightforwardly if we assume that "light verb" v attracts V in English, but not in Japanese (see (8)). However, we still assume in Fukui and Takano 1998, that v exists in Japanese even though it does not have an ability to induce V-raising. In the case of nominal structures, we claim that D (which roughly corresponds to v in its relevant function in our account) actually does not exist at all in Japanese. The reason for this difference is that while there is some independent evidence for the existence of v in Japanese, there is simply no evidence internal to Japanese grammar for the existence of the functional head D in the language. Thus, guided by minimalist intuitions, we should conclude that there is no such functional head in Japanese (see Chomsky 1995b: 4.10, and Fukui 1995b for relevant discussions).

One might then wonder how the semantics of nominal expressions might work without postulating the functional head D, which plays a crucial role in the semantics of nominal expressions as a quantificational device. In fact, this has been a major objection from semanticists that one of the authors of the present article has been facing ever since he first put forth the hypothesis that Japanese lacks the functional head D (Fukui 1986). One persistent alternative has been that Japanese does have an "empty D system", even though there is no syntactic evidence for it, because such a D system, either overt or covert, is required by the semantics of nouns, which is presumably universal, not allowing any variation.

Recently, however, Gennaro Chierchia has developed an interesting framework of semantics that seems to put an appropriate cross-linguistic perspective on this issue (Chierchia 1998). It is simply impossible for us to go into the details of his proposals here, and we have to refer the reader to his original article for fuller expositions of the theory. In a nutshell, however, Chierchia proposes a system that allows for certain "semantic variation" in the way in which the reference of the syntactic category NP is set. More specifically, he proposes the "Nominal Mapping Parameter", according to which nouns can be characterized in terms of the two primitive features [±arg(ument)] and [±pred(icate)]. The postulation of these features is based on the observation that nouns seem to play a double role: on the one hand, they are restrictors of quantifiers (as in *every boy*) or predicates (as in *John and Mary are students*), and, on the other hand, they are devices for kind reference, i.e., arguments (as in *Dogs bark*). These options seem to be available in one way or another in every language. However, the actual implementation of these two options may be parametrized, i.e., they can be manifested in different ways in different languages. By using the above-mentioned features, Chierchia divides natural languages into three distinct types: (i) [−pred, +arg], (ii) [+pred, +arg], and (iii) [+pred, −arg]. (The [−pred, −arg] option is obviously excluded, because such a specification would prevent an NP from having any interpretation at all.) Chierchia offers a rather thorough cross-linguistic study regarding the parametrization of these two features, but let us focus on the type (i) languages, that is, languages where all noun phrases are argumental. Chinese and Japanese belong to this type, according to Chierchia.[21] In this type of languages, Chierchia argues, all nouns are, in some sense, mass, and therefore, are allowed to occur freely as bare nouns without a need for D. He then connects this property with the lack of plural morphology and the existence of a classifier system, both of which are attested in, say, Japanese.

If this type of "comparative semantics" is on the right track, Japanese is different from, say, English in the way of referring to kinds: all nouns in Japanese are kind denoting, whereas in English, only some nouns are kind denoting, preserving the "mass/count" distinction. Romance languages are of the type (iii), in which all nouns are predicates. Thus, nouns in Romance always require D, those in English sometimes (when they are predicative and not kind denoting), but not always, do, and nouns in Japanese never require D because they are always kind denoting. There is simply no need for D in Japanese as far as the semantics of nominal expressions is concerned, and the "empty D" proposal for the language thus appears to be *non sequitur* (see also Chomsky 1998 for a conceptual argument against postulating such an empty D).

Theories of (comparative) syntax and semantics have been shaped under the heavy influence of the studies of certain class(es) of languages (mostly "western" languages) whose properties do not seem to be shared by other types of languages including East Asian languages. Consequently, comparative studies have been so far carried out either between English and some other language (e.g., Japanese), or else within a single language family (Romance, Germanic, etc.), also in comparison with English. Given a vast number of accumulated results in both types of comparative studies, as well as the current development of linguistic theory, it seems to us that the time is ripe to make a serious attempt to truly integrate the valuable research results of comparative syntax, which have been scattered over particular circles of different language families and which have not always generated fruitful interactions among linguists working on different types of languages (particularly between linguists working on English and other European languages and those working on, say, East Asian languages).[22] This article can, then, be taken, along with the important work by Chierchia on "comparative semantics", as a small attempt at introducing a more balanced view on comparative syntax/semantics, which incorporates the properties of languages that have not been sufficiently taken into consideration when certain mechanisms of syntax/semantics are to be invented. Whether or not our attempt turns out to be on the right track, of course, remains to be seen in future research.

12 Phrase structure

1 Introduction

That sentences and phrases in human language have abstract hierarchical structure, not merely sequences of words and formatives, is one of the fundamental discoveries of modern linguistics. Accordingly, any theory of human language must have a component or device that deals with its "phrase structure", regardless of the analyses it offers for other properties of language (such as transformations). In this sense, the theory of phrase structure is a kind of backbone for contemporary linguistic theory.

In earlier generative traditions, the properties of phrase structure were coded in terms of the formal mechanism called "phrase structure rules" of the following form, where α is a single symbol and φ, ψ, and χ are strings of symbols (χ non-null; φ and ψ possibly null):

(1) $\varphi \alpha \psi \rightarrow \varphi \chi \psi$

Phrase structure rules express the basic structural facts of the language in the form of "phrase markers" they generate,[1] with terminal strings drawn from the lexicon. In particular, phrase markers generated by phrase structure rules express three kinds of information about syntactic representations:

(2) i. the hierarchical grouping of the "constituents" of the structure (Dominance);
     ii. the "type" of each constituent (Labeling);
     iii. the left-to-right order (linear order) of the constituents (Precedence).

For example, the phrase marker (3), generated by the phrase structure rules in (4), indicates that the largest constituent, whose label is S (the designated initial symbol), is made up of a constituent NP (Noun Phrase) preceding the other constituent VP (Verb Phrase); that the NP consists of two constituents, D(eterminer) and a N(oun), in this order; and that the VP is composed of V(erb) and NP (in this order), and so on:

(3)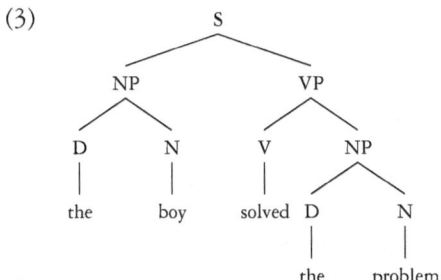

(4)   i.   S → NP VP
    ii.   VP → V NP
    iii. NP → D N
    iv. D → the
    v.   N → boy
    vi. N → problem
    vii. V → solved

Phrase structure rules of the kind represented by (4iv)–(4vii), which directly insert lexical items into appropriate places in the structure, were later abolished in favour of the lexicon with subcategorization features (Chomsky 1965). This separation of lexicon from the "computational system" (phrase structure rules) makes it possible to simplify the form of phrase structure rules for human language from the "context-sensitive" (1) to the "context-free" (5) (with φ, ψ necessarily null; other qualifications are the same):

(5)   α → χ

In (5), α is a single "nonterminal" symbol, and χ is either a non-null string of nonterminal symbols or the designated symbol "Δ", into which a lexical item is to be inserted in accordance with its subcategorization features (see Chomsky 1965 for details).

Thus, context-free phrase structure rules, coupled with the lexicon containing the information about idiosyncratic properties of each lexical item, were assumed in the "Standard Theory" of generative grammar (Chomsky 1965) to be responsible for expressing the properties of phrase structure. However, toward the end of the 1960s, it became apparent that certain important generalizations about the phrase structure of human language cannot be stated in terms of phrase structure rules alone. Recognition of the inadequacies of phrase structure rules, as we will see in the following section, led to the emergence and development of the general theory of phrase structure, "X′ theory", which is a main topic of this chapter.

The organization of this chapter is as follows. Section 2 discusses the basic insights of X′ theory. The section provides a brief explanation as to how this has emerged as an attempt to overcome the deficiencies of phrase structure rules in capturing the basic properties of phrase structure of human language, and summarizes the development of X′ theory from its inception to the Barriers version (Chomsky 1986a). Section 3 is concerned with the "post-Barriers" development of the theory of phrase structure, which can be characterized as minimizing the role of X′ theory as an independent principle of Universal Grammar (UG), while maintaining its basic insights, which led to the eventual elimination of X′ theory in the "minimalist program" (Chomsky 1994). It should be mentioned that the historical overview of these sections is by no means meant to be comprehensive, and the remarks to be made in the presentation are rather selective and schematic. It also goes without saying that the overview benefits from hindsight. Section 4 deals with one of the current issues in the theory of phrase structure, namely, the role of "linear order", in general, and that of the "head parameter", in particular. This section takes up some of the most recent works on the issue of linear order, and examines their basic claims. Section 5 is a summary and conclusion.

As the discussion proceeds, I will occasionally touch on some of the issues of movement (transformations) as well. This is because the theory of phrase structure and the theory of movement have been progressing side by side in the history of generative grammar. Transformations are formal operations applying to linguistic representations constructed in accordance with the general principles of phrase structure. Thus, a substantive change in the theory of phrase structure necessarily has important implications for the theory of transformations.

Throughout the chapter, I will basically confine myself to the discussion of the development of X′ theory, with only scattered references to other approaches to phrase structure, such as categorial grammars (Lambek 1958; see also Wood 1993 and references there), generalized phrase structure grammar (Gazdar et al. 1985) and its various ramifications (head-driven phrase structure grammar (Pollard and Sag 1994, for example)), lexical-functional grammar (Bresnan 1982), etc. This is of course not to dismiss the other approaches, but mainly to keep the discussion coherent and to manageable proportions. In addition, there are also more substantive reasons. First of all, the empirical insights offered by X′ theory are to be captured by any theory of phrase structure, regardless of the difference in formalism. Second, at least given the current version of "X′ theory" (this name may no longer be appropriate, as we will see later), there do not seem to be, as far as the treatment of phrase structure is concerned, so many fundamental differences between "X′ theory" and the other approaches mentioned above. The differences, if any, seem to be concerned only with the way other properties of language (the property of "displacement", for instance) are handled in a given framework.

2 From "Remarks" to *Barriers*: formulating and enriching X′ theory

The basic motivations for X′ theory come from the following two considerations:

(6) i. the notion of "possible phrase structure rules";
ii. cross-categorial generalizations.

The first consideration has to do with what counts as "a possible phrase structure rule" in natural languages. It is observed that while phrase structure rules of the kind in (7) (cf. also the phrase structure rules in (4) above) are widely attested in natural languages, those represented in (8) are systematically excluded in any grammar of human language:

(7) VP → V (NP) (PP)
NP → (Det) N (PP)
PP → P (NP)

(8) VP → N (PP)
NP → V (NP) (PP)
PP → N (VP)

In other words, structures such as those in (9), which are generated by the phrase structure rules in (7), are permitted in human language, whereas structures like those in (10), generated by the phrase structure rules in (8), are systematically excluded in human language:

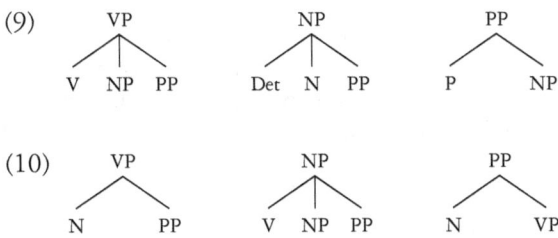

The reason for the impossibility of the phrase structure rules in (8) (and the corresponding structures in (10)) is intuitively clear. VP, for example, is a "Verb Phrase", rather than, say, a "Noun Phrase", and since it is a phrase of a verb, it must have a verb in it. However, the right-hand side of the phrase structure rule VP → N (PP) does not contain any verb. Hence the structure generated by such a phrase structure rule (i.e., the first structure in (10)) is ill-formed. The same is true for the other phrase structure rules in (8) (and the corresponding structures in (10)).

In general, an "XP" cannot be a "phrase of X" if there is no X. Put another way, phrase structure in human language is "endocentric", in the sense that it is constructed based on a certain central element (called the "head" of a phrase), which determines the essential properties of the phrase, accompanied by other non-central elements, thus forming a larger structure. This is the right intuition, but, as pointed out by Lyons (1968), the theory of phrase structure grammar simply cannot capture this. Recall that in the general scheme of context-free phrase structure rules in (5), reproduced here as (11), the only formal requirements are that α is a single nonterminal symbol and χ is a non-null string of nonterminal symbols (or the designated symbol Δ):

(11) $\alpha \rightarrow \chi$

The phrase structure rules in (7) (which are attested in human language) and those in (8) (which are excluded in human language) are no different as far as the formal "definitions" of phrase structure rules are concerned. Thus, in each of the phrase structure rules in (8), the left-hand side is a single nonterminal symbol ("VP", "NP", and "PP"), and the right-hand side of the rule is a non-null string of nonterminal symbols ("N (PP)", "V (NP) (PP)", and "N (VP)"). These are all legitimate phrase structure rules, satisfying the formal definitions of (context-free) phrase structure rules, just like the phrase structure rules in (7), despite the fact that only the latter type of phrase structure rule is permitted and the former type is never allowed (at least, has never been attested) in human language. Phrase structure rules are too "permissive" as a theory of phrase structure in human language in that they generate phrase structures that are indeed never permitted in human language. We thus need some other mechanism which correctly captures the endocentricity of phrase structure that appears to be a fundamental property of human language.

The second major motivation for X' theory is concerned with some observed parallelisms that exist across different categories. Historically, the discussion started out with the treatment of two types of nominal in English, as represented by the following examples:

(12) a. John's refusing the offer
     b. the enemy's destroying the city

(13) a. John's refusal of the offer
     b. the enemy's destruction of the city

Nominals of the type represented in (12) are called "gerundive nominals", whereas those shown in (13) are called "derived nominals". These two types of nominal were treated uniformly in terms of a "nominalization transformation", which derives nominals like, say, (12b) and (13b) from the same source, namely, (the underlying form of) the sentence "the enemy destroyed the city" (see Lees 1960 for details).

Chomsky (1970), however, refutes this "Transformationalist Hypothesis", and argues that the theory of grammar should not allow a nominalization transformation (or any other transformation with similar expressive power) because it performs various operations that are never observed in any other well-argued cases of transformations. Thus, the alleged nominalization transformation (i) changes category types (it changes S to NP and V to N), (ii) introduces the preposition *of*, (iii) changes the morphological shape of the element (*destroy* is changed to *destruction*; *refuse* is changed to *refusal*, etc.), (iv) deletes all auxiliaries, and so on. These are the operations that other well-attested transformations never perform, and hence should not be allowed, Chomsky argues, if we are to aim at restricting the class of possible grammars.

In particular, Chomsky points out (i) that derived nominals are really "noun-like", not sharing various essential properties with sentences, and (ii) that the relationship between derived nominals and their sentential counterparts is rather unsystematic and sometimes unpredictable (see Chomsky 1970 for more arguments establishing these points). He then concludes that derived nominals should be handled in the lexicon, rather than in terms of transformations which deal with formal and systematic relationships between phrase structure trees. This proposal defines the "Lexicalist Hypothesis", which has become standard for the analysis of derived nominals in particular, and for the characterization of transformations in general.

Once we adopt the Lexicalist Hypothesis, however, an important problem immediately arises as to how to capture certain similarities and parallelisms holding between verb/noun and sentence/nominal pairs. More specifically, the strict subcategorization properties of a verb generally carry over to the corresponding noun, and the identical grammatical relations are observed in both sentences and the corresponding nominals (see Lees 1960 and Chomsky 1970 for detailed illustrations of these points; see also van Riemsdijk and Williams 1986 for a lucid summary). Under the Transformationalist Hypothesis, these parallelisms are captured by the nominalization transformation. With the elimination of such a transformation under the Lexicalist Hypothesis, we now have to seek an alternative way to express the parallelisms in the grammar.

Chomsky (1970) proposes that these parallelisms can be successfully captured if the internal structure of noun phrases is made to be sufficiently similar to that of sentences so that the strict subcategorization properties and grammatical relations can be stated in such a general form as to apply to both verbs/sentences and nouns/nominals. As a concrete means to express these cross-categorial generalizations, Chomsky introduces a preliminary version of X' theory of the following kind (adapted from Chomsky 1970):

(14) a. $X' \rightarrow X \ldots$
b. $X'' \rightarrow [\text{Spec}, X'] \, X'$

The "X" in (14) is a variable ranging over the class of lexical categories

N(ouns), V(erbs), A(djectives), and (perhaps) P(repositions). The symbol X′ (called "X bar", although, for typographical reasons, it is common to use primes rather than bars) stands for a constituent (phrase) containing X as its "head" (the central and essential element of the phrase), as well as those elements appearing in the place indicated by "..." in (14a), the elements called the "complement" of X. The schema (14b) introduces a still larger phrase X″ (called "X double bar") containing X′ and pre-head elements associated with X′, called the "specifier" (Spec) of X′ (notated as [Spec, X′]).[2] Examples of specifiers include, according to Chomsky, determiners as [Spec, N′], auxiliary elements as [Spec, V′], comparative structures and elements like *very* as [Spec, A′], etc. X′ and X″, which share the basic properties of the head X, are called "projections" of X, with the latter (X″) referred to as the "maximal projection" of X (since it does not project any further).

The X′ schemata in (14) are proposed as a principle of UG on phrase structure, and express the manner in which phrases are constructed in human language. Note that given the X′ schemata, the problem concerning the "possible phrase structure rules" in human language discussed above is immediately resolved. That is, the "endocentricity" of phrases in human language is directly encoded in X′ theory as the generalization that phrases are all projections of their heads. Thus, the non-existing phrase structure rules in (8) are excluded on principled grounds as rules generating the illegitimate structures in (10), which contain phrases lacking the proper heads, in violation of X′ theory.

With respect to the problem of expressing cross-categorial parallelisms, X′ theory provides a generalized structure by which we can uniformly express basic grammatical relations. Thus, the notion of "object-of" X can be stated as an NP that is immediately dominated by X′, and the notion of "subject-of" X can be expressed as an NP that is immediately dominated by X″, where X in both cases ranges over V, N, etc. Likewise, the strict subcategorization properties of, say, verbs and nouns are stated uniformly in terms of the general X′ scheme. For example, if an X (a verb or a noun) has a subcategorization frame +[_ PP], then the PP is realized as the complement of X (the verb or noun).

However, the X′-theoretic generalizations were not complete at this stage of the development of the theory. This is because sentences did not quite fit into the general X′ scheme and were introduced by the following phrase structure rule, which does not really conform to X′ theory (see Chomsky 1970):

(15) S→N″ V″

Given the X′ schemata in (14) and the "S-introducing" phrase structure rule (15), the internal structures of noun phrases such as *the enemy's destruction of the city* and sentences like *the enemy destroyed the city* should be as follows (omitting much detail):

(16) a. Noun phrases

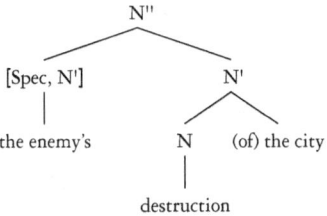

b. Sentences

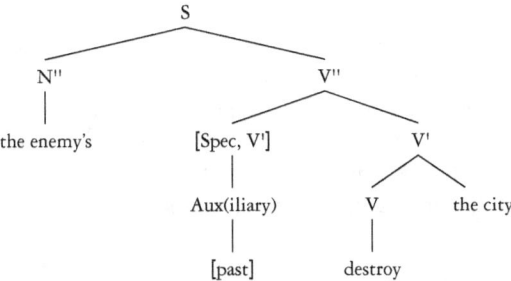

While these internal structures of noun phrases and sentences are sufficiently similar to permit a generalized cross-categorial formulation of grammatical relations and strict subcategorization properties for noun/verb pairs, it is also apparent that further (and rather complete) parallelism could be obtained if sentences are to be analysed as V″. This issue, however, turns out to be complex and controversial, and in fact motivates much of the subsequent development of X′ theory after Chomsky (1970), as we will see below.

A final tenet of Chomsky's X′ theory concerns the feature analysis of syntactic categories, according to which categories are defined in terms of the two primitive features [±N] (substantive) and [±V] (predicative). The major "lexical categories" are thus defined as follows, using these two primitive features:

(17) $N = [+N, -V]$
$A = [+N, +V]$
$P = [-N, -V]$
$V = [-N, +V]$

This feature analysis claims that categories in syntax are not really "atoms", but rather, they are decomposable feature complexes characterized by the primitive features, pretty much as "phonemes" are decomposed in terms of distinctive features in phonology. And, as in phonology, this approach makes it possible to define certain "natural classes" of syntactic category with respect to various syntactic operations and principles. Thus, we can capture the generalization that NPs and PPs behave in the same way (as opposed to VPs and APs) with respect to certain transformations, by attributing it to the feature specification [−V]; we can define the class of possible (structural) Case assigners, V and P (as opposed to N and A), by referring to the [−N] feature; we (correctly) predict that N and V never form a natural class because of their completely conflicting feature specifications, and so on (see, among many others, Bresnan 1977, Chomsky 1981a).

Summing up the discussion so far, the basic claims of X′ theory of Chomsky (1970) can be stated as follows:

(18) *The basic claims of X′ theory*
    a. Every phrase is "headed", i.e., has an endocentric structure, with the head X projecting to larger phrases.[3]
    b. Heads (categories) are not atomic elements; rather, they are feature complexes, consisting of the primitive features [±N] and [±V].
    c. UG provides the general X′ schemata of the following sort (cf. (14)), which govern the mode of projection of a head:
       X′ → X . . .
       X″ → [Spec, X′] X′

The version of X′ theory presented in Chomsky (1970) was in a preliminary form, and there certainly remained details to be worked out more fully. However, it is also true that all the crucial and fundamental insights of X′ theory were already presented in this study and have been subject to little substantive change in the following years. More specifically, the claims (18a) and (18b) above have survived almost in their original forms throughout the following development of grammatical theory and are still assumed in the current framework, while the claim (18c), the existence of the universal X′ schemata, has been subjected to critical scrutiny in recent years, as we will see in the next section.

The proposal of X′ theory was followed by a flux of research on phrase structure in the 1970s, trying to fix some technical problems associated with the initial version of the theory and to expand the scope of X′ theory to extensive descriptive material. The relevant literature in this era is too copious to mention in detail, but to name just a few: Siegel (1974), Bowers (1975), Bresnan (1976, 1977), Emonds (1976), Hornstein (1977), Selkirk (1977), and, perhaps most importantly, Jackendoff (1977). From our current perspectives, two important and interrelated problems emerged during this period. They are (i) the analysis of sentences (or clauses) *vis-à-vis* X′ theory, and (ii) the proper characterization of "Spec". Let us look at these issues in some detail.

As we saw above, the sentential structure was handled in Chomsky (1970) by the phrase structure rule (15), which does not conform to the general X' schemata in (14), thereby making the structure of a sentence a kind of an exception to X' theory. And this is the main reason for the rather incomplete parallelism between sentences and noun phrases as depicted by (16). Naturally, a proposal has been made, most notably by Jackendoff (1977) (cf. also Kayne 1981), that a sentence be analysed as the (maximal) projection of V, with its subject being treated as [Spec, V'] (or [Spec, V"] in Jackendoff's system, since he assumes that X''' is the maximal level for every category). While this proposal has the obvious advantage of making the internal structures of sentences and noun phrases (almost) completely parallel, there exists some evidence against this claim (see Hornstein 1977, among others). The most crucial evidence that counters the $S = V^{max}$ (the maximal projection of V) analysis comes from the close relationship holding between the subject of a sentence and I(nflectional elements, including the traditional notion of Aux) of that sentence. For example, it is the I of a sentence that assigns nominative Case to the subject, and it is also I that the subject agrees with (in terms of number, person, etc.). And this kind of formal relation cannot be straightforwardly stated if the subject is generated inside the projection of V, with I outside of that projection. Thus, even in Chomsky (1981a), S is still generated by the following phrase structure rule (adapted from Chomsky 1981a), where the subject N" is placed outside the maximal projection of V:

(19) S → N" I V"

Huang (1982) proposes (cf. also Stowell 1981b, Pesetsky 1982b) that S should in fact be analysed as the maximal projection of I, a natural extension of the spirit of X' theory. His arguments for this claim mainly come from considerations of the behaviour of the subject and I with respect to general principles such as the Empty Category Principle (ECP). In particular, Huang argues that I really behaves like a head in that it governs (but does not properly govern, at least in English) the subject (see Huang 1982 for much detailed discussion). The internal structure of a sentence now looks like the following, which conforms to X' theory:

(20)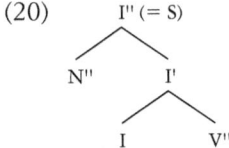

In (20), the subject is the [Spec, I'] and the sentential structure now looks quite "normal" in the sense that there is nothing special with it in light of X' theory, now extended to a "non-lexical" category I. Note, however, that the incompleteness of parallelism between sentences and noun phrases still remains even under this modified analysis: the subject of a noun phrase is inside its own projection, whereas the subject of a sentence is generated outside of the projection of a verb. This problem was resolved when the new analysis of subjects (called the "Predicate-Internal Subject Hypothesis") was introduced, as we will discuss in the following section.

Returning to the historical discussion of the analysis of sentences, Bresnan (1972), on the basis of extensive study of *wh*-movement phenomena, introduced a larger clausal unit that includes the core part of the sentence (S) and the "sentence-introducer", called C(omplementizer) (e.g., *that*, *for*, *whether*, etc.). Thus, the structure of a full clause (notated as S' (S-bar)) should be introduced by the following phrase structure rule (see Bresnan 1972 for details):

(21) S' → C S

Given the structure of S in (20), the structure of a full clause is:

(22)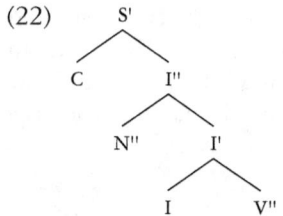

In (22), the top portion of the structure is still an exception to X' theory. S' is not headed by anything, but rather, branches to two co-ordinated elements, C and I" (=S). Evidence has been accumulated, however, to show that C functions as a head, in terms of, particularly, the ECP (Fassi Fehri 1980, Stowell 1981b, Lasnik and Saito 1984, among others). This led to the proposal of analysing C as the head of S', thus reanalysing the latter as C':

(23)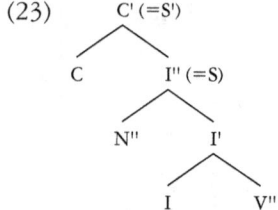

Now the clausal structure is made to fall under X' theory almost completely, the only problem being the "defectiveness" of the complementizer phrase, i.e., it projects only to C', not to C". To see how this final gap was filled, we should turn to the other major problem that motivated the development of X' theory, namely, the characterization of Spec.

In Chomsky's (1970) version of X' theory, "Spec" constituted a rather heterogeneous set, including a variety of "pre-head" elements. Thus, Chomsky suggested that [Spec, V'] includes auxiliary elements of various sorts (with time adverbials associated), [Spec, N'] is instantiated as determiners, [Spec, A'] contains the system of qualifying elements such as comparative structures, *very*, etc. As the research progressed, however, it became increasingly apparent that those pre-head elements can be classified into different types, and that the notion of Spec should be more narrowly defined to capture the true generalization. Accordingly, some elements that were initially identified as Spec were later reanalysed as heads (e.g., auxiliary elements, now analysed as instances of the head I), or "adjuncts" (modifiers) that are optionally generated to modify heads (e.g., *very*), although many descriptive questions remain (even now) with the analysis of the latter.

The notion of Spec that resulted from these efforts has the following properties: (i) it is typically an NP, and (ii) it bears a certain relationship with the head. Of the pre-head elements in English, the fronted *wh*-phrase, the subject of a sentence, and the subject of a noun phrase exhibit these properties. Thus, the subject of a sentence is identified as [Spec, I'], and the subject of a noun phrase (as in <u>*the enemy's destruction*</u>) is characterized as [Spec, N'].[4] The fronted *wh*-phrase apparently shows the two properties just discussed: it is typically an NP (or at least a maximal projection), and it bears a certain relationship with the head C (it is a [+wh] C that triggers *wh*-movement; see Bresnan 1972). Thus, it is well qualified to be [Spec, C'], patterning with the other Specs. However, to characterize a fronted *wh*-phrase as [Spec, C'] requires a reanalysis of *wh*-movement. Namely, *wh*-movement should now be analysed as "movement to [Spec, C']", rather than "movement to C", as has been long assumed ever since Bresnan's pioneering work (Bresnan 1972). This is in fact what Chomsky (1986a) proposes, with some additional arguments to support this conclusion (see Chomsky 1986a for details). If a fronted *wh*-phrase occupies [Spec, C'], then the structure of a full clause now looks like the following, with the projection of C completely on a par with other projections (i.e., no "defectiveness" of C^{max}):

(24)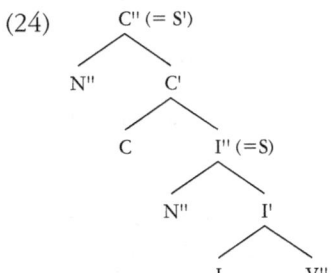

X' theory is now in full force, regulating the clausal structure, which has always been an exception to the theory in one way or another, as well as the structure of other phrases. The basic ideas of the version of X' theory presented in Chomsky (1986a) can be stated as follows:[5]

(25) X′ schemata (cf. Chomsky 1986a)
   a. X′ = X/X′ Y″
   b. X″ = Z″ X′/X″

In (25), X means X^0, a zero-level category (i.e., a head), the "/" sign between symbols indicates that there is a choice between them (e.g., either X or X′ can be chosen in (25a)), and X, Y, Z are variables ranging over possible categories (now including non-lexical categories). Notice that by allowing the same symbol (viz., X′ in (25a) and X″ in (25b)) to occur on both sides of the same equation, we permit "recursion" of the same bar-level structures in a phrase. For example, (25) licenses the following structure, where X′ and X″ each appear twice:

(26)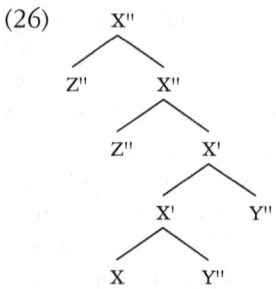

We call the lower Y″ in (26) the "complement" of X, the lower Z″ the "Spec" of X′ (or the Spec of X″ ([Spec, X″]); see note 2), and the upper Z″ an "adjunct" of X″. The status of the upper Y″ in (26) is ambiguous (it could be a "quasi-complement" or an adjunct, for instance), depending on further articulation of the theory of phrase structure (see Chomsky and Lasnik 1993). Note incidentally that these notions (complement, Spec, and adjunct) are "relational" notions defined in terms of their structural positions, not inherent and categorial ones (unlike notions such as "Noun Phrase", which are categorical). This is an assumption that has been pretty much constant throughout the history of X′ theory.

A few more general remarks are in order with respect to the X′ scheme in (25). First, one might notice the use of equations in (25), rather than X′ "rules" that have been exploited in previous works on X′ theory. In most earlier works, X′ theory was taken to be a principle of UG that provides the general "rule schemata" that regulate the general form of phrase structure rules of human language. This traditional conception of X′ theory collapsed when the very notion of phrase structure rules was subjected to critical scrutiny, and was eventually eliminated around 1980, when the "principles-and-parameters" approach was first set forth in a systematic way (see Chomsky 1981a). Specifically, it was pointed out that phrase structure rules are redundant and dubious devices, recapitulating the information that must be presented in the lexicon. For example, the fact that the verb *persuade* takes an NP and S′ (=C″) complement has to be stated as the verb's lexical property, quite independently from the phrase structure rule that generates the sequence V-NP-S'/C". And since descriptions of lexical properties in the lexicon are ineliminable, it is the phrase structure rules that ought to be eliminated. Subsequent work such as Stowell (1981b) showed that the other information expressed by phrase structure rules (most of which have to do with linear ordering) can in large part be determined by other general principles of UG (such as Case theory; see Stowell 1981b). Thus, it was generally believed in the principles-and-parameters approach that phrase structure rules could be entirely eliminated, apart from certain parameters of X' theory. With the notion of phrase structure rules eliminated from the grammar, X' theory has become a principle of UG that directly regulates phrase structure of human language.

Second, the X' scheme in (25) is formulated only in terms of the structural relation "dominance", and does not encode the information regarding linear order. Thus, of the three types of information listed in (2) before, i.e., (2i) Dominance, (2ii) Labeling, and (2iii) linear order (Precedence), only the first two ((2i) and (2ii)) are regulated by X' theory itself. The linear order of elements (2iii) is to be specified by the "parameter" (called the "head parameter") associated with X' theory. This is in accordance with the general guidelines of the principles-and-parameters approach, under which UG is conceived of as a finite set of invariant principles each of which is associated with a parameter whose value is to be fixed by experience. There are two values of the head parameter, "head initial" and "head last". If the parameter is set for the value "head initial", the English-type languages follow, in which complements generally follow their heads, whereas if the value is set as "head last", the Japanese-type languages obtain, where complements typically precede their heads.[6] With this move to parametrized X' theory, the phrase structure system for a particular language is largely restricted to the specification of the parameter(s) that determine(s) the linear ordering of elements.

Finally, given the narrower characterization of Spec as a place for a maximal projection (typically a noun phrase), we now have a much simplified theory of movement. Chomsky (1986a) proposes that there are two types of movement: (i) X^0-movement (movement of a head), and (ii) X'' (or X^{max})-movement (movement of a maximal projection). We put aside the discussion of X^0-movement (see Chomsky 1986a, 1995b; see also Roberts 2001 for much detailed discussion of this type of movement). Movement of a maximal projection is divided into two subtypes: (i) substitution, and (ii) adjunction. Chomsky then argues that, apart from X^0-movement to head position (which we put aside), various principles of UG ensure that substitution (NP-movement and *wh*-movement) always moves a maximal projection to a specifier position (see Chomsky 1986a for details).[7] Thus, the notion of "Spec" now receives a uniform characterization as a landing site for X^{max}-movement: [Spec, C'/C''] is the landing site for *wh*-movement, [Spec, I'/I''] is the landing site for NP-movement (passive and raising), and [Spec, N'/N''] is the landing site for "passive" in a noun phrase. We will return to adjunction later on.

To sum up, Chomsky's (1986a) version of X' theory has the following characteristics. First, it includes two "non-lexical" categories, I and C, as members of "X" relevant for X' theory, so that a full clausal structure is now in full conformity with the principles of X' theory and "sentences" are no longer exceptions to the theory, a great improvement over earlier versions of X' theory for which "sentences" have always been treated as exceptions. Second, X' theory is now parametrized in accordance with the general guidelines of the principles-and-parameters approach, and the theory no longer specifies the linear ordering of elements in the scheme. The ordering restrictions are determined by the value for the parameter (the head parameter) associated with X' theory, not by X' theory itself. And finally, the notion of Spec is further sharpened as a landing site for movement of a maximal projection (substitution), with a remarkable simplification of the theory of movement. Some important problems, however, remained open in this version of X' theory, which motivated further development of the theory in the decade that followed.

3 Minimizing and deriving X' theory

An obvious point in Chomsky's (1986a) version of X' theory that calls for further improvement is the incomplete parallelism it expresses between noun phrases and clauses/sentences. Compare the following structures which are assigned to noun phrases and clauses in this theory:

(27) a. Noun phrases

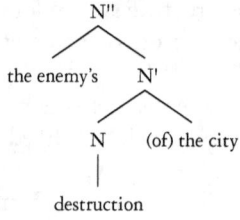

b. Clauses

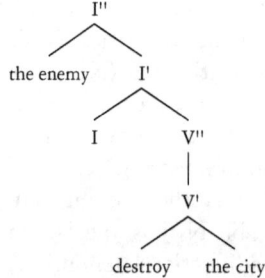

There are various problems with the structures in (27). The source of the problems is the fact that in (27a), all the "arguments" (subject and object) are located within the maximal projection of a single head (N = *destruction*), while in (27b), subject and object are split in two different projections. In other words, in a sentential structure (27b), there is an "additional" structure, due to the existence of the head I; in (27a), on the other hand, there is no such additional structure and all the arguments are located within the projection of N. From this discrepancy, a variety of problems arise. Why is the subject of a sentence located in [Spec, I″], a non-lexical category (I will henceforth follow a more recent practice to notate the Spec), whereas the subject of a noun phrase is located in [Spec, N″], a lexical category? A related question is: why does the "passive" in a sentence (e.g. *the city was destroyed (by the enemy)*) move a maximal projection to the specifier position of a non-lexical category ([Spec, I″]), but the corresponding passive in a noun phrase (e.g. *the city's destruction (by the enemy)*) move a maximal projection to the specifier position of a lexical category ([Spec, N″])? Also, why does V project from V′ to V″, without having Spec? And so on. The structures in (27) are clearly not parallel enough to capture the similarities between noun phrases and sentences.

Two proposals were made in the mid- to late 1980s which played important roles in resolving these problems. They are (i) the "DP-analysis" (Fukui and Speas 1986, Abney 1987; see also Brame 1981, 1982), and (ii) the "Predicate-Internal Subject" Hypothesis (see Hale 1978, Kitagawa 1986, Koopman and Sportiche 1991, Kuroda 1988, among others, for various versions of the "VP-Internal Subject" Hypothesis; see Fukui and Speas 1986 for a generalized form of the hypothesis as it is applied to all predicative categories).

The DP-analysis claims that "noun phrases" are in fact "determiner phrases" (DP) headed by the head D which takes a noun phrase as its complement. (See Longobardi 2001 for much relevant discussion, including detailed (cross-linguistic) analyses of the internal structure of noun phrases under this hypothesis.) According to this analysis, then, the internal structure of a noun phrase should be as follows:

(28)

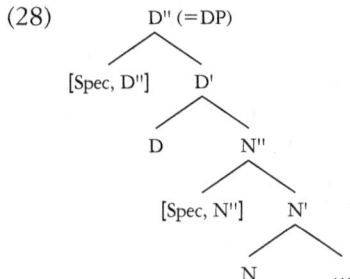

It was argued in the above-mentioned works that the DP-analysis is in fact supported by various syntactic considerations (see also Bernstein 2001 and

Longobardi 2001). Furthermore, the DP-analysis of noun phrases received much justification from the semantics of nominal expressions (a similar analysis had in fact been assumed in Montague semantics before the syntactic DP-analysis was proposed). Thus, this analysis has become more or less a standard analysis of noun phrases and is assumed in much current literature.

Notice that the DP-analysis provides a "two-story" structure for noun phrases that looks quite similar to the structure of sentences: in both structures, a non-lexical category (I in a sentence, D in a noun phrase) heads the whole phrase, taking a complement headed by a lexical category (V in a sentence, N in a noun phrase). Given the DP-analysis, then, the parallelism between sentences and noun phrases becomes much more visible and easy to capture than in the traditional analysis of noun phrases.

Where, then, is the subject located in these structures? Quite independently of the DP-analysis, it was proposed that the subject of a sentence should be generated in the projection of a verb (see the references cited above). In fact, the analysis that the subject of a sentence should be generated within a verb's projection is a rather traditional one (see, for example, Jackendoff 1977), which has been challenged by various evidence that the subject of a sentence is in a close relationship with I (see the discussion above). In other words, there seem to be two apparently conflicting sets of evidence regarding the status of the subject in a sentence: one type of evidence (most of which has to do with θ-theoretic considerations) indicates that the subject should be inside the verb's projection, while the other type of evidence (having to do with Case, agreement, government, etc.) suggests that the subject must occupy [Spec, I″]. The "VP-Internal Subject" Hypothesis was proposed mainly to reconcile these two types of evidence. The crucial and novel part of this hypothesis is the movement process that raises the subject (which is generated inside the verb's projection) to [Spec, I″]. This movement is driven by the need for Case assignment. Thus, the subject of a sentence is generated in [Spec, V″] (in some versions of the VP-Internal Subject Hypothesis, not in others), and then, is moved to [Spec, I″] in order to receive Case in that position. The D-structure position of the subject accounts for the subject's θ-theoretic status with respect to the verb, whereas its S-structure position (after the movement) accommodates the evidence indicating its close relationship with the inflectional head (I) (note that Case and agreement are S-structure (or at least non-D-structure) phenomena).

Combining the DP-analysis and the VP-Internal Subject Hypothesis (thus making the latter the "Predicate-Internal Subject" Hypothesis), we have completely parallel structures for noun phrases and clauses/sentences (Fukui and Speas 1986) (29). The subjects in both noun phrases and sentences are generated within the projection of the lexical category (N in a noun phrase and V in a sentence), receiving a θ-role in their original positions, and then are raised to the Spec positions of associated non-lexical categories (D in the case of noun phrases, I in sentences) to receive Case (genitive in noun phrases, nominative in sentences).[8] Passives in noun phrases (e.g. *the city's destruction (by the enemy)*) and those in sentences (e.g. *the city was destroyed (by the enemy)*) can be analysed uniformly as a process involving movement of an object from its base position (the complement position of a predicate N/V) to the Spec of an associated non-lexical category ([Spec, D"] in noun phrases and [Spec, I"] in sentences).

(29) a. Noun phrases

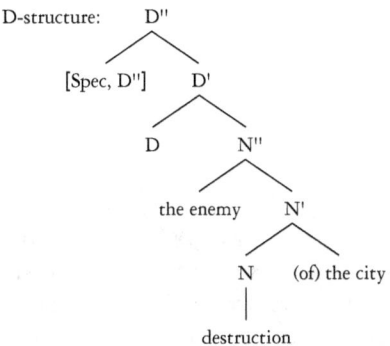

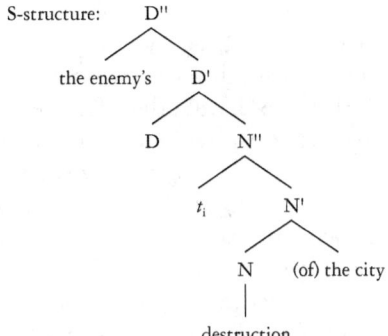

b. Clauses

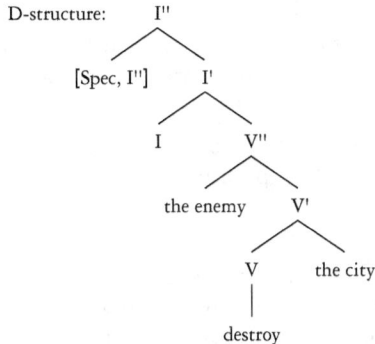

276 Phrase structure

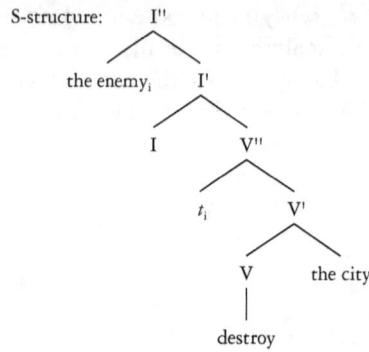

S-structure:

The integration of the DP-analysis and the Predicate-Internal Subject Hypothesis was based on the following ideas about the lexicon as it relates to syntactic computation. (See Fukui and Speas 1986, Abney 1987, for some preliminary discussions; see also Fukui 1986 for further discussion on this and related issues.) Items of the lexicon are divided into two major subtypes: lexical categories and "functional" categories. The latter type of categories roughly correspond to the traditional non-lexical categories, renamed in consideration of their nature. Lexical categories have substantive content, and include nouns, verbs, adjectives, etc. They typically enter into θ-marking. Functional categories do not have substantive content, and do not enter into θ-marking (although they do have other feature structures, including categorial features, agreement features, etc.). Lexical categories play an important role in interpretation of linguistic expressions, and indeed, most of the items in the lexicon belong to this type. Functional categories, on the other hand, do not play a comparable role in interpretation of linguistic expressions; their role is largely restricted to "grammatical" (or "computational") aspects of linguistic structure (although some of the proposed functional categories, e.g., I and D, may sometimes function as operators, bearing some "semantic" import). These categories constitute a small (and often closed) set, which include C, I, D (assuming the DP-analysis), and a few others.

Thus, the general view on the nature of these categories is the following division of labour for constructing linguistic expressions:

(30) (i) Lexical categories: the "conceptual" aspects of linguistic structure.
 (ii) Functional categories: the "computational" aspects of linguistic structure.

Lexical categories bear semantic features, including, in particular, features having to do with θ-roles ("θ-grids" in the sense of Stowell 1981b). They assign (or "discharge") θ-roles/features associated with them to other phrases, thereby forming larger structures that embed them. Functional categories do not bear θ-roles. Their role is largely restricted to purely formal and computational aspects of linguistic structure such as marking grammatical structures (nominals and clauses) or triggering movement operations. More specifically, some functional categories (functional heads) bear "agreement features", and these agreement features attract a maximal projection to their neighbourhoods (their specifier positions), in order for the latter to agree with the former. Thus, functional categories are indeed the "drive" for syntactic movement operations; lexical categories lack agreement features of this kind, and hence do not induce movement.

The idea of functional categories as the major driving force for movement opened up a new way of looking at cross-linguistic variation, and facilitated much subsequent work on comparative syntax in terms of properties of functional elements in languages. Given the nature and role of functional categories, it was proposed that language variation be restricted (apart from ordering restrictions) to the functional domain of the lexicon (Fukui 1986, 1988a; see also Borer 1984), and this proposal contributed to constructing a more restrictive theory of comparative syntax. At the same time, numerous "new" functional categories were proposed in the late 1980s, achieving tremendous descriptive success, although, from an explanatory point of view, it was clear that the class of possible functional categories has to be severely restricted in a principled way (Fukui 1988a, 1995b; see also Chomsky 1995b for a "Minimalist" critique of functional elements). See Belletti (2001) and Zanuttini (2001) and references there for much relevant discussion.

Explicit recognition of the division of labour between lexical and functional categories, as well as increasing emphasis on the importance of features in phrase structure composition, naturally led to a theory of phrase structure called "Relativized X' theory", which is an attempt to minimize the role of X' theory, while maintaining its basic insights.[9] The fundamental idea of Relativized X' theory, inspired by categorial grammars, can be summarized as follows:

(31) Phrase structure composition is driven by feature discharge.

Recall that lexical items have always been assumed, at least since Chomsky (1970), to be feature complexes (see the discussion in section 2). Given the fundamental difference between lexical and functional categories noted above, we can roughly assume the following feature specifications of these categories (see Chomsky 1995b for recent and much more elaborated discussion on features):

(32) (i) Lexical categories = [categorial features, θ-features (θ-roles/θ-grids), subcategorization features, phonological features, etc.].
 (ii) Functional categories = [categorial features, agreement features, subcategorization features, phonological features, etc.].

278 *Phrase structure*

The crucial difference, then, is that lexical categories bear θ-features but not agreement features, whereas functional categories lack θ-features but are associated with agreement features. And this crucial difference is directly reflected in their modes of projection in Relativized X′ theory. Thus, lexical categories project as they discharge their θ-features in the following manner.[10]

(33)

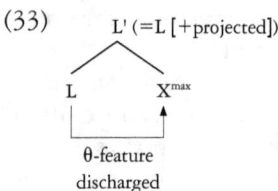

Lexical categories continue to project, forming larger structures, as they discharge their θ-features, until all the features have been discharged. In other words, the structure created in this process is recursive, and in this sense, the projection of a lexical category is never "closed". Note that in this system, the notion of "maximal projection" can no longer be defined in terms of "bar-levels", as in the standard X′ theory. Thus, maximal projection is defined as follows, in a way that is "relativized" to each head and configuration (see Muysken 1982 for an original proposal of this kind; see also Baltin 1989 for a similar approach):

(34) The "maximal projection" of X is a category X that does not project further in a given configuration.

The mode of projection of functional categories, although also governed by feature discharge, is different from that of lexical categories, since functional categories do not bear θ-features but instead have agreement features to discharge, and it is claimed that agreement is typically a one-to-one relation (Fukui 1986, Kuroda 1988). Thus, if a functional head F takes a maximal projection, discharging its subcategorization feature to the latter, and then takes another maximal projection for the purpose of agreement, its projection is "closed" at that point, owing to the one-to-one nature of agreement:

(35)

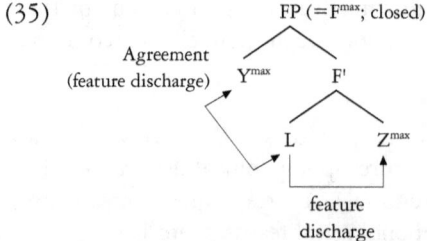

Once agreement occurs, therefore, the projection is closed (the closed projection of X is notated as "XP" in this theory, as in (35)), and no further projection is possible. As a closed category cannot project further, it is also a maximal projection. Notice that the reverse is not true. While a closed projection is always a maximal projection, being a maximal projection does not imply it is closed (by agreement). In fact, projections of lexical categories do have maximal projections, but they never have closed projections, simply because lexical heads do not have agreement features (therefore, there is no independent "LP", a closed lexical projection).

Recall that agreement features are the driving force for movement in syntax. Since only functional categories bear these features, it follows that only functional categories induce movement; lexical categories never trigger movement. And this is well in accord with the facts: NP-movement (passive and raising) moves a noun phrase to [Spec, I^{max}]; passive in a noun phrase is the process of moving a noun phrase to [Spec, D^{max}]; and *wh*-movement moves a *wh*-phrase to [Spec, C^{max}] (note that in Relativized X′ theory, maximal projections are not inherently related to bar-levels, even if the latter notion exists at all). It looks as though all typical movements (at least in English) are to the specifier position of a functional category. To sharpen the notion of "Spec" still further, Relativized X′ theory proposes that Spec be defined in terms of agreement:

(36) The specifier of X is a maximal projection that agrees with X.

Thus, a moved *wh*-phrase, the subject that agrees with I, etc. are all Specs, but lexical categories do not have Specs, since they do not have agreement features to license Specs. The definition of Spec in (36) clarifies the nature of Spec more than ever: Spec is the landing site for movement.

Relativized X′ theory has an important implication for the theory of movement. The issue, again, has to do with the notion of Spec. In the standard theory of movement, an empty category Δ is generated in the position of a specifier at D-structure (or in the course of a derivation; see Chomsky 1993a) as a target for substitution. However, it is impossible to justify this empty category in Relativized X′ theory. It is not licensed by θ-assignment, since a functional head never assigns a θ-role, and it is not licensed by agreement because it is the moved maximal projection, not an empty category, that agrees with the functional head. Also, the empty category never appears on the surface; it is there only to be replaced by a moved category, and it always has to be "erased" before the derivation ends. Therefore, such a superfluous empty category is eliminated in Relativized X′ theory, and, hence, substitution operations no longer exist as operations that "substitute for" some existing element. Formally, then, the operation that is involved in "substitution" is no different from Adjunction, in the sense that it does not substitute for anything.[11] Thus, the traditional notion of "substitution" transformation, with the dubious empty category Δ, is eliminated from the theory of grammar (but see note 11). And if phrase structure composition is also carried out by a formal operation Adjunction (whose application is driven by feature discharge), as we saw above, then it seems that there is one uniform operation which is responsible for both phrase structure building and movement, namely, Adjunction.[12]

Relativized X' theory minimized, in fact virtually eliminated, the need for an X' schema, which had been assumed throughout the previous development of X' theory. It takes seriously the notions (i) projection and (ii) feature discharge, and claims that every position in phrase structure must be licensed in terms of these notions. Since lexical and functional categories have different feature specifications – in particular, only the latter bears agreement features – the modes of projection of these two types of category must reflect the difference. Thus, only functional categories have Specs as a landing site for movement, triggered by agreement features associated with the functional heads, whereas lexical categories never have Specs and their projections are thus never closed. From this, it immediately follows that if a language lacks functional categories (or if its functional system is inert), then the phrase structure of the language is essentially based on the lexical system, phrasal projections in the language are never closed, and no syntactic movement is triggered. Fukui (1986, 1988a) argues that this is indeed the case in languages like Japanese, and demonstrates that a variety of typological properties of Japanese, e.g., the lack of *wh*-movement, the existence of multiple-nominative/genitive constructions, scrambling, and many others, are derived from this fundamental parametric property of the language.

The total elimination of X' theory was proposed and carried out by Chomsky's (1994) "bare phrase structure" theory (see also Kayne 1994 for a different approach). The bare theory is couched within the "minimalist program" (Chomsky 1993a), according to which all the principles and entities of grammar must be motivated and justified either by the properties of two "interface representations", LF and PF, or by considerations of economy (see Chomsky 1993a for details; see also Collins 2001). Most of the basic claims of Relativized X' theory carry over to the bare theory, except for a particular characterization of Spec in the former as an X^{max} agreeing with a head (see (36); also the next section for some relevant discussion).

Chomsky argues that (the standard) X' theory specifies much redundant information, while the only structural information needed is that a "head" and a "non-head" combine to create a unit. He then proposes that a phrase structure is constructed in a bottom-up fashion by a uniform operation called "Merge", which combines two elements, say α and β, and projects one of them as the head. This is illustrated in (37), where the prime simply means the category is projected (see note 10):

(37) α β $\xrightarrow[\text{Merge}]{}$ if α projects   α' (= α [+projected])
                                  /\
                                 α   β

              if β projects   β' (= β [+projected])
                                  /\
                                 α   β

Since Merge does not specify the linear order of α and β, the tree structures in (37) can be more formally, and more accurately, represented as in (38):

(38) K = [γ, [α, β]], where γ ∈ [α, β]

(38) states that Merge forms a new object K by combining two objects α and β, and specifies one of them as the projecting element (hence the head of K). Merge applies recursively to form a new structure.

Chomsky further argues that Merge is involved in both phrase structure composition and movement processes. Suppose that Merge is to apply to α and K, to form a new unit L, with K projecting:

(39) αK $\xrightarrow[\text{Merge}]{}$ L (=K')
                              /\
                             α   K

The only difference between simple phrase structure building and movement is whether α in (39) comes from the lexicon (or from the Numeration, in current terms), as in the case of phrase structure building, or from within K (leaving its copy in the original place), as in the case of movement. Thus, the bare theory unifies phrase structure composition and movement in terms of the single operation Merge (which is somewhat reminiscent of Adjunction in Relativized X' theory).

A "maximal projection" is also defined relationally in the bare theory: a category that does not project any further in a given configuration is a maximal projection. The terms "complement" and "specifier" are defined in the usual way. Note that the definition of the latter concept (Spec) in the bare theory is different from that of Spec in Relativized X' theory. In Relativized X' theory, Spec is defined in terms of agreement (cf. (36)), with the consequence that only functional categories have Specs. In the bare theory, on the other hand, agreement does not play any significant role in defining Spec, and hence Spec is defined in the traditional way as a phrase that is immediately dominated by a maximal projection. This (and the associated distinction between X^{max} (a simple maximal projection) and XP (a closed maximal projection)) seems to be the only substantive difference, apart from details, between Relativized X' theory and the bare theory. See Fukui

(1991), Fukui and Saito (1992), and Saito and Fukui (1998) for some arguments for the necessity of X^{max}/XP distinction. See also the next section for some relevant discussion.

With Chomsky's bare theory, X' theory is now completely eliminated as an independent module of grammar. The basic insights of X' theory, in particular, the insight that every phrase is headed in human language (cf. (18a)), is straightforwardly expressed as a fundamental property of the operation Merge, without postulating an additional "principle".

However, of the three kinds of information about syntactic representations listed in (2), i.e., (2i) Dominance, (2ii) Labeling, and (2iii) linear order (Precedence), the last kind of information is not encoded at all in Chomsky's formulation of Merge given above. In fact, whether or not the theory of phrase structure should specify the linear order of elements still remains open in current research, to which we now turn.

4 Linear order in phrase structure

The concept of linear order in a phrase marker was never questioned in an earlier framework of generative grammar. In fact, it was, as stated in (2), one of the few crucial primitive concepts in the theory of phrase structure, and a variety of grammatical rules was formulated with a crucial reference to linear order (see, for example, "pronominalization" transformation in the 1960s). However, it has been increasingly less obvious that linear order plays a role at all in language computation, apart from phonology. Thus, virtually all the principles and conditions assumed in the principles-and-parameters theory in the 1980s are formulated purely in hierarchical terms (in terms of domination and c-command), without referring to linear order. The "head parameter" (and its variants) seems to be the only notion in linguistic theory which crucially refers to linear order.

Kayne (1994) challenges this notion of head parameter. He proposes a universal principle, the Linear Correspondence Axiom (LCA), which states essentially that asymmetric c-command imposes a linear ordering of terminal elements. More specifically, the LCA dictates that if a nonterminal X asymmetrically c-commands a nonterminal Y in a given phrase marker P, then all terminals dominated by X must precede or follow all terminals dominated by Y in P. Kayne takes the relevant ordering to be precedence, rather than subsequence (following), based on his assumptions about the relation between terminals and "time slots" (see Kayne 1994 for more details). Thus, within Kayne's theory, asymmetric c-command relations uniquely map into precedence relations: all terminals dominated by X precede all terminals dominated by Y, in the configuration stated above. It then follows, given Kayne's formulation, that there is a universal S(pecifier)-H(ead)-C(omplement) order (in particular, S(ubject)-V(erb)-O(bject)), with other orders (S-C-H/S-O-V, for example) being derived via movement. With the universal S-H-C order, the head parameter is entirely eliminated.

Note that in Kayne's theory, linear order still plays a role in the core computation of language, though redundantly, because it is entirely determined by asymmetric c-command relations. In other words, Kayne proposes that linear order is not parametrized and that it is uniquely determined by asymmetric c-command relations, given his LCA, which he claims to apply at every syntactic level. But linear order is still defined and remains visible throughout the derivation and could conceivably play a role in the core computation of language.

Chomsky (1994, 1995b), adopting and incorporating the basic insights of Kayne's LCA into his bare theory, makes a step further toward complete elimination of linear order from the core of language computation. As we saw in the preceding section, Chomsky's bare theory, the recursive procedure Merge in particular, does not encode any information regarding linear order of syntactic elements. This is based on his understanding that there is no clear evidence that linear order plays a role at LF or in the core computation of human language.[13] Thus, he assumes that linear order is not defined and hence does not play a role in the core computation of language, and suggests that ordering is a property of the phonological component, a proposal that has been occasionally made in various forms in the literature. Specifically, he claims that a modified version of the LCA applies as a principle of the phonological component to the output of Morphology, a subcomponent of the phonological component (see Chomsky 1995b for detailed discussion). Thus, under Chomsky's proposal, phrase structure is defined without reference to linear order in the core computational part of human language, and will later be assigned linear order by (a modified version of) the LCA in the phonological component.

By contrast, Saito and Fukui (1998) (see also Fukui 1993b, Fukui and Saito 1992) claim that linear order indeed plays an important role in the core computational part of human language, and argue that the head parameter, or more precisely a modified version of it, should be maintained. One way, proposed in Saito and Fukui (1998), to incorporate the head parameter into the bare theory is to replace the set notation $[\alpha, \beta]$ in (38), reproduced here as (40), by an ordered pair $<\alpha, \beta>$, thereby specifying which of the two elements projects in a given language. Thus, we have (41) instead of (40):

(40) Chomsky's Merge: $K = [\gamma, [\alpha, \beta]]$, where $\gamma[[\alpha, \beta]$

(41) Saito and Fukui's parametrized Merge: $K = [\gamma, <\alpha, \beta>]$, where $\gamma[[\alpha, \beta]$

If γ takes the value "α", we have a "head-initial/left-headed" language such as English, whereas if $\gamma = \beta$, a "head-last/right-headed" language like Japanese is defined. Thus, in left-headed English, elements can be merged only on the *right* side of a head, whereas, in right-headed Japanese, Merge occurs only on the *left* side of a head. If something is to be introduced on the opposite side of the structure (i.e., on the left side of a head in English, and on the right side of a head in Japanese), it must be "adjoined" to the target, creating a multisegment structure (see Chomsky 1986a, 1995b, for relevant discussion on substitution v. adjunction). A case in point is the status of subjects in these languages. The subject in English is in an adjoined position because it appears on the left side of the head, where projection of the target is prohibited by (41) as it is parametrized for English. The subject in Japanese, on the other hand, is introduced into phrase structure by Merge (i.e., substitution; see below), since it shows up on the left side of the head, where merger is possible (Japanese is a right-headed language). See Saito and Fukui (1998) for more detailed discussion, as well as illustrations of this point.

Saito and Fukui argue that given the parametrized version of Merge (41), it becomes possible to characterize the traditional "adjunction" operation, viz., scrambling in Japanese and Heavy NP Shift in English, as paradigm cases of Merge (i.e., as substitution, in the sense that they always accompany projection of the target),[14] and hence, given the costless nature of Merge (Chomsky 1995b), the optionality of these operations, a matter that has been quite disturbing for the general economy approach to movement (Chomsky 1991b), is also straightforwardly accounted for. On the other hand, traditional "substitution" operations (*wh*-movement and NP-movement) are analysed in this system as genuine adjunction since they never induce projection of the target, creating a multisegment structure of the target (see Saito and Fukui 1998 for much detail). Further, they point out that the "directionality" of these optional movements correlates with the "directionality" of projection in the language. Thus, head-initial/left-headed English has rightward Heavy NP Shift, whereas head-last/right-headed Japanese exhibits leftward scrambling, but no other combination is allowed. It is clear that such a correlation can be captured only by a parametrized Merge embodying linear order, as in (41). Saito and Fukui show that a number of other differences between English and Japanese also follow from their theory of phrase structure.

The parametrized Merge has an important implication for the theory of locality on movement. It has been known since Cattell (1976), Kayne (1981), and Huang (1982) that a non-complement maximal projection forms an island for movement (see also Rizzi 2001 for some relevant discussion). Thus, extraction out of subjects and adverbial adjuncts results in ungrammaticality, as shown in (42):

(42) a. ?*Who$_i$ did [a picture of t_i] please John
 b. ?*Who$_i$ did John go home [because he saw t_i]

The effects illustrated by (42a) and (42b) are called the Subject Condition effects and the Adjunct Condition effects, respectively. There are two important problems with respect to these effects. One is how to unify them in a natural way. The other problem has to do with the cross-linguistic considerations of these effects. The Adjunct Condition effects are generally assumed to be universal, whereas the Subject Condition effects are known to show cross-linguistic variation. Specifically, it appears that while SVO languages generally exhibit the Subject Condition effects, SOV languages systematically lack the effects (Kayne 1984; see also Aissen 1996 for related discussion). Huang (1982) proposes the Condition on Extraction Domain (CED), which unifies the Subject and Adjunct Condition effects in terms of the notion of "proper government", and suggests a possible way of accounting for the observed cross-linguistic difference with respect to the Subject Condition effects (see Huang 1982 for details). Huang's CED was later incorporated into Chomsky's (1986a) barriers theory as a central ingredient of the latter system.

Takahashi (1994a), working under the general "economy" guidelines (see Collins 2001) and extending Chomsky (1986a) and Chomsky and Lasnik (1993), proposes to derive these effects from the Minimal Link Condition (MLC) and constraints on adjunction sites. The former condition, when interpreted derivationally, requires that movement go through every possible landing site. If any XP dominating the moved elements is a potential adjunction site in the case of A'-movement, this implies that the *wh*-phrases in (42) must adjoin to every maximal position that intervenes between their initial positions and the matrix [Spec, CP]. In particular, *who* must adjoin to the subject DP in (42a), and the adverbial CP in (42b). But if adjunction to subjects and adjuncts/modifiers is prohibited, as argued in Chomsky (1986a), then the moved *wh*-phrase must skip a possible landing site in these examples. Hence, (42a–b) both violate the MLC.

The remaining problem is to derive the constraints on adjunction sites. There have been some proposals that treat the subject case and the adjunct (modifier) case separately. (See, for example, Chomsky 1986a, Takahashi 1994a.) However, Saito and Fukui argue that their parametrized Merge approach opens up a refreshingly new way to unify these two cases. Suppose, following a standard assumption, that an adjunct (modifier) appears in a position adjoined to a maximal projection.[15] Then, descriptively, what is prohibited in the adjunct (modifier) case is adjunction to an adjoined phrase. And this extends automatically to the subject case, since a subject in English (or SVO languages generally) is in an adjoined position, as we discussed above. The explanation for the lack of the Subject Condition effects in Japanese (or SOV languages generally) is straightforward: subjects in this language are not in an adjoined position, but rather are introduced into structure by Merge (substitution). The question, thus, reduces to why adjunction to an adjoined position is disallowed.

Saito and Fukui propose that this is due to the indeterminacy of the adjunction site that arises in the relevant case. Consider the following configuration:

(43)

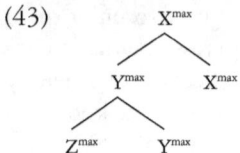

Both X^{max} and Y^{max} neither dominate nor exclude Z^{max} (see Chomsky 1986a for the definitions of these structural notions). Hence, if "adjunction" is defined as in (44), then Z^{max} in (43) is adjoined simultaneously to X^{max} and Y^{max}:

(44) α *is adjoined to* β = $_{def}$ neither α nor β dominates the other and β does not exclude α.

Adjunction to adjoined phrases, then, is excluded by the following plausible condition:

(45) An adjunction site must be unique.

Saito and Fukui argue that the condition (45) need not be stipulated as an independent condition on adjunction site, but rather is an instance of the general uniqueness condition on the licensing of (nonroot) elements in a phrase marker. (See Saito and Fukui 1998 for a precise formulation of the principle as well as much detailed discussion on relevant points.) Thus, their parametrized Merge, which incorporates the notion of linear order (the head parameter, in particular), unifies, without having recourse to such notions as "proper government" (Huang 1982) and "L-marking" (Chomsky 1986a), the classical cases of CED (the Subject and the Adjunct Condition effects), offering a natural explanation for the parametric variation associated with the Subject Condition effects.

The issue of linear order in phrase structure (and movement) is a complex matter and remains open for future research. It is probably conceptually desirable if we can eliminate the concept of linear order from the core part of human language computation, and locate it in the phonological component, where the importance of linear order is firmly established. On the other hand, if the evidence presented in Saito and Fukui's work is real, then it constitutes a rather strong reason for postulating linear order in the portion of grammar where the theory of economy (cf. their arguments with respect to optionality) and that of locality (recall their reunification of CED) are relevant. See also Fukui and Takano (1998) for related discussion on this issue.

5 Summary and conclusion

This chapter has discussed the development of the theory of phrase structure in generative grammar. Phrase structure of human language was described in terms of phrase structure rules; context-sensitive phrase structure rules in an earlier theory of generative grammar, and then context-free phrase structure rules with an enriched lexicon in the Standard Theory. X′ theory was proposed in the late 1960s on the basis of the recognition of the observed deficiencies of phrase structure rules as a means for explaining the nature of phrase structure of human language: (i) phrase structure rules are "too permissive", in that they allow rules generating various structures that are actually never attested, and (ii) phrase structure rules cannot capture certain systematically observed "cross-categorial" generalizations. X′ theory, as an invariant principle of UG, overcomes these problems by claiming (i) that every phrase is "headed" (i.e., has an endocentric structure), with the head X projecting to larger phrases, (ii) that heads (categories) are not atoms, but rather complexes of universal features, and (iii) that projection of heads conforms to the general "X′ schemata" provided by UG. (See (18a–c) in section 2.)

The development of X′ theory from its inception up until the mid-1980s can be characterized as a process of sharpening and elaborating the format of X′ schemata, in such a way as to expand the scope of X′ theory to extensive descriptive material. As we saw in section 2, during this period, the structure of clauses was reanalysed so as to fall under the scope of X′ theory, and the notion of "Spec" was gradually narrowed down to directly express its nature in phrase markers.

The subsequent development of X′ theory from the mid-1980s to the present can be described, as we discussed in section 3, as an accumulated attempt to minimize the role of X′ schemata, while maintaining the basic insight of X′ theory. Along the way, some novel analyses of particular constructions in phrase structure were proposed (the DP-analysis and the Predicate-Internal Subject Hypothesis), yielding numerous important empirical (cross-linguistic) studies concerning the structure of clauses and noun phrases. Relativized X′ theory makes a fundamental distinction between lexical categories and functional categories, and claims that phrase structure building is essentially feature driven. A "relativized" notion of maximal projection and the further sharpening of the concept of "Spec" in terms of agreement are also major claims of this theory. Motivated by the minimalist program, the "bare phrase structure" theory completely eliminates the X′ schemata, in terms of the recursive procedure Merge, keeping the major insight of X′ theory almost intact.

Thus, at the current stage of the theory, of the three basic claims of the classical X′ theory (i)–(iii) stated above, (i) and (ii) are preserved in the bare theory, while the claim (iii), i.e., the existence of the X′ schemata, is explicitly denied. In this sense, there seem to be few fundamental differences between the bare theory and other approaches to phrase structure. Various approaches to phrase structure appear to have started converging and fruitfully influencing each other. For instance, given the foremost importance of features in the theory of phrase structure (and in the minimalist program generally), the explicit mechanisms of feature systems developed in other approaches (e.g., in the GPSG/HPSG traditions) may well have an important impact on further development of the bare theory.

There are of course numerous remaining problems in the theory of phrase structure, many of which, including the influential "shell" structure proposed by Larson (1988), I could not discuss in this chapter. Section 4 briefly discussed one theoretical problem that remains open, i.e., the status of linear order. Various other theoretical questions remain, and as always, vast numbers of descriptive problems keep challenging the current theory of phrase structure. The theory of phrase structure, in my view, will continue to be one of the central topics of linguistic theory for years to come.

13 The Visibility Guideline for functional categories

Verb-raising in Japanese and related issues

with Hiromu Sakai

1 Introduction

Although the traditional term "function words" or Chomsky's (1970) notion of "non-lexical categories" has much in common with the contemporary notion of "functional categories", it seems fair to say that it is since the mid-1980s, when a class of elements was given the name "functional categories/elements" (Fukui 1986, Speas 1986, Abney 1987, among others) and their properties were first discussed in detail, that these elements have been a focus of much attention within the context of universal grammar (UG). The importance of these elements for the theory of grammar comes from the fact that (i) they are taken to be the sources of driving force for movement transformations, and (ii) they are also identified as a locus of cross-linguistic variation. Thus, ever since the notion was (re-)introduced in the mid-1980s, much syntactic discussion has been centring on the nature and properties of functional categories as they pertain to UG as well as to characterization of particular grammars. Japanese syntax is no exception, which is why we wish to discuss in this article some of the main issues concerning "functional categories in Japanese".

Section 2 of this article is devoted to a general discussion of functional categories. A brief historical overview of the development of the notion of functional categories in linguistic theory is presented in section 2.1, and in section 2.2 various hypotheses concerning the functional categories in Japanese are discussed. As a general theoretical guideline for a fruitful discussion of functional categories, the "Visibility Guideline for Functional Categories" is proposed, which dictates that functional categories be detected in the primary linguistic data. Various past proposals concerning the functional categories in Japanese are examined in light of this guideline.

Section 3 focuses on the issue of verb-raising in Japanese as a representative case of the debates concerning functional categories in Japanese syntax. Koizumi's (2000) arguments in favour of the existence of (string vacuous) overt verb-raising in the language are taken up and critically examined in detail. And it is concluded that, quite interesting though they are, none of his arguments is convincing enough to draw the conclusion that Japanese has the process of overt verb-raising.

The discussion in section 3 calls for an alternative analysis of coordination in Japanese, which is one of the central cases of Koizumi's arguments for overt verb-raising in the language. Section 4 offers such an alternative analysis, which claims that the construction is formed in the PF (Phonetic Form) component (or the "phonological" component) by means of a reduction or deletion of identical predicates and a reanalysis of adjacent elements into a single constituent.

Section 5 extends our discussion to case marking in Japanese. After a brief review of the past analyses of Japanese case marking which have developed side by side with general linguistic theory (the standard theory, the "government-binding" theory, and the minimalist program), it is suggested that case marking in a language like Japanese should take place in the PF component, essentially along the lines of Kuroda (1965, 1978, among others; see also Fukui and Takano, 1998), and contrary to much recent work on Japanese case marking.

Section 6 further pursues the issues of case marking in Japanese, and presents some evidence in favour of the PF analysis of case marking. Interactions between PF reanalysis and case marking are considered, and it is argued that the "syntactic case marking" approach (i.e., the assumption that Japanese case marking takes place in the narrow syntax) faces various problems. The discussion is then extended to the so-called light verb construction, and the same conclusion is reached based on the properties of this construction.

Section 7 summarizes the discussion in this paper, and makes some concluding remarks on functional categories in UG and in Japanese. A tentative view on the overall picture of Japanese syntax that emerges from our discussion is also presented.

2 General discussion

In this section, we first briefly go over the historical development of functional categories in linguistic theory, and, as a basis for the discussion that follows, we propose the "Visibility Guideline for Functional Categories" (section 2.1). We then go on to discuss various issues concerning the functional categories in Japanese as they have appeared in the past literature, and examine the previous proposals in light of the Visibility Guideline (section 2.2).

2.1 *Functional categories in universal grammar*

The concept of functional categories (or functional elements) started attracting much attention in linguistic theory around the mid-1980s. There are two major reasons for the upheaval of functional categories in this era. One has to do with the theory of phrase structure and movement, and the other is concerned with comparative syntax, i.e., the study of cross-linguistic variation. Let us consider these matters in some detail.

Modifying the previous analyses of *wh*-movement, Chomsky (1986a) proposes that *wh*-movement be analysed as an operation which moves a *wh*-phrase into the specifier position of a complementizer (notated as [Spec, C]), in the sense of X′ theory. Given this analysis of *wh*-movement, all movement (substitution, in particular) operations, apart from head movement, are now analysed as movement into Spec positions. Thus, Passive/Raising (so-called NP-movement) is a movement into [Spec, I] (where I stands for inflectional elements), Passive in a noun phrase is a movement into [Spec, N] (N is a Noun), and *wh*-movement, which has long been assumed to be a movement into a C position, is now analysed as a movement into [Spec, C]. Other options are independently excluded by principles of UG, and the theory of movement is now greatly simplified.

Around the same time, the basic properties of functional categories were identified (Fukui and Speas 1986, Abney 1987), and two major proposals were made with respect to phrase structure analyses. One is the so-called "DP (Determiner Phrase) analysis", which takes a determiner (D) to be the head of a nominal expression (Fukui and Speas 1986, Abney 1987, and references cited therein). The other is the "Predicate-Internal Subject Hypothesis", according to which all arguments, including crucially the subject (external) argument, are base-generated within the predicate's own projection (see, among others, Fukui 1986, Kitagawa 1986, Koopman and Sportiche 1991, Kuroda 1988, Speas 1986). There are variants of these (now well-known) analyses with diverse consequences. One variant, developed by Fukui's series of works since 1986 (see also Speas 1990, for a different development based on the same ideas), incorporates these analyses into the theory of phrase structure that he develops (the so-called Relativized X′ theory), which essentially eliminates the need for stipulating the X′ schemata, minimizing the role of X′ theory in phrase structure composition while maintaining its basic descriptive effects.

The core idea of Relativized X′ theory is that phrase structure composition is on a par with movement in that it is also driven by feature discharge. It has been assumed, at least since Chomsky (1970), that lexical items in the lexicon are bundles of features such as [±N], [±V], etc. Relativized X′ theory takes this idea seriously and claims that features are actually the driving force for constructing phrase structure. Items of the lexicon are divided into two major subtypes: lexical categories and functional categories. The latter type of categories roughly corresponds to the traditional non-lexical categories, renamed in consideration of their nature. Lexical categories have substantive content, and include noun, verbs, adjectives, etc. They typically enter into θ-marking (leading, eventually, to the construction of predicate-argument structure at LF (Logical Form)). Functional categories do not have substantive content, and do not enter into θ-marking, although they do have other feature structures, including categorial features, agreement features, etc. Lexical categories play an important role in interpretation of linguistic expressions, and indeed, most of the items in the lexicon belong to this type. Functional categories, on the other hand, do not play a comparable role in interpretation of linguistic expressions; their role is largely restricted to "grammatical" (or "computational") aspects of linguistic structure.[1] These categories constitute a small, and often closed, set, which include C, I, D, and a few others.

Thus, there exists a general division of labour between lexical and functional categories as to their roles in linguistic expressions:

(1) (i) Lexical categories: the conceptual aspects of linguistic expressions.
 (ii) Functional categories: the computational aspects of linguistic expressions.

Lexical categories bear semantic features, including in particular features having to do with θ-roles. They assign (or "discharge") θ-roles or features associated with them to other phrases, thereby forming larger structures that embed them. Functional categories do not bear θ-roles, their role being restricted to purely formal and computational aspects of linguistic structure such as marking grammatical structures or triggering movement operations. Some functional heads bear "agreement features", and these agreement features attract a maximal projection to their neighbourhoods (their Specs), in order for the latter to agree with the former. Thus, functional categories are indeed the "drive" for syntactic movement operations in the Relativized X' theory. Lexical categories, in contrast, lack agreement features of this kind, and hence do not induce movement. Furthermore, since [Spec, X] is defined in the Relativized X' theory as a maximal projection that agrees with the head X, it follows that only functional categories with agreement features have an ability to license the Spec positions; lexical categories (and functional categories with no agreement features) never license Spec positions.

The idea of functional categories as the major driving force for movement opened up a new way of looking at cross-linguistic variation, and facilitated much subsequent work on comparative syntax in terms of the properties of functional elements in various languages. Given the nature and role of functional categories, it was proposed that language variation be restricted (apart from ordering restrictions) to the functional domain of the lexicon (Fukui, 1986, 1988a; see also Borer, 1984, particularly for an illuminating discussion on the role of inflectional elements in language variation), and this proposal contributed significantly to constructing a more restrictive theory of comparative syntax. At the same time, numerous "new" functional categories were proposed in the late 1980s and in the early 1990s (initiated in part by J.-Y. Pollock's influential article (Pollock 1989)), achieving tremendous descriptive success,[2] although from an explanatory point of view, it was clear that the class of possible functional categories has to be severely restricted in a principled way.

There are various reasons for the emergence of "new" functional categories in the late 1980s. One reason is certainly "descriptive pressure", i.e., to achieve descriptive adequacy, it often seems necessary to enrich the descriptive apparatus that is permitted by UG. This is reminiscent of the situation of generative transformational grammar up to the early 1970s, where new transformations were added one after another as new phenomena were discovered, so to speak. Like transformations, functional categories are a useful descriptive tool whose attractiveness may be irresistible as one faces descriptive problems. They create new structures, with possibilities of additional movement operations (either head movement or movement of a maximal projection, or both).

Another reason is the absence of a general theory of functional categories in UG. There have been proposals as to the class of possible lexical categories in UG (see Chomsky 1970, Jackendoff 1977, among many others). Thus, if one assumes with Chomsky (1970) that all lexical categories are defined in terms of the [$\pm$N] and [$\pm$V] features, then there will be, in principle, only four possible lexical categories. By contrast, there was no widely assumed proposal in the late 1980s or early 1990s concerning the "possible functional categories in UG", and this led to the situation where one was tempted to create a "new functional category" when the phenomenon at hand seemed to require a new structure (and a movement).

The general theoretical trend in the 1980s constitutes another motivation for proposing "new" functional categories. Since the crystallization of the principles-and-parameters approach around 1980, efforts have been concentrated on enriching the content of UG, in an attempt to shift the descriptive burden from particular grammars to UG. Thus, during this period of "expanding UG", it was, at least implicitly, considered desirable to add new entities (new principles, new elements, etc.) to UG. Creation of "new" functional categories occurred as part of this general theoretical tendency and it was considered warranted.

Against this general trend, an attempt was indeed made from the outset to make it clear that postulated functional categories have to be fully justified by the evidence. Thus, Fukui (1986, 1988a) argues that a language like Japanese, in the absence of overt evidence in the language, lacks (active) functional categories in the lexicon, and he goes on to demonstrate that from this fundamental "parametric" property, various seemingly unrelated properties of Japanese are deductively derived (given Relativized X′ theory). The basic view on functional categories behind this proposal can be summarized as follows.

(2) The existence of a functional category has to be detected from overt evidence.

Under this view, the inventory of functional categories in UG cannot be assumed a priori, but rather, each functional category has to be justified based on the evidence. If there is no such evidence, the functional category in question has to be non-existent in the language. The core idea of this proposal was effectively adopted by Radford (1990) and was applied to the study of language acquisition. But the acquisition study of functional categories along these lines was overwhelmed by the proposal that UG is equipped with a full inventory of functional categories (Poeppel and Wexler 1993, Wexler 1994, among others). Iatridou (1990) examines that nature of "Agr" (a "newly created" functional head in the late 1980s) in the context of the theory of functional categories in general, and reaches a conclusion similar to (2). Fukui (1995b, written in 1992) further pursues a restrictive theory of functional categories in UG, and proposes that functional categories, like lexical categories, be characterized in terms of the [±N] and [±V] features (in addition to [±lexical] and [±functional] features; see Fukui 1995b, for details). He also suggests that the "genuine" functional categories are invisible at LF, and those LF-invisible functional categories can be completely missing in the lexicon of a given language (unless there is overt evidence at PF (Phonetic Form)).

The "minimalist program" was set forth in the early 1990s (Chomsky 1993a), which takes seriously the fact that language is embedded within other cognitive systems (conceptual-intentional and sensorimotor systems, in particular), apparently satisfying the "requirements" of the neighbouring cognitive systems in an optimal way. This research program specifically addresses the question of how many of the properties of UG can be explained "on principled grounds", i.e., in terms of the conditions imposed on language by the other cognitive systems (the "interface conditions") or in terms of the general principles of "economy/optimality" that regulate the properties of organisms including the human language faculty. In the minimalist program, every device in UG (entity, principle, etc.) that is employed in characterizing languages has to be closely and critically examined to determine to what extent it can be eliminated in favour of a principled account based on the interface conditions or general principles of economy or optimality. Thus, functional categories, too, should face such a minimalist critique.

The minimalist program effectively puts an end to the above-mentioned strong tendency toward enriching the devices of UG, including, in particular, functional categories. Applying minimalist guidelines to functional categories, Chomsky (1995b: 240) claims that "[p]ostulation of a functional category has to be justified, either by output [i.e., interface; N.F.] conditions (phonetic and semantic interpretation) or by theory-internal arguments. It bears a burden of proof, which is often not so easy to meet." Continuing to rest on the works mentioned so far (cf. (2)), we would like to modify Chomsky's remarks slightly, and propose the following guideline.[3]

(3) *The Visibility Guideline for Functional Categories*
A functional category has to be visible (i.e., detectable) in the primary linguistic data.

We hold that the nature of functional categories is to "drive" syntactic operations (by having "uninterpretable features" in current terminology). While it is true that functional categories may play a role at LF, we take this to be "accidental", not directly bearing on the nature of these categories. For example, the semantic notion of "specificity/referentiality" may be represented by the functional category D, but it may also be represented in some other way (see Chierchia 1998). There is no reason that the mood or force of a sentence must be indicated by the functional category C; it can be indicated by a lexical head or a particle, for example. The concept of negation can be encoded into a given language in various ways that are permitted by UG; the use of a functional category may not be even an option. We therefore maintain a narrower notion of functional categories that these elements have in principle no bearing on semantic interpretation (invisible at LF). If this is true, the Visibility Guideline for Functional Categories (the Visibility Guideline, henceforth) in (3) simply dictates that a functional category be visible/detectable at PF.

There are three ways that a functional category becomes visible or detectable at PF. One is to bear phonetic content by itself (and to be pronounced). Having phonetic content, then, the functional category becomes visible in its own right at PF. Another is to influence the morphological shape of a neighbouring lexical category (a verb, for example). A third way for a functional category to become visible or detectable is to trigger a movement of a maximal projection into its neighbourhood, thereby affecting the "canonical word order" of a given language, which in turn signals that a syntactic movement has occurred. The first possibility (i.e., its having phonetic content) is a direct way of becoming visible or detectable at PF. The other two possibilities represent an indirect signalling of a functional category in that it is not the functional category itself that is visible at PF, but its existence can be detected from other indications in a linguistic expression.

Furthermore, the direct signalling (the first possibility) and the indirect signalling (the second and the third possibilities) seem to be mutually exclusive (see Fukui 1986 for an early observation to this effect). Thus, Fukui and Takano (1998: 55) make the following generalization:

(4)   A functional head H enters into feature checking only if H lacks phonetic content.

Assuming that the second and third possibilities are driven by some sort of feature checking (or its equivalent, e.g., feature matching), statement (4) implies that an overt functional category never triggers feature checking (and hence movement). This prediction seems to be borne out in a wide variety of cross-linguistic cases. See Fukui and Takano (1998) for further discussion.

In the remainder of this article, we will consider various proposals concerning functional categories and related phenomena in Japanese in light of the Visibility Guideline (3), coupled with the generalization (4).

2.2 Functional categories and Japanese syntax

The status of "functional categories" in Japanese has a rather ironical history. As soon as the theory of functional categories was put forth in the mid-1980s, it was hypothesized that Japanese lacks active functional categories. In fact, in Fukui's (1986) system of phrase structure, this parametric statement about functional categories in Japanese was an integral part of his efforts to construct a comparative model which derives major differences between the Japanese-type languages and the English-type languages.[4] Thus, even though an initial theory of functional categories was proposed in the context of a comparative syntax of English and Japanese, the study of Japanese syntax did not play any substantive role in the subsequent developments of the theory of functional categories.

Fukui's hypothesis that Japanese lacks active functional categories was challenged by Tonoike (1987), who claims that Japanese possesses a set of functional categories but with no agreement features, a proposal which is along the lines of Kuroda (1988).[5] Fukui (1988a) argues that it is extremely difficult, if possible at all, to distinguish between a hypothesis that a given language lacks functional categories, and another hypothesis that the language possesses functional categories which are not "active" in the sense that they do not bear any agreement features. Given the Visibility Guideline, if a candidate "functional category" bears phonetic content, it is visible at PF and hence could be justified as an existing functional category in the language. And from the generalization (4) above, it follows that the functional category never enters into feature checking (agreement).

There are, however, at least two problems that arise in this connection. First, identifying a certain element in a language with a member of functional categories is no easy task. Thus, while it is true that the Japanese -*to* has a role of introducing some sort of a clause, it is another matter to determine whether or not it should be identified with the functional category C (attested in English, for example). One has to closely examine the properties of -*to* to see if this element exhibits various properties that justify its status as C in Japanese. The same holds true of other candidates for "functional categories" in Japanese. It is well known that Japanese has numerous elements that are not quite attested in English and other European languages (e.g., various kinds of particles). Simply classifying some of them as instances of "functional categories" (that do not induce agreement or feature checking) is just an arbitrary decision which does not contribute to a real understanding of the language (and UG). The second problem has to do with the "nature" of those alleged "functional categories" in Japanese. If the functional categories are present in a language, but they are not active, what does their existence mean exactly? Some of those functional categories do play a role in determining semantic interpretation. For example, -*ka* determines the scope of *wh*-phrases, and as such, it would be reasonable to analyse this element as a kind of "Question morpheme". It is a different matter, however, to claim that -*ka* is the Japanese counterpart of the complementizer in English (see Fukui 1986, 1988a for relevant discussion).

In the absence of a substantive general theory of functional categories, none of these (and many more) problems can even be properly addressed at this point. And this is why a number of efforts in the past fifteen years or so to "identify" functional categories in Japanese seem to have all failed. It is simply premature to try to "discover" functional categories in Japanese. It seems to us, then, that a meaningful question that can be asked at the present stage of our understanding is the following.

(5) Does Japanese exhibit formal and mechanical "feature checking phenomena" which are comparable in nature to those attested in other languages (such as English and other European languages)?

The "feature checking phenomena" here include those that are captured by a mechanism such as Agree/Match (see Chomsky 2000, 2001a, b) and those that are handled (controversially) by head movement. The problem is totally empirical, and the evidence has to be found by carefully examining the facts about Japanese syntax. Thus, when a certain "dependency" relation is found in Japanese, one cannot simply "assume" that this is a phenomenon to be handled by Agree/Match, without examining the nature of the dependency relation. It has to be shown that the dependency relation is indeed of a formal and mechanical nature that should be characterized by the operation Agree/Match.

Also, one cannot "assume" (without evidence) that Japanese has agreement (or feature checking) because English and other languages have been argued to exhibit agreement phenomena. Chomsky's remark of the following kind (cf. also Hattori 1971) is sometimes used (implicitly or explicitly) to justify assuming the set of functional categories and associated feature checking in Japanese. "One general working hypothesis that has proven very fruitful is that if some phenomenon is observed overtly in certain languages, then it probably applies covertly (i.e., without overt expressions at PF) in all languages in some manner" (Chomsky 1987: 69). It is certainly true that the research strategy guided by the working hypothesis in the above quote has been extremely successful in the development of linguistic theory in the past twenty years or so (C.-T. James Huang's work on "LF *wh*-movement" is a classical example). However, in all the successful cases, the relevant phenomena are carefully argued for, not just assumed. Thus, Huang (1982) examines the properties of *wh*-questions in English (where *wh*-phrases are overtly moved) and those of *wh*-questions in Chinese (where *wh*-phrases are not overtly moved), and he discovers various intricate similarities and differences between these two (types of) languages with respect to the behaviour of *wh*-questions. Then, he proposes that a unified account of these similarities and differences is readily available if it is assumed that *wh*-phrases in Chinese-type languages, even though they do not move overtly, actually undergo movement in the LF component. Here, the "assumption" is in fact argued for, and its plausibility is reasonably justified. Similar arguments are scarcely provided for the postulation of functional categories and associated feature checking phenomena in Japanese.

Furthermore, a word of caution is in order as to how to interpret the "working hypothesis" mentioned in the above quote. Following the current framework of generative grammar, let us assume that UG consists of two subcomponents, the lexicon and the computational system. With respect to the computational system, the "working hypothesis" makes good sense. If it is discovered that an operation (Merge, Agree/Match, etc.) is employed in one language, it means that the operation is "wired in" and is made available by UG. Thus, it is reasonable to expect that the operation is available to any human language and can be employed either overtly or covertly. However, the situation is not so clear with the lexicon. Suppose that a certain lexical item is attested in a language. Is it reasonable, then, to assume that every human language possesses this lexical item (either overtly or covertly)? This is a moot point even for those lexical elements (typically lexical categories) which generally play a role in semantic interpretation, thereby fulfilling interface conditions. For example, given the fact that Japanese has a variety of particles which contribute to the interpretation of a linguistic expression, is it reasonable to assume that English also has these particles (covertly)? The answer to this question is unclear, but no serious attempt has been made to justify "null particles" in English.[6] In the case of (genuine) functional categories playing no role in semantic interpretation, a reasonable conclusion is clear: One cannot assume the "universal" existence of functional categories. Each candidate for a functional category in each language has to have its existence justified on the basis of empirical evidence (available in the primary linguistic data, according to the Visibility Guideline).

Thus, we conclude that functional categories in Japanese and the phenomena associated with features of these categories have to be carefully justified in terms of empirical evidence in accordance with the Visibility Guideline (3). When a certain element is observed in Japanese with an LF function similar to that of a functional category in English (C, T, D, etc.), it is premature, without independent evidence, to identify the element in Japanese with the functional category in English, because the same LF role can be assumed by different categories (and not necessarily functional categories) across different languages. The lack of a substantive general theory of functional categories also makes it premature to identify "functional categories in Japanese". If a phenomenon related to a functional category (either a movement of a maximal projection or a head movement) is to be identified in Japanese, it is necessary to determine whether the given phenomenon is of the same nature as attested cases of agreement/movement induced by a functional category, i.e., whether it is of a formal and mechanical nature that should be handled by Agree/Match or head movement. In the next section, we will take up the case of T (Tense) in Japanese and will address these questions.

3 Verb-raising in Japanese: a case study

Among the functional categories attested in English and other European languages (C, T, D, etc.), we focus on the status of the category T in Japanese. This is mainly because a number of recent works on Japanese syntax (Watanabe 1993, 1996a, b, Ura 1994b, 1996, 1999, 2000, Kishimoto 2001, Koizumi 1995, 2000, Miyagawa 1997, 2001, among others) crucially assume that the category T exists as an independent functional head and that it plays various important roles in syntactic phenomena of Japanese, such as its verbal morphology, case marking, scrambling, and so on. If their arguments are convincing (based on compelling evidence), the category T is indeed visible in the narrow syntax of Japanese as well as in English. By contrast, Fukui (1986, 1995a: 109) argues that Japanese T (or I) is very defective and plays no vital role in narrow syntax except as a mere "place holder" for tense morphemes such as -*ru* (non-past) and -*ta* (past). In accordance with the Visibility Guideline introduced above, Fukui's claim can be interpreted to mean that the Japanese T, even though it is allowed to exist in the language, is visible only "on the PF side".

In recent literature on the syntax of European languages, it is widely assumed that the category T plays two significant roles in syntax. First, it hosts the V-to-T raising in overt V-raising languages such as French or Icelandic. Second, T is assumed to be a licenser of the nominative Case feature of a subject noun phrase in a finite clause. In an attempt to show that the same holds of Japanese, Otani and Whitman (1991), Koizumi (1995, 2000), and Miyagawa (2001), among others, argue for the existence of V-to-T raising in Japanese. As for the second role of T, Takezawa (1987, 1998), Watanabe (1993), Ura (1994b, 1996, 1999, 2000), and Miyagawa (1997), to name a few, claim that T plays an important role in licensing nominative Case (*ga*-marking) in Japanese. In this section, we focus on the arguments for V-to-T raising in Japanese proposed in the literature. We will show that a careful examination of verbal morphology in Japanese reveals that these previous arguments for V-to-T raising in Japanese are either inadequate or premature. Then, we present a piece of evidence that the Japanese V-T complex is actually created by a PF operation, i.e., so-called Morphological Merger proposed by Marantz (1988) and Halle and Marantz (1993). The issues surrounding nominative case marking in Japanese will be discussed in the following sections (particularly sections 5 and 6).

3.1 V-to-T raising in Japanese: a quick overview

Verb-raising phenomena have been extensively studied from the very beginning of the history of contemporary generative grammar. Thus, Chomsky (1957) presents a simple and elegant account for the complex properties of English verbal morphology in terms of Affix-Hopping and other transformations. Emonds (1978) also makes a significant contribution to the study of verbal morphology, by showing that systematic differences in finite verb positions between English and French are nicely accounted for on the basis of the presence or absence of overt verb-raising in these languages. Numerous works on verb second phenomena in Germanic languages also contribute to the study of verb-raising as it relates to inflectional morphology.

It should be noted in this connection that in the great majority of cases of European verb-raising languages, the result of verb-raising can be readily detected from the surface position of finite verbs. For instance, the position of a finite verb is clearly marked by its relative order with respect to adverbs and negation in languages like English or French. By contrast, in Japanese, which is a strict head-last language, the existence of verb-raising is not overtly manifested at all, i.e., it is always a case of "string vacuous" movement.[7]

Although earlier work on Japanese syntax often assumes "predicate raising" transformations, they are postulated just for the purpose of deriving surface/phonetic representations of complex predicates. This is because transformations are primarily motivated for deriving surface structure, which serves as an input for phonetic interpretation in the standard theory. In more recent frameworks in which the power of transformations is severely restricted, phonological or morphological reasons are not sufficient in motivating syntactic verb-raising, because Morphological Merger is also available for deriving the correct phonological or morphological structures of complex predicates.[8] Thus, many proposed arguments for the existence of "string vacuous" V-to-T raising in Japanese attempt to show either (i) that the remnant of V-to-T movement forms a syntactic constituent or (ii) that V-to-T raising has some sort of semantic effect. Otani and Whitman (1991) is a pioneering work of this type. They argue that the remnant of V-to-T movement undergoes VP ellipsis, and as a result of this, various apparent null-argument structures show the properties of VP ellipsis in Japanese. Hoji (1998c), however, argues against Otani and Whitman's (1991) claim, by demonstrating that the readings obtained in the alleged VP ellipsis constructions are in fact quite different from the readings associated with the VP ellipsis constructions in English.

While Hoji's arguments do not quite prove that Japanese lacks V-to-T raising, his refutation effectively reveals Otani and Whitman's argument to be inadequate (see also Koizumi 2000: 280 (note 1) for relevant discussion). Next, Koizumi (1995, 2000) takes over Otani and Whitman's idea that the remnant of V-to-T raising forms a syntactic constituent, and he presents a number of interesting empirical arguments in favour of the postulation of V-to-T raising in Japanese. Additional arguments are also presented for V-to-T raising, or V-to-v raising in more recent studies, such as Miyagawa (2001) and Kishimoto (2001), based on scope interpretation phenomena in Japanese. These arguments are unfortunately quite controversial because the primary data with respect to the scope interpretations do not seem to be solid enough. Sakai (2000a) actually reaches the opposite conclusion that general properties of scope interpretation of sentence-final elements indicate that there is indeed no syntactic verb-raising in Japanese. He also points out that the scope arguments presented in the above-mentioned works have inherent limitations because they cannot directly test the syntactic constituency in question. For these reasons, we will, in the following two subsections, focus on Koizumi's arguments and examine the validity of his analyses.

3.2 *String vacuous V-to-T raising*

Koizumi's (2000) argument for the existence of overt verb-raising in Japanese goes as follows. Suppose Japanese clauses have the structure in (6) (irrelevant details are omitted). The subject is base-generated in the [Spec, *v*] position, and is later overtly raised into the [Spec, T] position, leaving its trace in the original site. Now notice that none of the subject (SUB), the indirect object (IO), and the direct object (DO) in (6) forms a constituent with the others. In other words, no combination of these elements alone constitutes a syntactic constituent. For example, the DO/IO combination is not a constituent, nor is the DO/IO/SUB combination. Rather, it is the whole VP or TP that is a constituent, containing [V, DO, IO] in the former case, and [V, DO, IO, *v*, t_{SUB}, T, SUB] in the latter case. Given the general assumption that syntactic operations can only affect syntactic constituents, it is then predicted that if there are syntactic processes that seem to operate on, say, the DO/IO combination or the DO/IO/SUB combination, they in fact operate on VP (or *v*P) or TP, respectively, even though verbs are not visible on the surface, i.e., the processes in question operate on the "remnant" VP (or *v*P)/TP headed by an empty verb (=the trace of a verb left by the string vacuous verb-raising). Thus, to create a remnant VP (or *v*P)/TP, verbs have to have raised to T and C, respectively.

(6)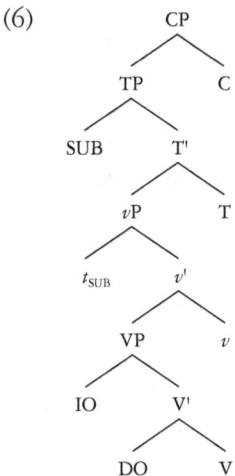

Koizumi argues that there are indeed three such processes in Japanese, (i) coordination, (ii) (pseudo-)cleft, and (iii) scrambling, thereby supporting the existence of string vacuous verb-raising in the language.

There are several assumptions in Koizumi's account that are not fully justified. For example, he assumes, following Nemoto (1993) and Miyagawa (2001), that the subject raises to [Spec, T] in the overt syntax of Japanese. However, it has been widely known since Fukui (1986) and Kuroda (1988) that certain properties of the subject in Japanese suggest that the subject in this language stays (or at least is able to stay) in its original position (either in [Spec, V] or [Spec, *v*]). Thus, unless the evidence is compelling, the assumption that the subject raises to [Spec, T] in Japanese is by no means innocuous and should not be put forward without careful discussion.

In fact, the assumption just mentioned is not really crucial for Koizumi's argument, as he himself notes (cf. his note 4 and Appendix B). If the subject in Japanese indeed stays in its original position, then there will be no argument for overt verb-raising to C, but the presented arguments for overt verb-raising to T (or *v*) remain valid. The crucial assumption for Koizumi's whole argument is that the constituency of the relevant element is due to verb-raising and that the element in question is headed by the trace of a raised verb. This central assumption, however, is highly dubious. First, Koizumi claims that in the following example (cf. his (36)), the scrambled element is actually a VP headed by the trace of a raised verb (NOM = Nominative, ACC = Accusative, DAT = Dative).

(7) [$_{VP}$ Hawai-de Masami-ni   purezento-o t_V]$_i$ John-ga [Kiyomi-ga t_i
     Hawaii-at   -DAT present   -ACC   -NOM   -NOM
     katta$_V$ to] omotteiru.
     bought that believe

Lit. "[A present for Masami in Hawaii] John believes that Kiyomi bought."
"John believes that Kiyomi bought a present for Masami in Hawaii."

In (7), one could hypothesize that the whole VP (with an unpronounced verb trace) is fronted. However, it is systematically possible to scramble a "portion" of an alleged VP. Consider the following representative examples.

(8) a. [Hawai-de Masami-ni] John-ga [Kiyomi-ga purezento-o katta to] omotteiru.
     b. [Masami-ni purezento-o] John-ga [Kiyomi-ga Hawai-de katta to] omotteiru.

In fact, it is possible to scramble any portion of the Sub-IO-DO sequence, as long as the legitimate parsing is somehow assured. Koizumi (2000) claims that examples like (8) are deviant (see his judgments for his (33c) and (33d)), but he also notes that "the acceptability of a sentence with multiple instances of scrambling will improve significantly if it is parsed in such a way that the scrambled elements form an intonation phrase" (Koizumi 2000: 239) and cites the example (7) above (his (34 = 36)) as an instance of acceptable multiple scrambling. He does not discuss the acceptability of multiple scrambling which affects only a portion of the set of arguments or adjuncts of a predicate. We agree with Koizumi that (particularly in the case of multiple scrambling) a scrambled element must form an intonation phrase (to facilitate proper parsing), which in turn suggests that a scrambled element must form some sort of constituent. But we do not accept his conclusion that the constituent has to be a VP headed by the trace of a raised verb. The existence of examples like those in (8) strongly suggests that the fronted element, although it is a constituent, is not a VP, since it is simply impossible to form a VP by picking only a portion of the verb's arguments or adjuncts, leaving the rest behind in the embedded clause.

Furthermore, there are numerous cases in Japanese where kinds of "constituents" that are not attested in languages like English are indeed observed, quite independently of the possibility of verb-raising. To cite just one example (see also the discussion in section 3.3.4 below), consider the following situation. Suppose the speaker A asks the question (TOP = Topic, GEN = Genitive, Q = Question Morpheme, PRT = Particle):

(9) Kono kurasu no hitotati-wa dooyuu purezento-kookan-o
 this class-GEN people -TOP what kind gift -exchange-ACC
 kono aida-no paatii-de yatta no? Gutaitekini agete mite yo.
 the other day-GEN party-at did Q Concretely list-try-PRT

"What kind of gift-exchanges did the people in this class do at the party the other day? Please tell me some concrete cases."

This question can be answered in various ways; for example, by uttering the following sentence. (CL = Classifier, CON = Conjunction Marker)

(10) Taroo-ga [Hanako-ni mannenhitu-o 2-hon] to [Tomoko-ni
 -NOM -to fountain pen-ACC -CL CON -to
 tokei -o 2-tu], sorekara, Ziroo-ga [Hanako-ni hon-o
 watch-ACC -CL and -NOM -to book-ACC
 1-satu] to [Tomoko-ni syasinsyuu -o 2-satu], ato, Hanako-mo
 -CL CON -to photo album-ACC -CL and -also
 [Taroo-ni syasinsyuu -o 1-satu] to [Ziroo-ni hon-o
 -to photo album-ACC -CL CON -ACC book-ACC
 1-satu] da-yo.
 -CL be-PRT

Lit. "It was that Taro, [two fountain pens to Hanako] and [two watches to Tomoko], and Ziro, [one book to Hanako] and [two photo albums to Tomoko], and also Hanako, [one photo album to Taro] and [one book to Ziro]."

"(The situation was such that:) Taro gave two fountain pens to Hanako, and two watches to Tomoko. Ziro gave a book to Hanako and two photo albums to Tomoko. And also, Hanako gave a photo album to Taro, and a book to Ziro."

According to Koizumi's analysis, all the bracketed phrases in (10) are VPs (or vPs) headed by the trace of a verb which has been raised in an across-the-board fashion. But it is simply impossible to come up with the relevant verb here. It is not clear which verb is to be stipulated; there is no candidate in (10), not even in the previous sentence (9).

Given these considerations (along with many others, some of which are to be discussed below), the reasonable conclusion is that verb-raising has nothing to do with the constituency of the relevant elements. While we maintain with Koizumi that the relevant elements must be constituents of some sort, we conclude that they are not VPs/vPs and that the postulated verb-raising has nothing to do with their constituency. Therefore, the data discussed in Koizumi (2000) cannot constitute compelling evidence for the existence of string vacuous V-to-T raising in Japanese.

In the remaining subsections, we examine more specific aspects of Koizumi's arguments. Of his three arguments mentioned above ((i) coordination, (ii) pseudo-cleft, and (iii) scrambling), the argument based on coordination (or the connective particle constructions) seems most revealing and significant. Thus, we examine the properties of connective particles in Japanese separately later in section 3.2.3, after a brief discussion of the other two arguments in sections 3.2.1 and 3.2.2.

3.2.1 Pseudo-cleft constructions

Koizumi argues that the remnant of V-to-T raising can be the focus of a pseudo-cleft construction, as shown in (11) (NL = Nominalizer).

(11) a.   Mary-ga   John-ni   ringo-o   3-tu age-ta.
         -NOM   -DAT apple-ACC -CL   gave

   "Mary gave three apples to John."

   b.   Mary-ga   age-ta no -wa   [John -ni   ringo-o   3-tu] da.
        -NOM gave   NL-TOP [-DAT apple-ACC -CL] is

   Lit. "It is [three apples to John] that Mary gave."

   c.   [Op$_i$ [SUB t_i V-v-T]] no-wa [$_{vP}$ IO DO (3-CL) [$_V$ e]]$_i$ da

In (11b), the indirect object *John-ni* "to John" and the direct object *ringo-o* "apples", along with the numeral quantifier *3-tu* "three", are located in the focus position. Koizumi hypothesizes that (11b) has the schematic structure (11c), where elements in the focus position constitute a syntactic constituent coindexed with the operator in the topic phrase. Koizumi argues that the indirect and the direct object form a syntactic constituent, namely a remnant VP headed by the trace(s) of a verb, as a result of the string vacuous V-to-T movement that he postulates.

The validity of his argument depends crucially on the analysis of pseudo-cleft constructions presented above.[9] However, at the present level of our understanding of this construction, it is still unclear whether the elements located in the focus position of pseudo-cleft constructions (the bracketed portion of (11b) above) must be a single constituent. Alternatively, we can analyse the structure as an instance of topicalization of nominalized clause as shown in (12).

(12) a. Mary-ga   age-ta no -wa [John-ni   ringo-o   3-tu] da
         -NOM gave NL-TOP [-DAT apple-ACC -CL] is

   Lit. "It is [three apples to John] that Mary gave."

   b. [SUB t_j t_k age-ta]-no$_i$-wa IO$_j$ DO$_k$ 3-tu [$_S$ e]$_i$ da

The representation in (12b) indicates that the topic part of the pseudo-cleft construction in (12a) is moved to the front of the sentence as an instance of topicalization.

Sakai (2000b, 2001) presents the same line of analysis for other closely related constructions in Japanese. He points out that the particle *-no* overtly marks the process of predicate nominalization, which has the effect of de-focusing the predicate. According to this analysis, nominalization by the particle *-no* plays an important role in predicate ellipsis phenomena in Japanese, as in (13).

(13) a. Taroo-wa Hanako-ni   ringo-o   age-ta.
         -TOP   -DAT apple-ACC gave

   "Taro gave an apple to Hanako."

   Kumiko-ni   -mo da.
   -DAT-also is

   "(Taro gave an apple) To Kumiko, too."

   b. Taroo-wa dareka -ni   ringo-o   age-ta.
       -TOP someone-DAT apple-ACC gave

   "Taro gave an apple to someone."

> Demo, dare-ni da-ka wakara-nai.
> but whom-DAT is-Q know-not

"But I don't know/it is unknown to whom."

Sakai argues that so-called pseudo-gapping constructions such as (13a), discussed by Kim (1997) and Kim and Sohn (1998) (or stripping by Hoji 1997), or sluicing constructions like (13b), analysed by Takahashi (1994b), Nishiyama et al. (1996), and Fukaya and Hoji (1999), are derived by the deletion of nominalized predicates, as depicted in (14).

(14) a. Kumiko-ni -mo da.
 -DAT-also is

"(Taro gave an apple) To Kumiko, too."

 b. Demo, dare-ni da-ka wakara-nai.
 but whom-DAT is-Q know-not

"But I don't know/it is unknown to whom."

Sakai argues that this analysis is in fact supported by the theory of focus of negation/question sentences proposed by Kuno (1983) and Takubo (1985). These authors observe that the unmarked focus of negation/question is assigned to the predicate in Japanese, and that the predicate must be nominalized by the particle *-no* if the other (non-predicate) elements in a sentence are to be assigned a focus interpretation. Predicate nominalization, therefore, has an effect of defocusing the predicate in Japanese. Since deletion is not allowed for focused elements, as pointed out by Kuno (1978a), predicate nominalization applies and defocuses a predicate, thereby making the predicate available to the ellipsis process. The predicate nominalization analysis has a clear advantage over alternative analyses in accounting for the obligatory presence of the copula *-da* in (14):[10] copula is required because there is a nominalized predicate before ellipsis applies. On the other hand, the obligatory presence of the copula *-da* remains a mystery in other approaches.

The pseudo-cleft constructions can be regarded as a subcase of predicate nominalization constructions, i.e., if the nominalized predicates undergo topicalization instead of deletion, we obtain the pseudo-cleft constructions. The relationship between these constructions is schematically represented in (15).

(15) a. Taroo-mo ringo-o tabe-ta.
 -also apple-ACC ate

"Taro also ate apples."

Predicate Nominalization → Taroo-mo ringo-o tabeta-no da.
　　　　　　　　　　　　　　-also apple-ACC ate-NL is

b.　Taroo-mo ringo-o　　tabeta-no da.
　　-also apple-ACC ate　-NL is

Predicate Ellipsis → Taroo-mo　　　　 da.
　　　　　　　　　-also apple-ACC ate-NL is

Predicate Topicalization → [Ringo-o　 tabe-ta-no]$_i$-wa Taroo-mo
　　　　　　　　　　　　apple-ACC ate-NL-TOP　　　　-also
t_i da.
　is

Given this analysis of pseudo-cleft constructions, it is not surprising at all that elements in the focus position do not form a syntactic constituent. They are in fact remnants of predicate topicalization. The following example provides an additional piece of support for this analysis (Aux = Auxiliary).

(16) a.　Taroo-ga　　Hanako-ni　Russell-no　hon -o　　yomu-yooni
　　　　-NOM　　　-DAT　　　-GEN book-ACC read -AUX
　　　　nessin-ni susume-ta.
　　　　earnestly recommended

"Taro earnestly recommended Hanako to read Russell's books."

b.　Taroo-ga　　yomu-yooni nessin-ni susumeta　　　-no -wa
　　-NOM read　-AUX earnestly recommended-NL-TOP
　　Russell-no　hon -o　　　Hanako-ni　da.
　　-GEN book-ACC　　　　-DAT is

Lit. "It is Russell's books, to Hanako, that Taro earnestly recommended to read."

Both the matrix argument *Hanako-ni* and the embedded argument *Russell-no hon-o* are located in the focus position of (16b). In order to make these elements form a constituent by V-to-T raising, the embedded predicate would have to raise to the position of the matrix T. However, the embedded predicate does not raise to the matrix T, as clearly shown by the intervening adverbial expression *nessin-ni*. Elements in the focus position therefore cannot be a constituent even if the V-to-T raising is assumed. These kinds of examples abound, and they clearly indicate that elements in the focus position of pseudo-cleft constructions are not necessarily a single syntactic constituent, or at the very least, that the alleged V-to-T raising has nothing to do with their "constituency". Therefore, Koizumi's argument based on pseudo-cleft constructions cannot be a convincing argument for string vacuous V-to-T raising in Japanese.

3.2.2 Remnant scrambling

Another argument presented by Koizumi is concerned with scrambling of a remnant VP (see our discussion in section 3.2 above). Koizumi first points out that application of more than one long-distance movement from within the same clause violates the Subjacency Condition as it is formulated by Chomsky (1986a) and Lasnik and Saito (1992). However, Japanese allows so-called multiple scrambling out of a single clause, as illustrated in the following examples.

(17) a. Hanako-ga   Taroo-ga   Ziroo-ni   sono hon-o   watasi-ta
     -NOM   -NOM   -DAT that book-ACC handed
     to   omotte-iru.
     that think

  "Hanako thinks that Taro handed that book to Ziro."

  b. Ziroo-ni $_i$ sono hon-o $_j$ Hanako-ga   Taroo-ga t_i t_j watasi-ta
     -DAT that book-ACC   -NOM   -NOM handed
     to   omotte-iru.
     that think

In (17b), both the direct object and the indirect object of the embedded clause are scrambled to the beginning of the matrix clause, and the sentence is still acceptable. Koizumi suggests that the possibility of multiple scrambling can be readily explained if we assume that the fronted elements in the multiple scrambling cases actually form a single constituent, a "remnant" VP headed by the trace of a raised verb. In support of this analysis, he points out that certain conditions are imposed on multiple long-distance scrambling (see our discussion in section 3.2). Thus, multiple scrambling is degraded if scrambled phrases do not form an intonation phrase, and floated numeral quantifiers cannot be "scrambled" if they are not accompanied by the object they are associated with.[11] (Judgments are Koizumi's. See note 12.)

(18) a. Taroo-ga   Hanako-ga   hon-o   3-satu katta   to
     -NOM   -NOM book-ACC -CL   bought that
     omotte-iru.
     think

  "Taro thinks that Hanako bought three books."

  b. *3-satu $_i$ Taroo-ga   Hanako-ga   hon-o t_i katta   to
     -CL   -NOM   -NOM book-ACC   bought that
     omotte-iru.
     think

  c. Hon -o $_i$ 3 -satu $_j$ Taroo -ga Hanako-ga t_i t_j katta   to   omotte-iru.
     book-ACC-CL   -NOM   -NOM bought that think

Koizumi points out that the ungrammaticality of example (18b) is naturally explained if multiple long-distance scrambling is actually an instance of scrambling of a remnant VP. The remnant VP is scrambled as a whole in (18c), whereas only a portion of the VP is scrambled in (18b), leading to the ungrammaticality (but see our discussion in section 3.2).

Koizumi's argument based on scrambling is rather theory-internal and hinges on various (factual and theoretical) assumptions, including a particular interpretation of the Subjacency Condition. Furthermore, although the requirement that a scrambled element be a constituent seems well-grounded, it is highly questionable that the constituent is a (remnant) VP, as we discussed in section 3.2 above. An alternative view, which dates back to Fukui (1986) and which, in our view, still seems plausible, is that Japanese is equipped with a "free merger" mechanism which, subject to other syntactic and interpretive constraints, freely merges (or "adjoins" in the older terms used in Fukui's earlier works) an element with an existing element, creating a new constituent. Thus, Japanese phrases are "never closed", to use Fukui's (1986) terms. Applications of this "free merger" mechanism are severely restricted in a language like English, perhaps owing to the existence/properties of functional categories. In other words, Japanese, thanks to the lack of agreement-inducing functional heads, makes maximal use of Merge, made available by UG. Complex constituents such as *hon-o 3-satu* (in (18c)) and *Hawai-de Masami-ni* (in (8a)) are created by Merge (or "pair-Merge", i.e., "adjunction"), and then undergo other processes like scrambling.[12] In fact, Sohn (1994) argues that adjunction of an argument to another argument is possible in languages like Korean and Japanese. If this type of adjunction to arguments is possible, the moved constituent in the relevant examples would be an NP instead of a VP, having no bearing on the verb-raising issue.[13]

Summarizing so far, Koizumi's (2000) arguments based on cleft and scrambling constructions are not convincing enough to draw any conclusion regarding the existence of string vacuous V-to-T raising in Japanese. In the next subsection, we examine his argument based on coordination.

3.2.3 Coordination and connective particles

In Japanese, a set of particles are used for conjunctive or disjunctive connections of more than one element. Koizumi presents a most direct and interesting argument for the postulated string vacuous V-to-T raising based on the structure created by one such connective particle.

Koizumi (1995, 2000) points out that a remnant VP can be connected by one of these particles, *-to*. Consider first the following examples in English and Japanese.

(19) *Mary three apples and Susan two bananas, John gave for breakfast.

(20) [Hanako-ni   ringo-o   3-tu] to
       -DAT apple-ACC -CL CON

   [Kumiko-ni   banana-o   2-hon] Taroo-ga   age-ta.
    -DAT banana-ACC -CL   -NOM   gave

   Lit. "Three apples to Hanako and two bananas to Kumiko, Taro gave."

The ungrammaticality of example (19) indicates that the DO/IO combination, *Mary three apples* or *Susan two bananas*, does not form a constituent, because coordination is allowed only if co-ordinated elements are syntactic constituents (of the same type), as originally pointed out by Chomsky (1957). In (20), by contrast, the DO/IO combinations *Hanako-ni ringo-o 3-tu* and *Kumiko-ni banana-o 2-hon* can be connected by the particle *-to* and the resulting structure is in fact grammatical.[14]

Koizumi argues that the possibility of such constituents in Japanese indicates the existence of string vacuous V-to-T raising in the language. As we have briefly discussed in section 3.2, he claims that V is moved to the position of T by across-the-board V-to-T raising, as illustrated in (21) below.

(21) Taroo-ga   [Hanako-ni   ringo-o   3-tu t_V] to
       -NOM   -DAT apple-ACC -CL   CON
   [Kumiko-ni   banana-o   2-hon t_V] age$_V$ -ta.
    -DAT banana-ACC -CL   give -PAST

   Lit. "Taro gave three apples to Hanako and two bananas to Kumiko."

In (21), the DO/IO combinations accompanied by a numeral quantifier ("*Hanako-ni ringo-o 3-tu*" and "*Kumiko-ni banana-o 2-hon*") form a constituent headed by the trace of a raised verb, i.e., a remnant VP. It is these remnant VPs, according to Koizumi, that are connected by the particle *-to*.

Koizumi argues that the adjunction-to-argument analysis has difficulty in handling the connective particle constructions, since it is usually not possible to move elements into coordinated constituents. He also points out that this type of connective construction can be scrambled or clefted as illustrated by the following examples, indicating that the DO/IO combinations constitute syntactic constituents.

(22) a.   Taroo-ga   [Hanako-ni   ringo-o   3-tu] to
            -NOM   -DAT apple-ACC -CL CON
       [Kumiko-ni   banana-o   2-hon] age-ta.
        -DAT banana-ACC -CL   gave

       Lit. "Taro gave three apples to Hanako and two bananas to Kumiko."

b. [Hanako-ni ringo-o 3-tu to Kumiko-ni banana-o
   -DAT apple-ACC -CL CON -DAT banana-ACC
   2-hon]ᵢ Taroo-ga tᵢ age-ta.
   -CL -NOM gave
c. Taroo-ga age-ta-no-wa [Hanako-ni ringo-o 3-tu to
   -NOM gave-NL-TOP -DAT apple-ACC -CL CON
   Kumiko-ni banana-o 2-hon] da.
   -DAT banana-ACC -CL is

   Lit. "It is [three apples to Hanako and two bananas to Kumiko] that Taro gave."

Putting these observations together, Koizumi concludes that there is sufficient evidence for the existence of string vacuous V-to-T raising in Japanese.

Koizumi's argument offers quite interesting observations on some of the properties of connective particle constructions. However, it seems premature to draw any definite conclusion from his argument with respect to the existence of string vacuous V-to-T raising in Japanese. In the following subsection, we point out that Koizumi's analysis in fact faces serious problems if we consider a broader range of data from connective particle constructions in Japanese.

3.3 Problems with Koizumi's analysis of connective constructions

Despite its initial appeal, Koizumi's analysis faces at least four serious problems, apart from the general problem that we discussed in section 3.2. We go over these problems in this subsection and show that Japanese connective particle constructions exhibit rather peculiar properties.

3.3.1 The particle -mo "also"

The Japanese language has another kind of connective particle, -mo "also" as illustrated in (23) below.[15]

(23) a. Taroo-ga ringo-to banana (-to) -o tabe-ta.[16]
     -NOM apple-CON banana (-CON)-ACC ate

   "Taro ate apples and bananas."

   b. Taroo-ga ringo-mo banana-mo tabe-ta.
      -NOM apple-also banana-also ate

   "Taro ate apples and bananas."

In these examples, both the particle -to and the particle -mo play a role in connecting two constituents. Despite its functional similarities to the particle *-to, -mo* cannot connect the direct and indirect objects. Observe the following examples.[17]

(24) a. *Taroo-ga [Hanako-ni   ringo-o   3-tu] mo
             -NOM   -DAT apple-ACC-CL also
    [Kumiko-ni   banana-o   2-hon] mo age-ta.
             -DAT banana-ACC -CL   also gave

   Lit. "Taro gave three apples to Hanako and two bananas to Kumiko."

  b. Taroo-ga   [Hanako-ni   ringo-o   3-tu age] mo
              -NOM   -DAT apple-ACC -CL gave also
     [Kumiko-ni   banana-o   2-hon age] mo si-ta.
              -DAT banana-ACC -CL give also did
  c. Sono hi -ni Taroo-wa [hon-o   5-satu yomi] mo
     that day-on   -TOP book-ACC -CL   read   also
     [sake-o   4-hon nomi] mo si-ta.
      sake-ACC -CL drink also did

   "On that day, Taro read five books and (also) drank four bottles of sake."

The particle *-mo* shows rather striking differences in these examples. First, coordination by *-mo* is not constrained by the categorial status of the co-ordinated elements. Thus, as in (24b), it is possible to combine two (or more) VPs if the verbal stem is repeated in the second conjunct. Furthermore, the verbs of the connected VPs need not be identical, as illustrated by example (24c), which we take to be a case of genuine VP-coordination where verbal stems clearly stay in their original positions. Now it is not at all clear how Koizumi's analysis can be extended to these properties of *-mo*, since, in his account, all of these cases are on a par with the cases of the particle *-to*, i.e., they are uniformly analysed as cases of "VP-coordination."

3.3.2 *The particle* -katu *"and"*

Japanese also has a set of elements which are used exclusively for predicate coordination. The particle *-katu* "and" is one such element. Consider the following examples.

(25) a. Taroo-ga   [zyuusu-o   nomi] katu [okasi-o   tabe] ta.
            -NOM juice   -ACC drink and   cake -ACC eat   PAST

   "Taro drank (a glass of) juice and ate (a piece of) cake."

b. Taroo-ga   [Hanako-ni   ringo-o   3-tu age] katu
      -NOM   -DAT apple-ACC   -CL give and
   [Kumiko-ni   banana-o   2-hon age] ta.
       -DAT banana-ACC   -CL   give PAST

   Lit. "Taro gave three apples to Hanako and gave two bananas to Kumiko."

In (25a), the particle -*katu* connects the direct object and the verbal stem. Example (25b) is a case in which the direct object, the indirect object, and the verbal stem are connected by -*katu*. The meaning of these examples clearly indicates that a single past tense morpheme takes both of the two VPs as a complement, which in turn suggests that the verbal stem stays within the VPs connected by the particle -*katu*. If string vacuous V-to-T raising is obligatory, as in the case of European languages, it is rather surprising that the verbal stems stay within VPs in this kind of construction.[18] This poses another problem for Koizumi's claim that verbs in Japanese (obligatorily) raise into T (and then to C). As we noted in the preceding subsection, the particle -*mo* also connects two VPs with the verbal stem staying inside the VPs. Taken together, these cases provide an extremely serious problem for Koizumi's string vacuous V-to-T raising analysis.

3.3.3 *Case particles*

As we have seen, Koizumi's analysis crucially assumes that the categorial status of constituents connected by the particle -*to* is VP. However, as the following examples indicate, case particles can be assigned to the connected constituents.[19]

(26) a. Taroo-ga   [Hanako-ni   ringo 3-tu to
        -NOM   -DAT apple   -CL CON
     Kumiko-ni   banana 2-hon (to)]   -o   age-ta.
         -DAT banana   -CL   (CON)-ACC gave

   Lit. "Taro gave [three apples to Hanako] and [two bananas to Kumiko]."

b. [Tookyoo-kara daigakusei   3-nin to
        -from college student   -CL CON
    Oosaka-kara kookoosei   2-ri (to)]   -ga   ki-ta.
        -from high school student -CL (CON)-NOM came

   Lit. "[From Tokyo three college students] and [from Osaka two high school students] came."

There are strict restrictions on the assignment of case particles in Japanese. In particular, the nominative particle -*ga* can be assigned only to nominal categories (noun phrases, postpositional phrases, and some instances of clausal projections headed by a nominal element such as *-ka* "Q"; see Fukui (1986) for more detailed discussion), and the accusative particle *-o* can be assigned only to noun phrases (and some clausal projections headed by a nominal head). There is simply no attested case in which these case particles are assigned to a VP. Thus, the grammaticality of the examples in (26) strongly suggests that the phrases connected by the particle *-to* are not VPs, but rather, some sort of nominal constituents.

3.3.4 *Infinitival complements and NP complements*

Finally, the particle *-to* can connect elements which appear not to be syntactic constituents in a wide variety of cases. They are not limited to the contexts of V-to-T raising, as shown in the following examples.

(27) a. Taroo-ga   [Hanako-ni   ringo-o   3-tu] to
        -NOM   -DAT apple-ACC -CL CON
     [Kumiko-ni   banana-o   2-hon] katte-kuru -yooni (teinei-ni)
           -DAT banana-ACC   -CL   buy -bring-AUX (politely)
     tanon-da.
     asked

   Lit. "Taro (politely) asked Hanako to buy and bring three apples and Kumiko to buy and bring two bananas."

b. Hahaoya-ga   [Hanako-ni   ringo(-o)   3-tu] to
   mother -NOM   -DAT apple(-ACC) -CL CON
   [Kumiko-ni   banana(-o)   2-hon]-no   oyatu-o   age-ta.
        -DAT banana(-ACC)   -CL   -GEN snack-ACC gave

   "Their/someone's mother gave a snack of three apples to Hanako and (a snack of) two bananas to Kumiko."

In (27a), the particle *-to* connects *Hanako-ni*, an argument of the matrix verb *tanomu* "ask", and *ringo-o 3-tu* "three apples", which is the direct object of the embedded predicate *katte-kuru* "buy-bring". These two arguments could not possibly form a constituent even if the embedded verb string-vacuously raised to the embedded T.[20] Note that the raising of the embedded V to the matrix T is highly unlikely, given the fact that adverbial expressions such as *teinei-ni* "politely" can freely intervene between the two predicates. In (27b), the particle connects an argument of the verb *ageru* "give" (viz., *Hanako-ni* and *Kumiko-ni*) and an argument of the noun *oyatu* "snack" (viz., *ringo(-o) 3-tu* and *banana(-o) 2-hon*). In this type of example, verb-raising is simply irrelevant and there is no way to form a constituent containing one argument from a predicate and another from a noun.

3.4 Summary and conclusion

In this section, we have examined in detail Koizumi's (2000) arguments for the existence of string vacuous V-to-T (to C) raising in Japanese. We first pointed out that his arguments are based on certain assumptions that may not be warranted. Specifically, all of his arguments hinge on the central assumption that certain "syntactic" processes operate on a syntactic constituent, and that the constituent in question is a VP. Koizumi argues that there are at least three such processes in Japanese, (i) coordination, (ii) (pseudo-)clefts, and (iii) scrambling. We have examined each case closely and have shown that in all of these cases, Koizumi's analysis faces serious problems. In particular, we have argued that there is mounting evidence that it is not a VP, but rather a certain nominal category, that undergoes the processes Koizumi discusses. This result effectively nullifies his arguments for the existence of string vacuous V-to-T raising in Japanese.

It has also been shown in our discussion that there are even cases in which verb-raising should not be postulated. For example, if we deny the existence of syntactic V-to-T raising, the impossibility of connecting the direct and the indirect object by the particle -*mo* is expected, because these elements do not form a syntactic constituent. The presence of a verbal stem within a VP in the case of connection by -*katu* is also not surprising at all, if we assume that the V-T complex is formed in the "phonological (PF) component" as a result of Morphological Merger in a theory which does not postulate string vacuous V-to-T raising in the narrow syntax of Japanese.

Thus, we must conclude that Koizumi's arguments for the presence of overt verb-raising in Japanese do not hold, and that there is still no compelling evidence for overt verb-raising in the language. In the absence of such supporting evidence, we should continue to assume that there is no overt verb-raising, and, given the Visibility Guideline introduced in section 2, that there is no active functional head T in Japanese.

Having established these points, we will go on in the following section to explore briefly alternative analyses of the phenomena Koizumi discusses, particularly the coordination cases involving -*to*.[21]

4 A reduction analysis and constituencies in the PF component

In this section, we present an alternative account for connective constructions with the particle -*to*, based on the idea that these constructions are formed by PF operations.[22] Specifically, we propose that (i) they involve reduction or deletion of identical predicates and (ii) a string of elements is reanalysed into a constituent by Phrase-Level Merger in the PF component.

A considerable number of recent works on conjunction/disjunction structure (Wilder 1997, Schwartz 1999, among many others) propose the so-called "reduction analysis", according to which a set of elements in one of the conjuncts can be deleted under certain identity conditions. In the reduction analysis, a set of elements which do not form a syntactic constituent appear to form a constituent connected by conjunction/disjunction markers in the surface form. Koizumi (1995, 2000) considers the reduction analysis for structures associated with -*to*, which claims, when applied to this construction, that examples like (20) above can be derived from the deletion of identical predicates as depicted in (28).

(28) Taroo-ga   [Hanako-ni   ringo-o   3-tu ~~age~~] to
         -NOM   -DAT apple-ACC   -CL give CON
     [Kumiko -ni   banana-o   2-hon age]-ta.
              -DAT banana-ACC   -CL give-PAST

Lit. "Taro gave three apples to Hanako and two bananas to Kumiko."

Koizumi rejects the reduction analysis on the basis of the fact that the constituent connected by the particle -*to* can be scrambled or clefted, as shown in (29) below.

(29) a. [Hanako-ni   ringo-o   3-tu to   Kumiko-ni   banana-o
                -DAT apple-ACC -CL CON   -DAT banana-ACC
         2-hon]$_i$ Masao-ga [Taroo-ga t_i age-ta] to   it-ta.
         -CL   -NOM   -NOM   gave   that said

   Lit. "Three apples to Hanako and two bananas to Kumiko, Masao said that Taro gave."

   b. Taroo-ga   age-ta no -wa [Hanako-ni   ringo-o
         -NOM gave   NL-TOP [-DAT apple-ACC
       3-tu] to   Kumiko-ni   banana-o   2-hon] da.
       -CL] CON   -DAT banana-ACC   -CL   is

   Lit. "It is [three apples to Hanako] and [two bananas to Kumiko] that Taro gave."

Here, we focus on the scrambling construction in (29a), because we have already argued in section 3.3 that elements in the focus position of pseudocleft constructions (29b) need not be a single constituent. The fronted elements in (29a) do not form a syntactic constituent of the usual kind according to the reduction analysis. The constituent connected by the particle -*to* contains the verbal stem *age-* in the structure represented in (28). Given the standard assumption that only constituents can undergo movement, the reduction analysis should be rejected, Koizumi argues.

Recent developments of the theory of scrambling, however, enable us to take a fresh look at the situation. Ueyama (1999) and Hayashishita (2000) (cf. also Saito 1989) claim that some instances of scrambling have no effect in LF and thus should be analysed as a PF operation.[23] If their analysis is tenable, the elements fronted by scrambling need not be a constituent of the usual kind during the narrow syntax. Marantz (1984, 1988, 1989) and Halle and Marantz (1993) propose that there is an operation called Morphological Merger, which combines two morphological units into a single unit in the PF component. We propose that the same operation applies to a sequence of phrase-level units and reanalyses them into a single constituent in the PF component. After the Phrase-Level Merger, or "PF reanalysis", scrambling applies to the reanalysed constituent and a structure like (29a) is derived in the PF component.[24]

The idea that constituent structures are not exactly identical in the narrow syntax and in the PF component is also supported by the recent development of the theory of linear order advanced by Kayne (1994), Chomsky (1995b), and Fukui and Takano (1998), among others. These works assume that constituent structures in the syntactic component (narrow syntax and LF) do not contain information on the linear (temporal) order of constituents (but see Saito and Fukui 1998 for an opposing view; see also Fukui 2001 for a general overview on the issue of linear order in phrase structure).

The linearization algorithm determines the surface order of constituents based on their structural properties. In other words, constituent structures based on hierarchical dependencies without linear order are re-interpreted in the PF component as constituent structures based primarily on linear order with little or no hierarchical structure. It is thus not at all surprising that a string of elements which does not form a constituent in the narrow syntax is reanalysed during the process of linearization.

As an operation in the PF component, Phrase-Level Merger/PF reanalysis must satisfy conditions on the linear order of constituents. Although in-depth explorations into the nature of PF derivations are a topic for future research, we can assume that at least the following two conditions hold. A string of elements is a PF constituent only if (i) they are string adjacent, and (ii) the derived constituent complies with the head parameter. Notice that these conditions are fulfilled in the following structure only if identical elements including the predicate *age-* "give" are deleted and the derived constituent is headed by the nominal *3-tu* "three" or *2-hon* "two".

(30) Taroo-ga [$_{VP}$ Hanako-ni   ringo-o   3-tu ~~age~~] to
           -NOM   -DAT apple-ACC -CL give CON
     [Kumiko-ni   banana-o   2-hon age]-ta.
            -DAT banana-ACC -CL give-PAST
     → Taroo-ga [$_{NP}$ Hanako-ni   ringo-o   3-tu ~~age~~] to
            -NOM   -DAT apple-ACC -CL give CON
     [$_{NP}$ Kumiko-ni   banana-o   2-hon] age-ta.
            -DAT banana-ACC -CL   give-PAST

The case assignment pattern shown in (31) strongly supports the PF reanalysis account, because case particles are assigned to the reanalysed constituents.

(31) Taroo-ga [vp [vp Hanako-ni   ringo 3-tu ~~age~~] to
       -NOM   -DAT apple -CL give CON
     [vp Kumiko-ni   banana 2-hon age]-ta]
            -DAT banana -CL give-PAST
  → Taroo-wa [NP [NP Hanako-ni   ringo 3-tu ~~age~~] to
       -TOP   -DAT apple -CL give CON
     [NP Kumiko-ni   banana 2-hon] (to)] -o   age-ta.
            -DAT banana -CL (CON)-ACC give-PAST

Notice that the case particle *-o* is assigned to the whole string of elements connected by the particle *-to*, i.e., *Hanako-ni ringo 3-tu to Kumiko-ni banana 2-hon (to)*. As we discussed above (section 3.3.3), Koizumi's analysis cannot explain this fact, since coordinated elements are remnant VPs under his analysis and the case particle *-o* can only be assigned to a nominal element, never to a VP. Given the PF reanalysis just proposed, we can now claim that case particles are assigned to the reanalysed NPs, along the lines of morphological case marking originally proposed by Kuroda (1965, 1978, among others).

The advantage of the PF reanalysis account becomes even more evident if we consider the other problematic cases for Koizumi's analysis. First, the PF reanalysis account naturally explains why these "unusual" constituents cannot be connected by the connective particle *-mo*. The particle *-mo* differs from the particle *-to* in that it carries clear quantificational force and must therefore be present in the LF representation, whereas the particle *-to* has no comparable semantic content. Thus, coordinate structures with the particle *-mo* have to be created in the narrow syntax. The DO/IO combinations, however, do not form a "real" constituent in the narrow syntax. The structure is thus ruled out as illegitimate.

Second, the fact that the connective particle *-katu* connects VPs with the verbal stem(s) in situ (cf. (25)) is not at all surprising under the PF reanalysis approach. The fact simply indicates that Japanese does not have V-to-T raising in the narrow syntax and that a V-T complex is formed by Morphological Merger as argued by Fukui and Takano (1998), Aoyagi (1998a, b), and Sakai (1996, 1998, 2000a). See Yoon (1994) for the claim that Korean does not have V-to-T raising. Sells (1995) also presents some arguments that there is no V-to-T raising, from a different (i.e., lexicalist) perspective.

Finally and most importantly, the reduction-and-reanalysis account correctly predicts the grammaticality of examples involving no V-to-T raising, which is a mystery under Koizumi's analysis. The relevant examples in (27) are repeated here as (32).

(32) a. Taroo-ga [Hanako-ni   ringo-o   3-tu] to
           -NOM   -DAT apple-ACC -CL CON

[Kumiko-ni   banana-o   2-hon] katte-kuru -yooni (teinei-ni)
    -DAT banana-ACC -CL   buy -bring-AUX (politely)
tanon-da.
asked

Lit. "Taro (politely) asked Hanako to buy and bring three apples and Kumiko to buy and bring two bananas."

b. Hahaoya-ga   [Hanako-ni   ringo(-o)   3-tu] to
   mother -NOM   -DAT apple(-ACC) -CL CON
   [Kumiko-ni   banana(-o)   2-hon]-no   oyatu-o   age-ta.
        -DAT banana(-ACC) -CL   -GEN snack-ACC gave

"Their/someone's mother gave a snack of three apples to Hanako and (a snack of) two bananas to Kumiko."

These examples contain typical contexts for deletion of identical predicates. Consider the following English examples.

(33) a. Mary [forced Tom [to go to Cambridge] and [forced John [[to go to Oxford]].

(Kuno 1976a)

b. Ugliness [is one of [the symptoms of disease]], and beauty [is one of [the symptoms of health]].

(Terazu 1975)

As indicated, example (33a) represents a case of deletion of a matrix predicate (*forced*) accompanied by the embedded infinitival predicate (*to go*). In (33b), the matrix predicate and part of a complement NP get deleted, as depicted above. Observe further that predicate ellipsis is prohibited across a finite clause boundary, as illustrated by the ungrammaticality of (34) below. Correspondingly, it is also impossible to connect more than one constituent by -*to* across a finite clause boundary, as shown by the ungrammaticality of example (35).

(34) *John thinks that Bill will see Susan and Harry [thinks [that Bill will see Mary]].

(Abe and Hoshi 1997)

(35) *Taroo-wa   [Hanako-ga   [ringo-ga   3-tu] to
        -TOP   -NOM apple-NOM -CL CON
    [Kumiko-ga   [banana-ga   2-hon aru] to   itta to   omotta.
        -NOM banana-NOM -CL   are that said that thought

Lit. "Taro thought that [Hanako (said that there are) three apples] and [Kumiko said that there are two bananas]."

(Adapted from Koizumi 2000)

These parallelisms strongly suggest that the same mechanism is at work in deriving both the Japanese examples in (32) and the English examples in (33), in support of our PF analysis.

In summary, the PF reduction analysis has clear advantages over the string vacuous V-to-T raising analysis. Empirical observations indicate serious drawbacks of V-to-T raising, and they strongly support the view that a V-T complex is derived by Morphological Merger in Japanese. This result suggests that the category T plays a quite different role in Japanese syntax compared to the functional head T attested in European languages. The category T in Japanese is never "visible" in the narrow syntax, inducing no verb-raising.

5 Case marking in Japanese

The mechanism of assignment of case particles has been one of the central topics in generative studies on the Japanese language from the very beginning of their history. Kuno (1973) proposes a set of transformational rules for assignment of case particles. Kuroda (1965, 1978) argues that the patterns of case marking in Japanese can be explained in terms of the basic sentence types and the linear order of noun phrases.

These earlier proposals were further refined and elaborated considerably as generative studies on Japanese advanced in the 1980s and the 1990s. In this section, we present a quick overview of these developments.

5.1 Japanese case system in the principles-and-parameters approach

The phenomena of morphological case have attracted much attention from classical grammarians and traditional linguists over the centuries. Within the framework of generative grammar, the most significant contribution is an invention of the theory of (abstract) structural Case proposed by Rouveret and Vergnaud (1980) and Chomsky (1981a). The theory of structural Case distinguishes between the abstract notion of structural Case and the concept of morphological case. Structural Case is motivated mainly for explaining the distribution of overt noun phrases. All overt noun phrases are supposed to be assigned Case even though the Case may not have any phonetic realizations. If a noun phrase does not receive Case, the structure containing it will be ruled out (the "Case Filter"). It is generally assumed in the literature that the functional head I(nfl) (inflectional elements, which consist of T and Agr) assigns nominative Case under government (or Spec-head agreement). Transitive verbs assign accusative Case and prepositions assign oblique Case, both under government.

Takezawa (1987, 1998) is a representative attempt at applying the theory of structural Case to nominative case marking in Japanese. Takezawa points out an interesting correlation between the distribution of nominative case particles and the existence of tense morphemes, and he argues that the theory of structural Case successfully accounts for the distribution of nominative case markers and tense morphemes. Consider the following examples.

(36) a. Taro-wa   Hanako-ga/o   totemo meewaku-da-to
         -TOP   -NOM/ACC   very   annoying-is-that
    omotte-iru.
    think

   "Taro thinks that Hanako is very annoying."

   b. Taroo-wa   Hanako-*ga/o   totemo meewaku-ni omotte-iru.
         -TOP   -NOM/ACC very   annoying-as think

   "Taro considers Hanako (to be) very annoying."

The embedded predicate has the present tense form of the copula -*da* in (36a), and the embedded subject *Hanako* can be marked either by the nominative case particle -*ga* or the accusative case particle -*o*. In (36b), by contrast, the predicate nominal is bare and it is accompanied by no tense particle, in which case the embedded subject NP (*Hanako*) can be marked only by the accusative case particle. Based on observations of this kind, Takezawa claims that assignment of the nominative case particle in Japanese hinges on the presence of a tense morpheme, and that Japanese nominative case is assigned by the functional head I (or T in current terms) in pretty much the same way that nominative Case is assigned by I in English.

While Takezawa's account is successful in capturing certain important correlations between nominative case particles and tense morphemes in Japanese, it leaves a number of peculiar properties of Japanese case marking unexplained. Consider, for example, multiple identical case constructions, which is one of the most notable properties of Japanese case marking (see Fukui 1986 and references therein for more discussion).

(37) a. Hiroshima-ga   huyu-ga   kaki-ga   oisii.
           -NOM   winter-NOM oyster-NOM be delicious

   "In Hiroshima, oysters are delicious in winter."

   b. Yamada kyoozyu-no   sensyuu -no   gengogaku-no   koogi
         professor-GEN last week-GEN linguistics-GEN lecture

   Lit. "Professor Yamada's last week's linguistics('s) lecture"

Notice that nominative case particle -*ga* and the genitive case particle -*no* appear more than once within the domain of relevant "functional heads" in these examples (I/T for nominative, and D or its equivalent for genitive, according to the "standard" analysis).

Another peculiar property of Japanese case marking is a free alternation of case particles, as illustrated in (38) below (cf. also (36a) above).[25]

(38) a. Taroo-ga   Kumiko-ga/o   kawaii to omot-ta.
       -NOM   -NOM/ACC pretty that thought

"Taro thought Kumiko is pretty./Taro considered Kumiko to be pretty."

b. Hanako-ga/no   siranai   koto-o   Taroo-ga   sitte-iru.
   -NOM/GEN not-know thing-ACC   -NOM knows

"Taro knows something that Hanako does not know."

Since English and other European languages do not generally exhibit these properties (multiple case marking and case alternations), the Japanese phenomena cannot be readily integrated into the government-based Case theory. Thus, earlier attempts to apply Case theory to Japanese have to introduce a number of stipulations in order to accommodate these properties in terms of the government-based Case theory.[26]

In the face of these peculiar properties of Japanese case assignment, other researchers have explored a different approach toward Japanese case marking within the context of an overall comparative syntax of English and Japanese. They do not apply the English-type structural Case theory directly to Japanese. Rather, on the basis of the facts of Japanese case marking, they propose a somewhat different mechanism which seems to be descriptively more adequate for the language. Thus, Saito (1982, 1983) argues that the particle *-ga* is assigned as a default case and *-o* is assigned as a marker of inherent case. Fukui (1986) claims that both *-ga* and *-no* are default cases which are assigned within VP and NP, respectively. Kuroda (1978, 1983, 1986) refines his earlier proposals and proposes the Linear Case Marking mechanism, which, applying cyclically, handles the distribution of case particles in terms of the canonical sentence patterns and the linear order of noun phases. Fukui and Nishigauchi (1992) develop a system of case marking according to which case is "licensed" (but not assigned) under government (which can be one-to-many, unlike Spec-head agreement), and they try to connect the case alternation phenomena in Japanese with the optionality of scrambling in the language.

In all of these analyses, assignment of case particles in Japanese does not involve Spec-head agreement, which was then standardly assumed to be one-to-one. (For more recent discussion on the possibility of "multiple agreement", see, among others, Chomsky 2001a, b and Hiraiwa 2001a, b.) Thus, assignment of multiple identical case is not a mystery in these approaches. Free alternation is also expected because case marking in Japanese does not involve an obligatory operation of Spec-head agreement.

It is important to note that in the approaches represented by the works just discussed, the above-mentioned peculiar properties of Japanese case marking are not regarded as isolated properties of the language. Rather, these properties are to be derived from deeper parametric differences between, say, the English-type languages and the Japanese-type languages. Thus, Kuroda (1988) attributes a set of differences between English and Japanese to the obligatoriness or optionality of agreement, i.e., agreement (or "Agreement", in his terms) is obligatory in English, while it is optional in Japanese, from which the other properties of the languages follow. Fukui (1986, 1988a, 1995a, b) argues that the major typological differences (including the properties of case marking) observed between Japanese and English (and other similar languages) can be deduced from different feature compositions of the functional heads in the lexicons of the languages. Japanese represents a rather extreme case, in which the role of "functional heads" in this language is almost zero, as far as "agreement" is concerned (see the discussion in section 2.2). He points out that one of the major roles of a functional head is, from the point of view of phrase structure composition, to "close off" a phrasal projection by means of its agreement features. Since Japanese does not really have active functional categories with agreement features, he argues, the phrases or projections in Japanese are never closed. Thus, additional elements are rather freely merged with a lexical projection (viz., verb phrases and noun phrases), and they are marked by case particles by the default rules, either by -*ga* in the case of a clausal projection, or by -*no* in the case of a nominal projection. (See also the discussion in section 3.2.2.) The existence of multiple identical case (or the existence of case alternations, for that matter) is not a parameter by itself. It is a property of a language which is correlated with other properties of the language and which is to be derived from deeper parametric properties of the language in question (such as the feature compositions of functional heads).

5.2 *Case marking in the minimalist program*

As we have discussed in section 2.1, the minimalist program was advanced in the early 1990s, addressing the question: "To what extent is the human language faculty an optimal solution to minimal design specifications, conditions that must be satisfied for language to be usable at all?" (adapted from Chomsky 2001a: 1). For reasons discussed in section 2, this research program forces us to examine all the concepts and mechanisms employed in UG against interface conditions and/or economy considerations, to see if they are truly motivated by these factors. As a result of these "minimalist scrutinies", many of the concepts and mechanisms assumed in earlier versions of the principles-and-parameters model have been eliminated. Consider, for example, the concept of government, which plays a crucial role in Case theory. In the following configuration (where XP is the maximal projection of X, and YP is an arbitrary maximal projection distinct from XP):

(39) $[_{XP} A [X [_{YP} \ldots B \ldots]]]$

X governs (i) A, (ii) YP, and (iii) B, in the classical theory of government. In case (i), X governs A if the notion of government is based on "m-command" (cf. Chomsky 1986a, among others) rather than c-command. X governs YP, representing the "core" case of government (case (ii)). In case (iii), X governs B if YP (or any other intervening maximal projection) is not a "barrier" for B. Of these three subcases of government, case (ii) remains valid even in the minimalist program, as an instance of sisterhood (defined by Merge, via a "more primitive" notion of "Immediately-Contain"). Case (iii) represents a non-local relation and ought to be eliminated in the minimalist program. Case (i) is a local relation holding within the same maximal projection, and therefore, can be maintained (at least for the moment).[27]

Given the minimalist re-examination of government, Case theory is reformulated in terms of "feature checking" holding between a head and its Spec, based on the structural relation depicted as case (i) in (39).[28] It is also proposed in earlier minimalist analyses of Case theory that Case be checked within a projection of the functional head Agr, an abstract functional category that is responsible for checking agreement features of noun phrases (see section 2.1). This version of Case theory is immediately applied to Japanese, with the crucial assumption that Japanese has the functional category Agr. Tada (1992), Watanabe (1993, 1996a), and Koizumi (1995) are a few of the representative works of this kind, but many other works on Japanese syntax in the late 1980s and the early 1990s also assume the existence of Agr in Japanese. Each of these works makes interesting observations and presents intriguing analyses, contributing greatly to the study of Japanese syntax (and UG). A common feature of these works, however, is that the existence of Agr in Japanese is somewhat aprioristically assumed and no empirical evidence is presented for its existence in the language.

In a more recent framework, Chomsky (1995b) argues, partly on the basis of earlier proposals by Fukui (1995b, written in 1992), Iatridou (1990), and Thráinsson (1996, written in 1994),[29] that the category Agr be eliminated from UG, since it does not fulfill the interface conditions and its existence in the theory of grammar is not justified. The so-called "Agr-less Case theory" is developed, based on Chomsky's claim that Agr should not exist in UG. According to this theory, Case features of nominative noun phrases and accusative noun phrases are checked by T and the "light verb" v, respectively. Couched in this framework, Ura (1994b, 1996, 1999, 2000) develops a version of the theory of multiple feature checking (see also Chomsky 1995b), which does not require a one-to-one correspondence between a functional head and its Spec, allowing multiple Specs per head. Ura proposes that UG provides the feature [±multiple] and that the values for this feature are parametrized. If a language selects the [+] value for this feature, multiple Specs are allowed in the language; if, on the other hand, the [−] value is selected, the one-to-one correspondence is required between a head and its Spec. The former case is manifested in a language like Japanese, whereas English represents the latter case. Ura (1996) argues that cross-linguistic variation in raising constructions can be nicely handled under this proposal. Ura (1999, 2000) goes on to point out that dative subject phenomena are also elegantly accounted for in terms of his theory of multiple feature checking.

It should be noted that the theory of multiple feature checking virtually introduces two distinct checking mechanisms to narrow syntax. A careful consideration is thus called for to determine whether each of the two mechanisms is well-motivated as an ingredient of narrow syntax. It is also important to note that, once the feature [±multiple] is introduced and parametrized, the existence of multiple identical case in a given language is stipulated as such, rather than characterized as a phenomenon to be derived from something more fundamental, a possibility that has been explored in earlier works by Fukui (1986, 1988a, 1995a, b) and Kuroda (1988), where the existence of "multiple specifiers" in Japanese, along with numerous other properties of the language, is shown to be derived from the lack of active functional heads in the language's lexicon.[30]

6 Case in the PF component

In this section we present pieces of empirical evidence for an alternative approach to Japanese case marking, essentially along the lines of Kuroda's series of works mentioned before (see also Fukui and Takano 1998, for relevant discussion). This approach treats the Japanese case marking system as a morphological mechanism operating in the PF component. We demonstrate that a target of case particle assignment in the language is not a syntactic constituent but a phonological or morphological constituent.

6.1 PF reanalysis and case marking

In section 4, we presented a set of examples which involve assignment of case particles to apparent syntactic non-constituents. Observe further the following examples (Pl = Plural marker).[31]

(40) a. [[Zimintoo   -kara gaimu-daizin   -ni
       Liberal Democratic Party-from minister of foreign affairs-DAT
       Yamada-si]   to [Hosyutoo   -kara zaimu-daizin
             -Mr/Ms CON Conservative Party-from minister of finance
       -ni   Suzuki-si]   (-to) -ga   syuunin-si-ta.
       -DAT   -Mr/Ms (CON)-NOM assumed

   Lit. "[From the Liberal Democratic Party, Mr Yamada (assumed) the minister of foreign affairs] and [from the Conservative Party, Mr Suzuki assumed the minister of finance]."

   b. [[Kinoo   kono-heya-de suugaku   -no   gakusei-tati] to
       yesterday this room -in mathematics-GEN student-PL   CON

[ototoi   ano-heya-de buturi-no   sensei-tati] (-to)] -ga
the day before that room-in physics-GEN teacher-PL (CON)-NOM
kono atarasii konpyuutaa-o   tukatta.
this new   computer-ACC used.

Lit. "[Yesterday in this room, math students] and [the day before in that room, physics teachers] used this new computer."

In these examples, the nominative particle *-ga* is assigned to a sequence of elements which appear to be syntactic non-constituents. Recall that if our analysis of connective particle constructions is right, these "constituents" are formed by an application of Phrase-Level Merger in the PF component. Thus, the possibility of assigning case particles to these "phonological/morphological constituents" indicates that case marking indeed takes place after Phrase-Level Merger applies, i.e., in the PF component. The Case (feature) checking mechanism of the normal kind (which is assumed to take place in the narrow syntax) cannot be involved in these examples, because the alleged target of Case (feature) checking does not form a constituent in narrow syntax.

As also noted in section 3.3.1, the fact that these PF constituents are never connected by the particle *-mo* provides an additional piece of support for our analysis.

(41) a. *[Zimintoo   -kara gaimu-daizin   -ni
       Liberal Democratic Party-from minister of foreign affairs-DAT
       Yamada-si]   mo [Hosyutoo   -kara zaimu-daizin
       -Mr/Ms also Conservative Party-from minister of
       -ni   Suzuki-si]   mo syuunin-si-ta.
       finance-DAT   -Mr/Ms also assumed
    b. *[Kinoo   kono-heya-de suugaku   -no gakusei-tati] mo
       yesterday this room -in mathematics-GEN student-PL   also
       [ototoi   ano-heya -de buturi -no   sensei-tati] mo kono
       the day before that room-in physics-GEN teacher-PL also this
       atarasii conpyuutaa-o   tukatta.
       new   computer -ACC used

As we argued in section 4, the particle *-mo* must be present in the LF representation because it has its own semantic content. This implies that the elements connected by the particle *-mo* have to be a constituent in the narrow syntax (i.e., the derivation of LF). The ungrammaticality of the examples in (41), as opposed to the grammaticality of the corresponding examples (cf. (40)), indicates that the bracketed portions are PF constituents but not syntactic constituents, to which case particles can be attached.

Note also that unlike case particles, postpositional particles such as *-kara* "from" or *-de* "in" cannot be attached to these PF constituents, as shown in (42).

(42) a. *[Gaimu-daizin   -ni   Yamada-si   -ga
         minister of foreign affairs-DAT   -Mr/Ms-NOM
       Zimintoo]   to   [zaimu-daizin   -ni
       Liberal Democratic Party CON minister of finance-DAT
       Suzuki-si-ga   Hosyutoo   (-to)] -kara syuunin-sita.
         -Mr/Ms-NOM Conservative Party-(CON)-from assumed
   b. *[Kinoo   suugaku   -no gakusei-ga   kono-heya] to
         yesterday mathematics-GEN student-NOM this room   CON
       [ototoi buturi   -no   sensei -ga   ano-heya (-to)]
       the day before physics-GEN teacher-NOM that room (CON)
       -de kono atarasii konpyuutaa-o   tukat-ta.
       -in this new   computer -ACC used

This pattern is again expected under our approach, since the postpositional particles have clear semantic content and must be present in the LF representation. Thus, they cannot take syntactic non-constituents as their complements in the narrow syntax.

Given the general assumption that feature checking/agreement is a structural relation holding between a syntactic constituent and a head, the facts we just pointed out constitute a serious challenge to any approach that takes Japanese case marking as an instance of feature checking/agreement applying in the narrow syntax. Furthermore, the bracketed elements in these examples do not even occupy a unique checking position since they do not form a constituent in the narrow syntax.[32]

On the other hand, these peculiar properties of Japanese case marking receive a natural explanation if we analyse the case marking mechanism in the language as a morphological process in the PF component: Case particles can be assigned to a constituent formed by an application of Phrase-Level Merger/PF reanalysis in the PF component. Thus, examples like those in (40)–(42) can be handled without any difficulty under this approach.

6.2 Case marking in light verb constructions

Another piece of evidence for the PF case marking analysis is found in the light verb construction. Grimshaw and Mester (1988) point out some interesting properties of the Japanese light verb construction, as illustrated below.

(43) a. Taroo-ga   Amerika-ni ryokoo-si-ta.
            -NOM America-to travel -did

   "Taro took a trip to the United States."

   b. Taroo-ga   Amerika-ni ryokoo-o   si-ta.
            -NOM America-to travel -ACC did

In (43a), the verbal noun *ryokoo* "travel" is incorporated into the light verb -*suru* (the past form of this verb is -*sita*, as in the examples above), forming a complex predicate *ryokoo-suru*, which assigns a θ-role to the locative argument *Amerika-ni* "to the United States". In (43b), on the other hand, the verbal noun is not incorporated into the light verb *-suru*, as evidenced by the accusative case marker *-o* attached to the verbal noun. However, the θ-role is assigned in the same way to the locative argument. This poses a problem for the Projection Principle of Chomsky (1981a) (or for the Uniformity of Theta Assignment Hypothesis in Baker 1988), which essentially requires that identical thematic relationships between items are represented by identical structural relationships between those items.

To resolve this problem, Grimshaw and Mester propose a mechanism of "argument transfer", which transfers the θ-role structure associated with the verbal noun to the light verb *-suru*. Extending this analysis further, a series of recent works by Saito and Hoshi (2000), Hoshi (1999, 2001), and Saito (2000) develop a new line of approach to the light verb construction within the framework of minimalism.[33] Since neither the level of D-structure nor the Projection Principle is maintained in the minimalist program, θ-roles can in principle be assigned derivationally in the course of the derivation. Thus, Hoshi and Saito argue that the verbal noun is incorporated into the light verb by covert verb-raising, and that θ-role assignment to the locative noun phrase is carried out derivationally, as schematically represented in (44).

(44) Taroo-ga   Amerika-ni t_i ryokoo$_i$-si-ta.
     -NOM America-to   travel did

This "LF verb incorporation" analysis is theoretically superior to the argument transfer analysis in that by employing the general mechanism of head movement, it is not necessary to have recourse to the special additional mechanism of "argument transfer" only for the particular purposes of the light verb construction. However, the LF verb incorporation analysis faces a problem in accounting for the following examples, which involve the coordination of an argument and a verbal noun by the particles *-to* or *-mo*.

(45) a.   Taroo-ga   kotosi -no   natu   [Amerika-ni ryokoo] to
                  -NOM this year-GEN summer America-to travel   CON
           [Doitu -ni ryuugaku] (-to)   -o   sita
           Germany-to study abroad (-CON)-ACC did

   Lit. "This summer, Taro did [a travel to the United States and a study abroad in Germany]."

   b.   Taroo-ga   kotosi -no   natu   [Amerika-ni ryokoo] mo
                  -NOM this year-GEN summer America-to travel   also
         [Doitu   -ni ryuugaku]   -mo sita.
         Germany-to study abroad-also did

Lit. "This summer, Taro did [a travel to the United States and also a study abroad in Germany]."

In these examples, sequences of an argument and a verbal noun are connected by the connective particles -*to* (in (45a)) and -*mo* (in (45b)). The fact that both of these particles can be used in these constructions (particularly, the possibility of using -*mo* as a connective particle; see our discussion in section 4) indicates that the coordination structure in question is created in the narrow syntax. And if the coordination structure is created in the narrow syntax, it is not possible in these constructions for the verbal noun to incorporate into the light verb -*suru* by covert verb-raising. The general theory of movement prohibits an across-the-board movement of different elements into a single landing site. Notice that overt incorporation of two heads into a single host is excluded, as shown by the ungrammaticality of the following example (with the intended meaning equivalent to that of (45b)).

(46) *Taroo-ga   kotosi -no   natu   [Amerika-ni t_i -mo]
     -NOM this year-GEN summer America-to   also
     [Doitu   -ni t_j -mo] ryokoo$_i$-ryuugaku$_j$ -sita.
     Germany-to   also travel -study abroad-did

Even if such a dubious movement operation were somehow allowed in LF (as opposed to overt syntax, in which the movement is clearly prohibited, as shown by the ungrammaticality of (46)), there would be no way of assuring the correct assignment of θ-roles to argument noun phrases, because they are dispersed in different conjuncts in the coordination. Thus, there is no way to ensure that the structure in (46) will lead to a proper LF representation.

In general, the light verb construction remains problematic for any theory which takes case marking and/or complex predicate formation to be processes within the narrow syntax. By contrast, if we assume that complex predicate formation and case particle assignment are PF operations (in the broader sense; see note 22), all of the problems discussed so far disappear. Based on the observation that the verbal noun and the argument noun phrase form a syntactic constituent, we claim that the light verb constructions are instances of small clauses. That is, examples (43a) and (43b) have an identical syntactic structure in the narrow syntax, represented by (47a) below.

(47) a.   Taroo [$_{\text{Small Clause}}$ Amerika-ni ryokoo] si-ta.
                      America-to travel   did
     b.   Morphological Merger → Taroo Amerika-ni ryokoo-si-ta.
                             America-to travel -did
     (After Nominative Case Marking: Taroo-ga Amerika-ni ryokoo-si-ta.)

c. Accusative Case Marking → Taroo Amerika-ni ryokoo-o si-ta.
America-to travel-ACC did
(After Nominative Case Marking: Taroo-ga Amerika-ni ryokoo-o si-ta.)

No verb-raising is required in the derivations shown in (47), and the verbal noun *ryokoo* assigns its θ-role to the argument in an ordinary fashion. As the structure enters the PF component, there are two options to choose from. One is to apply Morphological Merger to the verbal noun and the light verb, yielding *ryokoo-si-ta* (as in (47b)). The other option is to apply Accusative case marking, assigning *-o* to the verbal noun, as shown in (47c). In short, the structures in (43a/47b) and (43b/47c) are just PF variants of an identical syntactic/LF structure. Note that, in this account, there is no difficulty in explaining the uniformity of θ-role assignment because the variants have exactly the same LF output. The coordination structure in (45) is also not problematic. It is just a normal case of two small clause constituents being connected by the particles.

Finally, Kishimoto (2001) presents an interesting observation that the argument noun phrase in the light verb construction is inside the scope of a quantificational particle *-mo* attached to the verbal noun. Consider the following examples.

(48) a. Taroo-wa Hanako-ni [dare -ga warui-to] -mo
-TOP -DAT anyone-NOM fault -that-MO
iwanakat-ta.
did not say

Lit. "Taro did not say to Hanako that anyone was wrong."

b. *Taroo-wa dare -ni [Hanako-ga warui-to]-mo
-TOP anyone-DAT -NOM fault-that-MO
iwanakat-ta.
did not say

Lit. "Taro did not say to anyone that Hanako was wrong."

c. Taroo-wa doko -ni ryokoo-mo si-nakat-ta.
-TOP anywhere-to travel -MO did not

Lit. "Taro did not travel to anywhere."

As shown in the contrast between (48a) and (48b), the indefinite pronoun *dare* "anyone" must be in the scope of both the negation and the quantificational particle *-mo*. In the grammatical example (48a), the particle *-mo* is attached to the embedded clause and the indefinite pronoun is located inside the embedded clause. Example (48b) violates the condition, since the indefinite pronoun is located in the matrix clause and hence is outside the scope of the quantificational particle attached to the embedded clause. The grammatical status of example (48c) therefore indicates that the argument *doko-ni* "to anywhere" is located inside the scope of *-mo*, attached to the verbal noun *ryokoo* "travel". Based on this observation, Kishimoto argues that the particle *-mo* is indeed incorporated into the light verb along with the verbal noun. How is the necessary "incorporation" carried out, then? As we have already argued above, the covert incorporation analysis faces a serious problem in explaining coordination structures. Furthermore, it is not easy to answer the question of why only covert incorporation can pied-pipe the particle *-mo*, as opposed to overt incorporation, which never pied-pipes quantificational particles.

Again, if case marking takes place in the phonological component, as we have suggested, there is no problem in explaining this kind of example. The argument noun phrase and the verbal noun form a small clause constituent in the narrow syntax, and the quantificational particle is attached to this small clause as depicted in (49) below.

(49) Taroo-wa [$_{\text{Small Clause}}$ doko   -ni ryokoo]-mo si-nakat-ta.
     -TOP   anywhere-to travel -MO did not

Note that the argument *doko-ni* is located inside the scope of *-mo* in (49). Since the particle blocks adjacency between the verbal noun and the light verb, Morphological Merger does not apply to these elements. The reason why the particle is attached to the verbal noun in PF is that it is a clitic, as argued by Aoyagi (1998a, b). Thus, the observation made by Kishimoto (2001) provides still another piece of evidence for the PF case marking approach to Japanese.

Summarizing, we have seen that there are cases where case particles are attached to a constituent which is presumably formed by PF reanalysis. Thus, to the extent that our PF reanalysis is correct, these cases constitute evidence that case marking in Japanese takes place in the phonological component, i.e., case marking in the language must apply after PF reanalysis has taken place. Various properties of the light verb construction in Japanese were also examined in this section with regard to case marking, and we have argued that a careful examination of the properties of this construction also leads to the same conclusion that case particles in Japanese are assigned in the PF component.

7 Concluding remarks

The notion of functional categories plays an extremely important role in current linguistic theory, both with respect to universal principles and parametric variation. Yet, there is virtually no substantive general theory of these categories, which makes the discussion on these categories somewhat obscure. This paper is an attempt to clarify some of the central issues concerning functional categories, particularly as these elements pertain to Japanese syntax.

After briefly going over the major developments of the concept of functional categories in linguistic theory, we have proposed, based on various earlier works (see the discussion in section 2.1), the following general guideline for postulation of functional categories in a given language.

(3)   *The Visibility Guideline for Functional Categories*
A functional category has to be visible (i.e., detectable) in the primary linguistic data.

There are three ways that a functional category can be visible in the primary linguistic data. One is to have phonetic content and to be pronounced, thereby becoming directly visible at PF. The other two ways are indirect ways of becoming detectable in the overt data. That is, a functional category can be detectable indirectly, either by triggering a movement of a phrasal projection (and thus affecting the canonical word order), or by affecting the shape of a neighbouring head (via head movement, generally). We have also noted (see (4)) that the first possibility (direct detectability) and the other two (indirect detectability) seem to be mutually exclusive, i.e., a functional category can be visible either directly or indirectly, but not in both ways. From this generalization, it follows that, if a functional head has phonetic content, it doesn't induce feature checking, triggering no head or phrasal movement.

We then discussed the issues concerning functional categories in Japanese. As soon as the notion of functional categories was put forth in the mid-1980s, it was hypothesized that Japanese does not have active functional categories in the lexicon (Fukui 1986). On the other hand, much recent work on Japanese syntax (either in the "government-binding" framework or in the minimalist program) simply assumes the existence of functional categories in the language. We have argued that in the absence of a substantive general theory of functional categories, a meaningful question to be addressed at the present stage of our understanding is the following empirical question.

(5)   Does Japanese exhibit formal and mechanical "feature checking phenomena" which are comparable in nature to those attested in other languages (such as English and other European languages)?

Thus, if a phenomenon seemingly related to a functional category (either phrasal movement, head movement, or some sort of "agreement") is to be identified in Japanese, it is necessary to determine whether the given phenomenon is of the same nature as the attested cases of agreement or movement induced by a functional category, i.e., whether it is of formal and mechanical nature that should be handled by Agree (or some such mechanism) or head movement.

In fact, very few arguments have ever been put forward in favour of the existence of active functional categories in Japanese in the relevant sense just defined (in (5)), despite the fact that many researchers working on Japanese syntax simply "assume" their existence. Koizumi (2000) is one of the few such serious attempts. We examined in detail his arguments for string vacuous overt V-to-T(-to-C) raising in Japanese, and argued that his arguments suffer from various empirical problems (see section 3). An alternative approach in terms of PF reanalysis was proposed and the discussion was then extended to the issues of case marking in Japanese. We have argued that case particles in Japanese are assigned to the elements created by PF reanalysis (Morphological Merger), which entails that case marking in the language takes place in the phonological component rather than in the narrow syntax.

Thus, we must conclude that the empirical arguments for the existence of active functional categories in Japanese have yet to be presented. In the absence of compelling evidence for postulating a formal and mechanical "feature checking" mechanism in Japanese, we must at this point answer negatively question (5) above, and the minimalist guidelines (particularly the Visibility Guideline (3)) force us to continue to assume that Japanese lacks active functional categories. The hypothesis that Japanese lacks active (agreement-inducing) functional categories is advanced by Kuroda (1988) and Fukui's series of works, and essentially the same conclusion is independently reached in recent works by Hoji (1998a, b, 2002) based on a careful examination of the phenomena in Japanese that are not covered in this paper. Our discussion in this paper confirms the conclusion that there is no compelling reason yet for questioning the hypothesis.

We have focused the discussion on the functional head T, and have not delved into the issues concerning the other possible functional categories in Japanese. But our discussion can readily be extended to the other candidates for functional categories in the language (cf. also the discussion in section 2.1). The elements in Japanese which can be reasonable candidates for these functional heads (e.g., *-ka* for C, *-ga* for K(ase), *-no* for D, etc.) have invariable phonetic shape, and there is no known evidence that these elements trigger agreement/feature checking phenomena. In fact, if Fukui and Takano's (1998) generalization (see (4) in section 2.1) is tenable, these elements in Japanese should not participate in agreement or feature checking (because they have invariant phonetic shape). Thus, we are again led to the (tentative) conclusion that Japanese lacks active functional categories in the lexicon.

What does this conclusion tell us about the overall picture of Japanese grammar, as it relates to UG? Our discussion in this paper suggests that many of the processes taking place in the narrow syntax of English and other similar languages are found in the phonological component of Japanese grammar. More precisely, the role of narrow syntactic mechanisms seems to be transferred to the mechanisms in the phonological component (case marking is a case in point). Interestingly enough, Takeda (1999) argues that the formation of relative clauses in Japanese takes place not in the form of feature checking (operator movement) in narrow syntax, but rather, in terms of type-shifting in the "semantic component". Fukui and Takano (2000) argue that various differences between English and Japanese noun phrases, particularly the relative clause structures, receive a unified account if Japanese, as opposed to English, lacks the N-to-D raising process (owing to the lack of D in its lexicon), inducing no relevant "feature checking".[34] Ono (2002) examines the properties of exclamatory sentences in English and Japanese, and argues that this construction involves a kind of feature checking in English, while no such operation takes place in Japanese, owing to the existence in the latter (and the lack thereof in the former) of an overt element (*no da*) that marks the construction. If the analyses presented in these works are on the right track, then the role of narrow syntactic operations is transferred not only to the phonological component, as we have suggested in this paper, but also to the "semantic component" in the grammar of Japanese, particularly with respect to "operator movement" constructions. That is, more important processes occur in Japanese grammar "closer to" semantic and phonetic representations, as compared to the corresponding processes in English.[35]

This situation arises because the operation Agree apparently does not apply in Japanese, owing to the lack of the features that trigger its application (uninterpretable features). Thus, although Agree is made available by UG (and hence available in Japanese grammar as well), the operation remains (almost) totally unused in Japanese. Although it is unclear at this point whether this situation is natural or strange (calling for some discussion), let us consider some of the related issues here.

Agree is an operation in narrow syntax that is responsible for feature checking (see Chomsky 2000, 2001a, b). The need for this operation (and also the need for uninterpretable features) is grounded on the existence of the dislocation property (transformations) in natural languages. Chomsky often suggests (see Chomsky 1965, 2000, among many others) that interface conditions require that such notions as "topic-comment", "presupposition", "focus", "new/old information", etc. (collectively called the "surface structure" properties) be encoded into a linguistic expression produced by the human language system. These properties often involve the "edge" of constructions, which in turn requires the relevant element to be at the "edge" of a phrase or clause, yielding the need for dislocation of elements. The existence of uninterpretable features is required as a drive for dislocation or movement, and the formal operation Agree is called upon to handle feature checking.

While the first step of this reasoning seems universally true (i.e., the interface conditions require such notions as "topic-comment", etc.), there is no a priori reason that every language has to meet the requirement exactly in the same way, for example by placing the element at the "edge". Thus, Japanese has a specific element to mark the topic (*-wa*), which nullifies the need for marking a topic by placing it at the beginning of a sentence.

Although we cannot go into the details here, various case particles supplied by the Japanese lexicon (as well as the mechanism of complex predicate formation, in some cases) can actually express the other "surface" properties mentioned above. If so, there is simply no need in these respects for "dislocation" in Japanese; hence no need for uninterpretable features as a drive for movement. Thus, the operation Agree need not (and perhaps does not) apply in the narrow syntax of Japanese.

However, this does not mean that Agree is unavailable to the speakers of Japanese. To the extent that the operation is made available by UG, it should be available even in Japanese. In fact, a classical work by Harada (1973a, see also Harada 1972) demonstrates that the relationship between the Q-marker *-ka* and *wh*-phrases in Japanese exhibits properties very similar to those of Agree, though with important differences which show that the phenomenon does not belong to narrow syntax.[36] Thus, the grammar of Japanese makes use of a formal operation very similar in nature to Agree, although the operation does not seem to apply in narrow syntax. This suggests that what UG provides is a general (downward) "search mechanism" which meets specific locality conditions, and that the particular operation Agree as it is formulated for feature checking purposes in narrow syntax is a realization of this general search mechanism when it applies to a specialized relation (feature checking) in a specific component of grammar (narrow syntax). Japanese happens to lack this particular realization of the mechanism, but it is nevertheless equipped with the general search procedure, applying in a different component of the grammar.

As we briefly discussed in section 2, earlier work by Fukui and Kuroda shows that various characteristics of Japanese can be deduced from the fundamental parametric property of the language, i.e., the lack of formal agreement. Chomsky (2000: 131, 2001a, b) suggests that the operation Spell-Out is associated with agreement. More specifically, the timing of Spell-Out is related to the existence (and deletion) of uninterpretable features. Given the existence of uninterpretable features, Agree must apply to delete the features, and then Spell-Out must apply at the following phase level. Thus, if a language does not have the relevant uninterpretable features, then the timing of Spell-Out is not narrowly constrained and the operation can apply rather freely in the derivation (to the extent that the derivation will not crash). A case in point is Japanese. It is fairly clear that noun phrases in Japanese lack (interpretable) ϕ-features, which results in the non-existence of uninterpretable ϕ-features of T (see also Zushi 2002, for related discussion). Furthermore, Fukui and Takano (1998) argue that Japanese noun phrases do not have uninterpretable Case features to be deleted under feature checking. With overt case particles available in the lexicon, noun phrases in Japanese do not have to undergo feature checking to delete Case features (see Fukui and Takano 1998 for details). If this is indeed the case, and if the class of "phases" include (some) noun phrases (and possibly some adpositional phrases as well), then it follows that Spell-Out can optionally apply either, say, at the object noun phrase level (spelling it out to the phonological component, prior to the rest of the sentence), or at the *v*P/CP level. The former option yields a "scrambled" sentence (such as *pizza-o Taroo-ga tabeta* "Taro ate pizza"), while the latter option leads to a "canonical" SOV order (such as *Taroo-ga pizza-o tabeta* "Taro ate pizza"). In this way, the plausibility of the hypothesis that agreement does not take place in Japanese (or that Agree does not apply in the narrow syntax of Japanese) is further increased by showing that by interacting with other well-motivated principles and properties of Japanese, the hypothesis elegantly accounts for another salient property of the language, i.e., the existence of scrambling.[37]

The issues are all empirical. Thus, the conclusions discussed in this section are all tentative, subject to further empirical investigation. The existence of active functional categories/formal and mechanical feature checking in Japanese is still open to discussion, calling for novel empirical discoveries about the nature and properties of Japanese grammar. At the present stage of our understanding, however, the facts about Japanese seem to lead us to the conclusions that we have arrived at in this paper.

Appendix
On the nature of economy in language

This paper argues that there are rather unexpected fundamental connections to be made between the principles of language and the laws governing the inorganic world. After summarizing the major development of economy principles in physics and the basic results of discrete optimization problems in combinatorial mathematics, I will argue that the economy principles which theoretical linguists are currently trying to discover in the theory of language are something comparable to the Principle of Least Action in physics. This provides us with a concrete interpretation of the point Chomsky has repeatedly made (Chomsky 1991a, b, *passim*), i.e., language, despite its biological nature, shares the fundamental property of the inorganic world; it is designed for "elegance", not for efficient use. I will then discuss the nature of two types of economy principles of language proposed in the literature, "economy of derivation" and "economy of representation", from the point of view of the theory of computational complexity, and claim that the two economy principles exhibit quite different properties with respect to their computational complexities: economy of representation is efficiently solvable and therefore seems to be in the complexity class P in the sense of the theory of computational complexity, whereas economy of derivation is fundamentally computationally intractable and appears to belong to the class NP-P. How, then, can language ever be used, if its fundamental property (economy of derivation) poses an intractable optimization problem? I will suggest that language is equipped with certain mechanisms, the real-world counterparts of the "heuristic algorithms" studied in the theory of optimization, that facilitate its efficient use. Thus, to the extent that these mechanisms are available, language becomes usable, despite its fundamental computational intractability.

Considerations of "economy" in language have entered discussion within the theory of generative grammar since virtually the outset of the theory as part of the evaluation metric in the form of a "simplicity measure" (Chomsky 1951, 1955 (chapter 4); see also Chomsky 1965 (chapter 1, section 7) and Chomsky and Halle 1968 (chapter 9) for some relevant discussion). As the theory of generative grammar has advanced, however, the role of an evaluation metric in linguistic theory has declined, and with the advent of the principles-and-parameters approach in the early 1980s, the notion of an evaluation metric has generally been assumed to be completely dispensable, since the principles of Universal Grammar (UG) now seem sufficiently restrictive so that a language can be uniquely determined by the theory of UG on the basis of primary linguistic data (Chomsky 1981a). Nevertheless, as inquiry into the nature of language has progressed, it has also become clear that something that might be called "principles of economy" do play a significant role in determining the fundamental properties of language. Thus, Chomsky (1991b) suggested that there are some overarching economy principles that seem to have the effect of deriving most, if not all, of the existing "principles" of UG such as the Empty Category Principle (ECP), the Subjacency Condition, etc. Since then, the role of economy in the entire system of grammar has been significantly increased and the nature of economy principles in language has been the focus of much recent discussion in the linguistic literature.

The purpose of this paper is to explore the deeper nature of such economy principles in language in an attempt to place them in a wider intellectual context. In the next section, I will discuss "economy principles" in physics and show how these economy considerations crystallized to take the form of the Principle of Least Action in the eighteenth century. In section 2, I will go on to discuss so-called "discrete optimization problems" in various fields of combinatorial mathematics and overview what major results have been achieved in this area, particularly with respect to the theory of computational complexity. These considerations of economy in physics and combinatorial mathematics offer a number of quite interesting implications for the general design of language, if language indeed exhibits the property of economy as suggested by Chomsky. I will discuss these implications in detail in section 3. Section 4 gives a summary of our discussion and offers some conclusions.

1 Economy principles in physics

"Economy principles" have long been noted by scientists working on laws of nature. For example, Hero, a Greek mathematician in the first century, asserted that when a ray comes from point A to another point B reflecting at the point P on the surface of a mirror, the actual path that the ray takes is the *shortest possible* one that anything can take in going from A to the mirror and then to B. Scientists after Greek times claimed, primarily on the basis of such discoveries as Hero's, that nature acts in the shortest possible way. Thus, Olympiodorus (in the sixth century) said in his *Catoptrica* that "nature does nothing superfluous or any unnecessary work", a claim that was later echoed by Leonardo da Vinci, who asserted that "nature is economical".[1] In medieval times, the idea that nature is fundamentally "economical" was commonly accepted (see Kline 1972 for more detailed discussions).

The next big step toward the proper characterization of economy principles of nature was made by Pierre de Fermat in 1657. Fermat noted that, although Hero's law is true for reflection in a homogeneous material, the law is not applicable to a ray leaving a point A, refracting at an interface, and arriving at B in the transmitting medium. In this case, the shortest distance is a straight line from A to B, and that is certainly not the path taken by light. In other words, Fermat observed that Hero's law does not hold for cases in which light travels from a point in one uniform medium to a point in another, different medium. It then appeared as though reflection and refraction of light are governed by different principles. However, Fermat went on to claim that this is not the case and discovered that there is a unifying principle governing both reflection and refraction of light. He stated this principle as follows: A ray of light in traversing a route from one point to another follows the path which requires the *least time* (rather than the shortest distance). According to him, then, a light ray starting from one point and headed for another point considers all possible paths and then chooses the one that "economizes" most on time.[2] This is the principle now known as *Fermat's Principle of Least Time*.

By the early eighteenth century, there had been a few important attempts at elaborating on the description of the nature of economy in the physical world (e.g., Huygens's elaboration of Fermat's Principle of Least Time), but the next important step after Fermat's work was clearly the one done by Pierre-Louis Moreau de Maupertuis in 1744. Maupertuis argued that the principle of economy of nature is best satisfied not by time of transit (as Fermat claims), but by a scalar quantity that he called (somewhat misleadingly, from the current point of view) "action", mathematically the integral of the product of mass, velocity, and distance traversed by a moving object. He then proposed a principle called the *Principle of Least Action*, which states that any changes in nature, including the travel of light and motion of bodies, are such as to make the action *least*, thereby incorporating Fermat's Principle of Least Time into Newtonian mechanics, and furthermore, deriving, say, Newton's second law of motion. Again, it is as though each body (or particle) considers all possible paths laid out before it, and chooses the one along which its action changes minimally.

Almost at the same time as Maupertuis discovered his Principle of Least Action, Leonhard Euler arrived at the same conclusion and gave it a precise mathematical formulation. Euler's method, refined further by Joseph-Louis Comte de Lagrange, is called the *calculus of variations*. Because of its technical complexities, we cannot go into the details of the calculus of variations here, but the following discussion should suffice for our present concern.[3] Euler sharpened the mathematical formulation of the Principle of Least Action and derived the form of the differential equation ("Euler's equation") that constitutes the necessary conditions for the paths of particles and light rays to fulfill in order to make the action least. Lagrange then proposed the method of the calculus of variations (the term is actually Euler's) to give a mathematically elegant form of the Principle of Least Action, so that we can apply the Principle to more dynamical problems and, consequently, can replace the Newtonian laws of motion by the Principle of Least Action and the law of conservation of energy.

To see the fundamental idea of the Euler-Lagrange method, let us consider the situation in which the two points (x_1, y_1) and (x_2, y_2) are connected by a tentative path P. This path, chosen as an arbitrary continuous curve, will, in all probability, *not* coincide with the *actual* path that nature chooses for the motion. But, we can gradually *modify* our tentative solution and eventually arrive at the curve that is chosen as the actual path of motion, by considering the changes associated with an integral (an "action integral"; see above) that are due to conceptually possible displacements from the path that describes the actual history of the system (i.e., by looking at the "variations").[4] Notice that the changes in an integral (the "value" of each integral) varies from path to path. Some paths have greater values, for others the values come out smaller. Mathematically, it can be said that all possible paths have been examined. Also, there must exist one definite path for which the value of an integral is minimum.

Now the Principle of Least Action can be stated as the assertion that this particular path *with a minimum value of an action integral* be the one chosen by nature as the *actual* path of motion. By this method of the calculus of variations and the precise formulation of the Principle of Least Action, Euler and Lagrange laid out the solid foundation for a new field known as *analytical mechanics*, which is based on two fundamental scalar quantities, "kinetic energy" and "potential energy", as opposed to the classical Newtonian mechanics that is based on such vectors as "force" and "momentum".

William Rowan Hamilton then investigated the nature of Fermat's Principle of Least Time and Maupertuis's Principle of Least Action, and noted the similarity between the two principles. He then proceeded to claim that a kind of geometrical optical theory of mechanics could be developed in such a way that the laws of optics (e.g., Fermat's Principle of Least Time) and those of mechanics (e.g., The Principle of Least Action) can be combined and represented by the same, unifying minimum principle of action, now called *Hamilton's Principle*. Briefly put, Hamilton's Principle states that the action integral of the difference between the kinetic energy of an object and its potential energy over the interval of time during which the motion takes place must be a *minimum* for the path actually chosen by nature.

Hamilton's Principle was regarded as a final product of efforts in pursuit of the economy principle of nature (although, of course, there were important subsequent works, such as Jacobi's; see, for example, Lanczos 1970=1986 for much detailed discussion), and was taken to be the single, fundamental unifying minimum principle in physics from which numerous laws in various subfields of physics can be deduced, including the laws of mechanics, optics, electricity, and magnetism. Although twentieth-century physics, viz., electromagnetic theory, the theory of relativity, and quantum mechanics, has dramatically changed our view on the relevant physical phenomena, and hence Hamilton's Principle no longer suffices to unify all physical phenomena in as straightforward a way as it seemed to, it still stands as a basic principle for many branches of physics.

A few remarks are in order about the nature of the economy principle of physics in relation to the economy principle in language to be discussed below. First, the common feature of "economy principles" in physics can be summarized as follows: (i) find the relevant quantity Q; (ii) then, the principle is stated in the form "minimize Q", that is, in the form of a minimum principle. If the fundamental principle of language is shown to be stated essentially in this form, as I will argue below, it is a rather surprising discovery which indicates a remarkable similarity between the inorganic world and language, a similarity that is by no means expected, given the biological nature of language. This holds true even though there are differences with respect to the properties of Q and the method of minimization between the inorganic world and language (see the following sections for details).

Secondly, the economy principle in physics is fundamentally "global" in nature (the term will be made precise in section 3). For example, in order to apply Hamilton's Principle to an actual case of physical phenomena, say, the motion of an object starting at time t_1 and ending at time t_2, we must know the initial condition of the motion at t_1 and the final condition of the motion at t_2; more specifically, we must know the kinetic energy and the potential energy that the object possesses at t_1 and t_2, and must calculate the difference between the kinetic and potential energies. In fact, we can say that while Newtonian mechanics approaches physical phenomena in a "local" fashion in terms of differentiation, the Hamiltonian approach provides us with a "global" alternative for the description of physical phenomena, in terms of "action integrals". This point will become important when we consider the "global" nature of economy of derivation in language, as we will see later in section 3. We must note, however, that there is also an important difference between the Principle of Least Action and economy of derivation, as Takao Gunji points out (personal communication; see also Gunji 1994): in the former case, it is always possible (under certain conditions) to obtain a "differential", i.e., "local", counterpart of the Principle (the Euler-Lagrange equations), whereas in the latter case there is no known algorithm to formulate an equivalent local principle corresponding to economy of derivation (but see the discussion in section 4). This difference stems from the fact that the Principle of Least Action deals with continua, whereas economy of derivation is a property of a discrete system, where the calculus of variations cannot be used. Despite this and other possible differences due to the nature of the quantity Q in the two areas of inquiry, our main point still seems to hold, as we will see in the discussion that follows.

2 Discrete optimization problems

In section 1, we presented a brief historical overview of the development of the principle of economy in physics. Since language is a discrete system, and our major concern in this paper is the nature of economy in language, perhaps a more direct analogy can be made to so-called "discrete optimization problems", studied in the field of discrete mathematics and theoretical computer science.[5] Let us first examine what "optimization" means in its most general form. Optimization involves finding the variable x (called the *decision variable*) that minimizes[6] the function (called the *objective function*) $f(x)$ under some constraints. Let the variable x be an n-dimensional vector $x = (x_1, \ldots, x_n)'$. Then, an optimization problem can be stated as follows.

(1) Optimization Problem
    Objective function: $f(x)$
    Constraints: $x \in S$
    Problem: Minimize $(f(x))$

where the objective function f is defined over an appropriately chosen set $X (\supseteq S)$. The set S, which is a subset of X, is called the *feasible region* of the optimization problem, in which the variable x can take its value. The feasible region S is often given by a set of equations and/or inequalities with respect to x, though there are many cases in which the factors determining the feasible region are so complex that such equational specifications become hard to obtain. If x satisfies the constraints $x \in S$, it is called a feasible solution of the optimization problem (1). And if a feasible solution $x^*(x^* \in S)$ fulfills the condition (in the case of minimization):

(2) $f(x^*) \leq f(x)$, where $x \in S$,

it is called the *optimal solution* of an optimization problem (1). Given a neighbourhood set $U(x^*)$ that includes a feasible solution $x^* \in S$, x^* is called a *local optimal solution* if the following relation holds.

(3) $f(x^*) \leq f(x)$, where $x \in S \cap U(x^*)$

The feasible solution x^* in (2) is sometimes called a *global* optimal solution, when we need to distinguish it from the local optimal solution characterized in (3). A global optimal solution is always a local optimal solution, but the converse is not necessarily true. An optimization problem is to find an optimal solution which minimizes the value of an objective function under the given constraints.

Optimization problems can be classified based on the type of the variable, the objective function, and the constraints. If the variable takes a continuous real-number value, the optimization problem is called a *continuous* optimization problem. If the variable takes a discrete value (such as an integer), the problem is called a *discrete* optimization problem. So-called variational principles in physics, including Hamilton's Principle discussed in section 1, fall under the class of continuous optimization problems, in which the calculus of variations plays a central role. Discrete optimization problems include various combinatorial problems studied in combinatorial mathematics, and are further divided into different subtypes, depending on the form of constraints ("integer programming problems", "network flow problems", etc.; see, for instance, Ibaraki and Fukushima 1993 for a detailed discussion of various optimization problems). As we will see in the following section, economy principles in language are best characterized as instances of a discrete optimization problem.

Optimization problems are also classified from the viewpoint of the theory of computational complexity. Complexity theory deals with the classification of problems as to their intrinsic computational difficulty in terms of time, space, or other resources needed to solve the problems.[8] A great deal of progress has been made in classifying problems into general *complexity classes* which characterize their inherent computational difficulties in terms of time and space. Among those complexity classes, the most important classes for our present purposes are the classes P and NP. The class P is defined as the class of decision problems solvable within a polynomial-time-bound on a deterministic Turing machine. Technical details aside (see, for example, Hopcroft and Ullman 1979), the particular importance of this class of problems is due to the generally held thesis (Edmonds 1965, Garey and Johnson 1979), comparable in its status to Church's Thesis on computable functions, that the class P defines the class of problems that can be solved *efficiently*.

The class NP is defined as the class of decision problems solvable within a polynomial-time-bound on a nondeterministic Turing machine. The class NP trivially contains the class P (P $\subseteq$ NP) since deterministic Turing machines are special cases of nondeterministic Turing machines. However, it appears to be the case, yet to be proved though, that the class NP contains much more than P, i.e., the inclusion is proper (P $\neq$ NP), because nondeterminism generally adds significant power to time-bounded computations. An important property of the class NP is that, informally, it represents the class of decision problems that are *computationally intractable*. A decision problem in this class does not appear to have an efficient algorithm for its solution.

However, it is also known that a problem in the class NP is not always too hard to solve, in the sense that, although there is no efficient algorithm, it often allows for an easy "guess-and-check" procedure yielding a shortcut to what would otherwise seem to be an unavoidably exponential-time search. A problem in this class, in other words, is "easier" than a problem requiring exponential time for its solution (which is completely intractable and nonfeasible), but is "harder" than a problem which requires polynomial time with one processor (i.e., a problem in P). In short, a problem in this complexity class is intractable, but not always *too* intractable; it is hard to solve, but there is, in most cases, a way out, and, once the solution is found, it is easy to verify. See the references mentioned in note 8 for more detailed discussions. See also Johnson (1990) for a comprehensive overview of the classification of problems with respect to complexity classes.

A wide variety of problems that can be formulated as optimization problems are known to be in the class P. Perhaps the most famous (and significant) result is that the linear programming problem, which is a special case of continuous optimization problems, belongs to this complexity class. Some of the combinatorial optimization problems are also known to be in P.

The class NP contains various decision problems, including some of the well-known optimization problems such as the integer programming problem and the travelling salesperson problem. As we just discussed, optimization problems in this complexity class do not seem to have efficient algorithms and therefore appear to be computationally intractable. But, as stated above, they often allow for guess-and-check procedures to obtain "approximate optimal solutions". Various algorithms have been proposed to get approximate optimal solutions for optimization problems that are known to be in NP, e.g., the greedy method, the neighbourhood search, the genetic algorithm, to name a few (see Ibaraki and Fukushima 1993, see also Cormen et al. 1990 for much detailed discussion about what these methods are and how they work for concrete optimization problems). All of these "heuristic algorithms" share a common important property: they all attempt to make a good guess about the global optimal solution by examining, in one way or another, a local optimal solution, thereby bypassing the "globality" of the problem which is characteristic of a decision problem belonging to the class NP. This point will be taken up again when we consider the nature of economy of language in the next section.

3 Implications for language design

In the preceding sections, I have briefly discussed how the idea of economy of the natural world has evolved and crystallized to take the form of the Principle of Least Action in physics and how the problem of optimization (minimization) has been formalized and studied in discrete mathematics and the theory of computational complexity. In this section, I will explore the implications of the results accumulated in these fields for the nature of economy in language.

Let us first briefly summarize the current framework of generative grammar as it is outlined in Chomsky (1993a, 1994, 1995b), a framework called the "minimalist program" (or "minimalism"). The theory of generative grammar takes a biological approach to language, in which language is taken to be part of the natural world (the mind/brain). One component of the human brain, the *language faculty*, is responsible for the use of language. The language faculty provides a specific mapping system, a generative procedure called an "I-language"[9] (Chomsky 1986b), that generates a set of *structural descriptions*, each of which contains "semantic" and "phonetic" properties. The structural descriptions so generated are called the *expressions* of the language. A structural description, i.e., a linguistic expression, is a sequence of representations, one for each *linguistic level*, a symbolic system of a particular type.

Since language is obviously embedded in performance systems which enable its expressions to be used for various purposes, a structural description must contain at least two *interface levels* for different types of performance systems, the articulatory-perceptual and the conceptual-intentional systems, providing instructions for each of these systems. The minimalist program takes these two interface levels to be the *only* linguistic levels in the language, and identifies them as PF (phonetic form) for the articulatory-perceptual performance system, and LF (logical form) for the conceptual-intentional system. Thus, each structural description has a pair (π, λ), representations at PF and LF, respectively, and each language determines a set of pairs, $[(\pi, \lambda)]$, drawn from the interface levels.

A general assumption is that a language consists of two distinct components: (i) a lexicon, and (ii) a computational system. The lexicon provides an array of items with their idiosyncratic properties (a set of (sets of) features), i.e., it provides the inputs for the computational system. More specifically, the computational system (C_{HL}) selects some array of lexical choices and maps them to the pair (π, λ). Following Chomsky (1994: 7), let us assume that "some array of lexical choices" at least indicates what the lexical choices are and how many times each is selected from the lexicon. Call it *numeration* (N): $N = [(\underline{l}, \underline{n})]$ where $\underline{l}$ is an item of the lexicon and $\underline{n}$ is its index, understood to be the number of times that $\underline{l}$ is selected from the lexicon. Then, what the computational system C_{HL}, a mapping from N to (π, λ), carries out are: (1) selects an item $\underline{l}$ from N, (2) reduces its index $\underline{n}$ by 1, (3) performs a permissible computation, and (4) continues until $\underline{n}$ becomes 0, forming a *derivation* which leads to the pair (π, λ).[10]

A derivation D *converges* if it yields a "legitimate" structural description (π, λ);[11] otherwise it *crashes*. "Legitimacy" of π and λ are determined at PF and LF, respectively, in terms of interface conditions. Thus, some of the interface conditions are *convergence conditions*. One of the convergence conditions, or perhaps *the* convergence condition, is the condition on *economy of representation* (or the condition of "Full Interpretation"), which states that an interface representation be constituted entirely of legitimate objects, that is, "elements that have a uniform, language-independent interpretation at the interface" (Chomsky 1993a: 26). If π/λ satisfies the condition on economy of representation, the derivation D that formed it converges at PF/LF; otherwise, it crashes at PF/LF. The minimalist program asserts that conditions on representations "hold only at the interface, and are motivated by properties of the interface, perhaps properly understood as modes of interpretation by performance systems" (Chomsky 1993a: 4).

Under the minimalist conception of language we are considering, each linguistic expression (a structural description) is a formal object that is the *optimal* realization of the interface conditions. "Optimality", then, is determined by the principles of economy. The condition on economy of representation, which dictates that an interface representation consist of only legitimate objects, is one such economy principle. The linguistic expressions, however, must also meet another type of economy principle: the condition on *economy of derivation*. The condition on economy of derivation requires that interface representations have the "most economical" (or "least costly") derivation that formed them, where the "cost" of derivation is determined by some general metric defined by UG. Thus, there are two kinds of "economy" conditions in language; the condition on economy of representation and the condition on economy of derivation. And these economy conditions determine what counts as "optimal" in language.

Let us now explore implications of our discussions in the previous sections for the theory of language. Most importantly, the results in physics discussed in section 1 confirm the point that Chomsky has repeatedly made in his writings. Thus, at the very end of Chomsky (1991b), he states, referring to economy principles: "what we seem to discover are some intriguing and unexpected features of language design, not unlike those that have been discovered throughout the inquiry into the nature of language, though unusual among biological systems of the natural world" (Chomsky 1991b: 448). Chomsky further claims that the property of language as represented by principles of economy "is the kind of property that one seeks in core areas of the natural sciences" (Chomsky 1991a: 49). Given our discussion in section 1, we now have a concrete interpretation of what Chomsky suggests. The principle of language which linguists are now trying to discover is the same kind of minimum principle that physics has discovered in search of a unifying principle governing the laws of nature; that is, the linguistic version of Hamilton's Principle of Least Action.[12] If we compare Hamilton's Principle and the condition on economy of derivation, the similarities between the two principles are obvious; they both have the effect of minimizing the value of a function (or a functional), both principles require some form of "globality", etc. The analogy does not seem to be so straightforward in the case of the condition on economy of representation, as we will see shortly.

The discussion on discrete optimization problems in section 2 sheds more light on the nature of economy principles in language. Let us consider first the condition on economy of derivation, which essentially requires a derivation to be minimal in cost. The optimization problem posed by this condition obviously requires "globality". For example, to determine the status of an interface representation λ (we put aside the discussion of the "PF-side" for the moment) in this respect, one must determine whether the derivation forming it is minimal in cost, i.e., less costly than *any other possible* convergent derivation. As Chomsky claims (Chomsky 1991b, 1993a), this yields a serious computational burden, requiring "global" information.

To make our exposition straightforward, let us be a little bit more precise about what global/local means in the case of language. The clarification seems necessary since the terms "local" and "global" are used somewhat inconsistently in linguistics and the theory of computational complexity. We say a condition C is *local* if we can determine whether C is fulfilled or not by inspecting a *single* Phrase-marker; otherwise it is *global*.

We further say that a condition C is *strictly local* if we can determine whether it is met or not by inspecting a certain well-defined subdomain of a Phrase-marker (without paying attention to what happens in other parts of the same Phrase-marker), where a "certain subdomain" is generally taken to be the "minimal domain" of a given head.[13] Notice that the inspection with respect to a "strictly local" condition can and must be carried out in isolation of other conditions, whereas the inspection for a "local" (but not "strictly local") condition does not necessarily have this property. In other words, "strict locality" requires that a (local) condition does not essentially interact with other (local) conditions. This requirement does not generally hold for local (but not strictly local) conditions.[14] Given these characterizations of "(strict) locality/globality", it is clear that the condition on economy of derivation is a global condition, since, to determine whether it is satisfied or not, we have to inspect more than one Phrase-marker or perhaps even more than one derivation.

Let us consider now the condition on economy of representation, the other type of economy principle in language. As we saw above, this condition is the convergence condition, to be fulfilled at the interface levels. To see if the condition on economy of representation is met, we must inspect an interface representation λ, which is a Phrase-marker, *but nothing more*. Unlike economy of derivation, economy of representation is totally determined by inspecting a single interface representation. Therefore, the condition on economy of representation is a local condition, according to the characterization of locality/globality of a condition given above. Furthermore, notice that most of the interface conditions determining the legitimate objects are "strictly local" in the sense that we can determine whether they are satisfied or not by looking at a very local subdomain (the minimal domain) of a Phrase-marker, without considering other parts of the Phrase-marker.[15] It is then reasonable to characterize the condition on economy of representation as a strictly local condition.

We have just concluded that the condition on economy of derivation is a global condition, sharing basically the same "globality" with Hamilton's Principle of Least Action, whereas the condition on economy of representation appears to be a strictly local condition. Let us now consider the two economy conditions from the point of view of the theory of computational complexity.[16] As we saw in the preceding section, it is generally assumed in the complexity theory that "globality" is the major factor that induces a certain type of computational intractability; if a problem requires global information for its solution, then it is highly unlikely that the problem belongs to the class P (it most likely belongs to the class NP-P or a harder class).

Thus, if we formulate an optimization problem based on considerations having to do with economy of derivation, it is reasonable to conjecture, given the global nature of economy of derivation just discussed, that the problem does not belong to the class P. For concreteness, let us define a binary relation $R = [<(\pi, \lambda), D> | (\pi, \lambda)$ is a structural description of a linguistic expression, and D is a convergent derivation that forms it]. We can think of economy considerations as a *cost function* $C_D: R \rightarrow I$, where I is a nonnegative integer, called the *cost* of R. Then, the condition on economy of derivation can be formulated as an optimization problem which takes the cost function C_D as the objective function to minimize (Minimize (C_D)). Let us call the problem so defined Deconomy, and make the following conjecture.

(4) Deconomy $\in$ NP-P[17]

Note that Deconomy is an empirical problem. To solve this optimization problem, we have to specify the basic properties of a structural description (π, λ) and derivation D, and the nature of the cost function C_D, as well as other properties of language that may impose the "constraints" (in the sense discussed in section 2) of this problem.[18] All of these require much more extensive, empirical studies of language. Given the present stage of the understanding of basic properties of language, any attempt at further formalization and at proving the proposition (4) is probably premature. Nevertheless, empirical results that have been accumulated so far in theoretical linguistics strongly support the plausibility of the conjecture (4).

Ristad (1990, 1993) has shown that some specific problems of language that he formulates are "NP-complete" problems (cf. note 17), which implies, as he argues, that any adequate linguistic theory must encompass these hard problems (see also the references in note 16). Our conjecture (4) about the optimization problem Deconomy is clearly consistent with his results. Furthermore, our conjecture claims that not only some problems of language are hard to solve, as Ristad has shown, but language itself is *fundamentally* computationally intractable. This is a much stronger result, if true, since empirical studies to date strongly suggest that Deconomy reflects the basic nature of language; no matter how other specific linguistic problems may be sorted out and reformulated in future work, Deconomy will remain as a core problem of grammar, as long as the notion of "derivation" continues to exist (cf. note 10).

Turning to the problem of economy of representation, the condition on economy of representation is a local condition, as discussed above. This, however, does not guarantee that the corresponding optimization problem is in the class P. Ristad (1990, 1993) shows that some local problems, that is, problems that can be stated and solved within a single Phrase-marker, do not belong to the class P. Therefore, being local does not seem to ensure a membership in P. However, we have seen that most of the interface conditions, especially those having to do with economy of representation, are not only local but also strictly local.[19] We take this "strict locality" to be a necessary condition for computational feasibility, i.e., membership in the class P. Thus, to the extent that the condition on economy of representation is a strictly local condition, the corresponding optimization problem, call it Reconomy, appears to be in the complexity class P. We can easily formulate the problem as a problem to minimize the cost function C_R, which maps a structural description (π, λ) to a nonnegative integer $(C_R(\pi, \lambda) \in I)$. So, without going into details, we just state the hypothesis as the following conjecture.

(5)   Reconomy $\in$ P

Unlike Deconomy, then, Reconomy can be solved efficiently, by mutually independent inspections of strictly local domains (i.e., minimal domains of heads) of a single Phrase-marker, and induces no computational intractability.

We have seen that the condition on economy of derivation and the condition on economy of representation are quite different with respect to their complexity properties. Economy of derivation and economy of representation differ in still another respect. Recall that in the minimalist program there are a set of invariant principles. These principles are divided into two distinct types. One type of principle includes interpretive conditions at the interface, which "are motivated by properties of the interface, perhaps properly understood as modes of interpretation by performance systems" (Chomsky 1993a: 4). Let us call this type of principles or conditions *external* conditions (or *bare output* conditions, to use the term introduced by Chomsky 1995b: 2). The other type of principles include such conditions as the "extension requirement" on substitution (cf. Chomsky 1993b) and "X' theory"[20] which are not interface conditions, and are probably not motivated by properties of performance systems. These types of principles or conditions are *internal* conditions.[21]

Consider now the conditions on economy. As we have seen, the condition on economy of representation is an interface condition (the convergence condition), and hence belongs to the first type of principles of language, i.e., the external conditions. The condition on economy of derivation, on the other hand, is not an interface condition. It is a condition determining a proper structural description, and does not appear to be motivated by performance factors; it is a condition that is purely inherent to language. Therefore, economy of derivation is an internal condition. Notice incidentally that the economy conditions are the only conditions in language that "fall apart" with respect to the external/internal dichotomy, though what this fact means is not entirely clear at this point (see the discussion below).

Thus, economy of representation and economy of derivation seem to show fundamental differences in several respects. We can think of the condition on economy of derivation as a kind of linguistic counterpart of such minimum principles in physics as Hamilton's Principle of Least Action. As we have discussed, economy of derivation requires "globality", inducing a certain type of computational intractability, and perhaps belongs to the complexity class NP-P. By contrast, the analogy to the minimum principle in physics cannot be straightforwardly extended to economy of representation. It could be a rather trivial principle which requires an interface representation to be minimal, containing only legitimate objects. It presents an optimization problem that is easy to solve, the one which appears to belong to the class P. Finally, as we just pointed out, economy of representation is an external condition at the interface, whereas economy of derivation is an internal condition.

These fundamental differences cast some doubt on the implicit assumption in the minimalist program that economy of representation and economy of derivation are two instances of something general, as their names suggest, and should fall under the same "economy" condition. At the same time, however, we can certainly detect a common property shared by the two conditions, that is, both hold that there be nothing superfluous in language: no superfluous symbols in representations (economy of representation), and no superfluous steps in derivations (economy of derivation). It, then, seems premature to try to settle this issue at this point, so we leave it open here for future research, merely noting that the two economy conditions in language exhibit what appear to be fundamental differences.

To conclude our discussion on the design of language, we have shown that language shares a fundamental property of the natural, inorganic world: Principles of Economy. Although its actual formulation appears to be highly particular to language, the condition on economy of derivation can be regarded as the linguistic (and hence discrete) version of the Principle of Least Action in physics. This provides us with a concrete interpretation of Chomsky's suggestion that language appears to show the kind of property that we expect in core areas of the natural sciences. Results in the theory of optimization problems that we summarized in section 2 suggest that considerations of economy of derivation are formulable as a discrete optimization problem. Because of its "globality", we conjectured that the problem, Deconomy, belongs to the class of problems that do not generally have an efficient algorithm for their solutions, i.e., Deconomy $\in$ NP-P. This conjecture, if right, implies that language is computationally intractable precisely because of its nature, and therefore fundamentally "unusable" for the most part; language is designed for "elegance", just like the inorganic world, quite independently of considerations of "efficient use", a point repeatedly made by Chomsky (1991a, b, 1993a) (see also Barton, Berwick, and Ristad 1987).

How, then, can language ever be used in spite of its computational intractability? Recall that we discussed in section 2 that problems in the complexity class NP-P are computationally intractable, but not too intractable. They appear to have no efficient algorithm for their solutions, but often allow for "heuristic algorithms" which make it possible to obtain approximate optimal solutions, reducing the global burden of the problem to local search. For example, the greedy heuristic aims at obtaining a globally optimal solution to a problem by making a sequence of locally optimal (greedy) choices. See, for example, Cormen et al. (1990) for a comprehensive discussion of this and other heuristic algorithms. This, again, seems to be exactly what happens in language. Chomsky (1991a) puts this situation as follows:[22] "(language) is designed for elegance, not for use, though *with features that enable it to be used sufficiently for the purposes of normal life*" (Chomsky 1991a: 49; italics added). Chomsky calls these features "computational tricks" (Chomsky 1991b), and claims that properties like "Greed" (in the technical sense, see Chomsky 1993a, 1994) and "Procrastinate" embedded in economy of derivation have the function of facilitating usability of language, reducing the inherent globality to local properties. To illustrate how, say, Greed helps reducing the global burden, let us consider the following example discussed by Chomsky (1993a: 33).

(6) a. _____ seems to [a strange man] [that it is raining outside]
    b. *[a strange man]$_i$ seems to t_i [that it is raining outside]
    c. it seems to a strange man that it is raining outside

The "Extended Projection Principle" (Chomsky 1982) requires the underlined position in (6a) to be filled by some element. We cannot, however, save the structure by moving *a strange man* to the underlined position, yielding (6b) with the meaning (6c). This movement, then, should be blocked as a "costly" process. But to evaluate the cost of the derivation, we will have to compare the derivation with another derivation which does not involve the movement of *a strange man*. This requires a global computation, inducing intractability, as we have seen. However, Greed, which dictates that movement of α be permitted only if morphological properties (e.g., Case features) of α itself would not otherwise be satisfied in the derivation (Chomsky 1994: 14), helps us know that the movement of *a strange man* in (6a) is barred: we cannot move *a strange man* in (6a) since its morphological features, viz., Case features, are already satisfied in the present place (in the complement position of a preposition *to*, which assigns Case to *a strange man*). Thus, without having to carry out a global computation, we know that the movement is barred in the computational system by inspecting the local neighbourhood of *a strange man* in (6a). See Chomsky (1993a, 1994) for much relevant discussion.[23]

In our terms, these "computational tricks" suggested by Chomsky can be formally characterized as heuristic algorithms studied in the theory of computational complexity (with respect to optimization problems). Language is designed for elegance with an intractable optimization problem (economy of derivation) embedded within it and hence fundamentally unusable to some extent, but, it is equipped with certain mechanisms that facilitate efficient use (such as Greed and Procrastinate). To the extent that these mechanisms are available, language can be used; otherwise, it is simply unusable. Note that language is a real-world object that requires empirical inquiry, unlike other combinatorial optimization problems studied in discrete mathematics.

As far as we can see, it is the only real-world object, outside of the inorganic world, that exhibits the fundamental property of economy, presenting quite an interesting and intricate empirical optimization problem on the horizon.

4 Summary and conclusions

The purpose of this paper has been to place considerations of "economy" in language in a wider intellectual context, in an attempt to show that there are connections to be made between the study of language and the natural sciences. After summarizing major developments of economy principles in physics and the basic results of "discrete optimization problems" in combinatorial mathematics (sections 1 and 2), I argued that the economy principle which linguists are currently trying to discover in the theory of language is exactly the linguistic version of the Principle of Least Action in physics. This gives us a rather concrete interpretation of the point Chomsky has repeatedly made (Chomsky 1991a, b), i.e., language, for unknown reasons, shares the fundamental property of the inorganic world; it is designed for elegance, not for efficient use. In other words, our discussion supports the view that language is a "perfect" system (Chomsky 1994), a surprising discovery, if true, since it is widely known that complex biological systems, language being one of them, are "imperfect" and "unpredictable" (cf. Jantsch and Waddington 1975).

I then discussed the nature of two types of economy principles of language that Chomsky (1991b) proposes, economy of derivation and economy of representation, from the point of view of the theory of computational complexity, and claimed that the two economy principles exhibit quite different properties with respect to their computational complexities: economy of representation is efficiently solvable and therefore seems to be in the complexity class P in the sense of the theory of computational complexity, whereas economy of derivation, which has clear "global" characteristics, is fundamentally computationally intractable and appears to belong to the class NP-P. Given the nature of the Principle of Least Action in physics discussed in section 1, this indicates that economy of derivation is the fundamental principle of language reflecting its deep nature shared by the inorganic world, whereas economy of representation could be an independent (and perhaps rather trivial) property of language which requires representations to be non-redundant.

Finally, it was argued that although language seems to be computationally intractable by its very nature (economy of derivation), it is equipped with certain features that facilitate its "efficient use". I argued that these "computational tricks" can be best analysed as biological counterparts of the "heuristic algorithms" studied in the theory of optimization, showing the property of reducing the global burden of an optimization problem to local search.

In closing our discussion, let us briefly consider a recent proposal made by Chomsky (1995b) concerning economy of derivation. One component of the condition on economy of derivation is called the *Minimal Link Condition* (MLC), which requires each step of movement to be minimal/shortest (see Chomsky 1993a for details). It is easy to show that this economy condition induces globality, and creates a difficult problem for computational feasibility. Thus, Chomsky points out that "If MLC is an economy condition selecting among derivations, OP [a certain operation] will be permissible only if no other convergent derivation has shorter links. It is hard to see even how to formulate such a condition, let alone to apply it in some computationally feasible way; for example, how do we compare derivations with shorter links in different places?" (Chomsky 1995b: 26). To solve this problem, he proposes that MLC be part of the definition of Move, rather than an independent economy condition; violation of MLC is not a legitimate move in the first place. Thus, at a given stage of a derivation, Move just picks a closest target, making a link minimal or shortest.[24] Other "options" simply do not exist, and we do not have to compare competing convergent derivations as far as MLC is concerned.

It is not clear at this point that we can entirely eliminate the need for "comparing derivations" by incorporating MLC into the definition of Move, nor is it obvious that other parts of economy of derivation do not induce similar globality. But Chomsky's proposal certainly has the effect of avoiding excessive computational complexity. If the "globality" embedded in economy of derivation is left unconstrained, it is even possible that Deconomy induces "exponential blowup", in which case it would not even belong to NP-P, but is in a more difficult complexity class. Language, then, would be completely computationally intractable and totally unusable, surely a wrong conclusion. Thus, the "globality" of economy of derivation must be somehow constrained, and Chomsky's recent proposal briefly mentioned above can be taken as an attempt to achieve such a goal.

On the other hand, economy of derivation, which has to do with the properties of Move, is certainly not a strictly local condition, as we have argued before. If we take "strict-locality" to be a necessary condition for membership in the class P (as we claimed), then Deconomy, as opposed to Reconomy (which we claim to be a strictly local condition, and hence to be in the class P), cannot be in P.

If attempts such as the one mentioned above turn out to be successful, Deconomy should not be as hard as problems requiring exponential time solutions. Deconomy, which is imposed by the displacement property of language (i.e., Move), "is restricted by language design so as to avoid excessive computational complexity" (Chomsky 1995b: 6).

Our conjecture (4), therefore, makes even more sense now. Deconomy is harder than problems in P, but is not (and should not be) as hard as those inducing exponential explosion: It is located "somewhere in-between", that is, in the class NP-P.

Notes

1 Specifiers and projection

For comments, criticism and encouragement, we are grateful to Andy Barss, Noam Chomsky, Ken Hale, Kyle Johnson, Richard Kayne, Mary Laughren, Tova Rapoport, Betsy Ritter, Doug Saddy, Gabriel Segal, and Tarald Taraldsen. All errors and oversights are our own.

1. There have been various proposals in the literature that Infl weakly bears these features in one way or another, but even these proposals have not attributed a θ-grid to Infl.
2. and preposition, in Abney's view.
3. These last three were pointed out by Abney (1986).
4. The absence of Det in Japanese is obvious. It is argued in Whitman (1984) that Infl should be regarded as a verbal complex, rather than as an independent syntactic unit. Fukui (1986) argues that what have traditionally been regarded as complementizers (e.g., *to* "that", *ka* "Q", etc.) should not be considered to be a single functional category Comp, but should instead be analysed as a postposition (*to*), a noun (*ka*), etc. See Fukui (1986) for details.
5. Even in English, there are a small number of marked cases where a pronoun is modified, e.g., *the real you, my former self, he who casts the first stone*, etc. The existence of such marginal N' (or N) pro-forms in English does not affect our argument, however. The crucial fact for our argument here is that there are no non-modifiable pro-forms in Japanese.
6. The spirit of this "subject raising" in the clausal case can be traced back to Fillmore's (1968) "subjectivalization" rule in the framework of Case Grammar, and McCawley's (1970) proposal that English is underlyingly VSO. Within the GB framework, similar proposals have been made by various people. Ken Hale suggested the idea in 1983 (personal communication). Lumsden (1984) has suggested that the subject of a clause should be considered an A' position. Koopman and Sportiche (1985, 1986b), Kuroda (1988) and Johnson (1985) have independently proposed subject-raising analyses, but in orientations quite different from ours. See Koopman and Sportiche (1986b) for some arguments for the "subject raising".
7. See Anderson (1984) and Larson (1985) for suggested accounts of the apparent caselessness of certain NP adverbs in phrases like "the destruction of the city yesterday".
8. See section 2.3 for a more detailed account of *wanna*-contraction under our system.
9. In particular, it is generally assumed that the node created by Chomsky-adjunction is identical in both category and bar level to the category adjoined to. The

node which dominates the Spec of a functional category, on the other hand, is a higher bar-level than the sister of the Spec.
10 This intuition is behind the proposal for the representation of Aux elements made by Oehrle (1981), and seems also to be found in the work of Ross (1967), McCawley (1970), Kayne (1983a), and Emonds (1985).
11 We believe that it is unproblematic to suppose that all modifiers are also within X', so that "VP adjuncts" are positionally similar to subjects. Detailed investigation of the status of modifiers is beyond the scope of this paper.
12 We are assuming that there exist phonetically null lexical items, and that traces count as "filling" a given position.
13 The definition of "barrier" will be discussed in section 3.
14 Chomsky (1986a) suggests that this definition should actually be phrased in terms of exclusion. Evaluation of the evidence for this move is beyond the scope of this paper.
15 Chomsky (1986a) suggests that Infl might θ-mark (but not L-mark) its complement, but then goes on to reject the suggestion, based on evidence that long-distance V-raising yields an ECP violation.
16 We are assuming that PRO would not be governed by Infl, since only lexical heads may govern down into their complements.
17 Pointed out to us by Noam Chomsky (personal communication).
18 Cf. Jaeggli (1980), Chomsky (1981a), Aoun and Lightfoot (1984), among others.
19 Cf. Pesetsky (1982b) and Chomsky (1986b).
20 See section 3 for arguments that in (18b) there is no I" and I' is not a barrier.
21 It is not clear whether the complement of *want* is a projection of Infl or of Comp. Our account of long-distance movement allows for either possibility (see section 3). Regardless of the labels on the intermediate nodes, under our system there would be no empty categories between *want* and *to* in the contraction case.
22 Somehow we need to insure that N projects to N', so that it is not a sister to the "external" argument. This problem crops up again in the treatment of intransitive sentences.
23 The equivalence between α and β must be established in terms of a path projecting from a given head, in order to avoid the problems mentioned in section 2.5.
24 We are assuming, following Koopman (1984) and Travis (1984), that Subject-Aux inversion involves movement of Infl to Comp, as a subcase of general head-to-head movement.
25 It is not clear whether the F-features in this case come from the verb *wonder* or from some *wh*-feature in the head Comp.
26 If prepositions are functional heads, as Abney (1985) proposes, then prepositions would share this property (among others) with complementizers.
27 Richard Kayne (personal communication) has pointed out a potential problem if we cannot make such a distinction. In a sentence like "Who believes who to have been arrested", the movement of *who* from object of the passive verb to the position of surface subject of the embedded clause must be accounted for.
28 Sentences with *whether* are generally considered in the literature to be weakly ungrammatical. If such sentences are to be ruled out by subjacency, it may be the case that *wonder* does not really L-mark its complement, but that, as suggested by Chomsky (1986a), *whether* is generated in the head of Comp, and moves into the Spec at some point in the derivation, eliminating whatever is in that Spec.
29 We predict that (37b) should be as bad as (36b), but actually (36b) seems much worse. The contrast may be due to the multiple variables in (36b). We leave this question open.

30 For Pullum, the term "lexical categories" includes both major and minor (what we call functional) categories.
31 Pullum, working in the GPSG framework, defines minor lexical categories as those with a subcat value but no bar value.
32 This bit of evidence is weaker than the others, for two reasons. First of all, the anaphoric status of *zibun* is not completely clear (see Fukui 1984). Second, it seems to be the case that there are languages which have both long-distance reflexives and functional categories; Icelandic and Italian are two examples.

2 LF extraction of *naze*: some theoretical implications

Preparation of this material was supported by the MIT Center for Cognitive Science under a grant from the A. P. Sloan Foundation's program in Cognitive Science. Portions of this paper were presented to the Workshop on Oriental Linguistics at the University of Massachusetts, Amherst, and in a colloquium at Cornell University. The audiences provided me with a number of suggestions that helped improve the content of this paper. I would like to thank Noam Chomsky, Ken Hale, Howard Lasnik, Luigi Rizzi, Mamoru Saito, and three anonymous reviewers of *NLLT* for valuable comments and suggestions. I am also indebted to Andy Barss, Kazuko Harada, Shin Oshima, Tova Rapoport, and Peggy Speas for helpful comments and discussions. All the shortcomings that may remain are of course my own.

1 The characterization of L-marking given in (1) is slightly different from the one given in Chomsky (1986a), and is close to Chomsky's modified formulation presented in his class lectures (Fall, 1986).
2 The notion of government will be given a precise definition below.
3 The definition of *exclude* is given as follows:

(i) α *excludes* β if no segment of α dominates β. (Chomsky 1986a: 9)

Notice that in Chomsky's (1986a) theory (cf. also May 1985), a category β consists of a sequence of nodes (segments) $(\beta_1, \ldots, \beta_n)$, where β_i immediately dominates β_{i+1}. Though in most cases a category consists of only one segment, a structure of the form (ii), a typical adjunction structure in which α is adjoined to β, presents a crucially differentiating case.

(ii) $[\beta_1 \, \alpha \, [\beta_2 \ldots]]$

The distinction becomes most relevant when the notion "dominate" is considered. May (1985) proposes a definition of "dominate" in (iii) in order to ensure that α is not dominated by β in an adjunction structure such as (ii).

(iii) α *is dominated by* β only if it is dominated by every segment of β.

Thus, in (ii), α is not dominated by a category β which consists of two segments β_1 and β_2, since a segment of β, namely β_2, does not dominate α. The term "dominate" used in the text and in the definition of "exclude" in (i) above should be understood in this sense. As we noted above, the distinction between category and its segments becomes relevant only when adjunction structures such as (ii) are considered, and is largely irrelevant to our present concern. I will simply assume this distinction without going into technical details. The reader is referred to May (1985) and Chomsky (1986a) for much detailed discussions on this issue.
4 I assume with Belletti and Rizzi (1981) that if α governs β, then α also governs the head of β.
5 Whether or not the distribution of empty complementizers should ultimately be accounted for in terms of the ECP is another issue. For example, one might

assume, contrary to Stowell, that the distribution of empty complementizers has nothing directly to do with the ECP itself, but rather should be handled by some kind of general identification principle which dictates, roughly, that empty elements (other than PRO) be lexically governed (not necessarily properly governed in the sense relevant to the ECP). See Kayne (1981), Stowell (1981a, b), Saito (1984), Chomsky (1986a), among others, for much relevant discussion. In any event, what is important to our present concern is Stowell's observation that, in our terms, bridge verbs L-mark the clauses which follow, taking them as complements, whereas nonbridge verbs do not.

6 An anonymous reviewer suggests the following way of handling this case within a theory in which the relevant barrier is defined in terms of category types (NP or S'); for example, the one represented by Lasnik and Saito (1984). Suppose for the sake of argument that if a complementizer cannot be deleted on the surface, then it also cannot be deleted in LF. Then, if we assume the structure (21b) for (20b), and if, in addition, *because* is in the head position of Comp, then the intermediate trace cannot be the head of Comp and cannot antecedent-govern the initial trace of an adjunct, since *because* is never deletable on the surface and therefore is never deletable in LF as well. Notice however that this account hinges crucially on two assumptions: (i) that (21b) is the correct structure for (20b), and (ii) that the *wh*-element is moved into Comp, and the Comp indexing mechanism (Aoun, Hornstein, and Sportiche 1981) comes into play to license the initial trace. Thus, if the account based on these assumptions really works, then the status of evidence for Chomsky's (1986a) approach to antecedent-government reported in the text becomes more theory-internal. It is not clear at this point that both of the above-mentioned assumptions can be fully justified. See Chomsky (1986a) for some arguments against the second assumption.

7 The structure of adjunct clauses in Japanese is not clear. The *kara* "because" clause might form a PP with an empty complementizer, rather than S', as with *because* clauses in English:

(i) [$_{PP}$ [$_{S'}$ [$_S$ Mary-ga nani-o katta] e] kara]

However, this problem, i.e., whether or not there is a PP node, does not affect our discussion below, since, in either case, our approach correctly predicts that extraction of an adjunct out of an adjunct *kara* clause is impossible.

8 A question arises as to how we should treat a root sentence like *John left*. I tentatively assume here that declarative root sentences are IPs, rather than CPs, in the sense of Chomsky (1986a), lacking a complementizer, so that the question of licensing an empty complementizer does not arise.

9 The assumption that *to-yuu*, which consists of a complementizer *to* "that" and the verb *yuu* "say", is a complementizer may be a controversial one. See Nakau (1973) for arguments that *to-yuu* is a syntactically unanalysable unit, i.e., a complementizer, rather than a "complementizer-verb".

10 Our discussion here is by no means intended to be comprehensive. There are various other factors involved in the empty complementizer phenomenon (particularly in nominals) in Japanese that I will momentarily put aside here. See Josephs (1976), Teramura (1980), among others, for extensive discussion on this and related matters.

11 As Howard Lasnik (personal communication) pointed out to me, a question still remains regarding the treatment of nominals such as *proof*, where we cannot say that the associated clause is a statement about the content of "proof" (cf. *the proof that English is not context-free*).

12 Thus, the impossibility of an empty complementizer in (26) is parallel to the

impossibility of empty complementizers in English complex noun phrases such as *the rumour *(that) John is a genius*, *the claim *(that) the earth is round*, etc., if these constructions are, as Stowell (1981b) argues, a kind of appositive. Then, a question naturally arises as to why these constructions generally induce a weaker island effect than relative clauses with respect to subjacency, if they are appositives and contain no L-marking relationship inside. One possible way to handle this might be to claim that in noun-complement constructions such as *the rumour that John is a genius*, where no empty operator movement is involved, the vacant specifier position of the associated clause somehow functions as an escape hatch for a *wh*-element to be extracted, whereas, in relative clauses, the specifier position is not available as an escape hatch, having been already filled by an empty operator. I will not pursue this possible solution here, leaving the problem open for future research. See Chomsky (1986a) for some discussion on this issue. Also see Stowell (1981b), Hornstein and Lightfoot (1984), Levin (1984), among others, for detailed discussion on *that*-deletion phenomena in complex NPs.

13 Another well-known factor affecting acceptability judgements regarding subjacency violations is the tensed-nontensed distinction. That is, extraction out of tensed clauses induces a stronger subjacency violation than that out of nontensed clauses. The following contrast seems to indicate that the tensed-nontensed distinction in some manner also affects acceptability judgements concerning *naze* "why" extraction, though the nature of tensedness in Japanese is not clear at this point. See Fukui (1995a) for discussion.

(i) ?Kimi-wa[Taroo-ga naze kaisya- o yame- reba]
you -TOP -NOM why company-ACC resign (nontensed) if
manzokusuru no?
be satisfied Q

"Why will you be satisfied if Taro resigns from his company t?"

(ii) *?Kimi-wa [Taroo-ga naze kaisya-o yameta kara] sonnani
resigned (tensed) because so
okotte-iru no?
much be angry

"Why are you so angry because Taro resigned from his company t?"

14 I am indebted to Noam Chomsky (personal communication) for this suggestion.
15 It might be possible to generalize statement (35) by modifying slightly the definition of government in such a way that L-contained positions will be governed by a lexical head. Then, we might characterize a D-structure non-adjunct position (or A-position) in a general way as follows.

(i) α is a *non-adjunct* at D-structure iff it is lexically governed, i.e., governed by a lexical head.

16 See Fukui (1995a) for further discussion.
17 See Huang (1982) for much relevant discussion. Cf. also Pesetsky (1987), Nishigauchi (1986) for some attempts to overcome the problems of LF subjacency pointed out by Huang (1982) in terms of their pied-piping mechanism. Fukui (1995a) makes another attempt to solve the problems along quite different lines. In any event, the issue seems to me far from being settled at this point.

3 Strong and weak barriers: remarks on the proper characterization of barriers

This paper is an interim report of ongoing research. A larger work which will incorporate the content of this paper is now in preparation. The ideas contained in this paper were presented orally in various forms at the special forum "Cognitive Revolution: Approaches from Language" (1988) held in honour of Noam Chomsky's receiving the Kyoto Prize, and at colloquia in 1989 at the University of Pennsylvania, the University of Massachusetts at Amherst, the University of Texas at Austin, and Rutgers University. I am indebted to the audiences of these colloquia for valuable comments and suggestions. I would also like to express my deepest appreciation to Beatrice Santorini for her very useful comments, and to Heizo Nakajima for his warm encouragement and incomparable patience. Any shortcomings are of course my own.

1 The characterization of L-marking given in (1) is slightly different from that given in Chomsky (1986a), and is close to Chomsky's modified formulation presented in his class lectures (Fall, 1986).
2 Note that this formulation of the subjacency condition is neutral on the issue of whether the subjacency condition is a condition on movement or on the resulting representation.
3 Here, we take adjuncts to be CP. The category type of adjuncts is not relevant to our present discussion, however.
4 Certain functional categories, e.g., I and D (see below), may function as "operators" in LF, but this is essentially different from predicative relations in which lexical categories play a central role.
5 For arguments that lexical projections must allow recursion at the single-bar level, see Fukui (1986: Chapter 2) and the references cited there.
6 It might be that the problem has to do with the obscure status of P with regard to lexical/functional distinction. Other problems also arise regarding the status of P.
7 We will rather freely use the traditional symbols S', S, and NP when their exact categorial status and internal (X' theoretical) structures are not directly relevant to our present discussion.
8 Independent evidence that (standard) X' theory holds at D- and S-structures is presented in Chomsky's series of lectures (Tokyo, 1987) and in van Riemsdijk (1989).

4 Parameters and optionality

I gratefully acknowledge the following people for valuable and inspiring comments and discussions relevant to the present article: Lisa Cheng, Caroline Heycock, Jim Huang, Kyle Johnson, Chisato Kitagawa, Robert May, Masaru Nakamura, Mamoru Saito, Beatrice Santorini, Peggy Speas, Daiko Takahashi, Moira Yip, and two anonymous *Linguistic Inquiry* reviewers. Portions of the material in this article were presented at the 10th Workshop on Theoretical East Asian Linguistics held at the University of California, Irvine, at a colloquium at Hokkaido University, and in my syntax seminar (Spring 1992, UC Irvine). The questions and suggestions of these audiences have led to numerous improvements. The research represented here was supported in part by a UC Irvine Faculty Research Fellowship (1990–1991) and a Faculty Career Development Award (1991–1992).

1 Or the directionality parameter for θ-marking and Case marking (Koopman 1984, Travis 1984). The choice between the two proposed parameters is not directly relevant to present concerns.
2 An alternative way of expressing the same idea would be to assume, following the suggestion made by Huang (1982: chap. 2), that the head parameter is fixed not only at the lowest level of X' projection, but at each level of projection (possibly in different ways). To work out this idea, suppose that there is no Spec

position at D-structure, external arguments being "adjoined" to the single-bar projections of their heads (predicates) (Fukui 1986, Fukui and Speas 1986, Uriagereka 1988). Suppose also that in English an external argument (subject) is adjoined to the *right* of the X'-level of a predicate projection. Then English clauses, at the core, are strictly head-initial at every level of their projections. Thus, any adjunction to the right will be "structure-preserving" (or "X'-compatible" in the sense of Fukui and Saito 1992) and hence costless. Now suppose that "substitution into Spec" is actually adjunction to the left (in English), the notion "Spec" being defined contextually via "Spec-head agreement" at S-structure and/or at LF after movement takes place (for detailed discussion see Fukui 1995a and Fukui and Saito 1992). Then "substitution" in English will not be "X'-compatible" and hence will be a costly operation. Quite the opposite is the case in Japanese, under the assumption that this language is head-final at every level of projection, an external argument (subject) being adjoined to the left of the X'-level of a predicate projection. Thus, any kind of leftward adjunction is "X'-compatible" and therefore costless, whereas rightward adjunction is not "X'-compatible" and thus is costly. In this way, we may calculate the cost of Move α by using X' theory as a kind of derivational constraint applying at each step of a derivation. This approach seems to be conceptually more desirable than the one proposed in the text, in that it need not introduce an extra concept, "canonical precedence relation". However, the approach just suggested would make some counterfactual predictions. For instance, it may wrongly predict that leftward scrambling of object in Chinese clauses is possible (see the discussion in section 4), since the value of the head parameter at the single-bar level in Chinese is head-final (see Huang 1982). Because of this and other difficulties that I cannot go into here, I will not adopt this alternative in this article and will continue to assume the approach proposed in the text, merely noting the possibility of a conceptually more desirable alternative.

3 I add *koto* "the fact that" in order to avoid the unnaturalness sometimes caused by the lack of a topic in independent clauses in Japanese. I ignore it in the translations, though.

4 For the former type of analysis of Case marking in Japanese, see, among others, Kuroda (1978), Takezawa (1987), and Fukui and Nishigauchi (1992). For the latter approach see Saito (1982), Fukui (1986), Miyagawa (1989), and Tada (1991), among others. Note incidentally that, as a reviewer points out, if nominative Case in Japanese is assigned within the projection of a verb (see Fukui 1986), then passive becomes indistinguishable in the relevant respects from scrambling.

5 Whether this positional restriction is a universal condition or a parametric property of Japanese is not relevant to the present discussion.

6 For the rest of the article the indicated judgements on topicalization examples are those of speakers who allow topicalization quite freely.

7 Saito (1989) assumes the following definition of binding:

(i) α *binds* β iff (i) α and β are coindexed, and (ii) α c-commands β.
α *c-commands* β iff the branching node most immediately dominating α also dominates β.

8 The exact formulation of these requirements is not of concern here. They may have to be stated in some other way, depending on one's analysis of the "Q-morpheme" *ka* and *wh*-movement in Japanese. In this article I am not committed to any specific proposal concerning this issue.

9 It is well known that in English, (S-structure) *wh*-movement can apply only once per clause:

(i) a John wonders who$_i$ t_i bought what.
   b. *John wonders what$_j$ who$_i$ t_i bought t_j.

10 It remains to be seen whether extraposition and Heavy NP Shift in English behave the same way as scrambling in Japanese with respect to the two properties we have discussed. Guéron and May (1984) observe that multiple applications of extraposition (from NP) are allowed, subject to various independent conditions as in the derivation of (ib) from (ia) (Guéron and May's (65)–(66)).

(i) a. [$_{NP}$[$_{NP}$ many books [$_{PP}$ by Chomsky]] which I've enjoyed reading] have been published recently.
   b. Many books have been published recently [by Chomsky] [which I've enjoyed reading].

Heavy NP Shift, on the other hand, seems to generally resist multiple applications for unclear reasons (but see Webelhuth 1989 for some cases where multiple applications of Heavy NP Shift are in fact possible). In this article I focus on the optionality of Move α, leaving these and other important properties of each movement operation for future research.

11 The element *de*, glossed here as DE, is a marker of a prehead modifier, which is somewhat analogous in its function to *no* in Japanese. See Huang (1982), Kitagawa and Ross (1982), among others, for some discussion on the parallelism and differences between these elements.

12 I am indebted to Lisa Cheng for providing me with the relevant Chinese examples. The distinction between complements and noncomplements in Chinese noun phrases is not as clear as that in English noun phrases. Jim Huang (personal communication) points out that there is even a possibility that no such distinction is made in Chinese. Here, just for the sake of exposition, I assume that all the prenominal phrases in (25) have the same status with respect to complementhood. See Huang (1992) for much relevant discussion.

13 Likewise, as Peggy Speas points out (personal communication), the PVP measure would predict that rightward "scrambling" is in principle possible in noun phrases in English, since the CPR = $N^0 > Y^{max}$ will be preserved under such processes. This prediction is borne out, as indicated by the grammaticality of examples such as (ib) and (iib), although there are additional conditions (the "heaviness" of the *of*-phrase (cf. Heavy NP Shift in clauses), argument/adjunct status, etc.) governing the actual applicability of rightward "scrambling" in this case, as illustrated by the awkwardness of (iiib). (I am indebted to Caroline Heycock and Beatrice Santorini for useful discussion on this matter and for providing me with their judgements.)

(i) a. a student of some obscure dialect of Ainu from Japan
    b. (?)a student t_i from Japan [of some obscure dialect of Ainu]$_i$
(ii) a. a teacher of modern post-realist literature from France
    b. (?)a teacher t_i from France [of modern post-realist literature]$_i$
(iii) a. a student of mathematics from Japan
    b. *?a student t_i from Japan [of mathematics]$_i$

14 I am grateful to Jim Huang (personal communication) for bringing to my attention the relevance of the VSO languages for the PVP measure.

15 The "preference" for surface VSO order over surface VOS order in Chamorro calls for an independent explanation. In other words, a question still remains as to why "scrambling" of object in an SOV language like Japanese is truly optional, whereas application of a similar operation in a VOS language like

Chamorro (rightward "scrambling" of object or subject adjunction), though still optional as predicted by the PVP measure, seems to be "preferred". More broadly, a question remains as to how to explain Greenberg's Universal 1, which states that on the surface "in declarative sentences with nominal subject and object, the dominant order is almost always one in which the subject precedes the object" (Greenberg 1963: 77). See Chung (1990) for some suggestions concerning this matter.

16 The only exception I am aware of is an apparently optional rightward movement of a prepositional phrase over a verb in Dutch, discussed by Koster (1974). I have no clear explanation for this fact. Also, as a reviewer points out, facts in Hindi might not be accounted for solely on the basis of the PVP. Hindi has the basic word order SOV and allows apparently alternating SVO, OSV, OVS, VOS, and VSO surface orders. It may well be, as Mahajan (1990) argues, that some of these surface orders are created by a grammatical process driven by Spec-head agreement of some sort, in which case these word order patterns are independent of the validity of the PVP measure. See Mahajan (1990) for much relevant discussion.

5 A note on improper movement

Portions of the material in this paper were presented at various stages of development at colloquia in 1993 at Université du Québec à Montreal, McGill University, and Tohoku University. I thank the audiences on these occasions for their questions and comments. I am indebted to Lisa Cheng, Noam Chomsky, Jim Huang, Chisato Kitagawa, Utpal Lahiri, Mamoru Saito, Daiko Takahashi, Akira Watanabe, and especially Kyle Johnson, for inspiring comments and suggestions. Comments of the anonymous referees of this journal are also gratefully acknowledged.

1 The examples in (8) are adapted from Chomsky (1992: 21). Chomsky puts empty categories in the input representation in the positions corresponding to t_i and *John* in (8b), indicating the landing sites of the targeted element. I assume here that there are no such empty categories in the input representation for Form-Chain, but rather that those empty categories, if any, are created by Form-Chain itself.

2 One might suspect that the Uniformity Condition (7) would incorrectly exclude examples such as follows, since they appear to contain non-uniform chains.

(i) [who$_i$ [t_i' seems [t_i to win]]]
(ii) [who$_i$ do [you think [t_i'' [t_i' seems [t_i to win]]]]]

There is of course no such problem. In these examples, Form-Chain applies twice, rather than once, so there are two independent chains. Take (ii) for example. Form-Chain applies, being triggered by Agr$_S$ in the embedded clause, to create a chain $C = (t_i', t_i)$, which is a uniform A-chain. Then, Form-Chain applies again, to form a uniform A'-chain $C = (who_i, t_i'', t_i)$. Both of these applications of Form-Chain are in accordance with the Uniformity Condition (7).

3 The possibility of adjunction to Agr$_S^{max}$, which is stipulated to be impossible in Chomsky (1986a), remains open, depending on whether the Agr$_S^{max}$-adjoined position shares the relevant property with Spec of C. Also, it is not entirely clear at this point whether intermediate adjunctions are allowed in the case of A-movement. This all depends on how to characterize the V^{max}-adjoined position and the Spec-of-Agr$_S$ position with respect to the relevant property, say, L-relatedness. I leave this problem open here. See below for some relevant discussion.

4 See Frampton (1991), Law (1991), and Chomsky (1992) for similar proposals.

See also Takahashi (1993a) for an interesting attempt to derive the effect of barriers along the lines suggested in the text.
5 Frampton (1990) proposes a similar condition on adjunction based on canonical government (Kayne 1984) to the effect that a *wh*-phrase can only be adjoined to a maximal projection from a position that is canonically governed by its head. Frampton's condition shares many (but not all) of the empirical effects with Takahashi's formulation of the condition. I take Takahashi's formulation here as a starting point for further discussion because it expresses more straightforwardly the idea that some notion of distance plays a role in constraining adjunction. The points I will raise in the following discussion, however, apply, *mutatis mutandis*, to Frampton's formulation as well.
6 *Koto* "the fact that" is added in order to avoid the unnaturalness sometimes caused by the lack of topic in independent clauses in Japanese. I ignore it in translations, though.
7 Saito (1985) argues that the subject cannot be scrambled long-distance, on the basis of examples like (12c, d), rather than the corresponding example **Mary-ga$_i$ John-ga [t$_i$ Bill-ni sono hon-o watasita to] omotte-iru (koto)* "John thinks that Mary handed that book to Bill", which is, as indicated, in fact unacceptable. This is to exclude the possibility that the sentence under consideration becomes unacceptable owing to some extragrammatical factors such as Kuno's (1980) "anti-ambiguity" device. See Saito (1985) for much detailed discussion.
8 See Fukui and Saito (1993) for extensive discussions about the lack of Agr in Japanese, and for the analysis that Japanese clauses are a projection of T. This particular assumption does not crucially affect our argument here, though.
9 I assume that adjuncts are base-generated in a position adjoined to X'. See the discussion above.
10 I am indebted to Akira Watanabe for bringing these references to my attention.
11 After this paper had reached the final stage of its publication, I came to know that Mamoru Saito independently arrived at a condition on adjunction which is quite similar to (14), based on considerations different from ours. I refer the reader to Saito and Murasugi (1993) for details of his proposal.

6 The principles-and-parameters approach: a comparative syntax of English and Japanese

Portions of the material in this paper were presented in my lectures at the University of California, Irvine (spring, 1992) and at Hokkaido University (summer, 1992). I have benefited from discussions with participants in these lectures. The facts reported in section 4 of the present paper are largely taken from my earlier writing (Fukui 1988a). The research represented here was supported in part by UC Irvine Faculty Research Fellowship (1990–1991) and Faculty Career Development Award (1991–1992).

1 Our discussion here is by no means intended to be exhaustive. For more comprehensive and detailed discussions of the parameters proposed in the principles-and-parameters framework see Shibatani (1989) and Freidin (1991), among others.
2 See Fukui (1986), Speas (1986, 1990), Abney (1987), Pollock (1989), Chomsky (1991b), and references cited in these works for more detailed discussion of functional elements. I ignore some of the functional elements proposed in the literature, e.g., Neg(ative element), for ease of exposition.
3 Further refinement of the organization of the lexicon seems to be possible. That is, in addition to the feature [$\pm$F], there might be the feature [$\pm$L(exical)] in the universal lexicon. Combinations of these two features divide categories in the lexicon into four subtypes:

[+F, −L]: "pure" functional elements
[+F, +L]: functional elements with lexical nature
[−F, +L]: lexical categories (substantive elements)
[−F, −L]: "minor categories" (particles, etc.)

It seems that "pure" functional elements are functional categories observed in English and other European languages. Elements specified as [+F, +L] are functional elements which retain, to varying degrees, their characteristics as lexical categories, assuming that functional elements emerge from lexical categories (cf. Guilfoyle and Noonan 1988, Kornfilt 1989, and Radford 1990 for related discussions). Instantiations of this type of category may be found in languages like Japanese and other East Asian languages. Also, some types of preposition may be characterized as belonging to this class. Characterizations of lexical categories and "minor" categories as [−F, +L] and [−F, −L], respectively, do not seem to need further comment. With this refinement of the structure of the lexicon, the functional parametrization hypothesis might be restated in either of the following ways:

(i) *Functional Parametrization Hypothesis* (I)
Only [+F] elements (i.e., two kinds of functional elements) in the lexicon are subject to parametric variation.
(ii) *Functional Parametrization Hypothesis* (II)
Only [−L] elements (i.e. "pure" functional elements and "minor" categories) in the lexicon are subject to parametric variation.

The choice between these two versions of the functional parametrization hypothesis requires detailed and deeper investigations of cross-linguistic (and acquisitional) evidence, which is far beyond the scope of this paper; I leave this for future research.
4 Technically, "clauses" in Japanese are not projections of V *per se*, but projections of T, i.e., T' (see Fukui 1986 and the discussion in section 5). However, this does not affect our point here, since T is basically a feature of V and, unlike Agr, does not have nominal features (cf. (16)).
5 I assume that X' freely iterates. For arguments that recursion is necessary at the single-bar level see Fukui (1986, ch. 2) and references cited there.
6 It is virtually impossible for F' to iterate when the functional head induces agreement. I assume that this is due to the locality condition imposed on agreement which requires that an agreement-inducing functional head and its Spec be in the same "local domain". Thus, it is only those elements that cannot enter into an agreement relation (adverbs and the like) that may intervene between two agreeing elements (a functional head and its Spec). Also, we may want to deploy, among other standardly assumed features, the two features proposed by Muysken (1982), [±projected] and [±maximal], to distinguish base-generated "adjunction structures" from those created by adjunction operations. I put these matters aside here. See Fukui and Saito (1994) for more detailed discussions on the locality of agreement, and Chomsky and Lasnik (1993) for the latter point.
7 See Heycock and Santorini (1992) for a similar proposal, based on quite different considerations.
8 It is not entirely clear how this explanation captures the case of head-substitution, i.e., "substitution into a head".
9 The only difference between "substitution" and "adjunction" that may resist this account is the one with respect to the strict cycle, discussed in Chomsky (1993a), if there are indeed cases of "non-cyclic adjunction". See Fukui and Saito (1994) for further discussions on this issue.

10 Tokieda's originals are in Japanese. Translations are intended to give the reader a rough idea about what he claims, and should not be taken to be direct translations.
11 The idea that subject is generated inside the "core" of a proposition and later is attracted by a modal element can be traced back to the process of "subjectivalization" proposed in the framework of Case grammar (Fillmore 1968).
12 I add *koto* "fact" to avoid the unnaturalness sometimes caused by the lack of topic in independent clauses in Japanese. I ignore it in the translations, though.
13 In Fukui (1988a: 260), I also explore an alternative possibility, that Japanese does have all (or some) of the functional categories but none of them is "active" in the language, i.e., functional categories in Japanese do not induce Spec-head agreement. This alternative hypothesis is considered to be "equally plausible" in Fukui (1988a) but is here put aside since it is "extremely difficult to come up with decisive evidence between the two hypotheses" and "it is even not clear whether they make different empirical predictions concerning the parametric syntax of English and Japanese". This remark also holds of the discussion in the present paper. Under relativized X' theory, it is extremely difficult to distinguish, given a functional head F, the claim that F does not exist in a language L, from the claim that F does exist in L, but never induces agreement.
14 It is occasionally claimed that honorification might be an instance of subject-verb agreement in Japanese. I put aside this possibility, mainly because honorification does not involve φ-feature (person, number, gender) agreement, which is a typical property of agreement phenomena generally attributed to the Agr element. Cf. Fukui (1986, ch. 4).
15 See Chomsky (1993a) and references cited there for this possibility.
16 Koster (1978) argues that clauses generally cannot appear in subject position, and that so-called subject sentences should be analysed as "satellite sentences" binding an empty category in Comp. Even under his analysis, the difference between *to* and *that* will remain: *that*-clauses can be "satellite sentences", while *to*-sentences cannot. See also Stowell (1981b) for some relevant discussion.
17 Incidentally, in order for the examples in (42) to become grammatical, one has to use the "formal noun" *koto* "fact" and change the proposition into a noun phrase.
18 Under this account, it remains to be seen how to accommodate the fact reported in Saito (1987b) that in some western dialects of Japanese, *te* "that", apparently a dialectal variant of *to*, can actually drop under roughly the same condition as that for *that*-deletion in English.
19 The possibility that Case-particles in Japanese play a role comparable to that of D in the English-type languages is mentioned by Fukui (1986, ch. 4, note 11), essentially along the lines of "K(ase)P(hrase)" analysis proposed by Ken Hale (MIT class lectures, 1985), and is further explored by Tateishi (1988) and Tonoike (1991). I put this possibility aside here.
20 Saito and Murasugi (1989), on the basis of detailed examinations of N^{max}-deletion phenomena in Japanese, present some evidence that Japanese has empty D (or its equivalent; see the text) that functions as a proper governor.
21 To block unwanted free leftward adjunction of object to V' in English, yielding, for instance, *John the book$_i$ read t_i*, Fukui (1988a: 262) claims that leftward adjunction to V' is banned in English because it necessarily breaks the adjacency between a verb and T/Agr imposed by the adjacency condition on V-raising in English. Under the current approach, adjunction of object to the left of V' is independently excluded because of the PVP measure.
22 The reason why it cannot be adjunction to V' has to do with Case-realization. See below.
23 It remains to be seen how this account can be extended to, or made compatible

24 Takezawa (1987) proposes a similar mechanism. The crucial difference between Takezawa's analysis and the mechanism I'm assuming here is that, for Takezawa, nominative Case is actually "assigned" by T^0 (I^0 in his framework), just as accusative Case is assigned by V^0, whereas our system makes it clear that nominative Case (and genitive Case; see the discussion below in the text), unlike accusative Case, is not "assigned" by anything – that is, nominative Case-marking is not a process of discharging inherent features of a lexical item. See Fukui and Nishigauchi (1992) for more detailed discussion. Note incidentally that the Case-marking system proposed in Fukui and Nishigauchi (1992) strongly suggests that "m-command" plays no role in the definition of government, and perhaps in the theory of grammar in general.

25 Note that subject still can optionally move to the left, since such a movement in Japanese is costless (cf. the discussion on scrambling above).

26 In this case, it is not clear at this point why English cannot have "double", though not "multiple", genitives, one in the Spec-D and the other in the Spec-Agr. This is related to the problem of why movement cannot "stop" in the position of Spec-D without proceeding. Notice that exactly the same problem arises in the case of clauses for the relationship between Spec-T and Spec-Agr.

27 Following Saito (1985) and Murasugi (1991) (cf. also Sakai 1990), we assume that relative clauses in Japanese are T^{max} (I^{max} in their terms), rather than C^{max}, and that a null operator in Japanese relative clause structure is adjoined to T^{max} (T' under our current assumptions) to take scope. Note that this assumption is quite consistent with our discussion on the properties of *to* in Japanese (cf. (44)).

28 This account does not preclude the possibility that Japanese has *optional* syntactic *wh*-movement, since leftward movement of a *wh*-phrase is costless in the language and therefore can in principle freely occur. See Takahashi (1991) and Watanabe (1992) for relevant discussion.

29 Cheng (1991) proposes an interesting alternative account for the cross-linguistic distribution of syntactic *wh*-movement on the basis of the existence of overt Question markers (overt "Q-morphemes"), coupled with the theory of "clausal-typing" that she develops. One of the consequences of her theory is the prediction that languages without an overt Q-morpheme (e.g., English) have obligatory syntactic *wh*-movement, while languages with such an element (e.g., Japanese) do not have obligatory syntactic *wh*-movement. Cheng argues, through detailed examinations of cross-linguistic data, that this prediction is indeed confirmed. See Cheng (1991) for details of her theory. Note that her account is also consistent with our restrictive theory of parametric variation, assuming that Q-morpheme is a kind of a functional element.

30 Another possibility is to analyse elements like *sase* (causative) and *rare* (passive), which trigger verb movement, as some kind of functional elements. This analysis, however, seems difficult to maintain, since functional elements generally do not have anything to do with θ-structure, but *sase* and *rare* do affect the θ-structure of the predicate to which they are attached.

31 The Subject Condition effect can be checked with *wh*-movement in English, but cannot be checked with the same operation in Japanese, since the language lacks overt *wh*-movement. Thus, in (60), the effect is checked with scrambling.

32 Crucially, there is no subject-object symmetry in Japanese with respect to extractability. If a phrase is scrambled out of an object phrase, the result is exactly the same as that of scrambling out of subject. See Saito (1985) for detailed discussion.

7 Symmetry in syntax: Merge and Demerge

We are thankful to the following people for valuable and inspiring comments and discussions relevant to the present article: Jun Abe, Brian Agbayani, Yoshio Endo, Nobuko Hasegawa, Koji Hoshi, James Huang, Toshiaki Inada, Daisuke Inagaki, Kazuko Inoue, Sige-Yuki Kuroda, Roger Martin, Toshifusa Oka, Tsutomu Sakamoto, Yoko Sugioka, Hiroaki Tada, Daiko Takahashi, Kazue Takeda, Yukinori Takubo, Chris Tancredi, Shigeo Tonoike, Saeko Urushibara, Hiroyuki Ura, Akira Watanabe, Mihoko Zushi, and three anonymous reviewers of the *Journal of East Asian Linguistics*. Portions of this article were presented at Kanda University of International Studies, Kyushu University, Sophia University, the Tokyo Area Circle of Linguistics (TACL), and Yokohama National University. The questions and suggestions of these audiences have led to numerous improvements, for which we are grateful. Some of the materials of sections 3 and 4 are drawn from chapter 2 of Takano (1996), with radical and substantial revisions throughout. The research reported in this article was supported in part by the University of California's Pacific Rim Research Program (Naoki Fukui: Principal Investigator).

1. There are several other less obvious cases. The "leftness condition" of Chomsky (1976), carried over into the principles-and-parameters theory in the form of "weak crossover", is one such example.
2. In fact, Kayne's LCA, as he argues, also has this important function of eliminating the standard X' theory. See Kayne (1994) for much relevant discussion.
3. We use X, X', etc. only for expository purposes just to indicate X itself, the first projection of X, etc. These notations have nothing to do with the notion of "bar levels", which has significance in the standard X' theory but has no place at all in the bare theory. We also use XP to indicate a "maximal projection" of X, when subtle clarifications are not directly important. See Chomsky (1995b) and Fukui (1986, 1995b) for much more precise discussions of these notions in the theory of phrase structure.
4. While it is clear that the head-parameter is abandoned under Kayne's approach, Chomsky does not make an explicit statement about the head-parameter. Like Kayne's LCA, Chomsky's modified version of it clearly predicts, as he claims (Chomsky 1995b, 340), the universal S-H-C order. It is still possible, however, that this version of the LCA can be parametrized with respect to the order in which the abstract asymmetric c-command relations are "read off" from a phrase-marker (whether from left to right or from right to left). The resulting "head-parameter" will be a parameter in the phonological component, something similar to a parameter in stress assignment proposed in phonology, and will be quite different in nature from a classical head-parameter of the kind maintained in, say, Fukui and Saito (1996).
5. A familiar qualification about the Japanese examples is in order. Japanese examples containing nominative subjects in matrix clauses sometimes sound awkward when used in isolation, owing to lack of topic in a language like Japanese with "topic-orientation". We sometimes add *koto* "the fact that" to avoid the unnaturalness caused by the lack of topic but omit it in the English translations.
6. In Fukui and Saito's system, Spec is defined by agreement. Thus, the directionality of agreement is equivalent to the directionality of Spec.
7. Our description of the relevant part of the "minimalist" conception of language is necessarily quite sketchy and imprecise. See Chomsky's works cited in the text for more precise expositions.
8. In this sense, both the $N \rightarrow$ Spell-Out computation and Linearization are strictly "derivational", forming expressions step by step by applying their operations to objects.

9 Note that the conclusion remains the same when the complement (Y of K in (10)) is a terminal. Chomsky (1994, 1995b), adapting Kayne's LCA within the bare phrase structure framework, is forced to conclude that the complement Y of the head H necessarily incorporates to H when Y is a terminal. This is because the LCA, incorporated into the bare theory, cannot determine the order between Y and H when Y is a terminal. On the other hand, under the approach put forth in this article, the relation between Y and H need not be treated as an exception: Linearization assigns the Y-H order, regardless of whether or not Y is a terminal.

Note also that our approach does not force the conclusion that specifiers are adjoined elements, as does Kayne's LCA. It is an automatic consequence of the present theory that a specifier of H precedes both H and a complement of H.

10 Strictly speaking, Linearization applies to the root element, which corresponds to the tree rooted at vP.

11 In the bare phrase structure theory, a two-segmented category formed by adjunction has an ordered pair as its label (Chomsky 1994, 1995b). Thus, the two-segmented category $[v_1, v_2]$ is formally represented as in (i).

(i) $[v_1, v_2] = [<v, v>, [V, v]]$

12 Since V-raising is "substitution", the higher v' in (20) is a full projection, rather than a segment, of the lower v'. Thus, vP in (20) has "multiple Specs", allowed in the bare phrase structure theory (see Chomsky 1995b for discussion). The same qualification applies to other tree structures given below.

13 Note that the proposed system does not always determine a unique derivation that linearizes a given object Σ. Suppose that Σ has (i), where YP and ZP are complex, containing elements other than their heads:

(i)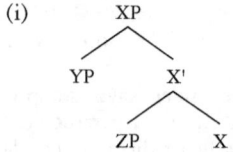

Linearization requires YP to be detached before ZP, but it does not say anything about the order of detachment of the constituents of YP and detachment of constituents of ZP. Thus, after both YP and ZP are detached, yielding YP + ZP + X, Linearization may apply to either YP or ZP, thereby causing an ambiguity of derivation. If we want to eliminate this kind of ambiguity of derivation in the application of Linearization (note that the core computation in the N→Spell-Out mapping also has this property), one possibility, suggested by James Huang (personal communication), is to incorporate into Linearization some notion of "Immediate Satisfaction" (or "Nonprocrastination"), developed by Ishii (1997) in connection with the theory of barriers, which, by appropriate extensions, requires that Linearization operate in such a way as to produce a pronounceable string of terminals as soon as possible. Then, in the above case, YP must be fully linearized before ZP is detached from X'. In general, Immediate Satisfaction has the effect of forcing K detached from Σ to be fully linearized before any other element is detached from ($\Sigma - K$). See Ishii (1997) for much detailed discussion of this principle.

14 On independent grounds, Oka (1996) proposes that head movement sometimes takes the form of substitution into Spec, claiming that the difference between Icelandic and French with respect to the existence of overt object shift follows under the hypothesis that the verb raises to Spec, T in Icelandic but adjoins to T in French.

15 Here we assume that attachment of FF(α) to H is exempt from the "root condition" on Merge. We may simply assume (with Chomsky 1995a, 1996) that Merge operates on categories alone and that feature attachment is carried out by an operation different from Merge.
16 The minimal domain of the head H is the checking domain of H plus the complement of H (Chomsky 1993a).
17 A reviewer points out that our discussion here and below assumes a certain "ordering" associated with feature checking and claims that is a problem for our analysis. While we certainly agree with the reviewer that the "ordering of feature checking" should eventually be eliminated from grammar for theoretical reasons, the problem here is a general one, not particular to our analysis. Thus, it is claimed in traditional approaches that V raises to C in German and Irish, to T in French, to v in English, etc. because of the properties of C, T, and v, but it is never clear how these properties follow from something more fundamental. Furthermore, if we follow Chomsky (1995b) in allowing "multiple Specs" in principle, a problem immediately arises as to how we guarantee the "correct order" of Specs of the same head. Given our present understanding of the issue, all we can say at this point is that it is determined by the properties of the head. Note that this problem is inherent to all approaches that allow multiple Specs and must be seriously addressed and resolved in future research as we understand the nature of the problem more fully.
18 Under the substitution analysis of head movement proposed here, various cases of incorporation discussed, say, by Baker (1988) must be reconsidered and reanalysed either as involving head movement to Spec or as being formed in the lexicon or the phonological component, rather than in the core computation, though we must leave detailed discussions of this matter for future research. We also assume that modals in English are in Spec, T, either moved from a lower position or inserted by "direct merger". Other elements that show head-initial order must be analysed along similar lines. See below (cf. also Chomsky 1995b) for the possibility that an element is inserted into Spec by direct merger, rather than by movement, for the purpose of feature checking.
19 Chinese also patterns with English in that it has no Case particles. This property falls out under the proposal about Case systems that we will discuss in section 4.1.
20 Strictly speaking, what enters in a checking relation with D and Deg are the formal features of determiners and degree words, given the checking theory of section 3.3. The same reservation applies to other cases to be discussed later.
21 Here we assume that there is no functional category between D and NP. However, several proposals have been made to claim that there is some functional category there. For example, Bernstein (1991) argues that there is a functional head, called Num(ber), that takes NP as its complement and that the N-A order in French and the A-N order in Walloon result from N-raising to Num in the former and lack of it in the latter (see also Picallo 1991 and references cited in these works). If there is indeed a projection of Num between D and NP, our proposal can be modified so that the H-C order in English derives from N-raising to Spec, Num.
22 See also Sells (1995) for the claim that Korean and Japanese do not have verb-raising.
23 We will return to inherent Case below. Chomsky (1995b) proposes a more complex theory of checking in terms of the operations "deletion" and "erasure". The simple conception of checking adopted here is sufficient for present purposes. Here we use the term "elimination" as a cover term for the operation that makes formal features invisible to the computation and the interpretation at LF.

24 While we assume that the feature [assign accusative Case] is located in the "main verb" V rather than the "light verb" v, a reviewer objects that the feature should be in v, claiming that v is a "transitivizer" and that this view has the advantage of directly deriving Burzio's generalization (that a verb assigns no structural Case if it has no external θ-role). However, it also raises the question why not all verbs with an external θ-role assign structural Case (e.g., *John spoke to Mary*, *John ran*, etc.). As we will show shortly, if we adopt the view that V has [assign accusative Case], we can derive far-reaching consequences for comparative syntax. We take this result to constitute an argument for our view.

25 Here we assume, essentially following Chomsky (1995b), that raising of V to v always takes place overtly and that there is no covert variant of it. Chomsky suggests that this is because verb-raising is triggered by the feature $[-V]$ of v and that $[-V]$ is "affixal" in nature. Under the present approach, we interpret this requirement as meaning that if v has the "affixal" (or "morphological") feature $[-V]$, v must have FF(V) within its "extended head" in the phonological component. Thus, if v has $[-V]$, FF(V) must raise to attach to v before Spell-Out (causing overt verb-raising); if v does not have $[-V]$, no raising of FF(V) (and hence no verb-raising) takes place. Alternatively, given the generalization (35) discussed before, we might claim that v does not enter into feature checking (overt or covert) in Japanese because of the existence of phonetically realized v in the language. See below for more relevant discussion.

26 Given that Japanese does not have an equivalent of *the* or *a* in English, we assume that K takes NP rather than DP as complement in Japanese (cf. Fukui 1986, 1988a).

27 Note that what our proposal actually says about languages without verb-raising is that Case cannot be checked by v in those languages, so either the subject or the object must have a Case particle. If the object has the particle, we have accusative languages. If, on the other hand, the subject has the particle, ergative languages result. In this case, the object is unmarked for Case and is subject to checking (overt or covert) by T if T has the ability to check. This approach to ergativity is thus close in spirit to Murasugi's (1992) proposal that T checks the Case of the object in ergative languages.

28 We might ask whether the difference between Japanese and Turkish or Tamil results from an arbitrary choice between the checking system and the particle system for nominative Case. On the basis of some historical considerations, Takano (1996) suggests that the particle system for nominative Case in modern Japanese may in fact be a "marked" option, forced by some language-specific properties. See Takano (1996) for details.

29 An alternative is that v or V has the feature, linked to some θ-role, just as V has the feature [assign accusative Case], linked (typically) to a theme/patient role. The story becomes complicated, given that a nominative phrase can be an agent (as in active sentences) or a theme or patient (as in passive sentences). The text assumption is much simpler and is also preferable, given the fact that the nominative marker can attach to adverbial elements functioning as foci, as extensively discussed by Saito (1982).

30 The mechanism of "head movement" proposed in Fukui and Nishigauchi's (1992) analysis of Case-making in Japanese cannot be maintained as a syntactic movement (verb-raising) under the present approach and would have to be reanalysed as a process occurring in the phonological component, as suggested earlier in Fukui (1986).

31 Ura (1994a, 1996), working within the framework of Chomsky (1995b), proposes an alternative analysis in which multiple subjects result from multiple feature checking by a single head. Japanese allows such multiple checking while English does not. He also proposes to unify super-raising phenomena and A-

scrambling under this analysis. For other approaches to Japanese Case phenomena see Takezawa (1987), Tada (1992), Miyagawa (1993), and Watanabe (1994), among others.

32 Takano (1996) claims that the relevant movement is scrambling.
33 See Watanabe (1992) and Takahashi (1993c) for different claims about overt *wh*-movement in Japanese.
34 Here we depart from Chomsky (1995b), who argues that [+Q] is interpretable and hence need not be eliminated. See Takano (1996) for further discussion of this matter.
35 In colloquial speech, the particle *no* can also be used in root questions. The particle *ka* can be omitted in root questions but not in embedded questions.
36 Here we assume with Chomsky (1995b) that the *wh*-feature of *wh*-phrases need not be checked. We also follow Chomsky (1995b) and Tsai (1994) in assuming that *wh*-phrases in situ are licensed by unselective binding by C in the sense of Heim (1982).
37 Chinese has overt verb-raising (hence the VO order and the lack of Case particles) but lacks overt *wh*-movement. This is obviously not a problem for our approach but simply suggests that Chinese has some language-particular factor (independent of Case) that prevents it from having a checking system for elimination of [+Q]. See Takano (1996) for relevant discussion.
38 As Cheng (1991) observes, some languages with *wh*-in-situ have no overt particle for *wh*-questions. Cheng also points out that all *wh*-in-situ languages have a particle for yes-no questions. One possibility then is that all *wh*-in-situ languages invoke the particle system for elimination of [+Q] but that some of them necessarily delete the question particle in the phonological component, except in yes-no questions. Another possibility is that some *wh*-in-situ languages have a way of eliminating [+Q] that does not involve Spell-Out.
39 English has another element that checks [−Q] of C, namely a phonetically null counterpart of *that* (as in *John thinks Mary left*), which we put aside.
40 A variety of mechanisms have been proposed in the literature to account for *that*-trace effects. For such proposals see Chomsky and Lasnik (1977), Chomsky (1980, 1981a), Pesetsky (1982a, 1982b), Kayne (1984), Aoun et al. (1987), Rizzi (1990), Lasnik and Saito (1992), Fukui (1993a), and Watanabe (1993), among many others. The argument here is neutral as to the choice among these proposals.
41 Basque is an apparent exception to this generalization. Basque has clause-final complementizers (realized as suffixes to subordinate verbs) but requires overt movement of *wh*-phrases. More investigation of general properties of Basque is necessary to draw any definite conclusion about the implications of the language for the generalization in question. For discussion of Basque *wh*-movement in this light, see Ormazabal, Uriagereka, and Uribe-Etxebarria (1994).
42 Discussion of the nature of scrambling involves a number of complicated issues and is beyond the scope of this paper. See Fukui and Saito (1996), Takano (1996), and references cited there for much relevant discussion. Other properties that Fukui (1986, 1988a, 1995b) discusses include the presence or absence of expletives, the Subject-Aux Inversion (SAI), and complex predicate formation. The fact that English has SAI, while Japanese does not, easily falls out from our hypothesis that only English has head movement. The fact that only Japanese has productive complex predicate formation may follow from our claim that the lack of verb-raising allows Japanese to have word formation in the phonological component (via "cliticization") whereas the presence of short verb-raising in English prevents the same type of word formation. We leave open for future research more detailed investigation of these matters.
43 More precisely, the Spell-Out → Morphology computation in the phonological

component, on the assumption that linearized elements function as input to Morphology.
44 There are of course some notable differences as well. One such difference, pointed out by Kazue Takeda (personal communication), is that pushdown automata generally allow "pushing" and "popping" operations to occur in a "mixed way" while language computation disallows such mixed applications: Demerge cannot apply until all applications of Merge have completed. We simply leave for future research more comprehensive comparisons of language computation and pushdown automata.
45 As Fukui (1996b) argues, it is suggestive to observe in this connection that scrambling does not exhibit the crucial property of Attract (i.e., it does not obey the Minimal Link Condition/Relativized Minimality), but it seems to show island-sensitivity in other cases. For example, scrambling seems to obey the Adjunct Condition. See Fukui and Saito (1996) and references cited there for relevant discussion.

8 Order in phrase structure and movement

This is a radically extended version of Fukui and Saito (1992). The initial version was presented at MIT, McGill University, Tohoku University, and the Fukuoka Linguistics Circle, and this extended version at Universität Frankfurt am Main, Sophia University, and University of Connecticut. We would like to thank Yasuaki Abe, Hiroshi Aoyagi, Željko Bošković, Noam Chomsky, João Costa, Danny Fox, Günther Grewendorf, Hiroto Hoshi, Richard Kayne, Rhanghyeyun Lee, Shigeru Miyagawa, Keiko Murasugi, Hiroaki Tada, Daiko Takahashi, Yuji Takano, Kazue Takeda, Akira Watanabe, Kazuko Yatsushiro, and anonymous *LI* reviewers for helpful comments and discussion. As is usually the case, the grammatical judgements in this article are given to illustrate contrasts that we believe are significant, and are not meant to be absolute. The research reported in this article was supported in part by the University of California's Pacific Rim Research Program (Fukui) and by the University of Connecticut Research Foundation (Saito).

1 As Last Resort (Chomsky 1993a) apparently excludes optionality in movement, interesting attempts have been made to reanalyse scrambling, or some types of scrambling, as movement motivated by feature checking. (See, for example, Miyagawa 1994, 1997, Kikuchi, Oishi, and Yusa 1994, and Kitahara 1994.) However, as far as we can see, they have not been able to accommodate successfully the kinds of facts discussed by Tada and also below.
2 We add *koto* "fact" at the end of some examples to avoid the unnaturalness resulting from the absence of a topic in a matrix sentence. Since it is not important for the discussion, we ignore it in the translations. In some cases we also substitute the rough structure of the Japanese example for its translation. The category labels in examples are given only for expository purposes and should not be taken to mean, unless so indicated, that we are committed to the specific categorial analysis of Japanese lexical elements.
3 See Saito (1994b) and Lee (1994) for discussions of the precise mechanism for "undoing" scrambling at LF.
4 We abstract away from the marginality of the example, which is due to Subjacency.
5 Here, we follow Authier (1992) and Watanabe (1993), and tentatively assume that topicalization is movement to an A'-Spec. See also Chomsky (1977) for relevant discussion.
6 Variants of this hypothesis can be found, for example, in Tada (1990) and Saito (1992a). As far as we know, no clear alternative has been proposed in the literature.

7 See also Tada (1990, 1993) and Fukui (1993b) for more detailed discussion of this point. Examples (2b) and (3b), which were employed to show the radical reconstruction property, involve long-distance scrambling. On the other hand, it has been shown (see Mahajan 1990 and Tada 1990, among others) that clause-internal scrambling and long-distance scrambling have different binding properties. Thus, only a phrase preposed by clause-internal scrambling can serve as the binder of a lexical anaphor, as shown in (i).

(i) a. ?[$_{IP}$ Karera-o$_i$ [[otagai -no$_i$ sensei] -ga t_i hihansita]] (koto).
     they-ACC each other-GEN teacher-NOM criticized fact

   "Them$_i$, each other$_i$'s teachers criticized t_i."

b. *[$_{IP}$ Karera-o$_i$ [[otagai -no$_i$ sensei] -ga [$_{CP}$ John-ga t_i
     they -ACC each other-GEN teacher-NOM John-NOM
   hihansita to] itta]] (koto).
   criticized that said fact

   "Them$_i$, each other$_i$'s teachers said [that John criticized t_i]."

Here, following Tada (1990), we maintain that this difference derives from locality and does not imply that there are two distinct operations. For detailed arguments for the optionality of clause-internal scrambling see Tada (1990, 1993). (See also Saito 1992a and Nemoto 1993 for relevant discussion.)

8 The number of scrambled phrases is by no means limited to two. In principle, any number of phrases can be moved to sentence-initial position, as shown in (i) and (ii).

(i) [$_{IP}$ Soko-de$_k$ [John-ni$_j$ [sono hon -o$_i$ [Bill-ga [$_{CP}$[$_{IP}$ Mary-ga t_k t_j t_i
    there-at John-to that book-ACC Bill-NOM Mary-NOM
    watasital to] sinziteiru]]]] (koto).
    handed that believe fact

    "[There$_k$ [to John$_j$ [that book$_i$ [Bill believes [that Mary handed t_i t_j t_k]]]]."

(ii) [$_{IP}$ Mikka -mae -ni$_l$ [soko-de$_k$ [John-ni$_j$ [sono hon-o$_i$
     three days-before-at there-at John-to that book-ACC
     [Bill-ga [$_{CP}$[$_{IP}$ Mary-ga t_l t_k t_j t_i. watasita] to] sinziteiru]]]] (koto).
     Bill-NOM Mary-NOM handed that believe fact

     "[Three days ago$_l$ [there$_k$ [to John$_j$ [that book$_i$ [Bill believes [that Mary handed t_i t_j t_k t_l]]]]]."

9 See Saito (1985) for an attempt to explain the adjunction pattern under the standard X$'$ theory.

10 XP is defined as the projection of X "closed off" by specifier-head agreement (i.e., X$''$) in Fukui (1995b). Here we use it interchangeably with X^{max}, the highest projection of X, for the purpose of exposition.

11 In this article we do not assume the kind of "shell structure" proposed by Larson (1988). As an anonymous reviewer notes, it would be interesting to see how our proposals fare with respect to Larson's analysis. Unfortunately, this topic is beyond the scope of the article.

12 See Takahashi (1994a) for much relevant discussion. Takahashi presents strong arguments based on the analysis of island effects that movement to Spec indeed involves adjunction. Note also that the adjunction + projection analysis of the classical cases of substitution has a conceptual advantage: it eliminates the need for the dubious "empty category", Δ, whose sole function is to mark the landing

site in the traditional theory of substitution. See Fukui and Saito (1992) for a more detailed discussion of this point.

13. In these works a rule of *ga*-insertion, parallel to *of*-insertion of Chomsky (1981a) and Stowell (1981b), is suggested. Alternatively, it is possible that a phrase with *ga* is simply licensed, or even "feature-checked", in a position sister to an I projection. We leave the precise mechanism of *ga*-licensing open. What is important for present purposes is that it is not licensed via specifier-head agreement.

14. See Kuroda (1988), Ura (1994a), and Koizumi (1994), among others, for different views on nominative Case assignment or checking in Japanese. We will present more evidence for the absence of specifier-head agreement in Japanese IPs in section 5.

15. This analysis of the multiple-subject construction and scrambling is an alternative to Kuroda's (1988) theory, which assumes multiple Specs in Japanese. We will return briefly to Kuroda's analysis in section 6.

16. See Fukui (1986: chap. 3) and Speas (1986) for discussion of this point.

17. Here, we assume that not only those genitive phrases that are θ-marked by N, but also possessor genitives, are moved to [Spec, DP] from within the N projection. See also Torrego (1986), Stowell (1989), Ormazabal (1991), Saito and Murasugi (1990, 1993), and the references cited there for relevant discussion of this topic and the DP hypothesis in general.

18. One question that remains is how to derive this apparently universal directionality requirement on agreement. See Kayne (1994) and Fukui and Takano (1998) for much relevant discussion.

19. Another similar characterization of optionality, which was also entertained in Fukui and Saito (1992), is that "structure-preserving" movement need not have a driving force. Scrambling and Heavy NP Shift do not affect the existing phrase structure, since they only add a segment to an existing category. On the other hand, *wh*-movement and NP-movement result in the projection of the target X′ to X″ and hence are "structure-building". But we will not pursue this characterization here. In fact, in the following section we will propose a theory that is diametrically opposed to it.

20. In the structure in (30), the higher α is a projection of the lower α and hence is an independent category. Merge simply combines α and β, chooses one of them as the projecting element, and creates a larger constituent with the chosen element as its head. This structure is to be distinguished from an adjunction structure, where the two α's would be segments of a single category. Below, we sometimes use notations like X, X′, and X″ for expository purposes just to indicate X itself, the first projection of X, and the second projection of X. With these notations, (30) can be written as (i) or (ii), for example.

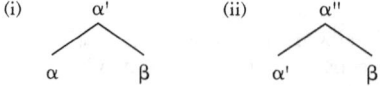

Note that these notations have nothing to do with "bar levels", which are significant in the standard X′ theory but have no place in the bare phrase structure theory.

21. Note that under this theory, a genuine adjunction structure, if it exists at all, cannot be formed with Merge and must be treated separately, since it involves a multisegmented category and no projection of the head. We discuss cases of genuine adjunction in section 4.

22. Here, we depart from Kayne (1994), where it is proposed that the head parameter be eliminated.

23 α projects in (33) exactly as in (30). Thus, (33), like (30), does not represent an adjunction structure. (See note 20.)
24 See, among others, Tada (1993) and Fukui (1993a) for more discussion of this point. The question remains why (34c) and (35c) are not as bad as (36). One possibility suggested in Saito (1994b) is that those examples are in fact completely unacceptable with VP-adjunction scrambling, but they can marginally be construed with the following structure:

(i) $[_{IP}$ John$_j$-ga XP$_i$ [pro$_j$ [$_{VP}$ ... t_i ...

Japanese sentences can have multiple subjects as shown in (25); further, they allow *pro* in any argument position. (See, among others, Kuroda 1965, Hoji 1985, and Murasugi 1991 on the latter point.) Thus, *John-ga* "John-Nom" in those examples can be in a higher subject position of the matrix clause, the regular subject position being occupied by *pro*. To the extent that this structure is possible, the scrambling in those examples can take place across the regular subject position and hence can be "IP-adjunction scrambling". If this speculation is correct, the marginality of (34c) and (35c) reflects the difficulty of construing those examples with the structure in (i).

25 Or, more generally, any position that is sister to and is dominated by projections of a single lexical category is an A-position.
26 See Murasugi and Saito (1995) and Saito (1994b) for the precise characterization of A/A'-positions implied by this analysis. It is proposed there that the position created by "IP-adjunction scrambling", as in (34b) and (35b), is completely within the I projection, but that this position is construed as an A-position only after V raises to I. If V-to-I movement applies in LF in Japanese, then "IP-adjunction scrambling", as an operation, need not be A-movement. Further, as the scrambled phrase can be "radically reconstructed" in LF before V-to-I movement applies, "IP-adjunction scrambling" need not create an A-chain at any level. See also Tada (1990) and Saito (1992a) for much relevant discussion.

We tentatively assume here that intermediate adjunction does not enter into the "calculation" of optionality. That is, scrambling and Heavy NP Shift are considered subcases of Merge even if they involve intermediate adjunction, as long as the final target of the movement is projected.

27 See Kayne (1994) and Takahashi (1994a) for similar proposals. Kayne proposes that there is no structural difference between the Spec and the adjoined position. On the other hand, as mentioned in note 12, Takahashi presents strong arguments based on locality effects that movement to Spec involves adjunction, basically along the lines proposed in Fukui and Speas (1986) and Fukui and Saito (1992). His analysis is consistent with our hypothesis here that movement to Spec not only is adjunction but also involves no projection of the target phrase.
28 This is consistent with the Last Resort characteristics of head movement, illustrated in (i).

(i) a. John wonders what Mary would say.
     b. *John wonders what would Mary say.

The ungrammaticality of (ib) shows that the adjunction of I to C in the embedded clause is not optional. Since head movement is adjunction and does not conform to (39), it needs to be triggered.

29 The embedded [Spec, IP] must be an intermediate landing site, since the movement to this position by itself does not satisfy Last Resort, as illustrated in (i).

(i) a. There$_i$ is likely [$_{IP}$ t_i to be a man there].
     b. *There is likely [$_{IP}$ a man$_i$ to be t_i there].

See Chomsky (1993a) and Bošković (1995), among others, for detailed discussion.

30 Note that this analysis does not necessarily depend on the presence of Agr_O. It is valid even if the object NP checks its features at the VP-adjoined position against the head V. The same point applies to the discussion of French participle agreement below.

31 See Ishii (1997) for relevant discussion of this assumption. Ishii proposes that it should be considered a consequence of a general principle on derivation, which he calls the Immediate Satisfaction Principle.

We leave open whether an adjunct (modifier) is directly generated in an adjoined position, or moved there. Under either hypothesis, if follows that an adjunct (modifier) is checked for a feature (the "adverb feature") at the adjoined position, as proposed by Oka (1993) and Lee (1994). (See also Travis 1988 for relevant discussion.) Since adjunction cannot be a subcase of Merge, it is subject to Last Resort. If an adjunct (modifier) is moved to an adjoined position, we tentatively assume here that the movement is overt. Note that "adverbial feature checking" differs in some respects from feature checking via specifier-head agreement. For example, as multiple adverbs are allowed (as opposed to multiple subjects), "adverbial feature checking" clearly does not require a one-to-one relation with the head. Further, an adverb apparently can appear on either side of a maximal projection; hence, the checking does not seem to have any directionality requirement. See Lee (1994) for detailed discussion of the nature of "adverbial feature checking".

32 This also excludes adjunction of a head to an already adjoined head as in (i).

(i)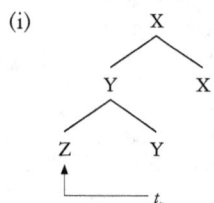

As Masao Ochi (personal communication) and others have pointed out, (51) must be a constraint on operations, not on representations, since the relevant configuration obtains in examples like (ii).

(ii) a. John's mother left.
     b. $[_I{}^{max} [_D{}^{max}$ John's $[_D{}^{max}$ mother$]] [_I{}^{max} \ldots]]$

Here, *John* adjoins to D^{max} before *John's mother* adjoins to I^{max}. Hence, the example does not violate (51) if the condition applies only to operations. Takahashi (1994a) proposes this type of analysis for examples like (ii) and also for relativization examples like (iii).

(iii) [the man $[_C{}^{max}$ who$_i$ $[_C{}^{max}$ John saw $t_i]]]$

According to him, the adjunction of *John* to D^{max} in (ii) does not count as an adjunction to a subject since it applies before the D^{max} moves to the subject position. In (iii) the relative operator *who* adjoins to the relative clause C^{max}, an adjunct (modifier). But since this operation applies before the relative clause is embedded under the complex NP, it does not count as an adjunction to an adjunct (modifier). See also Murasugi (1993) for a similar analysis proposed for Japanese relative clauses.

33 Here, we assume the following standard definition:

   (i) α dominates β =$_{def}$ every segment of α dominates β.

34 A problem remains here with respect to extraction out of a [Spec, CP], as pointed out by an anonymous reviewer. Since *wh*-phrases in [Spec, CP] are adjoined to C^{max}, we predict this type of extraction to be ruled out. But as Chomsky (1986a) notes, attributing the observation to Esther Torrego, it is far better than extraction out of a subject or an adverbial adjunct. The following example is from Lasnik and Saito (1992):

   (i) ??Who$_i$ do you wonder [which picture of t_i]$_j$ Mary bought t_j?

   Takahashi (1994a) argues that phrases in [Spec, CP] do form islands, though their effects are weak. But, like him, we have no account for why their effects are weaker than expected.

35 Given the adjunction analysis of movement to Spec, it may not be necessary to stipulate that specifier-head agreement, or adjunction, closes off a projection. If the I^{max} in (55) is projected further, then the two-segment category is no longer a maximal projection. And it is suggested in Chomsky (1994) that only heads and maximal projections are "visible". Then, it is plausible that the adjunction structure itself cannot be identified once the two-segment category projects. Hence, if the specifier-head configuration, as in (40a), should be "visible" at LF, then the effect of specifier-head agreement on projection may follow.

36 See also Kikuchi (1989), where it is shown that Japanese comparative deletion exhibits the same pattern of island effects even more clearly.

37 An anonymous reviewer points out that our theory may make an incorrect prediction for English with respect to *wh*-movement out of an NP moved rightward by Heavy NP Shift. A relevant example is shown in (i).

   (i) ?*What$_i$ did you give t_j to John [a book about t_i]$_j$?

   Having analysed Heavy NP Shift on a par with scrambling, we do predict that the heavy object NP in (i) is not an island for movement. We assume, as in Saito (1987a) and Lasnik and Saito (1992), that examples of this kind are ruled out independently as instances of "crossing" as formulated in Baker (1977).

38 See Saito (1994a) for further discussion of the "additional-*wh* effect" in Japanese.

39 More extensive research is needed to determine the exact class of functional categories Japanese has. We will leave the issue open, but see below for some related discussion.

40 See Saito and Murasugi (1993) and Kimura (1994) for further discussion of "N'-deletion" in Japanese. The argument is generalized to Japanese sluicing in Takahashi (1994b).

41 Note that this problem does not arise with Kuroda's (1988) theory, since, according to him, Japanese allows multiple Specs and specifier-head agreement is optional in this language. *Oya-e-no* and *kodomo-no* in the second conjunct of (72b) can both be in [Spec, DP], and only the latter can agree with the D head. See Kimura (1994) for relevant discussion of this particular point.

9 An A-over-A perspective on locality

I gratefully acknowledge the comments and suggestions made by the following colleagues: Brian Agbayani, Robert Freidin, Heizo Nakajima, Yuji Takano, Kazue Takeda, Akira Watanabe, and the reviewers of this volume. The research reported in this article was supported in part by the University of California's Pacific Rim Grant. An earlier version of this paper was published in a preliminary form as Fukui (1997).

1 I assume with Chomsky (1995b) that interpretable features such as *wh*-feature, D-feature and φ-features remain accessible or visible to further computation even after checking, while Case feature, which is uninterpretable, becomes inaccessible or invisible to computation when checked. But see note 9 below.
2 In fact, Kuroda (1988) calls checking/agreement (his "Agreement") a "feature-sharing" phenomenon. See also Stowell (1981b) for a similar view. There is some independent evidence for this "feature-sharing" view. Thus, as noted by Chomsky (1995b), when a DP enters into a checking relation with T, the φ-features of the DP specifier commonly show up both on the DP and the verbal head incorporating the T. This overt pattern, however, cannot straightforwardly extend to other cases of checking, although similar observations have been made about "*wh*-agreement" manifested on a complementizer when *wh*-movement is involved (see Chung 1994 and references cited therein). Percolation mechanisms based on ideas similar to the one discussed in the text have been proposed in various forms, especially with regard to [Spec, CP], in an attempt to account for pied-piping phenomena (including the "clausal pied-piping" phenomenon in languages like Basque). See, among others, Webelhuth (1989) and Ortiz de Urbina (1990) for relevant discussion.
3 Our account here is reminiscent of Chomsky's (1968) suggestion that, in the case of *wh*-island, "the process of *wh*-placement ... assigns the element *wh*- [i.e., [+wh]] not only to 'the book' [the moved element] ... but also to the proposition containing it" (Chomsky 1968: 53).
4 The intuition behind this claim is somewhat reminiscent of Lasnik and Saito's (1984) "Comp accessibility" proviso in their definition of antecedent-government, which exempts a CP from becoming a barrier to antecedent-government of a trace when it immediately dominates the trace in question (which they assume to occupy the head C position). Formalization of this notion of transparency is straightforward, assuming the dominance relation (with respect to the A-over-A Principle) to be irreflexive, where identity is defined in terms of relevant features.
5 The only other case mentioned by Chomsky (1995b) that might fall under the case is "superiority". Although it might not be totally impossible to account for superiority phenomenon in terms of the A-over-A Principle (by, for example, modifying slightly the mechanism of feature-sharing), such a move, which is not desirable for theoretical reasons alone, does not seem to be well-motivated at this point. Also, as Chomsky (1995b: 387) points out, the nature of superiority phenomenon is far from clear, and it may well fall outside the scope of the locality of language computation we are considering. Thus, I will leave the treatment of the superiority phenomenon open here, pending further research.
6 This is true even though Attract is regarded as a component of UG, rather than a "rule" of a particular grammar. Adding the "minimality" condition to the definition of Attract (as in (1)) is, in my opinion, similar to, say, stipulating as a particular property of Move α that it can only "raise" a category but can never "lower" one.
7 The literature on island constraints is too vast to mention. See Chomsky (1986a) and references cited there for much detailed discussion. I will put aside the Left Branch Condition and the Co-ordinate Structure Constraint of Ross (1967), since the nature of these phenomena is not entirely clear at this point (though, prima facie, the Left Branch Condition may be handled by the A-over-A Principle).
8 In the relative clause case, extraction of *who* may violate the A-over-A Principle twice; in addition to the case of A = categorial features, it may also violate the principle with A = operator feature (including the *wh*-feature), if we follow the

standard assumption that a relative clause formation involves an operator movement. This may account for the difference in degradation between the two cases of CNPC.

9 The Subject Condition case of (12a) in fact violates both the A-over-A Principle (as mentioned above) and CED (which is reduced to the theory of phrase structure theory), and hence the deviance is stronger than the Adjunct Condition effect (12b). This is not the case in languages like Japanese, where the subject is generated by substitution (Merge) and there is no subject-verb agreement: Extraction from subject in Japanese, therefore, violates neither the A-over-A Principle (due to the lack of agreement) nor the CED (because the subject is generated by substitution). As a reviewer points out, this situation might suggest that the parametric difference between English and Japanese in this respect should be attributed solely to the A-over-A Principle effect associated with subjects, without redundantly having recourse to the ban on multiple adjunctions, as in Saito and Fukui (1998). Note also that Saito and Fukui's account of CED assumes the MLC to be present as an economy principle of UG, quite independently from the treatment of the Relativized Minimality cases discussed above. It remains to be seen whether the effect of the MLC employed in their account can (and should) be derived from factors having to do with the A-over-A Principle.

10 This account assumes that a *wh*-feature at least optionally becomes inaccessible or invisible when checked, which is different from our previous assumption that a *wh*-feature, being interpretable, remains accessible even after checking. While the interpretability of D-feature and φ-features is relatively uncontroversial (as well as uninterpretability of Case feature), the interpretability of *wh*-feature seems to be far from clear at this point. I leave for future research more thorough investigations of the nature of these features. See Chomsky (1995b) for much relevant discussion.

10 The uniqueness parameter

I would like to thank Brian Agbayani, Cedric Boeckx, Koji Cho, Kazue Takeda, Mihoko Zushi, as well as an anonymous reviewer, for valuable comments and suggestions.

11 Nominal structure: an extension of the Symmetry Principle

Part of the material in this article has been presented by one of the authors (Fukui) at Linguistics and Phonetics Conference 1998 (Ohio State University), a syntax seminar at the University of California, Irvine (Spring 1999), a keynote speech at the 118th Semi-annual meeting of the Linguistic Society of Japan (Tokyo Metropolitan University, 1999), and at colloquia at Tokyo Metropolitan University, Nanzan University and Sophia University (all in 1999). We would like to thank the audiences of these occasions for their valuable comments and suggestions. We are particularly grateful for their useful comments to Jun Abe, Yasuaki Abe, Hiroshi Aoyagi, Peter Culicover, Osamu Fujimura, Koji Fujita, Koji Hoshi, Brian Joseph, Yasuhiko Kato, Heizo Nakajima, Peter Svenonius, Ken-ichi Takami, Kazue Takeda, and Sze-Wing Tang.

1 By "linear order", we mean "temporal order" throughout the discussion in this article.
2 There are in fact a few versions of generative grammar (widely construed) in which linear order (precedence) is not postulated as a primitive notion. Šaumjan's "applicational grammar" immediately comes to mind as a variant of

such a model. Versions of relational grammar and categorial grammar seem to share the same spirit. See also Chomsky (1965: 123–125) for some relevant discussion on this matter.

3 Watanabe (1998) presents interesting additional evidence for the hypothesis based on considerations of denominal verb formation, while casting some doubts about Fukui and Takano's (1998) uniform treatment of phrasal movement and head movement.

4 The same claim that (S-)C-H/(S-)O-V is "basic" is independently made on quite different grounds by Haider's series of works, dating back to his 1992 paper. See Haider (2000) and the references cited therein.

5 As we summarized briefly above, in Fukui and Takano's analysis of head movement, head movement is treated as "substitution into Spec" (i.e., a projection-creating operation in the terms of bare phrase structure theory of Chomsky 1995b) rather than adjunction to head. See Fukui and Takano (1998) for details.

6 Throughout this paper, we represent hierarchical structures in terms of tree diagrams. However, the reader should keep in mind that those tree structures are used just for expository reasons and they are by no means intended to imply anything about linear order of the elements.

7 Here we assume with Fukui (1986, 1988a) that Japanese lacks the functional category D. We also assume, for the sake of simplicity, that there is no functional projection between D and N. Note that the projection of D in the English nominal structure in (11) involves multiple specifiers occupied by the determiner and the raised N. The structure should not be confused with an adjunction structure.

8 See also Hoshi (1997) for an extension of the basic ideas proposed in Fukui and Takano (1998) to a parametric account of differences between English and Japanese concerning adjectival modification within the nominal structure.

9 Note that the lower segment is a trace or copy of the raised N. This means that we need to assume, contrary to Kayne (1994) and Chomsky (1995b), that a segment can undergo movement. Or we might adopt Chomsky's (1993a) claim that adjunction can be noncyclic, which entails that in the derivation, the relative clause adjoins to the trace or copy of the raised nominal head after raising to SpecD.

10 Structures in which an XP is adjoined to an X^0 have traditionally been excluded, because of the (plausible) morphological requirement that a word-level category consist only of X^0-elements. We can maintain this intuition by distinguishing a nonmaximal minimal category (pure X^0) and a maximal minimal category (the case in (14)). In the bare theory, a category is minimal if it is not a projection of anything. Then, traditional intuition states that the following structure, where ZP is a complement of $[X_1, X_1]$, is banned because of the morphological requirement in question:

(i)

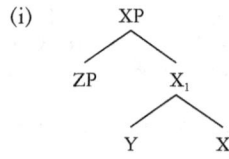

(i) is crucially different from (14) in the text in that in (i) $[X_1, X_1]$ is a nonmaximal minimal category (the maximal category there is XP), whereas in (14) $[N_1, N_1]$ is a maximal minimal category.

11 It is standardly assumed that the relative clause is predicated of the relative head. We take this to be a licensing condition on the relative clause containing

a relative pronoun that creates an open proposition. Note that if the condition in (15) is met, the predication condition is automatically satisfied as well with the open position in the relative clause identified with the relative head.

12 One might wonder how this analysis carries over to cases in which the relative head has a complement, as in (i).

(i) a picture of Mary which John saw yesterday

The intuition about (i) is that the relative pronoun is identified with *picture of Mary*, not just *picture*. We then analyse (i) as follows:

(ii)

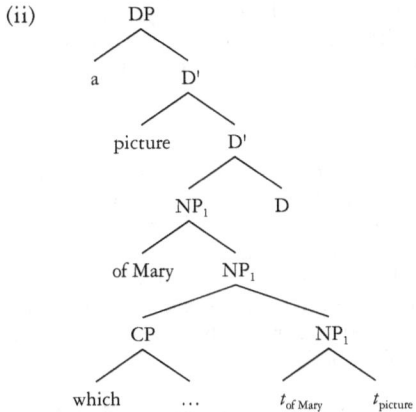

Following Takano (1996, 1998), we assume that *of Mary* has scrambled over the relative clause (if this scrambling did not happen, the derivation would crash; see Takano (1998) for details). In effect, we claim that *picture* and *of Mary* in (i) do not form a constituent (they form a constituent only in the "base structure"). However, both c-command the relative pronoun in (ii), which we take to be sufficient to ensure that the relative pronoun is identified with *picture of Mary*.

13 Here we are tentatively assuming that the Japanese relative clause is CP. We will recast this assumption in 3.4.

14 The "co-reference" relation between the object *pro* and the relative head should be a free option. However, if the object *pro* is interpreted as referring to something other than the relative head, the relative clause will fail to meet the "aboutness" condition.

15 Here we are neutral as to whether the overt raising of the relative pronoun is induced by some syntactic feature of C of the relative clause, or whether it is due to some other (possibly, semantic) force.

16 The claim that CP is lacking in the Japanese relative clause is compatible with Fukui's (1986, 1988a, 1995b) theory of parametric variation, which states that the functional categories C and Agr, having no semantic content, can be lacking in some languages.

17 A variety of analyses have been proposed for the structure of internally headed relative clauses in Japanese. See Kuroda (1998) for a summary of those analyses. Kuroda (1998) proposes an alternative to the analysis in which the internally headed relative has an invisible external head, arguing that what appears in the object position of the matrix verb in (31) is a headless relative clause and that the matrix verb directly θ-marks the internal head in the headless relative clause.

18 See Johnson (1997) for a general review of Kayne's (1994) work.
19 Feature attraction is in the form of "adjunction to head", not to be confused with movement of a head to another head, which is reanalysed as "substitution into Spec" in our framework.
20 The situation is reminiscent of the traditional intuition that the existence of overt Case-particles somehow makes it possible for an argument (e.g., direct object) to show up in a position that is remote from where it is θ-marked, i.e., scrambling. See Fukui and Takano (1998) for some relevant discussion.
21 Slavic/Germanic languages (including English) belong to type (ii), and the Romance languages in general belong to type (iii), according to Chierchia.
22 Integration of Romance comparative syntax and Japanese syntax seems to be particularly interesting in this light. See Fukui et al. (in preparation) for a rather comprehensive study on "Japanese syntax in a Romance perspective".

12 Phrase structure

Portions of the material contained in this article were presented in my lectures ("Phrase Structure and Movement") at the 1997 Linguistic Society of America's Summer Linguistic Institute (Cornell University). I would like to thank the audience there for many valuable questions and suggestions. I am also grateful to the editors and an anonymous reviewer of the *Handbook of contemporary syntactic theory*, Takao Gunji, and Heizo Nakajima for useful comments and suggestions. The research reported in this article was supported in part by the University of California's Pacific Rim Research Grant (PI: Naoki Fukui).

1 It is not implied here that phrase structure rules directly generate phrase markers. In fact, the standard assumption is that phrase structure rules generate "derivations", from which there is an algorithm to construct phrase markers. See Chomsky (1955, 1959) and especially McCawley (1968) for much relevant discussion on the nature of phrase structure rules and their relation to phrase markers.
2 It is now standard to call these elements the specifier of X'', rather than the specifier of X', and, accordingly, notate them as [Spec, X''].
3 Ideas of this sort were explored and developed in structural linguistics in terms of discovery procedures of constituent analysis (Harris 1946, 1951).
4 The determiners (such as *the*, *a*, etc.) are also analysed as [Spec, N']. As it is hard to analyse determiners as maximal projections (noun phrases, in particular), the identification of determiners as Spec elements poses a problem for the uniform characterization of Spec discussed in the text. This problem was later resolved by the "DP-analysis", as we will see in the next section.
5 The X' scheme in (25) is my interpretation of what is intended in the proposal of Chomsky (1986a). Chomsky's original formulation is as follows (Chomsky 1986a: 3):

X' schemata
a. $X' = X\ X''*$
b. $X'' = X''*\ X'$ (where $X*$ stands for zero or more occurrences of some maximal projection and $X = X^0$)

The crucial differences between (25) and Chomsky's original formulation is that the latter allows "flat" and multiple branching structures at both the single-bar and double-bar levels, whereas the former (i.e., (25)), while permitting "recursion", never allows flat and multiple branching structures, in accordance with Kayne's (1984) binary branching hypothesis. It seems to me that the schemata in (25) express more properly what was intended by the proposal of Chomsky (1986a).

6 There are of course more complex cases. Whether or not the other linear ordering in the X' scheme (viz., the Spec-head and head-adjunct order) is subject to parametrization is a complex issue that remains open. See among others Chomsky and Lasnik (1993) and references there for further discussion. We will return to the issue of the head parameter in section 4.
7 The converse is not implied in Chomsky's theory. That is, while X^{max}-movement (substitution) is always to a Spec position, it is not claimed that Spec is always a landing site for X^{max}-movement. Such a claim, which implies further sharpening of the notion of Spec, is in fact put forth in Relativized X' theory, to be discussed in section 3 below.
8 Details differ in various analyses. For example, we put aside the issue of whether all the subjects of noun phrases are generated within a noun's projection, or some subjects are base generated in [Spec, D'']. There are other problems that remain open. See Longobardi (2001).
9 Relativized X' theory was first presented in a preliminary form in Fukui and Speas (1986), and was later developed, in slightly different ways and directions, in Fukui (1986) and Speas (1986, 1990). The following exposition is largely based on Fukui (1986).
10 The formal operation building the structure is assumed to be "Adjunction". Note that Adjunction here is somewhat different from the standard notion of adjunction, which, when applied, creates a multisegment structure of the target. Adjunction, unlike adjunction, induces a projection of the target element (see the discussion in section 4 of this chapter). Note also that the notion of "bar-level" does not play any significant role in this theory. Thus, X' merely means that X is projected. See also Muysken (1982).
11 To the extent that "substitution" transformations and "adjunction" transformations must be distinguished with respect to their empirical properties, we have to make a distinction somehow, but differently from the traditional definitions. Fukui (1986) attempts to offer appropriate definitions of "substitution" and "adjunction" without having recourse to the empty category Δ, based on the idea that "substitution" is an operation that creates a legitimate structure licensed by (Relativized) X' theory, whereas "adjunction" creates a structure that is never licensed at the base (in terms of X' theory). See Fukui (1986: ch. 4). Note incidentally that under these definitions, some instances of Adjunction (see the preceding note), including, for example, scrambling in Japanese, which had been assumed to be adjunction (Saito 1985), should indeed be analysed as substitution.
12 Notice that this operation includes the traditional "substitution" and the operation that is in charge of building structures, but does not include, perhaps, the traditional "adjunction", which creates a "non-standard" multisegment structure. See notes 10 and 11. See also the discussion in the next section.
13 There are some potentially problematic cases for this claim. The "leftness condition" of Chomsky (1976), carried over into the principles-and-parameters approach in the form of "weak crossover", is one such.
14 Recall that the term "substitution" loses its traditional meaning in the bare theory (as well as in Relativized X' theory), since the dubious category Δ is eliminated from the theory of movement. See note 11.
15 See Ishii (1997) for relevant discussion on this assumption. He proposes that it should be considered a consequence of a general principle on derivation, which he calls the immediate satisfaction principle. It is left open in Saito and Fukui (1998) whether an adjunct (modifier) is directly generated in an adjoined position, or moved there. Under either hypothesis, it follows that an adjunct (modifier) is checked for a feature (the "adverb feature") at the adjoined position, as proposed by Oka (1993) and Lee (1994). (See also Travis 1988 for relevant

discussion.) Note finally that, since adjunction cannot be a subcase of Merge, it is subject to the Last Resort Principle, as Saito and Fukui argue. See Saito and Fukui (1998) for other details.

13 The Visibility Guideline for functional categories: verb-raising in Japanese and related issues

We would like to thank Jun Abe, Kazuhiko Fukushima, Naomi Harada, Ken Hiraiwa, Hiroto Hoshi, Andy Martin, and particularly Yukinori Takubo and Mihoko Zushi, for their helpful comments and suggestions.

1 Some of the proposed functional categories have been claimed to bear certain semantic import. This point will be taken up again later.
2 Relevant works are too numerous to mention. See the chapters in part IV (Functional Projections) of Baltin and Collins (2001) and references cited there.
3 See also Thráinsson (1996) for a proposal along similar lines, as well as a novel analysis of inflectional (tense and agreement) elements.
4 The same holds true, *mutatis mutandis*, of Kuroda's (1988) attempt at a comparative syntax of English and Japanese.
5 A preliminary version of this article was written in 1985.
6 Ken Hale's proposal (made in the mid-1980s) of the functional category K (for Case) (see Bittner and Hale 1996 for a written version), which is overt in Japanese but covert in English, is perhaps the only exception, though this alleged category is not a lexical category and has nothing to do with semantic interpretation of a linguistic expression. Ross's (1970) performative analysis can be taken as an attempt to propose a linguistic device that is overtly manifested (as sentence-final particles) in a language like Japanese, for an analysis of a language like English where there is no overt manifestation (although the analogy is not quite accurate).
7 The V-to-T raising in Germanic SOV languages can be taken as an instance of string vacuous verb-raising akin to the Japanese case. However, the situation in these languages is different from the case of Japanese in that a subsequent verb-raising to C makes visible the effect of the V-to-T raising. See Johnson (1994), Vikner (1995), Zwart (1997), and Roberts (2001) for an overview of verb-raising in Germanic languages.
8 For related discussions on English verbal morphology see Halle and Marantz (1993), Lasnik (1995), and Bobaljik (1995), among others.
9 See also Kuwabara (1996) for an analysis of cleft constructions similar to Koizumi's.
10 The presence of *-ka* seems to have the function of saving the structure without *-da*. Thus, example (14b) (as opposed to (14a)) is only a little bit degraded (but not totally ungrammatical) if there is no *-da*.
11 Koizumi attributes this observation to Miyagawa (1989).
12 We maintain that the deviance of examples like (18b) is due to the difficulty of associating the fronted numeral quantifier in the matrix clause and the noun phrase in the embedded clause that it is supposed to modify, rather than due to the "non-constituency" of the fronted elements. While the exact mechanism of this interpretive association is yet to be worked out, it is clear that the nature of the deviance exhibited by examples like (18b) is not caused by purely syntactic factors such as constituency. In fact, we would not assign a "*" to (18b) (although it is certainly hard to associate the two elements in this particular example), and lexical adjustments would surely improve the acceptability of the example. Note also that no arguments have ever been put forth, to the best of our knowledge, that a "fronted" numeral quantifier such as *3-satu* in (18b) has

been actually "moved/scrambled" from the trace position in the embedded clause. Instead, the numeral quantifier could have been simply merged at the beginning of the sentence, and then submitted for interpretation. This remark applies to alleged "scrambling" of non-arguments generally.
13 Koizumi takes up Sohn's analysis and argues against it (Koizumi 2000: 248–257). Sohn's work is based on Saito's (1994a) adjunction analysis of "LF saving effect", and is mainly concerned with the distribution of *wh*-phrases. Koizumi's criticism is directed toward this particular aspect of an "adjunction" analysis, and it does not argue against the general "free merger" view advocated by Fukui (1986) and subsequent works.
14 The presence of numeral quantifiers seems to have an important factor in legitimizing these co-ordinate structures. Koizumi (1995, 2000) attributes this effect to the morphological properties of connective particles which require a nominal host.
15 The study of the particle *-mo* has a long history in the generative study of Japanese. See Kuroda (1965, 1970) for a detailed analysis of syntactic and/or semantic properties of the particles *-mo* "also", *-dake* "only", and *-sae* "even". See also Nishigauchi (1990), Kawashima (1994), Aoyagi (1998a, b), among others, for more recent developments on the analysis of these elements.
16 As can be seen from these examples, there are certain differences between these particles with respect to their distributional properties. For instance, the occurrence of the particle *-to* after the second conjunct is optional, whereas the second occurrence of *-mo* is obligatory.
17 There is another particle *-mo* "as much as", which is homophonous with the particle *-mo* "also" under discussion. The example (24a) is grammatical if the particle *-mo* in these examples is taken to mean "as much as". The particle *-mo* in this sense has nothing to do with coordination, as shown by the fact that it can be used in a sentence like *Taroo-ga gohan-o 4-hai mo tabeta* "Taro ate as much as four bowls of rice", where there is simply no coordination structure.
18 It is not the case that the verbal stem stays within VP in order to satisfy the morphological property of *-katu*. In the following examples, the verbal stems stay within VP quite independently of the morphological properties of the particle *-katu*.
 (i) Taroo-ga   syokudoo -o   pikapika-ni katu daidokoro-o
       -NOM dining room-ACC shining   and kitchen   -ACC
     seiketu-ni soozi-si-ta.
     clean   cleaned

    "Taro made the dining room shiny and the kitchen clean."

 (ii) Taroo-ga   syokudoo-o   pikapika-ni-soozi-si katu daidokoro-o
       -NOM dining   -ACC shiny-clean   and kitchen   -ACC
     seiketu-ni soozi-si-ta.
     clean   cleaned

    Lit. "Taro cleaned the dining room shiny and cleaned the kitchen clean."

The example (i) indicates that an element like *pikapika-ni* "shining(ly)" can be followed by *-katu*. The example (ii) shows that a verb (*soozi-suru* "clean") need not raise to T even in this construction.
19 Fukushima (2003) independently observes this fact and argues that the connected constituents are NPs rather than VPs. He further proposes that these NP constituents are base-generated as such and that the correct interpretations of these constructions can be obtained by the semantic rules he postulates. We leave a close examination of possibilities of this kind for future research.
20 Koizumi (1995, 2000) presents an example which indicates that the matrix

argument and the embedded argument cannot be connected by *-to* if the embedded clause is finite. But this restriction does not hold in the case of infinitival complements. We return to the case of finite subordinate clauses in section 4.

21 For the other two cases (viz., the cases of scrambling and pseudo-clefts), we have already suggested (see section 3.2.2) an alternative analysis of unusual constituencies in Japanese in terms of the "free merger/adjunction" mechanism of Fukui (1986).

22 By "PF" (or the "phonological component"), we mean the components of grammar "on the PF side", i.e., the set of operations applying after Transfer/Spell-Out (cf. Chomsky 2001a, b), including (part of) this operation itself, which eventually lead the derivation to the interface PF expression. There are different sub-components of the "phonological component", with various distinct properties, but we put side the details here and continue to use the term "PF" to refer to the collection of operations which are performed outside of the narrow syntax.

23 The idea that scrambling is a PF operation is not at all new. Ross (1967) originally proposes scrambling as a rule in the stylistic (i.e., part of the PF) component (see Inoue 1978 for a similar view). There have been occasional "PF analyses of scrambling" proposed in the literature (see, for example, Chomsky 1995b: chapter 4, section 5.7.3). On the other hand, Harada (1977) and Saito (1985), among others, present empirical evidence that at least some instances of scrambling involve movement in the narrow syntax. However, as far as we are aware, no strong argument has been presented for the claim that scrambling *must* be exclusively a (narrow) syntactic operation. One possible objection to the PF analysis of scrambling comes from the fact (which, incidentally, is by no means clear and which requires much closer examination) that scrambling appears to obey at least some of the island constraints. However, the status of island constraints is far from clear in the current framework, and there is even a possibility that some of these constraints are operative in the PF component. See Agbayani (1998) and Hoshi (2000) for observations that PF operations obey island constraints. See also Fukui (1996b) and Kasai and Takahashi (2001) for arguments that the Subjacency Condition applies in PF.

24 The idea of PF reanalysis (or "readjustment rules" in the phonological component) has numerous predecessors in the history of generative grammar. See Chomsky and Halle (1968), Chomsky (1977), Hornstein and Weinberg (1981), and Kayne (1981), among many others.

25 See Kuno (1973, 1976a) and Harada (1971, 1976) for earlier discussions on case alternation phenomena in Japanese. See Sakai (1994) for an attempt to provide a unified account for case alternation (or "case conversion") phenomena in Japanese. More recent treatments within the minimalist program include Watanabe (1996b), Ochi (2001) and Hiraiwa (2001a, b), among others.

26 For example, Takezawa (1987, 1998) suggests that the possibility of licensing multiple case is parametrized, or that an object NP can be assigned a nominative Case because the VP projection of a stative V is "transparent" with respect to Case assignment. To the extent that these statements are descriptively adequate, we would certainly want them to be derived from more fundamental parametric properties.

27 It is an extension of a core local relation directly derived from the properties of Merge (such as "Immediately-Contain" or "Contain"). Thus, this, too, should be eventually eliminated if we strictly keep to minimalist assumptions, in which case the notion of "Spec-head relation" should also be re-examined.

28 The other logical possibility, in fact a more desirable one (see the preceding note), is the case (ii) in (39). That is, theoretically, it would be even more desirable if Case theory can be reformulated on the basis of sisterhood alone, elimin-

ating the need for the Spec-head relation. See Chomsky (2001b) for some relevant discussion.
29 These authors do not claim the total elimination of Agr from UG. Their specific claims vary, but the common point among these authors is that a functional head like Agr needs to be fully justified for each particular language, rather than just "assumed" as a universal entity.
30 Further applications of "Agr-less Case theory" to Japanese syntax are explored in recent works. Thus, Hiraiwa (2001a, b) proposes an analysis of case alternations in Japanese in terms of "multiple Agree", and argues that a phrase entering into a Case checking relation does not always raise to a Spec position of the relevant functional head in the narrow syntax (see Miyagawa 1993 for a similar suggestion), implying that the operation Agree alone is in fact sufficient for Case checking.
31 Whether the element -*tati* is a plural marker or not is actually unclear. For example, -*tati* can be attached to a proper noun as in *Taroo-tati* meaning "Taro and others", which indicates that it is not really a plural marker (plural markers do not attach to proper nouns). The exact nature of this element does not concern us here, of course.
32 Notice that these elements also exhibit case alternations as illustrated below.

(i) Kokumin-wa [gaimu-daizin   -ni Yamada-si   -to
    people -TOP the minister of foreign affairs-as   -Mr/Ms-CON
    zaimu-daizin   -ni Suzuki-si   (-to)] -ga/o   husawasii-to
    minister of finance-as   -Mr/Ms (CON)-NOM/ACC suitable -that
    omotte-iru.
    think

Lit. "People think/consider [Mr Yamada as the minister of foreign affairs] and [Mr Suzuki as the minister of finance] to be suitable."

(ii) [Kinoo   suugaku-no   gakusei -to   ototoi   buturi -no sensei]
      yesterday math   -GEN students-CON the day before physics-gen teacher
    -ga/no
    -NOM/GEN
    tukatte-ita atarasii konpyuutaa-ga   kesa   kyuu-ni
    used   new   computer -NOM this morning suddenly
    kowarete-simat-ta.
    broke down

Lit. "The new computer which [yesterday maths students] and [the day before physics teachers] used suddenly broke down this morning."

Given the general assumption that Move does not apply to non-constituents, these examples indicate that the case alternation phenomena at hand cannot readily be accounted for in terms of Move.
33 See Kuroda (2002) for a detailed discussion of their analysis.
34 Harada (2002) presents some acquisition data that support the analysis of relative clauses presented in Fukui and Takano (2000). See Watanabe (2002) for an overview of various issues concerning "operator constructions" in Japanese.
35 It has been occasionally claimed among Japanese linguists that "Japanese is a 'discourse-oriented' language where discourse principles play much more prominent roles than grammatical principles do", that "there is no 'grammar' of Japanese, only morphology" etc. Of course, these claims cannot be accepted as

such. As it turns out, however, the discussion in this paper suggests that there may be some truth to these remarks, although our conclusion by no means decreases the importance of formal syntactic approaches to Japanese. It is also worth pointing out that the general characteristics of Japanese grammar we are entertaining in the paper have much in common with the ideas of the "configurationality parameter" proposed by Hale (1980a, 1982, 1983).
36 For example, the linking between -*ka* and a *wh*-phrase does not exhibit island effects, and is sensitive to some sort of semantic factors (his "monkey wrench predicate constraint"). See Fukui (2000) for relevant discussion.
37 See Kasai (2002) for an analysis of scrambling along the lines sketched here.

Appendix: on the nature of economy in language

I would like to thank the following people for their comments, suggestions, and warm encouragement: Joseph Aoun, Robert Berwick, Sylvain Bromberger, Koji Cho, Noam Chomsky, Robert Freidin, Takao Gunji, Ken Hale, Kyle Johnson, Toshifusa Oka, Carlos Otero, Ken Safir, Mamoru Saito, Barry Schein, Ed Stabler, Jean-Roger Vergnaud, and Juan Uriagereka. I am particularly grateful to Robert Freidin, Takao Gunji, Toshifusa Oka, Juan Uriagereka, and two anonymous reviewers of *Cognitive Studies* for detailed written comments, from which I greatly benefited in revising earlier versions of the paper. Portions of the material in this article were presented at the 65th General Meeting of the English Literary Society of Japan (Special Symposium "On the Minimalist Program") held at the University of Tokyo (May 1993), and at colloquia at Kyoto University (June 1994, School of Engineering), the University of Connecticut (October 1994, Department of Linguistics), and the University of Southern California (April 1995, Department of Linguistics). I also presented the content of the paper in my lectures and seminars at the University of California, Irvine (1992–1993, 1993–1994), Osaka University (June 1994) and Kyushu University (June 1994). The questions and suggestions of these audiences have led to numerous improvements, for which I am grateful. Needless to say, all the shortcomings and inadequacies that (surely) remain are my own.

1 Both are quoted by Kline (1972: 580).
2 Stating the content of the Principle of Least Time this way may imply an introduction of "teleological", rather than "causal", explanations to scientific inquiry, which has bothered some physicists. Thus, Richard Feynman expresses his concern about the nature of the Principle of Least Time as follows: "the principle of least time is a completely different philosophical principle about the way nature works. Instead of saying it is a causal thing, that when we do one thing, something else happens, and so on, it says this: we set up the situation, and *light* decides which is the shortest time, or the extreme one, and chooses that path. But *what* does it do, *how* does it find out? Does it *smell* the nearby paths, and check them against each other? The answer is, yes, it does, in a way" (Feynman et al. 1963, volume 1: 26–27; emphases original). We refrain from the discussion of the "philosophical" nature of optimality principles in sciences. The fundamental issue seems to be whether the observed optimality is the nature of the object of inquiry or it merely reflects a specific mode of inquiry taken typically in the natural sciences. An interested reader is referred to Schoemaker (1991) (and commentaries in the same issue of the journal) for much relevant discussion. See also Chomsky (1993a: 2) for a very brief remark on this issue in the case of linguistics.
3 The calculus of variations is now part of the standard curriculum of analytic mechanics, and is explained in detail in any textbook of the field. See, for example, Arfken (1985), Feynman et al. (1963) (volumes 1 and 2), and Gold-

stein (1980). A classical discussion on the calculus of variations can be found in Courant and Hilbert (1924–1989; chapter IV). Lanczos (1970–1986) contains a quite readable, yet accurate, discussion about the history of its development, as well as technical details. Kline (1959; chapter 25) and Kline (1972; Chapter 24) present concise historical surveys of the development of mathematics and physics that are directly relevant to our discussion in the text.

4 It should be noted that the notion of "conceptually possible displacements" is reminiscent of the concept of "virtual displacement" in d'Alembert's principle.

5 See, for example, Papadimitriou and Steiglitz (1982) for much detailed expositions of optimization (especially, discrete optimization) problems. The classical literature in this field includes Bellman (1957) and Dreyfus (1965).

6 Or maximizes, depending on the nature of the problem. Since maximization of an objective function f is equivalent to minimization of the same function f multiplied by -1, and hence any results for minimization problems can be reexpressed for maximization problems, we will focus on the minimization problem in the following discussion.

7 The decision variable can itself be a function, in which case the objective function is defined over a class of functions and is technically called a *functional*. The integral used in the calculus of variations discussed above is a typical example of such functionals.

8 Our discussion here about this fast-growing field is quite brief and informal. See standard textbooks such as Hopcroft and Ullman (1979: chapter 12) for more precise explanations. See also Garey and Johnson (1979) and van Leeuwen, ed. (1990), for more technical discussions.

9 We will henceforth use the term "language" to mean "I-language", unless otherwise noted. For the concept of I-language and its relevance for linguistic theory, see Chomsky (1986b).

10 For expository purposes, we assume with Chomsky (1993a, 1994) that the mapping performed by C_{HL} is strictly derivational. This assumption, however, is not an uncontroversial one, and the fundamental issue concerning the general design of language seems to exist here. See Rizzi (1986b) and Prince and Smolensky (1993) for arguments in favour of the "non-derivational" view; see Chomsky (1994, 1995b) for some arguments in defence of the "derivational" view.

11 The notion of "convergence" in this sense should not be confused with the standard usage of the term in mathematics.

12 We are of course not suggesting that the economy principles of language are "reducible" to the Principle of Least Action. The actual formulation of the principles appears to be highly specific to language. Nevertheless, the fundamental similarity between language and the inorganic world in this respect is so striking that it suggests that there is something deep in common between the two areas of inquiry. See Chomsky (1991a) for some relevant discussion.

13 For a head α, take $Max(\alpha)$ to be the least full-category maximal projection dominating α (a "maximal projection" is a category that does not further project). The *domain* of a head α is the set of nodes contained in $Max(\alpha)$ that are distinct from and do not contain α. The *minimal domain* of α is its smallest domain. These definitions are informal and only for ease of exposition. For more precise definitions, see Chomsky (1993a, 1995b). "Phrase-marker" is a formal object that can be defined in set-theoretic terms. Cf. Chomsky (1994, 1995b).

14 I am indebted to a reviewer of *Cognitive Studies* for pointing out the need for this clarification. The reviewer further points out (correctly, I think) that the total computational complexity of a set of strictly-local conditions is just the *sum* of the local complexities, whereas in a more difficult case, say, the case of non-strictly-local conditions, the total complexity can be the *product* of the local ones.

15 While it is clear that all "feature-checking" conditions are strictly local, there are some proposed interface conditions that do not seem strictly local. For example, the Uniformity Condition on Chains probably requires non-strictly-local information. If we are to characterize all the interface conditions as strictly local conditions, the Uniformity Condition on Chains will have to be reformulated accordingly, perhaps as a derivational condition on Form-Chain (cf. Fukui 1993a). Also, the status of the binding theory remains unclear in the minimalist program. It is currently assumed to be one of the interface conditions (cf. Chomsky 1993a), but it is certainly not a feature-checking condition, nor does it seem to have anything to do with the determination of legitimate objects. Furthermore, it appears to be a non-strictly-local condition. Thus, if the above-mentioned move is to be taken, the binding theory will also have to be reformulated. Chomsky (1986b) suggests that Condition A of the binding theory should be reduced to ECP (and hence to the condition on economy of derivation, in minimalist terms). It is not clear, however, how we can eliminate the other two clauses from the class of interface conditions, and we will not pursue this issue further here. See Reinhart (1983) for some relevant discussions on the status of Conditions B and C of the binding theory.

16 There has been much important work in the study of human language from the viewpoint of the theory of computational complexity, notably those works done by Robert Berwick and his group. Some of their results are directly relevant to the points we are going to make in the following discussion. See, among others, Barton, Berwick, and Ristad (1987), Berwick (1991), and Ristad (1990, 1993) for detailed discussions of some of the results achieved in their research project.

17 If this conjecture turns out to be correct, it is probably possible to strengthen the proposition to (i), and then to (ii).

(i) Deconomy is NP-hard.
(ii) Deconomy is NP-complete.

Informally, a problem is said to be NP-*hard* if it is at least as hard as any problem in NP; a problem is called NP-*complete* if it is both in NP and NP-hard. See the references in note 8 for more accurate definitions of these notions.

18 A reviewer suggests that some notion of "semantic content" might be a plausible candidate for such "constraints". I simply leave the matter open here, pending further empirical research.

19 Note that the problems that Ristad has shown to belong to the class NP-P, e.g., the problem of anaphora, the problem of ellipsis, etc., are not related to economy of representation as the convergence condition.

20 Chomsky (1994) proposes that "X' theory" be eliminated from the theory of grammar (see also Fukui 1986, Fukui and Saito 1994, Kayne 1994) and suggests that the "extension requirement" on substitution be also eliminable. If this is a right move, then economy of derivation is the only internal condition of language (apart from the recursive concatenation procedure for phrase structure building; see Chomsky 1995b and Fukui and Saito 1994 for discussion on the precise nature of this procedure), an interesting and, I think, also desired result under minimalist assumptions.

21 The terms "external/internal" have been suggested to me by Noam Chomsky (personal communication).

22 See also Berwick (1991) for a similar conclusion.

23 Chomsky (1995b) proposes a further refinement of the notion of Last Resort (and consequently, Greed), by introducing a new interpretation of Move(ment), one of the permissible computations in language, such that Move does not target a category as a whole, as has been assumed so far in the literature, but rather it targets an unchecked feature, with obligatory pied-piping of a category

when it occurs in overt syntax. If we adopt this proposal, our discussion about Greed in the text will have to be modified. The main point of our discussion, however, remains intact.

24 Actually, this proposal is coupled with another modification of the theory of movement, which is also to avoid excessive computational intractability. See Chomsky (1995b) for a fuller discussion.

References

Abe, Jun. 1993. Binding conditions and scrambling without A/A' distinction. Doctoral dissertation, University of Connecticut, Storrs.

Abe, Jun, and Hiroto Hoshi. 1997. Gapping and P-stranding. *Journal of East Asian Linguistics* 6: 101–136.

Abney, Steven. 1985. Functional elements and licensing: Toward an elimination of the base component. Ms., MIT, Cambridge, Mass.

Abney, Steven. 1986. Functional elements and licensing. Paper presented at GLOW conference, Barcelona.

Abney, Steven. 1987. The English noun phrase in its sentential aspect. Doctoral dissertation, MIT, Cambridge, Mass.

Agbayani, Brian. 1998. Feature attraction and category movement. Doctoral dissertation, University of California, Irvine.

Aissen, Judith. 1996. Pied-piping, abstract agreement, and functional projections in Tzotzil. *Natural Language and Linguistic Theory* 14: 447–491.

Anderson, Mona. 1984. Prenominal genitive NPs. *The Linguistic Review* 3: 1–24.

Aoun, Joseph, Norbert Hornstein, and Dominique Sportiche. 1981. Some aspects of wide scope quantification. *Journal of Linguistic Research* 1: 69–95.

Aoun, Joseph, Norbert Hornstein, David Lightfoot, and Amy Weinberg. 1987. Two types of locality. *Linguistic Inquiry* 18: 537–577.

Aoun, Joseph, and David Lightfoot. 1984. Government and contraction. *Linguistic Inquiry* 15: 465–473.

Aoyagi, Hiroshi. 1998a. On the nature of particles in Japanese and its theoretical implications. Doctoral dissertation, University of Southern California.

Aoyagi, Hiroshi. 1998b. Particles as adjunct clitics. In *NELS* 28: 17–31. GLSA, University of Massachusetts, Amherst.

Arfken, George. 1985. *Mathematical methods for physicists*. San Diego: Academic Press.

Authier, J.-Marc. 1992. Iterated CPs and embedded topicalization. *Linguistic Inquiry* 23: 329–336.

Bach, Emmon. 1971. Questions. *Linguistic Inquiry* 2: 153–166.

Baker, C. L. 1970. Notes on the description of English questions: The role of an abstract question morpheme. *Foundations of Language* 6: 197–219.

Baker, C. L. 1977. Comments on the paper by Culicover and Wexler. In *Formal syntax*, ed. Peter W. Culicover, Thomas Wasow, and Adrian Akmajian, 61–70. New York: Academic Press.

Baker, Mark. 1988. *Incorporation: A theory of grammatical function changing*. Chicago: University of Chicago Press.

Baltin, Mark. 1982. A landing site theory of movement rules. *Linguistic Inquiry* 13: 1–38.

Baltin, Mark. 1983. Extraposition: Bounding versus government-binding. *Linguistic Inquiry* 14: 155–162.

Baltin, Mark. 1989. Heads and projections. In *Alternative conceptions of phrase structure*, ed. Mark Baltin and Anthony Kroch, 1–16. Chicago: University of Chicago Press.

Baltin, Mark, and Chris Collins, eds. 2001. *The handbook of contemporary syntactic theory*. Oxford: Blackwell.

Barss, Andrew. 1986. Chains and anaphoric dependencies. Doctoral dissertation, MIT, Cambridge, Mass.

Barton, Edward, Robert Berwick, and Eric Sven Ristad. 1987. *Computational complexity and natural language*. Cambridge, Mass.: MIT Press.

Bedell, George. 1972. On *no*. In *UCLA papers in syntax No. 3: Studies in East Asian syntax*, ed. George Bedell, 101–122. University of California, Los Angeles.

Belletti, Adriana, 2001. Agreement projections. In *The handbook of contemporary syntactic theory*, ed. Mark Baltin and Chris Collins, 483–510. Oxford: Blackwell.

Belletti, Adriana, and Luigi Rizzi. 1981. The syntax of *ne*: some theoretical implications. *The Linguistic Review* 1: 117–154.

Bellman, Richard. 1957. *Dynamic programming*. Princeton: Princeton University Press.

Bergvall, Victoria. 1987. Focus in Kikuyu. Doctoral dissertation, Harvard University, Cambridge, Mass.

Bernstein, Judy. 1991. DPs in French and Walloon: Evidence for parametric variation in nominal head movement. *Probus* 3.2: 101–126.

Bernstein, Judy. 2001. The DP hypothesis: Identifying clausal properties in the nominal domain. In *The handbook of contemporary syntactic theory*, ed. Mark Baltin and Chris Collins, 536–561. Oxford: Blackwell.

Berwick, Robert. 1991. Computational complexity theory and natural language: A paradox resolved. *Theoretical Linguistics* 19: 123–157.

Besten, Hans den, and Gert Webelhuth. 1987. Remnant topicalization and the constituent structure of VP in the Germanic SOV languages. Paper presented at GLOW colloquium, Venice.

Bittner, Maria and Kenneth Hale. 1996. The structural determination of case and agreement. *Linguistic Inquiry* 27: 1–68.

Bobaljik, Jonathan. 1995. Morphosyntax: The syntax of verbal inflection. Doctoral dissertation, MIT, Cambridge, Mass.

Bobaljik, Jonathan and Andrew Carnie. 1994. A minimalist approach to some problems of Irish word order. Ms., MIT, Cambridge, Mass.

Borer, Hagit. 1984. *Parametric syntax: Case studies in Semitic and Romance languages*. Dordrecht: Foris.

Borer, Hagit. 1986. I-subjects. *Linguistic Inquiry* 17: 375–416.

Bošković, Željko. 1993. On certain violations of the superiority condition, Agr_O, and economy of derivation. Ms., University of Connecticut, Storrs.

Bošković, Željko. 1995. Principles of economy in nonfinite complementation. Doctoral dissertation, University of Connecticut, Storrs.

Bowers, John. 1975. Adjectives and adverbs in English. *Foundations of Language* 13: 529–562.

Brame, Michael. 1981. The general theory of binding and fusion. *Linguistic Analysis* 7: 277–325.

Brame, Michael. 1982. The head-selector theory of lexical specifications and the nonexistence of coarse categories. *Linguistic Analysis* 10: 321–325.

Branigan, Phil. 1992. Subjects and complementizers. Doctoral dissertation, MIT, Cambridge, Mass.

Bresnan, Joan. 1970. On complementizers: Toward a syntactic theory of complement types. *Foundations of Language* 6: 297–321.

Bresnan, Joan. 1972. Theory of complementation in English syntax. Doctoral dissertation, MIT Cambridge, Mass.

Bresnan, Joan. 1976. On the form and functioning of transformations. *Linguistic Inquiry* 7: 3–40.

Bresnan, Joan. 1977. Variables in the theory of transformations. In *Formal Syntax*, ed. Peter W. Culicover, Thomas Wasow, and Adrian Akmajian, 157–196. New York: Academic Press.

Bresnan, Joan, ed. 1982. *The mental representation of grammatical relations*. Cambridge, Mass.: MIT Press.

Browning, Marguarite. 1987. Null operator constructions. Doctoral dissertation, MIT, Cambridge, Mass.

Cattell, Ray. 1976. Constraints on movement rules. *Language* 52: 18–50.

Chao, Wynn, and Peter Sells. 1983. On the interpretation of resumptive pronouns. In *NELS* 13: 47–61. GLSA, University of Massachusetts, Amherst.

Cheng, Lisa L.-S. 1991. On the typology of *wh*-questions. Doctoral dissertation, MIT, Cambridge, Mass.

Chierchia, Gennaro. 1998. Reference to kinds across languages. *Natural Language Semantics* 6: 339–405.

Choe, Hyon Sook. 1987a. An SVO analysis of VSO languages and parametrization: A study of Berber. In *Studies in Berber syntax*, ed. Mohamed Guerssel and Kenneth Hale, 121–158. (Lexicon project working papers 14.) Center for Cognitive Science, MIT, Cambridge, Mass.

Choe, Hyon Sook. 1987b. Syntactic adjunction, A-chain and the ECP – multiple identical case construction in Korean. In *NELS* 17: 100–121. GLSA, University of Massachusetts, Amherst.

Chomsky, Noam. 1951. The morphophonemics of modern Hebrew. Master's thesis. University of Pennsylvania, Philadelphia. [Revised version published by Garland, New York, 1979.]

Chomsky, Noam. 1955. The logical structure of linguistic theory. Ms., Harvard University. [Revised 1956 version published in part by Plenum, New York, 1975; University of Chicago Press, 1985.]

Chomsky, Noam. 1957. *Syntactic structures*. The Hague: Mouton.

Chomsky, Noam. 1959. On certain formal properties of grammars. *Information and Control* 2: 137–167. [Reprinted (1965) in *Readings in mathematical psychology, vol. II*, ed. R. D. Luce, R. Bush, and E. Galanter. New York: Wiley.]

Chomsky, Noam. 1964. *Current issues in linguistic theory*. The Hague: Mouton.

Chomsky, Noam. 1965. *Aspects of the theory of syntax*. Cambridge, Mass.: MIT Press.

Chomsky, Noam. 1968. *Language and mind*. New York: Harcourt Brace Jovanovich. [Page references are made to the 1972 Enlarged Edition.]

Chomsky, Noam. 1970. Remarks on nominalization. In *Readings in English transformational grammar*, ed. Roderick A. Jacobs and Peter S. Rosenbaum, 184–221. Waltham, Mass.: Ginn and Co.

Chomsky, Noam. 1973. Conditions on transformations. In *A festschrift for Morris*

Halle, ed. Stephen R. Anderson and Paul Kiparsky, 232–286. New York: Holt, Rinehart and Winston.

Chomsky, Noam. 1976. Conditions on rules of grammar. *Linguistic Analysis* 2: 303–351.

Chomsky, Noam. 1977. On *wh*-movement. In *Formal syntax*, ed. Peter W. Culicover, Thomas Wasow, and Adrian Akmajian, 71–132. New York: Academic Press.

Chomsky, Noam. 1980. On binding. *Linguistic Inquiry* 11: 1–46.

Chomsky, Noam. 1981a. *Lectures on government and binding*. Dordrecht: Foris.

Chomsky, Noam. 1981b. Principles and parameters in syntactic theory. In *Explanation in Linguistics: The logical problem of language acquisition*, ed. Norbert Hornstein and David Lightfoot, 32–75. Harlow: Longman.

Chomsky, Noam. 1982. *Some concepts and consequences of the theory of government and binding*. Cambridge, Mass.: MIT Press.

Chomsky, Noam. 1986a. *Barriers*. Cambridge, Mass.: MIT Press.

Chomsky, Noam. 1986b. *Knowledge of language: Its nature, origin, and use*. New York: Praeger.

Chomsky, Noam. 1987. Transformational grammar: past, present and future. In *Generative grammar: Its basis, development and prospects*, 33–80. Kyoto: Kyoto University of Foreign Studies.

Chomsky, Noam. 1988. *Language and problems of knowledge: The Managua lectures*. Cambridge, Mass.: MIT Press.

Chomsky, Noam. 1991a. Linguistics and cognitive science: Problems and mysteries. In *The Chomskyan turn*, ed. Asa Kasher, 26–53. Oxford: Blackwell.

Chomsky, Noam. 1991b. Some notes on economy of derivation and representation. In *Principles and parameters in comparative grammar*, ed. Robert Freidin, 417–454. Cambridge, Mass.: MIT Press.

Chomsky, Noam. 1992. A minimalist program for linguistic theory. *MIT occasional papers in linguistics* 1. Department of Linguistics and Philosophy, MIT, Cambridge, Mass.

Chomsky, Noam. 1993a. A minimalist program for linguistic theory. In *The view from Building 20: Essays in linguistics in honor of Sylvain Bromberger*, ed. Kenneth Hale and Samuel Jay Keyser, 1–52. Cambridge, Mass.: MIT Press.

Chomsky, Noam. 1993b. Prospects for minimalism. Paper given at the University of California, Irvine.

Chomsky, Noam. 1994. Bare phrase structure. *MIT occasional papers in linguistics* 5. Department of Linguistics and Philosophy, MIT, Cambridge, Mass. [Published in *Government and binding theory and the minimalist program*, ed. Gert Webelhuth, 383–439. Oxford: Blackwell (1995)]

Chomsky, Noam. 1995a. Fall Lectures. Department of Linguistics and Philosophy, MIT; transcribed and edited by Robert Freidin.

Chomsky, Noam. 1995b. *The minimalist program*. Cambridge, Mass.: MIT Press.

Chomsky, Noam. 1996. Some observations on economy in generative grammar. Ms., MIT, Cambridge, Mass.

Chomsky, Noam. 1998. Minimalist inquiries: The framework. *MIT occasional papers in linguistics* 15. Department of Linguistics and Philosophy, MIT, Cambridge, Mass.

Chomsky, Noam. 2000. Minimalist inquiries: The framework. In *Step by step: Essays on minimalist syntax in honor of Howard Lasnik*, ed. Roger Martin, David Michaels, and Juan Uriagereka, 89–155. Cambridge, Mass.: MIT Press.

Chomsky, Noam. 2001a. Derivation by phase. In *Ken Hale: A life in language*, ed. Michael Kenstowicz, 1–52. Cambridge, Mass.: MIT Press.

Chomsky, Noam. 2001b. Beyond explanatory adequacy. *MIT occasional papers in linguistics* 20. Department of Linguistics and Philosophy, MIT, Cambridge, Mass.

Chomsky, Noam, and Morris Halle. 1968. *The sound pattern of English*. New York: Harper & Row.

Chomsky, Noam, and Howard Lasnik. 1977. Filters and control. *Linguistic Inquiry* 8: 425–504.

Chomsky, Noam, and Howard Lasnik. 1993. Principles and parameters theory. In *Syntax: An international handbook of contemporary research*, ed. J. Jacobs, A. von Stechow, W. Sternefeld, and T. Vennemann, 506–569. Berlin: Walter de Gruyter.

Chung, Sandra. 1990. VP's and verb movement in Chamorro. *Natural Language and Linguistic Theory* 8: 559–619.

Chung, Sandra. 1994. *Wh*-agreement and "referentiality" in Chamorro. *Linguistic Inquiry* 25: 1–44.

Cole, Peter. 1987. The structure of internally headed relative clauses. *Natural Language and Linguistic Theory* 5: 277–302.

Collins, Chris. 1994. Economy of derivation and the generalized proper binding condition. *Linguistic Inquiry* 25: 45–62.

Collins, Chris. 2001. Economy conditions in syntax. In *The handbook of contemporary syntactic theory*, ed. Mark Baltin and Chris Collins, 45–61. Oxford: Blackwell.

Cormen, Thomas, Charles Leiserson, and Ronald Rivest. 1990. *Introduction to algorithms*. Cambridge, Mass.: MIT Press.

Courant, Richard, and D. Hilbert. 1924–1989. *Methods of mathematical physics*, 1. New York: John Wiley and Sons.

Culicover, Peter W. 1993. The adverb effect: Evidence against ECP accounts of the *that*-t effect. In *NELS* 23: 97–111, GLSA, University of Massachusetts, Amhurst.

Culicover, Peter, and Kenneth Wexler. 1973. Three further applications of the freezing principle in English. *Social science working papers* 48. University of California, Irvine.

Di Sciullo, Ann Marie. 1980. N and X-bar theory. In *NELS* 10, Cahiers Linguistique d'Ottawa 9. Department of Linguistics, University of Ottawa.

Diesing, Molly. 1990. Verb-second in Yiddish and the nature of the subject position. *Natural Language and Linguistic Theory* 8: 41–79.

Dreyfus, Stuart. 1965. *Dynamic programming and the calculus of variations*. New York: Academic Press.

Edmonds, Jack. 1965. Paths, trees, and flowers. *Canadian Journal of Mathematics* 17: 449–467.

Emonds, Joseph. 1976. *A transformational approach to English syntax: Root, structure-preserving and local transformations*. New York: Academic Press.

Emonds, Joseph. 1978. The verbal complex V'-V in French. *Linguistic Inquiry* 9: 151–175.

Emonds, Joseph. 1979. Word order in generative grammar. In *Explorations in linguistics: Papers in honor of Kazuko Inoue*, ed. George Bedell, Eichi Kobayashi, and Masatake Muraki, 58–88. Tokyo: Kenkyusha.

Emonds, Joseph. 1985. *A unified theory of syntactic categories*. Dordrecht: Foris.

Epstein, Samuel. 1995. The derivation of syntactic relations. Ms., Harvard University.

Fabb, Nigel. 1984. Syntactic affixation. Doctoral dissertation, MIT, Cambridge, Mass.

Fassi Fehri, Abdelkader. 1980. Some complement phenomena in Arabic, lexical grammar, the complementizer phrase hypothesis and the non-accessibility condition. Ms., University of Rabat.

Feynman, Richard, Ralf Leighton, and Matthew Sands, M. 1963. *The Feynman lectures on physics*, vols. 1 and 2. Reading, Mass.: Addison-Wesley.

Fiengo, Robert. 1974. Semantic conditions on surface structure. Doctoral dissertation, MIT, Cambridge, Mass.

Fiengo, Robert. 1977. On trace theory. *Linguistic Inquiry* 8: 35–61.

Fillmore, Charles. 1968. The case for case. In *Universals in linguistic theory*, ed. Emmon Bach and Robert Harms, 1–88. London and New York: Holt, Rinehart, and Winston.

Flynn, Michael. 1983. A categorial theory of structure building. In *Order, concord and constituency*, ed. Gerald Gazder, Ewan Klein, and Geoffrey Pullum, 138–174. Dordrecht: Foris.

Frampton. John. 1990. Parasitic gaps and the theory of *wh*-chains. *Linguistic Inquiry* 21: 49–77.

Frampton, John. 1991. Relativized minimality: A review. *The Linguistic Review* 8: 1–46.

Freidin, Robert, ed. 1991. *Principles and parameters in comparative grammar*. Cambridge, Mass.: MIT Press.

Fukaya, Teruhiko, and Hajime Hoji. 1999. Stripping and sluicing in Japanese and some implications. In *WCCFL* 18: 145–158. Somerville, Mass.: Cascadilla Press.

Fukui, Naoki. 1984. Studies on Japanese anaphora I. Ms., MIT, Cambridge, Mass.

Fukui, Naoki. 1986. A theory of category projection and its applications. Doctoral dissertation, MIT, Cambridge, Mass. [Revised version published as *Theory of projection in syntax*. Stanford, Calif.: CSLI Publications (1995). Distributed by University of Chicago Press.]

Fukui, Naoki. 1988a. Deriving the differences between English and Japanese: A case study in parametric syntax. *English Linguistics* 5: 249–270.

Fukui, Naoki. 1988b. LF extraction of *naze*: Some theoretical implications. *Natural Language and Linguistic Theory* 6: 503–526.

Fukui, Naoki. 1990. Problems of the phrase structure of Japanese: A historical survey. In *Proceedings of the International Symposium on Japanese Teaching*, ed. Masashi Sakamoto and Yasuaki Abe, 261–272. Nanzan University, Nagoya.

Fukui, Naoki. 1991. Strong and weak barriers: Remarks on the proper characterization of barriers. In *Current English linguistics in Japan*, ed. Heizo Nakajima, 249–270. Berlin: Mouton de Gruyter.

Fukui, Naoki. 1993a. A note on improper movement. *The Linguistic Review* 10: 111–126.

Fukui, Naoki. 1993b. Parameters and optionality. *Linguistic Inquiry* 24: 399–420.

Fukui, Naoki. 1995a. *Theory of projection in syntax*. CSLI Publications, Stanford.

Fukui, Naoki. 1995b. The principles-and-parameters approach: A comparative syntax of English and Japanese. In *Approaches to language typology*, ed. Masayoshi Shibatani and Theodora Bynon, 327–372. Oxford: Oxford University Press.

Fukui, Naoki. 1996a. On the nature of economy in language. *Cognitive Studies* 3: 51–71.

Fukui, Naoki. 1996b. On the status of island constraints in the minimalist program. Paper presented at the symposium "Locality and Minimality" held at the 68th General Meeting of the English Literary Society of Japan, Rissho University, Tokyo.

Fukui, Naoki. 1997. Attract and the A-over-A principle. In *UCI working papers in linguistics* 3, ed. Luther C.-S. Liu and Kazue Takeda, 51–67, University of California, Irvine.

Fukui, Naoki. 2000. WH gimonbun no bunseki (An analysis of *wh*-questions). In *Syntax and meaning: S.I. Harada collected works in linguistics*, ed. Naoki Fukui, 817–830. Tokyo: Taishukan.

Fukui, Naoki. 2001. Phrase structure. In *The handbook of contemporary syntactic theory*, ed. Mark Baltin and Chris Collins, 374–406. Oxford: Blackwell.

Fukui, Naoki. In preparation. *Transformational grammar*. Ms., Sophia University, Tokyo.

Fukui, Naoki, and Taisuke Nishigauchi. 1992. Head-movement and case-marking in Japanese. *Journal of Japanese Linguistics* 14: 1–35.

Fukui, Naoki, and Mamoru Saito. 1992. Spec-head agreement, X-bar compatibility, and optionality. Paper presented at MIT Colloquium, MIT, Cambridge, Mass.

Fukui, Naoki, and Mamoru Saito. 1993. Agreement, X'-compatibility, and the theory of movement. Ms., University of California, Irvine, and University of Connecticut, Storrs.

Fukui, Naoki, and Mamoru Saito. 1994. Order in the theory of phrase structure and movement. Ms., University of California, Irvine, and University of Connecticut.

Fukui, Naoki, and Mamoru Saito. 1996. Order in phrase structure and movement. Ms., University of California, Irvine, and Nanzan University.

Fukui, Naoki, and Margaret Speas. 1986. Specifiers and projection. In *MIT working papers in linguistics 8: Papers in theoretical linguistics*, 128–172. Department of Linguistics and Philosophy, MIT, Cambridge, Mass.

Fukui, Naoki, and Yuji Takano. 1998. Symmetry in syntax: Merge and Demerge. *Journal of East Asian Linguistics* 7: 27–86.

Fukui, Naoki, and Yuji Takano. 2000. Nominal structure: An extension of the symmetry principle. In *The derivation of VO and OV*, ed. Peter Svenonius, 219–254. Amsterdam and Philadelphia: John Benjamins.

Fukui, Naoki, Akira Watanabe, and Mihoko Zushi. In preparation. Japanese syntax in a Romance perspective. Ms., Sophia University, University of Tokyo, and Kanagawa University.

Fukushima, Kazuhiko. 2003. Verb-raising and numeral classifiers in Japanese: Incompatible bedfellows. *Journal of East Asian Linguistics* 12: 313–347.

Gazdar, Gerald, Ewan Klein, Geoffrey Pullum, and Ivan Sag. 1985. *Generalized phrase structure grammar*. Cambridge, Mass.: Harvard University Press.

Garey, Michael, and David Johnson. 1979. *Computers and intractability: A guide to the theory of NP-completeness*. San Francisco: Freeman.

George, Leland. 1980. Analogical generalization in natural language syntax. Doctoral dissertation, MIT, Cambridge, Mass.

Goldstein, Herbert. 1980. *Classical mechanics*, 2nd edition. Menlo Park: Addison-Wesley.

Greenberg, Joseph. 1963. Some universals of grammar with particular reference to the order of meaningful elements. In *Universals of language*, ed. Joseph Greenberg, 73–113. Cambridge, Mass.: MIT Press.

Greenberg, Joseph, ed. 1966. *Universals of language*, 2nd edition. Cambridge, Mass.: MIT Press.

Grimshaw, Jane, and Armin Mester. 1988. Light verbs and θ-marking. *Linguistic Inquiry* 19: 205–232.

Guéron, Jacqueline, and Robert May. 1984. Extraposition and Logical Form. *Linguistic Inquiry* 15: 1–31.

Guilfoyle, Eithne, and Maire Noonan. 1988. Functional categories and language acquisition. Ms., McGill University, Montreal.

Gunji, Takao. 1994. Riron-gengogaku no mukatteiru hookoo (Trends of theoretical linguistics). *Ninti Kagaku* (Cognitive studies: Bulletin of the Japanese cognitive science society) 1. 1: 31–42.

Haegeman, Liliane. 1991. *Introduction to government and binding theory*. Oxford: Basil Blackwell.

Haider, Hubert. 1992. Branching and discharge. In Working Papers of the Sonderforschungsbereich 340 23: 1–31. Universities of Stuttgart and Tübingen.

Haider, Hubert. 2000. OV is more basic than VO. In *The derivation of VO and OV*, ed. Peter Svenonius, 45–67. Amsterdam and Philadelphia: John Benjamins.

Haïk, Isabelle. 1985. The syntax of operators. Doctoral dissertation, MIT, Cambridge, Mass.

Hale, Kenneth. 1978. The structure of English sentences. Ms., MIT, Cambridge, Mass.

Hale, Kenneth. 1980a. Remarks on Japanese phrase structure: Comments on the papers on Japanese syntax. In *MIT working papers in linguistics* 21: ed. Ann Farmer and Yukio Otsu. 185–203. MIT, Cambridge, Mass.

Hale, Kenneth. 1980b The position of Warlbiri in a typology of the base. Indiana University Linguistic Club.

Hale, Kenneth. 1982. Preliminary remarks on configurationality. In *NELS* 12: 86–96. GLSA, University of Massachusetts, Amherst.

Hale, Kenneth. 1983. Warlpiri and the grammar of non-configurational languages. *Natural Language and Linguistic Theory* 1: 5–47.

Hale, Kenneth. 1990. Scrambling and adjunction: Toward a comparative grammar of two free word order languages. Ms., MIT, Cambridge, Mass

Hale, Kenneth and Samuel J. Keyser. 1993. On argument structure and the lexical expression of syntactic relations. In *The view from Building 20: Essays in linguistics in honor of Sylvain Bromberger*, ed. Kenneth Hale and Samuel J. Keyser, 53–109. Cambridge, Mass.: MIT Press.

Halle, Morris and Alec Marantz. 1993. Distributed morphology and the pieces of inflection. In *The view from Building 20: Essays in linguistics in honor of Sylvain Bromberger*, ed. Kenneth Hale and Samuel J. Keyser, 111–176. Cambridge, Mass.: MIT Press.

Harada, Kazuko I. 1972. Constraints on *wh*-Q binding. *Studies in descriptive and applied linguistics* 5: 180–206. Division of Languages, International Christian University, Tokyo.

Harada, Kazuko I. 2002. On the acquisition of Japanese relatives. *Kinjo Gakuin Daigaku Ronsyuu* (Kinjo Gakuin University research papers) vol. 43: 279–301. Kinjo Gakuin University, Nagoya.

Harada, Naomi. 1998. Interactions of functional and lexical categories: A theory of the lexicon in UG. Ms., University of California, Irvine.

Harada, S. I. 1971. Ga-No conversion and idiolectal variations in Japanese. *Gengo Kenkyu*, 60: 25–38. [Reprinted in *Syntax and meaning: S. I. Harada collected works in linguistics*, ed. Naoki Fukui, 75–87. Tokyo: Taishukan.]

Harada, S. I. 1973a. Constraints on binding. *Studies in English literature*, English No. 1973, 41–72. [Reprinted in *Syntax and meaning: S. I. Harada collected works in linguistics*, ed. Naoki Fukui, 130–157. Tokyo, Taishukan.]

Harada, S. I. 1973b. Counter equi NP deletion. *Annual Bulletin* 7: 113–147. Research Institute of Logopedics and Phoniatrics, University of Tokyo, Tokyo. [Reprinted in *Syntax and meaning: S. I. Harada collected works in linguistics*, ed. Naoki Fukui, 181–215. Tokyo: Taishukan.]

Harada, S. I. 1976. Ga-No conversion revisited: A reply to Shibatani. *Gengo Kenkyu* 70: 23–38. [Reprinted in *Syntax and meaning: S. I. Harada collected works in linguistics*, ed. Naoki Fukui, 346–358. Tokyo, Taishukan.]

Harada, S. I. 1977. Nihongo-ni henkei-wa hituyoo-da (There are transformations in Japanese). *Gengo* 6.10: 88–95, 6.11: 96–103. [Reprinted in *Syntax and meaning: S. I. Harada collected works in linguistics*, ed. Naoki Fukui, 545–566. Tokyo, Taishukan.]

Harris, Zelig. 1946. From morpheme to utterance. *Language* 22: 161–183.

Harris, Zelig. 1951. *Methods in structural linguistics*. Chicago: University of Chicago Press.

Hasegawa, Kinsuke. 1974. Generalized A-over-A principle. *Eigo Seinen* 119.11: 736–737; 119.12: 808–810.

Hattori, Shiro. 1971. Gengo to gengogaku to fuhensei (Language, linguistics, and universals). *Gengo* 1: 2–3.

Hayashishita, J.-R. 2000. Scope ambiguity and "scrambling". In *WCCFL* 19: 204–217. Somerville, Mass.: Cascadilla Press.

Heim, Irene. 1982. The semantics of definite and indefinite noun phrases. Doctoral dissertation, University of Massachusetts, Amherst.

Heycock, Caroline, and Beatrice Santorini. 1992. Head movement and the licensing of nonthematic positions. In *WCCFL* 11: 262–276. Stanford: Stanford Linguistics Association.

Higginbotham, James. 1985. On semantics. *Linguistic Inquiry* 16: 547–594.

Hinds, John. 1973. On the status of VP node in Japanese. *Language Research* 9: 44–57.

Hiraiwa, Ken. 2001a. Multiple Agree and the defective intervention constraint in Japanese. In *MIT working papers in linguistics* 40: *Proceedings of HUMIT 2000*, ed. Ova Matushansky, Albert Costa, Javier Martin-Gonzalez, Lance Nathan, and Adam S. Szczegialniak, 67–80. Department of Linguistics and Philosophy, MIT, Cambridge, Mass.

Hiraiwa, Ken. 2001b. Move or Agree?: Case and raising in Japanese. Ms., MIT, Cambridge, Mass.

Hoji, Hajime. 1985. Logical form constraints and configurational structures in Japanese. Doctoral dissertation, University of Washington, Seattle.

Hoji, Hajime. 1987. Japanese clefts and chain binding/reconstruction effects. Paper presented at WCCFL 6.

Hoji, Hajime. 1995. Null object and sloppy identity in Japanese. Ms., University of Southern California, Los Angeles.

Hoji, Hajime. 1997. Sloppy identity and principle B. In *Atomism and binding*, ed. Hans Bennis, Pierre Pica, and Johan Rooryck, 205–235. Dordrecht: Foris.

Hoji, Hajime. 1998a. Formal dependency, organization of grammar and Japanese demonstratives. In *Japanese/Korean Linguistics* 7: 649–677. CSLI Publications, Stanford.

Hoji, Hajime. 1998b. A review of *Japanese syntax and semantics* by S.-Y. Kuroda. *Language* 74: 146–152.

Hoji, Hajime. 1998c. Null object and sloppy identity in Japanese. *Linguistic Inquiry* 29: 127–152.

Hoji, Hajime. 2002. Falsifiability and repeatability in generative grammar: A case study of anaphora and scope dependency in Japanese. Ms., University of Southern California, Los Angeles. [Published in *Lingua (special issue): Formal Japanese syntax and universal grammar: The past 20 years*, ed. Naoki Fukui, 377–446 (2003).]

Hopcroft, John, and Jeffrey Ullman. 1979. *Introduction to automata theory, languages, and computation*. Menlo Park: Addison-Wesley.

Hornstein, Norbert. 1977. S and X' convention. *Linguistic Analysis* 3: 137–176.

Hornstein, Norbert, and Amy Weinberg. 1981. Case theory and preposition stranding. *Linguistic Inquiry* 12: 55–91.

Hornstein, Norbert, and David Lightfoot. 1984. Rethinking predication. Ms., University of Maryland, College Park.

Hoshi, Hidehito, 2000. Displacement and local economy. Doctoral dissertation, University of California, Irvine.

Hoshi, Hiroto, 1999. Complex predicate formation in Japanese: A (non-)configurational theory. In *SOAS working papers in linguistics and phonetics*, 427–473. SOAS, University of London, London.

Hoshi, Hiroto, 2001. Relations between thematic structure and syntax: A study on the nature of predicates in Japanese. In *SOAS working papers in linguistics and phonetics*, 203–247. SOAS, University of London, London.

Hoshi, Hiroto, and Mamoru Saito. 1993. The Japanese light verb construction: A case of LF theta marking. Ms., University of Connecticut, Storrs.

Hoshi, Koji. 1997. Deriving the differences of nominal modification: A comparative syntax of English and Japanese. *Language, culture and communication* 19: 92–114. Keio University, Tokyo.

Huang, C.-T. James. 1982. Logical relations in Chinese and the theory of grammar. Doctoral dissertation, MIT, Cambridge, Mass.

Huang, C.-T. James. 1984. On the distribution and reference of empty pronouns. *Linguistic Inquiry* 15: 531–574.

Huang, C.-T. James. 1992. Chinese word order revisited. Ms., University of California, Irvine.

Huang, C.-T. James. 1997. On lexical structure and syntactic projection. *Chinese Languages and Linguistics* 3: 45–89.

Iatridou, Sabine. 1990. About AgrP. *Linguistic Inquiry* 21: 551–576.

Ibaraki, Toshihide, and Masao Fukushima. 1993. *Saitekika no syuhoo* (Methods of optimization). Tokyo: Kyoritsu Shuppan.

Inoue, Kazuko. 1978. *Nihongo no bunpoo kisoku* (Grammatical rules in Japanese). Tokyo: Taishukan.

Ishii, Toru. 1997. An asymmetry in the composition of phrase structure and its consequences. Doctoral dissertation, University of California, Irvine.

Ishii, Yasuo. 1991. Operators and empty categories in Japanese. Doctoral dissertation, University of Connecticut, Storrs.

Jackendoff, Ray. 1977. *X' Syntax: A study of phrase structure*. Cambridge, Mass.: MIT Press.

Jaeggli, Osvaldo. 1980. Remarks on *to*-contraction. *Linguistic Inquiry* 11: 239–245.

Jaeggli, Osvaldo. 1982. *Topics in Romance syntax*. Dordrecht: Foris.

Jaeggli, Osvaldo, and Kenneth Safir, ed. 1989. *The null subject parameter*. Dordrecht: Kluwer Academic Publishers.

Jantsch, Erich, and Conrad Waddington. 1975. *Evolution and consciousness*. Reading, Mass: Addison-Wesley.

Johnson, David. 1990. A catalog of complexity classes. In *Handbook of theoretical computer science, vol. A*, ed. Jan van Leeuwen, 69–161. Cambridge, Mass.: MIT Press/Elsevier.

Johnson, Kyle. 1985. A case for movement. Doctoral dissertation, MIT, Cambridge, Mass.

Johnson, Kyle. 1992. Extraposition from NP is extraposition of NP. Talk given at the University of California, Irvine.

Johnson, Kyle. 1994. Head movement, word order, and inflection. In *Head movement: The interface between morphology and syntax*, ed. S.-H Park, and J.-Y. Yoon, 1–81. Seoul: Hankuk Publishing Company.

Johnson, Kyle. 1997. A review of *The antisymmetry of syntax*. *Lingua* 102: 21–53.

Josephs, Lewis S. 1976. Complementation. In *Syntax and Semantics 5: Japanese generative grammar*, ed. Masayoshi Shibatani, 307–369. New York: Academic Press.

Kasai, Hironobu. 2002. Eliminating "scrambling". Ms., University of California, Irvine.

Kasai, Hironobu, and Shoichi Takahashi. 2001. Where is subjacency? In *Papers from the 18th national conference of the English linguistic society of Japan*, 51–60.

Kawashima, Ruriko. 1994. The structure of noun phrases and the interpretation of quantificational NPs in Japanese. Doctoral dissertation, Cornell University, Ithaca.

Kayne, Richard. 1981. ECP extensions. *Linguistic Inquiry* 12: 93–133.

Kayne, Richard. 1983a. Chains, categories external to S and French complex inversion. *Natural Language and Linguistic Theory* 1: 107–139.

Kayne, Richard. 1983b. Connectedness. *Linguistic Inquiry* 14: 223–249.

Kayne, Richard 1984. *Connectedness and binary branching*. Dordrecht: Foris.

Kayne, Richard. 1986. Participles, agreement, auxiliaries, *se/si* and PRO. Ms., MIT, Cambridge, Mass.

Kayne, Richard. 1989. Facets of Romance past participle agreement. In *Dialect variation and the theory of grammar*, ed. Paola Benincà, 85–103. Dordrecht: Foris.

Kayne, Richard. 1994. *The antisymmetry of syntax*. Cambridge, Mass.: MIT Press.

Kikuchi, Akira. 1989. Comparative deletion in Japanese. Ms., Yamagata University, Yamagata.

Kikuchi, Akira, Masayuki Oishi, and Noriaki Yusa. 1994. Scrambling and relativized L-relatedness. In *MIT working papers in linguistics 24: Formal approaches to Japanese linguistics 1*, ed. Masatoshi Koizumi and Hiroyuki Ura, 141–158. Department of Linguistics and Philosophy, MIT, Cambridge, Mass.

Kim, Jeong-Seok. 1997. Syntactic focus movement and ellipsis: A minimalist approach. Doctoral dissertation, University of Connecticut, Storrs.

Kim, Jeong-Seok, and Keun-Won Sohn. 1998. Focusing effects in Korean/Japanese ellipsis. *Japanese/Korean Linguistics* 8: 459–470. CSLI Publications, Stanford.

Kim, Soowon. 1996. Issues on verb raising. Paper presented at UCI Colloquium. University of California, Irvine.

Kimura, Norimi, 1994. Multiple specifiers and long distance anaphora. In *MIT working papers in linguistics 24: Formal approaches to Japanese linguistics 1*, ed. Masatoshi Koizumi and Hiroyuki Ura, 159–178. Department of Linguistics and Philosophy, MIT, Cambridge, Mass.

Kishimoto, Hideki. 2001. Binding of indeterminate pronouns and clause structure in Japanese. *Linguistic Inquiry* 32: 597–633.

Kitagawa, Chisato, and Claudia N. G. Ross. 1982. Prenominal modification in Chinese and Japanese. *Linguistic Analysis* 9: 19–53.

Kitagawa, Yoshihisa. 1986. Subjects in Japanese and English. Doctoral dissertation, University of Massachusetts, Amherst. [Published in 1994, New York: Garland.]

Kitahara, Hisatsugu. 1994. Target α: A unified theory of movement and structure-building. Doctoral dissertation, Harvard University, Cambridge, Mass.

Kline, Morris. 1959. *Mathematics and the physical world.* New York: Dover.

Kline, Morris. 1972. *Mathematical thought from ancient to modern times 2*. New York: Oxford University Press.

Koizumi, Masatoshi. 1994. Nominative objects: The role of TP in Japanese. In *MIT working papers in linguistics 24: Formal approaches to Japanese linguistics 1*, ed. Masatoshi Koizumi and Hiroyuki Ura, 211–230. Department of Linguistics and Philosophy, MIT, Cambridge, Mass.

Koizumi, Masatoshi. 1995. Phrase structure in minimalist syntax. Doctoral dissertation, MIT, Cambridge, Mass.

Koizumi, Masatoshi. 2000. String vacuous overt verb raising. *Journal of East Asian Linguistics* 9: 227–285.

Koopman, Hilda. 1984. *The syntax of verbs*. Dordrecht: Foris.

Koopman, Hilda, and Dominique Sportiche. 1985. θ-theory and extraction. Paper presented at GLOW meeting, Brussels.

Koopman, Hilda, and Dominique Sportiche. 1986a. A note on long extraction in Vata and the ECP. *Natural Language and Linguistic Theory* 4: 357–373.

Koopman, Hilda, and Dominique Sportiche. 1986b. ECP and subjects. Talk presented at MIT, Cambridge, Mass.

Koopman, Hilda, and Dominique Sportiche. 1988. Subjects. Ms., University of California, Los Angeles.

Koopman, Hilda, and Dominique Sportiche. 1991. The position of subjects. *Lingua* 85: 211–258.

Kornfilt, Jaklin. 1989. Functional categories and syntactic change. In *MIT working papers in linguistics 10: Functional heads and clause structure*, ed. Itziar Laka and Anoop Mahajan, 147–193. Department of Linguistics and Philosophy, MIT, Cambridge, Mass.

Kornfilt, Jaklin. 1991. A case for emerging functional categories. In *Syntax and semantics* 25, ed. Susan Rothstein, 11–35. New York: Academic Press.

Koster, Jan. 1974. PP over V en de theorie van J. Emonds. *Spectator* 2: 294–309.

Koster, Jan. 1978. Why subject sentences don't exist. In *Recent transformational studies in European languages*, ed. Samuel J. Keyser, 53–64. Cambridge, Mass.: MIT Press.

Kuno, Susumu. 1972. Pronominalization, reflexivization, and direct discourse. *Linguistic Inquiry* 3: 161–196.

Kuno, Susumu. 1973. *The structure of the Japanese language*. Cambridge, Mass.: MIT Press.

Kuno, Susumu. 1976a. Gapping: A functional analysis. *Linguistic Inquiry* 7: 300–318.

Kuno, Susumu. 1976b. Subject raising. In *Syntax and semantics 5: Japanese generative grammar*, ed. Masayoshi Shibatani, 17–49. New York: Academic Press.

Kuno, Susumu. 1978a. *Danwa no bunpoo* (A Grammar of Discourse). Tokyo: Taishukan.

Kuno, Susumu. 1978b. Japanese: A characteristic OV language. In *Syntactic typology*, ed. Winfred P. Lehmann, 57–138. Austin: University of Texas Press.

Kuno, Susumu. 1980. A further note on Tonoike's intra-subjectivization hypothesis. In *MIT working papers in linguistics* 2, ed. Ann Farmer and Yukio Otsu, 171–184. Department of Linguistics and Philosophy, MIT, Cambridge, Mass.

Kuno, Susumu. 1983. *Sin nihon bunpoo kenkyuu* (New studies on Japanese grammar). Tokyo: Taishukan.

Kuroda, S.-Y. 1965. Generative grammatical studies in the Japanese language. Doctoral dissertation, MIT, Cambridge, Mass.

Kuroda, S.-Y. 1970. Remarks on the notion of subject with reference to words like *also*, *even*, and *only*. *Annual bulletin, Research Institute of Logopedics and Phoniatrics* 3: 111–129; 4: 127–152. [Reprinted in Kuroda, 1992, 78–113.]

Kuroda, S.-Y. 1978. Case-marking, canonical sentence patterns, and counter equi in Japanese. In *Problems in Japanese syntax and semantics*, ed. John Hinds and Irwin Howard, 30–51. Tokyo: Kaitakusha. [Reprinted in Kuroda, 1992, 78–113.]

Kuroda, S.-Y. 1983. What can Japanese say about government and binding? In *WCCFL* 2: 153–164. Stanford Linguistics Association, Stanford. [Reprinted in Kuroda, 1992, 40–52.]

Kuroda, S.-Y. 1986. Movement of noun phrases in Japanese. In *Issues in Japanese linguistics*, ed. Takashi Imai and Mamoru Saito, 229–271. Dordrecht: Foris. [Reprinted in Kuroda 1992, 253–292.]

Kuroda, S.-Y. 1988. Whether we agree or not: A comparative syntax of English and Japanese. In *Papers from the second international workshop on Japanese syntax*, ed. William J. Poser, 103–143. CSLI, Stanford University, Stanford, California. [Reprinted in Kuroda, 1992, 315–357.]

Kuroda, S.-Y. 1992. *Japanese syntax and semantics: Collected papers*. Dordrecht: Kluwer.

Kuroda, S.-Y. 1998. Syubu naizai kankei setu (Head-internal relative clauses). In *Gengo-no naizai to gaizai* (Intentions and extensions of language), ed. Hideyuki Hirano and Masaru Nakamura, 1–79. Faculty of Literature, Tohoku University, Sendai.

Kuroda, S.-Y. 2002. Complex predicates and predicate raising. Ms., University of California, San Diego. [Published in *Lingua* (special issue), *Formal Japanese syntax and universal grammar: The past 20 years*, ed. Naoki Fukui, 447–480 (2003)]

Kuwabara, Kazuki. 1996. Multiple *wh*-phrases in elliptical clauses and some aspects of clefts with multiple foci. In *MIT working papers in linguistics 29: Formal approaches to Japanese linguistics 2*, ed. Masatoshi Koizumi, Masayuki Oishi, and Uli Sauerland, 97–116. Department of Linguistics and Philosophy, MIT, Cambridge, Mass.

Lambek, J. 1958. The mathematics of sentence structure. *American Mathematical Monthly* 65: 154–170. [Reprinted in *Categorial grammar*, ed. Wojciech Buszkowski, Witold Marciszewski and Johan van Benthem. Amsterdam: John Benjamins.]

Lamontagne, Greg, and Lisa Travis. 1987. The syntax of adjacency. *WCCFL* 6: 178–186. CSLI Publications, Stanford.

Lanczos, Cornelius. 1970–1986. *The variational principles in mechanics*, 4th edition. New York: Dover.

Larson, Richard. 1985. Bare NP adverbs. *Linguistic Inquiry* 16: 595–621.

Larson, Richard. 1988. On the double object construction. *Linguistic Inquiry* 19: 335–391.

Lasnik, Howard. 1989. *Essays on Anaphora*. Dordrecht: Kluwer.
Lasnik, Howard, 1995. Verbal morphology: *Syntactic structures* meets the minimalist program. In *Evolution and revolution in linguistic theory: Essays in honor of Carlos Otero*, ed. Héctor Campos and Paula Kempchinsky, 251–275. Washington DC: Georgetown University Press.
Lasnik, Howard, and Mamoru Saito. 1984. On the nature of proper government. *Linguistic Inquiry* 15: 235–289.
Lasnik, Howard, and Mamoru Saito. 1992. *Move α: Conditions on its application and output*. Cambridge, Mass.: MIT Press.
Law, Paul. 1991. Verb movement, expletive replacement, and head government. *The Linguistic Review* 8: 253–289.
Lee, Rhanghyeyun K. 1994. Economy of representation. Doctoral dissertation, University of Connecticut, Storrs.
Lee, Young-Suk. 1991. Scrambling and the adjoined argument hypothesis. Ms., University of Pennsylvania, Philadelphia.
Lees, Robert. 1960. *The grammar of English nominalization*. The Hague: Mouton & Co.
Lehmann, Thomas. 1993. *A grammar of modern Tamil*. Pondicherry, India: Pondicherry Institute of Linguistics and Culture.
Levin, Beth. 1983. On the nature of ergativity. Doctoral dissertation, MIT, Cambridge, Mass.
Levin, Juliette. 1984. Government relations and the distribution of empty operators. In *NELS* 14: 294–305. GLSA, University of Massachusetts, Amherst, Mass.
Lobeck, Anne. 1990. Functional heads as proper governors. In *NELS* 20: 348–362. GLSA, University of Massachusetts, Amherst, Mass.
Longobardi, Giuseppe. 2001. The structure of DPs: Some principles, parameters, and problems. In *The handbook of contemporary syntactic theory*, ed. Mark Baltin and Chris Collins, 562–603. Oxford: Blackwell.
Lumsden, John. 1984. A baroque theory of subjects. Ms., MIT, Cambridge, Mass.
Lyons, John. 1968. *Introduction to theoretical linguistics*. Cambridge: Cambridge University Press.
McCawley, James. 1968. Concerning the base component of a transformational grammar. *Foundations of language* 4: 243–269.
McCawley, James. 1970. English as a VSO language. *Language* 46: 286–299.
McCloskey, James. 1983. A VP in VSO language? In *Order, concord, and constituency*, ed. Gerald Gazdar, Ewan Klein, and Geoffrey Pullum, 9–55. Dordrecht: Foris.
McCloskey, James. 1990. Resumptive pronouns, A-bar binding, and levels of representation in Irish. In *The syntax of the modern Celtic languages*, ed. Randall Hendrick, 199–243. San Diego: Academic Press.
Mahajan, Anoop K. 1990. The A/A-bar distinction and movement theory. Doctoral dissertation, MIT, Cambridge, Mass.
Manzini, Maria Rita, and Kenneth Wexler. 1987. Parameters, binding theory, and learnability. *Linguistic Inquiry*, 18: 413–444.
Marantz, Alec. 1984. *On the nature of grammatical relations*. Cambridge, Mass.: MIT Press.
Marantz, Alec. 1988. Clitics, morphological merger, and the mapping to phonological structure. In *Theoretical morphology: Approaches in modern linguistics*, ed. Michael Hammond, and Michael Noonan, 253–270. San Diego: Academic Press.
Marantz, Alec. 1989. Clitics and phrase structure. In *Alternative conceptions of phrase*

structure, ed. Mark Baltin and Anthony Kroch, 99–116. Chicago: University of Chicago Press.

Martin, Samuel. 1975. *Reference grammar of Japanese*. New Haven, Conn.: Yale University Press.

May, Robert. 1977. The grammar of quantification. Doctoral dissertation, MIT, Cambridge, Mass.

May, Robert. 1979. Must COMP-to-COMP movement be stipulated? *Linguistic Inquiry* 10: 719–725.

May, Robert. 1985. *Logical form*, Cambridge, Mass.: MIT Press.

Miyagawa, Shigeru. 1989. *Syntax and semantics 22: Structure and case-marking in Japanese*. New York: Academic Press.

Miyagawa, Shigeru. 1991. Case realization and scrambling. Ms., MIT, Cambridge, Mass.

Miyagawa, Shigeru. 1993. LF case-checking and minimal link condition. In *MIT working papers in linguistics 19: Papers on case and agreement II*, ed. Colin Phillips, 213–254. Department of Linguistics and Philosophy, MIT, Cambridge, Mass.

Miyagawa, Shigeru. 1994. Nonconfigurationality within a configurational structure. Ms., MIT, Cambridge, Mass.

Miyagawa, Shigeru. 1997. Against optional scrambling. *Linguistic Inquiry* 28: 1–25.

Miyagawa, Shigeru. 2001. The EPP, scrambling, and *wh*-in-situ. In *Ken Hale: A life in language*, ed. Michael Kenstowicz, 293–338. Cambridge, Mass.: MIT Press.

Murasugi, Keiko. 1991. Noun phrases in Japanese and English: A study in syntax, learnability and acquisition. Doctoral dissertation, University of Connecticut, Storrs.

Murasugi, Keiko. 1993. The generalized transformation analysis of relative clauses and island effects in Japanese. *Journal of Japanese Linguistics* 15: 113–123.

Murasugi, Keiko, and Mamoru Saito. 1995. Adjunction and cyclicity. In *WCCFL* 13: 302–317. Stanford, Calif.: CSLI Publications.

Murasugi, Kumiko. 1992. Crossing and nested paths: NP movement in accusative and ergative languages. Doctoral dissertation, MIT, Cambridge, Mass.

Muysken, Pieter. 1982. Parametrizing the notion "Head". *Journal of Linguistic Research* 2.3: 57–76.

Nakau, Minoru. 1973. *Sentential complementation in Japanese*. Tokyo: Kaitakusha.

Nash, David. 1980. Topics in Warlpiri grammar. Doctoral dissertation, MIT, Cambridge, Mass.

Nemoto, Naoko. 1993. Chains and case positions: A study from scrambling in Japanese. Doctoral dissertation, University of Connecticut, Storrs.

Nishigauchi, Taisuke. 1986. Quantification in syntax. Doctoral dissertation, University of Massachusetts, Amherst.

Nishigauchi, Taisuke. 1990. *Quantification in the theory of grammar*. Dordrecht: Kluwer.

Nishiyama, Kunio. 1998. The morphosyntax and morphophonology of Japanese predicates. Doctoral dissertation, Cornell University, Ithaca.

Nishiyama, Kunio, John Whitman, and Eun-Young Yi. 1996. Syntactic movement of overt *wh*-phrases in Japanese and Korean. *Japanese/Korean Linguistics* 5: 337–351. CSLI Publications, Stanford.

Ochi, Masao. 2001. Move F and *ga/no* conversion in Japanese. *Journal of East Asian Linguistics* 10: 247–286.

Oehrle, Richard. 1981. Appendix A: AUX in English. In *The encyclopedia of AUX: A study of cross-linguistic equivalence*, ed. Susan Steele, 226–259. Cambridge, Mass.: MIT Press.

Oka, Toshifusa. 1988. Abstract Case and empty pronouns. In *Tsukuba English Studies* 7: 187–227, ed. Toshifusa Oka. Institute of Literature and Linguistics, University of Tsukuba, Tsukuba.

Oka, Toshifusa. 1993. Minimalism in syntactic derivation. Doctoral dissertation, MIT, Cambridge, Mass.

Oka, Toshifusa. 1996. Shift and Headedness. Paper presented at the Workshop on Economy, Kwansei Gakuin University, Nishinomiya.

Ono, Hajime. 2002. An emphatic particle *da* and exclamatory sentences in Japanese. Ms., University of California, Irvine.

Ormazabal, Javier, Juan Uriagereka, and Maria Uribe-Etxebarria. 1994. Word order and *wh*-movement: Towards a parametric account. Ms., University of Connecticut/UPV-EMU, University of Maryland, and University of Connecticut/MIT.

Ormazabal, Javier. 1991. Asymmetries in *wh*-movement and specific DPs. Ms., University of Connecticut, Storrs.

Ortiz de Urbina, Jon. 1990. Operator feature percolation and clausal pied-piping. In *MIT working papers in linguistics* 13: 193–208. Department of Linguistics and Philosophy, MIT, Cambridge, Mass.

Ostler, Nick. 1979. Case-linking: A theory of case and verbal diathesis applied to classical Sanskrit. Doctoral dissertation, MIT, Cambridge, Mass.

Otani, Kazuyo, and John Whitman. 1991. V-Raising and VP-ellipsis. *Linguistic Inquiry* 22: 345–358.

Papadimitriou, Christos, and Kenneth Steiglitz. 1982. *Combinatorial optimization: Algorithms and complexity*. Englewood Cliffs: Prentice-Hall.

Perlmutter, David M. 1972. Evidence for shadow pronouns in French relativization. In *The Chicago which hunt*, ed. Paul M. Peranteau et al., 73–105. Chicago: Chicago Linguistic Society.

Pesetsky, David. 1982a. Complementizer-trace phenomena and the nominative island condition. *The Linguistic Review* 1: 297–343.

Pesetsky, David. 1982b. Paths and categories. Doctoral dissertation, MIT, Cambridge, Mass.

Pesetsky, David. 1987. *Wh*-in-situ: Movement and unselective binding. In *The representation of (in)definiteness*, ed. Eric Reuland and Alice ter Meulen, 98–129. Cambridge, Mass.: MIT Press.

Picallo, M. Carme. 1991. Nominals and nominalizations in Catalan. *Probus* 3.3: 279–316.

Poeppel, David, and Kenneth Wexler. 1993. The full competence hypothesis of clause structure in early German. *Language* 69: 1–33.

Pollard, Carl, and Ivan Sag. 1994. *Head-driven phrase structure grammar*. Stanford and Chicago: CSLI and the University of Chicago Press.

Pollock, Jean-Yves. 1989. Verb movement, universal grammar, and the structure of IP. *Linguistic Inquiry* 20: 365–424.

Poser, William. 1981. The double-*o* constraint: Evidence for a direct object relation in Japanese? Ms., MIT, Cambridge, Mass.

Postal, Paul M. 1974. *On raising: One rule of English grammar and its theoretical implications*. Cambridge, Mass.: MIT Press.

Prince, Alan, and Paul Smolensky. 1993. Optimality theory: Constraint interaction in generative grammar. *Rutgers center for cognitive science technical report* 2. Rutgers University, New Brunswick.

Pullum, Geoffrey. 1985. Assuming some version of X' theory. *CLS* 21: 323–353.

Radford, Andrew. 1990. *Syntactic theory and the acquisition of English syntax*. Oxford: Basil Blackwell.

Reinhart, Tanya. 1983. *Anaphora and semantic interpretation*. London: Croom Helm.

Reuland, Eric. 1983. Governing -*ing*. *Linguistic Inquiry* 14: 101–136.

Riemsdijk, Henk van. 1989. Movement and regeneration. In *Dialect variation and the theory of grammar*, ed. P. Benincà, 105–136. Dordrecht: Foris.

Riemsdijk, Henk van, and Edwin Williams. 1981. NP-structure. *The Linguistic Review* 1: 171–217.

Riemsdijk, Henk van, and Edwin Williams. 1986. *Introduction to the theory of grammar*. Cambridge, Mass.: MIT Press.

Ristad, Eric Sven. 1990. Computational structure of human language. Doctoral dissertation. MIT, Cambridge, Mass.

Ristad, Eric Sven. 1993. *The language complexity game*. Cambridge, Mass.: MIT Press.

Rizzi, Luizi. 1982. *Issues in Italian syntax*. Dordrecht: Foris.

Rizzi, Luizi. 1986a. Null objects in Italian and the theory of *pro*. *Linguistic Inquiry* 17: 501–557.

Rizzi, Luizi. 1986b. On chain formation. In *Syntax and semantics 19: The grammar of pronominal clitics*, ed. Hagit Borer, 65–95. New York: Academic Press.

Rizzi, Luigi. 1990. *Relativized minimality*. Cambridge, Mass.: MIT Press.

Rizzi, Luigi. 2001. Relativized minimality effects. In *The handbook of contemporary syntactic theory*, ed. Mark Baltin and Chris Collins, 89–110. Oxford: Blackwell.

Roberts, Ian. 2001. Head movement. In *The handbook of contemporary syntactic theory*, ed. Mark Baltin and Chris Collins, 113–147. Oxford: Blackwell.

Rochemont, Michael. 1978. A theory of stylistic rules in English. Doctoral dissertation, University of Massachusetts, Amherst.

Roeper, Thomas. 1983. Implicit thematic roles in the lexicon and syntax. Ms., University of Massachusetts, Amherst.

Ross, John. 1967. Constraints on variables in syntax. Doctoral dissertation, MIT, Cambridge, Mass.

Ross, John. 1970. On declarative sentences. In *Readings in English transformational grammar*, ed. Roderick A. Jacobs and Peter S. Rosenbaum, 222–272. Waltham, Mass.: Ginn and Co.

Rothstein, Susan. 1983. The syntactic forms of predication. Doctoral dissertation, MIT, Cambridge, Mass.

Rouveret, Alain, and Jean-Roger Vergnaud, 1980. Specifying reference to the subject: French causatives and conditions on representations. *Linguistic Inquiry* 11: 97–202.

Saito, Mamoru. 1982. Case marking in Japanese: A preliminary study. Ms., MIT, Cambridge, Mass.

Saito, Mamoru. 1983. Case and government in Japanese. In *WCCFL* 2: 247–259. Stanford: CSLI Publications.

Saito, Mamoru. 1984. On the definition of c-command and government. In *NELS* 14: 402–417. GLSA, University of Massachusetts, Amherst.

Saito, Mamoru. 1985. Some asymmetries in Japanese and their theoretical implications. Doctoral dissertation, MIT, Cambridge, Mass.

Saito, Mamoru. 1986. LF effects of scrambling. Paper presented at Princeton Workshop on Comparative Grammar, Princeton University, Princeton.

Saito, Mamoru. 1987a. An extension of K. I. Harada's *wh*-Q binding analysis. Paper presented at the 5th Annual Meeting of the English Linguistic Society of Japan.

Saito, Mamoru. 1987b. Three notes on syntactic movement in Japanese. In *Issues in Japanese linguistics*, ed. Takashi Imai and Mamoru Saito, 301–350. Dordrecht: Foris.

Saito, Mamoru. 1989. Scrambling as semantically vacuous A'-movement. In *Alternative conceptions of phrase structure*, ed. Mark R. Baltin and Anthony S. Kroch, 182–200. Chicago: University of Chicago Press.

Saito, Mamoru. 1992a. Long distance scrambling in Japanese. *Journal of East Asian Linguistics* 1: 69–118.

Saito, Mamoru. 1992b. The additional-*wh* effects and the adjunction site theory. Ms., University of Connecticut, Storrs.

Saito, Mamoru. 1994a. Additional-*wh* effects and the adjunction site theory. *Journal of East Asian Linguistics* 3: 195–240.

Saito, Mamoru. 1994b. Improper adjunction. *MIT working papers in linguistics 24: Formal approaches to Japanese linguistics* 1, ed. Masatoshi Koizumi and Hiroyuki Ura, 263–293. Department of Linguistics and Philosophy, MIT, Cambridge, Mass.

Saito, Mamoru. 2000. Predicate raising and θ relations. In *Proceeding of the 2000 Seoul International Conference on Language and Computation*, 85–113. Seoul: The Linguistic Society of Korea.

Saito, Mamoru. 2002. A derivational approach to the interpretation of scrambling chains. Ms., Nanzan University. [Published in *Lingua (special issue), Formal Japanese syntax and universal grammar: The past 20 years*, ed. Naoki Fukui, 481–518 (2003).]

Saito, Mamoru, and Naoki Fukui. 1998. Order in phrase structure and movement. *Linguistic Inquiry* 29: 439–474.

Saito, Mamoru, and Hiroto Hoshi. 2000. Japanese light verb construction and the minimalist program. In *Step by step: Essays on minimalist syntax in honor of Howard Lasnik*, ed. Roger Martin, David Michaels, and Juan Uriagereka, 261–295. Cambridge, Mass.: MIT Press.

Saito, Mamoru, and Keiko Murasugi. 1989. N'-deletion in Japanese. In *UConn working papers in linguistics*, 87–107. University of Connecticut, Storrs.

Saito, Mamoru, and Keiko Murasugi. 1990. N'-deletion in Japanese: A preliminary study. *Japanese/Korean Linguistics* 1: 285–301. Stanford: CSLI Publications.

Saito, Mamoru, and Keiko Murasugi. 1993. Subject predication within IP and DP. Ms., University of Connecticut, Storrs, and Kinjo Gakuin University, Nagoya.

Sakai, Hiromu. 1990. Complex NP and case conversion in Japanese. Paper presented at the First Workshop on Theoretical East Asian Linguistics, University of California, Irvine.

Sakai, Hiromu. 1994. Complex NP Constraint and case conversion in Japanese. In *Current topics in English and Japanese*, ed. Masaru Nakamura, 179–203. Tokyo: Hituzi Syoboo.

Sakai, Hiromu. 1996. Derivational uniformity: A study of syntactic derivation in parametric setting. Doctoral dissertation, University of California, Irvine.

Sakai, Hiromu. 1998. Feature checking and morphological merger. *Japanese/Korean Linguistics* 8: 189–201. Stanford: CSLI Publications.

Sakai, Hiromu. 2000a. Kotenteki ruikeiron-to hikaku toogoron (Classical typology and comparative syntax). *Kyoto Daigaku Gengogaku Kenkyu* 19: 117–146. Department of Linguistics, Kyoto University, Kyoto.

Sakai, Hiromu. 2000b. Predicate ellipsis and nominalization. In *Proceedings of the 2000 Seoul International Conference on Language and Computation*, 85–113. Seoul: The Linguistic Society of Korea.

Sakai, Hiromu. 2001. Review of *Syntactic focus movement and ellipsis: A minimalist approach* by Jeong-Seok Kim. *Glot International* 5. 2: 67–73.

Santorini, Beatrice. 1991. Scrambling and INFL in German. Ms., University of Pennsylvania, Philadelphia.

Saxon, Leslie. 1986. Dogrib pronouns. Doctoral dissertation, University of California, San Diego.

Schachter, Paul. 1976. The subject in Philippine languages: Topic, actor, actor-topic, or none of the above. In *Subject and topic*, ed. Charles N. Li, 491–518. New York: Academic Press.

Schoemaker, Paul. 1991. The quest for optimality: A positive heuristic of science? *Behavioral and Brain Science* 14. 2: 205–245.

Schwartz, Bernhard. 1999. On the syntax of either... or. *Natural Language and Linguistic Theory* 17: 339–370.

Selkirk, Elisabeth. 1977. Some remarks on noun phrase structure. In *Formal syntax*, ed. Peter Culicover, Thomas Wasow, and Adrian Akmajian, 285–316. New York: Academic Press.

Sells, Peter. 1995. Korean and Japanese morphology from a lexical perspective. *Linguistic Inquiry* 26: 277–325.

Shibatani, Masayoshi. 1989. Gengo ruikeiron (Language typology). In *Eigogaku-no kanren-bunya* (Related Disciplines), ed. Masayoshi Shibatani, Yukio Otsu, and Aoi Tsuda, *Outline of English Linguistics*, vol. 6. Tokyo: Taishukan.

Shibatani, Masayoshi. 1990a. On parametric syntax. *Studies in generative grammar* 1: 243–270.

Shibatani, Masayoshi. 1990b. *The languages of Japan*. Cambridge: Cambridge University Press.

Siegel, Dorothy. 1974. Topics in English morphology. Doctoral dissertation, MIT, Cambridge, Mass.

Simpson, Jane. 1984. Aspects of Warlbiri morphology and syntax. Doctoral dissertation, MIT, Cambridge, Mass.

Sohn, Keun-Won. 1993. Additional argument effects, scrambling, and the ECP. Ms., University of Connecticut, Storrs.

Sohn, Keun-Won. 1994. Adjunction to argument, free ride, and the minimalist program. *MIT working papers in linguistics 24: Formal approaches to Japanese linguistics 1*, ed. Masatoshi Koizumi and Hiroyuki Ura, 315–334. Department of Linguistics and Philosophy, MIT, Cambridge, Mass.

Speas, Margaret. 1984. Saturation and phrase structure. In *MIT working papers in linguistics* 6: 174–198. MIT, Cambridge, Mass.

Speas, Margaret. 1986. Adjunctions and projections in syntax. Doctoral dissertation, MIT, Cambridge, Mass.

Speas, Margaret. 1990. *Phrase structure in natural language*. Dordrecht: Kluwer.

Sproat, Richard. 1985. Welsh syntax and VSO structure. *Natural Language and Linguistic Theory* 3: 173–216.

Stowell, Timothy. 1981a. Complementizers and the Empty Category Principle. In *NELS* 11: 345–363. GLSA, University of Massachusetts, Amherst.

Stowell, Timothy. 1981b. Origins of phrase structure. Doctoral dissertation, MIT, Cambridge, Mass.

Stowell, Timothy. 1982. Subject across categories. *The Linguistic Review* 2: 285–312.

Stowell, Timothy. 1989. Subjects, specifiers, and X-bar theory. In *Alternative conceptions of phrase structure*, ed. Mark R. Baltin and Anthony S. Kroch, 232–262. Chicago: University of Chicago Press.

Stuurman, Frits. 1985. *Phrase structure in generative grammar*. Dordrecht: Foris.

Szabolcsi, Anna. 1987. Functional categories in noun phrase. In *Approaches to Hungarian vol. 2*, ed. Istvan Kenesei and J. Szeged, 167–190. University of Budapest.

Tada, Hiroaki. 1990. Scrambling(s). Paper presented at Ohio Workshop on Japanese Syntax, Ohio State University, Columbus.

Tada, Hiroaki. 1991. Nominative objects in Japanese. Ms., MIT, Cambridge, Mass.

Tada, Hiroaki. 1992. Nominative objects in Japanese. *Journal of Japanese Linguistics* 14: 91–108.

Tada, Hiroaki. 1993. A/A-bar partition in derivation. Doctoral dissertation, MIT, Cambridge, Mass.

Tada, Hiroaki, and Mamoru Saito. 1991. VP-internal scrambling. Paper presented at University of Massachusetts Colloquium, University of Massachusetts, Amherst.

Takahashi, Daiko, 1991. "Move-*wh*" in Japanese. Ms., University of Connecticut, Storrs.

Takahashi, Daiko. 1992. Sluicing in Japanese. Ms., University of Connecticut, Storrs.

Takahashi, Daiko. 1993a. Barriers, relativized minimality, and economy of derivation. Paper presented at a symposium on the minimalist program, held during the 65th General Meeting of the English Literary Society of Japan, Tokyo.

Takahashi, Daiko. 1993b. Minimize chain links. Paper presented at the 11th Annual Meeting of the English Linguistic Society of Japan.

Takahashi, Daiko. 1993c. Movement of *wh*-phrases in Japanese. *Natural Language and Linguistic Theory* 11: 655–678.

Takashashi, Daiko. 1993d. On antecedent contained deletion. Ms., University of Connecticut, Storrs.

Takahashi, Daiko. 1994a. Minimality of movement. Doctoral dissertation, University of Connecticut, Storrs.

Takahashi, Daiko. 1994b. Sluicing in Japanese. *Journal of East Asian Linguistics* 3: 265–300.

Takano, Yuji. 1992. Proper binding: A minimalist approach. Ms., University of California, Irvine.

Takano, Yuji. 1995. Predicate fronting and internal subjects. *Linguistic Inquiry* 26: 327–340.

Takano, Yuji. 1996. Movement and parametric variations in syntax. Doctoral dissertation, University of California, Irvine.

Takano, Yuji. 1998. Object shift and scrambling. *Natural Language and Linguistic Theory* 16: 817–889.

Takeda, Kazue. 1999. Multiple-headed structures. Doctoral dissertation, University of California, Irvine.

Takezawa, Koichi. 1987. A configurational approach to case-marking in Japanese. Doctoral dissertation, University of Washington, Seattle.

Takezawa, Koichi. 1998. Kaku no yakuwari to koozoo (The role of case and the structure). In *Kaku to gozyun to toogo koozoo* (Case, word order, and syntactic structure), ed. Koichi Takezawa and John Whitman, 1–102. Tokyo: Kenkyusha.

Takubo, Yukinori. 1985. On the scope of negation and question in Japanese. *Papers in Japanese Linguistics* 10: 87–115.

Taraldsen, Tarald. 1978. On the NIC, vacuous application, and the *that*-trace filter. Ms., MIT, Cambridge, Mass. [Reproduced in 1980 by the Indiana University Linguistics Club as On the nominative island condition, vacuous application, and the *that*-trace filter].

Tateishi, Koichi. 1988. SPEC in Japanese and universality of X' theory. Ms., University of Massachusetts, Amherst.

Teramura, Hideo. 1980. Meisi syuusyokubu no hikaku (Noun modifying expressions: Comparison between English and Japanese). In *Niti-Eigo Hikaku Koza* 2, ed. Tetsuya Kunihiro, 221–266. Tokyo: Taishukan.

Terazu, Noriko. 1975. Coordinate deletion, gapping, and right node raising. *Studies in English Linguistics* 3: 19–65.

Thráinsson, Höskuldur. 1996. On the (non-) universality of functional categories. In *Minimal ideas: syntactic studies in the minimalist framework*, ed. Warner Abraham, Samuel Epstein, Höskuldur Thráinsson, and Jan-Wouter Zwart, 253–281. Philadelphia: John Benjamins.

Tokieda, Motoki. 1941. *Kokugogaku genron* (Foundations of Japanese linguistics). Tokyo: Iwanami Shoten.

Tokieda, Motoki. 1950. *Nihon bunpoo: Koogo-hen* (The grammar of spoken Japanese). Tokyo: Iwanami Shoten.

Tokieda, Motoki. 1978. *Nihon bunpoo: Koogo-hen* (The grammar of spoken Japanese), revised edition. Tokyo: Iwanami Shoten.

Tonoike, Shigeo. 1987. Nonlexical categories in Japanese. *Language and Culture* 4: 83–97. Meiji Gakuin University, Tokyo.

Tonoike, Shigeo. 1991. The comparative syntax of English and Japanese: Relating unrelated languages. In *Current English linguistics in Japan*, ed. Heizo Nakajima, 455–506. Berlin: Mouton de Gruyter.

Torrego, Esther. 1986. On empty categories in nominals. Ms., University of Massachusetts, Boston.

Travis, Lisa. 1984. Parameters and the effects of word order variation. Doctoral dissertation, MIT, Cambridge, Mass.

Travis, Lisa. 1988. The syntax of adverbs. In *McGill working papers in linguistics: Special issue on comparative Germanic syntax*, 280–311. Department of Linguistics, McGill University, Montreal.

Travis, Lisa. 1991. Parameters of phrase structure and verb-second phenomena. In *Principles and parameters in comparative grammar*, ed. Robert Freidin, 339–364. Cambridge, Mass.: MIT Press.

Tsai, Wei-Tien Dylan. 1994. On economizing the theory of A-bar dependencies. Doctoral dissertation, MIT, Cambridge, Mass.

Tsao, F. 1977. A functional study of topic in Chinese: The first step toward discourse analysis. Doctoral dissertation, University of Southern California, Los Angeles.

Ueda, Masanobu. 1991. Japanese phrase structure and parameter setting. Doctoral dissertation, University of Massachusetts, Amherst.

Ueyama, Ayumi. 1999. Two type of scrambling constructions in Japanese. Ms.,

Kyoto University of Foreign Studies. [Published in *Anaphora: A reference guide*, ed. Andrew Barss and Terence Langendoen, 23–71. Oxford, Blackwell]

Ura, Hiroyuki. 1994a. Superraising in Japanese. In *MIT working papers in linguistics 24: Formal approaches to Japanese linguistics 1*, ed. Masatoshi Koizumi and Hiroyuki Ura, 355–374. Department of Linguistics and Philosophy, MIT, Cambridge, Mass.

Ura, Hiroyuki. 1994b. Varieties of raising and the feature-based bare phrase structure theory. *MIT occasional papers in linguistics 7*. Department of Linguistics and Philosophy, MIT, Cambridge, Mass.

Ura, Hiroyuki. 1996. Multiple feature-checking: A theory of grammatical function splitting. Doctoral dissertation, MIT, Cambridge, Mass.

Ura, Hiroyuki. 1999. Checking theory and dative subject constructions in Japanese and Korean. *Journal of East Asian Linguistics* 9: 223–254.

Ura, Hiroyuki. 2000. *Checking theory and grammatical functions in universal grammar*. Oxford: Oxford University Press.

Uriagereka, Juan. 1988. On government. Doctoral dissertation, University of Connecticut, Storrs.

Urushibara, Saeko. 1993. Syntactic categories and extended projections in Japanese. Doctoral dissertation, Brandeis University, Waltham, Mass.

van Leeuwen, Jan. 1990. *Handbook of theoretical computer science, Volume A: Algorithms and complexity*. Cambridge, Mass.: MIT Press/Elsevier.

Vikner, Sten. 1995. *Verb movement and expletive constructions in the Germanic languages*. Oxford: Oxford University Press,

Watanabe, Akira. 1992. Subjacency and s-structure movement of *wh*-in-situ. *Journal of East Asian Linguistics* 1: 255–291.

Watanabe, Akira. 1993. Agr-based Case theory and its interaction with the A-bar system. Doctoral dissertation, MIT, Cambridge, Mass.

Watanabe, Akira. 1994. A crosslinguistic perspective on Japanese nominative-genitive conversion and its implications for Japanese syntax. In *Current topics in English and Japanese*, ed. Masaru Nakamura, 341–369. Tokyo: Hituzi Syobo.

Watanabe, Akira. 1996a. *Case-absorption and wh-agreemant*. Dordrecht: Kluwer.

Watanabe, Akira. 1996b. Nominative-genitive conversion and agreement in Japanese. *Journal of East Asian Linguistics* 4: 373–410.

Watanabe, Akira. 1998. Remarks on head movement within VP shell. Ms., University of Tokyo.

Watanabe, Akira. 2002. *Wh* and operator constructions in Japanese. Ms., University of Tokyo. [Published in *Lingua (special issue), Formal Japanese syntax and universal grammar: The past 20 years*, ed. Naoki Fukui, 519–558 (2003).]

Webelhuth, Gert. 1989. Syntactic saturation phenomena and the modem Germanic languages. Doctoral dissertation, University of Massachusetts, Amherst.

Webelhuth, Gert. 1992. Scrambling without functional heads. Talk given at University of California, Irvine.

Wexler, Kenneth. 1994. Optional infinitives, head movement and the economy of derivations in child grammar. In *Verb movement*, ed. David Lightfoot and Norbert Hornstein, 305–350. Cambridge: Cambridge University Press.

Wexler, Kenneth, and Peter Culicover. 1980. *Formal principles of language acquisition*. Cambridge, Mass.: MIT Press.

Whitman, John. 1984. Configurationality parameters. Ms., Harvard University, Cambridge, Mass. [Published in *Issues in Japanese linguistics*, ed. Takashi Imai and Mamoru Saito, 351–374. Dordrecht: Foris (1986)]

Wilder, Chris. 1997. Some properties of ellipsis in coordination. In *Studies on universal grammar and typological variation*, ed. Artemis Alexiadow, and Alan Hall, 59–107. Amsterdam: John Benjamins.

Williams, Edwin. 1980. Predication. *Linguistic Inquiry* 11: 203–238.

Williams, Edwin. 1981. Argument structure and morphology. *The Linguistic Review* 1: 81–114.

Williams, Edwin. 1985. PRO and subject of NP. *Natural Language and Linguistic Theory* 3: 271–296.

Wood, Mary McGee. 1993. *Categorial grammars*. London and New York: Routledge.

Yamada, Hiroshi. 1983. Notes on the "Det = PRO" analysis of English picture NP reflexives. In *Issues in syntax and semantics: Festschrift for Masatake Muraki*, ed. Kazuko Inoue, Eichi Kobayashi, and Richard Linde, 265–289. Tokyo: Sansyusya.

Yoon, H.-S. J., 1994. Korean verbal inflection and checking theory. In *MIT working papers in linguistics 22: The morphology-syntax connection*, ed. Heidi Harley and Colin Phillips, 251–270. Department of Linguistics and Philosophy, MIT, Cambridge, Mass.

Zagona, Karen. 1988. *Verb phrase syntax: A parametric study of English and Spanish*. Dordrecht: Kluwer.

Zanuttini, Raffaella. 2001. Sentential negation. In *The handbook of contemporary syntactic theory*, ed. Mark Baltin and Chris Collins, 511–535. Oxford: Blackwell.

Zubizarreta, Maria Luisa. 1982. On the relationship of the lexicon to the syntax, Doctoral dissertation, MIT, Cambridge, Mass.

Zushi, Mihoko. 2002. Null arguments: The case of Japanese and Romance. Ms., Aichi Prefectural University. [Published in *Lingua (special issue), Formal Japanese syntax and universal grammar: The past 20 years*, ed. Naoki Fukui, 559–604 (2003).]

Zwart, C. Jan-Wouter. 1997. *Morphosyntax of verb movement: A minimalist approach to the syntax of Dutch*. Dordrecht: Kluwer.

Index

φ-features 3, 211–13, 216–17, 222, 335, 365n14, 378n1

A-over-A principle: Attract 6, 210–17, 223; Complex NP Constraint 221; extensions 217–22; Proper Binding Condition 209; Relativized Minimality 212–13; transformation 216; *wh*-movement 222
Abe, J. 319
Abney, S. 12, 16–17, 155
aboutness relation 241, 243, 254
accusative Case 159, 160–1, 162–3, 165–6, 224–5
action *see* Least Action Principle
adjacency effects 67, 166–7
adjective phrase 155
adjunct 2, 43–5, 48, 52–3, 270; extraction 43, 44; *see also* argument-adjunct asymmetry
Adjunct Condition 219, 284–5
adjunction: bare phrase structure 189–93; base-generated 190; constraints on 58–60, 198; directionality 185–9; economy condition 92–9; Heavy NP Shift 185–6; intermediate 90; IP/VP 188; Japanese 309; maximal projection 220; Merge 136, 193; relativized X' theory 188; Saito 191; scrambling 185; Spec 95–6, 193, 194–5; structure 15; substitution 6, 116, 149, 179, 189, 205–6, 218–19, 271, 279–80, 284; θ-marking 60; topicalization 66; uniqueness 198–9, 220; vacuousness 96–8; VP-adjunction 9, 29–30, 32, 58, 191–3; X' theory 187
adjunction-to-head 147, 149, 152
adverbs 25
Affix-Hopping 299
Agbayani, B. 213, 214
Agr-less system 151, 159
Agr (subject-agreement) 106, 109, 111, 120, 130, 294, 324, 334
agreement 70, 225–6, 279, 296, 322; Kayne 179, 196, 197
agreement features 62, 64, 114–17, 127, 276–80, 291–2, 296, 323–4
analytical mechanics 340

antecedent-government 49, 54
Aoyagi, H. 318, 331
argument: implicit 24; predicate 61; verbal noun 329
argument-adjunct asymmetry 87–8, 91, 310–11
Attract 6, 152, 210–17, 223
Attract-F 150–1, 167

Bach, E. 170–1
Baker, C.L. 173
Baker, M. 8, 129, 328
Baltin, M. 66, 80
bare phrase structure theory: adjunction 189–93; Chomsky 134–5, 140, 142, 185, 190, 231–2, 280–2; head parameter 283–4; maximal projection 281–2; X' schema 287–8
barriers: Blocking Category 67; Chomsky 26, 27, 31–2, 38–41, 47, 49, 51, 55–9, 285; exclusion 58; inherited 29, 31, 40; L-marking 4, 56, 60, 68; long-distance movement 26–33; maximal projection 4, 56, 60; movement 87–8; problems 59–61; projection 68; relativized X' theory 55; X' theory 261–72
Barss, A. 20
BC *see* Blocking Category
Bedell, G. 127
Berber 84
Bergvall, V. 20
Berwick, R. 350, 388, 390n16
binding 35, 82
Binding Theory 5, 24, 35–6, 88–9, 99, 247
Blocking Category 27, 39, 56, 63, 65, 67
Bobaljik, J. 151
Borer, H. 107
Bošković, Ž. 195–6
bounding nodes 61, 105, 107
Bowers, J. 266
Brame, M. 12
Branigan, P. 196
Bresnan, J. 173, 266, 268

c-command 19; Attract 6; distance 211–12; Kayne 240; LCA 134; *naze* 202; PRO 21

C specification 109, 120–1, 123, 130; see also complementizers
canonical precedence relation see CPR
Carnie, A. 151
Case 159–64, 320–3; Chomsky 163, 320; English 171–2; feature checking 324; Japanese 163, 187; Kase 36; nominative 16, 163; noun phrases 335; PF 325; Spell-Out 160–1, 164–5
Case Filter 70, 73
Case-marking: adjacency 67; Japanese 72–3, 320–5; light verb construction 327–31; minimalist program 323–5; PF reanalysis 325–7; see also Exceptional Case Marking
Case particles 160–1, 176, 251, 313–14, 321–2
Cattell, R. 197, 284
CED (Condition on Extraction Domain) 51, 177–8, 285; Complex NP Constraint 217–21; L-marking 54; parametrized Merge 220–1; reunification 197–9; Subjacency 54–6, 57, 59
centrality 33, 34
chains 88, 89, 90–2, 94
Chamorro 69, 83–4, 85
Cheng, L.L.-S. 359, 361n12, 362
Chichewa 129
Chierchia, G. 255–6, 257
Chinese 69, 81–3, 104, 106, 297–8
Choe, H.S. 83–4
Chomsky, N. 8, 10; A-over-A principle 210; adjunction 29–30; Agr 324; Agr-less system 151, 159; antecedent-government 45; Attract 211–17; bare phrase structure theory 134–5, 140, 142, 185, 190, 231–2, 280–2; barriers 26, 27, 31–2, 38–41, 47, 49, 51, 55–9, 285; Case theory 163, 320; computational tricks 351; economy principles 69, 124, 210, 219; empty category 116; extension condition 149; Form-Chain 89–90; Free Movement Hypothesis 91; generative grammar 344; head movement 147; lexical categories 23–4, 293, 345; LF 110; linear order 317; Linearization 177; Merge 134–5, 149, 161, 190, 218, 231–2; Minimal Link Condition 50–1, 183, 209, 215–16; minimalist program 132, 294, 344–5; optionality 85, 177–8; parametric variation 133; specifiers 11, 268–9; Spell-Out 335–6; subjacency 21, 64, 308; superiority phenomenon 195–6; *that*-trace effect 92; θ-marking 22; topicalization 78–9, 94; transformation 263; Uniformity Condition 87–8, 99; Universal Grammar 100, 139; verb phrases 145; verb-raising 145, 299; *wh*-island constraint 105; *wh*-movement 181–2; *wh*-phrase 57–8, 60; X' theory 9, 40, 179, 263–4, 269–70
Chung, S. 83–4, 85
class NP 343–4
classifier system 6–7, 250–4, 254–5
clauses: noun phrases 110, 116–17; structure 66; subjacency 56–7; tensed 68; verbs 117; see also relative clauses

cliticization 158
Collins, C. 221, 222, 280, 384n3
coordination structure 312–13, 330
Cole, P. 246
combinatorial mathematics 337
Comp: Blocking 63; functional heads 12; Japanese 120–3; Kase 16–17; movement 29; non-bridge verbs 41; projection 31; questions 245; relative clause 60, 244; X' schema 10
Comp-to-Comp 90–1
comparative structure 65
comparative syntax 1, 5, 100–1, 112, 130–1, 225, 256–7
complement 47, 66–7, 136–7, 145–8, 270, 314; see also head-complement relation
Complementizer Substitution Universal 173–4
complementizers 171–3, 249–50, 268; empty 45–7
Complex NP Constraint 58, 60, 105, 217–21
computational complexity theory 343
computational systems 174–6, 259, 351, 352
Concatenate 141, 143–5, 148–9, 234
Condition on Extraction Domain see CED
configurationality parameter 103, 111, 145
connective particle 309–14, 318
Cormen, T. 351
CP see Comp
CPR (canonical precedence relation) 71, 72, 74, 75, 80–1
Culicover, P. 15

D specification 109, 130; see also Determiner Phrase (DP)
Deconomy 348, 350, 353
Deg 156–7
Demerge 5, 140, 144, 148, 229, 233–4; computation 175; Concatenate 141, 148–9; maximal projections 142–3; Merge 141–2
demonstratives 45, 123
dependency relation 297
derivation see economy of derivation; Symmetry Principle of Derivation
Determiner Phrase (DP) 109, 130, 258–9; adjunct positions 52–3; Case-marking 73; English 18–19; head-parameter 107; lexical/syntactic 10; PRO 23–4; projection 9, 34, 189; relative clauses 31; relativized X' theory 66; structure 12, 15–16, 21; subjects 79; surface order 18–19; see also DP-analysis
Di Sciullo, A.M. 34
Diesing, M. 245
directionality 73, 136, 185–9, 194, 219, 232
dominance 21, 23, 56–7, 134, 258, 271, 282
Double-*o* Constraint 166
DP-analysis 2, 63, 189, 207–8, 273–6, 291; see also Determiner Phrase
Dutch 86, 170

economy of derivation 337–8, 341, 346, 349, 350, 352–3

economy of representation 337–8, 348–9, 350, 352
economy principles 69, 92–9, 124, 210, 219, 337, 338–41
ECP (Empty Category Principle) 4, 38, 41, 51, 87–8, 267, 268, 337–8
ellipsis 207–8, 305–6
Emonds, J. 9, 34, 109, 266, 299–300
empty categories 20, 116, 193; *see also* ECP
endocentricity 262, 264, 287
English: Case features 171–2; movement 71, 72–80, 80, 125, 219; subjects 1–2, 201; SVO word order 102; topicalization 75, 78–9, 85–6, 93–4, 182; verb-raising 162; *wh*-movement 85–6, 117–18, 128, 167–71; *see also* English/Japanese comparison; head-initial; Heavy NP Shift
English/Japanese comparisons: head-complement relation 120; head parameter 69, 70–1, 120, 129, 179; noun phrases 256, 334; nouns 206; parametric variation 179; phrase structure 188–9; relativized X' theory 130; scrambling 118, 124; Symmetry Principle of Derivation 6; typological differences 117–19; VO/OV 148; *wh*-movement 2–3, 117–18, 167–71
EPP *see* Extended Projection Principle
Epstein, S. 141
Euler, L. 339, 340
Exceptional Case Marking 16, 19, 30–1
expletive elements 118
Extended Projection Principle 17, 19, 125, 195, 216, 351
extension condition 149
extraction 43–5, 197–9, 200–1
extraposition 66, 80

Fabb, N. 34
feature chains 150–1, 156
feature checking: agreement 225–6, 296; Case theory 324; Chomsky 150; head movement 148–53; Japanese 297, 333; movement 151
Feldman, D. 33
Fermat, P. de 338–9, 340
Feynman, R. 388n2
Fiengo, R. 221
Fillmore, C. 354, 365
Flynn, M. 35
Form-Chain 89–90
formal features (FF) 159, 214
Frampton, John 209
Freezing Principle 21
Freidin, R. 363n1, 377, 388
French 152, 196, 299
Fukaya, T. 306
Fukui, N.: Agr 324; Case marking 322; CED 217–18; comparative syntax 225; "Deriving the differences between English and Japanese" 2–3; directionality 194; ellipsis 207; functional categories 35, 137–8, 280, 293, 294; functional heads 157; generalization 333; head-parameter 129; Japanese specifiers 52; Japanese verbs 17, 322; lexical parametrization 107, 108; linear order 135–6, 283, 317; Linearization 177, 238, 240; maximal projection 214; Merge 229; Morphological Merger 318; nominatives 126, 163–4; noun phrases 335; parametrization 107, 108–9; parametrized Merge 219–20, 232, 285–6; phrase structure 185, 237–8, 242–3, 296; projection 187; PVP 124; relativized X' theory 55, 61–3, 68, 186; S-adjoined position 92; scrambling 94–5; Spec-head agreement 73, 79; Spell-out 126; Symmetry Principle 229–30, 232–7; tenses 129; *that/to* 172–3; *A Theory of Category Projection and Its Applications* 2; *wh*-movement 168; zero topic parameter 111
Fukushima, K. 343, 344
functional categories 7, 16–18, 290; classified 5; computation 292; descriptive pressure 292–3; feature specifications 109, 130; Fukui 35, 137–8, 200, 293, 294; interpretation 276–8; Japanese 2–3, 35, 293, 296–8, 331; LF 133, 294; overt evidence 293–4; PF 294; projection 9, 10–21, 278; relativized X' theory 61–2; Spec 10–11, 280; Universal Grammar 289, 290–5; Visibility Guideline 289, 294–5, 296, 315, 332–6
functional heads 12, 13, 36, 157
Functional Parametrization Hypothesis 108–9, 130
Functional Projection Theorem 27

ga/o 163–4
ga particle 127, 299, 313–14, 322
generalization 333; A-movement 191–2; Bach 170–1; D-structures 9; language acquisition 157; uniformity 34
generative grammar 8, 100, 259, 286–7, 337–8, 344
genitive Case 16, 95, 126, 127, 189
George, L. 34
German 86, 170
gerunds *see* verbal nouns
globality 346, 347, 349–50
government 22, 39, 40, 41, 45
greed 351
Greenberg, J. 138, 362n15
Grimshaw, J. 327, 328
Gunji, T. 341

H-C *see* head-complement relation
Haider, H. 380n4
Hale, K. 9, 26, 102–3, 104, 117, 145, 160
Halle, M. 299, 317
Hamilton, W.R. 340–1, 342, 346, 347, 349
Harada, K.I. 180, 335
Harada, S.I. 335
Hasegawa, K. 210, 367
Hattori, S. 297
Hayashishita, J.-R. 316

head-complement relation 138; Chomsky 190–1; English/Japanese comparison 120; linearization 154–7; PP 169–70; Symmetry of Derivation 175–8; word order 145–8; *see also* SCH; SHC
head-initial/-last 3–5, 101–2, 107, 120, 124, 171–2, 200, 271
head movement 147–53
head parameter: bare phrase structure theory 283–4; D-structures 107; English/Japanese comparison 69, 70–1, 120, 129, 179; Heavy NP Shift 111; Kayne 282–3; Merge 205; ordering 111, 134; X' theory 101–2, 271
Heavy NP Shift: adjunction 185–6, 284; English 80, 184–5; head parameter 191; optionality 177–8, 180–5; relativized X' theory 66; substitution 179
Hero 338–9
heuristic algorithms 337
Higginbotham, J. 10, 17–18
Hoji, H. 158, 300, 306, 333
Hornstein, N. 266
Hoshi, H. 165–6, 319, 328
how 88
Huang, C.-T.J.: Agr 106; argument-adjunct 91; binding 82; CED 55–6, 59, 197, 285; Chinese 81; computation 176; directionality 73; ECP 267; topicalization 93–4; verb-raising 153–4; *wh*-movement 107, 111, 201–2, 203; *wh*-questions 297–8; X' theory 40
Hungarian 228

I-language 344
Iatridou, S. 294, 324
Icelandic 299
infinitivals 68
Infl 244, 245; adjunction 188, 200, 206–7; Blocking Category 63; English 17; functional head 12; Japanese Case 320; Kase 16–18, 19, 23–4; lexical 66; Spec 203; structure 15–16; verb phrase 57, 58–9; X' schema 10
interface levels 345
interrogatives 104–5
Irish 69, 151
Ishii, T. 161, 368n13, 383n15
Ishii, Y. 243
Italian 105, 106
iterability 13, 14, 16

Jackendoff, R. 10, 266, 267, 274
Jaeggli, O. 196
Japanese: accusative Case 160–1; adjunction 309; Case 163, 187; Case markings 72–3, 320–5; Comp 120–3; configurationality 103; ellipsis 207–8; feature checking 297, 333; functional categories 2–3, 35, 293, 296–8, 331; genitive 127; iterability 14; leftward movement 71, 72–80, 125, 219; Merge 283–4; nominative Case 164–6, 187–8; NPs 13–14; null subject 106; numerals 250–5; particle system 163; postpositions 157; PVP 73; scrambling 5–6,
64–5, 75, 77, 86, 94–5, 225; SOV 102, 145; specifiers 52, 64, 73, 199–205; subjects 1–2, 14, 218; tenses 299–313; verb-raising 6–7, 153–4, 158, 174, 176, 289–90, 299–313; *wh*-movement 77–8; *wh*-phrases 180; *see also* English/Japanese comparisons; head-initial/-last
Johnson, D. 343
Johnson, K. 60, 80, 93

ka (Question marker) 123, 172, 335
kara (because) 45, 50, 54, 326–7
kare (he) 13–14
Kase 16–17, 18, 19, 21, 36
katu (and) 312–13, 315, 318
Kayne, R.: agreement 179, 196, 197; C-checker 173; c-command 240; empty categories 20; extraction 200–1; head parameter 282–3; LCA 134, 136, 138, 141, 175, 230–1, 233, 238, 248–50, 282–3; linear order 317; relative pronouns 249; SVO 136, 230–1
keisiki meisi (formal noun) 46–7
Keyser, S.J. 145
Kikuchi, A. 65
Kim, J.-S. 306
Kim, S. 158
kinetic energy 340, 341
Kishimoto, H. 300, 330–1, 331
Kitagawa, C. 359, 361n11, 362
Kitagawa, Y. 273, 291
Koizumi, M. 319; Case particles 313–14; connective particle 309–14; functional categories 333; pseudo-cleft constructions 304–5, 307; reduction analysis 316; remnant scrambling 308–9; verb-raising 157–8, 289–90, 299, 301–4, 315
kono (this) 123
Koopman, H. 54
Korean 86, 106, 158, 165–6, 309, 318
Kornfilt, J. 165
koto (fact) 46–7, 48–9, 50
Kuno, S. 15, 118, 121–2, 129, 241, 242, 243, 306
Kuroda, S.-Y.: accusative Case 224–5; agreement 323; comparative syntax 225; lack of functional category 296, 333; multiple objects 165–6; multiple specifiers 325; nominative Case 126, 162–3; noun phrases 159; PF 290; scrambling 206; Spec 179; *wh*-movement 168

L-marking: barriers 4, 56, 60, 68; defined 22, 27, 54; empty complementizers 45–7; lexical government 39; m-command 32; non-adjuncts 53; verb-raising 30–1
Labeling 258, 271, 282
Lagrange, J.-L. de 339–40
Lamontagne, G. 160
language 8, 227–8, 259; *see also* natural language
language acquisition 157
Larson, R. 288
Lasnik, H. 42, 241; A-position 88–9; Complex NP 43, 44; economy condition 219; empty

category 116; Minimal Link Condition 183; subjacency 308; topicalization 66, 93–4, 183–4; trace-deletion 91; Uniformity Condition 87–8, 99
Last Resort 185, 191, 194, 205
LCA (Linear Correspondence Axiom) 134, 136, 138, 141, 175, 230–1, 233, 238, 248–50, 282–3
Least Action Principle 7, 337–8, 340, 341, 346, 347, 349–50
Least Time Principle 340
Lee, R.K. 179, 182, 194–5, 195, 196, 197
leftward movement 71, 72–80, 125, 144–5, 186, 219
Leonardo da Vinci 338
lexical categories 9, 33, 34, 277–8; Chomsky 23–4, 293, 345; interpretation 276, 291–2; LF 110–11; projection 10–12, 278; relativized X' theory 61–2
Lexical Parametrization Hypothesis 107–8
Lexical Structure (LS) 102–3
Lexicalist Hypothesis 263
LF (Logical Form): Binding Theory 89; Chain Condition 87; Chomsky 110; functional categories 133, 294; lexical categories 110–11; *naze* (why) 38; and PF 139, 345; Projection Principle 15–16; θ-marking 291–2; verbs 42, 328–9; *wh*-movement 67
Linear Correspondence Axiom *see* LCA
linear order: Fukui and Saito 135–6, 218, 283, 317; Kayne 317; PF interface 140–1; phrase structure 6, 133–8, 230–2, 282–6; X' theory 101–2, 271; *see also* precedence; SVO
linearity 112, 130, 132–3
linearization 140–5, 233–6; algorithm 317; Chomsky 177; Concatenate 143–5; Fukui 177, 238, 240; head-complement 154–7; Saito 177; Spell-Out 252; verb-raising 146–7, 235–6; *see also* head-initial/-last
Lobeck, A. 207
locality theory 4, 347
Logical Form *see* LF
LS (Lexical Structure) 102–3
Lyons, J. 262

m-command 19, 21, 32
McCloskey, J. 83, 84
Mahajan, A.K. 362n16, 373n7
Manzini, M.R. 107
Marantz, A. 9, 299, 317
Maupertuis, P.-L. M. de 339, 340
maximal projection: adjunction 220; bare phrase structure theory 281–2; barriers 4, 56, 60; Chomsky 142; defined 28; Demerge 142–3; Fukui 214; movement 271; noncomplement 197; relativized X' theory 114–15, 279; sentence analysis 267; Spec 5, 144–5, 271; X' 25–6, 33, 34; X' theory 62–3
Merge: adjunction 136, 193; Chomsky 134–5, 149, 161, 190, 218, 231–2; computation 175;

conceptual argument 193–4; Demerge 5, 141–2; free merger mechanism 309; Fukui 229; head parameter 205; Japanese 283–4; Move 191; parametrized 6, 219–20, 232, 283–4, 285–6; phrase structure 280–2; Spell-Out 140; verb-raising 157–9; VP-Internal Subject Hypothesis 200
Mester, A. 327, 328
Minimal Link Condition 184, 192, 195–8, 285, 353; Chomsky 50–1, 183, 209, 215–16
minimalist program: bare phrase structure theory 280–2; Case markings 323–5; Chomsky 132, 294, 344–5; formal features 159; phrase structure 132, 174–5; Universal Grammar 260
minimality effects, relativized 182–5, 211, 212–13, 214, 215
Miyagawa, S. 299, 300, 302
-*mo* particle 311–12, 328–9, 330–1
Montague Grammar 35, 274
Morphological Merger 299, 300, 318, 330, 333
Morphology 231, 283
Move [alpha] 70, 72–3, 80, 82, 85, 104–5, 215; *see also* scrambling
movement: A-position 88–9; barriers 87–8; Comp 29; English 71, 72–80, 125, 269; feature checking 151; Free Movement Hypothesis 91; functional categories 277; head 147–53; improper 5, 87–99; islands of 67, 217–21, 284; long distance 26–33; optional 82–3, 177–8; relativized X' theory 279–80; Vacuous Movement Hypothesis 95; *see also* leftward movement; rightward movement
Murasugi, K. 191, 207, 241, 242, 243, 244
Muysken, P. 34, 142

natural language 3–4, 177, 261
Navaho 103
naze (why) 38, 41, 51, 53–4, 65, 202
negation sentences 306
Nemoto, N. 302
Newton, Sir I. 339, 340
Nishigauchi, T. 163, 322
Nishiyama, K. 306
-*no* particle 123, 305–6, 322
Nominal Mapping Parameter 256
nominal structures 6, 237–8, 262–3
nominalization transformation 263
Nominalizer (NL) 304–5
nominative Case 16, 126, 162–6, 187–8, 200
nominative particle 313–14
non-lexical categories 56–7, 272
non-zero-topic languages 112
nonconfigurationality 102, 103, 104
noun-complement constructions 42–3, 48, 49–50
noun phrases (NPs) 258–9; Abney 155; Case features 335; Chinese 81–2; class 343–4; clauses 110, 116–17; complements 136–7; demonstratives 45; determiner phrases 273–6; English/Japanese comparisons 256, 334; Fukui 335; genitive 95; head 49, 62, 81; internal

noun phrases (NPs) *contd.*
  structure 109, 229, 264–6; Japanese 13–14; movement 73, 291; parallelism 274; passive 274–5; subjects 1; Symmetry Principle 254; *see also* Complex NP Constraint; Determiner Phrase; Heavy NP Shift
null subject 105–6, 111
numerals 6–7, 250–5, 310, 317–18
Numeration 281

object agreement 196
objects, multiple 164–6
Ochi, M. 376n32
Oka, T. 242
Olympiodorus 338
optimality 345–6
optimization 341–4, 346, 352; continuous 342–4; discrete 341–4
optionality: Heavy NP Shift 179, 180, 232; movement 69, 82–3, 85, 177–8; scrambling 4–5, 179, 180, 232; X′ schema 33, 34
ordering restrictions 108, 112, 123–4
Otani, K. 157–8, 299, 300
OV languages 148, 162–3

Papago 86
parallelism 263–4, 272–3, 274, 320
parameter value preservation (PVP) 4–5, 69, 70; CPR 71, 80–1; Fukui 124; Japanese 73; optional movement 82–3; scrambling 72; topicalization 79
parametric syntax 2–3, 100–1, 112
parametric variation 235–6; English/Japanese compared 179; restrictive theory 130, 133–4, 175–6; Universal Grammar 7–8; verb-raising 158–9
parametrization 107–8, 148, 219–20, 232, 285–6; *see also* Functional Parametrization Hypothesis; Lexical Parametrization Hypothesis
participle agreement 196
particle system 162–3, 298, 309–14
passive 23, 24, 29–30, 274–5
Perlmutter, D.M. 242, 243
persuade 270–1
Pesetsky, D. 40, 56
PF (Phonetic Form) 139, 140–1, 290, 294, 315–20, 325, 345
PF reanalysis 7, 317, 318, 320, 325–7, 333
phonemes 265
phonology 265–6
Phrase Level Merger 315, 317, 326
phrase structure 2, 7, 36, 102–3, 185, 242–3; barriers 26; closure property 113; configurationality 102–3; context-free 259; endocentricity 262, 264, 287; English/Japanese compared 188–9; Fukui 185, 237–8, 242–3, 296; generative grammar 286–7; linear order 6, 133–8, 230–2, 282–6; Merge 280–2; minimalist program 132, 174–5; natural language 3–4; phrase markers 258–60, 347; principles-and-parameters approach 132–3; relativized X′ theory 2, 7, 291–2; rules 36, 261, 287; Stowell 36; X′ theory 113; *see also* bare phrase structure theory
physics 337, 338–41, 349
pied-piping 67, 150, 169, 331
Pollock, J.-Y. 66, 152, 153, 292
Postal, P.M. 192
postpositions 157
potential energy 340, 341
PP 156, 169–70
precedence 258, 271, 282
predicate: argument 61; coordination 312–13; complex 119, 129; ellipsis 305–6; head noun phrase 49; nominalized 306; projection 112; structures 116–17; transformation 300
Predicate-Internal Subject Hypothesis 2, 268, 273, 274, 276, 291; *see also* VP-Internal Subject Hypothesis
prepositions 156–7, 169–70
principles-and-parameters 5, 100–1; abstract features 130–1; Case system 320–3; cross-linguistic variation 101–12; generative grammar 337–8; null subject 105–6; phrase structure 132–3; X′ theory 270–1
pro-drop parameter 105–6
pro-forms 13–14
PRO theorem 22–4
Procrastinate 351
projection: agreement 279; barriers 68; Comp 31; directionality 136, 219; double-bar 26, 63–4; Fukui 187; functional categories 9, 10–21, 278; lexical categories 10–21, 278; minimal 142; specifier-head agreement 186–7; X′ schema 33–5; *see also* maximal projection
Projection Principle 9, 10, 15–16, 17, 34, 103, 125
pronominalization 282
Proper Binding Condition 76–8, 209, 221–2
pseudo-cleft constructions 304–7
Pullum, G. 33–4
PVP *see* parameter value preservation

Q-morpheme 173
Quantifier Float 253–4, 255
question particles 169
questions 104–5, 245, 296–8, 306, 335

Radford, A. 294
Reconomy 349
reduction analysis 315–20
Reinhart, T. 22, 390n15
relative clauses 6; aboutness relation 241, 243, 254; Comp 60, 244; complementizers 244–5; DPs 31; internally headed 245–6; noun-complement constructions 42–3, 48; properties 241–4; Takeda 333–4; variation 237–50
relative pronouns 238–40, 249
relativized X′ theory 2, 112–17; adjunction 188;

barriers 55; D/S structures 66; directionality 186; English/Japanese comparisons 130; Fukui 55, 61–3, 68, 186; lexical/functional categories 287; maximal projection 114–15, 279; movement 279–80; phrase structure 291–2; Predicate Internal Subject Hypothesis 2, 268, 273, 274, 276, 291; VP-Internal Subject Hypothesis 116–17
Reuland, E. 12
rightward movement 71, 72–80, 186, 219
Ristad, E.S. 348
Rizzi, L. 105, 107, 111, 183
Rochemont, M. 80
Romance languages 256
Ross, J. 80, 105, 192
Rothstein, S. 17
Rouveret, A. 320

Saito, M. 129, 165; accusative Case 160, 166; adjunct extraction 43, 44; adjunction 191, 192; CED 217–18; directionality 194; focalization 125; *ga* 322; linear order 135–6, 283; linearization 177; maximal projection 214; *naze* (why) 202; nominatives 126, 163–4; non-bridging verbs 42; parametrized Merge 219–20, 232, 285–6; phrase structure 185; Proper Binding Condition 221–2; S-adjoined position 92; scrambling 15, 64–5, 75–6, 79, 85–6, 94–5, 125, 180–2, 203–4; Spec-head 73; subjacency 308; topicalization 66–7, 75–6, 79, 85–6, 93–4, 183–4; ungrammaticality 131; verbal noun 328
Sakai, H. 244, 300–1, 305–6, 318
Saturation Principle 17–18, 19, 26–7, 36
Saussure, F. de 8
Saxon, L. 20
SCH (Specifier-Complement-Head) 145, 248–50
scrambling 3, 4–5, 316–17; adjunction 185; Chinese 81–3; English/Japanese comparisons 118, 124; Fukui 94–5; grammaticality 204; IP-adjunction 206–7; Japanese 5–6, 64–5, 75, 77, 86, 94–5, 225; Kuroda 206; leftwards 284; multiple 15, 182–3, 308; multiple subjects 224, 302–3; phrase positions 127; PVP 72; radical reconstruction 180–2; Saito 15, 64–5, 75–6, 79, 85–6, 94–5, 125, 180–2, 203–4; substitution 179; vacuousness 181; verb phrases 191–2, 302–3, 308–9
Selkirk, E. 266
Sells, P. 318
sentential structure 266–7
SHC (Specifier-Head Complement) 134, 230–1, 235, 236, 282–3
Shibatani, M. 129
Siegel, D. 266
Sohn, K.-W. 306, 309
sono (that) 123
sore (it) 13–14
SOV (Subject-Object-Verb) word order 102, 136, 145, 170–1, 236, 336

Spanish 105, 196
Speas, M. 2, 34–5, 63, 103, 186–7, 207
Spec-head agreement: absence in Japanese 203–5, 207–8; adjunction 95–6; Agr 120; Lee 179; obligatory 74–5; projection 186–8; PVP 70, 73; topicalization 78–9
Spec (specifiers) 2, 6; adjunction 95–6, 193, 194–5; Chomsky 11, 268–9; functional categories 10–11, 280; functional heads 12, 36; IP 203; iterability 16; Japanese 52, 64, 73, 199–205; Kase 17; Kuroda 179; leftness 5; lexical categories 10–12; maximal projection 5, 144–5, 271; multiple 324–5; properties 269; relational 270; Spec position 20–1; substitution 148–9, 272; X′ theory 113, 287
specificity phenomena 67–8
Specified Subject Condition 24
Specifier-Complement-Head *see* SCH
Specifier-Head-Complement *see* SHC
Spell-Out 139–40; Case 160–1, 164–5; Chomsky 335–6; computation 175; Linearization 233, 252; question particles 169; Universal Grammar 162; *wh*-movement 128
Sportiche, D. 54
Stowell, T. 9, 36, 41, 46, 47, 49, 271
Stuurman, F. 34
Subjacency 4, 40–1, 58, 338; argument-adjunct 87–8; CED 54; Chomsky 21, 308; classical conditions 61; clausal structure 56–7; violation 44, 182; zero 64; *see also* ECP (Empty Category Principle)
subject-agreement *see* agreement
subject-Aux inversion 119, 129
Subject Condition 95, 201, 219, 220, 284–5
subject raising 20–1
subjects: Adjunct Condition 219; D-structure 79, 274; English 1–2, 201; extraction 200–1; iterability 14–15; Japanese 1–2, 14, 218; multiple 54, 118–19, 126, 127, 164–6, 224
substitution 193; adjunction 6, 116, 149, 179, 189, 205–6, 218–19, 271, 279–80, 284; directionality 232; head movement 147–8; maximal projection 271; parametrized Merge 6; Spec 148–9, 272
superraising 211, 212, 213, 215–16, 221
surface structure properties 18–19, 36, 334–5
SVO (Subject-Verb-Object): English 102, 235; Kayne 136, 230–1; linear order 134; PVP 85; Subject Condition effects 219, 285; Symmetry Principle 236
Symmetry Principle of Derivation 138, 158–9, 175–8; Demerge 5, 140, 158–9, 175–8, 229–30, 232–7; English/Japanese comparisons 6; Fukui 229–30, 232–7; NP 254
syntactic objects 134–5

T specification 109, 129, 130, 299–313
Tada, H. 180, 192, 324
Tagalog 86

Index

Takahashi, D. 79, 160, 179, 192, 197, 201, 219, 285, 306
Takano, Y. 138, 158; generalization 333; head parameter 136; internal argument 166–7; linear order 317; Linearization 140, 238, 240; Merge 229; Morphological Merger 318; noun phrases 335; phrase structure 237–8, 242–3; scrambling 183; SOV 145; Symmetry Principle 229–30, 232–7; *that*-trace 250; verb-raising 146
Takeda, K. 226–7, 333–4
Takezawa, K. 299, 320–1
Takubo, Y. 306
Tamil 162–3, 170
that 120–3, 172–3, 244
that-trace 92, 98–9, 173, 176, 249–50
θ-features 60, 278
θ-marking 9, 10, 21, 22, 27, 60, 291–2
θ-role assignment 37, 160–1, 164, 292, 328
Thráinsson, H. 324
Tiwa, Southern 129
-to 120–3, 172, 309–11, 314, 316, 328–9
Tokieda, M. 117
Tonoike, S. 296
topicalization 5; adjunction 66; English 75, 78–9, 85–6, 93–4, 182; focalization 125; multiple 183–4; PVP 79; Saito 66–7, 75–6, 79, 85–6, 93–4, 183–4; Spec-head agreement 78–9
transformations 216, 260, 263, 282
Travis, L. 34, 153, 160
Tsai, W.-T.D. 202
Turkish 162–3, 165, 170

Ueyama, A. 316
uniformity 33, 34, 147
Uniformity Condition on Chains 87, 89–92, 99
Uniformity of Theta Assignment Hypothesis 328
uniqueness parameter 6, 198–9, 220, 224–8, 226–7
Universal Grammar 1, 100, 139, 228, 293; A-over-A principle 210; adjunction constraints 59–60; D-structure 21; functional categories 289, 290–5; lexicon/computational system 298; parametric differences 3, 7–8; phrase structures 132; principles of economy 337–8; Spell-Out 162; uniqueness parameter 6; X' theory 271; *see also* minimalist program; principles-and-parameters approach
Ura, H. 299, 324–5
Uriagereka, J. 63
uwasa (rumour) 46, 48–9, 50–1

Vacuous Movement Hypothesis 95
vacuousness 96–8, 181, 301–4, 310–11
Van Riemsdijk 76, 182
Verb Phrase *see* VP
verb-raising: Case-particles 251; Chomsky 145, 299; English 162; Japanese 6–7, 153–4, 158, 174, 176, 289–90, 299–313; Koizumi 157–8, 289–90, 299, 301–4, 315; L-marking 30–1; language typology 153–4; linearization 146–7,

235–6; scope arguments 301; string vacuousness 301–4, 310, 311; *-to* particle 314
verbal nouns 12, 327–8, 329
verbs: bridge/nonbridge 41–2, 47–8, 49; clauses 117; finite 300; LF 42, 328–9; light 255, 327–31; subcategorization 263; transitive 160–1, 163–4
Vergnaud, J.-R. 320
VO/OV order 148
VP-adjunction 9, 29–30, 32, 58, 191–3
VP-Internal Subject Hypothesis 116–17, 200, 274; *see also* Predicate-Internal Subject Hypothesis
VP (Verb Phrase) 258–9, 261; Chomsky 145; ellipsis 300; remnant 308–11; scrambling 191–2, 302–3, 308–9
VSO languages 69, 83–5, 151

Walpiri 103
wanna-contraction 24
Watanabe, A. 299, 324
Webelhuth, G. 184
Wexler, K. 15, 107
whether 172, 244
wh-island 88, 105, 211, 212, 213, 215–16
Whitman, J. 157–8, 299, 300
wh-movement: A-over-A principle 222; Bresnan 268; Case particles 176; Chinese 104–5; Chomsky 181–2, 291; Comp-to-Comp 90–1; English 73, 85–6, 104–5, 128; English/Japanese comparisons 2–3, 117–18, 167–71; Fukui 168; Huang 107, 111, 201–2, 203; Japanese 77–8; passive 29–30; reconstruction 181–2; SOV languages 170–1; Spanish 196; Spell-Out 128
whom 76, 182
wh-phrases 38, 57–8, 60, 104–5, 180, 197–8, 296–7, 335
wh-questions 180–1, 297–8
Williams, E. 22, 24, 34, 49, 76, 182
Winnebago 103
word order 36, 102, 225; free 82, 84; *see also* linearity; SOV; SVO; VO/OV

X' schema 3, 4, 9, 10, 16, 33–5, 264, 287–8
X' theory 266–7; adjunction 187; barriers 65–6, 261–2; Chomsky 9, 40, 179, 263–4, 269–70; development 260; generalization 264; incomplete parallelism 272–3; linear order free 70–1; maximal projection 25–6, 62–3, 114–15; non-lexical categories 56–7; phrase structure 113; principles-and-parameters approach 270–1; Spec 113, 287; standard 112–13; *see also* relativized X' theory

Yoon, H.-S.J. 318

zero topic parameter 106, 111
zibun (self) 2, 13–14, 36
Zushi, M. 8, 335, 367, 379, 384

For Product Safety Concerns and Information please contact our EU
representative GPSR@taylorandfrancis.com
Taylor & Francis Verlag GmbH, Kaufingerstraße 24, 80331 München, Germany

www.ingramcontent.com/pod-product-compliance
Lightning Source LLC
Chambersburg PA
CBHW052129010526
44113CB00034B/1026